GCC 7.0 GNU Compiler Collection Internals 1/2

A catalogue record for this book is available from the Hong Kong Public Libraries.

Published in Hong Kong by Samurai Media Limited.

Email: info@samuraimedia.org

ISBN 978-988-8406-98-2

Short Contents

Table of Contents

17   Target Description Macros and Functions

Introduction

This manual documents the internals of the GNU compilers, including how to port them
to new targets and some information about how to write front ends for new languages.
It corresponds to the compilers (GCC) version 7.0.0. The use of the GNU compilers is
documented in a separate manual. See Section "Introduction" in *Using the GNU Compiler
Collection (GCC)*.

This manual is mainly a reference manual rather than a tutorial. It discusses how to con-
tribute to GCC (see Chapter 1 [Contributing], page 3), the characteristics of the machines
supported by GCC as hosts and targets (see Chapter 2 [Portability], page 5), how GCC
relates to the ABIs on such systems (see Chapter 3 [Interface], page 7), and the characteristics of the languages for which GCC front ends are written (see Chapter 5 [Languages],
page 59). It then describes the GCC source tree structure and build system, some of the
interfaces to GCC front ends, and how support for a target system is implemented in GCC.

Additional tutorial information is linked to from http://gcc.gnu.org/readings.html.

1 Contributing to GCC Development

If you would like to help pretest GCC releases to assure they work well, current development sources are available by SVN (see `http://gcc.gnu.org/svn.html`). Source and binary snapshots are also available for FTP; see `http://gcc.gnu.org/snapshots.html`.

If you would like to work on improvements to GCC, please read the advice at these URLs:

```
http://gcc.gnu.org/contribute.html
http://gcc.gnu.org/contributewhy.html
```

for information on how to make useful contributions and avoid duplication of effort. Suggested projects are listed at `http://gcc.gnu.org/projects/`.

2 GCC and Portability

GCC itself aims to be portable to any machine where `int` is at least a 32-bit type. It aims to target machines with a flat (non-segmented) byte addressed data address space (the code address space can be separate). Target ABIs may have 8, 16, 32 or 64-bit `int` type. `char` can be wider than 8 bits.

GCC gets most of the information about the target machine from a machine description which gives an algebraic formula for each of the machine's instructions. This is a very clean way to describe the target. But when the compiler needs information that is difficult to express in this fashion, ad-hoc parameters have been defined for machine descriptions. The purpose of portability is to reduce the total work needed on the compiler; it was not of interest for its own sake.

GCC does not contain machine dependent code, but it does contain code that depends on machine parameters such as endianness (whether the most significant byte has the highest or lowest address of the bytes in a word) and the availability of autoincrement addressing. In the RTL-generation pass, it is often necessary to have multiple strategies for generating code for a particular kind of syntax tree, strategies that are usable for different combinations of parameters. Often, not all possible cases have been addressed, but only the common ones or only the ones that have been encountered. As a result, a new target may require additional strategies. You will know if this happens because the compiler will call `abort`. Fortunately, the new strategies can be added in a machine-independent fashion, and will affect only the target machines that need them.

3 Interfacing to GCC Output

GCC is normally configured to use the same function calling convention normally in use on the target system. This is done with the machine-description macros described (see Chapter 17 [Target Macros], page 433).

However, returning of structure and union values is done differently on some target machines. As a result, functions compiled with PCC returning such types cannot be called from code compiled with GCC, and vice versa. This does not cause trouble often because few Unix library routines return structures or unions.

GCC code returns structures and unions that are 1, 2, 4 or 8 bytes long in the same registers used for `int` or `double` return values. (GCC typically allocates variables of such types in registers also.) Structures and unions of other sizes are returned by storing them into an address passed by the caller (usually in a register). The target hook `TARGET_STRUCT_VALUE_RTX` tells GCC where to pass this address.

By contrast, PCC on most target machines returns structures and unions of any size by copying the data into an area of static storage, and then returning the address of that storage as if it were a pointer value. The caller must copy the data from that memory area to the place where the value is wanted. This is slower than the method used by GCC, and fails to be reentrant.

On some target machines, such as RISC machines and the 80386, the standard system convention is to pass to the subroutine the address of where to return the value. On these machines, GCC has been configured to be compatible with the standard compiler, when this method is used. It may not be compatible for structures of 1, 2, 4 or 8 bytes.

GCC uses the system's standard convention for passing arguments. On some machines, the first few arguments are passed in registers; in others, all are passed on the stack. It would be possible to use registers for argument passing on any machine, and this would probably result in a significant speedup. But the result would be complete incompatibility with code that follows the standard convention. So this change is practical only if you are switching to GCC as the sole C compiler for the system. We may implement register argument passing on certain machines once we have a complete GNU system so that we can compile the libraries with GCC.

On some machines (particularly the SPARC), certain types of arguments are passed "by invisible reference". This means that the value is stored in memory, and the address of the memory location is passed to the subroutine.

If you use `longjmp`, beware of automatic variables. ISO C says that automatic variables that are not declared `volatile` have undefined values after a `longjmp`. And this is all GCC promises to do, because it is very difficult to restore register variables correctly, and one of GCC's features is that it can put variables in registers without your asking it to.

4 The GCC low-level runtime library

GCC provides a low-level runtime library, 'libgcc.a' or 'libgcc_s.so.1' on some platforms. GCC generates calls to routines in this library automatically, whenever it needs to perform some operation that is too complicated to emit inline code for.

Most of the routines in libgcc handle arithmetic operations that the target processor cannot perform directly. This includes integer multiply and divide on some machines, and all floating-point and fixed-point operations on other machines. libgcc also includes routines for exception handling, and a handful of miscellaneous operations.

Some of these routines can be defined in mostly machine-independent C. Others must be hand-written in assembly language for each processor that needs them.

GCC will also generate calls to C library routines, such as memcpy and memset, in some cases. The set of routines that GCC may possibly use is documented in Section "Other Builtins" in *Using the GNU Compiler Collection (GCC)*.

These routines take arguments and return values of a specific machine mode, not a specific C type. See Section 13.6 [Machine Modes], page 241, for an explanation of this concept. For illustrative purposes, in this chapter the floating point type float is assumed to correspond to SFmode; double to DFmode; and long double to both TFmode and XFmode. Similarly, the integer types int and unsigned int correspond to SImode; long and unsigned long to DImode; and long long and unsigned long long to TImode.

4.1 Routines for integer arithmetic

The integer arithmetic routines are used on platforms that don't provide hardware support for arithmetic operations on some modes.

4.1.1 Arithmetic functions

int __ashlsi3 (*int* a, *int* b)   [Runtime Function]
long __ashldi3 (*long* a, *int* b)   [Runtime Function]
long long __ashlti3 (*long long* a, *int* b)   [Runtime Function]
  These functions return the result of shifting a left by b bits.

int __ashrsi3 (*int* a, *int* b)   [Runtime Function]
long __ashrdi3 (*long* a, *int* b)   [Runtime Function]
long long __ashrti3 (*long long* a, *int* b)   [Runtime Function]
  These functions return the result of arithmetically shifting a right by b bits.

int __divsi3 (*int* a, *int* b)   [Runtime Function]
long __divdi3 (*long* a, *long* b)   [Runtime Function]
long long __divti3 (*long long* a, *long long* b)   [Runtime Function]
  These functions return the quotient of the signed division of a and b.

int __lshrsi3 (*int* a, *int* b)   [Runtime Function]
long __lshrdi3 (*long* a, *int* b)   [Runtime Function]
long long __lshrti3 (*long long* a, *int* b)   [Runtime Function]
  These functions return the result of logically shifting a right by b bits.

int __modsi3 (*int* a, *int* b)   [Runtime Function]
long __moddi3 (*long* a, *long* b)   [Runtime Function]
long long __modti3 (*long long* a, *long long* b)   [Runtime Function]
> These functions return the remainder of the signed division of a and b.

int __mulsi3 (*int* a, *int* b)   [Runtime Function]
long __muldi3 (*long* a, *long* b)   [Runtime Function]
long long __multi3 (*long long* a, *long long* b)   [Runtime Function]
> These functions return the product of a and b.

long __negdi2 (*long* a)   [Runtime Function]
long long __negti2 (*long long* a)   [Runtime Function]
> These functions return the negation of a.

unsigned int __udivsi3 (*unsigned int* a, *unsigned int* b)   [Runtime Function]
unsigned long __udivdi3 (*unsigned long* a, *unsigned long* b)   [Runtime Function]
unsigned long long __udivti3 (*unsigned long long* a,   [Runtime Function]
> *unsigned long long* b)
>
> These functions return the quotient of the unsigned division of a and b.

unsigned long __udivmoddi4 (*unsigned long* a, *unsigned long*   [Runtime Function]
> b, *unsigned long* *c*)
unsigned long long __udivmodti4 (*unsigned long long* a,   [Runtime Function]
> *unsigned long long* b, *unsigned long long* *c*)
>
> These functions calculate both the quotient and remainder of the unsigned division
> of a and b. The return value is the quotient, and the remainder is placed in variable
> pointed to by c.

unsigned int __umodsi3 (*unsigned int* a, *unsigned int* b)   [Runtime Function]
unsigned long __umoddi3 (*unsigned long* a, *unsigned long* b)   [Runtime Function]
unsigned long long __umodti3 (*unsigned long long* a,   [Runtime Function]
> *unsigned long long* b)
>
> These functions return the remainder of the unsigned division of a and b.

4.1.2 Comparison functions

The following functions implement integral comparisons. These functions implement a low-level compare, upon which the higher level comparison operators (such as less than and greater than or equal to) can be constructed. The returned values lie in the range zero to two, to allow the high-level operators to be implemented by testing the returned result using either signed or unsigned comparison.

int __cmpdi2 (*long* a, *long* b)   [Runtime Function]
int __cmpti2 (*long long* a, *long long* b)   [Runtime Function]
> These functions perform a signed comparison of a and b. If a is less than b, they
> return 0; if a is greater than b, they return 2; and if a and b are equal they return 1.

int __ucmpdi2 (*unsigned long* a, *unsigned long* b)   [Runtime Function]
int __ucmpti2 (*unsigned long long* a, *unsigned long long* b)   [Runtime Function]
> These functions perform an unsigned comparison of a and b. If a is less than b, they
> return 0; if a is greater than b, they return 2; and if a and b are equal they return 1.

4.1.3 Trapping arithmetic functions

The following functions implement trapping arithmetic. These functions call the libc function `abort` upon signed arithmetic overflow.

`int __absvsi2 (`*int* `a)`   [Runtime Function]
`long __absvdi2 (`*long* `a)`   [Runtime Function]
> These functions return the absolute value of *a*.

`int __addvsi3 (`*int* `a,` *int* `b)`   [Runtime Function]
`long __addvdi3 (`*long* `a,` *long* `b)`   [Runtime Function]
> These functions return the sum of *a* and *b*; that is a + b.

`int __mulvsi3 (`*int* `a,` *int* `b)`   [Runtime Function]
`long __mulvdi3 (`*long* `a,` *long* `b)`   [Runtime Function]
> The functions return the product of *a* and *b*; that is a * b.

`int __negvsi2 (`*int* `a)`   [Runtime Function]
`long __negvdi2 (`*long* `a)`   [Runtime Function]
> These functions return the negation of *a*; that is -a.

`int __subvsi3 (`*int* `a,` *int* `b)`   [Runtime Function]
`long __subvdi3 (`*long* `a,` *long* `b)`   [Runtime Function]
> These functions return the difference between *b* and a; that is a - b.

4.1.4 Bit operations

`int __clzsi2 (`*unsigned int* `a)`   [Runtime Function]
`int __clzdi2 (`*unsigned long* `a)`   [Runtime Function]
`int __clzti2 (`*unsigned long long* `a)`   [Runtime Function]
> These functions return the number of leading 0-bits in a, starting at the most significant bit position. If *a* is zero, the result is undefined.

`int __ctzsi2 (`*unsigned int* `a)`   [Runtime Function]
`int __ctzdi2 (`*unsigned long* `a)`   [Runtime Function]
`int __ctzti2 (`*unsigned long long* `a)`   [Runtime Function]
> These functions return the number of trailing 0-bits in a, starting at the least significant bit position. If *a* is zero, the result is undefined.

`int __ffsdi2 (`*unsigned long* `a)`   [Runtime Function]
`int __ffsti2 (`*unsigned long long* `a)`   [Runtime Function]
> These functions return the index of the least significant 1-bit in *a*, or the value zero if *a* is zero. The least significant bit is index one.

`int __paritysi2 (`*unsigned int* `a)`   [Runtime Function]
`int __paritydi2 (`*unsigned long* `a)`   [Runtime Function]
`int __parityti2 (`*unsigned long long* `a)`   [Runtime Function]
> These functions return the value zero if the number of bits set in *a* is even, and the value one otherwise.

int __popcountsi2 (*unsigned int* a)   [Runtime Function]
int __popcountdi2 (*unsigned long* a)   [Runtime Function]
int __popcountti2 (*unsigned long long* a)   [Runtime Function]
> These functions return the number of bits set in *a*.

int32_t __bswapsi2 (*int32_t* a)   [Runtime Function]
int64_t __bswapdi2 (*int64_t* a)   [Runtime Function]
> These functions return the *a* byteswapped.

4.2 Routines for floating point emulation

The software floating point library is used on machines which do not have hardware support for floating point. It is also used whenever '-msoft-float' is used to disable generation of floating point instructions. (Not all targets support this switch.)

For compatibility with other compilers, the floating point emulation routines can be renamed with the DECLARE_LIBRARY_RENAMES macro (see Section 17.12 [Library Calls], page 511). In this section, the default names are used.

Presently the library does not support XFmode, which is used for long double on some architectures.

4.2.1 Arithmetic functions

float __addsf3 (*float* a, *float* b)   [Runtime Function]
double __adddf3 (*double* a, *double* b)   [Runtime Function]
long double __addtf3 (*long double* a, *long double* b)   [Runtime Function]
long double __addxf3 (*long double* a, *long double* b)   [Runtime Function]
> These functions return the sum of *a* and *b*.

float __subsf3 (*float* a, *float* b)   [Runtime Function]
double __subdf3 (*double* a, *double* b)   [Runtime Function]
long double __subtf3 (*long double* a, *long double* b)   [Runtime Function]
long double __subxf3 (*long double* a, *long double* b)   [Runtime Function]
> These functions return the difference between *b* and *a*; that is, $a - b$.

float __mulsf3 (*float* a, *float* b)   [Runtime Function]
double __muldf3 (*double* a, *double* b)   [Runtime Function]
long double __multf3 (*long double* a, *long double* b)   [Runtime Function]
long double __mulxf3 (*long double* a, *long double* b)   [Runtime Function]
> These functions return the product of *a* and *b*.

float __divsf3 (*float* a, *float* b)   [Runtime Function]
double __divdf3 (*double* a, *double* b)   [Runtime Function]
long double __divtf3 (*long double* a, *long double* b)   [Runtime Function]
long double __divxf3 (*long double* a, *long double* b)   [Runtime Function]
> These functions return the quotient of *a* and *b*; that is, a/b.

float __negsf2 (*float* a)   [Runtime Function]
double __negdf2 (*double* a)   [Runtime Function]
long double __negtf2 (*long double* a)   [Runtime Function]

long double __negxf2 (*long double* a)   [Runtime Function]
> These functions return the negation of a. They simply flip the sign bit, so they can produce negative zero and negative NaN.

4.2.2 Conversion functions

double __extendsfdf2 (*float* a)   [Runtime Function]
long double __extendsftf2 (*float* a)   [Runtime Function]
long double __extendsfxf2 (*float* a)   [Runtime Function]
long double __extenddftf2 (*double* a)   [Runtime Function]
long double __extenddfxf2 (*double* a)   [Runtime Function]
> These functions extend a to the wider mode of their return type.

double __truncxfdf2 (*long double* a)   [Runtime Function]
double __trunctfdf2 (*long double* a)   [Runtime Function]
float __truncxfsf2 (*long double* a)   [Runtime Function]
float __trunctfsf2 (*long double* a)   [Runtime Function]
float __truncdfsf2 (*double* a)   [Runtime Function]
> These functions truncate a to the narrower mode of their return type, rounding toward zero.

int __fixsfsi (*float* a)   [Runtime Function]
int __fixdfsi (*double* a)   [Runtime Function]
int __fixtfsi (*long double* a)   [Runtime Function]
int __fixxfsi (*long double* a)   [Runtime Function]
> These functions convert a to a signed integer, rounding toward zero.

long __fixsfdi (*float* a)   [Runtime Function]
long __fixdfdi (*double* a)   [Runtime Function]
long __fixtfdi (*long double* a)   [Runtime Function]
long __fixxfdi (*long double* a)   [Runtime Function]
> These functions convert a to a signed long, rounding toward zero.

long long __fixsfti (*float* a)   [Runtime Function]
long long __fixdfti (*double* a)   [Runtime Function]
long long __fixtfti (*long double* a)   [Runtime Function]
long long __fixxfti (*long double* a)   [Runtime Function]
> These functions convert a to a signed long long, rounding toward zero.

unsigned int __fixunssfsi (*float* a)   [Runtime Function]
unsigned int __fixunsdfsi (*double* a)   [Runtime Function]
unsigned int __fixunstfsi (*long double* a)   [Runtime Function]
unsigned int __fixunsxfsi (*long double* a)   [Runtime Function]
> These functions convert a to an unsigned integer, rounding toward zero. Negative values all become zero.

unsigned long __fixunssfdi (*float* a)   [Runtime Function]
unsigned long __fixunsdfdi (*double* a)   [Runtime Function]
unsigned long __fixunstfdi (*long double* a)   [Runtime Function]

`unsigned long __fixunsxfdi` (*long double* a)   [Runtime Function]
> These functions convert *a* to an unsigned long, rounding toward zero. Negative values all become zero.

`unsigned long long __fixunssfti` (*float* a)   [Runtime Function]
`unsigned long long __fixunsdfti` (*double* a)   [Runtime Function]
`unsigned long long __fixunstfti` (*long double* a)   [Runtime Function]
`unsigned long long __fixunsxfti` (*long double* a)   [Runtime Function]
> These functions convert *a* to an unsigned long long, rounding toward zero. Negative values all become zero.

`float __floatsisf` (*int* i)   [Runtime Function]
`double __floatsidf` (*int* i)   [Runtime Function]
`long double __floatsitf` (*int* i)   [Runtime Function]
`long double __floatsixf` (*int* i)   [Runtime Function]
> These functions convert *i*, a signed integer, to floating point.

`float __floatdisf` (*long* i)   [Runtime Function]
`double __floatdidf` (*long* i)   [Runtime Function]
`long double __floatditf` (*long* i)   [Runtime Function]
`long double __floatdixf` (*long* i)   [Runtime Function]
> These functions convert *i*, a signed long, to floating point.

`float __floattisf` (*long long* i)   [Runtime Function]
`double __floattidf` (*long long* i)   [Runtime Function]
`long double __floattitf` (*long long* i)   [Runtime Function]
`long double __floattixf` (*long long* i)   [Runtime Function]
> These functions convert *i*, a signed long long, to floating point.

`float __floatunsisf` (*unsigned int* i)   [Runtime Function]
`double __floatunsidf` (*unsigned int* i)   [Runtime Function]
`long double __floatunsitf` (*unsigned int* i)   [Runtime Function]
`long double __floatunsixf` (*unsigned int* i)   [Runtime Function]
> These functions convert *i*, an unsigned integer, to floating point.

`float __floatundisf` (*unsigned long* i)   [Runtime Function]
`double __floatundidf` (*unsigned long* i)   [Runtime Function]
`long double __floatunditf` (*unsigned long* i)   [Runtime Function]
`long double __floatundixf` (*unsigned long* i)   [Runtime Function]
> These functions convert *i*, an unsigned long, to floating point.

`float __floatuntisf` (*unsigned long long* i)   [Runtime Function]
`double __floatuntidf` (*unsigned long long* i)   [Runtime Function]
`long double __floatuntitf` (*unsigned long long* i)   [Runtime Function]
`long double __floatuntixf` (*unsigned long long* i)   [Runtime Function]
> These functions convert *i*, an unsigned long long, to floating point.

4.2.3 Comparison functions

There are two sets of basic comparison functions.

int __cmpsf2 (*float* a, *float* b)	[Runtime Function]
int __cmpdf2 (*double* a, *double* b)	[Runtime Function]
int __cmptf2 (*long double* a, *long double* b)	[Runtime Function]

These functions calculate $a <=> b$. That is, if a is less than b, they return -1; if a is greater than b, they return 1; and if a and b are equal they return 0. If either argument is NaN they return 1, but you should not rely on this; if NaN is a possibility, use one of the higher-level comparison functions.

int __unordsf2 (*float* a, *float* b)	[Runtime Function]
int __unorddf2 (*double* a, *double* b)	[Runtime Function]
int __unordtf2 (*long double* a, *long double* b)	[Runtime Function]

These functions return a nonzero value if either argument is NaN, otherwise 0.

There is also a complete group of higher level functions which correspond directly to comparison operators. They implement the ISO C semantics for floating-point comparisons, taking NaN into account. Pay careful attention to the return values defined for each set. Under the hood, all of these routines are implemented as

```
if (__unordXf2 (a, b))
   return E;
return __cmpXf2 (a, b);
```

where E is a constant chosen to give the proper behavior for NaN. Thus, the meaning of the return value is different for each set. Do not rely on this implementation; only the semantics documented below are guaranteed.

int __eqsf2 (*float* a, *float* b)	[Runtime Function]
int __eqdf2 (*double* a, *double* b)	[Runtime Function]
int __eqtf2 (*long double* a, *long double* b)	[Runtime Function]

These functions return zero if neither argument is NaN, and a and b are equal.

int __nesf2 (*float* a, *float* b)	[Runtime Function]
int __nedf2 (*double* a, *double* b)	[Runtime Function]
int __netf2 (*long double* a, *long double* b)	[Runtime Function]

These functions return a nonzero value if either argument is NaN, or if a and b are unequal.

int __gesf2 (*float* a, *float* b)	[Runtime Function]
int __gedf2 (*double* a, *double* b)	[Runtime Function]
int __getf2 (*long double* a, *long double* b)	[Runtime Function]

These functions return a value greater than or equal to zero if neither argument is NaN, and a is greater than or equal to b.

int __ltsf2 (*float* a, *float* b)	[Runtime Function]
int __ltdf2 (*double* a, *double* b)	[Runtime Function]
int __lttf2 (*long double* a, *long double* b)	[Runtime Function]

These functions return a value less than zero if neither argument is NaN, and a is strictly less than b.

int __lesf2 (*float* a, *float* b)   [Runtime Function]
int __ledf2 (*double* a, *double* b)   [Runtime Function]
int __letf2 (*long double* a, *long double* b)   [Runtime Function]
> These functions return a value less than or equal to zero if neither argument is NaN,
> and a is less than or equal to b.

int __gtsf2 (*float* a, *float* b)   [Runtime Function]
int __gtdf2 (*double* a, *double* b)   [Runtime Function]
int __gttf2 (*long double* a, *long double* b)   [Runtime Function]
> These functions return a value greater than zero if neither argument is NaN, and a is
> strictly greater than b.

4.2.4 Other floating-point functions

float __powisf2 (*float* a, *int* b)   [Runtime Function]
double __powidf2 (*double* a, *int* b)   [Runtime Function]
long double __powitf2 (*long double* a, *int* b)   [Runtime Function]
long double __powixf2 (*long double* a, *int* b)   [Runtime Function]
> These functions convert raise a to the power b.

complex float __mulsc3 (*float* a, *float* b, *float* c, *float* d)   [Runtime Function]
complex double __muldc3 (*double* a, *double* b, *double* c,   [Runtime Function]
> *double* d)
complex long double __multc3 (*long double* a, *long double*   [Runtime Function]
> b, *long double* c, *long double* d)
complex long double __mulxc3 (*long double* a, *long double*   [Runtime Function]
> b, *long double* c, *long double* d)
> These functions return the product of $a + ib$ and $c + id$, following the rules of C99
> Annex G.

complex float __divsc3 (*float* a, *float* b, *float* c, *float* d)   [Runtime Function]
complex double __divdc3 (*double* a, *double* b, *double* c,   [Runtime Function]
> *double* d)
complex long double __divtc3 (*long double* a, *long double*   [Runtime Function]
> b, *long double* c, *long double* d)
complex long double __divxc3 (*long double* a, *long double*   [Runtime Function]
> b, *long double* c, *long double* d)
> These functions return the quotient of $a + ib$ and $c + id$ (i.e., $(a + ib)/(c + id)$),
> following the rules of C99 Annex G.

4.3 Routines for decimal floating point emulation

The software decimal floating point library implements IEEE 754-2008 decimal floating
point arithmetic and is only activated on selected targets.

The software decimal floating point library supports either DPD (Densely Packed Decimal) or BID (Binary Integer Decimal) encoding as selected at configure time.

4.3.1 Arithmetic functions

_Decimal32 __dpd_addsd3 (_Decimal32 a, _Decimal32 b)   [Runtime Function]
_Decimal32 __bid_addsd3 (_Decimal32 a, _Decimal32 b)   [Runtime Function]
_Decimal64 __dpd_adddd3 (_Decimal64 a, _Decimal64 b)   [Runtime Function]
_Decimal64 __bid_adddd3 (_Decimal64 a, _Decimal64 b)   [Runtime Function]
_Decimal128 __dpd_addtd3 (_Decimal128 a, _Decimal128 b)   [Runtime Function]
_Decimal128 __bid_addtd3 (_Decimal128 a, _Decimal128 b)   [Runtime Function]
    These functions return the sum of a and b.

_Decimal32 __dpd_subsd3 (_Decimal32 a, _Decimal32 b)   [Runtime Function]
_Decimal32 __bid_subsd3 (_Decimal32 a, _Decimal32 b)   [Runtime Function]
_Decimal64 __dpd_subdd3 (_Decimal64 a, _Decimal64 b)   [Runtime Function]
_Decimal64 __bid_subdd3 (_Decimal64 a, _Decimal64 b)   [Runtime Function]
_Decimal128 __dpd_subtd3 (_Decimal128 a, _Decimal128 b)   [Runtime Function]
_Decimal128 __bid_subtd3 (_Decimal128 a, _Decimal128 b)   [Runtime Function]
    These functions return the difference between b and a; that is, $a - b$.

_Decimal32 __dpd_mulsd3 (_Decimal32 a, _Decimal32 b)   [Runtime Function]
_Decimal32 __bid_mulsd3 (_Decimal32 a, _Decimal32 b)   [Runtime Function]
_Decimal64 __dpd_muldd3 (_Decimal64 a, _Decimal64 b)   [Runtime Function]
_Decimal64 __bid_muldd3 (_Decimal64 a, _Decimal64 b)   [Runtime Function]
_Decimal128 __dpd_multd3 (_Decimal128 a, _Decimal128 b)   [Runtime Function]
_Decimal128 __bid_multd3 (_Decimal128 a, _Decimal128 b)   [Runtime Function]
    These functions return the product of a and b.

_Decimal32 __dpd_divsd3 (_Decimal32 a, _Decimal32 b)   [Runtime Function]
_Decimal32 __bid_divsd3 (_Decimal32 a, _Decimal32 b)   [Runtime Function]
_Decimal64 __dpd_divdd3 (_Decimal64 a, _Decimal64 b)   [Runtime Function]
_Decimal64 __bid_divdd3 (_Decimal64 a, _Decimal64 b)   [Runtime Function]
_Decimal128 __dpd_divtd3 (_Decimal128 a, _Decimal128 b)   [Runtime Function]
_Decimal128 __bid_divtd3 (_Decimal128 a, _Decimal128 b)   [Runtime Function]
    These functions return the quotient of a and b; that is, a/b.

_Decimal32 __dpd_negsd2 (_Decimal32 a)   [Runtime Function]
_Decimal32 __bid_negsd2 (_Decimal32 a)   [Runtime Function]
_Decimal64 __dpd_negdd2 (_Decimal64 a)   [Runtime Function]
_Decimal64 __bid_negdd2 (_Decimal64 a)   [Runtime Function]
_Decimal128 __dpd_negtd2 (_Decimal128 a)   [Runtime Function]
_Decimal128 __bid_negtd2 (_Decimal128 a)   [Runtime Function]
    These functions return the negation of a. They simply flip the sign bit, so they can
    produce negative zero and negative NaN.

4.3.2 Conversion functions

_Decimal64 __dpd_extendsddd2 (_Decimal32 a)   [Runtime Function]
_Decimal64 __bid_extendsddd2 (_Decimal32 a)   [Runtime Function]
_Decimal128 __dpd_extendsdtd2 (_Decimal32 a)   [Runtime Function]
_Decimal128 __bid_extendsdtd2 (_Decimal32 a)   [Runtime Function]

_Decimal128 __dpd_extendddtd2 (_Decimal64 a)	[Runtime Function]
_Decimal128 __bid_extendddtd2 (_Decimal64 a)	[Runtime Function]
_Decimal32 __dpd_truncddsd2 (_Decimal64 a)	[Runtime Function]
_Decimal32 __bid_truncddsd2 (_Decimal64 a)	[Runtime Function]
_Decimal32 __dpd_trunctdsd2 (_Decimal128 a)	[Runtime Function]
_Decimal32 __bid_trunctdsd2 (_Decimal128 a)	[Runtime Function]
_Decimal64 __dpd_trunctddd2 (_Decimal128 a)	[Runtime Function]
_Decimal64 __bid_trunctddd2 (_Decimal128 a)	[Runtime Function]

These functions convert the value a from one decimal floating type to another.

_Decimal64 __dpd_extendsfdd (float a)	[Runtime Function]
_Decimal64 __bid_extendsfdd (float a)	[Runtime Function]
_Decimal128 __dpd_extendsftd (float a)	[Runtime Function]
_Decimal128 __bid_extendsftd (float a)	[Runtime Function]
_Decimal128 __dpd_extenddftd (double a)	[Runtime Function]
_Decimal128 __bid_extenddftd (double a)	[Runtime Function]
_Decimal128 __dpd_extendxftd (long double a)	[Runtime Function]
_Decimal128 __bid_extendxftd (long double a)	[Runtime Function]
_Decimal32 __dpd_truncdfsd (double a)	[Runtime Function]
_Decimal32 __bid_truncdfsd (double a)	[Runtime Function]
_Decimal32 __dpd_truncxfsd (long double a)	[Runtime Function]
_Decimal32 __bid_truncxfsd (long double a)	[Runtime Function]
_Decimal32 __dpd_trunctfsd (long double a)	[Runtime Function]
_Decimal32 __bid_trunctfsd (long double a)	[Runtime Function]
_Decimal64 __dpd_truncxfdd (long double a)	[Runtime Function]
_Decimal64 __bid_truncxfdd (long double a)	[Runtime Function]
_Decimal64 __dpd_trunctfdd (long double a)	[Runtime Function]
_Decimal64 __bid_trunctfdd (long double a)	[Runtime Function]

These functions convert the value of a from a binary floating type to a decimal floating type of a different size.

float __dpd_truncddsf (_Decimal64 a)	[Runtime Function]
float __bid_truncddsf (_Decimal64 a)	[Runtime Function]
float __dpd_trunctdsf (_Decimal128 a)	[Runtime Function]
float __bid_trunctdsf (_Decimal128 a)	[Runtime Function]
double __dpd_extendsddf (_Decimal32 a)	[Runtime Function]
double __bid_extendsddf (_Decimal32 a)	[Runtime Function]
double __dpd_trunctddf (_Decimal128 a)	[Runtime Function]
double __bid_trunctddf (_Decimal128 a)	[Runtime Function]
long double __dpd_extendsdxf (_Decimal32 a)	[Runtime Function]
long double __bid_extendsdxf (_Decimal32 a)	[Runtime Function]
long double __dpd_extendddxf (_Decimal64 a)	[Runtime Function]
long double __bid_extendddxf (_Decimal64 a)	[Runtime Function]
long double __dpd_trunctdxf (_Decimal128 a)	[Runtime Function]
long double __bid_trunctdxf (_Decimal128 a)	[Runtime Function]
long double __dpd_extendsdtf (_Decimal32 a)	[Runtime Function]
long double __bid_extendsdtf (_Decimal32 a)	[Runtime Function]
long double __dpd_extendddtf (_Decimal64 a)	[Runtime Function]

long double __bid_extendddtf (_Decimal64 a)   [Runtime Function]
> These functions convert the value of a from a decimal floating type to a binary floating type of a different size.

_Decimal32 __dpd_extendsfsd (*float* a)   [Runtime Function]
_Decimal32 __bid_extendsfsd (*float* a)   [Runtime Function]
_Decimal64 __dpd_extenddfdd (*double* a)   [Runtime Function]
_Decimal64 __bid_extenddfdd (*double* a)   [Runtime Function]
_Decimal128 __dpd_extendtftd (*long double* a)   [Runtime Function]
_Decimal128 __bid_extendtftd (*long double* a)   [Runtime Function]
float __dpd_truncsdsf (_Decimal32 a)   [Runtime Function]
float __bid_truncsdsf (_Decimal32 a)   [Runtime Function]
double __dpd_truncdddf (_Decimal64 a)   [Runtime Function]
double __bid_truncdddf (_Decimal64 a)   [Runtime Function]
long double __dpd_trunctdtf (_Decimal128 a)   [Runtime Function]
long double __bid_trunctdtf (_Decimal128 a)   [Runtime Function]
> These functions convert the value of a between decimal and binary floating types of the same size.

int __dpd_fixsdsi (_Decimal32 a)   [Runtime Function]
int __bid_fixsdsi (_Decimal32 a)   [Runtime Function]
int __dpd_fixddsi (_Decimal64 a)   [Runtime Function]
int __bid_fixddsi (_Decimal64 a)   [Runtime Function]
int __dpd_fixtdsi (_Decimal128 a)   [Runtime Function]
int __bid_fixtdsi (_Decimal128 a)   [Runtime Function]
> These functions convert a to a signed integer.

long __dpd_fixsddi (_Decimal32 a)   [Runtime Function]
long __bid_fixsddi (_Decimal32 a)   [Runtime Function]
long __dpd_fixdddi (_Decimal64 a)   [Runtime Function]
long __bid_fixdddi (_Decimal64 a)   [Runtime Function]
long __dpd_fixtddi (_Decimal128 a)   [Runtime Function]
long __bid_fixtddi (_Decimal128 a)   [Runtime Function]
> These functions convert a to a signed long.

unsigned int __dpd_fixunssdsi (_Decimal32 a)   [Runtime Function]
unsigned int __bid_fixunssdsi (_Decimal32 a)   [Runtime Function]
unsigned int __dpd_fixunsddsi (_Decimal64 a)   [Runtime Function]
unsigned int __bid_fixunsddsi (_Decimal64 a)   [Runtime Function]
unsigned int __dpd_fixunstdsi (_Decimal128 a)   [Runtime Function]
unsigned int __bid_fixunstdsi (_Decimal128 a)   [Runtime Function]
> These functions convert a to an unsigned integer. Negative values all become zero.

unsigned long __dpd_fixunssddi (_Decimal32 a)   [Runtime Function]
unsigned long __bid_fixunssddi (_Decimal32 a)   [Runtime Function]
unsigned long __dpd_fixunsdddi (_Decimal64 a)   [Runtime Function]
unsigned long __bid_fixunsdddi (_Decimal64 a)   [Runtime Function]
unsigned long __dpd_fixunstddi (_Decimal128 a)   [Runtime Function]

unsigned long __bid_fixunstddi (_Decimal128 a)   [Runtime Function]
    These functions convert a to an unsigned long. Negative values all become zero.

_Decimal32 __dpd_floatsisd (int i)   [Runtime Function]
_Decimal32 __bid_floatsisd (int i)   [Runtime Function]
_Decimal64 __dpd_floatsidd (int i)   [Runtime Function]
_Decimal64 __bid_floatsidd (int i)   [Runtime Function]
_Decimal128 __dpd_floatsitd (int i)   [Runtime Function]
_Decimal128 __bid_floatsitd (int i)   [Runtime Function]
    These functions convert i, a signed integer, to decimal floating point.

_Decimal32 __dpd_floatdisd (long i)   [Runtime Function]
_Decimal32 __bid_floatdisd (long i)   [Runtime Function]
_Decimal64 __dpd_floatdidd (long i)   [Runtime Function]
_Decimal64 __bid_floatdidd (long i)   [Runtime Function]
_Decimal128 __dpd_floatditd (long i)   [Runtime Function]
_Decimal128 __bid_floatditd (long i)   [Runtime Function]
    These functions convert i, a signed long, to decimal floating point.

_Decimal32 __dpd_floatunssisd (unsigned int i)   [Runtime Function]
_Decimal32 __bid_floatunssisd (unsigned int i)   [Runtime Function]
_Decimal64 __dpd_floatunssidd (unsigned int i)   [Runtime Function]
_Decimal64 __bid_floatunssidd (unsigned int i)   [Runtime Function]
_Decimal128 __dpd_floatunssitd (unsigned int i)   [Runtime Function]
_Decimal128 __bid_floatunssitd (unsigned int i)   [Runtime Function]
    These functions convert i, an unsigned integer, to decimal floating point.

_Decimal32 __dpd_floatunsdisd (unsigned long i)   [Runtime Function]
_Decimal32 __bid_floatunsdisd (unsigned long i)   [Runtime Function]
_Decimal64 __dpd_floatunsdidd (unsigned long i)   [Runtime Function]
_Decimal64 __bid_floatunsdidd (unsigned long i)   [Runtime Function]
_Decimal128 __dpd_floatunsditd (unsigned long i)   [Runtime Function]
_Decimal128 __bid_floatunsditd (unsigned long i)   [Runtime Function]
    These functions convert i, an unsigned long, to decimal floating point.

4.3.3 Comparison functions

int __dpd_unordsd2 (_Decimal32 a, _Decimal32 b)   [Runtime Function]
int __bid_unordsd2 (_Decimal32 a, _Decimal32 b)   [Runtime Function]
int __dpd_unorddd2 (_Decimal64 a, _Decimal64 b)   [Runtime Function]
int __bid_unorddd2 (_Decimal64 a, _Decimal64 b)   [Runtime Function]
int __dpd_unordtd2 (_Decimal128 a, _Decimal128 b)   [Runtime Function]
int __bid_unordtd2 (_Decimal128 a, _Decimal128 b)   [Runtime Function]
    These functions return a nonzero value if either argument is NaN, otherwise 0.

   There is also a complete group of higher level functions which correspond directly to comparison operators. They implement the ISO C semantics for floating-point comparisons, taking NaN into account. Pay careful attention to the return values defined for each set. Under the hood, all of these routines are implemented as

```
if (__bid_unordXd2 (a, b))
  return E;
return __bid_cmpXd2 (a, b);
```

where E is a constant chosen to give the proper behavior for NaN. Thus, the meaning of the return value is different for each set. Do not rely on this implementation; only the semantics documented below are guaranteed.

int __dpd_eqsd2 (_Decimal32 a, _Decimal32 b)		[Runtime Function]
int __bid_eqsd2 (_Decimal32 a, _Decimal32 b)		[Runtime Function]
int __dpd_eqdd2 (_Decimal64 a, _Decimal64 b)		[Runtime Function]
int __bid_eqdd2 (_Decimal64 a, _Decimal64 b)		[Runtime Function]
int __dpd_eqtd2 (_Decimal128 a, _Decimal128 b)		[Runtime Function]
int __bid_eqtd2 (_Decimal128 a, _Decimal128 b)		[Runtime Function]

These functions return zero if neither argument is NaN, and a and b are equal.

int __dpd_nesd2 (_Decimal32 a, _Decimal32 b)		[Runtime Function]
int __bid_nesd2 (_Decimal32 a, _Decimal32 b)		[Runtime Function]
int __dpd_nedd2 (_Decimal64 a, _Decimal64 b)		[Runtime Function]
int __bid_nedd2 (_Decimal64 a, _Decimal64 b)		[Runtime Function]
int __dpd_netd2 (_Decimal128 a, _Decimal128 b)		[Runtime Function]
int __bid_netd2 (_Decimal128 a, _Decimal128 b)		[Runtime Function]

These functions return a nonzero value if either argument is NaN, or if a and b are unequal.

int __dpd_gesd2 (_Decimal32 a, _Decimal32 b)		[Runtime Function]
int __bid_gesd2 (_Decimal32 a, _Decimal32 b)		[Runtime Function]
int __dpd_gedd2 (_Decimal64 a, _Decimal64 b)		[Runtime Function]
int __bid_gedd2 (_Decimal64 a, _Decimal64 b)		[Runtime Function]
int __dpd_getd2 (_Decimal128 a, _Decimal128 b)		[Runtime Function]
int __bid_getd2 (_Decimal128 a, _Decimal128 b)		[Runtime Function]

These functions return a value greater than or equal to zero if neither argument is NaN, and a is greater than or equal to b.

int __dpd_ltsd2 (_Decimal32 a, _Decimal32 b)		[Runtime Function]
int __bid_ltsd2 (_Decimal32 a, _Decimal32 b)		[Runtime Function]
int __dpd_ltdd2 (_Decimal64 a, _Decimal64 b)		[Runtime Function]
int __bid_ltdd2 (_Decimal64 a, _Decimal64 b)		[Runtime Function]
int __dpd_lttd2 (_Decimal128 a, _Decimal128 b)		[Runtime Function]
int __bid_lttd2 (_Decimal128 a, _Decimal128 b)		[Runtime Function]

These functions return a value less than zero if neither argument is NaN, and a is strictly less than b.

int __dpd_lesd2 (_Decimal32 a, _Decimal32 b)		[Runtime Function]
int __bid_lesd2 (_Decimal32 a, _Decimal32 b)		[Runtime Function]
int __dpd_ledd2 (_Decimal64 a, _Decimal64 b)		[Runtime Function]
int __bid_ledd2 (_Decimal64 a, _Decimal64 b)		[Runtime Function]
int __dpd_letd2 (_Decimal128 a, _Decimal128 b)		[Runtime Function]

int __bid_letd2 (*_Decimal128* a, *_Decimal128* b)   [Runtime Function]
> These functions return a value less than or equal to zero if neither argument is NaN, and a is less than or equal to b.

int __dpd_gtsd2 (*_Decimal32* a, *_Decimal32* b)   [Runtime Function]
int __bid_gtsd2 (*_Decimal32* a, *_Decimal32* b)   [Runtime Function]
int __dpd_gtdd2 (*_Decimal64* a, *_Decimal64* b)   [Runtime Function]
int __bid_gtdd2 (*_Decimal64* a, *_Decimal64* b)   [Runtime Function]
int __dpd_gttd2 (*_Decimal128* a, *_Decimal128* b)   [Runtime Function]
int __bid_gttd2 (*_Decimal128* a, *_Decimal128* b)   [Runtime Function]
> These functions return a value greater than zero if neither argument is NaN, and a is strictly greater than b.

4.4 Routines for fixed-point fractional emulation

The software fixed-point library implements fixed-point fractional arithmetic, and is only activated on selected targets.

For ease of comprehension `fract` is an alias for the `_Fract` type, `accum` an alias for `_Accum`, and `sat` an alias for `_Sat`.

For illustrative purposes, in this section the fixed-point fractional type `short fract` is assumed to correspond to machine mode QQmode; `unsigned short fract` to UQQmode; `fract` to HQmode; `unsigned fract` to UHQmode; `long fract` to SQmode; `unsigned long fract` to USQmode; `long long fract` to DQmode; and `unsigned long long fract` to UDQmode. Similarly the fixed-point accumulator type `short accum` corresponds to HAmode; `unsigned short accum` to UHAmode; `accum` to SAmode; `unsigned accum` to USAmode; `long accum` to DAmode; `unsigned long accum` to UDAmode; `long long accum` to TAmode; and `unsigned long long accum` to UTAmode.

4.4.1 Arithmetic functions

short fract __addqq3 (*short fract* a, *short fract* b)   [Runtime Function]
fract __addhq3 (*fract* a, *fract* b)   [Runtime Function]
long fract __addsq3 (*long fract* a, *long fract* b)   [Runtime Function]
long long fract __adddq3 (*long long fract* a, *long long fract* b) [Runtime Function]
unsigned short fract __adduqq3 (*unsigned short fract* a, *unsigned short fract* b) [Runtime Function]
unsigned fract __adduhq3 (*unsigned fract* a, *unsigned fract* b)   [Runtime Function]
unsigned long fract __addusq3 (*unsigned long fract* a, *unsigned long fract* b)   [Runtime Function]
unsigned long long fract __addudq3 (*unsigned long long fract* a, *unsigned long long fract* b) [Runtime Function]
short accum __addha3 (*short accum* a, *short accum* b)   [Runtime Function]
accum __addsa3 (*accum* a, *accum* b)   [Runtime Function]
long accum __addda3 (*long accum* a, *long accum* b)   [Runtime Function]
long long accum __addta3 (*long long accum* a, *long long accum* b) [Runtime Function]

unsigned short accum __adduha3 (*unsigned short accum* a,   [Runtime Function]
      unsigned short accum b)

unsigned accum __addusa3 (*unsigned accum* a, *unsigned*   [Runtime Function]
      accum b)

unsigned long accum __adduda3 (*unsigned long accum* a,   [Runtime Function]
      unsigned long accum b)

unsigned long long accum __adduta3 (*unsigned long long*   [Runtime Function]
      accum a, *unsigned long long accum* b)

>   These functions return the sum of a and b.

short fract __ssaddqq3 (*short fract* a, *short fract* b)   [Runtime Function]

fract __ssaddhq3 (*fract* a, *fract* b)   [Runtime Function]

long fract __ssaddsq3 (*long fract* a, *long fract* b)   [Runtime Function]

long long fract __ssadddq3 (*long long fract* a, *long long*   [Runtime Function]
      fract b)

short accum __ssaddha3 (*short accum* a, *short accum* b)   [Runtime Function]

accum __ssaddsa3 (*accum* a, *accum* b)   [Runtime Function]

long accum __ssaddda3 (*long accum* a, *long accum* b)   [Runtime Function]

long long accum __ssaddta3 (*long long accum* a, *long long*   [Runtime Function]
      accum b)

>   These functions return the sum of a and b with signed saturation.

unsigned short fract __usadduqq3 (*unsigned short fract* a,   [Runtime Function]
      unsigned short fract b)

unsigned fract __usadduhq3 (*unsigned fract* a, *unsigned*   [Runtime Function]
      fract b)

unsigned long fract __usaddusq3 (*unsigned long fract* a,   [Runtime Function]
      unsigned long fract b)

unsigned long long fract __usaddudq3 (*unsigned long*   [Runtime Function]
      long fract a, *unsigned long long fract* b)

unsigned short accum __usadduha3 (*unsigned short accum*   [Runtime Function]
      a, *unsigned short accum* b)

unsigned accum __usaddusa3 (*unsigned accum* a, *unsigned*   [Runtime Function]
      accum b)

unsigned long accum __usadduda3 (*unsigned long accum* a,   [Runtime Function]
      unsigned long accum b)

unsigned long long accum __usadduta3 (*unsigned long*   [Runtime Function]
      long accum a, *unsigned long long accum* b)

>   These functions return the sum of a and b with unsigned saturation.

short fract __subqq3 (*short fract* a, *short fract* b)   [Runtime Function]

fract __subhq3 (*fract* a, *fract* b)   [Runtime Function]

long fract __subsq3 (*long fract* a, *long fract* b)   [Runtime Function]

long long fract __subdq3 (*long long fract* a, *long long fract*   [Runtime Function]
      b)

unsigned short fract __subuqq3 (*unsigned short fract* a,   [Runtime Function]
      unsigned short fract b)

unsigned fract __subuhq3 (*unsigned fract* **a**, *unsigned fract*   [Runtime Function]
       b)

unsigned long fract __subusq3 (*unsigned long fract* **a**,   [Runtime Function]
       unsigned long fract **b**)

unsigned long long fract __subudq3 (*unsigned long long*   [Runtime Function]
       fract **a**, *unsigned long long fract* **b**)

short accum __subha3 (*short accum* **a**, *short accum* **b**)   [Runtime Function]

accum __subsa3 (*accum* **a**, *accum* **b**)   [Runtime Function]

long accum __subda3 (*long accum* **a**, *long accum* **b**)   [Runtime Function]

long long accum __subta3 (*long long accum* **a**, *long long*   [Runtime Function]
       accum **b**)

unsigned short accum __subuha3 (*unsigned short accum* **a**,   [Runtime Function]
       unsigned short accum **b**)

unsigned accum __subusa3 (*unsigned accum* **a**, *unsigned*   [Runtime Function]
       accum **b**)

unsigned long accum __subuda3 (*unsigned long accum* **a**,   [Runtime Function]
       unsigned long accum **b**)

unsigned long long accum __subuta3 (*unsigned long long*   [Runtime Function]
       accum **a**, *unsigned long long accum* **b**)

      These functions return the difference of *a* and *b*; that is, **a - b**.

short fract __sssubqq3 (*short fract* **a**, *short fract* **b**)   [Runtime Function]

fract __sssubhq3 (*fract* **a**, *fract* **b**)   [Runtime Function]

long fract __sssubsq3 (*long fract* **a**, *long fract* **b**)   [Runtime Function]

long long fract __sssubdq3 (*long long fract* **a**, *long long*   [Runtime Function]
       fract **b**)

short accum __sssubha3 (*short accum* **a**, *short accum* **b**)   [Runtime Function]

accum __sssubsa3 (*accum* **a**, *accum* **b**)   [Runtime Function]

long accum __sssubda3 (*long accum* **a**, *long accum* **b**)   [Runtime Function]

long long accum __sssubta3 (*long long accum* **a**, *long long*   [Runtime Function]
       accum **b**)

      These functions return the difference of *a* and *b* with signed saturation; that is, **a -**
      b.

unsigned short fract __ussubuqq3 (*unsigned short fract* **a**,   [Runtime Function]
       unsigned short fract **b**)

unsigned fract __ussubuhq3 (*unsigned fract* **a**, *unsigned*   [Runtime Function]
       fract **b**)

unsigned long fract __ussubusq3 (*unsigned long fract* **a**,   [Runtime Function]
       unsigned long fract **b**)

unsigned long long fract __ussubudq3 (*unsigned long*   [Runtime Function]
       long fract **a**, *unsigned long long fract* **b**)

unsigned short accum __ussubuha3 (*unsigned short accum*   [Runtime Function]
       a, *unsigned short accum* **b**)

unsigned accum __ussubusa3 (*unsigned accum* **a**, *unsigned*   [Runtime Function]
       accum **b**)

unsigned long accum __ussubuda3 (*unsigned long accum* **a**,   [Runtime Function]
       unsigned long accum **b**)

unsigned long long accum __ussubuta3 (*unsigned long*   [Runtime Function]
      long long accum a, *unsigned long long accum* b)
> These functions return the difference of a and b with unsigned saturation; that is, a - b.

short fract __mulqq3 (*short fract* a, *short fract* b)   [Runtime Function]
fract __mulhq3 (*fract* a, *fract* b)   [Runtime Function]
long fract __mulsq3 (*long fract* a, *long fract* b)   [Runtime Function]
long long fract __muldq3 (*long long fract* a, *long long fract*   [Runtime Function]
      b)
unsigned short fract __muluqq3 (*unsigned short fract* a,   [Runtime Function]
      unsigned short fract b)
unsigned fract __muluhq3 (*unsigned fract* a, *unsigned fract*   [Runtime Function]
      b)
unsigned long fract __mulusq3 (*unsigned long fract* a,   [Runtime Function]
      unsigned long fract b)
unsigned long long fract __muludq3 (*unsigned long long*   [Runtime Function]
      fract a, *unsigned long long fract* b)
short accum __mulha3 (*short accum* a, *short accum* b)   [Runtime Function]
accum __mulsa3 (*accum* a, *accum* b)   [Runtime Function]
long accum __mulda3 (*long accum* a, *long accum* b)   [Runtime Function]
long long accum __multa3 (*long long accum* a, *long long*   [Runtime Function]
      accum b)
unsigned short accum __muluha3 (*unsigned short accum* a,   [Runtime Function]
      unsigned short accum b)
unsigned accum __mulusa3 (*unsigned accum* a, *unsigned*   [Runtime Function]
      accum b)
unsigned long accum __muluda3 (*unsigned long accum* a,   [Runtime Function]
      unsigned long accum b)
unsigned long long accum __muluta3 (*unsigned long long*   [Runtime Function]
      accum a, *unsigned long long accum* b)
> These functions return the product of a and b.

short fract __ssmulqq3 (*short fract* a, *short fract* b)   [Runtime Function]
fract __ssmulhq3 (*fract* a, *fract* b)   [Runtime Function]
long fract __ssmulsq3 (*long fract* a, *long fract* b)   [Runtime Function]
long long fract __ssmuldq3 (*long long fract* a, *long long*   [Runtime Function]
      fract b)
short accum __ssmulha3 (*short accum* a, *short accum* b)   [Runtime Function]
accum __ssmulsa3 (*accum* a, *accum* b)   [Runtime Function]
long accum __ssmulda3 (*long accum* a, *long accum* b)   [Runtime Function]
long long accum __ssmulta3 (*long long accum* a, *long long*   [Runtime Function]
      accum b)
> These functions return the product of a and b with signed saturation.

`unsigned short fract __usmuluqq3` (*unsigned short fract* **a**,   [Runtime Function]
   unsigned short fract **b**)

`unsigned fract __usmuluhq3` (*unsigned fract* **a**, *unsigned*   [Runtime Function]
   fract **b**)

`unsigned long fract __usmulusq3` (*unsigned long fract* **a**,   [Runtime Function]
   unsigned long fract **b**)

`unsigned long long fract __usmuludq3` (*unsigned long*   [Runtime Function]
   long fract **a**, *unsigned long long fract* **b**)

`unsigned short accum __usmuluha3` (*unsigned short accum*   [Runtime Function]
   a, *unsigned short accum* **b**)

`unsigned accum __usmulusa3` (*unsigned accum* **a**, *unsigned*   [Runtime Function]
   accum **b**)

`unsigned long accum __usmuluda3` (*unsigned long accum* **a**,   [Runtime Function]
   unsigned long accum **b**)

`unsigned long long accum __usmuluta3` (*unsigned long*   [Runtime Function]
   long accum **a**, *unsigned long long accum* **b**)

  These functions return the product of *a* and *b* with unsigned saturation.

`short fract __divqq3` (*short fract* **a**, *short fract* **b**)   [Runtime Function]
`fract __divhq3` (*fract* **a**, *fract* **b**)   [Runtime Function]
`long fract __divsq3` (*long fract* **a**, *long fract* **b**)   [Runtime Function]
`long long fract __divdq3` (*long long fract* **a**, *long long fract*   [Runtime Function]
   b)

`short accum __divha3` (*short accum* **a**, *short accum* **b**)   [Runtime Function]
`accum __divsa3` (*accum* **a**, *accum* **b**)   [Runtime Function]
`long accum __divda3` (*long accum* **a**, *long accum* **b**)   [Runtime Function]
`long long accum __divta3` (*long long accum* **a**, *long long*   [Runtime Function]
   accum **b**)

  These functions return the quotient of the signed division of *a* and *b*.

`unsigned short fract __udivuqq3` (*unsigned short fract* **a**,   [Runtime Function]
   unsigned short fract **b**)

`unsigned fract __udivuhq3` (*unsigned fract* **a**, *unsigned fract*   [Runtime Function]
   b)

`unsigned long fract __udivusq3` (*unsigned long fract* **a**,   [Runtime Function]
   unsigned long fract **b**)

`unsigned long long fract __udivudq3` (*unsigned long long*   [Runtime Function]
   fract **a**, *unsigned long long fract* **b**)

`unsigned short accum __udivuha3` (*unsigned short accum* **a**,   [Runtime Function]
   unsigned short accum **b**)

`unsigned accum __udivusa3` (*unsigned accum* **a**, *unsigned*   [Runtime Function]
   accum **b**)

`unsigned long accum __udivuda3` (*unsigned long accum* **a**,   [Runtime Function]
   unsigned long accum **b**)

`unsigned long long accum __udivuta3` (*unsigned long long*   [Runtime Function]
   accum **a**, *unsigned long long accum* **b**)

  These functions return the quotient of the unsigned division of *a* and *b*.

short fract __ssdivqq3 (*short fract* **a**, *short fract* **b**)   [Runtime Function]
fract __ssdivhq3 (*fract* **a**, *fract* **b**)   [Runtime Function]
long fract __ssdivsq3 (*long fract* **a**, *long fract* **b**)   [Runtime Function]
long long fract __ssdivdq3 (*long long fract* **a**, *long long*   [Runtime Function]
    fract **b**)
short accum __ssdivha3 (*short accum* **a**, *short accum* **b**)   [Runtime Function]
accum __ssdivsa3 (*accum* **a**, *accum* **b**)   [Runtime Function]
long accum __ssdivda3 (*long accum* **a**, *long accum* **b**)   [Runtime Function]
long long accum __ssdivta3 (*long long accum* **a**, *long long*   [Runtime Function]
    accum **b**)

> These functions return the quotient of the signed division of *a* and *b* with signed saturation.

unsigned short fract __usdivuqq3 (*unsigned short fract* **a**,   [Runtime Function]
    unsigned short fract **b**)
unsigned fract __usdivuhq3 (*unsigned fract* **a**, *unsigned*   [Runtime Function]
    fract **b**)
unsigned long fract __usdivusq3 (*unsigned long fract* **a**,   [Runtime Function]
    unsigned long fract **b**)
unsigned long long fract __usdivudq3 (*unsigned long*   [Runtime Function]
    long fract **a**, *unsigned long long fract* **b**)
unsigned short accum __usdivuha3 (*unsigned short accum*   [Runtime Function]
    a, *unsigned short accum* **b**)
unsigned accum __usdivusa3 (*unsigned accum* **a**, *unsigned*   [Runtime Function]
    accum **b**)
unsigned long accum __usdivuda3 (*unsigned long accum* **a**,   [Runtime Function]
    unsigned long accum **b**)
unsigned long long accum __usdivuta3 (*unsigned long*   [Runtime Function]
    long accum **a**, *unsigned long long accum* **b**)

> These functions return the quotient of the unsigned division of *a* and *b* with unsigned saturation.

short fract __negqq2 (*short fract* **a**)   [Runtime Function]
fract __neghq2 (*fract* **a**)   [Runtime Function]
long fract __negsq2 (*long fract* **a**)   [Runtime Function]
long long fract __negdq2 (*long long fract* **a**)   [Runtime Function]
unsigned short fract __neguqq2 (*unsigned short fract* **a**)   [Runtime Function]
unsigned fract __neguhq2 (*unsigned fract* **a**)   [Runtime Function]
unsigned long fract __negusq2 (*unsigned long fract* **a**)   [Runtime Function]
unsigned long long fract __negudq2 (*unsigned long long*   [Runtime Function]
    fract **a**)
short accum __negha2 (*short accum* **a**)   [Runtime Function]
accum __negsa2 (*accum* **a**)   [Runtime Function]
long accum __negda2 (*long accum* **a**)   [Runtime Function]
long long accum __negta2 (*long long accum* **a**)   [Runtime Function]
unsigned short accum __neguha2 (*unsigned short accum* **a**)   [Runtime Function]
unsigned accum __negusa2 (*unsigned accum* **a**)   [Runtime Function]
unsigned long accum __neguda2 (*unsigned long accum* **a**)   [Runtime Function]

unsigned long long accum __neguta2 (*unsigned long long*   [Runtime Function]
        accum a)
        These functions return the negation of *a*.

short fract __ssnegqq2 (*short fract* a)   [Runtime Function]
fract __ssneghq2 (*fract* a)   [Runtime Function]
long fract __ssnegsq2 (*long fract* a)   [Runtime Function]
long long fract __ssnegdq2 (*long long fract* a)   [Runtime Function]
short accum __ssnegha2 (*short accum* a)   [Runtime Function]
accum __ssnegsa2 (*accum* a)   [Runtime Function]
long accum __ssnegda2 (*long accum* a)   [Runtime Function]
long long accum __ssnegta2 (*long long accum* a)   [Runtime Function]
        These functions return the negation of *a* with signed saturation.

unsigned short fract __usneguqq2 (*unsigned short fract* a)   [Runtime Function]
unsigned fract __usneguhq2 (*unsigned fract* a)   [Runtime Function]
unsigned long fract __usnegusq2 (*unsigned long fract* a)   [Runtime Function]
unsigned long long fract __usnegudq2 (*unsigned long*   [Runtime Function]
        long fract a)
unsigned short accum __usneguha2 (*unsigned short accum*   [Runtime Function]
        a)
unsigned accum __usnegusa2 (*unsigned accum* a)   [Runtime Function]
unsigned long accum __usneguda2 (*unsigned long accum* a)   [Runtime Function]
unsigned long long accum __usneguta2 (*unsigned long*   [Runtime Function]
        long accum a)
        These functions return the negation of *a* with unsigned saturation.

short fract __ashlqq3 (*short fract* a, *int* b)   [Runtime Function]
fract __ashlhq3 (*fract* a, *int* b)   [Runtime Function]
long fract __ashlsq3 (*long fract* a, *int* b)   [Runtime Function]
long long fract __ashldq3 (*long long fract* a, *int* b)   [Runtime Function]
unsigned short fract __ashluqq3 (*unsigned short fract* a,   [Runtime Function]
        int b)
unsigned fract __ashluhq3 (*unsigned fract* a, *int* b)   [Runtime Function]
unsigned long fract __ashlusq3 (*unsigned long fract* a, *int*   [Runtime Function]
        b)
unsigned long long fract __ashludq3 (*unsigned long long*   [Runtime Function]
        fract a, *int* b)
short accum __ashlha3 (*short accum* a, *int* b)   [Runtime Function]
accum __ashlsa3 (*accum* a, *int* b)   [Runtime Function]
long accum __ashlda3 (*long accum* a, *int* b)   [Runtime Function]
long long accum __ashlta3 (*long long accum* a, *int* b)   [Runtime Function]
unsigned short accum __ashluha3 (*unsigned short accum* a,   [Runtime Function]
        int b)
unsigned accum __ashlusa3 (*unsigned accum* a, *int* b)   [Runtime Function]
unsigned long accum __ashluda3 (*unsigned long accum* a,   [Runtime Function]
        int b)

`unsigned long long accum __ashluta3` (*unsigned long long*   [Runtime Function]
    accum a, *int* b)
> These functions return the result of shifting a left by b bits.

`short fract __ashrqq3` (*short fract* a, *int* b)   [Runtime Function]
`fract __ashrhq3` (*fract* a, *int* b)   [Runtime Function]
`long fract __ashrsq3` (*long fract* a, *int* b)   [Runtime Function]
`long long fract __ashrdq3` (*long long fract* a, *int* b)   [Runtime Function]
`short accum __ashrha3` (*short accum* a, *int* b)   [Runtime Function]
`accum __ashrsa3` (*accum* a, *int* b)   [Runtime Function]
`long accum __ashrda3` (*long accum* a, *int* b)   [Runtime Function]
`long long accum __ashrta3` (*long long accum* a, *int* b)   [Runtime Function]
> These functions return the result of arithmetically shifting a right by b bits.

`unsigned short fract __lshruqq3` (*unsigned short fract* a,   [Runtime Function]
    int b)
`unsigned fract __lshruhq3` (*unsigned fract* a, *int* b)   [Runtime Function]
`unsigned long fract __lshrusq3` (*unsigned long fract* a, *int* [Runtime Function]
    b)
`unsigned long long fract __lshrudq3` (*unsigned long long*   [Runtime Function]
    fract a, *int* b)
`unsigned short accum __lshruha3` (*unsigned short accum* a,   [Runtime Function]
    int b)
`unsigned accum __lshrusa3` (*unsigned accum* a, *int* b)   [Runtime Function]
`unsigned long accum __lshruda3` (*unsigned long accum* a,   [Runtime Function]
    int b)
`unsigned long long accum __lshruta3` (*unsigned long long*   [Runtime Function]
    accum a, *int* b)
> These functions return the result of logically shifting a right by b bits.

`fract __ssashlhq3` (*fract* a, *int* b)   [Runtime Function]
`long fract __ssashlsq3` (*long fract* a, *int* b)   [Runtime Function]
`long long fract __ssashldq3` (*long long fract* a, *int* b)   [Runtime Function]
`short accum __ssashlha3` (*short accum* a, *int* b)   [Runtime Function]
`accum __ssashlsa3` (*accum* a, *int* b)   [Runtime Function]
`long accum __ssashlda3` (*long accum* a, *int* b)   [Runtime Function]
`long long accum __ssashlta3` (*long long accum* a, *int* b)   [Runtime Function]
> These functions return the result of shifting a left by b bits with signed saturation.

`unsigned short fract __usashluqq3` (*unsigned short fract*   [Runtime Function]
    a, *int* b)
`unsigned fract __usashluhq3` (*unsigned fract* a, *int* b)   [Runtime Function]
`unsigned long fract __usashlusq3` (*unsigned long fract* a,   [Runtime Function]
    int b)
`unsigned long long fract __usashludq3` (*unsigned long*   [Runtime Function]
    long fract a, *int* b)
`unsigned short accum __usashluha3` (*unsigned short accum*   [Runtime Function]
    a, *int* b)

`unsigned accum __usashlusa3` (*unsigned accum* **a**, *int* **b**)	[Runtime Function]
`unsigned long accum __usashluda3` (*unsigned long accum* **a**, *int* **b**)	[Runtime Function]
`unsigned long long accum __usashluta3` (*unsigned long long accum* **a**, *int* **b**)	[Runtime Function]

These functions return the result of shifting *a* left by *b* bits with unsigned saturation.

4.4.2 Comparison functions

The following functions implement fixed-point comparisons. These functions implement a low-level compare, upon which the higher level comparison operators (such as less than and greater than or equal to) can be constructed. The returned values lie in the range zero to two, to allow the high-level operators to be implemented by testing the returned result using either signed or unsigned comparison.

`int __cmpqq2` (*short fract* **a**, *short fract* **b**)	[Runtime Function]
`int __cmphq2` (*fract* **a**, *fract* **b**)	[Runtime Function]
`int __cmpsq2` (*long fract* **a**, *long fract* **b**)	[Runtime Function]
`int __cmpdq2` (*long long fract* **a**, *long long fract* **b**)	[Runtime Function]
`int __cmpuqq2` (*unsigned short fract* **a**, *unsigned short fract* **b**)	[Runtime Function]
`int __cmpuhq2` (*unsigned fract* **a**, *unsigned fract* **b**)	[Runtime Function]
`int __cmpusq2` (*unsigned long fract* **a**, *unsigned long fract* **b**)	[Runtime Function]
`int __cmpudq2` (*unsigned long long fract* **a**, *unsigned long long fract* **b**)	[Runtime Function]
`int __cmpha2` (*short accum* **a**, *short accum* **b**)	[Runtime Function]
`int __cmpsa2` (*accum* **a**, *accum* **b**)	[Runtime Function]
`int __cmpda2` (*long accum* **a**, *long accum* **b**)	[Runtime Function]
`int __cmpta2` (*long long accum* **a**, *long long accum* **b**)	[Runtime Function]
`int __cmpuha2` (*unsigned short accum* **a**, *unsigned short accum* **b**)	[Runtime Function]
`int __cmpusa2` (*unsigned accum* **a**, *unsigned accum* **b**)	[Runtime Function]
`int __cmpuda2` (*unsigned long accum* **a**, *unsigned long accum* **b**)	[Runtime Function]
`int __cmputa2` (*unsigned long long accum* **a**, *unsigned long long accum* **b**)	[Runtime Function]

These functions perform a signed or unsigned comparison of *a* and *b* (depending on the selected machine mode). If *a* is less than *b*, they return 0; if *a* is greater than *b*, they return 2; and if *a* and *b* are equal they return 1.

4.4.3 Conversion functions

`fract __fractqqhq2` (*short fract* **a**)	[Runtime Function]
`long fract __fractqqsq2` (*short fract* **a**)	[Runtime Function]
`long long fract __fractqqdq2` (*short fract* **a**)	[Runtime Function]
`short accum __fractqqha` (*short fract* **a**)	[Runtime Function]
`accum __fractqqsa` (*short fract* **a**)	[Runtime Function]
`long accum __fractqqda` (*short fract* **a**)	[Runtime Function]
`long long accum __fractqqta` (*short fract* **a**)	[Runtime Function]
`unsigned short fract __fractqquqq` (*short fract* **a**)	[Runtime Function]
`unsigned fract __fractqquhq` (*short fract* **a**)	[Runtime Function]

unsigned long fract __fractqqusq (*short fract* a)	[Runtime Function]
unsigned long long fract __fractqqudq (*short fract* a)	[Runtime Function]
unsigned short accum __fractqquha (*short fract* a)	[Runtime Function]
unsigned accum __fractqqusa (*short fract* a)	[Runtime Function]
unsigned long accum __fractqquda (*short fract* a)	[Runtime Function]
unsigned long long accum __fractqquta (*short fract* a)	[Runtime Function]
signed char __fractqqqi (*short fract* a)	[Runtime Function]
short __fractqqhi (*short fract* a)	[Runtime Function]
int __fractqqsi (*short fract* a)	[Runtime Function]
long __fractqqdi (*short fract* a)	[Runtime Function]
long long __fractqqti (*short fract* a)	[Runtime Function]
float __fractqqsf (*short fract* a)	[Runtime Function]
double __fractqqdf (*short fract* a)	[Runtime Function]
short fract __fracthqqq2 (*fract* a)	[Runtime Function]
long fract __fracthqsq2 (*fract* a)	[Runtime Function]
long long fract __fracthqdq2 (*fract* a)	[Runtime Function]
short accum __fracthqha (*fract* a)	[Runtime Function]
accum __fracthqsa (*fract* a)	[Runtime Function]
long accum __fracthqda (*fract* a)	[Runtime Function]
long long accum __fracthqta (*fract* a)	[Runtime Function]
unsigned short fract __fracthquqq (*fract* a)	[Runtime Function]
unsigned fract __fracthquhq (*fract* a)	[Runtime Function]
unsigned long fract __fracthqusq (*fract* a)	[Runtime Function]
unsigned long long fract __fracthqudq (*fract* a)	[Runtime Function]
unsigned short accum __fracthquha (*fract* a)	[Runtime Function]
unsigned accum __fracthqusa (*fract* a)	[Runtime Function]
unsigned long accum __fracthquda (*fract* a)	[Runtime Function]
unsigned long long accum __fracthquta (*fract* a)	[Runtime Function]
signed char __fracthqqi (*fract* a)	[Runtime Function]
short __fracthqhi (*fract* a)	[Runtime Function]
int __fracthqsi (*fract* a)	[Runtime Function]
long __fracthqdi (*fract* a)	[Runtime Function]
long long __fracthqti (*fract* a)	[Runtime Function]
float __fracthqsf (*fract* a)	[Runtime Function]
double __fracthqdf (*fract* a)	[Runtime Function]
short fract __fractsqqq2 (*long fract* a)	[Runtime Function]
fract __fractsqhq2 (*long fract* a)	[Runtime Function]
long long fract __fractsqdq2 (*long fract* a)	[Runtime Function]
short accum __fractsqha (*long fract* a)	[Runtime Function]
accum __fractsqsa (*long fract* a)	[Runtime Function]
long accum __fractsqda (*long fract* a)	[Runtime Function]
long long accum __fractsqta (*long fract* a)	[Runtime Function]
unsigned short fract __fractsquqq (*long fract* a)	[Runtime Function]
unsigned fract __fractsquhq (*long fract* a)	[Runtime Function]
unsigned long fract __fractsqusq (*long fract* a)	[Runtime Function]
unsigned long long fract __fractsqudq (*long fract* a)	[Runtime Function]
unsigned short accum __fractsquha (*long fract* a)	[Runtime Function]

unsigned accum `__fractsqusa` (*long fract* a)   [Runtime Function]
unsigned long accum `__fractsquda` (*long fract* a)   [Runtime Function]
unsigned long long accum `__fractsquta` (*long fract* a)   [Runtime Function]
signed char `__fractsqqi` (*long fract* a)   [Runtime Function]
short `__fractsqhi` (*long fract* a)   [Runtime Function]
int `__fractsqsi` (*long fract* a)   [Runtime Function]
long `__fractsqdi` (*long fract* a)   [Runtime Function]
long long `__fractsqti` (*long fract* a)   [Runtime Function]
float `__fractsqsf` (*long fract* a)   [Runtime Function]
double `__fractsqdf` (*long fract* a)   [Runtime Function]
short fract `__fractdqqq2` (*long long fract* a)   [Runtime Function]
fract `__fractdqhq2` (*long long fract* a)   [Runtime Function]
long fract `__fractdqsq2` (*long long fract* a)   [Runtime Function]
short accum `__fractdqha` (*long long fract* a)   [Runtime Function]
accum `__fractdqsa` (*long long fract* a)   [Runtime Function]
long accum `__fractdqda` (*long long fract* a)   [Runtime Function]
long long accum `__fractdqta` (*long long fract* a)   [Runtime Function]
unsigned short fract `__fractdquqq` (*long long fract* a)   [Runtime Function]
unsigned fract `__fractdquhq` (*long long fract* a)   [Runtime Function]
unsigned long fract `__fractdqusq` (*long long fract* a)   [Runtime Function]
unsigned long long fract `__fractdqudq` (*long long fract*   [Runtime Function]
        a)
unsigned short accum `__fractdquha` (*long long fract* a)   [Runtime Function]
unsigned accum `__fractdqusa` (*long long fract* a)   [Runtime Function]
unsigned long accum `__fractdquda` (*long long fract* a)   [Runtime Function]
unsigned long long accum `__fractdquta` (*long long fract*   [Runtime Function]
        a)
signed char `__fractdqqi` (*long long fract* a)   [Runtime Function]
short `__fractdqhi` (*long long fract* a)   [Runtime Function]
int `__fractdqsi` (*long long fract* a)   [Runtime Function]
long `__fractdqdi` (*long long fract* a)   [Runtime Function]
long long `__fractdqti` (*long long fract* a)   [Runtime Function]
float `__fractdqsf` (*long long fract* a)   [Runtime Function]
double `__fractdqdf` (*long long fract* a)   [Runtime Function]
short fract `__fracthaqq` (*short accum* a)   [Runtime Function]
fract `__fracthahq` (*short accum* a)   [Runtime Function]
long fract `__fracthasq` (*short accum* a)   [Runtime Function]
long long fract `__fracthadq` (*short accum* a)   [Runtime Function]
accum `__fracthasa2` (*short accum* a)   [Runtime Function]
long accum `__fracthada2` (*short accum* a)   [Runtime Function]
long long accum `__fracthata2` (*short accum* a)   [Runtime Function]
unsigned short fract `__fracthauqq` (*short accum* a)   [Runtime Function]
unsigned fract `__fracthauhq` (*short accum* a)   [Runtime Function]
unsigned long fract `__fracthausq` (*short accum* a)   [Runtime Function]
unsigned long long fract `__fracthaudq` (*short accum* a)   [Runtime Function]
unsigned short accum `__fracthauha` (*short accum* a)   [Runtime Function]
unsigned accum `__fracthausa` (*short accum* a)   [Runtime Function]

unsigned long accum __fracthauda (*short accum* a)   [Runtime Function]
unsigned long long accum __fracthauta (*short accum* a)   [Runtime Function]
signed char __fracthaqi (*short accum* a)   [Runtime Function]
short __fracthahi (*short accum* a)   [Runtime Function]
int __fracthasi (*short accum* a)   [Runtime Function]
long __fracthadi (*short accum* a)   [Runtime Function]
long long __fracthati (*short accum* a)   [Runtime Function]
float __fracthasf (*short accum* a)   [Runtime Function]
double __fracthadf (*short accum* a)   [Runtime Function]
short fract __fractsaqq (*accum* a)   [Runtime Function]
fract __fractsahq (*accum* a)   [Runtime Function]
long fract __fractsasq (*accum* a)   [Runtime Function]
long long fract __fractsadq (*accum* a)   [Runtime Function]
short accum __fractsaha2 (*accum* a)   [Runtime Function]
long accum __fractsada2 (*accum* a)   [Runtime Function]
long long accum __fractsata2 (*accum* a)   [Runtime Function]
unsigned short fract __fractsauqq (*accum* a)   [Runtime Function]
unsigned fract __fractsauhq (*accum* a)   [Runtime Function]
unsigned long fract __fractsausq (*accum* a)   [Runtime Function]
unsigned long long fract __fractsaudq (*accum* a)   [Runtime Function]
unsigned short accum __fractsauha (*accum* a)   [Runtime Function]
unsigned accum __fractsausa (*accum* a)   [Runtime Function]
unsigned long accum __fractsauda (*accum* a)   [Runtime Function]
unsigned long long accum __fractsauta (*accum* a)   [Runtime Function]
signed char __fractsaqi (*accum* a)   [Runtime Function]
short __fractsahi (*accum* a)   [Runtime Function]
int __fractsasi (*accum* a)   [Runtime Function]
long __fractsadi (*accum* a)   [Runtime Function]
long long __fractsati (*accum* a)   [Runtime Function]
float __fractsasf (*accum* a)   [Runtime Function]
double __fractsadf (*accum* a)   [Runtime Function]
short fract __fractdaqq (*long accum* a)   [Runtime Function]
fract __fractdahq (*long accum* a)   [Runtime Function]
long fract __fractdasq (*long accum* a)   [Runtime Function]
long long fract __fractdadq (*long accum* a)   [Runtime Function]
short accum __fractdaha2 (*long accum* a)   [Runtime Function]
accum __fractdasa2 (*long accum* a)   [Runtime Function]
long long accum __fractdata2 (*long accum* a)   [Runtime Function]
unsigned short fract __fractdauqq (*long accum* a)   [Runtime Function]
unsigned fract __fractdauhq (*long accum* a)   [Runtime Function]
unsigned long fract __fractdausq (*long accum* a)   [Runtime Function]
unsigned long long fract __fractdaudq (*long accum* a)   [Runtime Function]
unsigned short accum __fractdauha (*long accum* a)   [Runtime Function]
unsigned accum __fractdausa (*long accum* a)   [Runtime Function]
unsigned long accum __fractdauda (*long accum* a)   [Runtime Function]
unsigned long long accum __fractdauta (*long accum* a)   [Runtime Function]
signed char __fractdaqi (*long accum* a)   [Runtime Function]

short __fractdahi (*long accum* a)   [Runtime Function]

int __fractdasi (*long accum* a)   [Runtime Function]

long __fractdadi (*long accum* a)   [Runtime Function]

long long __fractdati (*long accum* a)   [Runtime Function]

float __fractdasf (*long accum* a)   [Runtime Function]

double __fractdadf (*long accum* a)   [Runtime Function]

short fract __fracttaqq (*long long accum* a)   [Runtime Function]

fract __fracttahq (*long long accum* a)   [Runtime Function]

long fract __fracttasq (*long long accum* a)   [Runtime Function]

long long fract __fracttadq (*long long accum* a)   [Runtime Function]

short accum __fracttaha2 (*long long accum* a)   [Runtime Function]

accum __fracttasa2 (*long long accum* a)   [Runtime Function]

long accum __fracttada2 (*long long accum* a)   [Runtime Function]

unsigned short fract __fracttauqq (*long long accum* a)   [Runtime Function]

unsigned fract __fracttauhq (*long long accum* a)   [Runtime Function]

unsigned long fract __fracttausq (*long long accum* a)   [Runtime Function]

unsigned long long fract __fracttaudq (*long long accum*   [Runtime Function]
    a)

unsigned short accum __fracttauha (*long long accum* a)   [Runtime Function]

unsigned accum __fracttausa (*long long accum* a)   [Runtime Function]

unsigned long accum __fracttauda (*long long accum* a)   [Runtime Function]

unsigned long long accum __fracttauta (*long long accum*   [Runtime Function]
    a)

signed char __fracttaqi (*long long accum* a)   [Runtime Function]

short __fracttahi (*long long accum* a)   [Runtime Function]

int __fracttasi (*long long accum* a)   [Runtime Function]

long __fracttadi (*long long accum* a)   [Runtime Function]

long long __fracttati (*long long accum* a)   [Runtime Function]

float __fracttasf (*long long accum* a)   [Runtime Function]

double __fracttadf (*long long accum* a)   [Runtime Function]

short fract __fractuqqqq (*unsigned short fract* a)   [Runtime Function]

fract __fractuqqhq (*unsigned short fract* a)   [Runtime Function]

long fract __fractuqqsq (*unsigned short fract* a)   [Runtime Function]

long long fract __fractuqqdq (*unsigned short fract* a)   [Runtime Function]

short accum __fractuqqha (*unsigned short fract* a)   [Runtime Function]

accum __fractuqqsa (*unsigned short fract* a)   [Runtime Function]

long accum __fractuqqda (*unsigned short fract* a)   [Runtime Function]

long long accum __fractuqqta (*unsigned short fract* a)   [Runtime Function]

unsigned fract __fractuqquhq2 (*unsigned short fract* a)   [Runtime Function]

unsigned long fract __fractuqqusq2 (*unsigned short fract*   [Runtime Function]
    a)

unsigned long long fract __fractuqqudq2 (*unsigned*   [Runtime Function]
    short fract a)

unsigned short accum __fractuqquha (*unsigned short fract*   [Runtime Function]
    a)

unsigned accum __fractuqqusa (*unsigned short fract* a)   [Runtime Function] unsigned long accum __fractuqquda (*unsigned short fract* **a**) [Runtime Function]

unsigned long long accum __fractuqquta (*unsigned short fract* **a**) [Runtime Function]

signed char __fractuqqqi (*unsigned short fract* **a**) [Runtime Function]

short __fractuqqhi (*unsigned short fract* **a**) [Runtime Function]

int __fractuqqsi (*unsigned short fract* **a**) [Runtime Function]

long __fractuqqdi (*unsigned short fract* **a**) [Runtime Function]

long long __fractuqqti (*unsigned short fract* **a**) [Runtime Function]

float __fractuqqsf (*unsigned short fract* **a**) [Runtime Function]

double __fractuqqdf (*unsigned short fract* **a**) [Runtime Function]

short fract __fractuhqqq (*unsigned fract* **a**) [Runtime Function]

fract __fractuhqhq (*unsigned fract* **a**) [Runtime Function]

long fract __fractuhqsq (*unsigned fract* **a**) [Runtime Function]

long long fract __fractuhqdq (*unsigned fract* **a**) [Runtime Function]

short accum __fractuhqha (*unsigned fract* **a**) [Runtime Function]

accum __fractuhqsa (*unsigned fract* **a**) [Runtime Function]

long accum __fractuhqda (*unsigned fract* **a**) [Runtime Function]

long long accum __fractuhqta (*unsigned fract* **a**) [Runtime Function]

unsigned short fract __fractuhquqq2 (*unsigned fract* **a**) [Runtime Function]

unsigned long fract __fractuhqusq2 (*unsigned fract* **a**) [Runtime Function]

unsigned long long fract __fractuhqudq2 (*unsigned fract* **a**) [Runtime Function]

unsigned short accum __fractuhquha (*unsigned fract* **a**) [Runtime Function]

unsigned accum __fractuhqusa (*unsigned fract* **a**) [Runtime Function]

unsigned long accum __fractuhquda (*unsigned fract* **a**) [Runtime Function]

unsigned long long accum __fractuhquta (*unsigned fract* **a**) [Runtime Function]

signed char __fractuhqqi (*unsigned fract* **a**) [Runtime Function]

short __fractuhqhi (*unsigned fract* **a**) [Runtime Function]

int __fractuhqsi (*unsigned fract* **a**) [Runtime Function]

long __fractuhqdi (*unsigned fract* **a**) [Runtime Function]

long long __fractuhqti (*unsigned fract* **a**) [Runtime Function]

float __fractuhqsf (*unsigned fract* **a**) [Runtime Function]

double __fractuhqdf (*unsigned fract* **a**) [Runtime Function]

short fract __fractusqqq (*unsigned long fract* **a**) [Runtime Function]

fract __fractusqhq (*unsigned long fract* **a**) [Runtime Function]

long fract __fractusqsq (*unsigned long fract* **a**) [Runtime Function]

long long fract __fractusqdq (*unsigned long fract* **a**) [Runtime Function]

short accum __fractusqha (*unsigned long fract* **a**) [Runtime Function]

accum __fractusqsa (*unsigned long fract* **a**) [Runtime Function]

long accum __fractusqda (*unsigned long fract* **a**) [Runtime Function]

long long accum __fractusqta (*unsigned long fract* **a**) [Runtime Function]

unsigned short fract __fractusquqq2 (*unsigned long fract* **a**) [Runtime Function]

unsigned fract __fractusquhq2 (*unsigned long fract* **a**) [Runtime Function]

`unsigned long long fract __fractusqudq2` (*unsigned long*   [Runtime Function]
       fract **a**)

`unsigned short accum __fractusquha` (*unsigned long fract*   [Runtime Function]
       a)

`unsigned accum __fractusqusa` (*unsigned long fract* **a**)   [Runtime Function]

`unsigned long accum __fractusquda` (*unsigned long fract* **a**) [Runtime Function]

`unsigned long long accum __fractusquta` (*unsigned long*   [Runtime Function]
       fract **a**)

`signed char __fractusqqi` (*unsigned long fract* **a**)   [Runtime Function]

`short __fractusqhi` (*unsigned long fract* **a**)   [Runtime Function]

`int __fractusqsi` (*unsigned long fract* **a**)   [Runtime Function]

`long __fractusqdi` (*unsigned long fract* **a**)   [Runtime Function]

`long long __fractusqti` (*unsigned long fract* **a**)   [Runtime Function]

`float __fractusqsf` (*unsigned long fract* **a**)   [Runtime Function]

`double __fractusqdf` (*unsigned long fract* **a**)   [Runtime Function]

`short fract __fractudqqq` (*unsigned long long fract* **a**)   [Runtime Function]

`fract __fractudqhq` (*unsigned long long fract* **a**)   [Runtime Function]

`long fract __fractudqsq` (*unsigned long long fract* **a**)   [Runtime Function]

`long long fract __fractudqdq` (*unsigned long long fract* **a**) [Runtime Function]

`short accum __fractudqha` (*unsigned long long fract* **a**)   [Runtime Function]

`accum __fractudqsa` (*unsigned long long fract* **a**)   [Runtime Function]

`long accum __fractudqda` (*unsigned long long fract* **a**)   [Runtime Function]

`long long accum __fractudqta` (*unsigned long long fract* **a**) [Runtime Function]

`unsigned short fract __fractudquqq2` (*unsigned long long*   [Runtime Function]
       fract **a**)

`unsigned fract __fractudquhq2` (*unsigned long long fract* **a**) [Runtime Function]

`unsigned long fract __fractudqusq2` (*unsigned long long*   [Runtime Function]
       fract **a**)

`unsigned short accum __fractudquha` (*unsigned long long*   [Runtime Function]
       fract **a**)

`unsigned accum __fractudqusa` (*unsigned long long fract* **a**) [Runtime Function]

`unsigned long accum __fractudquda` (*unsigned long long*   [Runtime Function]
       fract **a**)

`unsigned long long accum __fractudquta` (*unsigned long*   [Runtime Function]
       long fract **a**)

`signed char __fractudqqi` (*unsigned long long fract* **a**)   [Runtime Function]

`short __fractudqhi` (*unsigned long long fract* **a**)   [Runtime Function]

`int __fractudqsi` (*unsigned long long fract* **a**)   [Runtime Function]

`long __fractudqdi` (*unsigned long long fract* **a**)   [Runtime Function]

`long long __fractudqti` (*unsigned long long fract* **a**)   [Runtime Function]

`float __fractudqsf` (*unsigned long long fract* **a**)   [Runtime Function]

`double __fractudqdf` (*unsigned long long fract* **a**)   [Runtime Function]

`short fract __fractuhaqq` (*unsigned short accum* **a**)   [Runtime Function]

`fract __fractuhahq` (*unsigned short accum* **a**)   [Runtime Function]

`long fract __fractuhasq` (*unsigned short accum* **a**)   [Runtime Function]

`long long fract __fractuhadq` (*unsigned short accum* **a**)   [Runtime Function]

`short accum __fractuhaha` (*unsigned short accum* **a**)   [Runtime Function]

accum __fractuhasa (*unsigned short accum* a)   [Runtime Function]
long accum __fractuhada (*unsigned short accum* a)   [Runtime Function]
long long accum __fractuhata (*unsigned short accum* a)   [Runtime Function]
unsigned short fract __fractuhauqq (*unsigned short   [Runtime Function]
    accum* a)
unsigned fract __fractuhauhq (*unsigned short accum* a)   [Runtime Function]
unsigned long fract __fractuhausq (*unsigned short accum   [Runtime Function]
    a*)
unsigned long long fract __fractuhaudq (*unsigned short   [Runtime Function]
    accum* a)
unsigned accum __fractuhausa2 (*unsigned short accum* a)   [Runtime Function]
unsigned long accum __fractuhauda2 (*unsigned short   [Runtime Function]
    accum* a)
unsigned long long accum __fractuhauta2 (*unsigned   [Runtime Function]
    short accum* a)
signed char __fractuhaqi (*unsigned short accum* a)   [Runtime Function]
short __fractuhahi (*unsigned short accum* a)   [Runtime Function]
int __fractuhasi (*unsigned short accum* a)   [Runtime Function]
long __fractuhadi (*unsigned short accum* a)   [Runtime Function]
long long __fractuhati (*unsigned short accum* a)   [Runtime Function]
float __fractuhasf (*unsigned short accum* a)   [Runtime Function]
double __fractuhadf (*unsigned short accum* a)   [Runtime Function]
short fract __fractusaqq (*unsigned accum* a)   [Runtime Function]
fract __fractusahq (*unsigned accum* a)   [Runtime Function]
long fract __fractusasq (*unsigned accum* a)   [Runtime Function]
long long fract __fractusadq (*unsigned accum* a)   [Runtime Function]
short accum __fractusaha (*unsigned accum* a)   [Runtime Function]
accum __fractusasa (*unsigned accum* a)   [Runtime Function]
long accum __fractusada (*unsigned accum* a)   [Runtime Function]
long long accum __fractusata (*unsigned accum* a)   [Runtime Function]
unsigned short fract __fractusauqq (*unsigned accum* a)   [Runtime Function]
unsigned fract __fractusauhq (*unsigned accum* a)   [Runtime Function]
unsigned long fract __fractusausq (*unsigned accum* a)   [Runtime Function]
unsigned long long fract __fractusaudq (*unsigned   [Runtime Function]
    accum* a)
unsigned short accum __fractusauha2 (*unsigned accum* a)   [Runtime Function]
unsigned long accum __fractusauda2 (*unsigned accum* a)   [Runtime Function]
unsigned long long accum __fractusauta2 (*unsigned   [Runtime Function]
    accum* a)
signed char __fractusaqi (*unsigned accum* a)   [Runtime Function]
short __fractusahi (*unsigned accum* a)   [Runtime Function]
int __fractusasi (*unsigned accum* a)   [Runtime Function]
long __fractusadi (*unsigned accum* a)   [Runtime Function]
long long __fractusati (*unsigned accum* a)   [Runtime Function]
float __fractusasf (*unsigned accum* a)   [Runtime Function]
double __fractusadf (*unsigned accum* a)   [Runtime Function]
short fract __fractudaqq (*unsigned long accum* a)   [Runtime Function]

`fract __fractudahq` (*unsigned long accum* a)   [Runtime Function]

`long fract __fractudasq` (*unsigned long accum* a)   [Runtime Function]

`long long fract __fractudadq` (*unsigned long accum* a)   [Runtime Function]

`short accum __fractudaha` (*unsigned long accum* a)   [Runtime Function]

`accum __fractudasa` (*unsigned long accum* a)   [Runtime Function]

`long accum __fractudada` (*unsigned long accum* a)   [Runtime Function]

`long long accum __fractudata` (*unsigned long accum* a)   [Runtime Function]

`unsigned short fract __fractudauqq` (*unsigned long   [Runtime Function]
        accum* a)

`unsigned fract __fractudauhq` (*unsigned long accum* a)   [Runtime Function]

`unsigned long fract __fractudausq` (*unsigned long accum*   [Runtime Function]
        a)

`unsigned long long fract __fractudaudq` (*unsigned long   [Runtime Function]
        accum* a)

`unsigned short accum __fractudauha2` (*unsigned long   [Runtime Function]
        accum* a)

`unsigned accum __fractudausa2` (*unsigned long accum* a)   [Runtime Function]

`unsigned long long accum __fractudauta2` (*unsigned long   [Runtime Function]
        accum* a)

`signed char __fractudaqi` (*unsigned long accum* a)   [Runtime Function]

`short __fractudahi` (*unsigned long accum* a)   [Runtime Function]

`int __fractudasi` (*unsigned long accum* a)   [Runtime Function]

`long __fractudadi` (*unsigned long accum* a)   [Runtime Function]

`long long __fractudati` (*unsigned long accum* a)   [Runtime Function]

`float __fractudasf` (*unsigned long accum* a)   [Runtime Function]

`double __fractudadf` (*unsigned long accum* a)   [Runtime Function]

`short fract __fractutaqq` (*unsigned long long accum* a)   [Runtime Function]

`fract __fractutahq` (*unsigned long long accum* a)   [Runtime Function]

`long fract __fractutasq` (*unsigned long long accum* a)   [Runtime Function]

`long long fract __fractutadq` (*unsigned long long accum* a)   [Runtime Function]

`short accum __fractutaha` (*unsigned long long accum* a)   [Runtime Function]

`accum __fractutasa` (*unsigned long long accum* a)   [Runtime Function]

`long accum __fractutada` (*unsigned long long accum* a)   [Runtime Function]

`long long accum __fractutata` (*unsigned long long accum* a)   [Runtime Function]

`unsigned short fract __fractutauqq` (*unsigned long long   [Runtime Function]
        accum* a)

`unsigned fract __fractutauhq` (*unsigned long long accum* a)   [Runtime Function]

`unsigned long fract __fractutausq` (*unsigned long long   [Runtime Function]
        accum* a)

`unsigned long long fract __fractutaudq` (*unsigned long   [Runtime Function]
        long accum* a)

`unsigned short accum __fractutauha2` (*unsigned long long   [Runtime Function]
        accum* a)

`unsigned accum __fractutausa2` (*unsigned long long accum*   [Runtime Function]
        a)

`unsigned long accum __fractutauda2` (*unsigned long long   [Runtime Function]
        accum* a)

signed char __fractutaqi (*unsigned long long accum* a)   [Runtime Function]
short __fractutahi (*unsigned long long accum* a)   [Runtime Function]
int __fractutasi (*unsigned long long accum* a)   [Runtime Function]
long __fractutadi (*unsigned long long accum* a)   [Runtime Function]
long long __fractutati (*unsigned long long accum* a)   [Runtime Function]
float __fractutasf (*unsigned long long accum* a)   [Runtime Function]
double __fractutadf (*unsigned long long accum* a)   [Runtime Function]
short fract __fractqiqq (*signed char* a)   [Runtime Function]
fract __fractqihq (*signed char* a)   [Runtime Function]
long fract __fractqisq (*signed char* a)   [Runtime Function]
long long fract __fractqidq (*signed char* a)   [Runtime Function]
short accum __fractqiha (*signed char* a)   [Runtime Function]
accum __fractqisa (*signed char* a)   [Runtime Function]
long accum __fractqida (*signed char* a)   [Runtime Function]
long long accum __fractqita (*signed char* a)   [Runtime Function]
unsigned short fract __fractqiuqq (*signed char* a)   [Runtime Function]
unsigned fract __fractqiuhq (*signed char* a)   [Runtime Function]
unsigned long fract __fractqiusq (*signed char* a)   [Runtime Function]
unsigned long long fract __fractqiudq (*signed char* a)   [Runtime Function]
unsigned short accum __fractqiuha (*signed char* a)   [Runtime Function]
unsigned accum __fractqiusa (*signed char* a)   [Runtime Function]
unsigned long accum __fractqiuda (*signed char* a)   [Runtime Function]
unsigned long long accum __fractqiuta (*signed char* a)   [Runtime Function]
short fract __fracthiqq (*short* a)   [Runtime Function]
fract __fracthihq (*short* a)   [Runtime Function]
long fract __fracthisq (*short* a)   [Runtime Function]
long long fract __fracthidq (*short* a)   [Runtime Function]
short accum __fracthiha (*short* a)   [Runtime Function]
accum __fracthisa (*short* a)   [Runtime Function]
long accum __fracthida (*short* a)   [Runtime Function]
long long accum __fracthita (*short* a)   [Runtime Function]
unsigned short fract __fracthiuqq (*short* a)   [Runtime Function]
unsigned fract __fracthiuhq (*short* a)   [Runtime Function]
unsigned long fract __fracthiusq (*short* a)   [Runtime Function]
unsigned long long fract __fracthiudq (*short* a)   [Runtime Function]
unsigned short accum __fracthiuha (*short* a)   [Runtime Function]
unsigned accum __fracthiusa (*short* a)   [Runtime Function]
unsigned long accum __fracthiuda (*short* a)   [Runtime Function]
unsigned long long accum __fracthiuta (*short* a)   [Runtime Function]
short fract __fractsiqq (*int* a)   [Runtime Function]
fract __fractsihq (*int* a)   [Runtime Function]
long fract __fractsisq (*int* a)   [Runtime Function]
long long fract __fractsidq (*int* a)   [Runtime Function]
short accum __fractsiha (*int* a)   [Runtime Function]
accum __fractsisa (*int* a)   [Runtime Function]
long accum __fractsida (*int* a)   [Runtime Function]
long long accum __fractsita (*int* a)   [Runtime Function]

unsigned short fract __fractsiuqq (*int* a)   [Runtime Function]
unsigned fract __fractsiuhq (*int* a)   [Runtime Function]
unsigned long fract __fractsiusq (*int* a)   [Runtime Function]
unsigned long long fract __fractsiudq (*int* a)   [Runtime Function]
unsigned short accum __fractsiuha (*int* a)   [Runtime Function]
unsigned accum __fractsiusa (*int* a)   [Runtime Function]
unsigned long accum __fractsiuda (*int* a)   [Runtime Function]
unsigned long long accum __fractsiuta (*int* a)   [Runtime Function]
short fract __fractdiqq (*long* a)   [Runtime Function]
fract __fractdihq (*long* a)   [Runtime Function]
long fract __fractdisq (*long* a)   [Runtime Function]
long long fract __fractdidq (*long* a)   [Runtime Function]
short accum __fractdiha (*long* a)   [Runtime Function]
accum __fractdisa (*long* a)   [Runtime Function]
long accum __fractdida (*long* a)   [Runtime Function]
long long accum __fractdita (*long* a)   [Runtime Function]
unsigned short fract __fractdiuqq (*long* a)   [Runtime Function]
unsigned fract __fractdiuhq (*long* a)   [Runtime Function]
unsigned long fract __fractdiusq (*long* a)   [Runtime Function]
unsigned long long fract __fractdiudq (*long* a)   [Runtime Function]
unsigned short accum __fractdiuha (*long* a)   [Runtime Function]
unsigned accum __fractdiusa (*long* a)   [Runtime Function]
unsigned long accum __fractdiuda (*long* a)   [Runtime Function]
unsigned long long accum __fractdiuta (*long* a)   [Runtime Function]
short fract __fracttiqq (*long long* a)   [Runtime Function]
fract __fracttihq (*long long* a)   [Runtime Function]
long fract __fracttisq (*long long* a)   [Runtime Function]
long long fract __fracttidq (*long long* a)   [Runtime Function]
short accum __fracttiha (*long long* a)   [Runtime Function]
accum __fracttisa (*long long* a)   [Runtime Function]
long accum __fracttida (*long long* a)   [Runtime Function]
long long accum __fracttita (*long long* a)   [Runtime Function]
unsigned short fract __fracttiuqq (*long long* a)   [Runtime Function]
unsigned fract __fracttiuhq (*long long* a)   [Runtime Function]
unsigned long fract __fracttiusq (*long long* a)   [Runtime Function]
unsigned long long fract __fracttiudq (*long long* a)   [Runtime Function]
unsigned short accum __fracttiuha (*long long* a)   [Runtime Function]
unsigned accum __fracttiusa (*long long* a)   [Runtime Function]
unsigned long accum __fracttiuda (*long long* a)   [Runtime Function]
unsigned long long accum __fracttiuta (*long long* a)   [Runtime Function]
short fract __fractsfqq (*float* a)   [Runtime Function]
fract __fractsfhq (*float* a)   [Runtime Function]
long fract __fractsfsq (*float* a)   [Runtime Function]
long long fract __fractsfdq (*float* a)   [Runtime Function]
short accum __fractsfha (*float* a)   [Runtime Function]
accum __fractsfsa (*float* a)   [Runtime Function]
long accum __fractsfda (*float* a)   [Runtime Function]

`long long accum __fractsfta` (*float* a)	[Runtime Function]
`unsigned short fract __fractsfuqq` (*float* a)	[Runtime Function]
`unsigned fract __fractsfuhq` (*float* a)	[Runtime Function]
`unsigned long fract __fractsfusq` (*float* a)	[Runtime Function]
`unsigned long long fract __fractsfudq` (*float* a)	[Runtime Function]
`unsigned short accum __fractsfuha` (*float* a)	[Runtime Function]
`unsigned accum __fractsfusa` (*float* a)	[Runtime Function]
`unsigned long accum __fractsfuda` (*float* a)	[Runtime Function]
`unsigned long long accum __fractsfuta` (*float* a)	[Runtime Function]
`short fract __fractdfqq` (*double* a)	[Runtime Function]
`fract __fractdfhq` (*double* a)	[Runtime Function]
`long fract __fractdfsq` (*double* a)	[Runtime Function]
`long long fract __fractdfdq` (*double* a)	[Runtime Function]
`short accum __fractdfha` (*double* a)	[Runtime Function]
`accum __fractdfsa` (*double* a)	[Runtime Function]
`long accum __fractdfda` (*double* a)	[Runtime Function]
`long long accum __fractdfta` (*double* a)	[Runtime Function]
`unsigned short fract __fractdfuqq` (*double* a)	[Runtime Function]
`unsigned fract __fractdfuhq` (*double* a)	[Runtime Function]
`unsigned long fract __fractdfusq` (*double* a)	[Runtime Function]
`unsigned long long fract __fractdfudq` (*double* a)	[Runtime Function]
`unsigned short accum __fractdfuha` (*double* a)	[Runtime Function]
`unsigned accum __fractdfusa` (*double* a)	[Runtime Function]
`unsigned long accum __fractdfuda` (*double* a)	[Runtime Function]
`unsigned long long accum __fractdfuta` (*double* a)	[Runtime Function]

These functions convert from fractional and signed non-fractionals to fractionals and signed non-fractionals, without saturation.

`fract __satfractqqhq2` (*short fract* a)	[Runtime Function]
`long fract __satfractqqsq2` (*short fract* a)	[Runtime Function]
`long long fract __satfractqqdq2` (*short fract* a)	[Runtime Function]
`short accum __satfractqqha` (*short fract* a)	[Runtime Function]
`accum __satfractqqsa` (*short fract* a)	[Runtime Function]
`long accum __satfractqqda` (*short fract* a)	[Runtime Function]
`long long accum __satfractqqta` (*short fract* a)	[Runtime Function]
`unsigned short fract __satfractqquqq` (*short fract* a)	[Runtime Function]
`unsigned fract __satfractqquhq` (*short fract* a)	[Runtime Function]
`unsigned long fract __satfractqqusq` (*short fract* a)	[Runtime Function]
`unsigned long long fract __satfractqqudq` (*short fract* a)	[Runtime Function]
`unsigned short accum __satfractqquha` (*short fract* a)	[Runtime Function]
`unsigned accum __satfractqqusa` (*short fract* a)	[Runtime Function]
`unsigned long accum __satfractqquda` (*short fract* a)	[Runtime Function]
`unsigned long long accum __satfractqquta` (*short fract* a)	[Runtime Function]
`short fract __satfracthqqq2` (*fract* a)	[Runtime Function]
`long fract __satfracthqsq2` (*fract* a)	[Runtime Function]

`long long fract __satfracthqdq2 (`*fract* `a)`   [Runtime Function]

`short accum __satfracthqha (`*fract* `a)`   [Runtime Function]

`accum __satfracthqsa (`*fract* `a)`   [Runtime Function]

`long accum __satfracthqda (`*fract* `a)`   [Runtime Function]

`long long accum __satfracthqta (`*fract* `a)`   [Runtime Function]

`unsigned short fract __satfracthquqq (`*fract* `a)`   [Runtime Function]

`unsigned fract __satfracthquhq (`*fract* `a)`   [Runtime Function]

`unsigned long fract __satfracthqusq (`*fract* `a)`   [Runtime Function]

`unsigned long long fract __satfracthqudq (`*fract* `a)`   [Runtime Function]

`unsigned short accum __satfracthquha (`*fract* `a)`   [Runtime Function]

`unsigned accum __satfracthqusa (`*fract* `a)`   [Runtime Function]

`unsigned long accum __satfracthquda (`*fract* `a)`   [Runtime Function]

`unsigned long long accum __satfracthquta (`*fract* `a)`   [Runtime Function]

`short fract __satfractsqqq2 (`*long fract* `a)`   [Runtime Function]

`fract __satfractsqhq2 (`*long fract* `a)`   [Runtime Function]

`long long fract __satfractsqdq2 (`*long fract* `a)`   [Runtime Function]

`short accum __satfractsqha (`*long fract* `a)`   [Runtime Function]

`accum __satfractsqsa (`*long fract* `a)`   [Runtime Function]

`long accum __satfractsqda (`*long fract* `a)`   [Runtime Function]

`long long accum __satfractsqta (`*long fract* `a)`   [Runtime Function]

`unsigned short fract __satfractsquqq (`*long fract* `a)`   [Runtime Function]

`unsigned fract __satfractsquhq (`*long fract* `a)`   [Runtime Function]

`unsigned long fract __satfractsqusq (`*long fract* `a)`   [Runtime Function]

`unsigned long long fract __satfractsqudq (`*long fract* `a)`   [Runtime Function]

`unsigned short accum __satfractsquha (`*long fract* `a)`   [Runtime Function]

`unsigned accum __satfractsqusa (`*long fract* `a)`   [Runtime Function]

`unsigned long accum __satfractsquda (`*long fract* `a)`   [Runtime Function]

`unsigned long long accum __satfractsquta (`*long fract* `a)`   [Runtime Function]

`short fract __satfractdqqq2 (`*long long fract* `a)`   [Runtime Function]

`fract __satfractdqhq2 (`*long long fract* `a)`   [Runtime Function]

`long fract __satfractdqsq2 (`*long long fract* `a)`   [Runtime Function]

`short accum __satfractdqha (`*long long fract* `a)`   [Runtime Function]

`accum __satfractdqsa (`*long long fract* `a)`   [Runtime Function]

`long accum __satfractdqda (`*long long fract* `a)`   [Runtime Function]

`long long accum __satfractdqta (`*long long fract* `a)`   [Runtime Function]

`unsigned short fract __satfractdquqq (`*long long fract* `a)`   [Runtime Function]

`unsigned fract __satfractdquhq (`*long long fract* `a)`   [Runtime Function]

`unsigned long fract __satfractdqusq (`*long long fract* `a)`   [Runtime Function]

`unsigned long long fract __satfractdqudq (`*long long*   [Runtime Function]
        fract `a)`

`unsigned short accum __satfractdquha (`*long long fract* `a)`   [Runtime Function]

`unsigned accum __satfractdqusa (`*long long fract* `a)`   [Runtime Function]

`unsigned long accum __satfractdquda (`*long long fract* `a)`   [Runtime Function]

`unsigned long long accum __satfractdquta (`*long long*   [Runtime Function]
        fract `a)`

`short fract __satfracthaqq (`*short accum* `a)`   [Runtime Function]

`fract __satfracthahq (`*short accum* `a)`   [Runtime Function]

long fract __satfracthasq (*short accum* a)   [Runtime Function]
long long fract __satfracthadq (*short accum* a)   [Runtime Function]
accum __satfracthasa2 (*short accum* a)   [Runtime Function]
long accum __satfracthada2 (*short accum* a)   [Runtime Function]
long long accum __satfracthata2 (*short accum* a)   [Runtime Function]
unsigned short fract __satfracthauqq (*short accum* a)   [Runtime Function]
unsigned fract __satfracthauhq (*short accum* a)   [Runtime Function]
unsigned long fract __satfracthausq (*short accum* a)   [Runtime Function]
unsigned long long fract __satfracthaudq (*short accum*   [Runtime Function]
    a)
unsigned short accum __satfracthauha (*short accum* a)   [Runtime Function]
unsigned accum __satfracthausa (*short accum* a)   [Runtime Function]
unsigned long accum __satfracthauda (*short accum* a)   [Runtime Function]
unsigned long long accum __satfracthauta (*short accum*   [Runtime Function]
    a)
short fract __satfractsaqq (*accum* a)   [Runtime Function]
fract __satfractsahq (*accum* a)   [Runtime Function]
long fract __satfractsasq (*accum* a)   [Runtime Function]
long long fract __satfractsadq (*accum* a)   [Runtime Function]
short accum __satfractsaha2 (*accum* a)   [Runtime Function]
long accum __satfractsada2 (*accum* a)   [Runtime Function]
long long accum __satfractsata2 (*accum* a)   [Runtime Function]
unsigned short fract __satfractsauqq (*accum* a)   [Runtime Function]
unsigned fract __satfractsauhq (*accum* a)   [Runtime Function]
unsigned long fract __satfractsausq (*accum* a)   [Runtime Function]
unsigned long long fract __satfractsaudq (*accum* a)   [Runtime Function]
unsigned short accum __satfractsauha (*accum* a)   [Runtime Function]
unsigned accum __satfractsausa (*accum* a)   [Runtime Function]
unsigned long accum __satfractsauda (*accum* a)   [Runtime Function]
unsigned long long accum __satfractsauta (*accum* a)   [Runtime Function]
short fract __satfractdaqq (*long accum* a)   [Runtime Function]
fract __satfractdahq (*long accum* a)   [Runtime Function]
long fract __satfractdasq (*long accum* a)   [Runtime Function]
long long fract __satfractdadq (*long accum* a)   [Runtime Function]
short accum __satfractdaha2 (*long accum* a)   [Runtime Function]
accum __satfractdasa2 (*long accum* a)   [Runtime Function]
long long accum __satfractdata2 (*long accum* a)   [Runtime Function]
unsigned short fract __satfractdauqq (*long accum* a)   [Runtime Function]
unsigned fract __satfractdauhq (*long accum* a)   [Runtime Function]
unsigned long fract __satfractdausq (*long accum* a)   [Runtime Function]
unsigned long long fract __satfractdaudq (*long accum*   [Runtime Function]
    a)
unsigned short accum __satfractdauha (*long accum* a)   [Runtime Function]
unsigned accum __satfractdausa (*long accum* a)   [Runtime Function]
unsigned long accum __satfractdauda (*long accum* a)   [Runtime Function]
unsigned long long accum __satfractdauta (*long accum*   [Runtime Function]
    a)

short fract __satfracttaqq (*long long accum* a)   [Runtime Function]
fract __satfracttahq (*long long accum* a)   [Runtime Function]
long fract __satfracttasq (*long long accum* a)   [Runtime Function]
long long fract __satfracttadq (*long long accum* a)   [Runtime Function]
short accum __satfracttaha2 (*long long accum* a)   [Runtime Function]
accum __satfracttasa2 (*long long accum* a)   [Runtime Function]
long accum __satfracttada2 (*long long accum* a)   [Runtime Function]
unsigned short fract __satfracttauqq (*long long accum*   [Runtime Function]
        a)
unsigned fract __satfracttauhq (*long long accum* a)   [Runtime Function]
unsigned long fract __satfracttausq (*long long accum* a)   [Runtime Function]
unsigned long long fract __satfracttaudq (*long long*   [Runtime Function]
        accum a)
unsigned short accum __satfracttauha (*long long accum*   [Runtime Function]
        a)
unsigned accum __satfracttausa (*long long accum* a)   [Runtime Function]
unsigned long accum __satfracttauda (*long long accum* a)   [Runtime Function]
unsigned long long accum __satfracttauta (*long long*   [Runtime Function]
        accum a)
short fract __satfractuqqqq (*unsigned short fract* a)   [Runtime Function]
fract __satfractuqqhq (*unsigned short fract* a)   [Runtime Function]
long fract __satfractuqqsq (*unsigned short fract* a)   [Runtime Function]
long long fract __satfractuqqdq (*unsigned short fract* a)   [Runtime Function]
short accum __satfractuqqha (*unsigned short fract* a)   [Runtime Function]
accum __satfractuqqsa (*unsigned short fract* a)   [Runtime Function]
long accum __satfractuqqda (*unsigned short fract* a)   [Runtime Function]
long long accum __satfractuqqta (*unsigned short fract* a)   [Runtime Function]
unsigned fract __satfractuqquhq2 (*unsigned short fract* a)   [Runtime Function]
unsigned long fract __satfractuqqusq2 (*unsigned short*   [Runtime Function]
        fract a)
unsigned long long fract __satfractuqqudq2 (*unsigned*   [Runtime Function]
        short fract a)
unsigned short accum __satfractuqquha (*unsigned short*   [Runtime Function]
        fract a)
unsigned accum __satfractuqqusa (*unsigned short fract* a)   [Runtime Function]
unsigned long accum __satfractuqquda (*unsigned short*   [Runtime Function]
        fract a)
unsigned long long accum __satfractuqquta (*unsigned*   [Runtime Function]
        short fract a)
short fract __satfractuhqqq (*unsigned fract* a)   [Runtime Function]
fract __satfractuhqhq (*unsigned fract* a)   [Runtime Function]
long fract __satfractuhqsq (*unsigned fract* a)   [Runtime Function]
long long fract __satfractuhqdq (*unsigned fract* a)   [Runtime Function]
short accum __satfractuhqha (*unsigned fract* a)   [Runtime Function]
accum __satfractuhqsa (*unsigned fract* a)   [Runtime Function]
long accum __satfractuhqda (*unsigned fract* a)   [Runtime Function]
long long accum __satfractuhqta (*unsigned fract* a)   [Runtime Function]

unsigned short fract __satfractuhquqq2 (*unsigned fract*   [Runtime Function]
      a*)

unsigned long fract __satfractuhqusq2 (*unsigned fract*   [Runtime Function]
      a*)

unsigned long long fract __satfractuhqudq2 (*unsigned*   [Runtime Function]
      fract a*)

unsigned short accum __satfractuhquha (*unsigned fract*   [Runtime Function]
      a*)

unsigned accum __satfractuhqusa (*unsigned fract* a*)   [Runtime Function]

unsigned long accum __satfractuhquda (*unsigned fract* a*) [Runtime Function]

unsigned long long accum __satfractuhquta (*unsigned*   [Runtime Function]
      fract a*)

short fract __satfractusqqq (*unsigned long fract* a*)   [Runtime Function]

fract __satfractusqhq (*unsigned long fract* a*)   [Runtime Function]

long fract __satfractusqsq (*unsigned long fract* a*)   [Runtime Function]

long long fract __satfractusqdq (*unsigned long fract* a*) [Runtime Function]

short accum __satfractusqha (*unsigned long fract* a*)   [Runtime Function]

accum __satfractusqsa (*unsigned long fract* a*)   [Runtime Function]

long accum __satfractusqda (*unsigned long fract* a*)   [Runtime Function]

long long accum __satfractusqta (*unsigned long fract* a*) [Runtime Function]

unsigned short fract __satfractusquqq2 (*unsigned long*   [Runtime Function]
      fract a*)

unsigned fract __satfractusquhq2 (*unsigned long fract* a*) [Runtime Function]

unsigned long long fract __satfractusqudq2 (*unsigned*   [Runtime Function]
      long fract a*)

unsigned short accum __satfractusquha (*unsigned long*   [Runtime Function]
      fract a*)

unsigned accum __satfractusqusa (*unsigned long fract* a*) [Runtime Function]

unsigned long accum __satfractusquda (*unsigned long*   [Runtime Function]
      fract a*)

unsigned long long accum __satfractusquta (*unsigned*   [Runtime Function]
      long fract a*)

short fract __satfractudqqq (*unsigned long long fract* a*) [Runtime Function]

fract __satfractudqhq (*unsigned long long fract* a*)   [Runtime Function]

long fract __satfractudqsq (*unsigned long long fract* a*) [Runtime Function]

long long fract __satfractudqdq (*unsigned long long fract* [Runtime Function]
      a*)

short accum __satfractudqha (*unsigned long long fract* a*) [Runtime Function]

accum __satfractudqsa (*unsigned long long fract* a*)   [Runtime Function]

long accum __satfractudqda (*unsigned long long fract* a*) [Runtime Function]

long long accum __satfractudqta (*unsigned long long fract* [Runtime Function]
      a*)

unsigned short fract __satfractudquqq2 (*unsigned long*   [Runtime Function]
      long fract a*)

unsigned fract __satfractudquhq2 (*unsigned long long*   [Runtime Function]
      fract a*)

unsigned long fract __satfractudqusq2 (*unsigned long*   [Runtime Function]
        long fract a)

unsigned short accum __satfractudquha (*unsigned long*   [Runtime Function]
        long fract a)

unsigned accum __satfractudqusa (*unsigned long long fract*   [Runtime Function]
        a)

unsigned long accum __satfractudquda (*unsigned long*   [Runtime Function]
        long fract a)

unsigned long long accum __satfractudquta (*unsigned*   [Runtime Function]
        long long fract a)

short fract __satfractuhaqq (*unsigned short accum* a)   [Runtime Function]

fract __satfractuhahq (*unsigned short accum* a)   [Runtime Function]

long fract __satfractuhasq (*unsigned short accum* a)   [Runtime Function]

long long fract __satfractuhadq (*unsigned short accum* a)   [Runtime Function]

short accum __satfractuhaha (*unsigned short accum* a)   [Runtime Function]

accum __satfractuhasa (*unsigned short accum* a)   [Runtime Function]

long accum __satfractuhada (*unsigned short accum* a)   [Runtime Function]

long long accum __satfractuhata (*unsigned short accum* a)   [Runtime Function]

unsigned short fract __satfractuhauqq (*unsigned short*   [Runtime Function]
        accum a)

unsigned fract __satfractuhauhq (*unsigned short accum* a)   [Runtime Function]

unsigned long fract __satfractuhausq (*unsigned short*   [Runtime Function]
        accum a)

unsigned long long fract __satfractuhaudq (*unsigned*   [Runtime Function]
        short accum a)

unsigned accum __satfractuhausa2 (*unsigned short accum*   [Runtime Function]
        a)

unsigned long accum __satfractuhauda2 (*unsigned short*   [Runtime Function]
        accum a)

unsigned long long accum __satfractuhauta2 (*unsigned*   [Runtime Function]
        short accum a)

short fract __satfractusaqq (*unsigned accum* a)   [Runtime Function]

fract __satfractusahq (*unsigned accum* a)   [Runtime Function]

long fract __satfractusasq (*unsigned accum* a)   [Runtime Function]

long long fract __satfractusadq (*unsigned accum* a)   [Runtime Function]

short accum __satfractusaha (*unsigned accum* a)   [Runtime Function]

accum __satfractusasa (*unsigned accum* a)   [Runtime Function]

long accum __satfractusada (*unsigned accum* a)   [Runtime Function]

long long accum __satfractusata (*unsigned accum* a)   [Runtime Function]

unsigned short fract __satfractusauqq (*unsigned accum*   [Runtime Function]
        a)

unsigned fract __satfractusauhq (*unsigned accum* a)   [Runtime Function]

unsigned long fract __satfractusausq (*unsigned accum*   [Runtime Function]
        a)

unsigned long long fract __satfractusaudq (*unsigned*   [Runtime Function]
        accum a)

`unsigned short accum __satfractusauha2` (*unsigned*   [Runtime Function]
      accum `a`)

`unsigned long accum __satfractusauda2` (*unsigned accum*   [Runtime Function]
      `a`)

`unsigned long long accum __satfractusauta2` (*unsigned*   [Runtime Function]
      accum `a`)

`short fract __satfractudaqq` (*unsigned long accum* `a`)   [Runtime Function]

`fract __satfractudahq` (*unsigned long accum* `a`)   [Runtime Function]

`long fract __satfractudasq` (*unsigned long accum* `a`)   [Runtime Function]

`long long fract __satfractudadq` (*unsigned long accum* `a`) [Runtime Function]

`short accum __satfractudaha` (*unsigned long accum* `a`)   [Runtime Function]

`accum __satfractudasa` (*unsigned long accum* `a`)   [Runtime Function]

`long accum __satfractudada` (*unsigned long accum* `a`)   [Runtime Function]

`long long accum __satfractudata` (*unsigned long accum* `a`) [Runtime Function]

`unsigned short fract __satfractudauqq` (*unsigned long*   [Runtime Function]
      accum `a`)

`unsigned fract __satfractudauhq` (*unsigned long accum* `a`) [Runtime Function]

`unsigned long fract __satfractudausq` (*unsigned long*   [Runtime Function]
      accum `a`)

`unsigned long long fract __satfractudaudq` (*unsigned*   [Runtime Function]
      long accum `a`)

`unsigned short accum __satfractudauha2` (*unsigned long*   [Runtime Function]
      accum `a`)

`unsigned accum __satfractudausa2` (*unsigned long accum*   [Runtime Function]
      `a`)

`unsigned long long accum __satfractudauta2` (*unsigned*   [Runtime Function]
      long accum `a`)

`short fract __satfractutaqq` (*unsigned long long accum* `a`) [Runtime Function]

`fract __satfractutahq` (*unsigned long long accum* `a`)   [Runtime Function]

`long fract __satfractutasq` (*unsigned long long accum* `a`) [Runtime Function]

`long long fract __satfractutadq` (*unsigned long long*   [Runtime Function]
      accum `a`)

`short accum __satfractutaha` (*unsigned long long accum* `a`) [Runtime Function]

`accum __satfractutasa` (*unsigned long long accum* `a`)   [Runtime Function]

`long accum __satfractutada` (*unsigned long long accum* `a`) [Runtime Function]

`long long accum __satfractutata` (*unsigned long long*   [Runtime Function]
      accum `a`)

`unsigned short fract __satfractutauqq` (*unsigned long*   [Runtime Function]
      long accum `a`)

`unsigned fract __satfractutauhq` (*unsigned long long*   [Runtime Function]
      accum `a`)

`unsigned long fract __satfractutausq` (*unsigned long*   [Runtime Function]
      long accum `a`)

`unsigned long long fract __satfractutaudq` (*unsigned*   [Runtime Function]
      long long accum `a`)

`unsigned short accum __satfractutauha2` (*unsigned long*   [Runtime Function]
      long accum `a`)

`unsigned accum __satfractutausa2` (*unsigned long long*   [Runtime Function]
     accum a)

`unsigned long accum __satfractutauda2` (*unsigned long*   [Runtime Function]
     long accum a)

`short fract __satfractqiqq` (*signed char* a)   [Runtime Function]

`fract __satfractqihq` (*signed char* a)   [Runtime Function]

`long fract __satfractqisq` (*signed char* a)   [Runtime Function]

`long long fract __satfractqidq` (*signed char* a)   [Runtime Function]

`short accum __satfractqiha` (*signed char* a)   [Runtime Function]

`accum __satfractqisa` (*signed char* a)   [Runtime Function]

`long accum __satfractqida` (*signed char* a)   [Runtime Function]

`long long accum __satfractqita` (*signed char* a)   [Runtime Function]

`unsigned short fract __satfractqiuqq` (*signed char* a)   [Runtime Function]

`unsigned fract __satfractqiuhq` (*signed char* a)   [Runtime Function]

`unsigned long fract __satfractqiusq` (*signed char* a)   [Runtime Function]

`unsigned long long fract __satfractqiudq` (*signed char*   [Runtime Function]
     a)

`unsigned short accum __satfractqiuha` (*signed char* a)   [Runtime Function]

`unsigned accum __satfractqiusa` (*signed char* a)   [Runtime Function]

`unsigned long accum __satfractqiuda` (*signed char* a)   [Runtime Function]

`unsigned long long accum __satfractqiuta` (*signed char*   [Runtime Function]
     a)

`short fract __satfracthiqq` (*short* a)   [Runtime Function]

`fract __satfracthihq` (*short* a)   [Runtime Function]

`long fract __satfracthisq` (*short* a)   [Runtime Function]

`long long fract __satfracthidq` (*short* a)   [Runtime Function]

`short accum __satfracthiha` (*short* a)   [Runtime Function]

`accum __satfracthisa` (*short* a)   [Runtime Function]

`long accum __satfracthida` (*short* a)   [Runtime Function]

`long long accum __satfracthita` (*short* a)   [Runtime Function]

`unsigned short fract __satfracthiuqq` (*short* a)   [Runtime Function]

`unsigned fract __satfracthiuhq` (*short* a)   [Runtime Function]

`unsigned long fract __satfracthiusq` (*short* a)   [Runtime Function]

`unsigned long long fract __satfracthiudq` (*short* a)   [Runtime Function]

`unsigned short accum __satfracthiuha` (*short* a)   [Runtime Function]

`unsigned accum __satfracthiusa` (*short* a)   [Runtime Function]

`unsigned long accum __satfracthiuda` (*short* a)   [Runtime Function]

`unsigned long long accum __satfracthiuta` (*short* a)   [Runtime Function]

`short fract __satfractsiqq` (*int* a)   [Runtime Function]

`fract __satfractsihq` (*int* a)   [Runtime Function]

`long fract __satfractsisq` (*int* a)   [Runtime Function]

`long long fract __satfractsidq` (*int* a)   [Runtime Function]

`short accum __satfractsiha` (*int* a)   [Runtime Function]

`accum __satfractsisa` (*int* a)   [Runtime Function]

`long accum __satfractsida` (*int* a)   [Runtime Function]

`long long accum __satfractsita` (*int* a)   [Runtime Function]

`unsigned short fract __satfractsiuqq` (*int* a)   [Runtime Function]

unsigned fract __satfractsiuhq (*int* a)   [Runtime Function]
unsigned long fract __satfractsiusq (*int* a)   [Runtime Function]
unsigned long long fract __satfractsiudq (*int* a)   [Runtime Function]
unsigned short accum __satfractsiuha (*int* a)   [Runtime Function]
unsigned accum __satfractsiusa (*int* a)   [Runtime Function]
unsigned long accum __satfractsiuda (*int* a)   [Runtime Function]
unsigned long long accum __satfractsiuta (*int* a)   [Runtime Function]
short fract __satfractdiqq (*long* a)   [Runtime Function]
fract __satfractdihq (*long* a)   [Runtime Function]
long fract __satfractdisq (*long* a)   [Runtime Function]
long long fract __satfractdidq (*long* a)   [Runtime Function]
short accum __satfractdiha (*long* a)   [Runtime Function]
accum __satfractdisa (*long* a)   [Runtime Function]
long accum __satfractdida (*long* a)   [Runtime Function]
long long accum __satfractdita (*long* a)   [Runtime Function]
unsigned short fract __satfractdiuqq (*long* a)   [Runtime Function]
unsigned fract __satfractdiuhq (*long* a)   [Runtime Function]
unsigned long fract __satfractdiusq (*long* a)   [Runtime Function]
unsigned long long fract __satfractdiudq (*long* a)   [Runtime Function]
unsigned short accum __satfractdiuha (*long* a)   [Runtime Function]
unsigned accum __satfractdiusa (*long* a)   [Runtime Function]
unsigned long accum __satfractdiuda (*long* a)   [Runtime Function]
unsigned long long accum __satfractdiuta (*long* a)   [Runtime Function]
short fract __satfracttiqq (*long long* a)   [Runtime Function]
fract __satfracttihq (*long long* a)   [Runtime Function]
long fract __satfracttisq (*long long* a)   [Runtime Function]
long long fract __satfracttidq (*long long* a)   [Runtime Function]
short accum __satfracttiha (*long long* a)   [Runtime Function]
accum __satfracttisa (*long long* a)   [Runtime Function]
long accum __satfracttida (*long long* a)   [Runtime Function]
long long accum __satfracttita (*long long* a)   [Runtime Function]
unsigned short fract __satfracttiuqq (*long long* a)   [Runtime Function]
unsigned fract __satfracttiuhq (*long long* a)   [Runtime Function]
unsigned long fract __satfracttiusq (*long long* a)   [Runtime Function]
unsigned long long fract __satfracttiudq (*long long* a)   [Runtime Function]
unsigned short accum __satfracttiuha (*long long* a)   [Runtime Function]
unsigned accum __satfracttiusa (*long long* a)   [Runtime Function]
unsigned long accum __satfracttiuda (*long long* a)   [Runtime Function]
unsigned long long accum __satfracttiuta (*long long* a)   [Runtime Function]
short fract __satfractsfqq (*float* a)   [Runtime Function]
fract __satfractsfhq (*float* a)   [Runtime Function]
long fract __satfractsfsq (*float* a)   [Runtime Function]
long long fract __satfractsfdq (*float* a)   [Runtime Function]
short accum __satfractsfha (*float* a)   [Runtime Function]
accum __satfractsfsa (*float* a)   [Runtime Function]
long accum __satfractsfda (*float* a)   [Runtime Function]
long long accum __satfractsfta (*float* a)   [Runtime Function]

`unsigned short fract __satfractsfuqq` (*float* a)	[Runtime Function]
`unsigned fract __satfractsfuhq` (*float* a)	[Runtime Function]
`unsigned long fract __satfractsfusq` (*float* a)	[Runtime Function]
`unsigned long long fract __satfractsfudq` (*float* a)	[Runtime Function]
`unsigned short accum __satfractsfuha` (*float* a)	[Runtime Function]
`unsigned accum __satfractsfusa` (*float* a)	[Runtime Function]
`unsigned long accum __satfractsfuda` (*float* a)	[Runtime Function]
`unsigned long long accum __satfractsfuta` (*float* a)	[Runtime Function]
`short fract __satfractdfqq` (*double* a)	[Runtime Function]
`fract __satfractdfhq` (*double* a)	[Runtime Function]
`long fract __satfractdfsq` (*double* a)	[Runtime Function]
`long long fract __satfractdfdq` (*double* a)	[Runtime Function]
`short accum __satfractdfha` (*double* a)	[Runtime Function]
`accum __satfractdfsa` (*double* a)	[Runtime Function]
`long accum __satfractdfda` (*double* a)	[Runtime Function]
`long long accum __satfractdfta` (*double* a)	[Runtime Function]
`unsigned short fract __satfractdfuqq` (*double* a)	[Runtime Function]
`unsigned fract __satfractdfuhq` (*double* a)	[Runtime Function]
`unsigned long fract __satfractdfusq` (*double* a)	[Runtime Function]
`unsigned long long fract __satfractdfudq` (*double* a)	[Runtime Function]
`unsigned short accum __satfractdfuha` (*double* a)	[Runtime Function]
`unsigned accum __satfractdfusa` (*double* a)	[Runtime Function]
`unsigned long accum __satfractdfuda` (*double* a)	[Runtime Function]
`unsigned long long accum __satfractdfuta` (*double* a)	[Runtime Function]

The functions convert from fractional and signed non-fractionals to fractionals, with saturation.

`unsigned char __fractunsqqqi` (*short fract* a)	[Runtime Function]
`unsigned short __fractunsqqhi` (*short fract* a)	[Runtime Function]
`unsigned int __fractunsqqsi` (*short fract* a)	[Runtime Function]
`unsigned long __fractunsqqdi` (*short fract* a)	[Runtime Function]
`unsigned long long __fractunsqqti` (*short fract* a)	[Runtime Function]
`unsigned char __fractunshqqi` (*fract* a)	[Runtime Function]
`unsigned short __fractunshqhi` (*fract* a)	[Runtime Function]
`unsigned int __fractunshqsi` (*fract* a)	[Runtime Function]
`unsigned long __fractunshqdi` (*fract* a)	[Runtime Function]
`unsigned long long __fractunshqti` (*fract* a)	[Runtime Function]
`unsigned char __fractunssqqi` (*long fract* a)	[Runtime Function]
`unsigned short __fractunssqhi` (*long fract* a)	[Runtime Function]
`unsigned int __fractunssqsi` (*long fract* a)	[Runtime Function]
`unsigned long __fractunssqdi` (*long fract* a)	[Runtime Function]
`unsigned long long __fractunssqti` (*long fract* a)	[Runtime Function]
`unsigned char __fractunsdqqi` (*long long fract* a)	[Runtime Function]
`unsigned short __fractunsdqhi` (*long long fract* a)	[Runtime Function]
`unsigned int __fractunsdqsi` (*long long fract* a)	[Runtime Function]
`unsigned long __fractunsdqdi` (*long long fract* a)	[Runtime Function]
`unsigned long long __fractunsdqti` (*long long fract* a)	[Runtime Function]

unsigned char __fractunshaqi (*short accum* a)   [Runtime Function]
unsigned short __fractunshahi (*short accum* a)   [Runtime Function]
unsigned int __fractunshasi (*short accum* a)   [Runtime Function]
unsigned long __fractunshadi (*short accum* a)   [Runtime Function]
unsigned long long __fractunshati (*short accum* a)   [Runtime Function]
unsigned char __fractunssaqi (*accum* a)   [Runtime Function]
unsigned short __fractunssahi (*accum* a)   [Runtime Function]
unsigned int __fractunssasi (*accum* a)   [Runtime Function]
unsigned long __fractunssadi (*accum* a)   [Runtime Function]
unsigned long long __fractunssati (*accum* a)   [Runtime Function]
unsigned char __fractunsdaqi (*long accum* a)   [Runtime Function]
unsigned short __fractunsdahi (*long accum* a)   [Runtime Function]
unsigned int __fractunsdasi (*long accum* a)   [Runtime Function]
unsigned long __fractunsdadi (*long accum* a)   [Runtime Function]
unsigned long long __fractunsdati (*long accum* a)   [Runtime Function]
unsigned char __fractunstaqi (*long long accum* a)   [Runtime Function]
unsigned short __fractunstahi (*long long accum* a)   [Runtime Function]
unsigned int __fractunstasi (*long long accum* a)   [Runtime Function]
unsigned long __fractunstadi (*long long accum* a)   [Runtime Function]
unsigned long long __fractunstati (*long long accum* a)   [Runtime Function]
unsigned char __fractunsuqqqi (*unsigned short fract* a) [Runtime Function]
unsigned short __fractunsuqqhi (*unsigned short fract* a) [Runtime Function]
unsigned int __fractunsuqqsi (*unsigned short fract* a)   [Runtime Function]
unsigned long __fractunsuqqdi (*unsigned short fract* a) [Runtime Function]
unsigned long long __fractunsuqqti (*unsigned short fract*   [Runtime Function]
    a)
unsigned char __fractunsuhqqi (*unsigned fract* a)   [Runtime Function]
unsigned short __fractunsuhqhi (*unsigned fract* a)   [Runtime Function]
unsigned int __fractunsuhqsi (*unsigned fract* a)   [Runtime Function]
unsigned long __fractunsuhqdi (*unsigned fract* a)   [Runtime Function]
unsigned long long __fractunsuhqti (*unsigned fract* a)   [Runtime Function]
unsigned char __fractunsusqqi (*unsigned long fract* a)   [Runtime Function]
unsigned short __fractunsusqhi (*unsigned long fract* a) [Runtime Function]
unsigned int __fractunsusqsi (*unsigned long fract* a)   [Runtime Function]
unsigned long __fractunsusqdi (*unsigned long fract* a)   [Runtime Function]
unsigned long long __fractunsusqti (*unsigned long fract*   [Runtime Function]
    a)
unsigned char __fractunsudqqi (*unsigned long long fract* a) [Runtime Function]
unsigned short __fractunsudqhi (*unsigned long long fract*   [Runtime Function]
    a)
unsigned int __fractunsudqsi (*unsigned long long fract* a) [Runtime Function]
unsigned long __fractunsudqdi (*unsigned long long fract* a) [Runtime Function]
unsigned long long __fractunsudqti (*unsigned long long*   [Runtime Function]
    fract a)
unsigned char __fractunsuhaqi (*unsigned short accum* a)   [Runtime Function]
unsigned short __fractunsuhahi (*unsigned short accum* a) [Runtime Function]
unsigned int __fractunsuhasi (*unsigned short accum* a)   [Runtime Function]

`unsigned long __fractunsuhadi` (*unsigned short accum* a)   [Runtime Function]

`unsigned long long __fractunsuhati` (*unsigned short* [Runtime Function]
    accum a)

`unsigned char __fractunsusaqi` (*unsigned accum* a)   [Runtime Function]

`unsigned short __fractunsusahi` (*unsigned accum* a)   [Runtime Function]

`unsigned int __fractunsusasi` (*unsigned accum* a)   [Runtime Function]

`unsigned long __fractunsusadi` (*unsigned accum* a)   [Runtime Function]

`unsigned long long __fractunsusati` (*unsigned accum* a)   [Runtime Function]

`unsigned char __fractunsudaqi` (*unsigned long accum* a)   [Runtime Function]

`unsigned short __fractunsudahi` (*unsigned long accum* a)   [Runtime Function]

`unsigned int __fractunsudasi` (*unsigned long accum* a)   [Runtime Function]

`unsigned long __fractunsudadi` (*unsigned long accum* a)   [Runtime Function]

`unsigned long long __fractunsudati` (*unsigned long* [Runtime Function]
    accum a)

`unsigned char __fractunsutaqi` (*unsigned long long accum* [Runtime Function]
    a)

`unsigned short __fractunsutahi` (*unsigned long long accum* [Runtime Function]
    a)

`unsigned int __fractunsutasi` (*unsigned long long accum* a)   [Runtime Function]

`unsigned long __fractunsutadi` (*unsigned long long accum* [Runtime Function]
    a)

`unsigned long long __fractunsutati` (*unsigned long long* [Runtime Function]
    accum a)

`short fract __fractunsqiqq` (*unsigned char* a)   [Runtime Function]

`fract __fractunsqihq` (*unsigned char* a)   [Runtime Function]

`long fract __fractunsqisq` (*unsigned char* a)   [Runtime Function]

`long long fract __fractunsqidq` (*unsigned char* a)   [Runtime Function]

`short accum __fractunsqiha` (*unsigned char* a)   [Runtime Function]

`accum __fractunsqisa` (*unsigned char* a)   [Runtime Function]

`long accum __fractunsqida` (*unsigned char* a)   [Runtime Function]

`long long accum __fractunsqita` (*unsigned char* a)   [Runtime Function]

`unsigned short fract __fractunsqiuqq` (*unsigned char* a)   [Runtime Function]

`unsigned fract __fractunsqiuhq` (*unsigned char* a)   [Runtime Function]

`unsigned long fract __fractunsqiusq` (*unsigned char* a)   [Runtime Function]

`unsigned long long fract __fractunsqiudq` (*unsigned* [Runtime Function]
    char a)

`unsigned short accum __fractunsqiuha` (*unsigned char* a)   [Runtime Function]

`unsigned accum __fractunsqiusa` (*unsigned char* a)   [Runtime Function]

`unsigned long accum __fractunsqiuda` (*unsigned char* a)   [Runtime Function]

`unsigned long long accum __fractunsqiuta` (*unsigned* [Runtime Function]
    char a)

`short fract __fractunshiqq` (*unsigned short* a)   [Runtime Function]

`fract __fractunshihq` (*unsigned short* a)   [Runtime Function]

`long fract __fractunshisq` (*unsigned short* a)   [Runtime Function]

`long long fract __fractunshidq` (*unsigned short* a)   [Runtime Function]

`short accum __fractunshiha` (*unsigned short* a)   [Runtime Function]

`accum __fractunshisa` (*unsigned short* a)   [Runtime Function] long accum __fractunshida (*unsigned short* a)   [Runtime Function]

long long accum __fractunshita (*unsigned short* a)   [Runtime Function]

unsigned short fract __fractunshiuqq (*unsigned short* a)   [Runtime Function]

unsigned fract __fractunshiuhq (*unsigned short* a)   [Runtime Function]

unsigned long fract __fractunshiusq (*unsigned short* a)   [Runtime Function]

unsigned long long fract __fractunshiudq (*unsigned*   [Runtime Function]
        short a)

unsigned short accum __fractunshiuha (*unsigned short* a)   [Runtime Function]

unsigned accum __fractunshiusa (*unsigned short* a)   [Runtime Function]

unsigned long accum __fractunshiuda (*unsigned short* a)   [Runtime Function]

unsigned long long accum __fractunshiuta (*unsigned*   [Runtime Function]
        short a)

short fract __fractunssiqq (*unsigned int* a)   [Runtime Function]

fract __fractunssihq (*unsigned int* a)   [Runtime Function]

long fract __fractunssisq (*unsigned int* a)   [Runtime Function]

long long fract __fractunssidq (*unsigned int* a)   [Runtime Function]

short accum __fractunssiha (*unsigned int* a)   [Runtime Function]

accum __fractunssisa (*unsigned int* a)   [Runtime Function]

long accum __fractunssida (*unsigned int* a)   [Runtime Function]

long long accum __fractunssita (*unsigned int* a)   [Runtime Function]

unsigned short fract __fractunssiuqq (*unsigned int* a)   [Runtime Function]

unsigned fract __fractunssiuhq (*unsigned int* a)   [Runtime Function]

unsigned long fract __fractunssiusq (*unsigned int* a)   [Runtime Function]

unsigned long long fract __fractunssiudq (*unsigned int*   [Runtime Function]
        a)

unsigned short accum __fractunssiuha (*unsigned int* a)   [Runtime Function]

unsigned accum __fractunssiusa (*unsigned int* a)   [Runtime Function]

unsigned long accum __fractunssiuda (*unsigned int* a)   [Runtime Function]

unsigned long long accum __fractunssiuta (*unsigned int*   [Runtime Function]
        a)

short fract __fractunsdiqq (*unsigned long* a)   [Runtime Function]

fract __fractunsdihq (*unsigned long* a)   [Runtime Function]

long fract __fractunsdisq (*unsigned long* a)   [Runtime Function]

long long fract __fractunsdidq (*unsigned long* a)   [Runtime Function]

short accum __fractunsdiha (*unsigned long* a)   [Runtime Function]

accum __fractunsdisa (*unsigned long* a)   [Runtime Function]

long accum __fractunsdida (*unsigned long* a)   [Runtime Function]

long long accum __fractunsdita (*unsigned long* a)   [Runtime Function]

unsigned short fract __fractunsdiuqq (*unsigned long* a)   [Runtime Function]

unsigned fract __fractunsdiuhq (*unsigned long* a)   [Runtime Function]

unsigned long fract __fractunsdiusq (*unsigned long* a)   [Runtime Function]

unsigned long long fract __fractunsdiudq (*unsigned*   [Runtime Function]
        long a)

unsigned short accum __fractunsdiuha (*unsigned long* a)   [Runtime Function]

unsigned accum __fractunsdiusa (*unsigned long* a)   [Runtime Function]

unsigned long accum __fractunsdiuda (*unsigned long* a)   [Runtime Function]

`unsigned long long accum __fractunsdiuta` (*unsigned*   [Runtime Function]
      long a)
`short fract __fractunstiqq` (*unsigned long long* a)   [Runtime Function]
`fract __fractunstihq` (*unsigned long long* a)   [Runtime Function]
`long fract __fractunstisq` (*unsigned long long* a)   [Runtime Function]
`long long fract __fractunstidq` (*unsigned long long* a)   [Runtime Function]
`short accum __fractunstiha` (*unsigned long long* a)   [Runtime Function]
`accum __fractunstisa` (*unsigned long long* a)   [Runtime Function]
`long accum __fractunstida` (*unsigned long long* a)   [Runtime Function]
`long long accum __fractunstita` (*unsigned long long* a)   [Runtime Function]
`unsigned short fract __fractunstiuqq` (*unsigned long*   [Runtime Function]
      long a)
`unsigned fract __fractunstiuhq` (*unsigned long long* a)   [Runtime Function]
`unsigned long fract __fractunstiusq` (*unsigned long long*   [Runtime Function]
      a)
`unsigned long long fract __fractunstiudq` (*unsigned*   [Runtime Function]
      long long a)
`unsigned short accum __fractunstiuha` (*unsigned long*   [Runtime Function]
      long a)
`unsigned accum __fractunstiusa` (*unsigned long long* a)   [Runtime Function]
`unsigned long accum __fractunstiuda` (*unsigned long long*   [Runtime Function]
      a)
`unsigned long long accum __fractunstiuta` (*unsigned*   [Runtime Function]
      long long a)

These functions convert from fractionals to unsigned non-fractionals; and from unsigned non-fractionals to fractionals, without saturation.

`short fract __satfractunsqiqq` (*unsigned char* a)   [Runtime Function]
`fract __satfractunsqihq` (*unsigned char* a)   [Runtime Function]
`long fract __satfractunsqisq` (*unsigned char* a)   [Runtime Function]
`long long fract __satfractunsqidq` (*unsigned char* a)   [Runtime Function]
`short accum __satfractunsqiha` (*unsigned char* a)   [Runtime Function]
`accum __satfractunsqisa` (*unsigned char* a)   [Runtime Function]
`long accum __satfractunsqida` (*unsigned char* a)   [Runtime Function]
`long long accum __satfractunsqita` (*unsigned char* a)   [Runtime Function]
`unsigned short fract __satfractunsqiuqq` (*unsigned char*   [Runtime Function]
      a)
`unsigned fract __satfractunsqiuhq` (*unsigned char* a)   [Runtime Function]
`unsigned long fract __satfractunsqiusq` (*unsigned char*   [Runtime Function]
      a)
`unsigned long long fract __satfractunsqiudq`   [Runtime Function]
      (*unsigned char* a)
`unsigned short accum __satfractunsqiuha` (*unsigned char*   [Runtime Function]
      a)
`unsigned accum __satfractunsqiusa` (*unsigned char* a)   [Runtime Function]
`unsigned long accum __satfractunsqiuda` (*unsigned char*   [Runtime Function]
      a)

unsigned long long accum __satfractunsqiuta   [Runtime Function]
      (*unsigned char* a)

short fract __satfractunshiqq (*unsigned short* a)   [Runtime Function]

fract __satfractunshihq (*unsigned short* a)   [Runtime Function]

long fract __satfractunshisq (*unsigned short* a)   [Runtime Function]

long long fract __satfractunshidq (*unsigned short* a)   [Runtime Function]

short accum __satfractunshiha (*unsigned short* a)   [Runtime Function]

accum __satfractunshisa (*unsigned short* a)   [Runtime Function]

long accum __satfractunshida (*unsigned short* a)   [Runtime Function]

long long accum __satfractunshita (*unsigned short* a)   [Runtime Function]

unsigned short fract __satfractunshiuqq (*unsigned*   [Runtime Function]
      short a)

unsigned fract __satfractunshiuhq (*unsigned short* a)   [Runtime Function]

unsigned long fract __satfractunshiusq (*unsigned short*   [Runtime Function]
      a)

unsigned long long fract __satfractunshiudq   [Runtime Function]
      (*unsigned short* a)

unsigned short accum __satfractunshiuha (*unsigned*   [Runtime Function]
      short a)

unsigned accum __satfractunshiusa (*unsigned short* a)   [Runtime Function]

unsigned long accum __satfractunshiuda (*unsigned short*   [Runtime Function]
      a)

unsigned long long accum __satfractunshiuta   [Runtime Function]
      (*unsigned short* a)

short fract __satfractunssiqq (*unsigned int* a)   [Runtime Function]

fract __satfractunssihq (*unsigned int* a)   [Runtime Function]

long fract __satfractunssisq (*unsigned int* a)   [Runtime Function]

long long fract __satfractunssidq (*unsigned int* a)   [Runtime Function]

short accum __satfractunssiha (*unsigned int* a)   [Runtime Function]

accum __satfractunssisa (*unsigned int* a)   [Runtime Function]

long accum __satfractunssida (*unsigned int* a)   [Runtime Function]

long long accum __satfractunssita (*unsigned int* a)   [Runtime Function]

unsigned short fract __satfractunssiuqq (*unsigned int*   [Runtime Function]
      a)

unsigned fract __satfractunssiuhq (*unsigned int* a)   [Runtime Function]

unsigned long fract __satfractunssiusq (*unsigned int* a)   [Runtime Function]

unsigned long long fract __satfractunssiudq   [Runtime Function]
      (*unsigned int* a)

unsigned short accum __satfractunssiuha (*unsigned int*   [Runtime Function]
      a)

unsigned accum __satfractunssiusa (*unsigned int* a)   [Runtime Function]

unsigned long accum __satfractunssiuda (*unsigned int* a)   [Runtime Function]

unsigned long long accum __satfractunssiuta   [Runtime Function]
      (*unsigned int* a)

short fract __satfractunsdiqq (*unsigned long* a)   [Runtime Function]

fract __satfractunsdihq (*unsigned long* a)   [Runtime Function]

long fract __satfractunsdisq (*unsigned long* a)   [Runtime Function] `long long fract __satfractunsdidq` (*unsigned long* a)   [Runtime Function]

`short accum __satfractunsdiha` (*unsigned long* a)   [Runtime Function]

`accum __satfractunsdisa` (*unsigned long* a)   [Runtime Function]

`long accum __satfractunsdida` (*unsigned long* a)   [Runtime Function]

`long long accum __satfractunsdita` (*unsigned long* a)   [Runtime Function]

`unsigned short fract __satfractunsdiuqq` (*unsigned long*   [Runtime Function]
        a)

`unsigned fract __satfractunsdiuhq` (*unsigned long* a)   [Runtime Function]

`unsigned long fract __satfractunsdiusq` (*unsigned long*   [Runtime Function]
        a)

`unsigned long long fract __satfractunsdiudq`   [Runtime Function]
        (*unsigned long* a)

`unsigned short accum __satfractunsdiuha` (*unsigned long*   [Runtime Function]
        a)

`unsigned accum __satfractunsdiusa` (*unsigned long* a)   [Runtime Function]

`unsigned long accum __satfractunsdiuda` (*unsigned long*   [Runtime Function]
        a)

`unsigned long long accum __satfractunsdiuta`   [Runtime Function]
        (*unsigned long* a)

`short fract __satfractunstiqq` (*unsigned long long* a)   [Runtime Function]

`fract __satfractunstihq` (*unsigned long long* a)   [Runtime Function]

`long fract __satfractunstisq` (*unsigned long long* a)   [Runtime Function]

`long long fract __satfractunstidq` (*unsigned long long* a)   [Runtime Function]

`short accum __satfractunstiha` (*unsigned long long* a)   [Runtime Function]

`accum __satfractunstisa` (*unsigned long long* a)   [Runtime Function]

`long accum __satfractunstida` (*unsigned long long* a)   [Runtime Function]

`long long accum __satfractunstita` (*unsigned long long* a)   [Runtime Function]

`unsigned short fract __satfractunstiuqq` (*unsigned long*   [Runtime Function]
        long a)

`unsigned fract __satfractunstiuhq` (*unsigned long long* a)   [Runtime Function]

`unsigned long fract __satfractunstiusq` (*unsigned long*   [Runtime Function]
        long a)

`unsigned long long fract __satfractunstiudq`   [Runtime Function]
        (*unsigned long long* a)

`unsigned short accum __satfractunstiuha` (*unsigned long*   [Runtime Function]
        long a)

`unsigned accum __satfractunstiusa` (*unsigned long long* a)   [Runtime Function]

`unsigned long accum __satfractunstiuda` (*unsigned long*   [Runtime Function]
        long a)

`unsigned long long accum __satfractunstiuta`   [Runtime Function]
        (*unsigned long long* a)

    These functions convert from unsigned non-fractionals to fractionals, with saturation.

4.5 Language-independent routines for exception handling

document me!

`_Unwind_DeleteException`

```
_Unwind_Find_FDE
_Unwind_ForcedUnwind
_Unwind_GetGR
_Unwind_GetIP
_Unwind_GetLanguageSpecificData
_Unwind_GetRegionStart
_Unwind_GetTextRelBase
_Unwind_GetDataRelBase
_Unwind_RaiseException
_Unwind_Resume
_Unwind_SetGR
_Unwind_SetIP
_Unwind_FindEnclosingFunction
_Unwind_SjLj_Register
_Unwind_SjLj_Unregister
_Unwind_SjLj_RaiseException
_Unwind_SjLj_ForcedUnwind
_Unwind_SjLj_Resume
__deregister_frame
__deregister_frame_info
__deregister_frame_info_bases
__register_frame
__register_frame_info
__register_frame_info_bases
__register_frame_info_table
__register_frame_info_table_bases
__register_frame_table
```

4.6 Miscellaneous runtime library routines

4.6.1 Cache control functions

void __clear_cache (*char *beg, char *end*)   [Runtime Function]
> This function clears the instruction cache between *beg* and *end*.

4.6.2 Split stack functions and variables

void * __splitstack_find (*void *segment_arg, void *sp,*   [Runtime Function]
   size_t len, *void **next_segment, void **next_sp, void **initial_sp*)
> When using '-fsplit-stack', this call may be used to iterate over the stack segments.
> It may be called like this:

```
        void *next_segment = NULL;
        void *next_sp = NULL;
        void *initial_sp = NULL;
        void *stack;
        size_t stack_size;
        while ((stack = __splitstack_find (next_segment, next_sp,
                                     &stack_size, &next_segment,
                                     &next_sp, &initial_sp))
             != NULL)
      {
        /* Stack segment starts at stack and is
           stack_size bytes long.  */
      }
```

There is no way to iterate over the stack segments of a different thread. However, what is permitted is for one thread to call this with the *segment_arg* and *sp* arguments NULL, to pass *next_segment*, *next_sp*, and *initial_sp* to a different thread, and then to suspend one way or another. A different thread may run the subsequent `__splitstack_find` iterations. Of course, this will only work if the first thread is suspended while the second thread is calling `__splitstack_find`. If not, the second thread could be looking at the stack while it is changing, and anything could happen.

`__morestack_segments`   [Variable]
`__morestack_current_segment`   [Variable]
`__morestack_initial_sp`   [Variable]
    Internal variables used by the '`-fsplit-stack`' implementation.

5 Language Front Ends in GCC

The interface to front ends for languages in GCC, and in particular the `tree` structure (see Chapter 10 [GENERIC], page 133), was initially designed for C, and many aspects of it are still somewhat biased towards C and C-like languages. It is, however, reasonably well suited to other procedural languages, and front ends for many such languages have been written for GCC.

Writing a compiler as a front end for GCC, rather than compiling directly to assembler or generating C code which is then compiled by GCC, has several advantages:

- GCC front ends benefit from the support for many different target machines already present in GCC.

- GCC front ends benefit from all the optimizations in GCC. Some of these, such as alias analysis, may work better when GCC is compiling directly from source code then when it is compiling from generated C code.

- Better debugging information is generated when compiling directly from source code than when going via intermediate generated C code.

Because of the advantages of writing a compiler as a GCC front end, GCC front ends have also been created for languages very different from those for which GCC was designed, such as the declarative logic/functional language Mercury. For these reasons, it may also be useful to implement compilers created for specialized purposes (for example, as part of a research project) as GCC front ends.

6 Source Tree Structure and Build System

This chapter describes the structure of the GCC source tree, and how GCC is built. The user documentation for building and installing GCC is in a separate manual (http://gcc.gnu.org/install/), with which it is presumed that you are familiar.

6.1 Configure Terms and History

The configure and build process has a long and colorful history, and can be confusing to anyone who doesn't know why things are the way they are. While there are other documents which describe the configuration process in detail, here are a few things that everyone working on GCC should know.

There are three system names that the build knows about: the machine you are building on (*build*), the machine that you are building for (*host*), and the machine that GCC will produce code for (*target*). When you configure GCC, you specify these with '--build=', '--host=', and '--target='.

Specifying the host without specifying the build should be avoided, as `configure` may (and once did) assume that the host you specify is also the build, which may not be true.

If build, host, and target are all the same, this is called a *native*. If build and host are the same but target is different, this is called a *cross*. If build, host, and target are all different this is called a *canadian* (for obscure reasons dealing with Canada's political party and the background of the person working on the build at that time). If host and target are the same, but build is different, you are using a cross-compiler to build a native for a different system. Some people call this a *host-x-host*, *crossed native*, or *cross-built native*. If build and target are the same, but host is different, you are using a cross compiler to build a cross compiler that produces code for the machine you're building on. This is rare, so there is no common way of describing it. There is a proposal to call this a *crossback*.

If build and host are the same, the GCC you are building will also be used to build the target libraries (like `libstdc++`). If build and host are different, you must have already built and installed a cross compiler that will be used to build the target libraries (if you configured with '--target=foo-bar', this compiler will be called `foo-bar-gcc`).

In the case of target libraries, the machine you're building for is the machine you specified with '--target'. So, build is the machine you're building on (no change there), host is the machine you're building for (the target libraries are built for the target, so host is the target you specified), and target doesn't apply (because you're not building a compiler, you're building libraries). The configure/make process will adjust these variables as needed. It also sets `$with_cross_host` to the original '--host' value in case you need it.

The `libiberty` support library is built up to three times: once for the host, once for the target (even if they are the same), and once for the build if build and host are different. This allows it to be used by all programs which are generated in the course of the build process.

6.2 Top Level Source Directory

The top level source directory in a GCC distribution contains several files and directories that are shared with other software distributions such as that of GNU Binutils. It also contains several subdirectories that contain parts of GCC and its runtime libraries:

'boehm-gc'

> The Boehm conservative garbage collector, optionally used as part of the ObjC runtime library when configured with '--enable-objc-gc'.

'config'   Autoconf macros and Makefile fragments used throughout the tree.

'contrib'   Contributed scripts that may be found useful in conjunction with GCC. One of these, 'contrib/texi2pod.pl', is used to generate man pages from Texinfo manuals as part of the GCC build process.

'fixincludes'

> The support for fixing system headers to work with GCC. See 'fixincludes/README' for more information. The headers fixed by this mechanism are installed in 'libsubdir/include-fixed'. Along with those headers, 'README-fixinc' is also installed, as 'libsubdir/include-fixed/README'.

'gcc'   The main sources of GCC itself (except for runtime libraries), including optimizers, support for different target architectures, language front ends, and testsuites. See Section 6.3 [The 'gcc' Subdirectory], page 63, for details.

'gnattools'

> Support tools for GNAT.

'include'   Headers for the libiberty library.

'intl'   GNU libintl, from GNU gettext, for systems which do not include it in libc.

'libada'   The Ada runtime library.

'libatomic'

> The runtime support library for atomic operations (e.g. for __sync and __atomic).

'libcpp'   The C preprocessor library.

'libdecnumber'

> The Decimal Float support library.

'libffi'   The libffi library, used as part of the Go runtime library.

'libgcc'   The GCC runtime library.

'libgfortran'

> The Fortran runtime library.

'libgo'   The Go runtime library. The bulk of this library is mirrored from the master Go repository.

'libgomp'   The GNU Offloading and Multi Processing Runtime Library.

'libiberty'

> The libiberty library, used for portability and for some generally useful data structures and algorithms. See Section "Introduction" in GNU libiberty, for more information about this library.

'libitm'   The runtime support library for transactional memory.

'libobjc'   The Objective-C and Objective-C++ runtime library.

'libquadmath'
            The runtime support library for quad-precision math operations.

'libssp'   The Stack protector runtime library.

'libstdc++-v3'
            The C++ runtime library.

'lto-plugin'
            Plugin used by the linker if link-time optimizations are enabled.

'maintainer-scripts'
            Scripts used by the gccadmin account on gcc.gnu.org.

'zlib'   The zlib compression library, used for compressing and uncompressing GCC's
            intermediate language in LTO object files.

The build system in the top level directory, including how recursion into subdirectories works and how building runtime libraries for multilibs is handled, is documented in a separate manual, included with GNU Binutils. See Section "GNU configure and build system" in *The GNU configure and build system*, for details.

6.3 The 'gcc' Subdirectory

The 'gcc' directory contains many files that are part of the C sources of GCC, other files used as part of the configuration and build process, and subdirectories including documentation and a testsuite. The files that are sources of GCC are documented in a separate chapter. See Chapter 9 [Passes and Files of the Compiler], page 115.

6.3.1 Subdirectories of 'gcc'

The 'gcc' directory contains the following subdirectories:

'*language*'
            Subdirectories for various languages.   Directories containing a file 'config-lang.in' are language subdirectories.   The contents of the subdirectories 'c' (for C), 'cp' (for C++), 'objc' (for Objective-C), 'objcp' (for Objective-C++), and 'lto' (for LTO) are documented in this manual (see Chapter 9 [Passes and Files of the Compiler], page 115); those for other languages are not. See Section 6.3.8 [Anatomy of a Language Front End], page 71, for details of the files in these directories.

'common'   Source files shared between the compiler drivers (such as gcc) and the compilers proper (such as 'cc1'). If an architecture defines target hooks shared between those places, it also has a subdirectory in 'common/config'. See Section 17.1 [Target Structure], page 433.

'config'   Configuration files for supported architectures and operating systems. See Section 6.3.9 [Anatomy of a Target Back End], page 75, for details of the files in this directory.

'doc'   Texinfo documentation for GCC, together with automatically generated man
               pages and support for converting the installation manual to HTML. See
               Section 6.3.7 [Documentation], page 69.

'ginclude'
               System headers installed by GCC, mainly those required by the C standard of
               freestanding implementations. See Section 6.3.6 [Headers Installed by GCC],
               page 68, for details of when these and other headers are installed.

'po'   Message catalogs with translations of messages produced by GCC into various
               languages, '*language*.po'. This directory also contains 'gcc.pot', the template
               for these message catalogues, 'exgettext', a wrapper around **gettext** to ex-
               tract the messages from the GCC sources and create 'gcc.pot', which is run
               by 'make gcc.pot', and 'EXCLUDES', a list of files from which messages should
               not be extracted.

'testsuite'
               The GCC testsuites (except for those for runtime libraries). See Chapter 7
               [Testsuites], page 77.

6.3.2 Configuration in the 'gcc' Directory

The 'gcc' directory is configured with an Autoconf-generated script 'configure'. The
'configure' script is generated from 'configure.ac' and 'aclocal.m4'. From the files
'configure.ac' and 'acconfig.h', Autoheader generates the file 'config.in'. The file
'cstamp-h.in' is used as a timestamp.

6.3.2.1 Scripts Used by 'configure'

'configure' uses some other scripts to help in its work:

- The standard GNU 'config.sub' and 'config.guess' files, kept in the top level directory, are used.
- The file 'config.gcc' is used to handle configuration specific to the particular target
  machine. The file 'config.build' is used to handle configuration specific to the particular build machine. The file 'config.host' is used to handle configuration specific
  to the particular host machine. (In general, these should only be used for features
  that cannot reasonably be tested in Autoconf feature tests.) See Section 6.3.2.2 [The
  'config.build'; 'config.host'; and 'config.gcc' Files], page 64, for details of the
  contents of these files.
- Each language subdirectory has a file '*language*/config-lang.in' that is used for
  front-end-specific configuration. See Section 6.3.8.2 [The Front End 'config-lang.in'
  File], page 73, for details of this file.
- A helper script 'configure.frag' is used as part of creating the output of 'configure'.

6.3.2.2 The 'config.build'; 'config.host'; and 'config.gcc' Files

The 'config.build' file contains specific rules for particular systems which GCC is built
on. This should be used as rarely as possible, as the behavior of the build system can always
be detected by autoconf.

The 'config.host' file contains specific rules for particular systems which GCC will run
on. This is rarely needed.

The 'config.gcc' file contains specific rules for particular systems which GCC will generate code for. This is usually needed.

Each file has a list of the shell variables it sets, with descriptions, at the top of the file.

FIXME: document the contents of these files, and what variables should be set to control build, host and target configuration.

6.3.2.3 Files Created by `configure`

Here we spell out what files will be set up by 'configure' in the 'gcc' directory. Some other files are created as temporary files in the configuration process, and are not used in the subsequent build; these are not documented.

- 'Makefile' is constructed from 'Makefile.in', together with the host and target fragments (see Chapter 19 [Makefile Fragments], page 617) 't-*target*' and 'x-*host*' from 'config', if any, and language Makefile fragments '*language*/Make-lang.in'.

- 'auto-host.h' contains information about the host machine determined by 'configure'. If the host machine is different from the build machine, then 'auto-build.h' is also created, containing such information about the build machine.

- 'config.status' is a script that may be run to recreate the current configuration.

- 'configargs.h' is a header containing details of the arguments passed to 'configure' to configure GCC, and of the thread model used.

- 'cstamp-h' is used as a timestamp.

- If a language 'config-lang.in' file (see Section 6.3.8.2 [The Front End 'config-lang.in' File], page 73) sets **outputs**, then the files listed in **outputs** there are also generated.

The following configuration headers are created from the Makefile, using 'mkconfig.sh', rather than directly by 'configure'. 'config.h', 'bconfig.h' and 'tconfig.h' all contain the 'xm-*machine*.h' header, if any, appropriate to the host, build and target machines respectively, the configuration headers for the target, and some definitions; for the host and build machines, these include the autoconfigured headers generated by 'configure'. The other configuration headers are determined by 'config.gcc'. They also contain the typedefs for **rtx**, **rtvec** and **tree**.

- 'config.h', for use in programs that run on the host machine.

- 'bconfig.h', for use in programs that run on the build machine.

- 'tconfig.h', for use in programs and libraries for the target machine.

- 'tm_p.h', which includes the header '*machine*-protos.h' that contains prototypes for functions in the target '*machine*.c' file. The header '*machine*-protos.h' can include prototypes of functions that use rtl and tree data structures inside appropriate #ifdef RTX_CODE and #ifdef TREE_CODE conditional code segments. The '*machine*-protos.h' is included after the 'rtl.h' and/or 'tree.h' would have been included. The 'tm_p.h' also includes the header 'tm-preds.h' which is generated by 'genpreds' program during the build to define the declarations and inline functions for the predicate functions.

6.3.3 Build System in the 'gcc' Directory

FIXME: describe the build system, including what is built in what stages. Also list the various source files that are used in the build process but aren't source files of GCC itself and so aren't documented below (see Chapter 9 [Passes], page 115).

6.3.4 Makefile Targets

These targets are available from the 'gcc' directory:

all   This is the default target. Depending on what your build/host/target configuration is, it coordinates all the things that need to be built.

doc   Produce info-formatted documentation and man pages. Essentially it calls 'make man' and 'make info'.

dvi   Produce DVI-formatted documentation.

pdf   Produce PDF-formatted documentation.

html   Produce HTML-formatted documentation.

man   Generate man pages.

info   Generate info-formatted pages.

mostlyclean
              Delete the files made while building the compiler.

clean   That, and all the other files built by 'make all'.

distclean
              That, and all the files created by configure.

maintainer-clean
              Distclean plus any file that can be generated from other files. Note that additional tools may be required beyond what is normally needed to build GCC.

srcextra   Generates files in the source directory that are not version-controlled but should go into a release tarball.

srcinfo
srcman   Copies the info-formatted and manpage documentation into the source directory usually for the purpose of generating a release tarball.

install   Installs GCC.

uninstall
              Deletes installed files, though this is not supported.

check   Run the testsuite. This creates a 'testsuite' subdirectory that has various '.sum' and '.log' files containing the results of the testing. You can run subsets with, for example, 'make check-gcc'. You can specify specific tests by setting RUNTESTFLAGS to be the name of the '.exp' file, optionally followed by (for some tests) an equals and a file wildcard, like:

              make check-gcc RUNTESTFLAGS="execute.exp=19980413-*"

              Note that running the testsuite may require additional tools be installed, such as Tcl or DejaGnu.

The toplevel tree from which you start GCC compilation is not the GCC directory, but rather a complex Makefile that coordinates the various steps of the build, including bootstrapping the compiler and using the new compiler to build target libraries.

When GCC is configured for a native configuration, the default action for `make` is to do a full three-stage bootstrap. This means that GCC is built three times—once with the native compiler, once with the native-built compiler it just built, and once with the compiler it built the second time. In theory, the last two should produce the same results, which '`make compare`' can check. Each stage is configured separately and compiled into a separate directory, to minimize problems due to ABI incompatibilities between the native compiler and GCC.

If you do a change, rebuilding will also start from the first stage and "bubble" up the change through the three stages. Each stage is taken from its build directory (if it had been built previously), rebuilt, and copied to its subdirectory. This will allow you to, for example, continue a bootstrap after fixing a bug which causes the stage2 build to crash. It does not provide as good coverage of the compiler as bootstrapping from scratch, but it ensures that the new code is syntactically correct (e.g., that you did not use GCC extensions by mistake), and avoids spurious bootstrap comparison failures[1].

Other targets available from the top level include:

`bootstrap-lean`

> Like `bootstrap`, except that the various stages are removed once they're no longer needed. This saves disk space.

`bootstrap2`
`bootstrap2-lean`

> Performs only the first two stages of bootstrap. Unlike a three-stage bootstrap, this does not perform a comparison to test that the compiler is running properly. Note that the disk space required by a "lean" bootstrap is approximately independent of the number of stages.

`stageN-bubble` (N = 1...4, `profile`, `feedback`)

> Rebuild all the stages up to N, with the appropriate flags, "bubbling" the changes as described above.

`all-stageN` (N = 1...4, `profile`, `feedback`)

> Assuming that stage N has already been built, rebuild it with the appropriate flags. This is rarely needed.

`cleanstrap`

> Remove everything ('`make clean`') and rebuilds ('`make bootstrap`').

`compare` Compares the results of stages 2 and 3. This ensures that the compiler is running properly, since it should produce the same object files regardless of how it itself was compiled.

`profiledbootstrap`

> Builds a compiler with profiling feedback information. In this case, the second and third stages are named '`profile`' and '`feedback`', respectively. For more information, see Section "Building with profile feedback" in *Installing GCC*.

---

[1] Except if the compiler was buggy and miscompiled some of the files that were not modified. In this case, it's best to use `make restrap`.

restrap   Restart a bootstrap, so that everything that was not built with the system
            compiler is rebuilt.

stage*N*-start (*N* = 1...4, profile, feedback)
            For each package that is bootstrapped, rename directories so that, for example,
            'gcc' points to the stage*N* GCC, compiled with the stage*N-1* GCC[2].

            You will invoke this target if you need to test or debug the stage*N* GCC. If
            you only need to execute GCC (but you need not run 'make' either to rebuild it
            or to run test suites), you should be able to work directly in the 'stage*N*-gcc'
            directory. This makes it easier to debug multiple stages in parallel.

stage   For each package that is bootstrapped, relocate its build directory to indicate
            its stage. For example, if the 'gcc' directory points to the stage2 GCC, after
            invoking this target it will be renamed to 'stage2-gcc'.

If you wish to use non-default GCC flags when compiling the stage2 and stage3 compilers,
set BOOT_CFLAGS on the command line when doing 'make'.

Usually, the first stage only builds the languages that the compiler is written in: typically,
C and maybe Ada. If you are debugging a miscompilation of a different stage2 front-end (for
example, of the Fortran front-end), you may want to have front-ends for other languages in
the first stage as well. To do so, set STAGE1_LANGUAGES on the command line when doing
'make'.

For example, in the aforementioned scenario of debugging a Fortran front-end miscompilation caused by the stage1 compiler, you may need a command like

```
make stage2-bubble STAGE1_LANGUAGES=c,fortran
```

Alternatively, you can use per-language targets to build and test languages that are not
enabled by default in stage1. For example, make f951 will build a Fortran compiler even in
the stage1 build directory.

6.3.5 Library Source Files and Headers under the 'gcc' Directory

FIXME: list here, with explanation, all the C source files and headers under the 'gcc'
directory that aren't built into the GCC executable but rather are part of runtime libraries
and object files, such as 'crtstuff.c' and 'unwind-dw2.c'. See Section 6.3.6 [Headers
Installed by GCC], page 68, for more information about the 'ginclude' directory.

6.3.6 Headers Installed by GCC

In general, GCC expects the system C library to provide most of the headers to be used
with it. However, GCC will fix those headers if necessary to make them work with GCC,
and will install some headers required of freestanding implementations. These headers are
installed in '*libsubdir*/include'. Headers for non-C runtime libraries are also installed by
GCC; these are not documented here. (FIXME: document them somewhere.)

Several of the headers GCC installs are in the 'ginclude' directory. These
headers, 'iso646.h', 'stdarg.h', 'stdbool.h', and 'stddef.h', are installed in
'*libsubdir*/include', unless the target Makefile fragment (see Section 19.1 [Target
Fragment], page 617) overrides this by setting USER_H.

---

[2] Customarily, the system compiler is also termed the 'stage0' GCC.

In addition to these headers and those generated by fixing system headers to work with GCC, some other headers may also be installed in '*libsubdir*/include'. 'config.gcc' may set **extra_headers**; this specifies additional headers under '**config**' to be installed on some systems.

GCC installs its own version of <float.h>, from 'ginclude/float.h'. This is done to cope with command-line options that change the representation of floating point numbers.

GCC also installs its own version of <limits.h>; this is generated from 'glimits.h', together with 'limitx.h' and 'limity.h' if the system also has its own version of <limits.h>. (GCC provides its own header because it is required of ISO C freestanding implementations, but needs to include the system header from its own header as well because other standards such as POSIX specify additional values to be defined in <limits.h>.) The system's <limits.h> header is used via '*libsubdir*/include/syslimits.h', which is copied from 'gsyslimits.h' if it does not need fixing to work with GCC; if it needs fixing, 'syslimits.h' is the fixed copy.

GCC can also install <tgmath.h>. It will do this when 'config.gcc' sets **use_gcc_tgmath** to **yes**.

6.3.7 Building Documentation

The main GCC documentation is in the form of manuals in Texinfo format. These are installed in Info format; DVI versions may be generated by '**make dvi**', PDF versions by '**make pdf**', and HTML versions by '**make html**'. In addition, some man pages are generated from the Texinfo manuals, there are some other text files with miscellaneous documentation, and runtime libraries have their own documentation outside the '**gcc**' directory. FIXME: document the documentation for runtime libraries somewhere.

6.3.7.1 Texinfo Manuals

The manuals for GCC as a whole, and the C and C++ front ends, are in files 'doc/*.texi'. Other front ends have their own manuals in files '*language*/*.texi'. Common files 'doc/include/*.texi' are provided which may be included in multiple manuals; the following files are in 'doc/include':

'fdl.texi'
> The GNU Free Documentation License.

'funding.texi'
> The section "Funding Free Software".

'gcc-common.texi'
> Common definitions for manuals.

'gpl_v3.texi'
> The GNU General Public License.

'texinfo.tex'
> A copy of 'texinfo.tex' known to work with the GCC manuals.

DVI-formatted manuals are generated by '**make dvi**', which uses texi2dvi (via the Makefile macro $(TEXI2DVI)). PDF-formatted manuals are generated by '**make pdf**', which uses texi2pdf (via the Makefile macro $(TEXI2PDF)). HTML formatted manuals are generated by 'make html'. Info manuals are generated by 'make info' (which is run as part of a boot-strap); this generates the manuals in the source directory, using makeinfo via the Makefile macro $(MAKEINFO), and they are included in release distributions.

Manuals are also provided on the GCC web site, in both HTML and PostScript forms. This is done via the script 'maintainer-scripts/update_web_docs_svn'. Each manual to be provided online must be listed in the definition of MANUALS in that file; a file 'name.texi' must only appear once in the source tree, and the output manual must have the same name as the source file. (However, other Texinfo files, included in manuals but not them-selves the root files of manuals, may have names that appear more than once in the source tree.) The manual file 'name.texi' should only include other files in its own directory or in 'doc/include'. HTML manuals will be generated by 'makeinfo --html', PostScript manu-als by texi2dvi and dvips, and PDF manuals by texi2pdf. All Texinfo files that are parts of manuals must be version-controlled, even if they are generated files, for the generation of online manuals to work.

The installation manual, 'doc/install.texi', is also provided on the GCC web site. The HTML version is generated by the script 'doc/install.texi2html'.

6.3.7.2 Man Page Generation

Because of user demand, in addition to full Texinfo manuals, man pages are provided which contain extracts from those manuals. These man pages are generated from the Texinfo manuals using 'contrib/texi2pod.pl' and pod2man. (The man page for g++, 'cp/g++.1', just contains a '.so' reference to 'gcc.1', but all the other man pages are generated from Texinfo manuals.)

Because many systems may not have the necessary tools installed to generate the man pages, they are only generated if the 'configure' script detects that recent enough tools are installed, and the Makefiles allow generating man pages to fail without aborting the build. Man pages are also included in release distributions. They are generated in the source directory.

Magic comments in Texinfo files starting '@c man' control what parts of a Texinfo file go into a man page. Only a subset of Texinfo is supported by 'texi2pod.pl', and it may be necessary to add support for more Texinfo features to this script when generating new man pages. To improve the man page output, some special Texinfo macros are provided in 'doc/include/gcc-common.texi' which 'texi2pod.pl' understands:

@gcctabopt

Use in the form '@table @gcctabopt' for tables of options, where for printed output the effect of '@code' is better than that of '@option' but for man page output a different effect is wanted.

@gccoptlist

Use for summary lists of options in manuals.

@gol   Use at the end of each line inside '@gccoptlist'. This is necessary to avoid problems with differences in how the '@gccoptlist' macro is handled by dif-ferent Texinfo formatters.

FIXME: describe the 'texi2pod.pl' input language and magic comments in more detail.

6.3.7.3 Miscellaneous Documentation

In addition to the formal documentation that is installed by GCC, there are several other text files in the 'gcc' subdirectory with miscellaneous documentation:

'ABOUT-GCC-NLS'

>   Notes on GCC's Native Language Support. FIXME: this should be part of this manual rather than a separate file.

'ABOUT-NLS'

>   Notes on the Free Translation Project.

'COPYING'
'COPYING3'

>   The GNU General Public License, Versions 2 and 3.

'COPYING.LIB'
'COPYING3.LIB'

>   The GNU Lesser General Public License, Versions 2.1 and 3.

'*ChangeLog*'
'*/ChangeLog*'

>   Change log files for various parts of GCC.

'LANGUAGES'

>   Details of a few changes to the GCC front-end interface. FIXME: the information in this file should be part of general documentation of the front-end interface in this manual.

'ONEWS'   Information about new features in old versions of GCC. (For recent versions, the information is on the GCC web site.)

'README.Portability'

>   Information about portability issues when writing code in GCC. FIXME: why isn't this part of this manual or of the GCC Coding Conventions?

   FIXME: document such files in subdirectories, at least 'config', 'c', 'cp', 'objc', 'testsuite'.

6.3.8 Anatomy of a Language Front End

A front end for a language in GCC has the following parts:

- A directory 'language' under 'gcc' containing source files for that front end. See Section 6.3.8.1 [The Front End 'language' Directory], page 72, for details.
- A mention of the language in the list of supported languages in 'gcc/doc/install.texi'.
- A mention of the name under which the language's runtime library is recognized by '--enable-shared=package' in the documentation of that option in 'gcc/doc/install.texi'.
- A mention of any special prerequisites for building the front end in the documentation of prerequisites in 'gcc/doc/install.texi'.
- Details of contributors to that front end in 'gcc/doc/contrib.texi'. If the details are in that front end's own manual then there should be a link to that manual's list in 'contrib.texi'.

- Information about support for that language in 'gcc/doc/frontends.texi'.

- Information about standards for that language, and the front end's support for them, in 'gcc/doc/standards.texi'. This may be a link to such information in the front end's own manual.

- Details of source file suffixes for that language and '-x lang' options supported, in 'gcc/doc/invoke.texi'.

- Entries in default_compilers in 'gcc.c' for source file suffixes for that language.

- Preferably testsuites, which may be under 'gcc/testsuite' or runtime library directories. FIXME: document somewhere how to write testsuite harnesses.

- Probably a runtime library for the language, outside the 'gcc' directory. FIXME: document this further.

- Details of the directories of any runtime libraries in 'gcc/doc/sourcebuild.texi'.

- Check targets in 'Makefile.def' for the top-level 'Makefile' to check just the compiler or the compiler and runtime library for the language.

If the front end is added to the official GCC source repository, the following are also necessary:

- At least one Bugzilla component for bugs in that front end and runtime libraries. This category needs to be added to the Bugzilla database.

- Normally, one or more maintainers of that front end listed in 'MAINTAINERS'.

- Mentions on the GCC web site in 'index.html' and 'frontends.html', with any relevant links on 'readings.html'. (Front ends that are not an official part of GCC may also be listed on 'frontends.html', with relevant links.)

- A news item on 'index.html', and possibly an announcement on the gcc-announce@gcc.gnu.org mailing list.

- The front end's manuals should be mentioned in 'maintainer-scripts/update_web_docs_svn' (see Section 6.3.7.1 [Texinfo Manuals], page 69) and the online manuals should be linked to from 'onlinedocs/index.html'.

- Any old releases or CVS repositories of the front end, before its inclusion in GCC, should be made available on the GCC FTP site ftp://gcc.gnu.org/pub/gcc/old-releases/.

- The release and snapshot script 'maintainer-scripts/gcc_release' should be updated to generate appropriate tarballs for this front end.

- If this front end includes its own version files that include the current date, 'maintainer-scripts/update_version' should be updated accordingly.

6.3.8.1 The Front End 'language' Directory

A front end 'language' directory contains the source files of that front end (but not of any runtime libraries, which should be outside the 'gcc' directory). This includes documentation, and possibly some subsidiary programs built alongside the front end. Certain files are special and other parts of the compiler depend on their names:

'config-lang.in'

> This file is required in all language subdirectories. See Section 6.3.8.2 [The Front End 'config-lang.in' File], page 73, for details of its contents

'Make-lang.in'

> This file is required in all language subdirectories. See Section 6.3.8.3 [The Front End 'Make-lang.in' File], page 74, for details of its contents.

'lang.opt'

> This file registers the set of switches that the front end accepts on the command line, and their '--help' text. See Chapter 8 [Options], page 107.

'lang-specs.h'

> This file provides entries for default_compilers in 'gcc.c' which override the default of giving an error that a compiler for that language is not installed.

'language-tree.def'

> This file, which need not exist, defines any language-specific tree codes.

6.3.8.2 The Front End 'config-lang.in' File

Each language subdirectory contains a 'config-lang.in' file. This file is a shell script that may define some variables describing the language:

language This definition must be present, and gives the name of the language for some purposes such as arguments to '--enable-languages'.

lang_requires

> If defined, this variable lists (space-separated) language front ends other than C that this front end requires to be enabled (with the names given being their language settings). For example, the Obj-C++ front end depends on the C++ and ObjC front ends, so sets 'lang_requires="objc c++"'.

subdir_requires

> If defined, this variable lists (space-separated) front end directories other than C that this front end requires to be present. For example, the Objective-C++ front end uses source files from the C++ and Objective-C front ends, so sets 'subdir_requires="cp objc"'.

target_libs

> If defined, this variable lists (space-separated) targets in the top level 'Makefile' to build the runtime libraries for this language, such as target-libobjc.

lang_dirs

> If defined, this variable lists (space-separated) top level directories (parallel to 'gcc'), apart from the runtime libraries, that should not be configured if this front end is not built.

build_by_default

> If defined to 'no', this language front end is not built unless enabled in a '--enable-languages' argument. Otherwise, front ends are built by default, subject to any special logic in 'configure.ac' (as is present to disable the Ada front end if the Ada compiler is not already installed).

boot_language

> If defined to 'yes', this front end is built in stage1 of the bootstrap. This is only relevant to front ends written in their own languages.

compilers

> If defined, a space-separated list of compiler executables that will be run by the driver. The names here will each end with '\\\$(exeext)'.

outputs   If defined, a space-separated list of files that should be generated by 'configure' substituting values in them. This mechanism can be used to create a file 'language/Makefile' from 'language/Makefile.in', but this is deprecated, building everything from the single 'gcc/Makefile' is preferred.

gtfiles   If defined, a space-separated list of files that should be scanned by 'gengtype.c' to generate the garbage collection tables and routines for this language. This excludes the files that are common to all front ends. See Chapter 22 [Type Information], page 625.

6.3.8.3 The Front End 'Make-lang.in' File

Each language subdirectory contains a 'Make-lang.in' file. It contains targets *lang.hook* (where *lang* is the setting of **language** in 'config-lang.in') for the following values of *hook*, and any other Makefile rules required to build those targets (which may if necessary use other Makefiles specified in **outputs** in 'config-lang.in', although this is deprecated). It also adds any testsuite targets that can use the standard rule in 'gcc/Makefile.in' to the variable **lang_checks**.

all.cross
start.encap
rest.encap

> FIXME: exactly what goes in each of these targets?

tags   Build an **etags** 'TAGS' file in the language subdirectory in the source tree.

info   Build info documentation for the front end, in the build directory. This target is only called by 'make bootstrap' if a suitable version of **makeinfo** is available, so does not need to check for this, and should fail if an error occurs.

dvi   Build DVI documentation for the front end, in the build directory. This should be done using $(TEXI2DVI), with appropriate '-I' arguments pointing to directories of included files.

pdf   Build PDF documentation for the front end, in the build directory. This should be done using $(TEXI2PDF), with appropriate '-I' arguments pointing to directories of included files.

html   Build HTML documentation for the front end, in the build directory.

man   Build generated man pages for the front end from Texinfo manuals (see Section 6.3.7.2 [Man Page Generation], page 70), in the build directory. This target is only called if the necessary tools are available, but should ignore errors so as not to stop the build if errors occur; man pages are optional and the tools involved may be installed in a broken way.

install-common

> Install everything that is part of the front end, apart from the compiler executables listed in **compilers** in 'config-lang.in'.

install-info

> Install info documentation for the front end, if it is present in the source directory. This target should have dependencies on info files that should be installed.

install-man

> Install man pages for the front end. This target should ignore errors.

install-plugin

> Install headers needed for plugins.

srcextra   Copies its dependencies into the source directory. This generally should be used for generated files such as Bison output files which are not version-controlled, but should be included in any release tarballs. This target will be executed during a bootstrap if '--enable-generated-files-in-srcdir' was specified as a 'configure' option.

srcinfo
srcman   Copies its dependencies into the source directory. These targets will be executed during a bootstrap if '--enable-generated-files-in-srcdir' was specified as a 'configure' option.

uninstall

> Uninstall files installed by installing the compiler. This is currently documented not to be supported, so the hook need not do anything.

mostlyclean
clean
distclean
maintainer-clean

> The language parts of the standard GNU '*clean' targets. See Section "Standard Targets for Users" in *GNU Coding Standards*, for details of the standard targets. For GCC, maintainer-clean should delete all generated files in the source directory that are not version-controlled, but should not delete anything that is.

'Make-lang.in' must also define a variable *lang*_OBJS to a list of host object files that are used by that language.

6.3.9 Anatomy of a Target Back End

A back end for a target architecture in GCC has the following parts:

- A directory '*machine*' under 'gcc/config', containing a machine description '*machine*.md' file (see Chapter 16 [Machine Descriptions], page 303), header files '*machine*.h' and '*machine*-protos.h' and a source file '*machine*.c' (see Chapter 17 [Target Description Macros and Functions], page 433), possibly a target Makefile fragment 't-*machine*' (see Section 19.1 [The Target Makefile Fragment], page 617), and maybe some other files. The names of these files may be changed from the defaults given by explicit specifications in 'config.gcc'.

- If necessary, a file '*machine*-modes.def' in the '*machine*' directory, containing additional machine modes to represent condition codes. See Section 17.15 [Condition Code], page 521, for further details.

- An optional '*machine*.opt' file in the '*machine*' directory, containing a list of target-specific options. You can also add other option files using the extra_options variable in 'config.gcc'. See Chapter 8 [Options], page 107.

- Entries in 'config.gcc' (see Section 6.3.2.2 [The 'config.gcc' File], page 64) for the systems with this target architecture.

- Documentation in 'gcc/doc/invoke.texi' for any command-line options supported by this target (see Section 17.3 [Run-time Target Specification], page 440). This means both entries in the summary table of options and details of the individual options.

- Documentation in 'gcc/doc/extend.texi' for any target-specific attributes supported (see Section 17.24 [Defining target-specific uses of __attribute__], page 582), including where the same attribute is already supported on some targets, which are enumerated in the manual.

- Documentation in 'gcc/doc/extend.texi' for any target-specific pragmas supported.

- Documentation in 'gcc/doc/extend.texi' of any target-specific built-in functions supported.

- Documentation in 'gcc/doc/extend.texi' of any target-specific format checking styles supported.

- Documentation in 'gcc/doc/md.texi' of any target-specific constraint letters (see Section 16.8.5 [Constraints for Particular Machines], page 323).

- A note in 'gcc/doc/contrib.texi' under the person or people who contributed the target support.

- Entries in 'gcc/doc/install.texi' for all target triplets supported with this target architecture, giving details of any special notes about installation for this target, or saying that there are no special notes if there are none.

- Possibly other support outside the 'gcc' directory for runtime libraries. FIXME: reference docs for this. The libstdc++ porting manual needs to be installed as info for this to work, or to be a chapter of this manual.

If the back end is added to the official GCC source repository, the following are also necessary:

- An entry for the target architecture in 'readings.html' on the GCC web site, with any relevant links.

- Details of the properties of the back end and target architecture in 'backends.html' on the GCC web site.

- A news item about the contribution of support for that target architecture, in 'index.html' on the GCC web site.

- Normally, one or more maintainers of that target listed in 'MAINTAINERS'. Some existing architectures may be unmaintained, but it would be unusual to add support for a target that does not have a maintainer when support is added.

- Target triplets covering all 'config.gcc' stanzas for the target, in the list in 'contrib/config-list.mk'.

7 Testsuites

GCC contains several testsuites to help maintain compiler quality. Most of the runtime libraries and language front ends in GCC have testsuites. Currently only the C language testsuites are documented here; FIXME: document the others.

7.1 Idioms Used in Testsuite Code

In general, C testcases have a trailing '-*n*.c', starting with '-1.c', in case other testcases with similar names are added later. If the test is a test of some well-defined feature, it should have a name referring to that feature such as '*feature*-1.c'. If it does not test a well-defined feature but just happens to exercise a bug somewhere in the compiler, and a bug report has been filed for this bug in the GCC bug database, 'pr*bug-number*-1.c' is the appropriate form of name. Otherwise (for miscellaneous bugs not filed in the GCC bug database), and previously more generally, test cases are named after the date on which they were added. This allows people to tell at a glance whether a test failure is because of a recently found bug that has not yet been fixed, or whether it may be a regression, but does not give any other information about the bug or where discussion of it may be found. Some other language testsuites follow similar conventions.

In the 'gcc.dg' testsuite, it is often necessary to test that an error is indeed a hard error and not just a warning—for example, where it is a constraint violation in the C standard, which must become an error with '-pedantic-errors'. The following idiom, where the first line shown is line *line* of the file and the line that generates the error, is used for this:

```
/* { dg-bogus "warning" "warning in place of error" } */
/* { dg-error "regexp" "message" { target *-*-* } line } */
```

It may be necessary to check that an expression is an integer constant expression and has a certain value. To check that *E* has value *V*, an idiom similar to the following is used:

```
char x[((E) == (V) ? 1 : -1)];
```

In 'gcc.dg' tests, __typeof__ is sometimes used to make assertions about the types of expressions. See, for example, 'gcc.dg/c99-condexpr-1.c'. The more subtle uses depend on the exact rules for the types of conditional expressions in the C standard; see, for example, 'gcc.dg/c99-intconst-1.c'.

It is useful to be able to test that optimizations are being made properly. This cannot be done in all cases, but it can be done where the optimization will lead to code being optimized away (for example, where flow analysis or alias analysis should show that certain code cannot be called) or to functions not being called because they have been expanded as built-in functions. Such tests go in 'gcc.c-torture/execute'. Where code should be optimized away, a call to a nonexistent function such as link_failure () may be inserted; a definition

```
#ifndef __OPTIMIZE__
void
link_failure (void)
{
  abort ();
}
#endif
```

will also be needed so that linking still succeeds when the test is run without optimization. When all calls to a built-in function should have been optimized and no calls to the non-built-in version of the function should remain, that function may be defined as `static` to call `abort ()` (although redeclaring a function as static may not work on all targets).

All testcases must be portable. Target-specific testcases must have appropriate code to avoid causing failures on unsupported systems; unfortunately, the mechanisms for this differ by directory.

FIXME: discuss non-C testsuites here.

7.2 Directives used within DejaGnu tests

7.2.1 Syntax and Descriptions of test directives

Test directives appear within comments in a test source file and begin with `dg-`. Some of these are defined within DejaGnu and others are local to the GCC testsuite.

The order in which test directives appear in a test can be important: directives local to GCC sometimes override information used by the DejaGnu directives, which know nothing about the GCC directives, so the DejaGnu directives must precede GCC directives.

Several test directives include selectors (see Section 7.2.2 [Selectors], page 82) which are usually preceded by the keyword `target` or `xfail`.

7.2.1.1 Specify how to build the test

`{ dg-do do-what-keyword [{ target/xfail selector }] }`
>   *do-what-keyword* specifies how the test is compiled and whether it is executed. It is one of:

> `preprocess`
> >   Compile with '`-E`' to run only the preprocessor.

> `compile`   Compile with '`-S`' to produce an assembly code file.

> `assemble`   Compile with '`-c`' to produce a relocatable object file.

> `link`   Compile, assemble, and link to produce an executable file.

> `run`   Produce and run an executable file, which is expected to return an exit code of 0.

>   The default is `compile`. That can be overridden for a set of tests by redefining `dg-do-what-default` within the `.exp` file for those tests.

>   If the directive includes the optional '`{ target selector }`' then the test is skipped unless the target system matches the *selector*.

>   If *do-what-keyword* is `run` and the directive includes the optional '`{ xfail selector }`' and the selector is met then the test is expected to fail. The `xfail` clause is ignored for other values of *do-what-keyword*; those tests can use directive `dg-xfail-if`.

7.2.1.2 Specify additional compiler options

{ dg-options *options* [{ target *selector* }] }

> This DejaGnu directive provides a list of compiler options, to be used if the
> target system matches *selector*, that replace the default options used for this
> set of tests.

{ dg-add-options *feature* ... }

> Add any compiler options that are needed to access certain features. This
> directive does nothing on targets that enable the features by default, or that
> don't provide them at all. It must come after all **dg-options** directives. For
> supported values of *feature* see Section 7.2.4 [Add Options], page 95.

{ dg-additional-options *options* [{ target *selector* }] }

> This directive provides a list of compiler options, to be used if the target system
> matches *selector*, that are added to the default options used for this set of tests.

7.2.1.3 Modify the test timeout value

The normal timeout limit, in seconds, is found by searching the following in order:

- the value defined by an earlier **dg-timeout** directive in the test
- variable *tool_timeout* defined by the set of tests
- *gcc,timeout* set in the target board
- 300

{ dg-timeout *n* [{target *selector* }] }

> Set the time limit for the compilation and for the execution of the test to the
> specified number of seconds.

{ dg-timeout-factor *x* [{ target *selector* }] }

> Multiply the normal time limit for compilation and execution of the test by the
> specified floating-point factor.

7.2.1.4 Skip a test for some targets

{ dg-skip-if *comment* { *selector* } [{ *include-opts* } [{ *exclude-opts* }]] }

> Arguments *include-opts* and *exclude-opts* are lists in which each element is
> a string of zero or more GCC options. Skip the test if all of the following
> conditions are met:
>
> - the test system is included in *selector*
> - for at least one of the option strings in *include-opts*, every option from that
>   string is in the set of options with which the test would be compiled; use
>   '"*"' for an *include-opts* list that matches any options; that is the default
>   if *include-opts* is not specified
> - for each of the option strings in *exclude-opts*, at least one option from that
>   string is not in the set of options with which the test would be compiled;
>   use '""' for an empty *exclude-opts* list; that is the default if *exclude-opts*
>   is not specified
>
> For example, to skip a test if option **-Os** is present:

```
/* { dg-skip-if "" { *-*-* }  { "-Os" } { "" } } */
```

To skip a test if both options -O2 and -g are present:

```
/* { dg-skip-if "" { *-*-* }  { "-O2 -g" } { "" } } */
```

To skip a test if either -O2 or -O3 is present:

```
/* { dg-skip-if "" { *-*-* }  { "-O2" "-O3" } { "" } } */
```

To skip a test unless option -Os is present:

```
/* { dg-skip-if "" { *-*-* }  { "*" } { "-Os" } } */
```

To skip a test if either -O2 or -O3 is used with -g but not if -fpic is also present:

```
/* { dg-skip-if "" { *-*-* }  { "-O2 -g" "-O3 -g" } { "-fpic" } } */
```

`{ dg-require-effective-target` *keyword* `[{` *selector* `}] }`

>   Skip the test if the test target, including current multilib flags, is not covered by the effective-target keyword. If the directive includes the optional '{ *selector* }' then the effective-target test is only performed if the target system matches the *selector*. This directive must appear after any **dg-do** directive in the test and before any **dg-additional-sources** directive. See Section 7.2.3 [Effective-Target Keywords], page 82.

`{ dg-require-`*support* `args }`

>   Skip the test if the target does not provide the required support. These directives must appear after any **dg-do** directive in the test and before any **dg-additional-sources** directive. They require at least one argument, which can be an empty string if the specific procedure does not examine the argument. See Section 7.2.5 [Require Support], page 97, for a complete list of these directives.

7.2.1.5 Expect a test to fail for some targets

`{ dg-xfail-if` *comment* `{` *selector* `} [{` *include-opts* `} [{` *exclude-opts* `}]] }`

>   Expect the test to fail if the conditions (which are the same as for **dg-skip-if**) are met. This does not affect the execute step.

`{ dg-xfail-run-if` *comment* `{` *selector* `} [{` *include-opts* `} [{` *exclude-opts* `}]] }`

>   Expect the execute step of a test to fail if the conditions (which are the same as for **dg-skip-if**) are met.

7.2.1.6 Expect the test executable to fail

`{ dg-shouldfail` *comment* `[{` *selector* `} [{` *include-opts* `} [{` *exclude-opts* `}]]] }`

>   Expect the test executable to return a nonzero exit status if the conditions (which are the same as for **dg-skip-if**) are met.

7.2.1.7 Verify compiler messages

`{ dg-error` *regexp* `[comment [{` target/xfail *selector* `} [`line`] ]] }`

>   This DejaGnu directive appears on a source line that is expected to get an error message, or else specifies the source line associated with the message. If there is no message for that line or if the text of that message is not matched by *regexp* then the check fails and *comment* is included in the **FAIL** message. The check does not look for the string 'error' unless it is part of *regexp*.

`{ dg-warning regexp [comment [{ target/xfail selector } [line] ]] }`

> This DejaGnu directive appears on a source line that is expected to get a warning message, or else specifies the source line associated with the message. If there is no message for that line or if the text of that message is not matched by *regexp* then the check fails and *comment* is included in the `FAIL` message. The check does not look for the string 'warning' unless it is part of *regexp*.

`{ dg-message regexp [comment [{ target/xfail selector } [line] ]] }`

> The line is expected to get a message other than an error or warning. If there is no message for that line or if the text of that message is not matched by *regexp* then the check fails and *comment* is included in the `FAIL` message.

`{ dg-bogus regexp [comment [{ target/xfail selector } [line] ]] }`

> This DejaGnu directive appears on a source line that should not get a message matching *regexp*, or else specifies the source line associated with the bogus message. It is usually used with 'xfail' to indicate that the message is a known problem for a particular set of targets.

`{ dg-excess-errors comment [{ target/xfail selector }] }`

> This DejaGnu directive indicates that the test is expected to fail due to compiler messages that are not handled by 'dg-error', 'dg-warning' or 'dg-bogus'. For this directive 'xfail' has the same effect as 'target'.

`{ dg-prune-output regexp }`

> Prune messages matching *regexp* from the test output.

7.2.1.8 Verify output of the test executable

`{ dg-output regexp [{ target/xfail selector }] }`

> This DejaGnu directive compares *regexp* to the combined output that the test executable writes to 'stdout' and 'stderr'.

7.2.1.9 Specify additional files for a test

`{ dg-additional-files "filelist" }`

> Specify additional files, other than source files, that must be copied to the system where the compiler runs.

`{ dg-additional-sources "filelist" }`

> Specify additional source files to appear in the compile line following the main test file.

7.2.1.10 Add checks at the end of a test

`{ dg-final { local-directive } }`

> This DejaGnu directive is placed within a comment anywhere in the source file and is processed after the test has been compiled and run. Multiple 'dg-final' commands are processed in the order in which they appear in the source file. See Section 7.2.6 [Final Actions], page 98, for a list of directives that can be used within dg-final.

7.2.2 Selecting targets to which a test applies

Several test directives include *selector*s to limit the targets for which a test is run or to declare that a test is expected to fail on particular targets.

A selector is:

- one or more target triplets, possibly including wildcard characters; use '*-*-*' to match any target

- a single effective-target keyword (see Section 7.2.3 [Effective-Target Keywords], page 82)

- a logical expression

Depending on the context, the selector specifies whether a test is skipped and reported as unsupported or is expected to fail. A context that allows either '`target`' or '`xfail`' also allows '{ `target` *selector1* `xfail` *selector2* }' to skip the test for targets that don't match *selector1* and the test to fail for targets that match *selector2*.

A selector expression appears within curly braces and uses a single logical operator: one of '!', '&&', or '||'. An operand is another selector expression, an effective-target keyword, a single target triplet, or a list of target triplets within quotes or curly braces. For example:

```
{ target { ! "hppa*-*-* ia64*-*-*" } }
{ target { powerpc*-*-* && lp64 } }
{ xfail { lp64 || vect_no_align } }
```

7.2.3 Keywords describing target attributes

Effective-target keywords identify sets of targets that support particular functionality. They are used to limit tests to be run only for particular targets, or to specify that particular sets of targets are expected to fail some tests.

Effective-target keywords are defined in '`lib/target-supports.exp`' in the GCC testsuite, with the exception of those that are documented as being local to a particular test directory.

The '`effective target`' takes into account all of the compiler options with which the test will be compiled, including the multilib options. By convention, keywords ending in `_nocache` can also include options specified for the particular test in an earlier `dg-options` or `dg-add-options` directive.

7.2.3.1 Data type sizes

`ilp32`   Target has 32-bit `int`, `long`, and pointers.

`lp64`   Target has 32-bit `int`, 64-bit `long` and pointers.

`llp64`   Target has 32-bit `int` and `long`, 64-bit `long long` and pointers.

`double64` Target has 64-bit `double`.

`double64plus`
        Target has `double` that is 64 bits or longer.

`longdouble128`
        Target has 128-bit `long double`.

int32plus
>
> Target has `int` that is at 32 bits or longer.

int16   Target has `int` that is 16 bits or shorter.

long_neq_int
>
> Target has `int` and `long` with different sizes.

large_double
>
> Target supports `double` that is longer than `float`.

large_long_double
>
> Target supports `long double` that is longer than `double`.

ptr32plus
>
> Target has pointers that are 32 bits or longer.

size32plus
>
> Target supports array and structure sizes that are 32 bits or longer.

4byte_wchar_t
>
> Target has `wchar_t` that is at least 4 bytes.

floatn   Target has the `_Floatn` type.

floatnx   Target has the `_Floatnx` type.

floatn_runtime
>
> Target has the `_Floatn` type, including runtime support for any options added with `dg-add-options`.

floatnx_runtime
>
> Target has the `_Floatnx` type, including runtime support for any options added with `dg-add-options`.

floatn_nx_runtime
>
> Target has runtime support for any options added with `dg-add-options` for any `_Floatn` or `_Floatnx` type.

7.2.3.2 Fortran-specific attributes

fortran_integer_16
>
> Target supports Fortran `integer` that is 16 bytes or longer.

fortran_large_int
>
> Target supports Fortran `integer` kinds larger than `integer(8)`.

fortran_large_real
>
> Target supports Fortran `real` kinds larger than `real(8)`.

7.2.3.3 Vector-specific attributes

vect_condition
>
> Target supports vector conditional operations.

vect_cond_mixed
>
> Target supports vector conditional operations where comparison operands have different type from the value operands.

`vect_double`
> Target supports hardware vectors of `double`.

`vect_float`
> Target supports hardware vectors of `float`.

`vect_int`   Target supports hardware vectors of `int`.

`vect_long`
> Target supports hardware vectors of `long`.

`vect_long_long`
> Target supports hardware vectors of `long long`.

`vect_aligned_arrays`
> Target aligns arrays to vector alignment boundary.

`vect_hw_misalign`
> Target supports a vector misalign access.

`vect_no_align`
> Target does not support a vector alignment mechanism.

`vect_no_int_min_max`
> Target does not support a vector min and max instruction on `int`.

`vect_no_int_add`
> Target does not support a vector add instruction on `int`.

`vect_no_bitwise`
> Target does not support vector bitwise instructions.

`vect_char_mult`
> Target supports `vector char` multiplication.

`vect_short_mult`
> Target supports `vector short` multiplication.

`vect_int_mult`
> Target supports `vector int` multiplication.

`vect_extract_even_odd`
> Target supports vector even/odd element extraction.

`vect_extract_even_odd_wide`
> Target supports vector even/odd element extraction of vectors with elements `SImode` or larger.

`vect_interleave`
> Target supports vector interleaving.

`vect_strided`
> Target supports vector interleaving and extract even/odd.

`vect_strided_wide`
> Target supports vector interleaving and extract even/odd for wide element types.

`vect_perm`

> Target supports vector permutation.

`vect_shift`

> Target supports a hardware vector shift operation.

`vect_widen_sum_hi_to_si`

> Target supports a vector widening summation of **short** operands into **int** results, or can promote (unpack) from **short** to **int**.

`vect_widen_sum_qi_to_hi`

> Target supports a vector widening summation of **char** operands into **short** results, or can promote (unpack) from **char** to **short**.

`vect_widen_sum_qi_to_si`

> Target supports a vector widening summation of **char** operands into **int** results.

`vect_widen_mult_qi_to_hi`

> Target supports a vector widening multiplication of **char** operands into **short** results, or can promote (unpack) from **char** to **short** and perform non-widening multiplication of **short**.

`vect_widen_mult_hi_to_si`

> Target supports a vector widening multiplication of **short** operands into **int** results, or can promote (unpack) from **short** to **int** and perform non-widening multiplication of **int**.

`vect_widen_mult_si_to_di_pattern`

> Target supports a vector widening multiplication of **int** operands into **long** results.

`vect_sdot_qi`

> Target supports a vector dot-product of **signed char**.

`vect_udot_qi`

> Target supports a vector dot-product of **unsigned char**.

`vect_sdot_hi`

> Target supports a vector dot-product of **signed short**.

`vect_udot_hi`

> Target supports a vector dot-product of **unsigned short**.

`vect_pack_trunc`

> Target supports a vector demotion (packing) of **short** to **char** and from **int** to **short** using modulo arithmetic.

`vect_unpack`

> Target supports a vector promotion (unpacking) of **char** to **short** and from **char** to **int**.

`vect_intfloat_cvt`

> Target supports conversion from **signed int** to **float**.

`vect_uintfloat_cvt`

> Target supports conversion from **unsigned int** to **float**.

`vect_floatint_cvt`
>	Target supports conversion from `float` to `signed int`.

`vect_floatuint_cvt`
>	Target supports conversion from `float` to `unsigned int`.

`vect_max_reduc`
>	Target supports max reduction for vectors.

7.2.3.4 Thread Local Storage attributes

`tls`   Target supports thread-local storage.

`tls_native`
>	Target supports native (rather than emulated) thread-local storage.

`tls_runtime`
>	Test system supports executing TLS executables.

7.2.3.5 Decimal floating point attributes

`dfp`   Targets supports compiling decimal floating point extension to C.

`dfp_nocache`
>	Including the options used to compile this particular test, the target supports compiling decimal floating point extension to C.

`dfprt`   Test system can execute decimal floating point tests.

`dfprt_nocache`
>	Including the options used to compile this particular test, the test system can execute decimal floating point tests.

`hard_dfp` Target generates decimal floating point instructions with current options.

7.2.3.6 ARM-specific attributes

`arm32`   ARM target generates 32-bit code.

`arm_eabi` ARM target adheres to the ABI for the ARM Architecture.

`arm_fp_ok`
>	ARM target defines `__ARM_FP` using `-mfloat-abi=softfp` or equivalent options. Some multilibs may be incompatible with these options.

`arm_hf_eabi`
>	ARM target adheres to the VFP and Advanced SIMD Register Arguments variant of the ABI for the ARM Architecture (as selected with `-mfloat-abi=hard`).

`arm_hard_vfp_ok`
>	ARM target supports `-mfpu=vfp -mfloat-abi=hard`. Some multilibs may be incompatible with these options.

`arm_iwmmxt_ok`
>	ARM target supports `-mcpu=iwmmxt`. Some multilibs may be incompatible with this option.

`arm_neon`   ARM target supports generating NEON instructions.

`arm_tune_string_ops_prefer_neon`
              Test CPU tune supports inlining string operations with NEON instructions.

`arm_neon_hw`
              Test system supports executing NEON instructions.

`arm_neonv2_hw`
              Test system supports executing NEON v2 instructions.

`arm_neon_ok`
              ARM Target supports `-mfpu=neon -mfloat-abi=softfp` or compatible op-
              tions. Some multilibs may be incompatible with these options.

`arm_neonv2_ok`
              ARM Target supports `-mfpu=neon-vfpv4 -mfloat-abi=softfp` or compatible
              options. Some multilibs may be incompatible with these options.

`arm_fp16_ok`
              Target supports options to generate VFP half-precision floating-point instruc-
              tions. Some multilibs may be incompatible with these options. This test is
              valid for ARM only.

`arm_fp16_hw`
              Target supports executing VFP half-precision floating-point instructions. This
              test is valid for ARM only.

`arm_neon_fp16_ok`
              ARM Target supports `-mfpu=neon-fp16 -mfloat-abi=softfp` or compatible
              options, including `-mfp16-format=ieee` if necessary to obtain the `__fp16` type.
              Some multilibs may be incompatible with these options.

`arm_neon_fp16_hw`
              Test system supports executing Neon half-precision float instructions. (Implies
              previous.)

`arm_fp16_alternative_ok`
              ARM target supports the ARM FP16 alternative format. Some multilibs may
              be incompatible with the options needed.

`arm_fp16_none_ok`
              ARM target supports specifying none as the ARM FP16 format.

`arm_thumb1_ok`
              ARM target generates Thumb-1 code for `-mthumb`.

`arm_thumb2_ok`
              ARM target generates Thumb-2 code for `-mthumb`.

`arm_vfp_ok`
              ARM target supports `-mfpu=vfp -mfloat-abi=softfp`. Some multilibs may
              be incompatible with these options.

`arm_vfp3_ok`

>ARM target supports `-mfpu=vfp3 -mfloat-abi=softfp`. Some multilibs may be incompatible with these options.

`arm_v8_vfp_ok`

>ARM target supports `-mfpu=fp-armv8 -mfloat-abi=softfp`. Some multilibs may be incompatible with these options.

`arm_v8_neon_ok`

>ARM target supports `-mfpu=neon-fp-armv8 -mfloat-abi=softfp`. Some multilibs may be incompatible with these options.

`arm_v8_1a_neon_ok`

>ARM target supports options to generate ARMv8.1 Adv.SIMD instructions. Some multilibs may be incompatible with these options.

`arm_v8_1a_neon_hw`

>ARM target supports executing ARMv8.1 Adv.SIMD instructions. Some multilibs may be incompatible with the options needed. Implies arm_v8_1a_neon_ok.

`arm_acq_rel`

>ARM target supports acquire-release instructions.

`arm_v8_2a_fp16_scalar_ok`

>ARM target supports options to generate instructions for ARMv8.2 and scalar instructions from the FP16 extension. Some multilibs may be incompatible with these options.

`arm_v8_2a_fp16_scalar_hw`

>ARM target supports executing instructions for ARMv8.2 and scalar instructions from the FP16 extension. Some multilibs may be incompatible with these options. Implies arm_v8_2a_fp16_neon_ok.

`arm_v8_2a_fp16_neon_ok`

>ARM target supports options to generate instructions from ARMv8.2 with the FP16 extension. Some multilibs may be incompatible with these options. Implies arm_v8_2a_fp16_scalar_ok.

`arm_v8_2a_fp16_neon_hw`

>ARM target supports executing instructions from ARMv8.2 with the FP16 extension. Some multilibs may be incompatible with these options. Implies arm_v8_2a_fp16_neon_ok and arm_v8_2a_fp16_scalar_hw.

`arm_prefer_ldrd_strd`

>ARM target prefers `LDRD` and `STRD` instructions over `LDM` and `STM` instructions.

`arm_thumb1_movt_ok`

>ARM target generates Thumb-1 code for `-mthumb` with `MOVW` and `MOVT` instructions available.

`arm_thumb1_cbz_ok`

>ARM target generates Thumb-1 code for `-mthumb` with `CBZ` and `CBNZ` instructions available.

`arm_divmod_simode`

> ARM target for which divmod transform is disabled, if it supports hardware div instruction.

`arm_cmse_ok`

> ARM target supports ARMv8-M Security Extensions, enabled by the `-mcmse` option.

7.2.3.7 AArch64-specific attributes

`aarch64_asm_<ext>_ok`

> AArch64 assembler supports the architecture extension `ext` via the `.arch_extension` pseudo-op.

`aarch64_tiny`

> AArch64 target which generates instruction sequences for tiny memory model.

`aarch64_small`

> AArch64 target which generates instruction sequences for small memory model.

`aarch64_large`

> AArch64 target which generates instruction sequences for large memory model.

`aarch64_little_endian`

> AArch64 target which generates instruction sequences for little endian.

`aarch64_big_endian`

> AArch64 target which generates instruction sequences for big endian.

`aarch64_small_fpic`

> Binutils installed on test system supports relocation types required by -fpic for AArch64 small memory model.

7.2.3.8 MIPS-specific attributes

`mips64`   MIPS target supports 64-bit instructions.

`nomips16`   MIPS target does not produce MIPS16 code.

`mips16_attribute`

> MIPS target can generate MIPS16 code.

`mips_loongson`

> MIPS target is a Loongson-2E or -2F target using an ABI that supports the Loongson vector modes.

`mips_msa`   MIPS target supports `-mmsa`, MIPS SIMD Architecture (MSA).

`mips_newabi_large_long_double`

> MIPS target supports `long double` larger than `double` when using the new ABI.

`mpaired_single`

> MIPS target supports `-mpaired-single`.

7.2.3.9 PowerPC-specific attributes

dfp_hw   PowerPC target supports executing hardware DFP instructions.

p8vector_hw
> PowerPC target supports executing VSX instructions (ISA 2.07).

powerpc64
> Test system supports executing 64-bit instructions.

powerpc_altivec
> PowerPC target supports AltiVec.

powerpc_altivec_ok
> PowerPC target supports -maltivec.

powerpc_eabi_ok
> PowerPC target supports -meabi.

powerpc_elfv2
> PowerPC target supports -mabi=elfv2.

powerpc_fprs
> PowerPC target supports floating-point registers.

powerpc_hard_double
> PowerPC target supports hardware double-precision floating-point.

powerpc_htm_ok
> PowerPC target supports -mhtm

powerpc_p8vector_ok
> PowerPC target supports -mpower8-vector

powerpc_ppu_ok
> PowerPC target supports -mcpu=cell.

powerpc_spe
> PowerPC target supports PowerPC SPE.

powerpc_spe_nocache
> Including the options used to compile this particular test, the PowerPC target supports PowerPC SPE.

powerpc_spu
> PowerPC target supports PowerPC SPU.

powerpc_vsx_ok
> PowerPC target supports -mvsx.

powerpc_405_nocache
> Including the options used to compile this particular test, the PowerPC target supports PowerPC 405.

ppc_recip_hw
> PowerPC target supports executing reciprocal estimate instructions.

spu_auto_overlay

> SPU target has toolchain that supports automatic overlay generation.

vmx_hw   PowerPC target supports executing AltiVec instructions.

vsx_hw   PowerPC target supports executing VSX instructions (ISA 2.06).

7.2.3.10 Other hardware attributes

avx   Target supports compiling avx instructions.

avx_runtime

> Target supports the execution of avx instructions.

cell_hw   Test system can execute AltiVec and Cell PPU instructions.

coldfire_fpu

> Target uses a ColdFire FPU.

hard_float

> Target supports FPU instructions.

non_strict_align

> Target does not require strict alignment.

sqrt_insn

> Target has a square root instruction that the compiler can generate.

sse   Target supports compiling sse instructions.

sse_runtime

> Target supports the execution of sse instructions.

sse2   Target supports compiling sse2 instructions.

sse2_runtime

> Target supports the execution of sse2 instructions.

sync_char_short

> Target supports atomic operations on char and short.

sync_int_long

> Target supports atomic operations on int and long.

ultrasparc_hw

> Test environment appears to run executables on a simulator that accepts only EM_SPARC executables and chokes on EM_SPARC32PLUS or EM_SPARCV9 executables.

vect_cmdline_needed

> Target requires a command line argument to enable a SIMD instruction set.

pie_copyreloc

> The x86-64 target linker supports PIE with copy reloc.

divmod   Target supporting hardware divmod insn or divmod libcall.

divmod_simode

> Target supporting hardware divmod insn or divmod libcall for SImode.

7.2.3.11 Environment attributes

c   The language for the compiler under test is C.

c++   The language for the compiler under test is C++.

c99_runtime
               Target provides a full C99 runtime.

correct_iso_cpp_string_wchar_protos
               Target `string.h` and `wchar.h` headers provide C++ required overloads for
               `strchr` etc. functions.

dummy_wcsftime
               Target uses a dummy `wcsftime` function that always returns zero.

fd_truncate
               Target can truncate a file from a file descriptor, as used by
               'libgfortran/io/unix.c:fd_truncate'; i.e. `ftruncate` or `chsize`.

freestanding
               Target is 'freestanding' as defined in section 4 of the C99 standard. Effec-
               tively, it is a target which supports no extra headers or libraries other than
               what is considered essential.

init_priority
               Target supports constructors with initialization priority arguments.

inttypes_types
               Target has the basic signed and unsigned types in `inttypes.h`. This is for
               tests that GCC's notions of these types agree with those in the header, as some
               systems have only `inttypes.h`.

lax_strtofp
               Target might have errors of a few ULP in string to floating-point conversion
               functions and overflow is not always detected correctly by those functions.

mempcpy   Target provides `mempcpy` function.

mmap   Target supports `mmap`.

newlib   Target supports Newlib.

pow10   Target provides `pow10` function.

pthread   Target can compile using `pthread.h` with no errors or warnings.

pthread_h
               Target has `pthread.h`.

run_expensive_tests
               Expensive testcases (usually those that consume excessive amounts of CPU
               time) should be run on this target. This can be enabled by setting the `GCC_TEST_RUN_EXPENSIVE` environment variable to a non-empty string.

simulator
               Test system runs executables on a simulator (i.e. slowly) rather than hardware
               (i.e. fast).

stabs   Target supports the stabs debugging format.

stdint_types
                 Target has the basic signed and unsigned C types in `stdint.h`. This will be
                 obsolete when GCC ensures a working `stdint.h` for all targets.

stpcpy   Target provides `stpcpy` function.

trampolines
                 Target supports trampolines.

uclibc   Target supports uClibc.

unwrapped
                 Target does not use a status wrapper.

vxworks_kernel
                 Target is a VxWorks kernel.

vxworks_rtp
                 Target is a VxWorks RTP.

wchar   Target supports wide characters.

7.2.3.12 Other attributes

automatic_stack_alignment
                 Target supports automatic stack alignment.

cilkplus_runtime
                 Target supports the Cilk Plus runtime library.

cxa_atexit
                 Target uses `__cxa_atexit`.

default_packed
                 Target has packed layout of structure members by default.

fgraphite
                 Target supports Graphite optimizations.

fixed_point
                 Target supports fixed-point extension to C.

fopenacc   Target supports OpenACC via '`-fopenacc`'.

fopenmp   Target supports OpenMP via '`-fopenmp`'.

fpic   Target supports '`-fpic`' and '`-fPIC`'.

freorder   Target supports '`-freorder-blocks-and-partition`'.

fstack_protector
                 Target supports '`-fstack-protector`'.

gas   Target uses GNU `as`.

gc_sections
                 Target supports '`--gc-sections`'.

gld   Target uses GNU `ld`.

keeps_null_pointer_checks
               Target keeps null pointer checks, either due to the use of
               '-fno-delete-null-pointer-checks' or hardwired into the target.

lto   Compiler has been configured to support link-time optimization (LTO).

naked_functions
               Target supports the `naked` function attribute.

named_sections
               Target supports named sections.

natural_alignment_32
               Target uses natural alignment (aligned to type size) for types of 32 bits or less.

target_natural_alignment_64
               Target uses natural alignment (aligned to type size) for types of 64 bits or less.

nonpic   Target does not generate PIC by default.

pie_enabled
               Target generates PIE by default.

pcc_bitfield_type_matters
               Target defines `PCC_BITFIELD_TYPE_MATTERS`.

pe_aligned_commons
               Target supports '-mpe-aligned-commons'.

pie   Target supports '-pie', '-fpie' and '-fPIE'.

section_anchors
               Target supports section anchors.

short_enums
               Target defaults to short enums.

static   Target supports '-static'.

static_libgfortran
               Target supports statically linking '`libgfortran`'.

string_merging
               Target supports merging string constants at link time.

ucn   Target supports compiling and assembling UCN.

ucn_nocache
               Including the options used to compile this particular test, the target supports
               compiling and assembling UCN.

unaligned_stack
               Target does not guarantee that its `STACK_BOUNDARY` is greater than or equal to
               the required vector alignment.

vector_alignment_reachable
               Vector alignment is reachable for types of 32 bits or less.

`vector_alignment_reachable_for_64bit`
>   Vector alignment is reachable for types of 64 bits or less.

`wchar_t_char16_t_compatible`
>   Target supports `wchar_t` that is compatible with `char16_t`.

`wchar_t_char32_t_compatible`
>   Target supports `wchar_t` that is compatible with `char32_t`.

`comdat_group`
>   Target uses comdat groups.

7.2.3.13 Local to tests in `gcc.target/i386`

`3dnow`   Target supports compiling `3dnow` instructions.

`aes`   Target supports compiling `aes` instructions.

`fma4`   Target supports compiling `fma4` instructions.

`ms_hook_prologue`
>   Target supports attribute `ms_hook_prologue`.

`pclmul`   Target supports compiling `pclmul` instructions.

`sse3`   Target supports compiling `sse3` instructions.

`sse4`   Target supports compiling `sse4` instructions.

`sse4a`   Target supports compiling `sse4a` instructions.

`ssse3`   Target supports compiling `ssse3` instructions.

`vaes`   Target supports compiling `vaes` instructions.

`vpclmul`   Target supports compiling `vpclmul` instructions.

`xop`   Target supports compiling `xop` instructions.

7.2.3.14 Local to tests in `gcc.target/spu/ea`

`ealib`   Target `__ea` library functions are available.

7.2.3.15 Local to tests in `gcc.test-framework`

`no`   Always returns 0.

`yes`   Always returns 1.

7.2.4 Features for `dg-add-options`

The supported values of *feature* for directive `dg-add-options` are:

`arm_fp`   `__ARM_FP` definition. Only ARM targets support this feature, and only then in certain modes; see the [arm_fp_ok effective target keyword], page 86.

`arm_neon`   NEON support. Only ARM targets support this feature, and only then in certain modes; see the [arm_neon_ok effective target keyword], page 87.

`arm_fp16`   VFP half-precision floating point support. This does not select the FP16 format; for that, use [arm_fp16_ieee], page 96 or [arm_fp16_alternative], page 96 instead. This feature is only supported by ARM targets and then only in certain modes; see the [arm_fp16_ok effective target keyword], page 87.

`arm_fp16_ieee`

ARM IEEE 754-2008 format VFP half-precision floating point support. This feature is only supported by ARM targets and then only in certain modes; see the [arm_fp16_ok effective target keyword], page 87.

`arm_fp16_alternative`

ARM Alternative format VFP half-precision floating point support. This feature is only supported by ARM targets and then only in certain modes; see the [arm_fp16_ok effective target keyword], page 87.

`arm_neon_fp16`

NEON and half-precision floating point support. Only ARM targets support this feature, and only then in certain modes; see the [arm_neon_fp16_ok effective target keyword], page 87.

`arm_vfp3`   arm vfp3 floating point support; see the [arm_vfp3_ok effective target keyword], page 88.

`arm_v8_1a_neon`

Add options for ARMv8.1 with Adv.SIMD support, if this is supported by the target; see the [arm_v8_1a_neon_ok], page 88 effective target keyword.

`arm_v8_2a_fp16_scalar`

Add options for ARMv8.2 with scalar FP16 support, if this is supported by the target; see the [arm_v8_2a_fp16_scalar_ok], page 88 effective target keyword.

`arm_v8_2a_fp16_neon`

Add options for ARMv8.2 with Adv.SIMD FP16 support, if this is supported by the target; see the [arm_v8_2a_fp16_neon_ok], page 88 effective target keyword.

`bind_pic_locally`

Add the target-specific flags needed to enable functions to bind locally when using pic/PIC passes in the testsuite.

`c99_runtime`

Add the target-specific flags needed to access the C99 runtime.

`floatn`   Add the target-specific flags needed to use the _Floatn type.

`floatnx`   Add the target-specific flags needed to use the _Floatnx type.

`ieee`   Add the target-specific flags needed to enable full IEEE compliance mode.

`mips16_attribute`

`mips16` function attributes. Only MIPS targets support this feature, and only then in certain modes.

`tls`   Add the target-specific flags needed to use thread-local storage.

7.2.5 Variants of `dg-require-`*`support`*

A few of the **dg-require** directives take arguments.

dg-require-iconv *codeset*

> Skip the test if the target does not support iconv. *codeset* is the codeset to convert to.

dg-require-profiling *profopt*

> Skip the test if the target does not support profiling with option *profopt*.

dg-require-visibility *vis*

> Skip the test if the target does not support the **visibility** attribute. If *vis* is "", support for **visibility("hidden")** is checked, for **visibility("**_vis_**")** otherwise.

The original **dg-require** directives were defined before there was support for effective-target keywords. The directives that do not take arguments could be replaced with effective-target keywords.

dg-require-alias ""

> Skip the test if the target does not support the 'alias' attribute.

dg-require-ascii-locale ""

> Skip the test if the host does not support an ASCII locale.

dg-require-compat-dfp ""

> Skip this test unless both compilers in a 'compat' testsuite support decimal floating point.

dg-require-cxa-atexit ""

> Skip the test if the target does not support **__cxa_atexit**. This is equivalent to **dg-require-effective-target cxa_atexit**.

dg-require-dll ""

> Skip the test if the target does not support DLL attributes.

dg-require-fork ""

> Skip the test if the target does not support **fork**.

dg-require-gc-sections ""

> Skip the test if the target's linker does not support the **--gc-sections** flags. This is equivalent to **dg-require-effective-target gc-sections**.

dg-require-host-local ""

> Skip the test if the host is remote, rather than the same as the build system. Some tests are incompatible with DejaGnu's handling of remote hosts, which involves copying the source file to the host and compiling it with a relative path and **"-o a.out"**.

dg-require-mkfifo ""

> Skip the test if the target does not support **mkfifo**.

dg-require-named-sections ""

> Skip the test is the target does not support named sections. This is equivalent to **dg-require-effective-target named_sections**.

```
dg-require-weak ""
```
> Skip the test if the target does not support weak symbols.

```
dg-require-weak-override ""
```
> Skip the test if the target does not support overriding weak symbols.

7.2.6 Commands for use in `dg-final`

The GCC testsuite defines the following directives to be used within `dg-final`.

7.2.6.1 Scan a particular file

```
scan-file filename regexp [{ target/xfail selector }]
```
> Passes if *regexp* matches text in *filename*.

```
scan-file-not filename regexp [{ target/xfail selector }]
```
> Passes if *regexp* does not match text in *filename*.

```
scan-module module regexp [{ target/xfail selector }]
```
> Passes if *regexp* matches in Fortran module *module*.

7.2.6.2 Scan the assembly output

```
scan-assembler regex [{ target/xfail selector }]
```
> Passes if *regex* matches text in the test's assembler output.

```
scan-assembler-not regex [{ target/xfail selector }]
```
> Passes if *regex* does not match text in the test's assembler output.

```
scan-assembler-times regex num [{ target/xfail selector }]
```
> Passes if *regex* is matched exactly *num* times in the test's assembler output.

```
scan-assembler-dem regex [{ target/xfail selector }]
```
> Passes if *regex* matches text in the test's demangled assembler output.

```
scan-assembler-dem-not regex [{ target/xfail selector }]
```
> Passes if *regex* does not match text in the test's demangled assembler output.

```
scan-hidden symbol [{ target/xfail selector }]
```
> Passes if *symbol* is defined as a hidden symbol in the test's assembly output.

```
scan-not-hidden symbol [{ target/xfail selector }]
```
> Passes if *symbol* is not defined as a hidden symbol in the test's assembly output.

7.2.6.3 Scan optimization dump files

These commands are available for *kind* of `tree`, `rtl`, and `ipa`.

```
scan-kind-dump regex suffix [{ target/xfail selector }]
```
> Passes if *regex* matches text in the dump file with suffix *suffix*.

```
scan-kind-dump-not regex suffix [{ target/xfail selector }]
```
> Passes if *regex* does not match text in the dump file with suffix *suffix*.

```
scan-kind-dump-times regex num suffix [{ target/xfail selector }]
```
> Passes if *regex* is found exactly *num* times in the dump file with suffix *suffix*.

scan-*kind*-dump-dem *regex suffix* [{ target/xfail *selector* }]
>   Passes if *regex* matches demangled text in the dump file with suffix *suffix*.

scan-*kind*-dump-dem-not *regex suffix* [{ target/xfail *selector* }]
>   Passes if *regex* does not match demangled text in the dump file with suffix *suffix*.

7.2.6.4 Verify that an output files exists or not

output-exists [{ target/xfail *selector* }]
>   Passes if compiler output file exists.

output-exists-not [{ target/xfail *selector* }]
>   Passes if compiler output file does not exist.

7.2.6.5 Check for LTO tests

scan-symbol *regexp* [{ target/xfail *selector* }]
>   Passes if the pattern is present in the final executable.

7.2.6.6 Checks for gcov tests

run-gcov *sourcefile*
>   Check line counts in gcov tests.

run-gcov [branches] [calls] { *opts sourcefile* }
>   Check branch and/or call counts, in addition to line counts, in gcov tests.

7.2.6.7 Clean up generated test files

Usually the test-framework removes files that were generated during testing. If a testcase, for example, uses any dumping mechanism to inspect a passes dump file, the testsuite recognized the dump option passed to the tool and schedules a final cleanup to remove these files.

There are, however, following additional cleanup directives that can be used to annotate a testcase "manually".

cleanup-coverage-files
>   Removes coverage data files generated for this test.

cleanup-modules "*list-of-extra-modules*"
>   Removes Fortran module files generated for this test, excluding the module names listed in keep-modules. Cleaning up module files is usually done automatically by the testsuite by looking at the source files and removing the modules after the test has been executed.
>
>   ```
>   module MoD1
>   end module MoD1
>   module Mod2
>   end module Mod2
>   module moD3
>   end module moD3
>   module mod4
>   end module mod4
>   ! { dg-final { cleanup-modules "mod1 mod2" } } ! redundant
>   ! { dg-final { keep-modules "mod3 mod4" } }
>   ```

`keep-modules "`*`list-of-modules-not-to-delete`*`"`

> Whitespace separated list of module names that should not be deleted by
> cleanup-modules. If the list of modules is empty, all modules defined in this file
> are kept.

```
module maybe_unneeded
end module maybe_unneeded
module keep1
end module keep1
module keep2
end module keep2
! { dg-final { keep-modules "keep1 keep2" } } ! just keep these two
! { dg-final { keep-modules "" } } ! keep all
```

`dg-keep-saved-temps "`*`list-of-suffixes-not-to-delete`*`"`

> Whitespace separated list of suffixes that should not be deleted automatically
> in a testcase that uses '`-save-temps`'.

```
// { dg-options "-save-temps -fpch-preprocess -I." }
int main() { return 0; }
// { dg-keep-saved-temps ".s" } ! just keep assembler file
// { dg-keep-saved-temps ".s" ".i" } ! ... and .i
// { dg-keep-saved-temps ".ii" ".o" } ! or just .ii and .o
```

`cleanup-profile-file`

> Removes profiling files generated for this test.

`cleanup-repo-files`

> Removes files generated for this test for '`-frepo`'.

7.3 Ada Language Testsuites

The Ada testsuite includes executable tests from the ACATS testsuite, publicly available
at `http://www.ada-auth.org/acats.html`.

These tests are integrated in the GCC testsuite in the '`ada/acats`' directory, and enabled
automatically when running **make check**, assuming the Ada language has been enabled when
configuring GCC.

You can also run the Ada testsuite independently, using **make check-ada**, or run a subset
of the tests by specifying which chapter to run, e.g.:

```
$ make check-ada CHAPTERS="c3 c9"
```

The tests are organized by directory, each directory corresponding to a chapter of the
Ada Reference Manual. So for example, '`c9`' corresponds to chapter 9, which deals with
tasking features of the language.

The tests are run using two **sh** scripts: '`run_acats`' and '`run_all.sh`'. To run the
tests using a simulator or a cross target, see the small customization section at the top of
'`run_all.sh`'.

These tests are run using the build tree: they can be run without doing a **make install**.

7.4 C Language Testsuites

GCC contains the following C language testsuites, in the '`gcc/testsuite`' directory:

'gcc.dg'   This contains tests of particular features of the C compiler, using the more
             modern 'dg' harness. Correctness tests for various compiler features should go
             here if possible.

             Magic comments determine whether the file is preprocessed, compiled, linked
             or run. In these tests, error and warning message texts are compared against
             expected texts or regular expressions given in comments. These tests are run
             with the options '-ansi -pedantic' unless other options are given in the test.
             Except as noted below they are not run with multiple optimization options.

'gcc.dg/compat'
             This   subdirectory   contains   tests   for   binary   compatibility   using
             'lib/compat.exp', which in turn uses the language-independent support (see
             Section 7.8 [Support for testing binary compatibility], page 104).

'gcc.dg/cpp'
             This subdirectory contains tests of the preprocessor.

'gcc.dg/debug'
             This subdirectory contains tests for debug formats. Tests in this subdirectory
             are run for each debug format that the compiler supports.

'gcc.dg/format'
             This subdirectory contains tests of the '-Wformat' format checking. Tests in
             this directory are run with and without '-DWIDE'.

'gcc.dg/noncompile'
             This subdirectory contains tests of code that should not compile and does not
             need any special compilation options. They are run with multiple optimization
             options, since sometimes invalid code crashes the compiler with optimization.

'gcc.dg/special'
             FIXME: describe this.

'gcc.c-torture'
             This contains particular code fragments which have historically broken easily.
             These tests are run with multiple optimization options, so tests for features
             which only break at some optimization levels belong here. This also contains
             tests to check that certain optimizations occur. It might be worthwhile to
             separate the correctness tests cleanly from the code quality tests, but it hasn't
             been done yet.

'gcc.c-torture/compat'
             FIXME: describe this.

             This directory should probably not be used for new tests.

'gcc.c-torture/compile'
             This testsuite contains test cases that should compile, but do not need to link
             or run. These test cases are compiled with several different combinations of
             optimization options. All warnings are disabled for these test cases, so this
             directory is not suitable if you wish to test for the presence or absence of
             compiler warnings. While special options can be set, and tests disabled on

specific platforms, by the use of '.x' files, mostly these test cases should not contain platform dependencies. FIXME: discuss how defines such as `NO_LABEL_VALUES` and `STACK_SIZE` are used.

'gcc.c-torture/execute'

This testsuite contains test cases that should compile, link and run; otherwise the same comments as for 'gcc.c-torture/compile' apply.

'gcc.c-torture/execute/ieee'

This contains tests which are specific to IEEE floating point.

'gcc.c-torture/unsorted'

FIXME: describe this.

This directory should probably not be used for new tests.

'gcc.misc-tests'

This directory contains C tests that require special handling. Some of these tests have individual expect files, and others share special-purpose expect files:

'bprob*.c'

Test '-fbranch-probabilities' using 'gcc.misc-tests/bprob.exp', which in turn uses the generic, language-independent framework (see Section 7.7 [Support for testing profile-directed optimizations], page 104).

'gcov*.c' Test `gcov` output using 'gcov.exp', which in turn uses the language-independent support (see Section 7.6 [Support for testing gcov], page 103).

'i386-pf-*.c'

Test i386-specific support for data prefetch using 'i386-prefetch.exp'.

'gcc.test-framework'

'dg-*.c' Test the testsuite itself using 'gcc.test-framework/test-framework.exp'.

FIXME: merge in 'testsuite/README.gcc' and discuss the format of test cases and magic comments more.

7.5 Support for testing link-time optimizations

Tests for link-time optimizations usually require multiple source files that are compiled separately, perhaps with different sets of options. There are several special-purpose test directives used for these tests.

{ dg-lto-do *do-what-keyword* }

do-what-keyword specifies how the test is compiled and whether it is executed. It is one of:

assemble Compile with '-c' to produce a relocatable object file.

link   Compile, assemble, and link to produce an executable file.

run   Produce and run an executable file, which is expected to return an exit code of 0.

The default is **assemble**. That can be overridden for a set of tests by redefining **dg-do-what-default** within the .exp file for those tests.

Unlike **dg-do**, **dg-lto-do** does not support an optional 'target' or 'xfail' list. Use **dg-skip-if**, **dg-xfail-if**, or **dg-xfail-run-if**.

`{ dg-lto-options { { `*options*` } [{ `*options*` }] } [{ target `*selector*` }]}`

This directive provides a list of one or more sets of compiler options to override *LTO_OPTIONS*. Each test will be compiled and run with each of these sets of options.

`{ dg-extra-ld-options `*options*` [{ target `*selector*` }]}`

This directive adds *options* to the linker options used.

`{ dg-suppress-ld-options `*options*` [{ target `*selector*` }]}`

This directive removes *options* from the set of linker options used.

7.6 Support for testing gcov

Language-independent support for testing **gcov**, and for checking that branch profiling produces expected values, is provided by the expect file 'lib/gcov.exp'. gcov tests also rely on procedures in 'lib/gcc-dg.exp' to compile and run the test program. A typical **gcov** test contains the following DejaGnu commands within comments:

```
{ dg-options "-fprofile-arcs -ftest-coverage" }
{ dg-do run { target native } }
{ dg-final { run-gcov sourcefile } }
```

Checks of **gcov** output can include line counts, branch percentages, and call return percentages. All of these checks are requested via commands that appear in comments in the test's source file. Commands to check line counts are processed by default. Commands to check branch percentages and call return percentages are processed if the **run-gcov** command has arguments **branches** or **calls**, respectively. For example, the following specifies checking both, as well as passing '-b' to **gcov**:

```
{ dg-final { run-gcov branches calls { -b sourcefile } } }
```

A line count command appears within a comment on the source line that is expected to get the specified count and has the form **count(cnt)**. A test should only check line counts for lines that will get the same count for any architecture.

Commands to check branch percentages (**branch**) and call return percentages (**returns**) are very similar to each other. A beginning command appears on or before the first of a range of lines that will report the percentage, and the ending command follows that range of lines. The beginning command can include a list of percentages, all of which are expected to be found within the range. A range is terminated by the next command of the same kind. A command **branch(end)** or **returns(end)** marks the end of a range without starting a new one. For example:

```
if (i > 10 && j > i && j < 20)   /* branch(27 50 75) */
                                 /* branch(end) */
    foo (i, j);
```

For a call return percentage, the value specified is the percentage of calls reported to return. For a branch percentage, the value is either the expected percentage or 100 minus that value, since the direction of a branch can differ depending on the target or the optimization level.

Not all branches and calls need to be checked. A test should not check for branches that might be optimized away or replaced with predicated instructions. Don't check for calls inserted by the compiler or ones that might be inlined or optimized away.

A single test can check for combinations of line counts, branch percentages, and call return percentages. The command to check a line count must appear on the line that will report that count, but commands to check branch percentages and call return percentages can bracket the lines that report them.

7.7 Support for testing profile-directed optimizations

The file 'profopt.exp' provides language-independent support for checking correct execution of a test built with profile-directed optimization. This testing requires that a test program be built and executed twice. The first time it is compiled to generate profile data, and the second time it is compiled to use the data that was generated during the first execution. The second execution is to verify that the test produces the expected results.

To check that the optimization actually generated better code, a test can be built and run a third time with normal optimizations to verify that the performance is better with the profile-directed optimizations. 'profopt.exp' has the beginnings of this kind of support.

'profopt.exp' provides generic support for profile-directed optimizations. Each set of tests that uses it provides information about a specific optimization:

tool   tool being tested, e.g., gcc

profile_option
            options used to generate profile data

feedback_option
            options used to optimize using that profile data

prof_ext   suffix of profile data files

PROFOPT_OPTIONS
            list of options with which to run each test, similar to the lists for torture tests

{ dg-final-generate { *local-directive* } }
            This directive is similar to dg-final, but the *local-directive* is run after the generation of profile data.

{ dg-final-use { *local-directive* } }
            The *local-directive* is run after the profile data have been used.

7.8 Support for testing binary compatibility

The file 'compat.exp' provides language-independent support for binary compatibility testing. It supports testing interoperability of two compilers that follow the same ABI, or of multiple sets of compiler options that should not affect binary compatibility. It is intended to be used for testsuites that complement ABI testsuites.

A test supported by this framework has three parts, each in a separate source file: a main program and two pieces that interact with each other to split up the functionality being tested.

'`testname_main.suffix`'

>   Contains the main program, which calls a function in file '`testname_x.suffix`'.

'`testname_x.suffix`'

>   Contains at least one call to a function in '`testname_y.suffix`'.

'`testname_y.suffix`'

>   Shares data with, or gets arguments from, '`testname_x.suffix`'.

Within each test, the main program and one functional piece are compiled by the GCC under test. The other piece can be compiled by an alternate compiler. If no alternate compiler is specified, then all three source files are all compiled by the GCC under test. You can specify pairs of sets of compiler options. The first element of such a pair specifies options used with the GCC under test, and the second element of the pair specifies options used with the alternate compiler. Each test is compiled with each pair of options.

'`compat.exp`' defines default pairs of compiler options. These can be overridden by defining the environment variable `COMPAT_OPTIONS` as:

```
COMPAT_OPTIONS="[list [list {tst1} {alt1}]
   ...[list {tstn} {altn}]]"
```

where *tsti* and *alti* are lists of options, with *tsti* used by the compiler under test and *alti* used by the alternate compiler. For example, with [list [list {-g -O0} {-O3}] [list {-fpic} {-fPIC -O2}]], the test is first built with '`-g -O0`' by the compiler under test and with '`-O3`' by the alternate compiler. The test is built a second time using '`-fpic`' by the compiler under test and '`-fPIC -O2`' by the alternate compiler.

An alternate compiler is specified by defining an environment variable to be the full pathname of an installed compiler; for C define `ALT_CC_UNDER_TEST`, and for C++ define `ALT_CXX_UNDER_TEST`. These will be written to the '`site.exp`' file used by DejaGnu. The default is to build each test with the compiler under test using the first of each pair of compiler options from `COMPAT_OPTIONS`. When `ALT_CC_UNDER_TEST` or `ALT_CXX_UNDER_TEST` is `same`, each test is built using the compiler under test but with combinations of the options from `COMPAT_OPTIONS`.

To run only the C++ compatibility suite using the compiler under test and another version of GCC using specific compiler options, do the following from '`objdir/gcc`':

```
rm site.exp
make -k \
  ALT_CXX_UNDER_TEST=${alt_prefix}/bin/g++ \
  COMPAT_OPTIONS="lists as shown above" \
  check-c++ \
  RUNTESTFLAGS="compat.exp"
```

A test that fails when the source files are compiled with different compilers, but passes when the files are compiled with the same compiler, demonstrates incompatibility of the generated code or runtime support. A test that fails for the alternate compiler but passes for the compiler under test probably tests for a bug that was fixed in the compiler under test but is present in the alternate compiler.

The binary compatibility tests support a small number of test framework commands that appear within comments in a test file.

`dg-require-*`

>   These commands can be used in '`testname_main.suffix`' to skip the test if specific support is not available on the target.

`dg-options`

> The specified options are used for compiling this particular source file, appended to the options from `COMPAT_OPTIONS`. When this command appears in '*testname_main.suffix*' the options are also used to link the test program.

`dg-xfail-if`

> This command can be used in a secondary source file to specify that compilation is expected to fail for particular options on particular targets.

7.9 Support for torture testing using multiple options

Throughout the compiler testsuite there are several directories whose tests are run multiple times, each with a different set of options. These are known as torture tests. '`lib/torture-options.exp`' defines procedures to set up these lists:

`torture-init`

> Initialize use of torture lists.

`set-torture-options`

> Set lists of torture options to use for tests with and without loops. Optionally combine a set of torture options with a set of other options, as is done with Objective-C runtime options.

`torture-finish`

> Finalize use of torture lists.

The '`.exp`' file for a set of tests that use torture options must include calls to these three procedures if:

- It calls `gcc-dg-runtest` and overrides *DG_TORTURE_OPTIONS*.
- It calls *${tool}*`-torture` or *${tool}*`-torture-execute`, where *tool* is `c`, `fortran`, or `objc`.
- It calls `dg-pch`.

It is not necessary for a '`.exp`' file that calls `gcc-dg-runtest` to call the torture procedures if the tests should use the list in *DG_TORTURE_OPTIONS* defined in '`gcc-dg.exp`'.

Most uses of torture options can override the default lists by defining *TORTURE_OPTIONS* or add to the default list by defining *ADDITIONAL_TORTURE_OPTIONS*. Define these in a '`.dejagnurc`' file or add them to the '`site.exp`' file; for example

```
set ADDITIONAL_TORTURE_OPTIONS [list \
  { -O2 -ftree-loop-linear } \
  { -O2 -fpeel-loops } ]
```

8 Option specification files

Most GCC command-line options are described by special option definition files, the names of which conventionally end in `.opt`. This chapter describes the format of these files.

8.1 Option file format

Option files are a simple list of records in which each field occupies its own line and in which the records themselves are separated by blank lines. Comments may appear on their own line anywhere within the file and are preceded by semicolons. Whitespace is allowed before the semicolon.

The files can contain the following types of record:

- A language definition record. These records have two fields: the string 'Language' and the name of the language. Once a language has been declared in this way, it can be used as an option property. See Section 8.2 [Option properties], page 109.

- A target specific save record to save additional information. These records have two fields: the string 'TargetSave', and a declaration type to go in the `cl_target_option` structure.

- A variable record to define a variable used to store option information. These records have two fields: the string 'Variable', and a declaration of the type and name of the variable, optionally with an initializer (but without any trailing ';'). These records may be used for variables used for many options where declaring the initializer in a single option definition record, or duplicating it in many records, would be inappropriate, or for variables set in option handlers rather than referenced by `Var` properties.

- A variable record to define a variable used to store option information. These records have two fields: the string 'TargetVariable', and a declaration of the type and name of the variable, optionally with an initializer (but without any trailing ';'). 'TargetVariable' is a combination of 'Variable' and 'TargetSave' records in that the variable is defined in the `gcc_options` structure, but these variables are also stored in the `cl_target_option` structure. The variables are saved in the target save code and restored in the target restore code.

- A variable record to record any additional files that the 'options.h' file should include. This is useful to provide enumeration or structure definitions needed for target variables. These records have two fields: the string 'HeaderInclude' and the name of the include file.

- A variable record to record any additional files that the 'options.c' or 'options-save.c' file should include. This is useful to provide inline functions needed for target variables and/or `#ifdef` sequences to properly set up the initialization. These records have two fields: the string 'SourceInclude' and the name of the include file.

- An enumeration record to define a set of strings that may be used as arguments to an option or options. These records have three fields: the string 'Enum', a space-separated list of properties and help text used to describe the set of strings in '--help' output. Properties use the same format as option properties; the following are valid:

Name(*name*)

> This property is required; *name* must be a name (suitable for use in C identifiers) used to identify the set of strings in Enum option properties.

Type(*type*)

> This property is required; *type* is the C type for variables set by options using this enumeration together with Var.

UnknownError(*message*)

> The message *message* will be used as an error message if the argument is invalid; for enumerations without UnknownError, a generic error message is used. *message* should contain a single '%qs' format, which will be used to format the invalid argument.

- An enumeration value record to define one of the strings in a set given in an 'Enum' record. These records have two fields: the string 'EnumValue' and a space-separated list of properties. Properties use the same format as option properties; the following are valid:

Enum(*name*)

> This property is required; *name* says which 'Enum' record this 'EnumValue' record corresponds to.

String(*string*)

> This property is required; *string* is the string option argument being described by this record.

Value(*value*)

> This property is required; it says what value (representable as int) should be used for the given string.

Canonical

> This property is optional. If present, it says the present string is the canonical one among all those with the given value. Other strings yielding that value will be mapped to this one so specs do not need to handle them.

DriverOnly

> This property is optional. If present, the present string will only be accepted by the driver. This is used for cases such as '-march=native' that are processed by the driver so that 'gcc -v' shows how the options chosen depended on the system on which the compiler was run.

- An option definition record. These records have the following fields:
  1. the name of the option, with the leading "-" removed
  2. a space-separated list of option properties (see Section 8.2 [Option properties], page 109)
  3. the help text to use for '--help' (omitted if the second field contains the Undocumented property).

By default, all options beginning with "f", "W" or "m" are implicitly assumed to take a "no-" form. This form should not be listed separately. If an option beginning with one of these letters does not have a "no-" form, you can use the RejectNegative property to reject it.

The help text is automatically line-wrapped before being displayed. Normally the name of the option is printed on the left-hand side of the output and the help text is printed on the right. However, if the help text contains a tab character, the text to the left of the tab is used instead of the option's name and the text to the right of the tab forms the help text. This allows you to elaborate on what type of argument the option takes.

- A target mask record. These records have one field of the form 'Mask(x)'. The options-processing script will automatically allocate a bit in **target_flags** (see Section 17.3 [Run-time Target], page 440) for each mask name x and set the macro MASK_x to the appropriate bitmask. It will also declare a TARGET_x macro that has the value 1 when bit MASK_x is set and 0 otherwise.

  They are primarily intended to declare target masks that are not associated with user options, either because these masks represent internal switches or because the options are not available on all configurations and yet the masks always need to be defined.

8.2 Option properties

The second field of an option record can specify any of the following properties. When an option takes an argument, it is enclosed in parentheses following the option property name. The parser that handles option files is quite simplistic, and will be tricked by any nested parentheses within the argument text itself; in this case, the entire option argument can be wrapped in curly braces within the parentheses to demarcate it, e.g.:

```
Condition({defined (USE_CYGWIN_LIBSTDCXX_WRAPPERS)})
```

Common   The option is available for all languages and targets.

Target   The option is available for all languages but is target-specific.

Driver   The option is handled by the compiler driver using code not shared with the compilers proper ('cc1' etc.).

language   The option is available when compiling for the given language.

            It is possible to specify several different languages for the same option. Each *language* must have been declared by an earlier **Language** record. See Section 8.1 [Option file format], page 107.

RejectDriver
            The option is only handled by the compilers proper ('cc1' etc.) and should not be accepted by the driver.

RejectNegative
            The option does not have a "no-" form. All options beginning with "f", "W" or "m" are assumed to have a "no-" form unless this property is used.

Negative(*othername*)
            The option will turn off another option *othername*, which is the option name with the leading "-" removed. This chain action will propagate through the **Negative** property of the option to be turned off.

            As a consequence, if you have a group of mutually-exclusive options, their **Negative** properties should form a circular chain. For example, if options '-a', '-b' and '-c' are mutually exclusive, their respective **Negative** properties should be 'Negative(b)', 'Negative(c)' and 'Negative(a)'.

Joined

Separate   The option takes a mandatory argument. `Joined` indicates that the option and
            argument can be included in the same `argv` entry (as with `-mflush-func=name`,
            for example). `Separate` indicates that the option and argument can be separate
            `argv` entries (as with `-o`). An option is allowed to have both of these properties.

JoinedOrMissing
            The option takes an optional argument. If the argument is given, it will be part
            of the same `argv` entry as the option itself.

            This property cannot be used alongside `Joined` or `Separate`.

MissingArgError(*message*)
            For an option marked `Joined` or `Separate`, the message *message* will be used
            as an error message if the mandatory argument is missing; for options without
            `MissingArgError`, a generic error message is used. *message* should contain a
            single '`%qs`' format, which will be used to format the name of the option passed.

Args(*n*)   For an option marked `Separate`, indicate that it takes *n* arguments. The default
            is 1.

UInteger   The option's argument is a non-negative integer. The option parser will check
            and convert the argument before passing it to the relevant option handler.
            `UInteger` should also be used on options like `-falign-loops` where both `-falign-loops`
            and `-falign-loops=`*n* are supported to make sure the saved
            options are given a full integer.

ToLower   The option's argument should be converted to lowercase as part of putting it in
            canonical form, and before comparing with the strings indicated by any `Enum`
            property.

NoDriverArg
            For an option marked `Separate`, the option only takes an argument in the com-
            piler proper, not in the driver. This is for compatibility with existing options
            that are used both directly and via '`-Wp,`'; new options should not have this
            property.

Var(*var*) The state of this option should be stored in variable *var* (actually a macro for
            `global_options.x_var`). The way that the state is stored depends on the type
            of option:

            - If the option uses the `Mask` or `InverseMask` properties, *var* is the integer
              variable that contains the mask.

            - If the option is a normal on/off switch, *var* is an integer variable that is
              nonzero when the option is enabled. The options parser will set the variable
              to 1 when the positive form of the option is used and 0 when the "no-"
              form is used.

            - If the option takes an argument and has the `UInteger` property, *var* is an
              integer variable that stores the value of the argument.

            - If the option takes an argument and has the `Enum` property, *var* is a variable
              (type given in the `Type` property of the '`Enum`' record whose `Name` property

has the same argument as the `Enum` property of this option) that stores the value of the argument.

- If the option has the `Defer` property, *var* is a pointer to a `VEC(cl_deferred_option,heap)` that stores the option for later processing. (*var* is declared with type `void *` and needs to be cast to `VEC(cl_deferred_option,heap)` before use.)

- Otherwise, if the option takes an argument, *var* is a pointer to the argument string. The pointer will be null if the argument is optional and wasn't given.

The option-processing script will usually zero-initialize *var*. You can modify this behavior using `Init`.

`Var(var, set)`

> The option controls an integer variable *var* and is active when *var* equals *set*. The option parser will set *var* to *set* when the positive form of the option is used and `!`*set* when the "no-" form is used.
>
> *var* is declared in the same way as for the single-argument form described above.

`Init(value)`

> The variable specified by the `Var` property should be statically initialized to *value*. If more than one option using the same variable specifies `Init`, all must specify the same initializer.

`Mask(name)`

> The option is associated with a bit in the `target_flags` variable (see Section 17.3 [Run-time Target], page 440) and is active when that bit is set. You may also specify `Var` to select a variable other than `target_flags`.
>
> The options-processing script will automatically allocate a unique bit for the option. If the option is attached to '`target_flags`', the script will set the macro `MASK_name` to the appropriate bitmask. It will also declare a `TARGET_name` macro that has the value 1 when the option is active and 0 otherwise. If you use `Var` to attach the option to a different variable, the bitmask macro with be called `OPTION_MASK_name`.

`InverseMask(othername)`
`InverseMask(othername, thisname)`

> The option is the inverse of another option that has the `Mask(othername)` property. If *thisname* is given, the options-processing script will declare a `TARGET_thisname` macro that is 1 when the option is active and 0 otherwise.

`Enum(name)`

> The option's argument is a string from the set of strings associated with the corresponding '`Enum`' record. The string is checked and converted to the integer specified in the corresponding '`EnumValue`' record before being passed to option handlers.

`Defer`   The option should be stored in a vector, specified with `Var`, for later processing.

`Alias(`*opt*`)`
`Alias(`*opt*`, arg)`
`Alias(`*opt*`, `*posarg*`, `*negarg*`)`

> The option is an alias for '`-`*opt*' (or the negative form of that option, depending on `NegativeAlias`). In the first form, any argument passed to the alias is considered to be passed to '`-`*opt*', and '`-`*opt*' is considered to be negated if the alias is used in negated form. In the second form, the alias may not be negated or have an argument, and *posarg* is considered to be passed as an argument to '`-`*opt*'. In the third form, the alias may not have an argument, if the alias is used in the positive form then *posarg* is considered to be passed to '`-`*opt*', and if the alias is used in the negative form then *negarg* is considered to be passed to '`-`*opt*'.
>
> Aliases should not specify `Var` or `Mask` or `UInteger`. Aliases should normally specify the same languages as the target of the alias; the flags on the target will be used to determine any diagnostic for use of an option for the wrong language, while those on the alias will be used to identify what command-line text is the option and what text is any argument to that option.
>
> When an `Alias` definition is used for an option, driver specs do not need to handle it and no '`OPT_`' enumeration value is defined for it; only the canonical form of the option will be seen in those places.

`NegativeAlias`

> For an option marked with `Alias(`*opt*`)`, the option is considered to be an alias for the positive form of '`-`*opt*' if negated and for the negative form of '`-`*opt*' if not negated. `NegativeAlias` may not be used with the forms of `Alias` taking more than one argument.

`Ignore`   This option is ignored apart from printing any warning specified using `Warn`. The option will not be seen by specs and no '`OPT_`' enumeration value is defined for it.

`SeparateAlias`

> For an option marked with `Joined`, `Separate` and `Alias`, the option only acts as an alias when passed a separate argument; with a joined argument it acts as a normal option, with an '`OPT_`' enumeration value. This is for compatibility with the Java '`-d`' option and should not be used for new options.

`Warn(`*message*`)`

> If this option is used, output the warning *message*. *message* is a format string, either taking a single operand with a '`%qs`' format which is the option name, or not taking any operands, which is passed to the '`warning`' function. If an alias is marked `Warn`, the target of the alias must not also be marked `Warn`.

`Report`   The state of the option should be printed by '`-fverbose-asm`'.

`Warning`   This is a warning option and should be shown as such in '`--help`' output. This flag does not currently affect anything other than '`--help`'.

Optimization

> This is an optimization option. It should be shown as such in '--help' output, and any associated variable named using **Var** should be saved and restored when the optimization level is changed with **optimize** attributes.

Undocumented

> The option is deliberately missing documentation and should not be included in the '--help' output.

Condition(*cond***)**

> The option should only be accepted if preprocessor condition *cond* is true. Note that any C declarations associated with the option will be present even if *cond* is false; *cond* simply controls whether the option is accepted and whether it is printed in the '--help' output.

Save
> Build the **cl_target_option** structure to hold a copy of the option, add the functions **cl_target_option_save** and **cl_target_option_restore** to save and restore the options.

SetByCombined

> The option may also be set by a combined option such as '-ffast-math'. This causes the **gcc_options** struct to have a field **frontend_set_**_name_, where *name* is the name of the field holding the value of this option (without the leading **x_**). This gives the front end a way to indicate that the value has been set explicitly and should not be changed by the combined option. For example, some front ends use this to prevent '-ffast-math' and '-fno-fast-math' from changing the value of '-fmath-errno' for languages that do not use **errno**.

EnabledBy(*opt***)**
EnabledBy(*opt* || *opt2***)**
EnabledBy(*opt* && *opt2***)**

> If not explicitly set, the option is set to the value of '-*opt*'; multiple options can be given, separated by ||. The third form using && specifies that the option is only set if both *opt* and *opt2* are set. The options *opt* and *opt2* must have the **Common** property; otherwise, use **LangEnabledBy**.

LangEnabledBy(*language, opt***)**
LangEnabledBy(*language, opt, posarg, negarg***)**

> When compiling for the given language, the option is set to the value of '-*opt*', if not explicitly set. *opt* can be also a list of || separated options. In the second form, if *opt* is used in the positive form then *posarg* is considered to be passed to the option, and if *opt* is used in the negative form then *negarg* is considered to be passed to the option. It is possible to specify several different languages. Each *language* must have been declared by an earlier **Language** record. See Section 8.1 [Option file format], page 107.

NoDWARFRecord

> The option is omitted from the producer string written by '-grecord-gcc-switches'.

PchIgnore
> Even if this is a target option, this option will not be recorded / compared to determine if a precompiled header file matches.

CPP(*var*)   The state of this option should be kept in sync with the preprocessor option *var*. If this property is set, then properties `Var` and `Init` must be set as well.

CppReason(*CPP_W_Enum*)
> This warning option corresponds to `cpplib.h` warning reason code *CPP_W_Enum*. This should only be used for warning options of the C-family front-ends.

9 Passes and Files of the Compiler

This chapter is dedicated to giving an overview of the optimization and code generation passes of the compiler. In the process, it describes some of the language front end interface, though this description is no where near complete.

9.1 Parsing pass

The language front end is invoked only once, via `lang_hooks.parse_file`, to parse the entire input. The language front end may use any intermediate language representation deemed appropriate. The C front end uses GENERIC trees (see Chapter 10 [GENERIC], page 133), plus a double handful of language specific tree codes defined in 'c-common.def'. The Fortran front end uses a completely different private representation.

At some point the front end must translate the representation used in the front end to a representation understood by the language-independent portions of the compiler. Current practice takes one of two forms. The C front end manually invokes the gimplifier (see Chapter 11 [GIMPLE], page 179) on each function, and uses the gimplifier callbacks to convert the language-specific tree nodes directly to GIMPLE before passing the function off to be compiled. The Fortran front end converts from a private representation to GENERIC, which is later lowered to GIMPLE when the function is compiled. Which route to choose probably depends on how well GENERIC (plus extensions) can be made to match up with the source language and necessary parsing data structures.

BUG: Gimplification must occur before nested function lowering, and nested function lowering must be done by the front end before passing the data off to cgraph.

TODO: Cgraph should control nested function lowering. It would only be invoked when it is certain that the outer-most function is used.

TODO: Cgraph needs a gimplify_function callback. It should be invoked when (1) it is certain that the function is used, (2) warning flags specified by the user require some amount of compilation in order to honor, (3) the language indicates that semantic analysis is not complete until gimplification occurs. Hum... this sounds overly complicated. Perhaps we should just have the front end gimplify always; in most cases it's only one function call.

The front end needs to pass all function definitions and top level declarations off to the middle-end so that they can be compiled and emitted to the object file. For a simple procedural language, it is usually most convenient to do this as each top level declaration or definition is seen. There is also a distinction to be made between generating functional code and generating complete debug information. The only thing that is absolutely required for functional code is that function and data *definitions* be passed to the middle-end. For complete debug information, function, data and type declarations should all be passed as well.

In any case, the front end needs each complete top-level function or data declaration, and each data definition should be passed to `rest_of_decl_compilation`. Each complete type definition should be passed to `rest_of_type_compilation`. Each function definition should be passed to `cgraph_finalize_function`.

TODO: I know rest_of_compilation currently has all sorts of RTL generation semantics. I plan to move all code generation bits (both Tree and RTL) to compile_function. Should we hide cgraph from the front ends and move back to rest_of_compilation as the official interface? Possibly we should rename all three interfaces such that the names match in some meaningful way and that is more descriptive than "rest_of".

The middle-end will, at its option, emit the function and data definitions immediately or queue them for later processing.

9.2 Cilk Plus Transformation

If Cilk Plus generation (flag '-fcilkplus') is enabled, all the Cilk Plus code is transformed into equivalent C and C++ functions. Majority of this transformation occurs toward the end of the parsing and right before the gimplification pass.

These are the major components to the Cilk Plus language extension:

- Array Notations: During parsing phase, all the array notation specific information is stored in `ARRAY_NOTATION_REF` tree using the function `c_parser_array_notation`. During the end of parsing, we check the entire function to see if there are any array notation specific code (using the function `contains_array_notation_expr`). If this function returns true, then we expand them using either `expand_array_notation_exprs` or `build_array_notation_expr`. For the cases where array notations are inside conditions, they are transformed using the function `fix_conditional_array_notations`. The C language-specific routines are located in 'c/c-array-notation.c' and the equivalent C++ routines are in the file 'cp/cp-array-notation.c'. Common routines such as functions to initialize built-in functions are stored in 'array-notation-common.c'.

- Cilk keywords:

  - `_Cilk_spawn`: The `_Cilk_spawn` keyword is parsed and the function it contains is marked as a spawning function. The spawning function is called the spawner. At the end of the parsing phase, appropriate built-in functions are added to the spawner that are defined in the Cilk runtime. The appropriate locations of these functions, and the internal structures are detailed in `cilk_init_builtins` in the file 'cilk-common.c'. The pointers to Cilk functions and fields of internal structures are described in 'cilk.h'. The built-in functions are described in 'cilk-builtins.def'.

    During gimplification, a new "spawn-helper" function is created. The spawned function is replaced with a spawn helper function in the spawner. The spawned function-call is moved into the spawn helper. The main function that does these transformations is `gimplify_cilk_spawn` in 'c-family/cilk.c'. In the spawn-helper, the gimplification function `gimplify_call_expr`, inserts a function call `__cilkrts_detach`. This function is expanded by `builtin_expand_cilk_detach` located in 'c-family/cilk.c'.

  - `_Cilk_sync`: `_Cilk_sync` is parsed like a keyword. During gimplification, the function `gimplify_cilk_sync` in 'c-family/cilk.c', will replace this keyword with a set of functions that are stored in the Cilk runtime. One of the internal functions inserted during gimplification, `__cilkrts_pop_frame` must be expanded by the compiler and is done by `builtin_expand_cilk_pop_frame` in 'cilk-common.c'.

Documentation about Cilk Plus and language specification is provided under the "Learn" section in http://www.cilkplus.org/. It is worth mentioning that the current implementation follows ABI 1.1.

9.3 Gimplification pass

Gimplification is a whimsical term for the process of converting the intermediate representation of a function into the GIMPLE language (see Chapter 11 [GIMPLE], page 179). The term stuck, and so words like "gimplification", "gimplify", "gimplifier" and the like are sprinkled throughout this section of code.

While a front end may certainly choose to generate GIMPLE directly if it chooses, this can be a moderately complex process unless the intermediate language used by the front end is already fairly simple. Usually it is easier to generate GENERIC trees plus extensions and let the language-independent gimplifier do most of the work.

The main entry point to this pass is `gimplify_function_tree` located in 'gimplify.c'. From here we process the entire function gimplifying each statement in turn. The main workhorse for this pass is `gimplify_expr`. Approximately everything passes through here at least once, and it is from here that we invoke the `lang_hooks.gimplify_expr` callback.

The callback should examine the expression in question and return `GS_UNHANDLED` if the expression is not a language specific construct that requires attention. Otherwise it should alter the expression in some way to such that forward progress is made toward producing valid GIMPLE. If the callback is certain that the transformation is complete and the expression is valid GIMPLE, it should return `GS_ALL_DONE`. Otherwise it should return `GS_OK`, which will cause the expression to be processed again. If the callback encounters an error during the transformation (because the front end is relying on the gimplification process to finish semantic checks), it should return `GS_ERROR`.

9.4 Pass manager

The pass manager is located in 'passes.c', 'tree-optimize.c' and 'tree-pass.h'. It processes passes as described in 'passes.def'. Its job is to run all of the individual passes in the correct order, and take care of standard bookkeeping that applies to every pass.

The theory of operation is that each pass defines a structure that represents everything we need to know about that pass—when it should be run, how it should be run, what intermediate language form or on-the-side data structures it needs. We register the pass to be run in some particular order, and the pass manager arranges for everything to happen in the correct order.

The actuality doesn't completely live up to the theory at present. Command-line switches and `timevar_id_t` enumerations must still be defined elsewhere. The pass manager validates constraints but does not attempt to (re-)generate data structures or lower intermediate language form based on the requirements of the next pass. Nevertheless, what is present is useful, and a far sight better than nothing at all.

Each pass should have a unique name. Each pass may have its own dump file (for GCC debugging purposes). Passes with a name starting with a star do not dump anything. Sometimes passes are supposed to share a dump file / option name. To still give these unique names, you can use a prefix that is delimited by a space from the part that is used for the dump file / option name. E.g. When the pass name is "ud dce", the name used for dump file/options is "dce".

TODO: describe the global variables set up by the pass manager, and a brief description of how a new pass should use it. I need to look at what info RTL passes use first...

9.5 Tree SSA passes

The following briefly describes the Tree optimization passes that are run after gimplification and what source files they are located in.

- Remove useless statements

  This pass is an extremely simple sweep across the gimple code in which we identify obviously dead code and remove it. Here we do things like simplify `if` statements with constant conditions, remove exception handling constructs surrounding code that obviously cannot throw, remove lexical bindings that contain no variables, and other assorted simplistic cleanups. The idea is to get rid of the obvious stuff quickly rather than wait until later when it's more work to get rid of it. This pass is located in 'tree-cfg.c' and described by `pass_remove_useless_stmts`.

- OpenMP lowering

  If OpenMP generation ('-fopenmp') is enabled, this pass lowers OpenMP constructs into GIMPLE.

  Lowering of OpenMP constructs involves creating replacement expressions for local variables that have been mapped using data sharing clauses, exposing the control flow of most synchronization directives and adding region markers to facilitate the creation of the control flow graph. The pass is located in 'omp-low.c' and is described by `pass_lower_omp`.

- OpenMP expansion

  If OpenMP generation ('-fopenmp') is enabled, this pass expands parallel regions into their own functions to be invoked by the thread library. The pass is located in 'omp-low.c' and is described by `pass_expand_omp`.

- Lower control flow

  This pass flattens `if` statements (`COND_EXPR`) and moves lexical bindings (`BIND_EXPR`) out of line. After this pass, all `if` statements will have exactly two `goto` statements in its `then` and `else` arms. Lexical binding information for each statement will be found in `TREE_BLOCK` rather than being inferred from its position under a `BIND_EXPR`. This pass is found in 'gimple-low.c' and is described by `pass_lower_cf`.

- Lower exception handling control flow

  This pass decomposes high-level exception handling constructs (`TRY_FINALLY_EXPR` and `TRY_CATCH_EXPR`) into a form that explicitly represents the control flow involved. After this pass, `lookup_stmt_eh_region` will return a non-negative number for any statement that may have EH control flow semantics; examine `tree_can_throw_internal` or `tree_can_throw_external` for exact semantics. Exact control flow may be extracted from `foreach_reachable_handler`. The EH region nesting tree is defined in 'except.h' and built in 'except.c'. The lowering pass itself is in 'tree-eh.c' and is described by `pass_lower_eh`.

- Build the control flow graph

  This pass decomposes a function into basic blocks and creates all of the edges that connect them. It is located in 'tree-cfg.c' and is described by `pass_build_cfg`.

- Find all referenced variables

  This pass walks the entire function and collects an array of all variables referenced in the function, `referenced_vars`. The index at which a variable is found in the array is used as a UID for the variable within this function. This data is needed by the SSA rewriting routines. The pass is located in 'tree-dfa.c' and is described by `pass_referenced_vars`.

- Enter static single assignment form

  This pass rewrites the function such that it is in SSA form. After this pass, all `is_gimple_reg` variables will be referenced by `SSA_NAME`, and all occurrences of other variables will be annotated with `VDEFS` and `VUSES`; PHI nodes will have been inserted as necessary for each basic block. This pass is located in 'tree-ssa.c' and is described by `pass_build_ssa`.

- Warn for uninitialized variables

  This pass scans the function for uses of `SSA_NAME`s that are fed by default definition. For non-parameter variables, such uses are uninitialized. The pass is run twice, before and after optimization (if turned on). In the first pass we only warn for uses that are positively uninitialized; in the second pass we warn for uses that are possibly uninitialized. The pass is located in 'tree-ssa.c' and is defined by `pass_early_warn_uninitialized` and `pass_late_warn_uninitialized`.

- Dead code elimination

  This pass scans the function for statements without side effects whose result is unused. It does not do memory life analysis, so any value that is stored in memory is considered used. The pass is run multiple times throughout the optimization process. It is located in 'tree-ssa-dce.c' and is described by `pass_dce`.

- Dominator optimizations

  This pass performs trivial dominator-based copy and constant propagation, expression simplification, and jump threading. It is run multiple times throughout the optimization process. It is located in 'tree-ssa-dom.c' and is described by `pass_dominator`.

- Forward propagation of single-use variables

  This pass attempts to remove redundant computation by substituting variables that are used once into the expression that uses them and seeing if the result can be simplified. It is located in 'tree-ssa-forwprop.c' and is described by `pass_forwprop`.

- Copy Renaming

  This pass attempts to change the name of compiler temporaries involved in copy operations such that SSA->normal can coalesce the copy away. When compiler temporaries are copies of user variables, it also renames the compiler temporary to the user variable resulting in better use of user symbols. It is located in 'tree-ssa-copyrename.c' and is described by `pass_copyrename`.

- PHI node optimizations

  This pass recognizes forms of PHI inputs that can be represented as conditional expressions and rewrites them into straight line code. It is located in 'tree-ssa-phiopt.c' and is described by `pass_phiopt`.

- May-alias optimization

  This pass performs a flow sensitive SSA-based points-to analysis. The resulting may-alias, must-alias, and escape analysis information is used to promote variables from in-memory addressable objects to non-aliased variables that can be renamed into SSA form. We also update the `VDEF`/`VUSE` memory tags for non-renameable aggregates so that we get fewer false kills. The pass is located in 'tree-ssa-alias.c' and is described by `pass_may_alias`.

Interprocedural points-to information is located in 'tree-ssa-structalias.c' and described by `pass_ipa_pta`.

- Profiling

  This pass instruments the function in order to collect runtime block and value profiling data. Such data may be fed back into the compiler on a subsequent run so as to allow optimization based on expected execution frequencies. The pass is located in 'tree-profile.c' and is described by `pass_ipa_tree_profile`.

- Static profile estimation

  This pass implements series of heuristics to guess propababilities of branches. The resulting predictions are turned into edge profile by propagating branches across the control flow graphs. The pass is located in 'tree-profile.c' and is described by `pass_profile`.

- Lower complex arithmetic

  This pass rewrites complex arithmetic operations into their component scalar arithmetic operations. The pass is located in 'tree-complex.c' and is described by `pass_lower_complex`.

- Scalar replacement of aggregates

  This pass rewrites suitable non-aliased local aggregate variables into a set of scalar variables. The resulting scalar variables are rewritten into SSA form, which allows subsequent optimization passes to do a significantly better job with them. The pass is located in 'tree-sra.c' and is described by `pass_sra`.

- Dead store elimination

  This pass eliminates stores to memory that are subsequently overwritten by another store, without any intervening loads. The pass is located in 'tree-ssa-dse.c' and is described by `pass_dse`.

- Tail recursion elimination

  This pass transforms tail recursion into a loop. It is located in 'tree-tailcall.c' and is described by `pass_tail_recursion`.

- Forward store motion

  This pass sinks stores and assignments down the flowgraph closer to their use point. The pass is located in 'tree-ssa-sink.c' and is described by `pass_sink_code`.

- Partial redundancy elimination

  This pass eliminates partially redundant computations, as well as performing load motion. The pass is located in 'tree-ssa-pre.c' and is described by `pass_pre`.

  Just before partial redundancy elimination, if '-funsafe-math-optimizations' is on, GCC tries to convert divisions to multiplications by the reciprocal. The pass is located in 'tree-ssa-math-opts.c' and is described by `pass_cse_reciprocal`.

- Full redundancy elimination

  This is a simpler form of PRE that only eliminates redundancies that occur on all paths. It is located in 'tree-ssa-pre.c' and described by `pass_fre`.

- Loop optimization

  The main driver of the pass is placed in 'tree-ssa-loop.c' and described by pass_loop.

  The optimizations performed by this pass are:

  Loop invariant motion. This pass moves only invariants that would be hard to handle on RTL level (function calls, operations that expand to nontrivial sequences of insns). With '-funswitch-loops' it also moves operands of conditions that are invariant out of the loop, so that we can use just trivial invariantness analysis in loop unswitching. The pass also includes store motion. The pass is implemented in 'tree-ssa-loop-im.c'.

  Canonical induction variable creation. This pass creates a simple counter for number of iterations of the loop and replaces the exit condition of the loop using it, in case when a complicated analysis is necessary to determine the number of iterations. Later optimizations then may determine the number easily. The pass is implemented in 'tree-ssa-loop-ivcanon.c'.

  Induction variable optimizations. This pass performs standard induction variable optimizations, including strength reduction, induction variable merging and induction variable elimination. The pass is implemented in 'tree-ssa-loop-ivopts.c'.

  Loop unswitching. This pass moves the conditional jumps that are invariant out of the loops. To achieve this, a duplicate of the loop is created for each possible outcome of conditional jump(s). The pass is implemented in 'tree-ssa-loop-unswitch.c'.

  Loop splitting. If a loop contains a conditional statement that is always true for one part of the iteration space and false for the other this pass splits the loop into two, one dealing with one side the other only with the other, thereby removing one inner-loop conditional. The pass is implemented in 'tree-ssa-loop-split.c'.

  The optimizations also use various utility functions contained in 'tree-ssa-loop-manip.c', 'cfgloop.c', 'cfgloopanal.c' and 'cfgloopmanip.c'.

  Vectorization. This pass transforms loops to operate on vector types instead of scalar types. Data parallelism across loop iterations is exploited to group data elements from consecutive iterations into a vector and operate on them in parallel. Depending on available target support the loop is conceptually unrolled by a factor VF (vectorization factor), which is the number of elements operated upon in parallel in each iteration, and the VF copies of each scalar operation are fused to form a vector operation. Additional loop transformations such as peeling and versioning may take place to align the number of iterations, and to align the memory accesses in the loop. The pass is implemented in 'tree-vectorizer.c' (the main driver), 'tree-vect-loop.c' and 'tree-vect-loop-manip.c' (loop specific parts and general loop utilities), 'tree-vect-slp' (loop-aware SLP functionality), 'tree-vect-stmts.c' and 'tree-vect-data-refs.c'. Analysis of data references is in 'tree-data-ref.c'.

  SLP Vectorization. This pass performs vectorization of straight-line code. The pass is implemented in 'tree-vectorizer.c' (the main driver), 'tree-vect-slp.c', 'tree-vect-stmts.c' and 'tree-vect-data-refs.c'.

  Autoparallelization. This pass splits the loop iteration space to run into several threads. The pass is implemented in 'tree-parloops.c'.

  Graphite is a loop transformation framework based on the polyhedral model. Graphite stands for Gimple Represented as Polyhedra. The internals of this infrastructure are documented in `http://gcc.gnu.org/wiki/Graphite`. The passes working on this representation are implemented in the various '`graphite-*`' files.

- Tree level if-conversion for vectorizer

  This pass applies if-conversion to simple loops to help vectorizer. We identify if convertible loops, if-convert statements and merge basic blocks in one big block. The idea is to present loop in such form so that vectorizer can have one to one mapping between statements and available vector operations. This pass is located in '`tree-if-conv.c`' and is described by `pass_if_conversion`.

- Conditional constant propagation

  This pass relaxes a lattice of values in order to identify those that must be constant even in the presence of conditional branches. The pass is located in '`tree-ssa-ccp.c`' and is described by `pass_ccp`.

  A related pass that works on memory loads and stores, and not just register values, is located in '`tree-ssa-ccp.c`' and described by `pass_store_ccp`.

- Conditional copy propagation

  This is similar to constant propagation but the lattice of values is the "copy-of" relation. It eliminates redundant copies from the code. The pass is located in '`tree-ssa-copy.c`' and described by `pass_copy_prop`.

  A related pass that works on memory copies, and not just register copies, is located in '`tree-ssa-copy.c`' and described by `pass_store_copy_prop`.

- Value range propagation

  This transformation is similar to constant propagation but instead of propagating single constant values, it propagates known value ranges. The implementation is based on Patterson's range propagation algorithm (Accurate Static Branch Prediction by Value Range Propagation, J. R. C. Patterson, PLDI '95). In contrast to Patterson's algorithm, this implementation does not propagate branch probabilities nor it uses more than a single range per SSA name. This means that the current implementation cannot be used for branch prediction (though adapting it would not be difficult). The pass is located in '`tree-vrp.c`' and is described by `pass_vrp`.

- Folding built-in functions

  This pass simplifies built-in functions, as applicable, with constant arguments or with inferable string lengths. It is located in '`tree-ssa-ccp.c`' and is described by `pass_fold_builtins`.

- Split critical edges

  This pass identifies critical edges and inserts empty basic blocks such that the edge is no longer critical. The pass is located in '`tree-cfg.c`' and is described by `pass_split_crit_edges`.

- Control dependence dead code elimination

  This pass is a stronger form of dead code elimination that can eliminate unnecessary control flow statements. It is located in '`tree-ssa-dce.c`' and is described by `pass_cd_dce`.

- Tail call elimination

  This pass identifies function calls that may be rewritten into jumps. No code transformation is actually applied here, but the data and control flow problem is solved.

The code transformation requires target support, and so is delayed until RTL. In the meantime `CALL_EXPR_TAILCALL` is set indicating the possibility. The pass is located in 'tree-tailcall.c' and is described by `pass_tail_calls`. The RTL transformation is handled by `fixup_tail_calls` in 'calls.c'.

- Warn for function return without value

  For non-void functions, this pass locates return statements that do not specify a value and issues a warning. Such a statement may have been injected by falling off the end of the function. This pass is run last so that we have as much time as possible to prove that the statement is not reachable. It is located in 'tree-cfg.c' and is described by `pass_warn_function_return`.

- Leave static single assignment form

  This pass rewrites the function such that it is in normal form. At the same time, we eliminate as many single-use temporaries as possible, so the intermediate language is no longer GIMPLE, but GENERIC. The pass is located in 'tree-outof-ssa.c' and is described by `pass_del_ssa`.

- Merge PHI nodes that feed into one another

  This is part of the CFG cleanup passes. It attempts to join PHI nodes from a forwarder CFG block into another block with PHI nodes. The pass is located in 'tree-cfgcleanup.c' and is described by `pass_merge_phi`.

- Return value optimization

  If a function always returns the same local variable, and that local variable is an aggregate type, then the variable is replaced with the return value for the function (i.e., the function's DECL_RESULT). This is equivalent to the C++ named return value optimization applied to GIMPLE. The pass is located in 'tree-nrv.c' and is described by `pass_nrv`.

- Return slot optimization

  If a function returns a memory object and is called as `var = foo()`, this pass tries to change the call so that the address of `var` is sent to the caller to avoid an extra memory copy. This pass is located in `tree-nrv.c` and is described by `pass_return_slot`.

- Optimize calls to `__builtin_object_size`

  This is a propagation pass similar to CCP that tries to remove calls to `__builtin_object_size` when the size of the object can be computed at compile-time. This pass is located in 'tree-object-size.c' and is described by `pass_object_sizes`.

- Loop invariant motion

  This pass removes expensive loop-invariant computations out of loops. The pass is located in 'tree-ssa-loop.c' and described by `pass_lim`.

- Loop nest optimizations

  This is a family of loop transformations that works on loop nests. It includes loop interchange, scaling, skewing and reversal and they are all geared to the optimization of data locality in array traversals and the removal of dependencies that hamper optimizations such as loop parallelization and vectorization. The pass is located in 'tree-loop-linear.c' and described by `pass_linear_transform`.

- Removal of empty loops

  This pass removes loops with no code in them. The pass is located in
  'tree-ssa-loop-ivcanon.c' and described by pass_empty_loop.

- Unrolling of small loops

  This pass completely unrolls loops with few iterations. The pass is located in
  'tree-ssa-loop-ivcanon.c' and described by pass_complete_unroll.

- Predictive commoning

  This pass makes the code reuse the computations from the previous iterations of the
  loops, especially loads and stores to memory. It does so by storing the values of these
  computations to a bank of temporary variables that are rotated at the end of loop. To
  avoid the need for this rotation, the loop is then unrolled and the copies of the loop
  body are rewritten to use the appropriate version of the temporary variable. This pass
  is located in 'tree-predcom.c' and described by pass_predcom.

- Array prefetching

  This pass issues prefetch instructions for array references inside loops. The pass is
  located in 'tree-ssa-loop-prefetch.c' and described by pass_loop_prefetch.

- Reassociation

  This pass rewrites arithmetic expressions to enable optimizations that operate
  on them, like redundancy elimination and vectorization. The pass is located in
  'tree-ssa-reassoc.c' and described by pass_reassoc.

- Optimization of stdarg functions

  This pass tries to avoid the saving of register arguments into the stack on entry to
  stdarg functions. If the function doesn't use any va_start macros, no registers need
  to be saved. If va_start macros are used, the va_list variables don't escape the
  function, it is only necessary to save registers that will be used in va_arg macros.
  For instance, if va_arg is only used with integral types in the function, floating point
  registers don't need to be saved. This pass is located in tree-stdarg.c and described
  by pass_stdarg.

9.6 RTL passes

The following briefly describes the RTL generation and optimization passes that are run
after the Tree optimization passes.

- RTL generation

  The source files for RTL generation include 'stmt.c', 'calls.c', 'expr.c', 'explow.c',
  'expmed.c', 'function.c', 'optabs.c' and 'emit-rtl.c'. Also, the file 'insn-emit.c',
  generated from the machine description by the program genemit, is used in this pass.
  The header file 'expr.h' is used for communication within this pass.

  The header files 'insn-flags.h' and 'insn-codes.h', generated from the machine
  description by the programs genflags and gencodes, tell this pass which standard
  names are available for use and which patterns correspond to them.

- Generation of exception landing pads

  This pass generates the glue that handles communication between the exception handling library routines and the exception handlers within the function. Entry points in

the function that are invoked by the exception handling library are called *landing pads*. The code for this pass is located in 'except.c'.

- Control flow graph cleanup

  This pass removes unreachable code, simplifies jumps to next, jumps to jump, jumps across jumps, etc. The pass is run multiple times. For historical reasons, it is occasionally referred to as the "jump optimization pass". The bulk of the code for this pass is in 'cfgcleanup.c', and there are support routines in 'cfgrtl.c' and 'jump.c'.

- Forward propagation of single-def values

  This pass attempts to remove redundant computation by substituting variables that come from a single definition, and seeing if the result can be simplified. It performs copy propagation and addressing mode selection. The pass is run twice, with values being propagated into loops only on the second run. The code is located in 'fwprop.c'.

- Common subexpression elimination

  This pass removes redundant computation within basic blocks, and optimizes addressing modes based on cost. The pass is run twice. The code for this pass is located in 'cse.c'.

- Global common subexpression elimination

  This pass performs two different types of GCSE depending on whether you are optimizing for size or not (LCM based GCSE tends to increase code size for a gain in speed, while Morel-Renvoise based GCSE does not). When optimizing for size, GCSE is done using Morel-Renvoise Partial Redundancy Elimination, with the exception that it does not try to move invariants out of loops—that is left to the loop optimization pass. If MR PRE GCSE is done, code hoisting (aka unification) is also done, as well as load motion. If you are optimizing for speed, LCM (lazy code motion) based GCSE is done. LCM is based on the work of Knoop, Ruthing, and Steffen. LCM based GCSE also does loop invariant code motion. We also perform load and store motion when optimizing for speed. Regardless of which type of GCSE is used, the GCSE pass also performs global constant and copy propagation. The source file for this pass is 'gcse.c', and the LCM routines are in 'lcm.c'.

- Loop optimization

  This pass performs several loop related optimizations. The source files 'cfgloopanal.c' and 'cfgloopmanip.c' contain generic loop analysis and manipulation code. Initialization and finalization of loop structures is handled by 'loop-init.c'. A loop invariant motion pass is implemented in 'loop-invariant.c'. Basic block level optimizations— unrolling, and peeling loops— are implemented in 'loop-unroll.c'. Replacing of the exit condition of loops by special machine-dependent instructions is handled by 'loop-doloop.c'.

- Jump bypassing

  This pass is an aggressive form of GCSE that transforms the control flow graph of a function by propagating constants into conditional branch instructions. The source file for this pass is 'gcse.c'.

- If conversion

  This pass attempts to replace conditional branches and surrounding assignments with arithmetic, boolean value producing comparison instructions, and conditional move instructions. In the very last invocation after reload/LRA, it will generate predicated instructions when supported by the target. The code is located in 'ifcvt.c'.

- Web construction

  This pass splits independent uses of each pseudo-register. This can improve effect of the other transformation, such as CSE or register allocation. The code for this pass is located in 'web.c'.

- Instruction combination

  This pass attempts to combine groups of two or three instructions that are related by data flow into single instructions. It combines the RTL expressions for the instructions by substitution, simplifies the result using algebra, and then attempts to match the result against the machine description. The code is located in 'combine.c'.

- Mode switching optimization

  This pass looks for instructions that require the processor to be in a specific "mode" and minimizes the number of mode changes required to satisfy all users. What these modes are, and what they apply to are completely target-specific. The code for this pass is located in 'mode-switching.c'.

- Modulo scheduling

  This pass looks at innermost loops and reorders their instructions by overlapping different iterations. Modulo scheduling is performed immediately before instruction scheduling. The code for this pass is located in 'modulo-sched.c'.

- Instruction scheduling

  This pass looks for instructions whose output will not be available by the time that it is used in subsequent instructions. Memory loads and floating point instructions often have this behavior on RISC machines. It re-orders instructions within a basic block to try to separate the definition and use of items that otherwise would cause pipeline stalls. This pass is performed twice, before and after register allocation. The code for this pass is located in 'haifa-sched.c', 'sched-deps.c', 'sched-ebb.c', 'sched-rgn.c' and 'sched-vis.c'.

- Register allocation

  These passes make sure that all occurrences of pseudo registers are eliminated, either by allocating them to a hard register, replacing them by an equivalent expression (e.g. a constant) or by placing them on the stack. This is done in several subpasses:

  - The integrated register allocator (IRA). It is called integrated because coalescing, register live range splitting, and hard register preferencing are done on-the-fly during coloring. It also has better integration with the reload/LRA pass. Pseudo-registers spilled by the allocator or the reload/LRA have still a chance to get hard-registers if the reload/LRA evicts some pseudo-registers from hard-registers. The allocator helps to choose better pseudos for spilling based on their live ranges and to coalesce stack slots allocated for the spilled pseudo-registers. IRA is a regional register allocator which is transformed into Chaitin-Briggs allocator if there is one region. By default, IRA chooses regions using register pressure but the user can force it to use one region or regions corresponding to all loops.

    Source files of the allocator are 'ira.c', 'ira-build.c', 'ira-costs.c', 'ira-conflicts.c', 'ira-color.c', 'ira-emit.c', 'ira-lives', plus header files 'ira.h' and 'ira-int.h' used for the communication between the allocator and the rest of the compiler and between the IRA files.

- Reloading. This pass renumbers pseudo registers with the hardware registers numbers they were allocated. Pseudo registers that did not get hard registers are replaced with stack slots. Then it finds instructions that are invalid because a value has failed to end up in a register, or has ended up in a register of the wrong kind. It fixes up these instructions by reloading the problematical values temporarily into registers. Additional instructions are generated to do the copying.

  The reload pass also optionally eliminates the frame pointer and inserts instructions to save and restore call-clobbered registers around calls.

  Source files are 'reload.c' and 'reload1.c', plus the header 'reload.h' used for communication between them.

- This pass is a modern replacement of the reload pass. Source files are 'lra.c', 'lra-assign.c', 'lra-coalesce.c', 'lra-constraints.c', 'lra-eliminations.c', 'lra-lives.c', 'lra-remat.c', 'lra-spills.c', the header 'lra-int.h' used for communication between them, and the header 'lra.h' used for communication between LRA and the rest of compiler.

  Unlike the reload pass, intermediate LRA decisions are reflected in RTL as much as possible. This reduces the number of target-dependent macros and hooks, leaving instruction constraints as the primary source of control.

  LRA is run on targets for which TARGET_LRA_P returns true.

- Basic block reordering

  This pass implements profile guided code positioning. If profile information is not available, various types of static analysis are performed to make the predictions normally coming from the profile feedback (IE execution frequency, branch probability, etc). It is implemented in the file 'bb-reorder.c', and the various prediction routines are in 'predict.c'.

- Variable tracking

  This pass computes where the variables are stored at each position in code and generates notes describing the variable locations to RTL code. The location lists are then generated according to these notes to debug information if the debugging information format supports location lists. The code is located in 'var-tracking.c'.

- Delayed branch scheduling

  This optional pass attempts to find instructions that can go into the delay slots of other instructions, usually jumps and calls. The code for this pass is located in 'reorg.c'.

- Branch shortening

  On many RISC machines, branch instructions have a limited range. Thus, longer sequences of instructions must be used for long branches. In this pass, the compiler figures out what how far each instruction will be from each other instruction, and therefore whether the usual instructions, or the longer sequences, must be used for each branch. The code for this pass is located in 'final.c'.

- Register-to-stack conversion

Conversion from usage of some hard registers to usage of a register stack may be done at this point. Currently, this is supported only for the floating-point registers of the Intel 80387 coprocessor. The code for this pass is located in 'reg-stack.c'.

- Final

  This pass outputs the assembler code for the function. The source files are 'final.c' plus 'insn-output.c'; the latter is generated automatically from the machine description by the tool 'genoutput'. The header file 'conditions.h' is used for communication between these files.

- Debugging information output

  This is run after final because it must output the stack slot offsets for pseudo registers that did not get hard registers. Source files are 'dbxout.c' for DBX symbol table format, 'sdbout.c' for SDB symbol table format, 'dwarfout.c' for DWARF symbol table format, files 'dwarf2out.c' and 'dwarf2asm.c' for DWARF2 symbol table format, and 'vmsdbgout.c' for VMS debug symbol table format.

9.7 Optimization info

This section is describes dump infrastructure which is common to both pass dumps as well as optimization dumps. The goal for this infrastructure is to provide both gcc developers and users detailed information about various compiler transformations and optimizations.

9.7.1 Dump setup

A dump_manager class is defined in 'dumpfile.h'. Various passes register dumping pass-specific information via dump_register in 'passes.c'. During the registration, an optimization pass can select its optimization group (see Section 9.7.2 [Optimization groups], page 128). After that optimization information corresponding to the entire group (presumably from multiple passes) can be output via command-line switches. Note that if a pass does not fit into any of the pre-defined groups, it can select OPTGROUP_NONE.

Note that in general, a pass need not know its dump output file name, whether certain flags are enabled, etc. However, for legacy reasons, passes could also call dump_begin which returns a stream in case the particular pass has optimization dumps enabled. A pass could call dump_end when the dump has ended. These methods should go away once all the passes are converted to use the new dump infrastructure.

The recommended way to setup the dump output is via dump_start and dump_end.

9.7.2 Optimization groups

The optimization passes are grouped into several categories. Currently defined categories in 'dumpfile.h' are

OPTGROUP_IPA
        IPA optimization passes. Enabled by '-ipa'

OPTGROUP_LOOP
        Loop optimization passes. Enabled by '-loop'.

OPTGROUP_INLINE
        Inlining passes. Enabled by '-inline'.

`OPTGROUP_OPENMP`

> OpenMP passes. Enabled by '`-openmp`'.

`OPTGROUP_VEC`

> Vectorization passes. Enabled by '`-vec`'.

`OPTGROUP_OTHER`

> All other optimization passes which do not fall into one of the above.

`OPTGROUP_ALL`

> All optimization passes. Enabled by '`-all`'.

By using groups a user could selectively enable optimization information only for a group of passes. By default, the optimization information for all the passes is dumped.

9.7.3 Dump files and streams

There are two separate output streams available for outputting optimization information from passes. Note that both these streams accept **stderr** and **stdout** as valid streams and thus it is possible to dump output to standard output or error. This is specially handy for outputting all available information in a single file by redirecting **stderr**.

`pstream`   This stream is for pass-specific dump output. For example, '`-fdump-tree-vect=foo.v`' dumps tree vectorization pass output into the given file name '`foo.v`'. If the file name is not provided, the default file name is based on the source file and pass number. Note that one could also use special file names **stdout** and **stderr** for dumping to standard output and standard error respectively.

`alt_stream`

> This steam is used for printing optimization specific output in response to the '`-fopt-info`'. Again a file name can be given. If the file name is not given, it defaults to **stderr**.

9.7.4 Dump output verbosity

The dump verbosity has the following options

'`optimized`'

> Print information when an optimization is successfully applied. It is up to a pass to decide which information is relevant. For example, the vectorizer passes print the source location of loops which got successfully vectorized.

'`missed`'   Print information about missed optimizations. Individual passes control which information to include in the output. For example,

```
gcc -O2 -ftree-vectorize -fopt-info-vec-missed
```

> will print information about missed optimization opportunities from vectorization passes on stderr.

'`note`'   Print verbose information about optimizations, such as certain transformations, more detailed messages about decisions etc.

'`all`'   Print detailed optimization information. This includes *optimized*, *missed*, and *note*.

9.7.5 Dump types

`dump_printf`

This is a generic method for doing formatted output. It takes an additional argument `dump_kind` which signifies the type of dump. This method outputs information only when the dumps are enabled for this particular `dump_kind`. Note that the caller doesn't need to know if the particular dump is enabled or not, or even the file name. The caller only needs to decide which dump output information is relevant, and under what conditions. This determines the associated flags.

Consider the following example from 'loop-unroll.c' where an informative message about a loop (along with its location) is printed when any of the following flags is enabled

— optimization messages

— RTL dumps

— detailed dumps

```
int report_flags = MSG_OPTIMIZED_LOCATIONS | TDF_RTL | TDF_DETAILS;
dump_printf_loc (report_flags, locus,
                "loop turned into non-loop; it never loops.\n");
```

`dump_basic_block`

Output basic block.

`dump_generic_expr`

Output generic expression.

`dump_gimple_stmt`

Output gimple statement.

Note that the above methods also have variants prefixed with `_loc`, such as `dump_printf_loc`, which are similar except they also output the source location information.

9.7.6 Dump examples

```
gcc -O3 -fopt-info-missed=missed.all
```

outputs missed optimization report from all the passes into 'missed.all'.

As another example,

```
gcc -O3 -fopt-info-inline-optimized-missed=inline.txt
```

will output information about missed optimizations as well as optimized locations from all the inlining passes into 'inline.txt'.

If the *filename* is provided, then the dumps from all the applicable optimizations are concatenated into the 'filename'. Otherwise the dump is output onto 'stderr'. If *options* is omitted, it defaults to 'all-all', which means dump all available optimization info from all the passes. In the following example, all optimization info is output on to 'stderr'.

```
gcc -O3 -fopt-info
```

Note that '-fopt-info-vec-missed' behaves the same as '-fopt-info-missed-vec'.

As another example, consider

```
gcc -fopt-info-vec-missed=vec.miss -fopt-info-loop-optimized=loop.opt
```

Here the two output file names 'vec.miss' and 'loop.opt' are in conflict since only one output file is allowed. In this case, only the first option takes effect and the subsequent options are ignored. Thus only the 'vec.miss' is produced which containts dumps from the vectorizer about missed opportunities.

10 GENERIC

The purpose of GENERIC is simply to provide a language-independent way of representing an entire function in trees. To this end, it was necessary to add a few new tree codes to the back end, but almost everything was already there. If you can express it with the codes in `gcc/tree.def`, it's GENERIC.

Early on, there was a great deal of debate about how to think about statements in a tree IL. In GENERIC, a statement is defined as any expression whose value, if any, is ignored. A statement will always have `TREE_SIDE_EFFECTS` set (or it will be discarded), but a non-statement expression may also have side effects. A `CALL_EXPR`, for instance.

It would be possible for some local optimizations to work on the GENERIC form of a function; indeed, the adapted tree inliner works fine on GENERIC, but the current compiler performs inlining after lowering to GIMPLE (a restricted form described in the next section). Indeed, currently the frontends perform this lowering before handing off to `tree_rest_of_compilation`, but this seems inelegant.

10.1 Deficiencies

There are many places in which this document is incomplet and incorrekt. It is, as of yet, only *preliminary* documentation.

10.2 Overview

The central data structure used by the internal representation is the **tree**. These nodes, while all of the C type **tree**, are of many varieties. A **tree** is a pointer type, but the object to which it points may be of a variety of types. From this point forward, we will refer to trees in ordinary type, rather than in **this font**, except when talking about the actual C type **tree**.

You can tell what kind of node a particular tree is by using the `TREE_CODE` macro. Many, many macros take trees as input and return trees as output. However, most macros require a certain kind of tree node as input. In other words, there is a type-system for trees, but it is not reflected in the C type-system.

For safety, it is useful to configure GCC with '`--enable-checking`'. Although this results in a significant performance penalty (since all tree types are checked at run-time), and is therefore inappropriate in a release version, it is extremely helpful during the development process.

Many macros behave as predicates. Many, although not all, of these predicates end in '`_P`'. Do not rely on the result type of these macros being of any particular type. You may, however, rely on the fact that the type can be compared to 0, so that statements like

```
if (TEST_P (t) && !TEST_P (y))
  x = 1;
```

and

```
int i = (TEST_P (t) != 0);
```

are legal. Macros that return **int** values now may be changed to return **tree** values, or other pointers in the future. Even those that continue to return **int** may return multiple nonzero codes where previously they returned only zero and one. Therefore, you should not write code like

```
    if (TEST_P (t) == 1)
```
as this code is not guaranteed to work correctly in the future.

You should not take the address of values returned by the macros or functions described here. In particular, no guarantee is given that the values are lvalues.

In general, the names of macros are all in uppercase, while the names of functions are entirely in lowercase. There are rare exceptions to this rule. You should assume that any macro or function whose name is made up entirely of uppercase letters may evaluate its arguments more than once. You may assume that a macro or function whose name is made up entirely of lowercase letters will evaluate its arguments only once.

The `error_mark_node` is a special tree. Its tree code is `ERROR_MARK`, but since there is only ever one node with that code, the usual practice is to compare the tree against `error_mark_node`. (This test is just a test for pointer equality.) If an error has occurred during front-end processing the flag `errorcount` will be set. If the front end has encountered code it cannot handle, it will issue a message to the user and set `sorrycount`. When these flags are set, any macro or function which normally returns a tree of a particular kind may instead return the `error_mark_node`. Thus, if you intend to do any processing of erroneous code, you must be prepared to deal with the `error_mark_node`.

Occasionally, a particular tree slot (like an operand to an expression, or a particular field in a declaration) will be referred to as "reserved for the back end". These slots are used to store RTL when the tree is converted to RTL for use by the GCC back end. However, if that process is not taking place (e.g., if the front end is being hooked up to an intelligent editor), then those slots may be used by the back end presently in use.

If you encounter situations that do not match this documentation, such as tree nodes of types not mentioned here, or macros documented to return entities of a particular kind that instead return entities of some different kind, you have found a bug, either in the front end or in the documentation. Please report these bugs as you would any other bug.

10.2.1 Trees

All GENERIC trees have two fields in common. First, `TREE_CHAIN` is a pointer that can be used as a singly-linked list to other trees. The other is `TREE_TYPE`. Many trees store the type of an expression or declaration in this field.

These are some other functions for handling trees:

`tree_size`
> Return the number of bytes a tree takes.

`build0`
`build1`
`build2`
`build3`
`build4`
`build5`
`build6`
> These functions build a tree and supply values to put in each parameter. The basic signature is '`code, type, [operands]`'. `code` is the `TREE_CODE`, and `type` is a tree representing the `TREE_TYPE`. These are followed by the operands, each of which is also a tree.

10.2.2 Identifiers

An `IDENTIFIER_NODE` represents a slightly more general concept than the standard C or C++ concept of identifier. In particular, an `IDENTIFIER_NODE` may contain a '`$`', or other extraordinary characters.

There are never two distinct `IDENTIFIER_NODE`s representing the same identifier. Therefore, you may use pointer equality to compare `IDENTIFIER_NODE`s, rather than using a routine like `strcmp`. Use `get_identifier` to obtain the unique `IDENTIFIER_NODE` for a supplied string.

You can use the following macros to access identifiers:

`IDENTIFIER_POINTER`

> The string represented by the identifier, represented as a `char*`. This string is always NUL-terminated, and contains no embedded NUL characters.

`IDENTIFIER_LENGTH`

> The length of the string returned by `IDENTIFIER_POINTER`, not including the trailing NUL. This value of `IDENTIFIER_LENGTH (x)` is always the same as `strlen (IDENTIFIER_POINTER (x))`.

`IDENTIFIER_OPNAME_P`

> This predicate holds if the identifier represents the name of an overloaded operator. In this case, you should not depend on the contents of either the `IDENTIFIER_POINTER` or the `IDENTIFIER_LENGTH`.

`IDENTIFIER_TYPENAME_P`

> This predicate holds if the identifier represents the name of a user-defined conversion operator. In this case, the `TREE_TYPE` of the `IDENTIFIER_NODE` holds the type to which the conversion operator converts.

10.2.3 Containers

Two common container data structures can be represented directly with tree nodes. A `TREE_LIST` is a singly linked list containing two trees per node. These are the `TREE_PURPOSE` and `TREE_VALUE` of each node. (Often, the `TREE_PURPOSE` contains some kind of tag, or additional information, while the `TREE_VALUE` contains the majority of the payload. In other cases, the `TREE_PURPOSE` is simply NULL_TREE, while in still others both the `TREE_PURPOSE` and `TREE_VALUE` are of equal stature.) Given one `TREE_LIST` node, the next node is found by following the `TREE_CHAIN`. If the `TREE_CHAIN` is NULL_TREE, then you have reached the end of the list.

A `TREE_VEC` is a simple vector. The `TREE_VEC_LENGTH` is an integer (not a tree) giving the number of nodes in the vector. The nodes themselves are accessed using the `TREE_VEC_ELT` macro, which takes two arguments. The first is the `TREE_VEC` in question; the second is an integer indicating which element in the vector is desired. The elements are indexed from zero.

10.3 Types

All types have corresponding tree nodes. However, you should not assume that there is exactly one tree node corresponding to each type. There are often multiple nodes corresponding to the same type.

For the most part, different kinds of types have different tree codes. (For example, pointer types use a `POINTER_TYPE` code while arrays use an `ARRAY_TYPE` code.) However, pointers to member functions use the `RECORD_TYPE` code. Therefore, when writing a `switch` statement that depends on the code associated with a particular type, you should take care to handle pointers to member functions under the `RECORD_TYPE` case label.

The following functions and macros deal with cv-qualification of types:

`TYPE_MAIN_VARIANT`

> This macro returns the unqualified version of a type. It may be applied to an unqualified type, but it is not always the identity function in that case.

A few other macros and functions are usable with all types:

`TYPE_SIZE`

> The number of bits required to represent the type, represented as an `INTEGER_CST`. For an incomplete type, `TYPE_SIZE` will be `NULL_TREE`.

`TYPE_ALIGN`

> The alignment of the type, in bits, represented as an `int`.

`TYPE_NAME`

> This macro returns a declaration (in the form of a `TYPE_DECL`) for the type. (Note this macro does *not* return an `IDENTIFIER_NODE`, as you might expect, given its name!) You can look at the `DECL_NAME` of the `TYPE_DECL` to obtain the actual name of the type. The `TYPE_NAME` will be `NULL_TREE` for a type that is not a built-in type, the result of a typedef, or a named class type.

`TYPE_CANONICAL`

> This macro returns the "canonical" type for the given type node. Canonical types are used to improve performance in the C++ and Objective-C++ front ends by allowing efficient comparison between two type nodes in `same_type_p`: if the `TYPE_CANONICAL` values of the types are equal, the types are equivalent; otherwise, the types are not equivalent. The notion of equivalence for canonical types is the same as the notion of type equivalence in the language itself. For instance,
>
> When `TYPE_CANONICAL` is `NULL_TREE`, there is no canonical type for the given type node. In this case, comparison between this type and any other type requires the compiler to perform a deep, "structural" comparison to see if the two type nodes have the same form and properties.
>
> The canonical type for a node is always the most fundamental type in the equivalence class of types. For instance, `int` is its own canonical type. A typedef `I` of `int` will have `int` as its canonical type. Similarly, `I*` and a typedef `IP` (defined to `I*`) will has `int*` as their canonical type. When building a new type node, be sure to set `TYPE_CANONICAL` to the appropriate canonical type. If the new type is a compound type (built from other types), and any of those other types require structural equality, use `SET_TYPE_STRUCTURAL_EQUALITY` to ensure that the new type also requires structural equality. Finally, if for some reason you cannot guarantee that `TYPE_CANONICAL` will point to the canonical type, use `SET_TYPE_STRUCTURAL_EQUALITY` to make sure that the new type–and any type constructed based on it–requires structural equality. If you suspect

that the canonical type system is miscomparing types, pass --param verify-canonical-types=1 to the compiler or configure with --enable-checking to force the compiler to verify its canonical-type comparisons against the structural comparisons; the compiler will then print any warnings if the canonical types miscompare.

TYPE_STRUCTURAL_EQUALITY_P

This predicate holds when the node requires structural equality checks, e.g., when TYPE_CANONICAL is NULL_TREE.

SET_TYPE_STRUCTURAL_EQUALITY

This macro states that the type node it is given requires structural equality checks, e.g., it sets TYPE_CANONICAL to NULL_TREE.

same_type_p

This predicate takes two types as input, and holds if they are the same type. For example, if one type is a typedef for the other, or both are typedefs for the same type. This predicate also holds if the two trees given as input are simply copies of one another; i.e., there is no difference between them at the source level, but, for whatever reason, a duplicate has been made in the representation. You should never use == (pointer equality) to compare types; always use same_type_p instead.

Detailed below are the various kinds of types, and the macros that can be used to access them. Although other kinds of types are used elsewhere in G++, the types described here are the only ones that you will encounter while examining the intermediate representation.

VOID_TYPE

Used to represent the void type.

INTEGER_TYPE

Used to represent the various integral types, including char, short, int, long, and long long. This code is not used for enumeration types, nor for the bool type. The TYPE_PRECISION is the number of bits used in the representation, represented as an unsigned int. (Note that in the general case this is not the same value as TYPE_SIZE; suppose that there were a 24-bit integer type, but that alignment requirements for the ABI required 32-bit alignment. Then, TYPE_SIZE would be an INTEGER_CST for 32, while TYPE_PRECISION would be 24.) The integer type is unsigned if TYPE_UNSIGNED holds; otherwise, it is signed.

The TYPE_MIN_VALUE is an INTEGER_CST for the smallest integer that may be represented by this type. Similarly, the TYPE_MAX_VALUE is an INTEGER_CST for the largest integer that may be represented by this type.

REAL_TYPE

Used to represent the float, double, and long double types. The number of bits in the floating-point representation is given by TYPE_PRECISION, as in the INTEGER_TYPE case.

FIXED_POINT_TYPE

Used to represent the short _Fract, _Fract, long _Fract, long long _Fract, short _Accum, _Accum, long _Accum, and long long _Accum types. The number of bits in the fixed-point representation is given by `TYPE_PRECISION`, as in the `INTEGER_TYPE` case. There may be padding bits, fractional bits and integral bits. The number of fractional bits is given by `TYPE_FBIT`, and the number of integral bits is given by `TYPE_IBIT`. The fixed-point type is unsigned if `TYPE_UNSIGNED` holds; otherwise, it is signed. The fixed-point type is saturating if `TYPE_SATURATING` holds; otherwise, it is not saturating.

`COMPLEX_TYPE`

Used to represent GCC built-in `__complex__` data types. The `TREE_TYPE` is the type of the real and imaginary parts.

`ENUMERAL_TYPE`

Used to represent an enumeration type. The `TYPE_PRECISION` gives (as an `int`), the number of bits used to represent the type. If there are no negative enumeration constants, `TYPE_UNSIGNED` will hold. The minimum and maximum enumeration constants may be obtained with `TYPE_MIN_VALUE` and `TYPE_MAX_VALUE`, respectively; each of these macros returns an `INTEGER_CST`.

The actual enumeration constants themselves may be obtained by looking at the `TYPE_VALUES`. This macro will return a `TREE_LIST`, containing the constants. The `TREE_PURPOSE` of each node will be an `IDENTIFIER_NODE` giving the name of the constant; the `TREE_VALUE` will be an `INTEGER_CST` giving the value assigned to that constant. These constants will appear in the order in which they were declared. The `TREE_TYPE` of each of these constants will be the type of enumeration type itself.

`BOOLEAN_TYPE`

Used to represent the `bool` type.

`POINTER_TYPE`

Used to represent pointer types, and pointer to data member types. The `TREE_TYPE` gives the type to which this type points.

`REFERENCE_TYPE`

Used to represent reference types. The `TREE_TYPE` gives the type to which this type refers.

`FUNCTION_TYPE`

Used to represent the type of non-member functions and of static member functions. The `TREE_TYPE` gives the return type of the function. The `TYPE_ARG_TYPES` are a `TREE_LIST` of the argument types. The `TREE_VALUE` of each node in this list is the type of the corresponding argument; the `TREE_PURPOSE` is an expression for the default argument value, if any. If the last node in the list is `void_list_node` (a `TREE_LIST` node whose `TREE_VALUE` is the `void_type_node`), then functions of this type do not take variable arguments. Otherwise, they do take a variable number of arguments.

Note that in C (but not in C++) a function declared like `void f()` is an unprototyped function taking a variable number of arguments; the `TYPE_ARG_TYPES` of such a function will be `NULL`.

METHOD_TYPE

> Used to represent the type of a non-static member function. Like a FUNCTION_
> TYPE, the return type is given by the TREE_TYPE. The type of *this, i.e., the
> class of which functions of this type are a member, is given by the TYPE_METHOD_
> BASETYPE. The TYPE_ARG_TYPES is the parameter list, as for a FUNCTION_TYPE,
> and includes the this argument.

ARRAY_TYPE

> Used to represent array types. The TREE_TYPE gives the type of the elements
> in the array. If the array-bound is present in the type, the TYPE_DOMAIN is an
> INTEGER_TYPE whose TYPE_MIN_VALUE and TYPE_MAX_VALUE will be the lower
> and upper bounds of the array, respectively. The TYPE_MIN_VALUE will always
> be an INTEGER_CST for zero, while the TYPE_MAX_VALUE will be one less than
> the number of elements in the array, i.e., the highest value which may be used
> to index an element in the array.

RECORD_TYPE

> Used to represent struct and class types, as well as pointers to member
> functions and similar constructs in other languages. TYPE_FIELDS contains the
> items contained in this type, each of which can be a FIELD_DECL, VAR_DECL,
> CONST_DECL, or TYPE_DECL. You may not make any assumptions about the
> ordering of the fields in the type or whether one or more of them overlap.

UNION_TYPE

> Used to represent union types. Similar to RECORD_TYPE except that all FIELD_
> DECL nodes in TYPE_FIELD start at bit position zero.

QUAL_UNION_TYPE

> Used to represent part of a variant record in Ada. Similar to UNION_TYPE except
> that each FIELD_DECL has a DECL_QUALIFIER field, which contains a boolean
> expression that indicates whether the field is present in the object. The type
> will only have one field, so each field's DECL_QUALIFIER is only evaluated if none
> of the expressions in the previous fields in TYPE_FIELDS are nonzero. Normally
> these expressions will reference a field in the outer object using a PLACEHOLDER_
> EXPR.

LANG_TYPE

> This node is used to represent a language-specific type. The front end must
> handle it.

OFFSET_TYPE

> This node is used to represent a pointer-to-data member. For a data member
> X::m the TYPE_OFFSET_BASETYPE is X and the TREE_TYPE is the type of m.

There are variables whose values represent some of the basic types. These include:

void_type_node

> A node for void.

integer_type_node

> A node for int.

`unsigned_type_node`.

> A node for `unsigned int`.

`char_type_node`.

> A node for `char`.

It may sometimes be useful to compare one of these variables with a type in hand, using `same_type_p`.

10.4 Declarations

This section covers the various kinds of declarations that appear in the internal representation, except for declarations of functions (represented by `FUNCTION_DECL` nodes), which are described in Section 10.8 [Functions], page 163.

10.4.1 Working with declarations

Some macros can be used with any kind of declaration. These include:

`DECL_NAME`

> This macro returns an `IDENTIFIER_NODE` giving the name of the entity.

`TREE_TYPE`

> This macro returns the type of the entity declared.

`EXPR_FILENAME`

> This macro returns the name of the file in which the entity was declared, as a `char*`. For an entity declared implicitly by the compiler (like `__builtin_memcpy`), this will be the string `"<internal>"`.

`EXPR_LINENO`

> This macro returns the line number at which the entity was declared, as an `int`.

`DECL_ARTIFICIAL`

> This predicate holds if the declaration was implicitly generated by the compiler. For example, this predicate will hold of an implicitly declared member function, or of the `TYPE_DECL` implicitly generated for a class type. Recall that in C++ code like:
>
> ```
> struct S {};
> ```
>
> is roughly equivalent to C code like:
>
> ```
> struct S {};
> typedef struct S S;
> ```
>
> The implicitly generated `typedef` declaration is represented by a `TYPE_DECL` for which `DECL_ARTIFICIAL` holds.

The various kinds of declarations include:

`LABEL_DECL`

> These nodes are used to represent labels in function bodies. For more information, see Section 10.8 [Functions], page 163. These nodes only appear in block scopes.

CONST_DECL

These nodes are used to represent enumeration constants. The value of the constant is given by DECL_INITIAL which will be an INTEGER_CST with the same type as the TREE_TYPE of the CONST_DECL, i.e., an ENUMERAL_TYPE.

RESULT_DECL

These nodes represent the value returned by a function. When a value is assigned to a RESULT_DECL, that indicates that the value should be returned, via bitwise copy, by the function. You can use DECL_SIZE and DECL_ALIGN on a RESULT_DECL, just as with a VAR_DECL.

TYPE_DECL

These nodes represent typedef declarations. The TREE_TYPE is the type declared to have the name given by DECL_NAME. In some cases, there is no associated name.

VAR_DECL   These nodes represent variables with namespace or block scope, as well as static data members. The DECL_SIZE and DECL_ALIGN are analogous to TYPE_SIZE and TYPE_ALIGN. For a declaration, you should always use the DECL_SIZE and DECL_ALIGN rather than the TYPE_SIZE and TYPE_ALIGN given by the TREE_TYPE, since special attributes may have been applied to the variable to give it a particular size and alignment. You may use the predicates DECL_THIS_STATIC or DECL_THIS_EXTERN to test whether the storage class specifiers static or extern were used to declare a variable.

If this variable is initialized (but does not require a constructor), the DECL_INITIAL will be an expression for the initializer. The initializer should be evaluated, and a bitwise copy into the variable performed. If the DECL_INITIAL is the error_mark_node, there is an initializer, but it is given by an explicit statement later in the code; no bitwise copy is required.

GCC provides an extension that allows either automatic variables, or global variables, to be placed in particular registers. This extension is being used for a particular VAR_DECL if DECL_REGISTER holds for the VAR_DECL, and if DECL_ASSEMBLER_NAME is not equal to DECL_NAME. In that case, DECL_ASSEMBLER_NAME is the name of the register into which the variable will be placed.

PARM_DECL

Used to represent a parameter to a function. Treat these nodes similarly to VAR_DECL nodes. These nodes only appear in the DECL_ARGUMENTS for a FUNCTION_DECL.

The DECL_ARG_TYPE for a PARM_DECL is the type that will actually be used when a value is passed to this function. It may be a wider type than the TREE_TYPE of the parameter; for example, the ordinary type might be short while the DECL_ARG_TYPE is int.

DEBUG_EXPR_DECL

Used to represent an anonymous debug-information temporary created to hold an expression as it is optimized away, so that its value can be referenced in debug bind statements.

FIELD_DECL

These nodes represent non-static data members. The `DECL_SIZE` and `DECL_ALIGN` behave as for `VAR_DECL` nodes. The position of the field within the parent record is specified by a combination of three attributes. `DECL_FIELD_OFFSET` is the position, counting in bytes, of the `DECL_OFFSET_ALIGN`-bit sized word containing the bit of the field closest to the beginning of the structure. `DECL_FIELD_BIT_OFFSET` is the bit offset of the first bit of the field within this word; this may be nonzero even for fields that are not bit-fields, since `DECL_OFFSET_ALIGN` may be greater than the natural alignment of the field's type.

If `DECL_C_BIT_FIELD` holds, this field is a bit-field. In a bit-field, `DECL_BIT_FIELD_TYPE` also contains the type that was originally specified for it, while `DECL_TYPE` may be a modified type with lesser precision, according to the size of the bit field.

NAMESPACE_DECL

Namespaces provide a name hierarchy for other declarations. They appear in the `DECL_CONTEXT` of other `_DECL` nodes.

10.4.2 Internal structure

`DECL` nodes are represented internally as a hierarchy of structures.

10.4.2.1 Current structure hierarchy

struct tree_decl_minimal

This is the minimal structure to inherit from in order for common `DECL` macros to work. The fields it contains are a unique ID, source location, context, and name.

struct tree_decl_common

This structure inherits from `struct tree_decl_minimal`. It contains fields that most `DECL` nodes need, such as a field to store alignment, machine mode, size, and attributes.

struct tree_field_decl

This structure inherits from `struct tree_decl_common`. It is used to represent `FIELD_DECL`.

struct tree_label_decl

This structure inherits from `struct tree_decl_common`. It is used to represent `LABEL_DECL`.

struct tree_translation_unit_decl

This structure inherits from `struct tree_decl_common`. It is used to represent `TRANSLATION_UNIT_DECL`.

struct tree_decl_with_rtl

This structure inherits from `struct tree_decl_common`. It contains a field to store the low-level RTL associated with a `DECL` node.

struct tree_result_decl

This structure inherits from `struct tree_decl_with_rtl`. It is used to represent `RESULT_DECL`.

`struct tree_const_decl`

> This structure inherits from `struct tree_decl_with_rtl`. It is used to represent `CONST_DECL`.

`struct tree_parm_decl`

> This structure inherits from `struct tree_decl_with_rtl`. It is used to represent `PARM_DECL`.

`struct tree_decl_with_vis`

> This structure inherits from `struct tree_decl_with_rtl`. It contains fields necessary to store visibility information, as well as a section name and assembler name.

`struct tree_var_decl`

> This structure inherits from `struct tree_decl_with_vis`. It is used to represent `VAR_DECL`.

`struct tree_function_decl`

> This structure inherits from `struct tree_decl_with_vis`. It is used to represent `FUNCTION_DECL`.

10.4.2.2 Adding new DECL node types

Adding a new `DECL` tree consists of the following steps

Add a new tree code for the `DECL` node

> For language specific `DECL` nodes, there is a '`.def`' file in each frontend directory where the tree code should be added. For `DECL` nodes that are part of the middle-end, the code should be added to '`tree.def`'.

Create a new structure type for the `DECL` node

> These structures should inherit from one of the existing structures in the language hierarchy by using that structure as the first member.
>
> ```
> struct tree_foo_decl
> {
>    struct tree_decl_with_vis common;
> }
> ```
>
> Would create a structure name `tree_foo_decl` that inherits from `struct tree_decl_with_vis`.
>
> For language specific `DECL` nodes, this new structure type should go in the appropriate '`.h`' file. For `DECL` nodes that are part of the middle-end, the structure type should go in '`tree.h`'.

Add a member to the tree structure enumerator for the node

> For garbage collection and dynamic checking purposes, each `DECL` node structure type is required to have a unique enumerator value specified with it. For language specific `DECL` nodes, this new enumerator value should go in the appropriate '`.def`' file. For `DECL` nodes that are part of the middle-end, the enumerator values are specified in '`treestruct.def`'.

Update union `tree_node`

> In order to make your new structure type usable, it must be added to `union tree_node`. For language specific `DECL` nodes, a new entry should be added to the appropriate '.h' file of the form
>
> ```
> struct tree_foo_decl GTY ((tag ("TS_VAR_DECL"))) foo_decl;
> ```
>
> For `DECL` nodes that are part of the middle-end, the additional member goes directly into `union tree_node` in 'tree.h'.

Update dynamic checking info

> In order to be able to check whether accessing a named portion of `union tree_node` is legal, and whether a certain `DECL` node contains one of the enumerated `DECL` node structures in the hierarchy, a simple lookup table is used. This lookup table needs to be kept up to date with the tree structure hierarchy, or else checking and containment macros will fail inappropriately.
>
> For language specific `DECL` nodes, their is an `init_ts` function in an appropriate '.c' file, which initializes the lookup table. Code setting up the table for new `DECL` nodes should be added there. For each `DECL` tree code and enumerator value representing a member of the inheritance hierarchy, the table should contain 1 if that tree code inherits (directly or indirectly) from that member. Thus, a `FOO_DECL` node derived from `struct decl_with_rtl`, and enumerator value `TS_FOO_DECL`, would be set up as follows
>
> ```
> tree_contains_struct[FOO_DECL][TS_FOO_DECL] = 1;
> tree_contains_struct[FOO_DECL][TS_DECL_WRTL] = 1;
> tree_contains_struct[FOO_DECL][TS_DECL_COMMON] = 1;
> tree_contains_struct[FOO_DECL][TS_DECL_MINIMAL] = 1;
> ```
>
> For `DECL` nodes that are part of the middle-end, the setup code goes into 'tree.c'.

Add macros to access any new fields and flags

> Each added field or flag should have a macro that is used to access it, that performs appropriate checking to ensure only the right type of `DECL` nodes access the field.
>
> These macros generally take the following form
>
> ```
> #define FOO_DECL_FIELDNAME(NODE) FOO_DECL_CHECK(NODE)->foo_decl.fieldname
> ```
>
> However, if the structure is simply a base class for further structures, something like the following should be used
>
> ```
> #define BASE_STRUCT_CHECK(T) CONTAINS_STRUCT_CHECK(T, TS_BASE_STRUCT)
> #define BASE_STRUCT_FIELDNAME(NODE) \
>   (BASE_STRUCT_CHECK(NODE)->base_struct.fieldname
> ```
>
> Reading them from the generated 'all-tree.def' file (which in turn includes all the 'tree.def' files), 'gencheck.c' is used during GCC's build to generate the `*_CHECK` macros for all tree codes.

10.5 Attributes in trees

Attributes, as specified using the `__attribute__` keyword, are represented internally as a `TREE_LIST`. The `TREE_PURPOSE` is the name of the attribute, as an `IDENTIFIER_NODE`. The `TREE_VALUE` is a `TREE_LIST` of the arguments of the attribute, if any, or `NULL_TREE` if there are no arguments; the arguments are stored as the `TREE_VALUE` of successive entries in the list, and may be identifiers or expressions. The `TREE_CHAIN` of the attribute is the next attribute in a list of attributes applying to the same declaration or type, or `NULL_TREE` if there are no further attributes in the list.

Attributes may be attached to declarations and to types; these attributes may be accessed with the following macros. All attributes are stored in this way, and many also cause other changes to the declaration or type or to other internal compiler data structures.

`tree DECL_ATTRIBUTES (`*tree `decl`*`)`   [Tree Macro]
    This macro returns the attributes on the declaration *decl*.

`tree TYPE_ATTRIBUTES (`*tree `type`*`)`   [Tree Macro]
    This macro returns the attributes on the type *type*.

10.6 Expressions

The internal representation for expressions is for the most part quite straightforward. However, there are a few facts that one must bear in mind. In particular, the expression "tree" is actually a directed acyclic graph. (For example there may be many references to the integer constant zero throughout the source program; many of these will be represented by the same expression node.) You should not rely on certain kinds of node being shared, nor should you rely on certain kinds of nodes being unshared.

The following macros can be used with all expression nodes:

`TREE_TYPE`

        Returns the type of the expression. This value may not be precisely the same type that would be given the expression in the original program.

In what follows, some nodes that one might expect to always have type `bool` are documented to have either integral or boolean type. At some point in the future, the C front end may also make use of this same intermediate representation, and at this point these nodes will certainly have integral type. The previous sentence is not meant to imply that the C++ front end does not or will not give these nodes integral type.

Below, we list the various kinds of expression nodes. Except where noted otherwise, the operands to an expression are accessed using the `TREE_OPERAND` macro. For example, to access the first operand to a binary plus expression `expr`, use:

    `TREE_OPERAND (expr, 0)`

As this example indicates, the operands are zero-indexed.

10.6.1 Constant expressions

The table below begins with constants, moves on to unary expressions, then proceeds to binary expressions, and concludes with various other kinds of expressions:

`INTEGER_CST`

        These nodes represent integer constants. Note that the type of these constants is obtained with `TREE_TYPE`; they are not always of type `int`. In particular, `char` constants are represented with `INTEGER_CST` nodes. The value of the integer constant `e` is represented in an array of HOST_WIDE_INT. There are enough elements in the array to represent the value without taking extra elements for redundant 0s or -1. The number of elements used to represent e is available via `TREE_INT_CST_NUNITS`. Element i can be extracted by using `TREE_INT_CST_ELT (e, i)`. `TREE_INT_CST_LOW` is a shorthand for `TREE_INT_CST_ELT (e, 0)`.

The functions `tree_fits_shwi_p` and `tree_fits_uhwi_p` can be used to tell if the value is small enough to fit in a signed HOST_WIDE_INT or an unsigned HOST_WIDE_INT respectively. The value can then be extracted using `tree_to_shwi` and `tree_to_uhwi`.

REAL_CST

FIXME: Talk about how to obtain representations of this constant, do comparisons, and so forth.

FIXED_CST

These nodes represent fixed-point constants. The type of these constants is obtained with `TREE_TYPE`. `TREE_FIXED_CST_PTR` points to a **struct fixed_value**; `TREE_FIXED_CST` returns the structure itself. **struct fixed_value** contains **data** with the size of two `HOST_BITS_PER_WIDE_INT` and **mode** as the associated fixed-point machine mode for **data**.

COMPLEX_CST

These nodes are used to represent complex number constants, that is a **__complex__** whose parts are constant nodes. The `TREE_REALPART` and `TREE_IMAGPART` return the real and the imaginary parts respectively.

VECTOR_CST

These nodes are used to represent vector constants, whose parts are constant nodes. Each individual constant node is either an integer or a double constant node. The first operand is a `TREE_LIST` of the constant nodes and is accessed through `TREE_VECTOR_CST_ELTS`.

STRING_CST

These nodes represent string-constants. The `TREE_STRING_LENGTH` returns the length of the string, as an **int**. The `TREE_STRING_POINTER` is a **char*** containing the string itself. The string may not be NUL-terminated, and it may contain embedded NUL characters. Therefore, the `TREE_STRING_LENGTH` includes the trailing NUL if it is present.

For wide string constants, the `TREE_STRING_LENGTH` is the number of bytes in the string, and the `TREE_STRING_POINTER` points to an array of the bytes of the string, as represented on the target system (that is, as integers in the target endianness). Wide and non-wide string constants are distinguished only by the `TREE_TYPE` of the STRING_CST.

FIXME: The formats of string constants are not well-defined when the target system bytes are not the same width as host system bytes.

10.6.2 References to storage

ARRAY_REF

These nodes represent array accesses. The first operand is the array; the second is the index. To calculate the address of the memory accessed, you must scale the index by the size of the type of the array elements. The type of these expressions must be the type of a component of the array. The third and fourth operands are used after gimplification to represent the lower bound and component size but should not be used directly; call `array_ref_low_bound` and `array_ref_element_size` instead.

ARRAY_RANGE_REF

These nodes represent access to a range (or "slice") of an array. The operands are the same as that for `ARRAY_REF` and have the same meanings. The type of these expressions must be an array whose component type is the same as that of the first operand. The range of that array type determines the amount of data these expressions access.

TARGET_MEM_REF

These nodes represent memory accesses whose address directly map to an addressing mode of the target architecture. The first argument is `TMR_SYMBOL` and must be a `VAR_DECL` of an object with a fixed address. The second argument is `TMR_BASE` and the third one is `TMR_INDEX`. The fourth argument is `TMR_STEP` and must be an `INTEGER_CST`. The fifth argument is `TMR_OFFSET` and must be an `INTEGER_CST`. Any of the arguments may be NULL if the appropriate component does not appear in the address. Address of the `TARGET_MEM_REF` is determined in the following way.

```
&TMR_SYMBOL + TMR_BASE + TMR_INDEX * TMR_STEP + TMR_OFFSET
```

The sixth argument is the reference to the original memory access, which is preserved for the purposes of the RTL alias analysis. The seventh argument is a tag representing the results of tree level alias analysis.

ADDR_EXPR

These nodes are used to represent the address of an object. (These expressions will always have pointer or reference type.) The operand may be another expression, or it may be a declaration.

As an extension, GCC allows users to take the address of a label. In this case, the operand of the `ADDR_EXPR` will be a `LABEL_DECL`. The type of such an expression is `void*`.

If the object addressed is not an lvalue, a temporary is created, and the address of the temporary is used.

INDIRECT_REF

These nodes are used to represent the object pointed to by a pointer. The operand is the pointer being dereferenced; it will always have pointer or reference type.

MEM_REF   These nodes are used to represent the object pointed to by a pointer offset by a constant. The first operand is the pointer being dereferenced; it will always have pointer or reference type. The second operand is a pointer constant. Its type is specifying the type to be used for type-based alias analysis.

COMPONENT_REF

These nodes represent non-static data member accesses. The first operand is the object (rather than a pointer to it); the second operand is the `FIELD_DECL` for the data member. The third operand represents the byte offset of the field, but should not be used directly; call `component_ref_field_offset` instead.

10.6.3 Unary and Binary Expressions

`NEGATE_EXPR`

These nodes represent unary negation of the single operand, for both integer and floating-point types. The type of negation can be determined by looking at the type of the expression.

The behavior of this operation on signed arithmetic overflow is controlled by the `flag_wrapv` and `flag_trapv` variables.

`ABS_EXPR`   These nodes represent the absolute value of the single operand, for both integer and floating-point types. This is typically used to implement the `abs`, `labs` and `llabs` builtins for integer types, and the `fabs`, `fabsf` and `fabsl` builtins for floating point types. The type of abs operation can be determined by looking at the type of the expression.

This node is not used for complex types. To represent the modulus or complex abs of a complex value, use the `BUILT_IN_CABS`, `BUILT_IN_CABSF` or `BUILT_IN_CABSL` builtins, as used to implement the C99 `cabs`, `cabsf` and `cabsl` built-in functions.

`BIT_NOT_EXPR`

These nodes represent bitwise complement, and will always have integral type. The only operand is the value to be complemented.

`TRUTH_NOT_EXPR`

These nodes represent logical negation, and will always have integral (or boolean) type. The operand is the value being negated. The type of the operand and that of the result are always of `BOOLEAN_TYPE` or `INTEGER_TYPE`.

`PREDECREMENT_EXPR`
`PREINCREMENT_EXPR`
`POSTDECREMENT_EXPR`
`POSTINCREMENT_EXPR`

These nodes represent increment and decrement expressions. The value of the single operand is computed, and the operand incremented or decremented. In the case of `PREDECREMENT_EXPR` and `PREINCREMENT_EXPR`, the value of the expression is the value resulting after the increment or decrement; in the case of `POSTDECREMENT_EXPR` and `POSTINCREMENT_EXPR` is the value before the increment or decrement occurs. The type of the operand, like that of the result, will be either integral, boolean, or floating-point.

`FIX_TRUNC_EXPR`

These nodes represent conversion of a floating-point value to an integer. The single operand will have a floating-point type, while the complete expression will have an integral (or boolean) type. The operand is rounded towards zero.

FLOAT_EXPR

> These nodes represent conversion of an integral (or boolean) value to a floating-point value. The single operand will have integral type, while the complete expression will have a floating-point type.
>
> FIXME: How is the operand supposed to be rounded? Is this dependent on '-mieee'?

COMPLEX_EXPR

> These nodes are used to represent complex numbers constructed from two expressions of the same (integer or real) type. The first operand is the real part and the second operand is the imaginary part.

CONJ_EXPR

> These nodes represent the conjugate of their operand.

REALPART_EXPR
IMAGPART_EXPR

> These nodes represent respectively the real and the imaginary parts of complex numbers (their sole argument).

NON_LVALUE_EXPR

> These nodes indicate that their one and only operand is not an lvalue. A back end can treat these identically to the single operand.

NOP_EXPR These nodes are used to represent conversions that do not require any code-generation. For example, conversion of a `char*` to an `int*` does not require any code be generated; such a conversion is represented by a `NOP_EXPR`. The single operand is the expression to be converted. The conversion from a pointer to a reference is also represented with a `NOP_EXPR`.

CONVERT_EXPR

> These nodes are similar to `NOP_EXPR`s, but are used in those situations where code may need to be generated. For example, if an `int*` is converted to an `int` code may need to be generated on some platforms. These nodes are never used for C++-specific conversions, like conversions between pointers to different classes in an inheritance hierarchy. Any adjustments that need to be made in such cases are always indicated explicitly. Similarly, a user-defined conversion is never represented by a `CONVERT_EXPR`; instead, the function calls are made explicit.

FIXED_CONVERT_EXPR

> These nodes are used to represent conversions that involve fixed-point values. For example, from a fixed-point value to another fixed-point value, from an integer to a fixed-point value, from a fixed-point value to an integer, from a floating-point value to a fixed-point value, or from a fixed-point value to a floating-point value.

LSHIFT_EXPR
RSHIFT_EXPR

> These nodes represent left and right shifts, respectively. The first operand is the value to shift; it will always be of integral type. The second operand is

an expression for the number of bits by which to shift. Right shift should be treated as arithmetic, i.e., the high-order bits should be zero-filled when the expression has unsigned type and filled with the sign bit when the expression has signed type. Note that the result is undefined if the second operand is larger than or equal to the first operand's type size. Unlike most nodes, these can have a vector as first operand and a scalar as second operand.

`BIT_IOR_EXPR`
`BIT_XOR_EXPR`
`BIT_AND_EXPR`

These nodes represent bitwise inclusive or, bitwise exclusive or, and bitwise and, respectively. Both operands will always have integral type.

`TRUTH_ANDIF_EXPR`
`TRUTH_ORIF_EXPR`

These nodes represent logical "and" and logical "or", respectively. These operators are not strict; i.e., the second operand is evaluated only if the value of the expression is not determined by evaluation of the first operand. The type of the operands and that of the result are always of `BOOLEAN_TYPE` or `INTEGER_TYPE`.

`TRUTH_AND_EXPR`
`TRUTH_OR_EXPR`
`TRUTH_XOR_EXPR`

These nodes represent logical and, logical or, and logical exclusive or. They are strict; both arguments are always evaluated. There are no corresponding operators in C or C++, but the front end will sometimes generate these expressions anyhow, if it can tell that strictness does not matter. The type of the operands and that of the result are always of `BOOLEAN_TYPE` or `INTEGER_TYPE`.

`POINTER_PLUS_EXPR`

This node represents pointer arithmetic. The first operand is always a pointer/reference type. The second operand is always an unsigned integer type compatible with sizetype. This is the only binary arithmetic operand that can operate on pointer types.

`PLUS_EXPR`
`MINUS_EXPR`
`MULT_EXPR`

These nodes represent various binary arithmetic operations. Respectively, these operations are addition, subtraction (of the second operand from the first) and multiplication. Their operands may have either integral or floating type, but there will never be case in which one operand is of floating type and the other is of integral type.

The behavior of these operations on signed arithmetic overflow is controlled by the `flag_wrapv` and `flag_trapv` variables.

`MULT_HIGHPART_EXPR`

This node represents the "high-part" of a widening multiplication. For an integral type with b bits of precision, the result is the most significant b bits of the full $2b$ product.

RDIV_EXPR

>   This node represents a floating point division operation.

TRUNC_DIV_EXPR
FLOOR_DIV_EXPR
CEIL_DIV_EXPR
ROUND_DIV_EXPR

>   These nodes represent integer division operations that return an integer result.
>   TRUNC_DIV_EXPR rounds towards zero, FLOOR_DIV_EXPR rounds towards nega-
>   tive infinity, CEIL_DIV_EXPR rounds towards positive infinity and ROUND_DIV_
>   EXPR rounds to the closest integer. Integer division in C and C++ is truncating,
>   i.e. TRUNC_DIV_EXPR.
>
>   The behavior of these operations on signed arithmetic overflow, when dividing
>   the minimum signed integer by minus one, is controlled by the flag_wrapv and
>   flag_trapv variables.

TRUNC_MOD_EXPR
FLOOR_MOD_EXPR
CEIL_MOD_EXPR
ROUND_MOD_EXPR

>   These nodes represent the integer remainder or modulus operation. The integer
>   modulus of two operands a and b is defined as a - (a/b)*b where the division
>   calculated using the corresponding division operator. Hence for TRUNC_MOD_
>   EXPR this definition assumes division using truncation towards zero, i.e. TRUNC_
>   DIV_EXPR. Integer remainder in C and C++ uses truncating division, i.e. TRUNC_
>   MOD_EXPR.

EXACT_DIV_EXPR

>   The EXACT_DIV_EXPR code is used to represent integer divisions where the nu-
>   merator is known to be an exact multiple of the denominator. This allows the
>   backend to choose between the faster of TRUNC_DIV_EXPR, CEIL_DIV_EXPR and
>   FLOOR_DIV_EXPR for the current target.

LT_EXPR
LE_EXPR
GT_EXPR
GE_EXPR
EQ_EXPR
NE_EXPR   These nodes represent the less than, less than or equal to, greater than, greater
>   than or equal to, equal, and not equal comparison operators. The first and
>   second operands will either be both of integral type, both of floating type or
>   both of vector type. The result type of these expressions will always be of
>   integral, boolean or signed integral vector type. These operations return the
>   result type's zero value for false, the result type's one value for true, and a
>   vector whose elements are zero (false) or minus one (true) for vectors.
>
>   For floating point comparisons, if we honor IEEE NaNs and either operand is
>   NaN, then NE_EXPR always returns true and the remaining operators always
>   return false. On some targets, comparisons against an IEEE NaN, other than
>   equality and inequality, may generate a floating point exception.

ORDERED_EXPR
UNORDERED_EXPR

These nodes represent non-trapping ordered and unordered comparison operators. These operations take two floating point operands and determine whether they are ordered or unordered relative to each other. If either operand is an IEEE NaN, their comparison is defined to be unordered, otherwise the comparison is defined to be ordered. The result type of these expressions will always be of integral or boolean type. These operations return the result type's zero value for false, and the result type's one value for true.

UNLT_EXPR
UNLE_EXPR
UNGT_EXPR
UNGE_EXPR
UNEQ_EXPR
LTGT_EXPR

These nodes represent the unordered comparison operators. These operations take two floating point operands and determine whether the operands are unordered or are less than, less than or equal to, greater than, greater than or equal to, or equal respectively. For example, UNLT_EXPR returns true if either operand is an IEEE NaN or the first operand is less than the second. With the possible exception of LTGT_EXPR, all of these operations are guaranteed not to generate a floating point exception. The result type of these expressions will always be of integral or boolean type. These operations return the result type's zero value for false, and the result type's one value for true.

MODIFY_EXPR

These nodes represent assignment. The left-hand side is the first operand; the right-hand side is the second operand. The left-hand side will be a VAR_DECL, INDIRECT_REF, COMPONENT_REF, or other lvalue.

These nodes are used to represent not only assignment with '=' but also compound assignments (like '+='), by reduction to '=' assignment. In other words, the representation for 'i += 3' looks just like that for 'i = i + 3'.

INIT_EXPR

These nodes are just like MODIFY_EXPR, but are used only when a variable is initialized, rather than assigned to subsequently. This means that we can assume that the target of the initialization is not used in computing its own value; any reference to the lhs in computing the rhs is undefined.

COMPOUND_EXPR

These nodes represent comma-expressions. The first operand is an expression whose value is computed and thrown away prior to the evaluation of the second operand. The value of the entire expression is the value of the second operand.

COND_EXPR

These nodes represent ?: expressions. The first operand is of boolean or integral type. If it evaluates to a nonzero value, the second operand should be evaluated, and returned as the value of the expression. Otherwise, the third operand is evaluated, and returned as the value of the expression.

The second operand must have the same type as the entire expression, unless it unconditionally throws an exception or calls a noreturn function, in which case it should have void type. The same constraints apply to the third operand. This allows array bounds checks to be represented conveniently as (i >= 0 && i < 10) ? i : abort().

As a GNU extension, the C language front-ends allow the second operand of the ?: operator may be omitted in the source. For example, x ? : 3 is equivalent to x ? x : 3, assuming that x is an expression without side-effects. In the tree representation, however, the second operand is always present, possibly protected by SAVE_EXPR if the first argument does cause side-effects.

CALL_EXPR

These nodes are used to represent calls to functions, including non-static member functions. CALL_EXPRs are implemented as expression nodes with a variable number of operands. Rather than using TREE_OPERAND to extract them, it is preferable to use the specialized accessor macros and functions that operate specifically on CALL_EXPR nodes.

CALL_EXPR_FN returns a pointer to the function to call; it is always an expression whose type is a POINTER_TYPE.

The number of arguments to the call is returned by call_expr_nargs, while the arguments themselves can be accessed with the CALL_EXPR_ARG macro. The arguments are zero-indexed and numbered left-to-right. You can iterate over the arguments using FOR_EACH_CALL_EXPR_ARG, as in:

```
tree call, arg;
call_expr_arg_iterator iter;
FOR_EACH_CALL_EXPR_ARG (arg, iter, call)
  /* arg is bound to successive arguments of call.  */
  ...;
```

For non-static member functions, there will be an operand corresponding to the this pointer. There will always be expressions corresponding to all of the arguments, even if the function is declared with default arguments and some arguments are not explicitly provided at the call sites.

CALL_EXPRs also have a CALL_EXPR_STATIC_CHAIN operand that is used to implement nested functions. This operand is otherwise null.

CLEANUP_POINT_EXPR

These nodes represent full-expressions. The single operand is an expression to evaluate. Any destructor calls engendered by the creation of temporaries during the evaluation of that expression should be performed immediately after the expression is evaluated.

CONSTRUCTOR

These nodes represent the brace-enclosed initializers for a structure or an array. They contain a sequence of component values made out of a vector of constructor_elt, which is a (INDEX, VALUE) pair.

If the TREE_TYPE of the CONSTRUCTOR is a RECORD_TYPE, UNION_TYPE or QUAL_UNION_TYPE then the INDEX of each node in the sequence will be a FIELD_DECL and the VALUE will be the expression used to initialize that field.

If the `TREE_TYPE` of the `CONSTRUCTOR` is an `ARRAY_TYPE`, then the `INDEX` of each node in the sequence will be an `INTEGER_CST` or a `RANGE_EXPR` of two `INTEGER_CST`s. A single `INTEGER_CST` indicates which element of the array is being assigned to. A `RANGE_EXPR` indicates an inclusive range of elements to initialize. In both cases the `VALUE` is the corresponding initializer. It is re-evaluated for each element of a `RANGE_EXPR`. If the `INDEX` is `NULL_TREE`, then the initializer is for the next available array element.

In the front end, you should not depend on the fields appearing in any particular order. However, in the middle end, fields must appear in declaration order. You should not assume that all fields will be represented. Unrepresented fields will be cleared (zeroed), unless the CONSTRUCTOR_NO_CLEARING flag is set, in which case their value becomes undefined.

COMPOUND_LITERAL_EXPR

These nodes represent ISO C99 compound literals. The `COMPOUND_LITERAL_EXPR_DECL_EXPR` is a `DECL_EXPR` containing an anonymous `VAR_DECL` for the unnamed object represented by the compound literal; the `DECL_INITIAL` of that `VAR_DECL` is a `CONSTRUCTOR` representing the brace-enclosed list of initializers in the compound literal. That anonymous `VAR_DECL` can also be accessed directly by the `COMPOUND_LITERAL_EXPR_DECL` macro.

SAVE_EXPR

A `SAVE_EXPR` represents an expression (possibly involving side-effects) that is used more than once. The side-effects should occur only the first time the expression is evaluated. Subsequent uses should just reuse the computed value. The first operand to the `SAVE_EXPR` is the expression to evaluate. The side-effects should be executed where the `SAVE_EXPR` is first encountered in a depth-first preorder traversal of the expression tree.

TARGET_EXPR

A `TARGET_EXPR` represents a temporary object. The first operand is a `VAR_DECL` for the temporary variable. The second operand is the initializer for the temporary. The initializer is evaluated and, if non-void, copied (bitwise) into the temporary. If the initializer is void, that means that it will perform the initialization itself.

Often, a `TARGET_EXPR` occurs on the right-hand side of an assignment, or as the second operand to a comma-expression which is itself the right-hand side of an assignment, etc. In this case, we say that the `TARGET_EXPR` is "normal"; otherwise, we say it is "orphaned". For a normal `TARGET_EXPR` the temporary variable should be treated as an alias for the left-hand side of the assignment, rather than as a new temporary variable.

The third operand to the `TARGET_EXPR`, if present, is a cleanup-expression (i.e., destructor call) for the temporary. If this expression is orphaned, then this expression must be executed when the statement containing this expression is complete. These cleanups must always be executed in the order opposite to that in which they were encountered. Note that if a temporary is created on one branch of a conditional operator (i.e., in the second or third operand to a `COND_EXPR`), the cleanup must be run only if that branch is actually executed.

VA_ARG_EXPR

>	This node is used to implement support for the C/C++ variable argument-list mechanism. It represents expressions like va_arg (ap, type). Its TREE_TYPE yields the tree representation for type and its sole argument yields the representation for ap.

ANNOTATE_EXPR

>	This node is used to attach markers to an expression. The first operand is the annotated expression, the second is an INTEGER_CST with a value from enum annot_expr_kind.

10.6.4 Vectors

VEC_LSHIFT_EXPR
VEC_RSHIFT_EXPR

>	These nodes represent whole vector left and right shifts, respectively. The first operand is the vector to shift; it will always be of vector type. The second operand is an expression for the number of bits by which to shift. Note that the result is undefined if the second operand is larger than or equal to the first operand's type size.

VEC_WIDEN_MULT_HI_EXPR
VEC_WIDEN_MULT_LO_EXPR

>	These nodes represent widening vector multiplication of the high and low parts of the two input vectors, respectively. Their operands are vectors that contain the same number of elements (N) of the same integral type. The result is a vector that contains half as many elements, of an integral type whose size is twice as wide. In the case of VEC_WIDEN_MULT_HI_EXPR the high $N/2$ elements of the two vector are multiplied to produce the vector of $N/2$ products. In the case of VEC_WIDEN_MULT_LO_EXPR the low $N/2$ elements of the two vector are multiplied to produce the vector of $N/2$ products.

VEC_UNPACK_HI_EXPR
VEC_UNPACK_LO_EXPR

>	These nodes represent unpacking of the high and low parts of the input vector, respectively. The single operand is a vector that contains N elements of the same integral or floating point type. The result is a vector that contains half as many elements, of an integral or floating point type whose size is twice as wide. In the case of VEC_UNPACK_HI_EXPR the high $N/2$ elements of the vector are extracted and widened (promoted). In the case of VEC_UNPACK_LO_EXPR the low $N/2$ elements of the vector are extracted and widened (promoted).

VEC_UNPACK_FLOAT_HI_EXPR
VEC_UNPACK_FLOAT_LO_EXPR

>	These nodes represent unpacking of the high and low parts of the input vector, where the values are converted from fixed point to floating point. The single operand is a vector that contains N elements of the same integral type. The result is a vector that contains half as many elements of a floating point type whose size is twice as wide. In the case of VEC_UNPACK_HI_EXPR the high $N/2$

elements of the vector are extracted, converted and widened. In the case of `VEC_UNPACK_LO_EXPR` the low `N/2` elements of the vector are extracted, converted and widened.

`VEC_PACK_TRUNC_EXPR`

This node represents packing of truncated elements of the two input vectors into the output vector. Input operands are vectors that contain the same number of elements of the same integral or floating point type. The result is a vector that contains twice as many elements of an integral or floating point type whose size is half as wide. The elements of the two vectors are demoted and merged (concatenated) to form the output vector.

`VEC_PACK_SAT_EXPR`

This node represents packing of elements of the two input vectors into the output vector using saturation. Input operands are vectors that contain the same number of elements of the same integral type. The result is a vector that contains twice as many elements of an integral type whose size is half as wide. The elements of the two vectors are demoted and merged (concatenated) to form the output vector.

`VEC_PACK_FIX_TRUNC_EXPR`

This node represents packing of elements of the two input vectors into the output vector, where the values are converted from floating point to fixed point. Input operands are vectors that contain the same number of elements of a floating point type. The result is a vector that contains twice as many elements of an integral type whose size is half as wide. The elements of the two vectors are merged (concatenated) to form the output vector.

`VEC_COND_EXPR`

These nodes represent `?:` expressions. The three operands must be vectors of the same size and number of elements. The second and third operands must have the same type as the entire expression. The first operand is of signed integral vector type. If an element of the first operand evaluates to a zero value, the corresponding element of the result is taken from the third operand. If it evaluates to a minus one value, it is taken from the second operand. It should never evaluate to any other value currently, but optimizations should not rely on that property. In contrast with a `COND_EXPR`, all operands are always evaluated.

`SAD_EXPR`   This node represents the Sum of Absolute Differences operation. The three operands must be vectors of integral types. The first and second operand must have the same type. The size of the vector element of the third operand must be at lease twice of the size of the vector element of the first and second one. The SAD is calculated between the first and second operands, added to the third operand, and returned.

10.7 Statements

Most statements in GIMPLE are assignment statements, represented by `GIMPLE_ASSIGN`. No other C expressions can appear at statement level; a reference to a volatile object is converted into a `GIMPLE_ASSIGN`.

There are also several varieties of complex statements.

10.7.1 Basic Statements

ASM_EXPR

>   Used to represent an inline assembly statement. For an inline assembly state-
>   ment like:
>
>   asm ("mov x, y");
>
>   The ASM_STRING macro will return a STRING_CST node for "mov x, y". If
>   the original statement made use of the extended-assembly syntax, then ASM_
>   OUTPUTS, ASM_INPUTS, and ASM_CLOBBERS will be the outputs, inputs, and
>   clobbers for the statement, represented as STRING_CST nodes. The extended-
>   assembly syntax looks like:
>
>   asm ("fsinx %1,%0" : "=f" (result) : "f" (angle));
>
>   The first string is the ASM_STRING, containing the instruction template. The
>   next two strings are the output and inputs, respectively; this statement has no
>   clobbers. As this example indicates, "plain" assembly statements are merely
>   a special case of extended assembly statements; they have no cv-qualifiers,
>   outputs, inputs, or clobbers. All of the strings will be NUL-terminated, and will
>   contain no embedded NUL-characters.
>
>   If the assembly statement is declared volatile, or if the statement was not
>   an extended assembly statement, and is therefore implicitly volatile, then the
>   predicate ASM_VOLATILE_P will hold of the ASM_EXPR.

DECL_EXPR

>   Used to represent a local declaration. The DECL_EXPR_DECL macro can be
>   used to obtain the entity declared. This declaration may be a LABEL_DECL,
>   indicating that the label declared is a local label. (As an extension, GCC
>   allows the declaration of labels with scope.) In C, this declaration may be a
>   FUNCTION_DECL, indicating the use of the GCC nested function extension. For
>   more information, see Section 10.8 [Functions], page 163.

LABEL_EXPR

>   Used to represent a label. The LABEL_DECL declared by this statement can be
>   obtained with the LABEL_EXPR_LABEL macro. The IDENTIFIER_NODE giving the
>   name of the label can be obtained from the LABEL_DECL with DECL_NAME.

GOTO_EXPR

>   Used to represent a goto statement. The GOTO_DESTINATION will usually be
>   a LABEL_DECL. However, if the "computed goto" extension has been used, the
>   GOTO_DESTINATION will be an arbitrary expression indicating the destination.
>   This expression will always have pointer type.

RETURN_EXPR

>   Used to represent a return statement. Operand 0 represents the value to
>   return. It should either be the RESULT_DECL for the containing function, or
>   a MODIFY_EXPR or INIT_EXPR setting the function's RESULT_DECL. It will be
>   NULL_TREE if the statement was just
>
>   return;

LOOP_EXPR

> These nodes represent "infinite" loops. The LOOP_EXPR_BODY represents the body of the loop. It should be executed forever, unless an EXIT_EXPR is encountered.

EXIT_EXPR

> These nodes represent conditional exits from the nearest enclosing LOOP_EXPR. The single operand is the condition; if it is nonzero, then the loop should be exited. An EXIT_EXPR will only appear within a LOOP_EXPR.

SWITCH_STMT

> Used to represent a switch statement. The SWITCH_STMT_COND is the expression on which the switch is occurring. See the documentation for an IF_STMT for more information on the representation used for the condition. The SWITCH_STMT_BODY is the body of the switch statement. The SWITCH_STMT_TYPE is the original type of switch expression as given in the source, before any compiler conversions.

CASE_LABEL_EXPR

> Use to represent a case label, range of case labels, or a default label. If CASE_LOW is NULL_TREE, then this is a default label. Otherwise, if CASE_HIGH is NULL_TREE, then this is an ordinary case label. In this case, CASE_LOW is an expression giving the value of the label. Both CASE_LOW and CASE_HIGH are INTEGER_CST nodes. These values will have the same type as the condition expression in the switch statement.
>
> Otherwise, if both CASE_LOW and CASE_HIGH are defined, the statement is a range of case labels. Such statements originate with the extension that allows users to write things of the form:
>
> > case 2 ... 5:
>
> The first value will be CASE_LOW, while the second will be CASE_HIGH.

10.7.2 Blocks

Block scopes and the variables they declare in GENERIC are expressed using the BIND_EXPR code, which in previous versions of GCC was primarily used for the C statement-expression extension.

Variables in a block are collected into BIND_EXPR_VARS in declaration order through their TREE_CHAIN field. Any runtime initialization is moved out of DECL_INITIAL and into a statement in the controlled block. When gimplifying from C or C++, this initialization replaces the DECL_STMT. These variables will never require cleanups. The scope of these variables is just the body

Variable-length arrays (VLAs) complicate this process, as their size often refers to variables initialized earlier in the block and their initialization involves an explicit stack allocation. To handle this, we add an indirection and replace them with a pointer to stack space allocated by means of alloca. In most cases, we also arrange for this space to be reclaimed when the enclosing BIND_EXPR is exited, the exception to this being when there is an explicit call to alloca in the source code, in which case the stack is left depressed on exit of the BIND_EXPR.

A C++ program will usually contain more `BIND_EXPR`s than there are syntactic blocks in the source code, since several C++ constructs have implicit scopes associated with them. On the other hand, although the C++ front end uses pseudo-scopes to handle cleanups for objects with destructors, these don't translate into the GIMPLE form; multiple declarations at the same level use the same `BIND_EXPR`.

10.7.3 Statement Sequences

Multiple statements at the same nesting level are collected into a `STATEMENT_LIST`. Statement lists are modified and traversed using the interface in 'tree-iterator.h'.

10.7.4 Empty Statements

Whenever possible, statements with no effect are discarded. But if they are nested within another construct which cannot be discarded for some reason, they are instead replaced with an empty statement, generated by `build_empty_stmt`. Initially, all empty statements were shared, after the pattern of the Java front end, but this caused a lot of trouble in practice.

An empty statement is represented as `(void)0`.

10.7.5 Jumps

Other jumps are expressed by either `GOTO_EXPR` or `RETURN_EXPR`.

The operand of a `GOTO_EXPR` must be either a label or a variable containing the address to jump to.

The operand of a `RETURN_EXPR` is either `NULL_TREE`, `RESULT_DECL`, or a `MODIFY_EXPR` which sets the return value. It would be nice to move the `MODIFY_EXPR` into a separate statement, but the special return semantics in `expand_return` make that difficult. It may still happen in the future, perhaps by moving most of that logic into `expand_assignment`.

10.7.6 Cleanups

Destructors for local C++ objects and similar dynamic cleanups are represented in GIMPLE by a `TRY_FINALLY_EXPR`. `TRY_FINALLY_EXPR` has two operands, both of which are a sequence of statements to execute. The first sequence is executed. When it completes the second sequence is executed.

The first sequence may complete in the following ways:

1. Execute the last statement in the sequence and fall off the end.
2. Execute a goto statement (`GOTO_EXPR`) to an ordinary label outside the sequence.
3. Execute a return statement (`RETURN_EXPR`).
4. Throw an exception. This is currently not explicitly represented in GIMPLE.

The second sequence is not executed if the first sequence completes by calling `setjmp` or `exit` or any other function that does not return. The second sequence is also not executed if the first sequence completes via a non-local goto or a computed goto (in general the compiler does not know whether such a goto statement exits the first sequence or not, so we assume that it doesn't).

After the second sequence is executed, if it completes normally by falling off the end, execution continues wherever the first sequence would have continued, by falling off the end, or doing a goto, etc.

TRY_FINALLY_EXPR complicates the flow graph, since the cleanup needs to appear on every edge out of the controlled block; this reduces the freedom to move code across these edges. Therefore, the EH lowering pass which runs before most of the optimization passes eliminates these expressions by explicitly adding the cleanup to each edge. Rethrowing the exception is represented using RESX_EXPR.

10.7.7 OpenMP

All the statements starting with OMP_ represent directives and clauses used by the OpenMP API http://www.openmp.org/.

OMP_PARALLEL

> Represents #pragma omp parallel [clause1 ... clauseN]. It has four operands:

> Operand OMP_PARALLEL_BODY is valid while in GENERIC and High GIMPLE forms. It contains the body of code to be executed by all the threads. During GIMPLE lowering, this operand becomes NULL and the body is emitted linearly after OMP_PARALLEL.

> Operand OMP_PARALLEL_CLAUSES is the list of clauses associated with the directive.

> Operand OMP_PARALLEL_FN is created by pass_lower_omp, it contains the FUNCTION_DECL for the function that will contain the body of the parallel region.

> Operand OMP_PARALLEL_DATA_ARG is also created by pass_lower_omp. If there are shared variables to be communicated to the children threads, this operand will contain the VAR_DECL that contains all the shared values and variables.

OMP_FOR

> Represents #pragma omp for [clause1 ... clauseN]. It has six operands:

> Operand OMP_FOR_BODY contains the loop body.

> Operand OMP_FOR_CLAUSES is the list of clauses associated with the directive.

> Operand OMP_FOR_INIT is the loop initialization code of the form VAR = N1.

> Operand OMP_FOR_COND is the loop conditional expression of the form VAR {<,>,<=,>=} N2.

> Operand OMP_FOR_INCR is the loop index increment of the form VAR {+=,-=} INCR.

> Operand OMP_FOR_PRE_BODY contains side-effect code from operands OMP_FOR_INIT, OMP_FOR_COND and OMP_FOR_INC. These side-effects are part of the OMP_FOR block but must be evaluated before the start of loop body.

> The loop index variable VAR must be a signed integer variable, which is implicitly private to each thread. Bounds N1 and N2 and the increment expression INCR are required to be loop invariant integer expressions that are evaluated without any synchronization. The evaluation order, frequency of evaluation and side-effects are unspecified by the standard.

OMP_SECTIONS

> Represents #pragma omp sections [clause1 ... clauseN].

Operand `OMP_SECTIONS_BODY` contains the sections body, which in turn contains a set of `OMP_SECTION` nodes for each of the concurrent sections delimited by `#pragma omp section`.

Operand `OMP_SECTIONS_CLAUSES` is the list of clauses associated with the directive.

OMP_SECTION

Section delimiter for `OMP_SECTIONS`.

OMP_SINGLE

Represents `#pragma omp single`.

Operand `OMP_SINGLE_BODY` contains the body of code to be executed by a single thread.

Operand `OMP_SINGLE_CLAUSES` is the list of clauses associated with the directive.

OMP_MASTER

Represents `#pragma omp master`.

Operand `OMP_MASTER_BODY` contains the body of code to be executed by the master thread.

OMP_ORDERED

Represents `#pragma omp ordered`.

Operand `OMP_ORDERED_BODY` contains the body of code to be executed in the sequential order dictated by the loop index variable.

OMP_CRITICAL

Represents `#pragma omp critical [name]`.

Operand `OMP_CRITICAL_BODY` is the critical section.

Operand `OMP_CRITICAL_NAME` is an optional identifier to label the critical section.

OMP_RETURN

This does not represent any OpenMP directive, it is an artificial marker to indicate the end of the body of an OpenMP. It is used by the flow graph (`tree-cfg.c`) and OpenMP region building code (`omp-low.c`).

OMP_CONTINUE

Similarly, this instruction does not represent an OpenMP directive, it is used by `OMP_FOR` (and similar codes) as well as `OMP_SECTIONS` to mark the place where the code needs to loop to the next iteration, or the next section, respectively.

In some cases, `OMP_CONTINUE` is placed right before `OMP_RETURN`. But if there are cleanups that need to occur right after the looping body, it will be emitted between `OMP_CONTINUE` and `OMP_RETURN`.

OMP_ATOMIC

Represents `#pragma omp atomic`.

Operand 0 is the address at which the atomic operation is to be performed.

Operand 1 is the expression to evaluate. The gimplifier tries three alternative code generation strategies. Whenever possible, an atomic update built-in is

used. If that fails, a compare-and-swap loop is attempted. If that also fails, a
regular critical section around the expression is used.

OMP_CLAUSE

Represents clauses associated with one of the OMP_ directives. Clauses are
represented by separate subcodes defined in 'tree.h'. Clauses codes can be one
of: OMP_CLAUSE_PRIVATE, OMP_CLAUSE_SHARED, OMP_CLAUSE_FIRSTPRIVATE,
OMP_CLAUSE_LASTPRIVATE, OMP_CLAUSE_COPYIN, OMP_CLAUSE_COPYPRIVATE,
OMP_CLAUSE_IF,   OMP_CLAUSE_NUM_THREADS,   OMP_CLAUSE_SCHEDULE,
OMP_CLAUSE_NOWAIT,   OMP_CLAUSE_ORDERED,   OMP_CLAUSE_DEFAULT,
OMP_CLAUSE_REDUCTION,   OMP_CLAUSE_COLLAPSE,   OMP_CLAUSE_UNTIED,
OMP_CLAUSE_FINAL, and OMP_CLAUSE_MERGEABLE. Each code represents the
corresponding OpenMP clause.

Clauses associated with the same directive are chained together via
OMP_CLAUSE_CHAIN. Those clauses that accept a list of variables are restricted
to exactly one, accessed with OMP_CLAUSE_VAR. Therefore, multiple variables
under the same clause C need to be represented as multiple C clauses chained
together. This facilitates adding new clauses during compilation.

10.7.8 OpenACC

All the statements starting with OACC_ represent directives and clauses used by the OpenACC API http://www.openacc.org/.

OACC_CACHE

Represents #pragma acc cache (var ...).

OACC_DATA

Represents #pragma acc data [clause1 ... clauseN].

OACC_DECLARE

Represents #pragma acc declare [clause1 ... clauseN].

OACC_ENTER_DATA

Represents #pragma acc enter data [clause1 ... clauseN].

OACC_EXIT_DATA

Represents #pragma acc exit data [clause1 ... clauseN].

OACC_HOST_DATA

Represents #pragma acc host_data [clause1 ... clauseN].

OACC_KERNELS

Represents #pragma acc kernels [clause1 ... clauseN].

OACC_LOOP

Represents #pragma acc loop [clause1 ... clauseN].

See the description of the OMP_FOR code.

OACC_PARALLEL

Represents #pragma acc parallel [clause1 ... clauseN].

OACC_UPDATE

Represents #pragma acc update [clause1 ... clauseN].

10.8 Functions

A function is represented by a `FUNCTION_DECL` node. It stores the basic pieces of the function such as body, parameters, and return type as well as information on the surrounding context, visibility, and linkage.

10.8.1 Function Basics

A function has four core parts: the name, the parameters, the result, and the body. The following macros and functions access these parts of a `FUNCTION_DECL` as well as other basic features:

`DECL_NAME`

> This macro returns the unqualified name of the function, as an `IDENTIFIER_NODE`. For an instantiation of a function template, the `DECL_NAME` is the unqualified name of the template, not something like `f<int>`. The value of `DECL_NAME` is undefined when used on a constructor, destructor, overloaded operator, or type-conversion operator, or any function that is implicitly generated by the compiler. See below for macros that can be used to distinguish these cases.

`DECL_ASSEMBLER_NAME`

> This macro returns the mangled name of the function, also an `IDENTIFIER_NODE`. This name does not contain leading underscores on systems that prefix all identifiers with underscores. The mangled name is computed in the same way on all platforms; if special processing is required to deal with the object file format used on a particular platform, it is the responsibility of the back end to perform those modifications. (Of course, the back end should not modify `DECL_ASSEMBLER_NAME` itself.)

> Using `DECL_ASSEMBLER_NAME` will cause additional memory to be allocated (for the mangled name of the entity) so it should be used only when emitting assembly code. It should not be used within the optimizers to determine whether or not two declarations are the same, even though some of the existing optimizers do use it in that way. These uses will be removed over time.

`DECL_ARGUMENTS`

> This macro returns the `PARM_DECL` for the first argument to the function. Subsequent `PARM_DECL` nodes can be obtained by following the `TREE_CHAIN` links.

`DECL_RESULT`

> This macro returns the `RESULT_DECL` for the function.

`DECL_SAVED_TREE`

> This macro returns the complete body of the function.

`TREE_TYPE`

> This macro returns the `FUNCTION_TYPE` or `METHOD_TYPE` for the function.

`DECL_INITIAL`

> A function that has a definition in the current translation unit will have a non-`NULL` `DECL_INITIAL`. However, back ends should not make use of the particular value given by `DECL_INITIAL`.

It should contain a tree of `BLOCK` nodes that mirrors the scopes that variables are bound in the function. Each block contains a list of decls declared in a basic block, a pointer to a chain of blocks at the next lower scope level, then a pointer to the next block at the same level and a backpointer to the parent `BLOCK` or `FUNCTION_DECL`. So given a function as follows:

```
void foo()
{
  int a;
  {
    int b;
  }
  int c;
}
```

you would get the following:

```
tree foo = FUNCTION_DECL;
tree decl_a = VAR_DECL;
tree decl_b = VAR_DECL;
tree decl_c = VAR_DECL;
tree block_a = BLOCK;
tree block_b = BLOCK;
tree block_c = BLOCK;
BLOCK_VARS(block_a) = decl_a;
BLOCK_SUBBLOCKS(block_a) = block_b;
BLOCK_CHAIN(block_a) = block_c;
BLOCK_SUPERCONTEXT(block_a) = foo;
BLOCK_VARS(block_b) = decl_b;
BLOCK_SUPERCONTEXT(block_b) = block_a;
BLOCK_VARS(block_c) = decl_c;
BLOCK_SUPERCONTEXT(block_c) = foo;
DECL_INITIAL(foo) = block_a;
```

10.8.2 Function Properties

To determine the scope of a function, you can use the `DECL_CONTEXT` macro. This macro will return the class (either a `RECORD_TYPE` or a `UNION_TYPE`) or namespace (a `NAMESPACE_DECL`) of which the function is a member. For a virtual function, this macro returns the class in which the function was actually defined, not the base class in which the virtual declaration occurred.

In C, the `DECL_CONTEXT` for a function maybe another function. This representation indicates that the GNU nested function extension is in use. For details on the semantics of nested functions, see the GCC Manual. The nested function can refer to local variables in its containing function. Such references are not explicitly marked in the tree structure; back ends must look at the `DECL_CONTEXT` for the referenced `VAR_DECL`. If the `DECL_CONTEXT` for the referenced `VAR_DECL` is not the same as the function currently being processed, and neither `DECL_EXTERNAL` nor `TREE_STATIC` hold, then the reference is to a local variable in a containing function, and the back end must take appropriate action.

`DECL_EXTERNAL`

> This predicate holds if the function is undefined.

`TREE_PUBLIC`

> This predicate holds if the function has external linkage.

`TREE_STATIC`

>   This predicate holds if the function has been defined.

`TREE_THIS_VOLATILE`

>   This predicate holds if the function does not return normally.

`TREE_READONLY`

>   This predicate holds if the function can only read its arguments.

`DECL_PURE_P`

>   This predicate holds if the function can only read its arguments, but may also read global memory.

`DECL_VIRTUAL_P`

>   This predicate holds if the function is virtual.

`DECL_ARTIFICIAL`

>   This macro holds if the function was implicitly generated by the compiler, rather than explicitly declared. In addition to implicitly generated class member functions, this macro holds for the special functions created to implement static initialization and destruction, to compute run-time type information, and so forth.

`DECL_FUNCTION_SPECIFIC_TARGET`

>   This macro returns a tree node that holds the target options that are to be used to compile this particular function or `NULL_TREE` if the function is to be compiled with the target options specified on the command line.

`DECL_FUNCTION_SPECIFIC_OPTIMIZATION`

>   This macro returns a tree node that holds the optimization options that are to be used to compile this particular function or `NULL_TREE` if the function is to be compiled with the optimization options specified on the command line.

10.9 Language-dependent trees

Front ends may wish to keep some state associated with various GENERIC trees while parsing. To support this, trees provide a set of flags that may be used by the front end. They are accessed using `TREE_LANG_FLAG_n` where 'n' is currently 0 through 6.

If necessary, a front end can use some language-dependent tree codes in its GENERIC representation, so long as it provides a hook for converting them to GIMPLE and doesn't expect them to work with any (hypothetical) optimizers that run before the conversion to GIMPLE. The intermediate representation used while parsing C and C++ looks very little like GENERIC, but the C and C++ gimplifier hooks are perfectly happy to take it as input and spit out GIMPLE.

10.10 C and C++ Trees

This section documents the internal representation used by GCC to represent C and C++ source programs. When presented with a C or C++ source program, GCC parses the program, performs semantic analysis (including the generation of error messages), and then produces the internal representation described here. This representation contains a complete representation for the entire translation unit provided as input to the front end. This representation is then typically processed by a code-generator in order to produce machine code, but could also be used in the creation of source browsers, intelligent editors, automatic documentation generators, interpreters, and any other programs needing the ability to process C or C++ code.

This section explains the internal representation. In particular, it documents the internal representation for C and C++ source constructs, and the macros, functions, and variables that can be used to access these constructs. The C++ representation is largely a superset of the representation used in the C front end. There is only one construct used in C that does not appear in the C++ front end and that is the GNU "nested function" extension. Many of the macros documented here do not apply in C because the corresponding language constructs do not appear in C.

The C and C++ front ends generate a mix of GENERIC trees and ones specific to C and C++. These language-specific trees are higher-level constructs than the ones in GENERIC to make the parser's job easier. This section describes those trees that aren't part of GENERIC as well as aspects of GENERIC trees that are treated in a language-specific manner.

If you are developing a "back end", be it is a code-generator or some other tool, that uses this representation, you may occasionally find that you need to ask questions not easily answered by the functions and macros available here. If that situation occurs, it is quite likely that GCC already supports the functionality you desire, but that the interface is simply not documented here. In that case, you should ask the GCC maintainers (via mail to gcc@gcc.gnu.org) about documenting the functionality you require. Similarly, if you find yourself writing functions that do not deal directly with your back end, but instead might be useful to other people using the GCC front end, you should submit your patches for inclusion in GCC.

10.10.1 Types for C++

In C++, an array type is not qualified; rather the type of the array elements is qualified. This situation is reflected in the intermediate representation. The macros described here will always examine the qualification of the underlying element type when applied to an array type. (If the element type is itself an array, then the recursion continues until a non-array type is found, and the qualification of this type is examined.) So, for example, CP_TYPE_CONST_P will hold of the type const int ()[7], denoting an array of seven ints.

The following functions and macros deal with cv-qualification of types:

cp_type_quals

> This function returns the set of type qualifiers applied to this type. This value is TYPE_UNQUALIFIED if no qualifiers have been applied. The TYPE_QUAL_CONST bit is set if the type is const-qualified. The TYPE_QUAL_VOLATILE bit is set if the type is volatile-qualified. The TYPE_QUAL_RESTRICT bit is set if the type is restrict-qualified.

CP_TYPE_CONST_P

> This macro holds if the type is const-qualified.

CP_TYPE_VOLATILE_P

> This macro holds if the type is volatile-qualified.

CP_TYPE_RESTRICT_P

>   This macro holds if the type is **restrict**-qualified.

CP_TYPE_CONST_NON_VOLATILE_P

>   This predicate holds for a type that is **const**-qualified, but *not* **volatile**-qualified; other cv-qualifiers are ignored as well: only the **const**-ness is tested.

A few other macros and functions are usable with all types:

TYPE_SIZE

>   The number of bits required to represent the type, represented as an **INTEGER_CST**. For an incomplete type, **TYPE_SIZE** will be **NULL_TREE**.

TYPE_ALIGN

>   The alignment of the type, in bits, represented as an **int**.

TYPE_NAME

>   This macro returns a declaration (in the form of a **TYPE_DECL**) for the type. (Note this macro does *not* return an **IDENTIFIER_NODE**, as you might expect, given its name!) You can look at the **DECL_NAME** of the **TYPE_DECL** to obtain the actual name of the type. The **TYPE_NAME** will be **NULL_TREE** for a type that is not a built-in type, the result of a typedef, or a named class type.

CP_INTEGRAL_TYPE

>   This predicate holds if the type is an integral type. Notice that in C++, enumerations are *not* integral types.

ARITHMETIC_TYPE_P

>   This predicate holds if the type is an integral type (in the C++ sense) or a floating point type.

CLASS_TYPE_P

>   This predicate holds for a class-type.

TYPE_BUILT_IN

>   This predicate holds for a built-in type.

TYPE_PTRDATAMEM_P

>   This predicate holds if the type is a pointer to data member.

TYPE_PTR_P

>   This predicate holds if the type is a pointer type, and the pointee is not a data member.

TYPE_PTRFN_P

>   This predicate holds for a pointer to function type.

TYPE_PTROB_P

>   This predicate holds for a pointer to object type. Note however that it does not hold for the generic pointer to object type **void ***. You may use **TYPE_PTROBV_P** to test for a pointer to object type as well as **void ***.

The table below describes types specific to C and C++ as well as language-dependent info about GENERIC types.

POINTER_TYPE

> Used to represent pointer types, and pointer to data member types. If `TREE_TYPE` is a pointer to data member type, then `TYPE_PTRDATAMEM_P` will hold. For a pointer to data member type of the form 'T X::*', `TYPE_PTRMEM_CLASS_TYPE` will be the type X, while `TYPE_PTRMEM_POINTED_TO_TYPE` will be the type T.

RECORD_TYPE

> Used to represent **struct** and **class** types in C and C++. If `TYPE_PTRMEMFUNC_P` holds, then this type is a pointer-to-member type. In that case, the `TYPE_PTRMEMFUNC_FN_TYPE` is a `POINTER_TYPE` pointing to a `METHOD_TYPE`. The `METHOD_TYPE` is the type of a function pointed to by the pointer-to-member function. If `TYPE_PTRMEMFUNC_P` does not hold, this type is a class type. For more information, see Section 10.10.3 [Classes], page 169.

UNKNOWN_TYPE

> This node is used to represent a type the knowledge of which is insufficient for a sound processing.

TYPENAME_TYPE

> Used to represent a construct of the form **typename T::A**. The `TYPE_CONTEXT` is T; the `TYPE_NAME` is an `IDENTIFIER_NODE` for A. If the type is specified via a template-id, then `TYPENAME_TYPE_FULLNAME` yields a `TEMPLATE_ID_EXPR`. The `TREE_TYPE` is non-NULL if the node is implicitly generated in support for the implicit typename extension; in which case the `TREE_TYPE` is a type node for the base-class.

TYPEOF_TYPE

> Used to represent the `__typeof__` extension. The `TYPE_FIELDS` is the expression the type of which is being represented.

10.10.2 Namespaces

The root of the entire intermediate representation is the variable `global_namespace`. This is the namespace specified with :: in C++ source code. All other namespaces, types, variables, functions, and so forth can be found starting with this namespace.

However, except for the fact that it is distinguished as the root of the representation, the global namespace is no different from any other namespace. Thus, in what follows, we describe namespaces generally, rather than the global namespace in particular.

A namespace is represented by a `NAMESPACE_DECL` node.

The following macros and functions can be used on a `NAMESPACE_DECL`:

DECL_NAME

> This macro is used to obtain the `IDENTIFIER_NODE` corresponding to the un-qualified name of the name of the namespace (see Section 10.2.2 [Identifiers], page 135). The name of the global namespace is '::', even though in C++ the global namespace is unnamed. However, you should use comparison with `global_namespace`, rather than `DECL_NAME` to determine whether or not a namespace is the global one. An unnamed namespace will have a `DECL_NAME` equal to `anonymous_namespace_name`. Within a single translation unit, all un-named namespaces will have the same name.

DECL_CONTEXT

> This macro returns the enclosing namespace. The DECL_CONTEXT for the global_namespace is NULL_TREE.

DECL_NAMESPACE_ALIAS

> If this declaration is for a namespace alias, then DECL_NAMESPACE_ALIAS is the namespace for which this one is an alias.

> Do not attempt to use cp_namespace_decls for a namespace which is an alias. Instead, follow DECL_NAMESPACE_ALIAS links until you reach an ordinary, non-alias, namespace, and call cp_namespace_decls there.

DECL_NAMESPACE_STD_P

> This predicate holds if the namespace is the special ::std namespace.

cp_namespace_decls

> This function will return the declarations contained in the namespace, including types, overloaded functions, other namespaces, and so forth. If there are no declarations, this function will return NULL_TREE. The declarations are connected through their TREE_CHAIN fields.

> Although most entries on this list will be declarations, TREE_LIST nodes may also appear. In this case, the TREE_VALUE will be an OVERLOAD. The value of the TREE_PURPOSE is unspecified; back ends should ignore this value. As with the other kinds of declarations returned by cp_namespace_decls, the TREE_CHAIN will point to the next declaration in this list.

> For more information on the kinds of declarations that can occur on this list, See Section 10.4 [Declarations], page 140. Some declarations will not appear on this list. In particular, no FIELD_DECL, LABEL_DECL, or PARM_DECL nodes will appear here.

> This function cannot be used with namespaces that have DECL_NAMESPACE_ALIAS set.

10.10.3 Classes

Besides namespaces, the other high-level scoping construct in C++ is the class. (Throughout this manual the term *class* is used to mean the types referred to in the ANSI/ISO C++ Standard as classes; these include types defined with the class, struct, and union keywords.)

A class type is represented by either a RECORD_TYPE or a UNION_TYPE. A class declared with the union tag is represented by a UNION_TYPE, while classes declared with either the struct or the class tag are represented by RECORD_TYPEs. You can use the CLASSTYPE_DECLARED_CLASS macro to discern whether or not a particular type is a class as opposed to a struct. This macro will be true only for classes declared with the class tag.

Almost all non-function members are available on the TYPE_FIELDS list. Given one member, the next can be found by following the TREE_CHAIN. You should not depend in any way on the order in which fields appear on this list. All nodes on this list will be 'DECL' nodes. A FIELD_DECL is used to represent a non-static data member, a VAR_DECL is used to represent a static data member, and a TYPE_DECL is used to represent a type. Note that the CONST_DECL for an enumeration constant will appear on this list, if the enumeration type was declared in the class. (Of course, the `TYPE_DECL` for the enumeration type will appear here as well.) There are no entries for base classes on this list. In particular, there is no `FIELD_DECL` for the "base-class portion" of an object.

The `TYPE_VFIELD` is a compiler-generated field used to point to virtual function tables. It may or may not appear on the `TYPE_FIELDS` list. However, back ends should handle the `TYPE_VFIELD` just like all the entries on the `TYPE_FIELDS` list.

The function members are available on the `TYPE_METHODS` list. Again, subsequent members are found by following the `TREE_CHAIN` field. If a function is overloaded, each of the overloaded functions appears; no `OVERLOAD` nodes appear on the `TYPE_METHODS` list. Implicitly declared functions (including default constructors, copy constructors, assignment operators, and destructors) will appear on this list as well.

Every class has an associated *binfo*, which can be obtained with `TYPE_BINFO`. Binfos are used to represent base-classes. The binfo given by `TYPE_BINFO` is the degenerate case, whereby every class is considered to be its own base-class. The base binfos for a particular binfo are held in a vector, whose length is obtained with `BINFO_N_BASE_BINFOS`. The base binfos themselves are obtained with `BINFO_BASE_BINFO` and `BINFO_BASE_ITERATE`. To add a new binfo, use `BINFO_BASE_APPEND`. The vector of base binfos can be obtained with `BINFO_BASE_BINFOS`, but normally you do not need to use that. The class type associated with a binfo is given by `BINFO_TYPE`. It is not always the case that `BINFO_TYPE (TYPE_BINFO (x))`, because of typedefs and qualified types. Neither is it the case that `TYPE_BINFO (BINFO_TYPE (y))` is the same binfo as `y`. The reason is that if `y` is a binfo representing a base-class B of a derived class D, then `BINFO_TYPE (y)` will be B, and `TYPE_BINFO (BINFO_TYPE (y))` will be B as its own base-class, rather than as a base-class of D.

The access to a base type can be found with `BINFO_BASE_ACCESS`. This will produce `access_public_node`, `access_private_node` or `access_protected_node`. If bases are always public, `BINFO_BASE_ACCESSES` may be `NULL`.

`BINFO_VIRTUAL_P` is used to specify whether the binfo is inherited virtually or not. The other flags, `BINFO_FLAG_0` to `BINFO_FLAG_6`, can be used for language specific use.

The following macros can be used on a tree node representing a class-type.

`LOCAL_CLASS_P`
> This predicate holds if the class is local class *i.e.* declared inside a function body.

`TYPE_POLYMORPHIC_P`
> This predicate holds if the class has at least one virtual function (declared or inherited).

`TYPE_HAS_DEFAULT_CONSTRUCTOR`
> This predicate holds whenever its argument represents a class-type with default constructor.

`CLASSTYPE_HAS_MUTABLE`
`TYPE_HAS_MUTABLE_P`
> These predicates hold for a class-type having a mutable data member.

`CLASSTYPE_NON_POD_P`
> This predicate holds only for class-types that are not PODs.

TYPE_HAS_NEW_OPERATOR
> This predicate holds for a class-type that defines `operator new`.

TYPE_HAS_ARRAY_NEW_OPERATOR
> This predicate holds for a class-type for which `operator new[]` is defined.

TYPE_OVERLOADS_CALL_EXPR
> This predicate holds for class-type for which the function call `operator()` is overloaded.

TYPE_OVERLOADS_ARRAY_REF
> This predicate holds for a class-type that overloads `operator[]`

TYPE_OVERLOADS_ARROW
> This predicate holds for a class-type for which `operator->` is overloaded.

10.10.4 Functions for C++

A function is represented by a `FUNCTION_DECL` node. A set of overloaded functions is sometimes represented by an `OVERLOAD` node.

An `OVERLOAD` node is not a declaration, so none of the 'DECL_' macros should be used on an `OVERLOAD`. An `OVERLOAD` node is similar to a `TREE_LIST`. Use `OVL_CURRENT` to get the function associated with an `OVERLOAD` node; use `OVL_NEXT` to get the next `OVERLOAD` node in the list of overloaded functions. The macros `OVL_CURRENT` and `OVL_NEXT` are actually polymorphic; you can use them to work with `FUNCTION_DECL` nodes as well as with overloads. In the case of a `FUNCTION_DECL`, `OVL_CURRENT` will always return the function itself, and `OVL_NEXT` will always be `NULL_TREE`.

To determine the scope of a function, you can use the `DECL_CONTEXT` macro. This macro will return the class (either a `RECORD_TYPE` or a `UNION_TYPE`) or namespace (a `NAMESPACE_DECL`) of which the function is a member. For a virtual function, this macro returns the class in which the function was actually defined, not the base class in which the virtual declaration occurred.

If a friend function is defined in a class scope, the `DECL_FRIEND_CONTEXT` macro can be used to determine the class in which it was defined. For example, in

```
class C { friend void f() {} };
```

the `DECL_CONTEXT` for `f` will be the `global_namespace`, but the `DECL_FRIEND_CONTEXT` will be the `RECORD_TYPE` for C.

The following macros and functions can be used on a `FUNCTION_DECL`:

DECL_MAIN_P
> This predicate holds for a function that is the program entry point `::code`.

DECL_LOCAL_FUNCTION_P
> This predicate holds if the function was declared at block scope, even though it has a global scope.

DECL_ANTICIPATED
> This predicate holds if the function is a built-in function but its prototype is not yet explicitly declared.

DECL_EXTERN_C_FUNCTION_P
> This predicate holds if the function is declared as an 'extern "C"' function.

DECL_LINKONCE_P

> This macro holds if multiple copies of this function may be emitted in various translation units. It is the responsibility of the linker to merge the various copies. Template instantiations are the most common example of functions for which DECL_LINKONCE_P holds; G++ instantiates needed templates in all translation units which require them, and then relies on the linker to remove duplicate instantiations.
>
> FIXME: This macro is not yet implemented.

DECL_FUNCTION_MEMBER_P

> This macro holds if the function is a member of a class, rather than a member of a namespace.

DECL_STATIC_FUNCTION_P

> This predicate holds if the function a static member function.

DECL_NONSTATIC_MEMBER_FUNCTION_P

> This macro holds for a non-static member function.

DECL_CONST_MEMFUNC_P

> This predicate holds for a const-member function.

DECL_VOLATILE_MEMFUNC_P

> This predicate holds for a volatile-member function.

DECL_CONSTRUCTOR_P

> This macro holds if the function is a constructor.

DECL_NONCONVERTING_P

> This predicate holds if the constructor is a non-converting constructor.

DECL_COMPLETE_CONSTRUCTOR_P

> This predicate holds for a function which is a constructor for an object of a complete type.

DECL_BASE_CONSTRUCTOR_P

> This predicate holds for a function which is a constructor for a base class sub-object.

DECL_COPY_CONSTRUCTOR_P

> This predicate holds for a function which is a copy-constructor.

DECL_DESTRUCTOR_P

> This macro holds if the function is a destructor.

DECL_COMPLETE_DESTRUCTOR_P

> This predicate holds if the function is the destructor for an object a complete type.

DECL_OVERLOADED_OPERATOR_P

> This macro holds if the function is an overloaded operator.

DECL_CONV_FN_P

> This macro holds if the function is a type-conversion operator.

DECL_GLOBAL_CTOR_P

> This predicate holds if the function is a file-scope initialization function.

DECL_GLOBAL_DTOR_P

> This predicate holds if the function is a file-scope finalization function.

DECL_THUNK_P

> This predicate holds if the function is a thunk.
>
> These functions represent stub code that adjusts the **this** pointer and then jumps to another function. When the jumped-to function returns, control is transferred directly to the caller, without returning to the thunk. The first parameter to the thunk is always the **this** pointer; the thunk should add THUNK_DELTA to this value. (The THUNK_DELTA is an **int**, not an INTEGER_CST.)
>
> Then, if THUNK_VCALL_OFFSET (an INTEGER_CST) is nonzero the adjusted **this** pointer must be adjusted again. The complete calculation is given by the following pseudo-code:
>
> ```
> this += THUNK_DELTA
> if (THUNK_VCALL_OFFSET)
>   this += (*((ptrdiff_t **) this))[THUNK_VCALL_OFFSET]
> ```
>
> Finally, the thunk should jump to the location given by DECL_INITIAL; this will always be an expression for the address of a function.

DECL_NON_THUNK_FUNCTION_P

> This predicate holds if the function is *not* a thunk function.

GLOBAL_INIT_PRIORITY

> If either DECL_GLOBAL_CTOR_P or DECL_GLOBAL_DTOR_P holds, then this gives the initialization priority for the function. The linker will arrange that all functions for which DECL_GLOBAL_CTOR_P holds are run in increasing order of priority before **main** is called. When the program exits, all functions for which DECL_GLOBAL_DTOR_P holds are run in the reverse order.

TYPE_RAISES_EXCEPTIONS

> This macro returns the list of exceptions that a (member-)function can raise. The returned list, if non NULL, is comprised of nodes whose TREE_VALUE represents a type.

TYPE_NOTHROW_P

> This predicate holds when the exception-specification of its arguments is of the form '()'.

DECL_ARRAY_DELETE_OPERATOR_P

> This predicate holds if the function an overloaded **operator delete[]**.

10.10.5 Statements for C++

A function that has a definition in the current translation unit will have a non-NULL DECL_INITIAL. However, back ends should not make use of the particular value given by DECL_INITIAL.

The DECL_SAVED_TREE macro will give the complete body of the function.

10.10.5.1 Statements

There are tree nodes corresponding to all of the source-level statement constructs, used within the C and C++ frontends. These are enumerated here, together with a list of the various macros that can be used to obtain information about them. There are a few macros that can be used with all statements:

STMT_IS_FULL_EXPR_P

> In C++, statements normally constitute "full expressions"; temporaries created during a statement are destroyed when the statement is complete. However, G++ sometimes represents expressions by statements; these statements will not have STMT_IS_FULL_EXPR_P set. Temporaries created during such statements should be destroyed when the innermost enclosing statement with STMT_IS_FULL_EXPR_P set is exited.

Here is the list of the various statement nodes, and the macros used to access them. This documentation describes the use of these nodes in non-template functions (including instantiations of template functions). In template functions, the same nodes are used, but sometimes in slightly different ways.

Many of the statements have substatements. For example, a `while` loop will have a body, which is itself a statement. If the substatement is NULL_TREE, it is considered equivalent to a statement consisting of a single ; , i.e., an expression statement in which the expression has been omitted. A substatement may in fact be a list of statements, connected via their TREE_CHAINs. So, you should always process the statement tree by looping over substatements, like this:

```
void process_stmt (stmt)
     tree stmt;
{
  while (stmt)
    {
      switch (TREE_CODE (stmt))
        {
        case IF_STMT:
          process_stmt (THEN_CLAUSE (stmt));
          /* More processing here.  */
          break;

          ...
        }

      stmt = TREE_CHAIN (stmt);
    }
}
```

In other words, while the `then` clause of an `if` statement in C++ can be only one statement (although that one statement may be a compound statement), the intermediate representation will sometimes use several statements chained together.

BREAK_STMT

> Used to represent a `break` statement. There are no additional fields.

CILK_SPAWN_STMT

>Used to represent a spawning function in the Cilk Plus language extension. This tree has one field that holds the name of the spawning function. _Cilk_spawn can be written in C in the following way:
>
>>_Cilk_spawn <function_name> (<parameters>);
>
>Detailed description for usage and functionality of _Cilk_spawn can be found at http://www.cilkplus.org

CILK_SYNC_STMT

>This statement is part of the Cilk Plus language extension. It indicates that the current function cannot continue in parallel with its spawned children. There are no additional fields. _Cilk_sync can be written in C in the following way:
>
>>_Cilk_sync;

CLEANUP_STMT

>Used to represent an action that should take place upon exit from the enclosing scope. Typically, these actions are calls to destructors for local objects, but back ends cannot rely on this fact. If these nodes are in fact representing such destructors, CLEANUP_DECL will be the VAR_DECL destroyed. Otherwise, CLEANUP_DECL will be NULL_TREE. In any case, the CLEANUP_EXPR is the expression to execute. The cleanups executed on exit from a scope should be run in the reverse order of the order in which the associated CLEANUP_STMTs were encountered.

CONTINUE_STMT

>Used to represent a continue statement. There are no additional fields.

CTOR_STMT

>Used to mark the beginning (if CTOR_BEGIN_P holds) or end (if CTOR_END_P holds of the main body of a constructor. See also SUBOBJECT for more information on how to use these nodes.

DO_STMT

>Used to represent a do loop. The body of the loop is given by DO_BODY while the termination condition for the loop is given by DO_COND. The condition for a do-statement is always an expression.

EMPTY_CLASS_EXPR

>Used to represent a temporary object of a class with no data whose address is never taken. (All such objects are interchangeable.) The TREE_TYPE represents the type of the object.

EXPR_STMT

>Used to represent an expression statement. Use EXPR_STMT_EXPR to obtain the expression.

FOR_STMT

>Used to represent a for statement. The FOR_INIT_STMT is the initialization statement for the loop. The FOR_COND is the termination condition. The FOR_EXPR is the expression executed right before the FOR_COND on each loop iteration; often, this expression increments a counter. The body of the loop is given by

FOR_BODY. Note that `FOR_INIT_STMT` and `FOR_BODY` return statements, while `FOR_COND` and `FOR_EXPR` return expressions.

HANDLER

Used to represent a C++ `catch` block. The `HANDLER_TYPE` is the type of exception that will be caught by this handler; it is equal (by pointer equality) to `NULL` if this handler is for all types. `HANDLER_PARMS` is the `DECL_STMT` for the catch parameter, and `HANDLER_BODY` is the code for the block itself.

IF_STMT

Used to represent an `if` statement. The `IF_COND` is the expression.

If the condition is a `TREE_LIST`, then the `TREE_PURPOSE` is a statement (usually a `DECL_STMT`). Each time the condition is evaluated, the statement should be executed. Then, the `TREE_VALUE` should be used as the conditional expression itself. This representation is used to handle C++ code like this:

C++ distinguishes between this and `COND_EXPR` for handling templates.

```
if (int i = 7) ...
```

where there is a new local variable (or variables) declared within the condition.

The `THEN_CLAUSE` represents the statement given by the `then` condition, while the `ELSE_CLAUSE` represents the statement given by the `else` condition.

SUBOBJECT

In a constructor, these nodes are used to mark the point at which a subobject of `this` is fully constructed. If, after this point, an exception is thrown before a `CTOR_STMT` with `CTOR_END_P` set is encountered, the `SUBOBJECT_CLEANUP` must be executed. The cleanups must be executed in the reverse order in which they appear.

SWITCH_STMT

Used to represent a `switch` statement. The `SWITCH_STMT_COND` is the expression on which the switch is occurring. See the documentation for an `IF_STMT` for more information on the representation used for the condition. The `SWITCH_STMT_BODY` is the body of the switch statement. The `SWITCH_STMT_TYPE` is the original type of switch expression as given in the source, before any compiler conversions.

TRY_BLOCK

Used to represent a `try` block. The body of the try block is given by `TRY_STMTS`. Each of the catch blocks is a `HANDLER` node. The first handler is given by `TRY_HANDLERS`. Subsequent handlers are obtained by following the `TREE_CHAIN` link from one handler to the next. The body of the handler is given by `HANDLER_BODY`.

If `CLEANUP_P` holds of the `TRY_BLOCK`, then the `TRY_HANDLERS` will not be a `HANDLER` node. Instead, it will be an expression that should be executed if an exception is thrown in the try block. It must rethrow the exception after executing that code. And, if an exception is thrown while the expression is executing, `terminate` must be called.

USING_STMT

> Used to represent a **using** directive. The namespace is given by USING_STMT_NAMESPACE, which will be a NAMESPACE_DECL. This node is needed inside template functions, to implement using directives during instantiation.

WHILE_STMT

> Used to represent a **while** loop. The WHILE_COND is the termination condition for the loop. See the documentation for an IF_STMT for more information on the representation used for the condition.
>
> The WHILE_BODY is the body of the loop.

10.10.6 C++ Expressions

This section describes expressions specific to the C and C++ front ends.

TYPEID_EXPR

> Used to represent a **typeid** expression.

NEW_EXPR
VEC_NEW_EXPR

> Used to represent a call to **new** and **new[]** respectively.

DELETE_EXPR
VEC_DELETE_EXPR

> Used to represent a call to **delete** and **delete[]** respectively.

MEMBER_REF

> Represents a reference to a member of a class.

THROW_EXPR

> Represents an instance of **throw** in the program. Operand 0, which is the expression to throw, may be NULL_TREE.

AGGR_INIT_EXPR

> An AGGR_INIT_EXPR represents the initialization as the return value of a function call, or as the result of a constructor. An AGGR_INIT_EXPR will only appear as a full-expression, or as the second operand of a TARGET_EXPR. AGGR_INIT_EXPRs have a representation similar to that of CALL_EXPRs. You can use the AGGR_INIT_EXPR_FN and AGGR_INIT_EXPR_ARG macros to access the function to call and the arguments to pass.
>
> If AGGR_INIT_VIA_CTOR_P holds of the AGGR_INIT_EXPR, then the initialization is via a constructor call. The address of the AGGR_INIT_EXPR_SLOT operand, which is always a VAR_DECL, is taken, and this value replaces the first argument in the argument list.
>
> In either case, the expression is void.

10.11 Java Trees

11 GIMPLE

GIMPLE is a three-address representation derived from GENERIC by breaking down GENERIC expressions into tuples of no more than 3 operands (with some exceptions like function calls). GIMPLE was heavily influenced by the SIMPLE IL used by the McCAT compiler project at McGill University, though we have made some different choices. For one thing, SIMPLE doesn't support `goto`.

Temporaries are introduced to hold intermediate values needed to compute complex expressions. Additionally, all the control structures used in GENERIC are lowered into conditional jumps, lexical scopes are removed and exception regions are converted into an on the side exception region tree.

The compiler pass which converts GENERIC into GIMPLE is referred to as the 'gimplifier'. The gimplifier works recursively, generating GIMPLE tuples out of the original GENERIC expressions.

One of the early implementation strategies used for the GIMPLE representation was to use the same internal data structures used by front ends to represent parse trees. This simplified implementation because we could leverage existing functionality and interfaces. However, GIMPLE is a much more restrictive representation than abstract syntax trees (AST), therefore it does not require the full structural complexity provided by the main tree data structure.

The GENERIC representation of a function is stored in the `DECL_SAVED_TREE` field of the associated `FUNCTION_DECL` tree node. It is converted to GIMPLE by a call to `gimplify_function_tree`.

If a front end wants to include language-specific tree codes in the tree representation which it provides to the back end, it must provide a definition of `LANG_HOOKS_GIMPLIFY_EXPR` which knows how to convert the front end trees to GIMPLE. Usually such a hook will involve much of the same code for expanding front end trees to RTL. This function can return fully lowered GIMPLE, or it can return GENERIC trees and let the main gimplifier lower them the rest of the way; this is often simpler. GIMPLE that is not fully lowered is known as "High GIMPLE" and consists of the IL before the pass `pass_lower_cf`. High GIMPLE contains some container statements like lexical scopes (represented by `GIMPLE_BIND`) and nested expressions (e.g., `GIMPLE_TRY`), while "Low GIMPLE" exposes all of the implicit jumps for control and exception expressions directly in the IL and EH region trees.

The C and C++ front ends currently convert directly from front end trees to GIMPLE, and hand that off to the back end rather than first converting to GENERIC. Their gimplifier hooks know about all the `_STMT` nodes and how to convert them to GENERIC forms. There was some work done on a genericization pass which would run first, but the existence of `STMT_EXPR` meant that in order to convert all of the C statements into GENERIC equivalents would involve walking the entire tree anyway, so it was simpler to lower all the way. This might change in the future if someone writes an optimization pass which would work better with higher-level trees, but currently the optimizers all expect GIMPLE.

You can request to dump a C-like representation of the GIMPLE form with the flag '`-fdump-tree-gimple`'.

11.1 Tuple representation

GIMPLE instructions are tuples of variable size divided in two groups: a header describing the instruction and its locations, and a variable length body with all the operands. Tuples are organized into a hierarchy with 3 main classes of tuples.

11.1.1 gimple (gsbase)

This is the root of the hierarchy, it holds basic information needed by most GIMPLE statements. There are some fields that may not be relevant to every GIMPLE statement, but those were moved into the base structure to take advantage of holes left by other fields (thus making the structure more compact). The structure takes 4 words (32 bytes) on 64 bit hosts:

Field	Size (bits)
code	8
subcode	16
no_warning	1
visited	1
nontemporal_move	1
plf	2
modified	1
has_volatile_ops	1
references_memory_p	1
uid	32
location	32
num_ops	32
bb	64
block	63
Total size	32 bytes

- `code` Main identifier for a GIMPLE instruction.

- `subcode` Used to distinguish different variants of the same basic instruction or provide flags applicable to a given code. The `subcode` flags field has different uses depending on the code of the instruction, but mostly it distinguishes instructions of the same family. The most prominent use of this field is in assignments, where subcode indicates the operation done on the RHS of the assignment. For example, a = b + c is encoded as `GIMPLE_ASSIGN <PLUS_EXPR, a, b, c>`.

- `no_warning` Bitflag to indicate whether a warning has already been issued on this statement.

- `visited` General purpose "visited" marker. Set and cleared by each pass when needed.

- `nontemporal_move` Bitflag used in assignments that represent non-temporal moves. Although this bitflag is only used in assignments, it was moved into the base to take advantage of the bit holes left by the previous fields.

- `plf` Pass Local Flags. This 2-bit mask can be used as general purpose markers by any pass. Passes are responsible for clearing and setting these two flags accordingly.

- `modified` Bitflag to indicate whether the statement has been modified. Used mainly by the operand scanner to determine when to re-scan a statement for operands.

- `has_volatile_ops` Bitflag to indicate whether this statement contains operands that have been marked volatile.

- `references_memory_p` Bitflag to indicate whether this statement contains memory references (i.e., its operands are either global variables, or pointer dereferences or anything that must reside in memory).

- `uid` This is an unsigned integer used by passes that want to assign IDs to every statement. These IDs must be assigned and used by each pass.

- `location` This is a `location_t` identifier to specify source code location for this statement. It is inherited from the front end.

- `num_ops` Number of operands that this statement has. This specifies the size of the operand vector embedded in the tuple. Only used in some tuples, but it is declared in the base tuple to take advantage of the 32-bit hole left by the previous fields.

- `bb` Basic block holding the instruction.

- `block` Lexical block holding this statement. Also used for debug information generation.

11.1.2 gimple_statement_with_ops

This tuple is actually split in two: `gimple_statement_with_ops_base` and `gimple_statement_with_ops`. This is needed to accommodate the way the operand vector is allocated. The operand vector is defined to be an array of 1 element. So, to allocate a dynamic number of operands, the memory allocator (`gimple_alloc`) simply allocates enough memory to hold the structure itself plus N − 1 operands which run "off the end" of the structure. For example, to allocate space for a tuple with 3 operands, `gimple_alloc` reserves `sizeof (struct gimple_statement_with_ops) + 2 * sizeof (tree)` bytes.

On the other hand, several fields in this tuple need to be shared with the `gimple_statement_with_memory_ops` tuple. So, these common fields are placed in `gimple_statement_with_ops_base` which is then inherited from the other two tuples.

gsbase	256
def_ops	64
use_ops	64
op	num_ops * 64
Total size	48 + 8 * num_ops bytes

- `gsbase` Inherited from `struct gimple`.

- `def_ops` Array of pointers into the operand array indicating all the slots that contain a variable written-to by the statement. This array is also used for immediate use chaining. Note that it would be possible to not rely on this array, but the changes required to implement this are pretty invasive.

- `use_ops` Similar to `def_ops` but for variables read by the statement.

- `op` Array of trees with `num_ops` slots.

11.1.3 gimple_statement_with_memory_ops

This tuple is essentially identical to `gimple_statement_with_ops`, except that it contains 4 additional fields to hold vectors related memory stores and loads. Similar to the previous case, the structure is split in two to accommodate for the operand vector (`gimple_statement_with_memory_ops_base` and `gimple_statement_with_memory_ops`).

Field	Size (bits)
`gsbase`	256
`def_ops`	64
`use_ops`	64
`vdef_ops`	64
`vuse_ops`	64
`stores`	64
`loads`	64
`op`	`num_ops` * 64
Total size	80 + 8 * `num_ops` bytes

- `vdef_ops` Similar to `def_ops` but for `VDEF` operators. There is one entry per memory symbol written by this statement. This is used to maintain the memory SSA use-def and def-def chains.

- `vuse_ops` Similar to `use_ops` but for `VUSE` operators. There is one entry per memory symbol loaded by this statement. This is used to maintain the memory SSA use-def chains.

- `stores` Bitset with all the UIDs for the symbols written-to by the statement. This is different than `vdef_ops` in that all the affected symbols are mentioned in this set. If memory partitioning is enabled, the `vdef_ops` vector will refer to memory partitions. Furthermore, no SSA information is stored in this set.

- `loads` Similar to `stores`, but for memory loads. (Note that there is some amount of redundancy here, it should be possible to reduce memory utilization further by removing these sets).

All the other tuples are defined in terms of these three basic ones. Each tuple will add some fields.

11.2 Class hierarchy of GIMPLE statements

The following diagram shows the C++ inheritance hierarchy of statement kinds, along with their relationships to **GSS_** values (layouts) and **GIMPLE_** values (codes):

```
gimple
    |     layout: GSS_BASE
    |     used for 4 codes: GIMPLE_ERROR_MARK
    |                       GIMPLE_NOP
    |                       GIMPLE_OMP_SECTIONS_SWITCH
    |                       GIMPLE_PREDICT
    |
    + gimple_statement_with_ops_base
    |   |     (no GSS layout)
    |   |
    |   + gimple_statement_with_ops
    |   |   |     layout: GSS_WITH_OPS
    |   |   |
    |   |   + gcond
    |   |   |     code: GIMPLE_COND
    |   |   |
    |   |   + gdebug
```

```
|   |   |       code: GIMPLE_DEBUG
|   |   |
|   |   + ggoto
|   |   |       code: GIMPLE_GOTO
|   |   |
|   |   + glabel
|   |   |       code: GIMPLE_LABEL
|   |   |
|   |   + gswitch
|   |           code: GIMPLE_SWITCH
|   |
|   + gimple_statement_with_memory_ops_base
|   |       layout: GSS_WITH_MEM_OPS_BASE
|   |
|   + gimple_statement_with_memory_ops
|   |   |       layout: GSS_WITH_MEM_OPS
|   |   |
|   |   + gassign
|   |   |     code GIMPLE_ASSIGN
|   |   |
|   |   + greturn
|   |         code GIMPLE_RETURN
|   |
|   + gcall
|   |           layout: GSS_CALL, code: GIMPLE_CALL
|   |
|   + gasm
|   |           layout: GSS_ASM, code: GIMPLE_ASM
|   |
|   + gtransaction
|           layout: GSS_TRANSACTION, code: GIMPLE_TRANSACTION
|
+ gimple_statement_omp
|   |       layout: GSS_OMP.  Used for code GIMPLE_OMP_SECTION
|   |
|   + gomp_critical
|   |       layout: GSS_OMP_CRITICAL, code: GIMPLE_OMP_CRITICAL
|   |
|   + gomp_for
|   |       layout: GSS_OMP_FOR, code: GIMPLE_OMP_FOR
|   |
|   + gomp_parallel_layout
|   |   |       layout: GSS_OMP_PARALLEL_LAYOUT
|   |   |
|   |   + gimple_statement_omp_taskreg
|   |   |   |
|   |   |   + gomp_parallel
|   |   |   |       code: GIMPLE_OMP_PARALLEL
|   |   |   |
|   |   |   + gomp_task
|   |   |           code: GIMPLE_OMP_TASK
|   |   |
|   |   + gimple_statement_omp_target
|   |           code: GIMPLE_OMP_TARGET
|   |
|   + gomp_sections
|   |       layout: GSS_OMP_SECTIONS, code: GIMPLE_OMP_SECTIONS
|   |
```

```
|    + gimple_statement_omp_single_layout
|    |      layout: GSS_OMP_SINGLE_LAYOUT
|    |
|    + gomp_single
|    |        code: GIMPLE_OMP_SINGLE
|    |
|    + gomp_teams
|             code: GIMPLE_OMP_TEAMS
|
+ gbind
|        layout: GSS_BIND, code: GIMPLE_BIND
|
+ gcatch
|        layout: GSS_CATCH, code: GIMPLE_CATCH
|
+ geh_filter
|        layout: GSS_EH_FILTER, code: GIMPLE_EH_FILTER
|
+ geh_else
|        layout: GSS_EH_ELSE, code: GIMPLE_EH_ELSE
|
+ geh_mnt
|        layout: GSS_EH_MNT, code: GIMPLE_EH_MUST_NOT_THROW
|
+ gphi
|        layout: GSS_PHI, code: GIMPLE_PHI
|
+ gimple_statement_eh_ctrl
|    |    layout: GSS_EH_CTRL
|    |
|    + gresx
|    |        code: GIMPLE_RESX
|    |
|    + geh_dispatch
|             code: GIMPLE_EH_DISPATCH
|
+ gtry
|        layout: GSS_TRY, code: GIMPLE_TRY
|
+ gimple_statement_wce
|        layout: GSS_WCE, code: GIMPLE_WITH_CLEANUP_EXPR
|
+ gomp_continue
|        layout: GSS_OMP_CONTINUE, code: GIMPLE_OMP_CONTINUE
|
+ gomp_atomic_load
|        layout: GSS_OMP_ATOMIC_LOAD, code: GIMPLE_OMP_ATOMIC_LOAD
|
+ gimple_statement_omp_atomic_store_layout
|    |    layout: GSS_OMP_ATOMIC_STORE_LAYOUT,
|    |    code: GIMPLE_OMP_ATOMIC_STORE
|    |
|    + gomp_atomic_store
|    |        code: GIMPLE_OMP_ATOMIC_STORE
|    |
|    + gomp_return
|             code: GIMPLE_OMP_RETURN
```

11.3 GIMPLE instruction set

The following table briefly describes the GIMPLE instruction set.

Instruction	High GIMPLE	Low GIMPLE
GIMPLE_ASM	x	x
GIMPLE_ASSIGN	x	x
GIMPLE_BIND	x	
GIMPLE_CALL	x	x
GIMPLE_CATCH	x	
GIMPLE_COND	x	x
GIMPLE_DEBUG	x	x
GIMPLE_EH_FILTER	x	
GIMPLE_GOTO	x	x
GIMPLE_LABEL	x	x
GIMPLE_NOP	x	x
GIMPLE_OMP_ATOMIC_LOAD	x	x
GIMPLE_OMP_ATOMIC_STORE	x	x
GIMPLE_OMP_CONTINUE	x	x
GIMPLE_OMP_CRITICAL	x	x
GIMPLE_OMP_FOR	x	x
GIMPLE_OMP_MASTER	x	x
GIMPLE_OMP_ORDERED	x	x
GIMPLE_OMP_PARALLEL	x	x
GIMPLE_OMP_RETURN	x	x
GIMPLE_OMP_SECTION	x	x
GIMPLE_OMP_SECTIONS	x	x
GIMPLE_OMP_SECTIONS_SWITCH	x	x
GIMPLE_OMP_SINGLE	x	x
GIMPLE_PHI		x
GIMPLE_RESX		x
GIMPLE_RETURN	x	x
GIMPLE_SWITCH	x	x
GIMPLE_TRY	x	

11.4 Exception Handling

Other exception handling constructs are represented using GIMPLE_TRY_CATCH. GIMPLE_TRY_CATCH has two operands. The first operand is a sequence of statements to execute. If executing these statements does not throw an exception, then the second operand is ignored. Otherwise, if an exception is thrown, then the second operand of the GIMPLE_TRY_CATCH is checked. The second operand may have the following forms:

1. A sequence of statements to execute. When an exception occurs, these statements are executed, and then the exception is rethrown.

2. A sequence of GIMPLE_CATCH statements. Each GIMPLE_CATCH has a list of applicable exception types and handler code. If the thrown exception matches one of the caught types, the associated handler code is executed. If the handler code falls off the bottom, execution continues after the original GIMPLE_TRY_CATCH.

3. A `GIMPLE_EH_FILTER` statement. This has a list of permitted exception types, and code to handle a match failure. If the thrown exception does not match one of the allowed types, the associated match failure code is executed. If the thrown exception does match, it continues unwinding the stack looking for the next handler.

Currently throwing an exception is not directly represented in GIMPLE, since it is implemented by calling a function. At some point in the future we will want to add some way to express that the call will throw an exception of a known type.

Just before running the optimizers, the compiler lowers the high-level EH constructs above into a set of 'goto's, magic labels, and EH regions. Continuing to unwind at the end of a cleanup is represented with a `GIMPLE_RESX`.

11.5 Temporaries

When gimplification encounters a subexpression that is too complex, it creates a new temporary variable to hold the value of the subexpression, and adds a new statement to initialize it before the current statement. These special temporaries are known as 'expression temporaries', and are allocated using `get_formal_tmp_var`. The compiler tries to always evaluate identical expressions into the same temporary, to simplify elimination of redundant calculations.

We can only use expression temporaries when we know that it will not be reevaluated before its value is used, and that it will not be otherwise modified[1]. Other temporaries can be allocated using `get_initialized_tmp_var` or `create_tmp_var`.

Currently, an expression like `a = b + 5` is not reduced any further. We tried converting it to something like

```
T1 = b + 5;
a = T1;
```

but this bloated the representation for minimal benefit. However, a variable which must live in memory cannot appear in an expression; its value is explicitly loaded into a temporary first. Similarly, storing the value of an expression to a memory variable goes through a temporary.

11.6 Operands

In general, expressions in GIMPLE consist of an operation and the appropriate number of simple operands; these operands must either be a GIMPLE rvalue (`is_gimple_val`), i.e. a constant or a register variable. More complex operands are factored out into temporaries, so that

```
a = b + c + d
```

becomes

```
T1 = b + c;
a = T1 + d;
```

The same rule holds for arguments to a `GIMPLE_CALL`.

The target of an assignment is usually a variable, but can also be a `MEM_REF` or a compound lvalue as described below.

---

[1] These restrictions are derived from those in Morgan 4.8.

11.6.1 Compound Expressions

The left-hand side of a C comma expression is simply moved into a separate statement.

11.6.2 Compound Lvalues

Currently compound lvalues involving array and structure field references are not broken down; an expression like `a.b[2] = 42` is not reduced any further (though complex array subscripts are). This restriction is a workaround for limitations in later optimizers; if we were to convert this to

```
T1 = &a.b;
T1[2] = 42;
```

alias analysis would not remember that the reference to `T1[2]` came by way of `a.b`, so it would think that the assignment could alias another member of `a`; this broke `struct-alias-1.c`. Future optimizer improvements may make this limitation unnecessary.

11.6.3 Conditional Expressions

A C `?:` expression is converted into an `if` statement with each branch assigning to the same temporary. So,

```
a = b ? c : d;
```

becomes

```
if (b == 1)
  T1 = c;
else
  T1 = d;
a = T1;
```

The GIMPLE level if-conversion pass re-introduces `?:` expression, if appropriate. It is used to vectorize loops with conditions using vector conditional operations.

Note that in GIMPLE, `if` statements are represented using `GIMPLE_COND`, as described below.

11.6.4 Logical Operators

Except when they appear in the condition operand of a `GIMPLE_COND`, logical 'and' and 'or' operators are simplified as follows: `a = b && c` becomes

```
T1 = (bool)b;
if (T1 == true)
  T1 = (bool)c;
a = T1;
```

Note that `T1` in this example cannot be an expression temporary, because it has two different assignments.

11.6.5 Manipulating operands

All gimple operands are of type `tree`. But only certain types of trees are allowed to be used as operand tuples. Basic validation is controlled by the function `get_gimple_rhs_class`, which given a tree code, returns an `enum` with the following values of type `enum gimple_rhs_class`

- `GIMPLE_INVALID_RHS` The tree cannot be used as a GIMPLE operand.
- `GIMPLE_TERNARY_RHS` The tree is a valid GIMPLE ternary operation.

- `GIMPLE_BINARY_RHS` The tree is a valid GIMPLE binary operation.
- `GIMPLE_UNARY_RHS` The tree is a valid GIMPLE unary operation.
- `GIMPLE_SINGLE_RHS` The tree is a single object, that cannot be split into simpler operands (for instance, `SSA_NAME`, `VAR_DECL`, `COMPONENT_REF`, etc).

  This operand class also acts as an escape hatch for tree nodes that may be flattened out into the operand vector, but would need more than two slots on the RHS. For instance, a `COND_EXPR` expression of the form `(a op b) ? x : y` could be flattened out on the operand vector using 4 slots, but it would also require additional processing to distinguish `c = a op b` from `c = a op b ? x : y`. Something similar occurs with `ASSERT_EXPR`. In time, these special case tree expressions should be flattened into the operand vector.

For tree nodes in the categories `GIMPLE_TERNARY_RHS`, `GIMPLE_BINARY_RHS` and `GIMPLE_UNARY_RHS`, they cannot be stored inside tuples directly. They first need to be flattened and separated into individual components. For instance, given the GENERIC expression

```
a = b + c
```

its tree representation is:

```
MODIFY_EXPR <VAR_DECL  <a>, PLUS_EXPR <VAR_DECL <b>, VAR_DECL <c>>>
```

In this case, the GIMPLE form for this statement is logically identical to its GENERIC form but in GIMPLE, the `PLUS_EXPR` on the RHS of the assignment is not represented as a tree, instead the two operands are taken out of the `PLUS_EXPR` sub-tree and flattened into the GIMPLE tuple as follows:

```
GIMPLE_ASSIGN <PLUS_EXPR, VAR_DECL <a>, VAR_DECL <b>, VAR_DECL <c>>
```

11.6.6 Operand vector allocation

The operand vector is stored at the bottom of the three tuple structures that accept operands. This means, that depending on the code of a given statement, its operand vector will be at different offsets from the base of the structure. To access tuple operands use the following accessors

unsigned gimple_num_ops (*gimple g*)   [GIMPLE function]
    Returns the number of operands in statement G.

tree gimple_op (*gimple g, unsigned i*)   [GIMPLE function]
    Returns operand I from statement G.

tree * gimple_ops (*gimple g*)   [GIMPLE function]
    Returns a pointer into the operand vector for statement G. This is computed using an internal table called `gimple_ops_offset_[]`. This table is indexed by the gimple code of G.

    When the compiler is built, this table is filled-in using the sizes of the structures used by each statement code defined in gimple.def. Since the operand vector is at the bottom of the structure, for a gimple code C the offset is computed as sizeof (struct-of C) - sizeof (tree).

    This mechanism adds one memory indirection to every access when using `gimple_op()`, if this becomes a bottleneck, a pass can choose to memoize the result from `gimple_ops()` and use that to access the operands.

11.6.7 Operand validation

When adding a new operand to a gimple statement, the operand will be validated according to what each tuple accepts in its operand vector. These predicates are called by the `gimple_name_set_...()`. Each tuple will use one of the following predicates (Note, this list is not exhaustive):

bool is_gimple_val (*tree t*)   [GIMPLE function]
> Returns true if t is a "GIMPLE value", which are all the non-addressable stack variables (variables for which `is_gimple_reg` returns true) and constants (expressions for which `is_gimple_min_invariant` returns true).

bool is_gimple_addressable (*tree t*)   [GIMPLE function]
> Returns true if t is a symbol or memory reference whose address can be taken.

bool is_gimple_asm_val (*tree t*)   [GIMPLE function]
> Similar to `is_gimple_val` but it also accepts hard registers.

bool is_gimple_call_addr (*tree t*)   [GIMPLE function]
> Return true if t is a valid expression to use as the function called by a `GIMPLE_CALL`.

bool is_gimple_mem_ref_addr (*tree t*)   [GIMPLE function]
> Return true if t is a valid expression to use as first operand of a `MEM_REF` expression.

bool is_gimple_constant (*tree t*)   [GIMPLE function]
> Return true if t is a valid gimple constant.

bool is_gimple_min_invariant (*tree t*)   [GIMPLE function]
> Return true if t is a valid minimal invariant. This is different from constants, in that the specific value of t may not be known at compile time, but it is known that it doesn't change (e.g., the address of a function local variable).

bool is_gimple_ip_invariant (*tree t*)   [GIMPLE function]
> Return true if t is an interprocedural invariant. This means that t is a valid invariant in all functions (e.g. it can be an address of a global variable but not of a local one).

bool is_gimple_ip_invariant_address (*tree t*)   [GIMPLE function]
> Return true if t is an `ADDR_EXPR` that does not change once the program is running (and which is valid in all functions).

11.6.8 Statement validation

bool is_gimple_assign (*gimple g*)   [GIMPLE function]
> Return true if the code of g is `GIMPLE_ASSIGN`.

bool is_gimple_call (*gimple g*)   [GIMPLE function]
> Return true if the code of g is `GIMPLE_CALL`.

bool is_gimple_debug (*gimple g*)   [GIMPLE function]
> Return true if the code of g is `GIMPLE_DEBUG`.

bool gimple_assign_cast_p (*const_gimple g*)   [GIMPLE function]
> Return true if g is a `GIMPLE_ASSIGN` that performs a type cast operation.

`bool gimple_debug_bind_p` (*gimple g*)   [GIMPLE function]
    Return true if g is a `GIMPLE_DEBUG` that binds the value of an expression to a variable.

`bool is_gimple_omp` (*gimple g*)   [GIMPLE function]
    Return true if g is any of the OpenMP codes.

11.7 Manipulating GIMPLE statements

This section documents all the functions available to handle each of the GIMPLE instructions.

11.7.1 Common accessors

The following are common accessors for gimple statements.

`enum gimple_code gimple_code` (*gimple g*)   [GIMPLE function]
    Return the code for statement G.

`basic_block gimple_bb` (*gimple g*)   [GIMPLE function]
    Return the basic block to which statement G belongs to.

`tree gimple_block` (*gimple g*)   [GIMPLE function]
    Return the lexical scope block holding statement G.

`tree gimple_expr_type` (*gimple stmt*)   [GIMPLE function]
    Return the type of the main expression computed by STMT. Return `void_type_node` if STMT computes nothing. This will only return something meaningful for `GIMPLE_ASSIGN`, `GIMPLE_COND` and `GIMPLE_CALL`. For all other tuple codes, it will return `void_type_node`.

`enum tree_code gimple_expr_code` (*gimple stmt*)   [GIMPLE function]
    Return the tree code for the expression computed by STMT. This is only meaningful for `GIMPLE_CALL`, `GIMPLE_ASSIGN` and `GIMPLE_COND`. If STMT is `GIMPLE_CALL`, it will return `CALL_EXPR`. For `GIMPLE_COND`, it returns the code of the comparison predicate. For `GIMPLE_ASSIGN` it returns the code of the operation performed by the RHS of the assignment.

`void gimple_set_block` (*gimple g, tree block*)   [GIMPLE function]
    Set the lexical scope block of G to `BLOCK`.

`location_t gimple_locus` (*gimple g*)   [GIMPLE function]
    Return locus information for statement G.

`void gimple_set_locus` (*gimple g, location_t locus*)   [GIMPLE function]
    Set locus information for statement G.

`bool gimple_locus_empty_p` (*gimple g*)   [GIMPLE function]
    Return true if G does not have locus information.

`bool gimple_no_warning_p` (*gimple stmt*)   [GIMPLE function]
    Return true if no warnings should be emitted for statement STMT.

void gimple_set_visited (*gimple stmt, bool visited_p*)   [GIMPLE function]
> Set the visited status on statement STMT to VISITED_P.

bool gimple_visited_p (*gimple stmt*)   [GIMPLE function]
> Return the visited status on statement STMT.

void gimple_set_plf (*gimple stmt, enum plf_mask plf, bool*   [GIMPLE function]
>   *val_p*)
> Set pass local flag PLF on statement STMT to VAL_P.

unsigned int gimple_plf (*gimple stmt, enum plf_mask plf*)   [GIMPLE function]
> Return the value of pass local flag PLF on statement STMT.

bool gimple_has_ops (*gimple g*)   [GIMPLE function]
> Return true if statement G has register or memory operands.

bool gimple_has_mem_ops (*gimple g*)   [GIMPLE function]
> Return true if statement G has memory operands.

unsigned gimple_num_ops (*gimple g*)   [GIMPLE function]
> Return the number of operands for statement G.

tree * gimple_ops (*gimple g*)   [GIMPLE function]
> Return the array of operands for statement G.

tree gimple_op (*gimple g, unsigned i*)   [GIMPLE function]
> Return operand I for statement G.

tree * gimple_op_ptr (*gimple g, unsigned i*)   [GIMPLE function]
> Return a pointer to operand I for statement G.

void gimple_set_op (*gimple g, unsigned i, tree op*)   [GIMPLE function]
> Set operand I of statement G to OP.

bitmap gimple_addresses_taken (*gimple stmt*)   [GIMPLE function]
> Return the set of symbols that have had their address taken by STMT.

struct def_optype_d * gimple_def_ops (*gimple g*)   [GIMPLE function]
> Return the set of DEF operands for statement G.

void gimple_set_def_ops (*gimple g, struct def_optype_d*   [GIMPLE function]
>   **def*)
> Set DEF to be the set of DEF operands for statement G.

struct use_optype_d * gimple_use_ops (*gimple g*)   [GIMPLE function]
> Return the set of USE operands for statement G.

void gimple_set_use_ops (*gimple g, struct use_optype_d*   [GIMPLE function]
>   **use*)
> Set USE to be the set of USE operands for statement G.

struct voptype_d * gimple_vuse_ops (*gimple g*)   [GIMPLE function]
> Return the set of VUSE operands for statement G.

void gimple_set_vuse_ops (*gimple g, struct voptype_d *ops*)   [GIMPLE function]
:   Set OPS to be the set of VUSE operands for statement G.

struct voptype_d * gimple_vdef_ops (*gimple g*)   [GIMPLE function]
:   Return the set of VDEF operands for statement G.

void gimple_set_vdef_ops (*gimple g, struct voptype_d *ops*)   [GIMPLE function]
:   Set OPS to be the set of VDEF operands for statement G.

bitmap gimple_loaded_syms (*gimple g*)   [GIMPLE function]
:   Return the set of symbols loaded by statement G. Each element of the set is the DECL_UID of the corresponding symbol.

bitmap gimple_stored_syms (*gimple g*)   [GIMPLE function]
:   Return the set of symbols stored by statement G. Each element of the set is the DECL_UID of the corresponding symbol.

bool gimple_modified_p (*gimple g*)   [GIMPLE function]
:   Return true if statement G has operands and the modified field has been set.

bool gimple_has_volatile_ops (*gimple stmt*)   [GIMPLE function]
:   Return true if statement STMT contains volatile operands.

void gimple_set_has_volatile_ops (*gimple stmt, bool volatilep*)   [GIMPLE function]
:   Return true if statement STMT contains volatile operands.

void update_stmt (*gimple s*)   [GIMPLE function]
:   Mark statement S as modified, and update it.

void update_stmt_if_modified (*gimple s*)   [GIMPLE function]
:   Update statement S if it has been marked modified.

gimple gimple_copy (*gimple stmt*)   [GIMPLE function]
:   Return a deep copy of statement STMT.

11.8 Tuple specific accessors

11.8.1 GIMPLE_ASM

gasm *gimple_build_asm_vec (*const char *string, vec<tree,*   [GIMPLE function]
    *va_gc> *inputs, vec<tree, va_gc> *outputs, vec<tree, va_gc> *clobbers,*
    *vec<tree, va_gc> *labels*)
:   Build a GIMPLE_ASM statement. This statement is used for building in-line assembly constructs. STRING is the assembly code. INPUTS, OUTPUTS, CLOBBERS and LABELS are the inputs, outputs, clobbered registers and labels.

unsigned gimple_asm_ninputs (*const gasm *g*)   [GIMPLE function]
:   Return the number of input operands for GIMPLE_ASM G.

unsigned gimple_asm_noutputs (*const gasm *g*)   [GIMPLE function]
:   Return the number of output operands for GIMPLE_ASM G.

unsigned gimple_asm_nclobbers (*const gasm *g*)   [GIMPLE function]
Return the number of clobber operands for `GIMPLE_ASM` G.

tree gimple_asm_input_op (*const gasm *g, unsigned index*)   [GIMPLE function]
Return input operand `INDEX` of `GIMPLE_ASM` G.

void gimple_asm_set_input_op (*gasm *g, unsigned index,*   [GIMPLE function]
    tree in_op)
Set `IN_OP` to be input operand `INDEX` in `GIMPLE_ASM` G.

tree gimple_asm_output_op (*const gasm *g, unsigned index*)   [GIMPLE function]
Return output operand `INDEX` of `GIMPLE_ASM` G.

void gimple_asm_set_output_op (*gasm *g, unsigned index,*   [GIMPLE function]
    tree out_op)
Set `OUT_OP` to be output operand `INDEX` in `GIMPLE_ASM` G.

tree gimple_asm_clobber_op (*const gasm *g, unsigned index*)   [GIMPLE function]
Return clobber operand `INDEX` of `GIMPLE_ASM` G.

void gimple_asm_set_clobber_op (*gasm *g, unsigned index,*   [GIMPLE function]
    tree clobber_op)
Set `CLOBBER_OP` to be clobber operand `INDEX` in `GIMPLE_ASM` G.

const char * gimple_asm_string (*const gasm *g*)   [GIMPLE function]
Return the string representing the assembly instruction in `GIMPLE_ASM` G.

bool gimple_asm_volatile_p (*const gasm *g*)   [GIMPLE function]
Return true if G is an asm statement marked volatile.

void gimple_asm_set_volatile (*gasm *g, bool volatile_p*)   [GIMPLE function]
Mark asm statement G as volatile or non-volatile based on `VOLATILE_P`.

11.8.2 GIMPLE_ASSIGN

gassign *gimple_build_assign (*tree lhs, tree rhs*)   [GIMPLE function]
Build a `GIMPLE_ASSIGN` statement. The left-hand side is an lvalue passed in lhs. The right-hand side can be either a unary or binary tree expression. The expression tree rhs will be flattened and its operands assigned to the corresponding operand slots in the new statement. This function is useful when you already have a tree expression that you want to convert into a tuple. However, try to avoid building expression trees for the sole purpose of calling this function. If you already have the operands in separate trees, it is better to use `gimple_build_assign` with `enum tree_code` argument and separate arguments for each operand.

gassign *gimple_build_assign (*tree lhs, enum tree_code*   [GIMPLE function]
    subcode, tree op1, tree op2, tree op3)
This function is similar to two operand `gimple_build_assign`, but is used to build a `GIMPLE_ASSIGN` statement when the operands of the right-hand side of the assignment are already split into different operands.

The left-hand side is an lvalue passed in lhs. Subcode is the `tree_code` for the right-hand side of the assignment. Op1, op2 and op3 are the operands.

`gassign *gimple_build_assign` (*tree lhs, enum tree_code*   [GIMPLE function]
         subcode, tree op1, tree op2)
> Like the above 5 operand `gimple_build_assign`, but with the last argument `NULL` -
> this overload should not be used for `GIMPLE_TERNARY_RHS` assignments.

`gassign *gimple_build_assign` (*tree lhs, enum tree_code*   [GIMPLE function]
         subcode, tree op1)
> Like the above 4 operand `gimple_build_assign`, but with the last argument `NULL`
> - this overload should be used only for `GIMPLE_UNARY_RHS` and `GIMPLE_SINGLE_RHS`
> assignments.

`gimple gimplify_assign` (*tree dst, tree src, gimple_seq*   [GIMPLE function]
         *seq_p)
> Build a new `GIMPLE_ASSIGN` tuple and append it to the end of `*SEQ_P`.

`DST`/`SRC` are the destination and source respectively. You can pass ungimplified trees in
`DST` or `SRC`, in which case they will be converted to a gimple operand if necessary.

This function returns the newly created `GIMPLE_ASSIGN` tuple.

`enum tree_code gimple_assign_rhs_code` (*gimple g*)   [GIMPLE function]
> Return the code of the expression computed on the `RHS` of assignment statement `G`.

`enum gimple_rhs_class gimple_assign_rhs_class`   [GIMPLE function]
         (*gimple g*)
> Return the gimple rhs class of the code for the expression computed on the rhs of
> assignment statement `G`. This will never return `GIMPLE_INVALID_RHS`.

`tree gimple_assign_lhs` (*gimple g*)   [GIMPLE function]
> Return the `LHS` of assignment statement `G`.

`tree * gimple_assign_lhs_ptr` (*gimple g*)   [GIMPLE function]
> Return a pointer to the `LHS` of assignment statement `G`.

`tree gimple_assign_rhs1` (*gimple g*)   [GIMPLE function]
> Return the first operand on the `RHS` of assignment statement `G`.

`tree * gimple_assign_rhs1_ptr` (*gimple g*)   [GIMPLE function]
> Return the address of the first operand on the `RHS` of assignment statement `G`.

`tree gimple_assign_rhs2` (*gimple g*)   [GIMPLE function]
> Return the second operand on the `RHS` of assignment statement `G`.

`tree * gimple_assign_rhs2_ptr` (*gimple g*)   [GIMPLE function]
> Return the address of the second operand on the `RHS` of assignment statement `G`.

`tree gimple_assign_rhs3` (*gimple g*)   [GIMPLE function]
> Return the third operand on the `RHS` of assignment statement `G`.

`tree * gimple_assign_rhs3_ptr` (*gimple g*)   [GIMPLE function]
> Return the address of the third operand on the `RHS` of assignment statement `G`.

void gimple_assign_set_lhs (*gimple g, tree lhs*)   [GIMPLE function]
 Set LHS to be the LHS operand of assignment statement G.

void gimple_assign_set_rhs1 (*gimple g, tree rhs*)   [GIMPLE function]
 Set RHS to be the first operand on the RHS of assignment statement G.

void gimple_assign_set_rhs2 (*gimple g, tree rhs*)   [GIMPLE function]
 Set RHS to be the second operand on the RHS of assignment statement G.

void gimple_assign_set_rhs3 (*gimple g, tree rhs*)   [GIMPLE function]
 Set RHS to be the third operand on the RHS of assignment statement G.

bool gimple_assign_cast_p (*const_gimple s*)   [GIMPLE function]
 Return true if S is a type-cast assignment.

11.8.3 GIMPLE_BIND

gbind *gimple_build_bind (*tree vars, gimple_seq body*)   [GIMPLE function]
 Build a GIMPLE_BIND statement with a list of variables in VARS and a body of statements in sequence BODY.

tree gimple_bind_vars (*const gbind *g*)   [GIMPLE function]
 Return the variables declared in the GIMPLE_BIND statement G.

void gimple_bind_set_vars (*gbind *g, tree vars*)   [GIMPLE function]
 Set VARS to be the set of variables declared in the GIMPLE_BIND statement G.

void gimple_bind_append_vars (*gbind *g, tree vars*)   [GIMPLE function]
 Append VARS to the set of variables declared in the GIMPLE_BIND statement G.

gimple_seq gimple_bind_body (*gbind *g*)   [GIMPLE function]
 Return the GIMPLE sequence contained in the GIMPLE_BIND statement G.

void gimple_bind_set_body (*gbind *g, gimple_seq seq*)   [GIMPLE function]
 Set SEQ to be sequence contained in the GIMPLE_BIND statement G.

void gimple_bind_add_stmt (*gbind *gs, gimple stmt*)   [GIMPLE function]
 Append a statement to the end of a GIMPLE_BIND's body.

void gimple_bind_add_seq (*gbind *gs, gimple_seq seq*)   [GIMPLE function]
 Append a sequence of statements to the end of a GIMPLE_BIND's body.

tree gimple_bind_block (*const gbind *g*)   [GIMPLE function]
 Return the TREE_BLOCK node associated with GIMPLE_BIND statement G. This is analogous to the BIND_EXPR_BLOCK field in trees.

void gimple_bind_set_block (*gbind *g, tree block*)   [GIMPLE function]
 Set BLOCK to be the TREE_BLOCK node associated with GIMPLE_BIND statement G.

11.8.4 GIMPLE_CALL

gcall *gimple_build_call (*tree fn, unsigned nargs, ...*)   [GIMPLE function]
    Build a GIMPLE_CALL statement to function FN. The argument FN must be either
    a FUNCTION_DECL or a gimple call address as determined by is_gimple_call_addr.
    NARGS are the number of arguments. The rest of the arguments follow the argument
    NARGS, and must be trees that are valid as rvalues in gimple (i.e., each operand is
    validated with is_gimple_operand).

gcall *gimple_build_call_from_tree (*tree call_expr*)   [GIMPLE function]
    Build a GIMPLE_CALL from a CALL_EXPR node. The arguments and the function are
    taken from the expression directly. This routine assumes that call_expr is already
    in GIMPLE form. That is, its operands are GIMPLE values and the function call
    needs no further simplification. All the call flags in call_expr are copied over to the
    new GIMPLE_CALL.

gcall *gimple_build_call_vec (*tree fn*, vec<tree> *args*)   [GIMPLE function]
    Identical to gimple_build_call but the arguments are stored in a vec<tree>.

tree gimple_call_lhs (*gimple g*)   [GIMPLE function]
    Return the LHS of call statement G.

tree * gimple_call_lhs_ptr (*gimple g*)   [GIMPLE function]
    Return a pointer to the LHS of call statement G.

void gimple_call_set_lhs (*gimple g, tree lhs*)   [GIMPLE function]
    Set LHS to be the LHS operand of call statement G.

tree gimple_call_fn (*gimple g*)   [GIMPLE function]
    Return the tree node representing the function called by call statement G.

void gimple_call_set_fn (*gcall *g, tree fn*)   [GIMPLE function]
    Set FN to be the function called by call statement G. This has to be a gimple value
    specifying the address of the called function.

tree gimple_call_fndecl (*gimple g*)   [GIMPLE function]
    If a given GIMPLE_CALL's callee is a FUNCTION_DECL, return it. Otherwise return NULL.
    This function is analogous to get_callee_fndecl in GENERIC.

tree gimple_call_set_fndecl (*gimple g, tree fndecl*)   [GIMPLE function]
    Set the called function to FNDECL.

tree gimple_call_return_type (*const gcall *g*)   [GIMPLE function]
    Return the type returned by call statement G.

tree gimple_call_chain (*gimple g*)   [GIMPLE function]
    Return the static chain for call statement G.

void gimple_call_set_chain (*gcall *g, tree chain*)   [GIMPLE function]
    Set CHAIN to be the static chain for call statement G.

unsigned gimple_call_num_args (*gimple g*)   [GIMPLE function]
  Return the number of arguments used by call statement G.

tree gimple_call_arg (*gimple g, unsigned index*)   [GIMPLE function]
  Return the argument at position INDEX for call statement G. The first argument is 0.

tree * gimple_call_arg_ptr (*gimple g, unsigned index*)   [GIMPLE function]
  Return a pointer to the argument at position INDEX for call statement G.

void gimple_call_set_arg (*gimple g, unsigned index, tree*   [GIMPLE function]
    arg)
  Set ARG to be the argument at position INDEX for call statement G.

void gimple_call_set_tail (*gcall *s*)   [GIMPLE function]
  Mark call statement S as being a tail call (i.e., a call just before the exit of a function).
  These calls are candidate for tail call optimization.

bool gimple_call_tail_p (*gcall *s*)   [GIMPLE function]
  Return true if GIMPLE_CALL S is marked as a tail call.

bool gimple_call_noreturn_p (*gimple s*)   [GIMPLE function]
  Return true if S is a noreturn call.

gimple gimple_call_copy_skip_args (*gcall *stmt, bitmap*   [GIMPLE function]
    args_to_skip)
  Build a GIMPLE_CALL identical to STMT but skipping the arguments in the positions
  marked by the set ARGS_TO_SKIP.

11.8.5 GIMPLE_CATCH

gcatch *gimple_build_catch (*tree types, gimple_seq handler*)   [GIMPLE function]
  Build a GIMPLE_CATCH statement. TYPES are the tree types this catch handles.
  HANDLER is a sequence of statements with the code for the handler.

tree gimple_catch_types (*const gcatch *g*)   [GIMPLE function]
  Return the types handled by GIMPLE_CATCH statement G.

tree * gimple_catch_types_ptr (*gcatch *g*)   [GIMPLE function]
  Return a pointer to the types handled by GIMPLE_CATCH statement G.

gimple_seq gimple_catch_handler (*gcatch *g*)   [GIMPLE function]
  Return the GIMPLE sequence representing the body of the handler of GIMPLE_CATCH
  statement G.

void gimple_catch_set_types (*gcatch *g, tree t*)   [GIMPLE function]
  Set T to be the set of types handled by GIMPLE_CATCH G.

void gimple_catch_set_handler (*gcatch *g, gimple_seq*   [GIMPLE function]
    handler)
  Set HANDLER to be the body of GIMPLE_CATCH G.

11.8.6 GIMPLE_COND

gcond *gimple_build_cond (*enum tree_code pred_code, tree*   [GIMPLE function]
      lhs, tree rhs, tree t_label, tree f_label)
> Build a GIMPLE_COND statement. A GIMPLE_COND statement compares LHS and RHS
> and if the condition in PRED_CODE is true, jump to the label in t_label, otherwise
> jump to the label in f_label. PRED_CODE are relational operator tree codes like
> EQ_EXPR, LT_EXPR, LE_EXPR, NE_EXPR, etc.

gcond *gimple_build_cond_from_tree (*tree cond, tree*   [GIMPLE function]
      t_label, tree f_label)
> Build a GIMPLE_COND statement from the conditional expression tree COND. T_LABEL
> and F_LABEL are as in gimple_build_cond.

enum tree_code gimple_cond_code (*gimple g*)   [GIMPLE function]
> Return the code of the predicate computed by conditional statement G.

void gimple_cond_set_code (*gcond *g, enum tree_code code*)   [GIMPLE function]
> Set CODE to be the predicate code for the conditional statement G.

tree gimple_cond_lhs (*gimple g*)   [GIMPLE function]
> Return the LHS of the predicate computed by conditional statement G.

void gimple_cond_set_lhs (*gcond *g, tree lhs*)   [GIMPLE function]
> Set LHS to be the LHS operand of the predicate computed by conditional statement G.

tree gimple_cond_rhs (*gimple g*)   [GIMPLE function]
> Return the RHS operand of the predicate computed by conditional G.

void gimple_cond_set_rhs (*gcond *g, tree rhs*)   [GIMPLE function]
> Set RHS to be the RHS operand of the predicate computed by conditional statement G.

tree gimple_cond_true_label (*const gcond *g*)   [GIMPLE function]
> Return the label used by conditional statement G when its predicate evaluates to true.

void gimple_cond_set_true_label (*gcond *g, tree label*)   [GIMPLE function]
> Set LABEL to be the label used by conditional statement G when its predicate evaluates
> to true.

void gimple_cond_set_false_label (*gcond *g, tree label*)   [GIMPLE function]
> Set LABEL to be the label used by conditional statement G when its predicate evaluates
> to false.

tree gimple_cond_false_label (*const gcond *g*)   [GIMPLE function]
> Return the label used by conditional statement G when its predicate evaluates to false.

void gimple_cond_make_false (*gcond *g*)   [GIMPLE function]
> Set the conditional COND_STMT to be of the form 'if (1 == 0)'.

void gimple_cond_make_true (*gcond *g*)   [GIMPLE function]
> Set the conditional COND_STMT to be of the form 'if (1 == 1)'.

11.8.7 GIMPLE_DEBUG

gdebug *gimple_build_debug_bind (*tree var, tree value,*   [GIMPLE function]
          gimple stmt)
> Build a GIMPLE_DEBUG statement with GIMPLE_DEBUG_BIND of subcode. The effect of this statement is to tell debug information generation machinery that the value of user variable var is given by value at that point, and to remain with that value until var runs out of scope, a dynamically-subsequent debug bind statement overrides the binding, or conflicting values reach a control flow merge point. Even if components of the value expression change afterwards, the variable is supposed to retain the same value, though not necessarily the same location.
>
> It is expected that var be most often a tree for automatic user variables (VAR_DECL or PARM_DECL) that satisfy the requirements for gimple registers, but it may also be a tree for a scalarized component of a user variable (ARRAY_REF, COMPONENT_REF), or a debug temporary (DEBUG_EXPR_DECL).
>
> As for value, it can be an arbitrary tree expression, but it is recommended that it be in a suitable form for a gimple assignment RHS. It is not expected that user variables that could appear as var ever appear in value, because in the latter we'd have their SSA_NAMEs instead, but even if they were not in SSA form, user variables appearing in value are to be regarded as part of the executable code space, whereas those in var are to be regarded as part of the source code space. There is no way to refer to the value bound to a user variable within a value expression.
>
> If value is GIMPLE_DEBUG_BIND_NOVALUE, debug information generation machinery is informed that the variable var is unbound, i.e., that its value is indeterminate, which sometimes means it is really unavailable, and other times that the compiler could not keep track of it.
>
> Block and location information for the newly-created stmt are taken from stmt, if given.

tree gimple_debug_bind_get_var (*gimple stmt*)   [GIMPLE function]
> Return the user variable var that is bound at stmt.

tree gimple_debug_bind_get_value (*gimple stmt*)   [GIMPLE function]
> Return the value expression that is bound to a user variable at stmt.

tree * gimple_debug_bind_get_value_ptr (*gimple stmt*)   [GIMPLE function]
> Return a pointer to the value expression that is bound to a user variable at stmt.

void gimple_debug_bind_set_var (*gimple stmt, tree var*)   [GIMPLE function]
> Modify the user variable bound at stmt to *var*.

void gimple_debug_bind_set_value (*gimple stmt, tree var*)   [GIMPLE function]
> Modify the value bound to the user variable bound at stmt to *value*.

void gimple_debug_bind_reset_value (*gimple stmt*)   [GIMPLE function]
> Modify the value bound to the user variable bound at stmt so that the variable becomes unbound.

bool gimple_debug_bind_has_value_p (*gimple stmt*)   [GIMPLE function]
    Return `TRUE` if `stmt` binds a user variable to a value, and `FALSE` if it unbinds the variable.

11.8.8 GIMPLE_EH_FILTER

geh_filter *gimple_build_eh_filter (*tree types,*   [GIMPLE function]
      gimple_seq failure)
    Build a `GIMPLE_EH_FILTER` statement. `TYPES` are the filter's types. `FAILURE` is a sequence with the filter's failure action.

tree gimple_eh_filter_types (*gimple g*)   [GIMPLE function]
    Return the types handled by `GIMPLE_EH_FILTER` statement G.

tree * gimple_eh_filter_types_ptr (*gimple g*)   [GIMPLE function]
    Return a pointer to the types handled by `GIMPLE_EH_FILTER` statement G.

gimple_seq gimple_eh_filter_failure (*gimple g*)   [GIMPLE function]
    Return the sequence of statement to execute when `GIMPLE_EH_FILTER` statement fails.

void gimple_eh_filter_set_types (*geh_filter *g, tree types*)   [GIMPLE function]
    Set `TYPES` to be the set of types handled by `GIMPLE_EH_FILTER` G.

void gimple_eh_filter_set_failure (*geh_filter *g,*   [GIMPLE function]
      gimple_seq failure)
    Set `FAILURE` to be the sequence of statements to execute on failure for `GIMPLE_EH_FILTER` G.

tree gimple_eh_must_not_throw_fndecl (*geh_mnt*   [GIMPLE function]
      *eh_mnt_stmt)
    Get the function decl to be called by the MUST_NOT_THROW region.

void gimple_eh_must_not_throw_set_fndecl (*geh_mnt*   [GIMPLE function]
      *eh_mnt_stmt, tree decl)
    Set the function decl to be called by GS to DECL.

11.8.9 GIMPLE_LABEL

glabel *gimple_build_label (*tree label*)   [GIMPLE function]
    Build a `GIMPLE_LABEL` statement with corresponding to the tree label, `LABEL`.

tree gimple_label_label (*const glabel *g*)   [GIMPLE function]
    Return the `LABEL_DECL` node used by `GIMPLE_LABEL` statement G.

void gimple_label_set_label (*glabel *g, tree label*)   [GIMPLE function]
    Set `LABEL` to be the `LABEL_DECL` node used by `GIMPLE_LABEL` statement G.

11.8.10 GIMPLE_GOTO

ggoto *gimple_build_goto (*tree dest*)   [GIMPLE function]
    Build a GIMPLE_GOTO statement to label DEST.

tree gimple_goto_dest (*gimple g*)   [GIMPLE function]
    Return the destination of the unconditional jump G.

void gimple_goto_set_dest (*ggoto *g, tree dest*)   [GIMPLE function]
    Set DEST to be the destination of the unconditional jump G.

11.8.11 GIMPLE_NOP

gimple gimple_build_nop (*void*)   [GIMPLE function]
    Build a GIMPLE_NOP statement.

bool gimple_nop_p (*gimple g*)   [GIMPLE function]
    Returns TRUE if statement G is a GIMPLE_NOP.

11.8.12 GIMPLE_OMP_ATOMIC_LOAD

gomp_atomic_load *gimple_build_omp_atomic_load (*tree*   [GIMPLE function]
    lhs, tree rhs)
    Build a GIMPLE_OMP_ATOMIC_LOAD statement. LHS is the left-hand side of the assignment. RHS is the right-hand side of the assignment.

void gimple_omp_atomic_load_set_lhs (*gomp_atomic_load* [GIMPLE function]
    g, tree lhs)
    Set the LHS of an atomic load.

tree gimple_omp_atomic_load_lhs (*const*   [GIMPLE function]
    *gomp_atomic_load *g*)
    Get the LHS of an atomic load.

void gimple_omp_atomic_load_set_rhs (*gomp_atomic_load* [GIMPLE function]
    g, tree rhs)
    Set the RHS of an atomic set.

tree gimple_omp_atomic_load_rhs (*const*   [GIMPLE function]
    *gomp_atomic_load *g*)
    Get the RHS of an atomic set.

11.8.13 GIMPLE_OMP_ATOMIC_STORE

gomp_atomic_store *gimple_build_omp_atomic_store ([GIMPLE function]
    tree val)
    Build a GIMPLE_OMP_ATOMIC_STORE statement. VAL is the value to be stored.

void gimple_omp_atomic_store_set_val ([GIMPLE function]
    *gomp_atomic_store *g, tree val*)
    Set the value being stored in an atomic store.

tree gimple_omp_atomic_store_val (*const*   [GIMPLE function]
        gomp_atomic_store *g)
      Return the value being stored in an atomic store.

11.8.14 GIMPLE_OMP_CONTINUE

gomp_continue *gimple_build_omp_continue (*tree*   [GIMPLE function]
        control_def, tree control_use)
      Build a GIMPLE_OMP_CONTINUE statement. CONTROL_DEF is the definition of the control variable. CONTROL_USE is the use of the control variable.

tree gimple_omp_continue_control_def (*const*   [GIMPLE function]
        gomp_continue *s)
      Return the definition of the control variable on a GIMPLE_OMP_CONTINUE in S.

tree gimple_omp_continue_control_def_ptr ([GIMPLE function]
        gomp_continue *s)
      Same as above, but return the pointer.

tree gimple_omp_continue_set_control_def ([GIMPLE function]
        gomp_continue *s)
      Set the control variable definition for a GIMPLE_OMP_CONTINUE statement in S.

tree gimple_omp_continue_control_use (*const*   [GIMPLE function]
        gomp_continue *s)
      Return the use of the control variable on a GIMPLE_OMP_CONTINUE in S.

tree gimple_omp_continue_control_use_ptr ([GIMPLE function]
        gomp_continue *s)
      Same as above, but return the pointer.

tree gimple_omp_continue_set_control_use ([GIMPLE function]
        gomp_continue *s)
      Set the control variable use for a GIMPLE_OMP_CONTINUE statement in S.

11.8.15 GIMPLE_OMP_CRITICAL

gomp_critical *gimple_build_omp_critical (*gimple_seq*   [GIMPLE function]
        body, tree name)
      Build a GIMPLE_OMP_CRITICAL statement. BODY is the sequence of statements for which only one thread can execute. NAME is an optional identifier for this critical block.

tree gimple_omp_critical_name (*const gomp_critical *g*)   [GIMPLE function]
      Return the name associated with OMP_CRITICAL statement G.

tree * gimple_omp_critical_name_ptr (*gomp_critical *g*)   [GIMPLE function]
      Return a pointer to the name associated with OMP critical statement G.

void gimple_omp_critical_set_name (*gomp_critical *g,*   [GIMPLE function]
        tree name)
      Set NAME to be the name associated with OMP critical statement G.

11.8.16 GIMPLE_OMP_FOR

gomp_for *gimple_build_omp_for (*gimple_seq body, tree*   [GIMPLE function]
        clauses, tree index, tree initial, tree final, tree incr, gimple_seq pre_body, enum
        tree_code omp_for_cond)
   Build a GIMPLE_OMP_FOR statement. BODY is sequence of statements inside the for
   loop. CLAUSES, are any of the loop construct's clauses. PRE_BODY is the sequence of
   statements that are loop invariant. INDEX is the index variable. INITIAL is the initial
   value of INDEX. FINAL is final value of INDEX. OMP_FOR_COND is the predicate
   used to compare INDEX and FINAL. INCR is the increment expression.

tree gimple_omp_for_clauses (*gimple g*)   [GIMPLE function]
   Return the clauses associated with OMP_FOR G.

tree * gimple_omp_for_clauses_ptr (*gimple g*)   [GIMPLE function]
   Return a pointer to the OMP_FOR G.

void gimple_omp_for_set_clauses (*gimple g, tree clauses*)   [GIMPLE function]
   Set CLAUSES to be the list of clauses associated with OMP_FOR G.

tree gimple_omp_for_index (*gimple g*)   [GIMPLE function]
   Return the index variable for OMP_FOR G.

tree * gimple_omp_for_index_ptr (*gimple g*)   [GIMPLE function]
   Return a pointer to the index variable for OMP_FOR G.

void gimple_omp_for_set_index (*gimple g, tree index*)   [GIMPLE function]
   Set INDEX to be the index variable for OMP_FOR G.

tree gimple_omp_for_initial (*gimple g*)   [GIMPLE function]
   Return the initial value for OMP_FOR G.

tree * gimple_omp_for_initial_ptr (*gimple g*)   [GIMPLE function]
   Return a pointer to the initial value for OMP_FOR G.

void gimple_omp_for_set_initial (*gimple g, tree initial*)   [GIMPLE function]
   Set INITIAL to be the initial value for OMP_FOR G.

tree gimple_omp_for_final (*gimple g*)   [GIMPLE function]
   Return the final value for OMP_FOR G.

tree * gimple_omp_for_final_ptr (*gimple g*)   [GIMPLE function]
   turn a pointer to the final value for OMP_FOR G.

void gimple_omp_for_set_final (*gimple g, tree final*)   [GIMPLE function]
   Set FINAL to be the final value for OMP_FOR G.

tree gimple_omp_for_incr (*gimple g*)   [GIMPLE function]
   Return the increment value for OMP_FOR G.

tree * gimple_omp_for_incr_ptr (*gimple g*)   [GIMPLE function]
   Return a pointer to the increment value for OMP_FOR G.

void gimple_omp_for_set_incr (*gimple g, tree incr*)   [GIMPLE function]
    Set INCR to be the increment value for OMP_FOR G.

gimple_seq gimple_omp_for_pre_body (*gimple g*)   [GIMPLE function]
    Return the sequence of statements to execute before the OMP_FOR statement G starts.

void gimple_omp_for_set_pre_body (*gimple g, gimple_seq*   [GIMPLE function]
        pre_body)
    Set PRE_BODY to be the sequence of statements to execute before the OMP_FOR statement G starts.

void gimple_omp_for_set_cond (*gimple g, enum tree_code*   [GIMPLE function]
        cond)
    Set COND to be the condition code for OMP_FOR G.

enum tree_code gimple_omp_for_cond (*gimple g*)   [GIMPLE function]
    Return the condition code associated with OMP_FOR G.

11.8.17 GIMPLE_OMP_MASTER

gimple gimple_build_omp_master (*gimple_seq body*)   [GIMPLE function]
    Build a GIMPLE_OMP_MASTER statement. BODY is the sequence of statements to be executed by just the master.

11.8.18 GIMPLE_OMP_ORDERED

gimple gimple_build_omp_ordered (*gimple_seq body*)   [GIMPLE function]
    Build a GIMPLE_OMP_ORDERED statement.

BODY is the sequence of statements inside a loop that will executed in sequence.

11.8.19 GIMPLE_OMP_PARALLEL

gomp_parallel *gimple_build_omp_parallel (*gimple_seq*   [GIMPLE function]
        body, tree clauses, tree child_fn, tree data_arg)
    Build a GIMPLE_OMP_PARALLEL statement.

BODY is sequence of statements which are executed in parallel. CLAUSES, are the OMP parallel construct's clauses. CHILD_FN is the function created for the parallel threads to execute. DATA_ARG are the shared data argument(s).

bool gimple_omp_parallel_combined_p (*gimple g*)   [GIMPLE function]
    Return true if OMP parallel statement G has the GF_OMP_PARALLEL_COMBINED flag set.

void gimple_omp_parallel_set_combined_p (*gimple g*)   [GIMPLE function]
    Set the GF_OMP_PARALLEL_COMBINED field in OMP parallel statement G.

gimple_seq gimple_omp_body (*gimple g*)   [GIMPLE function]
    Return the body for the OMP statement G.

void gimple_omp_set_body (*gimple g, gimple_seq body*)   [GIMPLE function]
    Set BODY to be the body for the OMP statement G.

tree `gimple_omp_parallel_clauses` (*gimple g*)   [GIMPLE function]
>   Return the clauses associated with `OMP_PARALLEL` G.

tree * `gimple_omp_parallel_clauses_ptr` (*gomp_parallel*   [GIMPLE function]
>   **g*)
>   Return a pointer to the clauses associated with `OMP_PARALLEL` G.

void `gimple_omp_parallel_set_clauses` (*gomp_parallel*   [GIMPLE function]
>   **g, tree clauses*)
>   Set `CLAUSES` to be the list of clauses associated with `OMP_PARALLEL` G.

tree `gimple_omp_parallel_child_fn` (*const gomp_parallel*   [GIMPLE function]
>   **g*)
>   Return the child function used to hold the body of `OMP_PARALLEL` G.

tree * `gimple_omp_parallel_child_fn_ptr` ([GIMPLE function]
>   *gomp_parallel *g*)
>   Return a pointer to the child function used to hold the body of `OMP_PARALLEL` G.

void `gimple_omp_parallel_set_child_fn` (*gomp_parallel*   [GIMPLE function]
>   **g, tree child_fn*)
>   Set `CHILD_FN` to be the child function for `OMP_PARALLEL` G.

tree `gimple_omp_parallel_data_arg` (*const gomp_parallel*   [GIMPLE function]
>   **g*)
>   Return the artificial argument used to send variables and values from the parent to
>   the children threads in `OMP_PARALLEL` G.

tree * `gimple_omp_parallel_data_arg_ptr` ([GIMPLE function]
>   *gomp_parallel *g*)
>   Return a pointer to the data argument for `OMP_PARALLEL` G.

void `gimple_omp_parallel_set_data_arg` (*gomp_parallel*   [GIMPLE function]
>   **g, tree data_arg*)
>   Set `DATA_ARG` to be the data argument for `OMP_PARALLEL` G.

11.8.20 `GIMPLE_OMP_RETURN`

gimple `gimple_build_omp_return` (*bool wait_p*)   [GIMPLE function]
>   Build a `GIMPLE_OMP_RETURN` statement. `WAIT_P` is true if this is a non-waiting return.

void `gimple_omp_return_set_nowait` (*gimple s*)   [GIMPLE function]
>   Set the nowait flag on `GIMPLE_OMP_RETURN` statement S.

bool `gimple_omp_return_nowait_p` (*gimple g*)   [GIMPLE function]
>   Return true if `OMP` return statement G has the `GF_OMP_RETURN_NOWAIT` flag set.

11.8.21 GIMPLE_OMP_SECTION

gimple gimple_build_omp_section (*gimple_seq body*)   [GIMPLE function]
> Build a GIMPLE_OMP_SECTION statement for a sections statement.

> BODY is the sequence of statements in the section.

bool gimple_omp_section_last_p (*gimple g*)   [GIMPLE function]
> Return true if OMP section statement G has the GF_OMP_SECTION_LAST flag set.

void gimple_omp_section_set_last (*gimple g*)   [GIMPLE function]
> Set the GF_OMP_SECTION_LAST flag on G.

11.8.22 GIMPLE_OMP_SECTIONS

gomp_sections *gimple_build_omp_sections (*gimple_seq*   [GIMPLE function]
    body, tree clauses)
> Build a GIMPLE_OMP_SECTIONS statement. BODY is a sequence of section statements.
> CLAUSES are any of the OMP sections construct's clauses: private, firstprivate, lastprivate, reduction, and nowait.

gimple gimple_build_omp_sections_switch (*void*)   [GIMPLE function]
> Build a GIMPLE_OMP_SECTIONS_SWITCH statement.

tree gimple_omp_sections_control (*gimple g*)   [GIMPLE function]
> Return the control variable associated with the GIMPLE_OMP_SECTIONS in G.

tree * gimple_omp_sections_control_ptr (*gimple g*)   [GIMPLE function]
> Return a pointer to the clauses associated with the GIMPLE_OMP_SECTIONS in G.

void gimple_omp_sections_set_control (*gimple g, tree*   [GIMPLE function]
    control)
> Set CONTROL to be the set of clauses associated with the GIMPLE_OMP_SECTIONS in G.

tree gimple_omp_sections_clauses (*gimple g*)   [GIMPLE function]
> Return the clauses associated with OMP_SECTIONS G.

tree * gimple_omp_sections_clauses_ptr (*gimple g*)   [GIMPLE function]
> Return a pointer to the clauses associated with OMP_SECTIONS G.

void gimple_omp_sections_set_clauses (*gimple g, tree*   [GIMPLE function]
    clauses)
> Set CLAUSES to be the set of clauses associated with OMP_SECTIONS G.

11.8.23 GIMPLE_OMP_SINGLE

gomp_single *gimple_build_omp_single (*gimple_seq body,*   [GIMPLE function]
    tree clauses)
> Build a GIMPLE_OMP_SINGLE statement. BODY is the sequence of statements that will
> be executed once. CLAUSES are any of the OMP single construct's clauses: private,
> firstprivate, copyprivate, nowait.

tree gimple_omp_single_clauses (*gimple g*)   [GIMPLE function]
> Return the clauses associated with OMP_SINGLE G.

tree * gimple_omp_single_clauses_ptr (*gimple g*)   [GIMPLE function]
> Return a pointer to the clauses associated with OMP_SINGLE G.

void gimple_omp_single_set_clauses (*gomp_single *g,*   [GIMPLE function]
> *tree clauses*)
> Set CLAUSES to be the clauses associated with OMP_SINGLE G.

11.8.24 GIMPLE_PHI

unsigned gimple_phi_capacity (*gimple g*)   [GIMPLE function]
> Return the maximum number of arguments supported by GIMPLE_PHI G.

unsigned gimple_phi_num_args (*gimple g*)   [GIMPLE function]
> Return the number of arguments in GIMPLE_PHI G. This must always be exactly the
> number of incoming edges for the basic block holding G.

tree gimple_phi_result (*gimple g*)   [GIMPLE function]
> Return the SSA name created by GIMPLE_PHI G.

tree * gimple_phi_result_ptr (*gimple g*)   [GIMPLE function]
> Return a pointer to the SSA name created by GIMPLE_PHI G.

void gimple_phi_set_result (*gphi *g, tree result*)   [GIMPLE function]
> Set RESULT to be the SSA name created by GIMPLE_PHI G.

struct phi_arg_d * gimple_phi_arg (*gimple g, index*)   [GIMPLE function]
> Return the PHI argument corresponding to incoming edge INDEX for GIMPLE_PHI G.

void gimple_phi_set_arg (*gphi *g, index, struct phi_arg_d **   [GIMPLE function]
> *phiarg*)
> Set PHIARG to be the argument corresponding to incoming edge INDEX for GIMPLE_PHI
> G.

11.8.25 GIMPLE_RESX

gresx *gimple_build_resx (*int region*)   [GIMPLE function]
> Build a GIMPLE_RESX statement which is a statement. This statement is a placeholder
> for _Unwind_Resume before we know if a function call or a branch is needed. REGION
> is the exception region from which control is flowing.

int gimple_resx_region (*const gresx *g*)   [GIMPLE function]
> Return the region number for GIMPLE_RESX G.

void gimple_resx_set_region (*gresx *g, int region*)   [GIMPLE function]
> Set REGION to be the region number for GIMPLE_RESX G.

11.8.26 GIMPLE_RETURN

greturn *gimple_build_return (*tree retval*)   [GIMPLE function]
>   Build a GIMPLE_RETURN statement whose return value is retval.

tree gimple_return_retval (*const greturn *g*)   [GIMPLE function]
>   Return the return value for GIMPLE_RETURN G.

void gimple_return_set_retval (*greturn *g, tree retval*)   [GIMPLE function]
>   Set RETVAL to be the return value for GIMPLE_RETURN G.

11.8.27 GIMPLE_SWITCH

gswitch *gimple_build_switch (*tree index, tree*   [GIMPLE function]
>   *default_label*, vec<tree> *args*)
>   Build a GIMPLE_SWITCH statement. INDEX is the index variable to switch on, and
>   DEFAULT_LABEL represents the default label. ARGS is a vector of CASE_LABEL_EXPR
>   trees that contain the non-default case labels. Each label is a tree of code CASE_
>   LABEL_EXPR.

unsigned gimple_switch_num_labels (*const gswitch *g*)   [GIMPLE function]
>   Return the number of labels associated with the switch statement G.

void gimple_switch_set_num_labels (*gswitch *g, unsigned*   [GIMPLE function]
>   *nlabels*)
>   Set NLABELS to be the number of labels for the switch statement G.

tree gimple_switch_index (*const gswitch *g*)   [GIMPLE function]
>   Return the index variable used by the switch statement G.

void gimple_switch_set_index (*gswitch *g, tree index*)   [GIMPLE function]
>   Set INDEX to be the index variable for switch statement G.

tree gimple_switch_label (*const gswitch *g, unsigned index*)   [GIMPLE function]
>   Return the label numbered INDEX. The default label is 0, followed by any labels in a
>   switch statement.

void gimple_switch_set_label (*gswitch *g, unsigned index,*   [GIMPLE function]
>   *tree label*)
>   Set the label number INDEX to LABEL. 0 is always the default label.

tree gimple_switch_default_label (*const gswitch *g*)   [GIMPLE function]
>   Return the default label for a switch statement.

void gimple_switch_set_default_label (*gswitch *g, tree*   [GIMPLE function]
>   *label*)
>   Set the default label for a switch statement.

11.8.28 `GIMPLE_TRY`

`gtry *gimple_build_try` (*gimple_seq eval, gimple_seq*   [GIMPLE function]
    cleanup, unsigned int kind)
> Build a `GIMPLE_TRY` statement. `EVAL` is a sequence with the expression to evaluate.
> `CLEANUP` is a sequence of statements to run at clean-up time. `KIND` is the enumeration
> value `GIMPLE_TRY_CATCH` if this statement denotes a try/catch construct or `GIMPLE_`
> `TRY_FINALLY` if this statement denotes a try/finally construct.

`enum gimple_try_flags gimple_try_kind` (*gimple g*)   [GIMPLE function]
> Return the kind of try block represented by `GIMPLE_TRY` G. This is either `GIMPLE_`
> `TRY_CATCH` or `GIMPLE_TRY_FINALLY`.

`bool gimple_try_catch_is_cleanup` (*gimple g*)   [GIMPLE function]
> Return the `GIMPLE_TRY_CATCH_IS_CLEANUP` flag.

`gimple_seq gimple_try_eval` (*gimple g*)   [GIMPLE function]
> Return the sequence of statements used as the body for `GIMPLE_TRY` G.

`gimple_seq gimple_try_cleanup` (*gimple g*)   [GIMPLE function]
> Return the sequence of statements used as the cleanup body for `GIMPLE_TRY` G.

`void gimple_try_set_catch_is_cleanup` (*gimple g, bool*   [GIMPLE function]
    catch_is_cleanup)
> Set the `GIMPLE_TRY_CATCH_IS_CLEANUP` flag.

`void gimple_try_set_eval` (*gtry *g, gimple_seq eval*)   [GIMPLE function]
> Set `EVAL` to be the sequence of statements to use as the body for `GIMPLE_TRY` G.

`void gimple_try_set_cleanup` (*gtry *g, gimple_seq cleanup*)   [GIMPLE function]
> Set `CLEANUP` to be the sequence of statements to use as the cleanup body for `GIMPLE_`
> `TRY` G.

11.8.29 `GIMPLE_WITH_CLEANUP_EXPR`

`gimple gimple_build_wce` (*gimple_seq cleanup*)   [GIMPLE function]
> Build a `GIMPLE_WITH_CLEANUP_EXPR` statement. `CLEANUP` is the clean-up expression.

`gimple_seq gimple_wce_cleanup` (*gimple g*)   [GIMPLE function]
> Return the cleanup sequence for cleanup statement G.

`void gimple_wce_set_cleanup` (*gimple g, gimple_seq cleanup*)   [GIMPLE function]
> Set `CLEANUP` to be the cleanup sequence for G.

`bool gimple_wce_cleanup_eh_only` (*gimple g*)   [GIMPLE function]
> Return the `CLEANUP_EH_ONLY` flag for a `WCE` tuple.

`void gimple_wce_set_cleanup_eh_only` (*gimple g, bool*   [GIMPLE function]
    eh_only_p)
> Set the `CLEANUP_EH_ONLY` flag for a `WCE` tuple.

11.9 GIMPLE sequences

GIMPLE sequences are the tuple equivalent of `STATEMENT_LIST`'s used in `GENERIC`. They are used to chain statements together, and when used in conjunction with sequence iterators, provide a framework for iterating through statements.

GIMPLE sequences are of type struct `gimple_sequence`, but are more commonly passed by reference to functions dealing with sequences. The type for a sequence pointer is `gimple_seq` which is the same as struct `gimple_sequence *`. When declaring a local sequence, you can define a local variable of type struct `gimple_sequence`. When declaring a sequence allocated on the garbage collected heap, use the function `gimple_seq_alloc` documented below.

There are convenience functions for iterating through sequences in the section entitled Sequence Iterators.

Below is a list of functions to manipulate and query sequences.

void **gimple_seq_add_stmt** (*gimple_seq *seq, gimple g*)   [GIMPLE function]
> Link a gimple statement to the end of the sequence *SEQ if G is not NULL. If *SEQ is NULL, allocate a sequence before linking.

void **gimple_seq_add_seq** (*gimple_seq *dest, gimple_seq src*)   [GIMPLE function]
> Append sequence SRC to the end of sequence *DEST if SRC is not NULL. If *DEST is NULL, allocate a new sequence before appending.

gimple_seq **gimple_seq_deep_copy** (*gimple_seq src*)   [GIMPLE function]
> Perform a deep copy of sequence SRC and return the result.

gimple_seq **gimple_seq_reverse** (*gimple_seq seq*)   [GIMPLE function]
> Reverse the order of the statements in the sequence SEQ. Return SEQ.

gimple **gimple_seq_first** (*gimple_seq s*)   [GIMPLE function]
> Return the first statement in sequence S.

gimple **gimple_seq_last** (*gimple_seq s*)   [GIMPLE function]
> Return the last statement in sequence S.

void **gimple_seq_set_last** (*gimple_seq s, gimple last*)   [GIMPLE function]
> Set the last statement in sequence S to the statement in LAST.

void **gimple_seq_set_first** (*gimple_seq s, gimple first*)   [GIMPLE function]
> Set the first statement in sequence S to the statement in FIRST.

void **gimple_seq_init** (*gimple_seq s*)   [GIMPLE function]
> Initialize sequence S to an empty sequence.

gimple_seq **gimple_seq_alloc** (*void*)   [GIMPLE function]
> Allocate a new sequence in the garbage collected store and return it.

void **gimple_seq_copy** (*gimple_seq dest, gimple_seq src*)   [GIMPLE function]
> Copy the sequence SRC into the sequence DEST.

bool gimple_seq_empty_p (*gimple_seq s*)   [GIMPLE function]
  Return true if the sequence S is empty.

gimple_seq bb_seq (*basic_block bb*)   [GIMPLE function]
  Returns the sequence of statements in BB.

void set_bb_seq (*basic_block bb, gimple_seq seq*)   [GIMPLE function]
  Sets the sequence of statements in BB to SEQ.

bool gimple_seq_singleton_p (*gimple_seq seq*)   [GIMPLE function]
  Determine whether SEQ contains exactly one statement.

11.10 Sequence iterators

Sequence iterators are convenience constructs for iterating through statements in a sequence. Given a sequence SEQ, here is a typical use of gimple sequence iterators:

```
gimple_stmt_iterator gsi;

for (gsi = gsi_start (seq); !gsi_end_p (gsi); gsi_next (&gsi))
  {
    gimple g = gsi_stmt (gsi);
    /* Do something with gimple statement G.  */
  }
```

Backward iterations are possible:

```
        for (gsi = gsi_last (seq); !gsi_end_p (gsi); gsi_prev (&gsi))
```

Forward and backward iterations on basic blocks are possible with `gsi_start_bb` and `gsi_last_bb`.

In the documentation below we sometimes refer to enum `gsi_iterator_update`. The valid options for this enumeration are:

- `GSI_NEW_STMT` Only valid when a single statement is added. Move the iterator to it.
- `GSI_SAME_STMT` Leave the iterator at the same statement.
- `GSI_CONTINUE_LINKING` Move iterator to whatever position is suitable for linking other statements in the same direction.

Below is a list of the functions used to manipulate and use statement iterators.

gimple_stmt_iterator gsi_start (*gimple_seq seq*)   [GIMPLE function]
  Return a new iterator pointing to the sequence SEQ's first statement. If SEQ is empty, the iterator's basic block is NULL. Use `gsi_start_bb` instead when the iterator needs to always have the correct basic block set.

gimple_stmt_iterator gsi_start_bb (*basic_block bb*)   [GIMPLE function]
  Return a new iterator pointing to the first statement in basic block BB.

gimple_stmt_iterator gsi_last (*gimple_seq seq*)   [GIMPLE function]
  Return a new iterator initially pointing to the last statement of sequence SEQ. If SEQ is empty, the iterator's basic block is NULL. Use `gsi_last_bb` instead when the iterator needs to always have the correct basic block set.

gimple_stmt_iterator gsi_last_bb (*basic_block bb*)   [GIMPLE function]
  Return a new iterator pointing to the last statement in basic block BB.

`bool gsi_end_p` (*gimple_stmt_iterator i*)   [GIMPLE function]
    Return `TRUE` if at the end of `I`.

`bool gsi_one_before_end_p` (*gimple_stmt_iterator i*)   [GIMPLE function]
    Return `TRUE` if we're one statement before the end of `I`.

`void gsi_next` (*gimple_stmt_iterator *i*)   [GIMPLE function]
    Advance the iterator to the next gimple statement.

`void gsi_prev` (*gimple_stmt_iterator *i*)   [GIMPLE function]
    Advance the iterator to the previous gimple statement.

`gimple gsi_stmt` (*gimple_stmt_iterator i*)   [GIMPLE function]
    Return the current stmt.

`gimple_stmt_iterator gsi_after_labels` (*basic_block bb*)   [GIMPLE function]
    Return a block statement iterator that points to the first non-label statement in block
    `BB`.

`gimple * gsi_stmt_ptr` (*gimple_stmt_iterator *i*)   [GIMPLE function]
    Return a pointer to the current stmt.

`basic_block gsi_bb` (*gimple_stmt_iterator i*)   [GIMPLE function]
    Return the basic block associated with this iterator.

`gimple_seq gsi_seq` (*gimple_stmt_iterator i*)   [GIMPLE function]
    Return the sequence associated with this iterator.

`void gsi_remove` (*gimple_stmt_iterator *i, bool remove_eh_info*)   [GIMPLE function]
    Remove the current stmt from the sequence. The iterator is updated to point to the
    next statement. When `REMOVE_EH_INFO` is true we remove the statement pointed to
    by iterator `I` from the `EH` tables. Otherwise we do not modify the `EH` tables. Generally,
    `REMOVE_EH_INFO` should be true when the statement is going to be removed from the
    `IL` and not reinserted elsewhere.

`void gsi_link_seq_before` (*gimple_stmt_iterator *i,*   [GIMPLE function]
        gimple_seq seq, enum gsi_iterator_update mode)
    Links the sequence of statements `SEQ` before the statement pointed by iterator `I`. `MODE`
    indicates what to do with the iterator after insertion (see `enum gsi_iterator_update`
    above).

`void gsi_link_before` (*gimple_stmt_iterator *i, gimple g,*   [GIMPLE function]
        enum gsi_iterator_update mode)
    Links statement `G` before the statement pointed-to by iterator `I`. Updates iterator `I`
    according to `MODE`.

`void gsi_link_seq_after` (*gimple_stmt_iterator *i,*   [GIMPLE function]
        gimple_seq seq, enum gsi_iterator_update mode)
    Links sequence `SEQ` after the statement pointed-to by iterator `I`. `MODE` is as in `gsi_`
    `insert_after`.

void **gsi_link_after** (*gimple_stmt_iterator *i, gimple g, enum*   [GIMPLE function]
  gsi_iterator_update mode)

  Links statement G after the statement pointed-to by iterator I. MODE is as in **gsi_insert_after**.

gimple_seq **gsi_split_seq_after** (*gimple_stmt_iterator i*)   [GIMPLE function]

  Move all statements in the sequence after I to a new sequence. Return this new sequence.

gimple_seq **gsi_split_seq_before** (*gimple_stmt_iterator *i*)   [GIMPLE function]

  Move all statements in the sequence before I to a new sequence. Return this new sequence.

void **gsi_replace** (*gimple_stmt_iterator *i, gimple stmt, bool*   [GIMPLE function]
  update_eh_info)

  Replace the statement pointed-to by I to STMT. If UPDATE_EH_INFO is true, the exception handling information of the original statement is moved to the new statement.

void **gsi_insert_before** (*gimple_stmt_iterator *i, gimple*   [GIMPLE function]
  stmt, enum gsi_iterator_update mode)

  Insert statement STMT before the statement pointed-to by iterator I, update STMT's basic block and scan it for new operands. MODE specifies how to update iterator I after insertion (see enum **gsi_iterator_update**).

void **gsi_insert_seq_before** (*gimple_stmt_iterator *i,*   [GIMPLE function]
  gimple_seq seq, enum gsi_iterator_update mode)

  Like **gsi_insert_before**, but for all the statements in SEQ.

void **gsi_insert_after** (*gimple_stmt_iterator *i, gimple stmt,*   [GIMPLE function]
  enum gsi_iterator_update mode)

  Insert statement STMT after the statement pointed-to by iterator I, update STMT's basic block and scan it for new operands. MODE specifies how to update iterator I after insertion (see enum **gsi_iterator_update**).

void **gsi_insert_seq_after** (*gimple_stmt_iterator *i,*   [GIMPLE function]
  gimple_seq seq, enum gsi_iterator_update mode)

  Like **gsi_insert_after**, but for all the statements in SEQ.

gimple_stmt_iterator **gsi_for_stmt** (*gimple stmt*)   [GIMPLE function]

  Finds iterator for STMT.

void **gsi_move_after** (*gimple_stmt_iterator *from,*   [GIMPLE function]
  gimple_stmt_iterator *to)

  Move the statement at FROM so it comes right after the statement at TO.

void **gsi_move_before** (*gimple_stmt_iterator *from,*   [GIMPLE function]
  gimple_stmt_iterator *to)

  Move the statement at FROM so it comes right before the statement at TO.

void **gsi_move_to_bb_end** (*gimple_stmt_iterator *from,*   [GIMPLE function]
  basic_block bb)

  Move the statement at FROM to the end of basic block BB.

`void gsi_insert_on_edge` (*edge e, gimple stmt*)   [GIMPLE function]
>   Add `STMT` to the pending list of edge `E`. No actual insertion is made until a call to
>   `gsi_commit_edge_inserts`() is made.

`void gsi_insert_seq_on_edge` (*edge e, gimple_seq seq*)   [GIMPLE function]
>   Add the sequence of statements in `SEQ` to the pending list of edge `E`. No actual
>   insertion is made until a call to `gsi_commit_edge_inserts`() is made.

`basic_block gsi_insert_on_edge_immediate` (*edge e,*   [GIMPLE function]
>   *gimple stmt*)
>   Similar to `gsi_insert_on_edge`+`gsi_commit_edge_inserts`. If a new block has to
>   be created, it is returned.

`void gsi_commit_one_edge_insert` (*edge e, basic_block*   [GIMPLE function]
>   **new_bb*)*
>   Commit insertions pending at edge `E`. If a new block is created, set `NEW_BB` to this
>   block, otherwise set it to `NULL`.

`void gsi_commit_edge_inserts` (*void*)   [GIMPLE function]
>   This routine will commit all pending edge insertions, creating any new basic blocks
>   which are necessary.

11.11 Adding a new GIMPLE statement code

The first step in adding a new GIMPLE statement code, is modifying the file `gimple.def`,
which contains all the GIMPLE codes. Then you must add a corresponding gimple subclass
located in `gimple.h`. This in turn, will require you to add a corresponding `GTY` tag in
`gsstruct.def`, and code to handle this tag in `gss_for_code` which is located in `gimple.c`.

In order for the garbage collector to know the size of the structure you created in
`gimple.h`, you need to add a case to handle your new GIMPLE statement in `gimple_size`
which is located in `gimple.c`.

You will probably want to create a function to build the new gimple statement in
`gimple.c`. The function should be called `gimple_build_new-tuple-name`, and should return the new tuple as a pointer to the appropriate gimple subclass.

If your new statement requires accessors for any members or operands it may have,
put simple inline accessors in `gimple.h` and any non-trivial accessors in `gimple.c` with a
corresponding prototype in `gimple.h`.

You should add the new statement subclass to the class hierarchy diagram in
`gimple.texi`.

11.12 Statement and operand traversals

There are two functions available for walking statements and sequences: `walk_gimple_stmt` and `walk_gimple_seq`, accordingly, and a third function for walking the operands in
a statement: `walk_gimple_op`.

tree walk_gimple_stmt (*gimple_stmt_iterator *gsi,*   [GIMPLE function]
    walk_stmt_fn callback_stmt, walk_tree_fn callback_op, struct walk_stmt_info
    *wi)

This function is used to walk the current statement in `GSI`, optionally using traversal state stored in `WI`. If `WI` is `NULL`, no state is kept during the traversal.

The callback `CALLBACK_STMT` is called. If `CALLBACK_STMT` returns true, it means that the callback function has handled all the operands of the statement and it is not necessary to walk its operands.

If `CALLBACK_STMT` is `NULL` or it returns false, `CALLBACK_OP` is called on each operand of the statement via `walk_gimple_op`. If `walk_gimple_op` returns non-`NULL` for any operand, the remaining operands are not scanned.

The return value is that returned by the last call to `walk_gimple_op`, or `NULL_TREE` if no `CALLBACK_OP` is specified.

tree walk_gimple_op (*gimple stmt, walk_tree_fn callback_op,*   [GIMPLE function]
    struct walk_stmt_info *wi)

Use this function to walk the operands of statement `STMT`. Every operand is walked via `walk_tree` with optional state information in `WI`.

`CALLBACK_OP` is called on each operand of `STMT` via `walk_tree`. Additional parameters to `walk_tree` must be stored in `WI`. For each operand `OP`, `walk_tree` is called as:

```
walk_tree (&OP, CALLBACK_OP, WI, PSET)
```

If `CALLBACK_OP` returns non-`NULL` for an operand, the remaining operands are not scanned. The return value is that returned by the last call to `walk_tree`, or `NULL_TREE` if no `CALLBACK_OP` is specified.

tree walk_gimple_seq (*gimple_seq seq, walk_stmt_fn*   [GIMPLE function]
    callback_stmt, walk_tree_fn callback_op, struct walk_stmt_info *wi)

This function walks all the statements in the sequence `SEQ` calling `walk_gimple_stmt` on each one. `WI` is as in `walk_gimple_stmt`. If `walk_gimple_stmt` returns non-`NULL`, the walk is stopped and the value returned. Otherwise, all the statements are walked and `NULL_TREE` returned.

12 Analysis and Optimization of GIMPLE tuples

GCC uses three main intermediate languages to represent the program during compilation: GENERIC, GIMPLE and RTL. GENERIC is a language-independent representation generated by each front end. It is used to serve as an interface between the parser and optimizer. GENERIC is a common representation that is able to represent programs written in all the languages supported by GCC.

GIMPLE and RTL are used to optimize the program. GIMPLE is used for target and language independent optimizations (e.g., inlining, constant propagation, tail call elimination, redundancy elimination, etc). Much like GENERIC, GIMPLE is a language independent, tree based representation. However, it differs from GENERIC in that the GIMPLE grammar is more restrictive: expressions contain no more than 3 operands (except function calls), it has no control flow structures and expressions with side-effects are only allowed on the right hand side of assignments. See the chapter describing GENERIC and GIMPLE for more details.

This chapter describes the data structures and functions used in the GIMPLE optimizers (also known as "tree optimizers" or "middle end"). In particular, it focuses on all the macros, data structures, functions and programming constructs needed to implement optimization passes for GIMPLE.

12.1 Annotations

The optimizers need to associate attributes with variables during the optimization process. For instance, we need to know whether a variable has aliases. All these attributes are stored in data structures called annotations which are then linked to the field `ann` in `struct tree_common`.

12.2 SSA Operands

Almost every GIMPLE statement will contain a reference to a variable or memory location. Since statements come in different shapes and sizes, their operands are going to be located at various spots inside the statement's tree. To facilitate access to the statement's operands, they are organized into lists associated inside each statement's annotation. Each element in an operand list is a pointer to a `VAR_DECL`, `PARM_DECL` or `SSA_NAME` tree node. This provides a very convenient way of examining and replacing operands.

Data flow analysis and optimization is done on all tree nodes representing variables. Any node for which `SSA_VAR_P` returns nonzero is considered when scanning statement operands. However, not all `SSA_VAR_P` variables are processed in the same way. For the purposes of optimization, we need to distinguish between references to local scalar variables and references to globals, statics, structures, arrays, aliased variables, etc. The reason is simple, the compiler can gather complete data flow information for a local scalar. On the other hand, a global variable may be modified by a function call, it may not be possible to keep track of all the elements of an array or the fields of a structure, etc.

The operand scanner gathers two kinds of operands: *real* and *virtual*. An operand for which `is_gimple_reg` returns true is considered real, otherwise it is a virtual operand. We also distinguish between uses and definitions. An operand is used if its value is loaded by the statement (e.g., the operand at the RHS of an assignment). If the statement assigns a new value to the operand, the operand is considered a definition (e.g., the operand at the LHS of an assignment).

Virtual and real operands also have very different data flow properties. Real operands are unambiguous references to the full object that they represent. For instance, given

```
{
  int a, b;
  a = b
}
```

Since `a` and `b` are non-aliased locals, the statement `a = b` will have one real definition and one real use because variable `a` is completely modified with the contents of variable `b`. Real definition are also known as *killing definitions*. Similarly, the use of `b` reads all its bits.

In contrast, virtual operands are used with variables that can have a partial or ambiguous reference. This includes structures, arrays, globals, and aliased variables. In these cases, we have two types of definitions. For globals, structures, and arrays, we can determine from a statement whether a variable of these types has a killing definition. If the variable does, then the statement is marked as having a *must definition* of that variable. However, if a statement is only defining a part of the variable (i.e. a field in a structure), or if we know that a statement might define the variable but we cannot say for sure, then we mark that statement as having a *may definition*. For instance, given

```
{
  int a, b, *p;

  if (...)
    p = &a;
  else
    p = &b;
  *p = 5;
  return *p;
}
```

The assignment `*p = 5` may be a definition of `a` or `b`. If we cannot determine statically where `p` is pointing to at the time of the store operation, we create virtual definitions to mark that statement as a potential definition site for `a` and `b`. Memory loads are similarly marked with virtual use operands. Virtual operands are shown in tree dumps right before the statement that contains them. To request a tree dump with virtual operands, use the '-vops' option to '-fdump-tree':

```
{
  int a, b, *p;

  if (...)
    p = &a;
  else
    p = &b;
  # a = VDEF <a>
  # b = VDEF <b>
  *p = 5;

  # VUSE <a>
  # VUSE <b>
  return *p;
}
```

Notice that **VDEF** operands have two copies of the referenced variable. This indicates that this is not a killing definition of that variable. In this case we refer to it as a *may definition* or *aliased store*. The presence of the second copy of the variable in the **VDEF** operand will become important when the function is converted into SSA form. This will be used to link all the non-killing definitions to prevent optimizations from making incorrect assumptions about them.

Operands are updated as soon as the statement is finished via a call to **update_stmt**. If statement elements are changed via **SET_USE** or **SET_DEF**, then no further action is required (i.e., those macros take care of updating the statement). If changes are made by manipulating the statement's tree directly, then a call must be made to **update_stmt** when complete. Calling one of the **bsi_insert** routines or **bsi_replace** performs an implicit call to **update_stmt**.

12.2.1 Operand Iterators And Access Routines

Operands are collected by 'tree-ssa-operands.c'. They are stored inside each statement's annotation and can be accessed through either the operand iterators or an access routine.

The following access routines are available for examining operands:

1. **SINGLE_SSA_{USE,DEF,TREE}_OPERAND**: These accessors will return NULL unless there is exactly one operand matching the specified flags. If there is exactly one operand, the operand is returned as either a **tree**, **def_operand_p**, or **use_operand_p**.

```
tree t = SINGLE_SSA_TREE_OPERAND (stmt, flags);
use_operand_p u = SINGLE_SSA_USE_OPERAND (stmt, SSA_ALL_VIRTUAL_USES);
def_operand_p d = SINGLE_SSA_DEF_OPERAND (stmt, SSA_OP_ALL_DEFS);
```

2. **ZERO_SSA_OPERANDS**: This macro returns true if there are no operands matching the specified flags.

```
if (ZERO_SSA_OPERANDS (stmt, SSA_OP_ALL_VIRTUALS))
    return;
```

3. **NUM_SSA_OPERANDS**: This macro Returns the number of operands matching 'flags'. This actually executes a loop to perform the count, so only use this if it is really needed.

```
int count = NUM_SSA_OPERANDS (stmt, flags)
```

If you wish to iterate over some or all operands, use the **FOR_EACH_SSA_{USE,DEF,TREE}_OPERAND** iterator. For example, to print all the operands for a statement:

```
void
print_ops (tree stmt)
{
  ssa_op_iter;
  tree var;

  FOR_EACH_SSA_TREE_OPERAND (var, stmt, iter, SSA_OP_ALL_OPERANDS)
    print_generic_expr (stderr, var, TDF_SLIM);
}
```

How to choose the appropriate iterator:

1. Determine whether you are need to see the operand pointers, or just the trees, and choose the appropriate macro:

```
Need          Macro:
----          -------
use_operand_p FOR_EACH_SSA_USE_OPERAND
```

```
def_operand_p      FOR_EACH_SSA_DEF_OPERAND
tree               FOR_EACH_SSA_TREE_OPERAND
```

2. You need to declare a variable of the type you are interested in, and an ssa_op_iter structure which serves as the loop controlling variable.

3. Determine which operands you wish to use, and specify the flags of those you are interested in. They are documented in 'tree-ssa-operands.h':

```
#define SSA_OP_USE            0x01      /* Real USE operands.  */
#define SSA_OP_DEF            0x02      /* Real DEF operands.  */
#define SSA_OP_VUSE           0x04      /* VUSE operands.  */
#define SSA_OP_VDEF           0x08      /* VDEF operands.  */

/* These are commonly grouped operand flags.  */
#define SSA_OP_VIRTUAL_USES (SSA_OP_VUSE)
#define SSA_OP_VIRTUAL_DEFS (SSA_OP_VDEF)
#define SSA_OP_ALL_VIRTUALS   (SSA_OP_VIRTUAL_USES | SSA_OP_VIRTUAL_DEFS)
#define SSA_OP_ALL_USES (SSA_OP_VIRTUAL_USES | SSA_OP_USE)
#define SSA_OP_ALL_DEFS (SSA_OP_VIRTUAL_DEFS | SSA_OP_DEF)
#define SSA_OP_ALL_OPERANDS (SSA_OP_ALL_USES | SSA_OP_ALL_DEFS)
```

So if you want to look at the use pointers for all the USE and VUSE operands, you would do something like:

```
use_operand_p use_p;
ssa_op_iter iter;

FOR_EACH_SSA_USE_OPERAND (use_p, stmt, iter, (SSA_OP_USE | SSA_OP_VUSE))
  {
    process_use_ptr (use_p);
  }
```

The TREE macro is basically the same as the USE and DEF macros, only with the use or def dereferenced via USE_FROM_PTR (use_p) and DEF_FROM_PTR (def_p). Since we aren't using operand pointers, use and defs flags can be mixed.

```
tree var;
ssa_op_iter iter;

FOR_EACH_SSA_TREE_OPERAND (var, stmt, iter, SSA_OP_VUSE)
  {
    print_generic_expr (stderr, var, TDF_SLIM);
  }
```

VDEFs are broken into two flags, one for the DEF portion (SSA_OP_VDEF) and one for the USE portion (SSA_OP_VUSE).

There are many examples in the code, in addition to the documentation in 'tree-ssa-operands.h' and 'ssa-iterators.h'.

There are also a couple of variants on the stmt iterators regarding PHI nodes.

FOR_EACH_PHI_ARG Works exactly like FOR_EACH_SSA_USE_OPERAND, except it works over PHI arguments instead of statement operands.

```
/* Look at every virtual PHI use.  */
FOR_EACH_PHI_ARG (use_p, phi_stmt, iter, SSA_OP_VIRTUAL_USES)
{
   my_code;
}

/* Look at every real PHI use.  */
```

```
FOR_EACH_PHI_ARG (use_p, phi_stmt, iter, SSA_OP_USES)
  my_code;

/* Look at every PHI use. */
FOR_EACH_PHI_ARG (use_p, phi_stmt, iter, SSA_OP_ALL_USES)
  my_code;
```

FOR_EACH_PHI_OR_STMT_{USE,DEF} works exactly like FOR_EACH_SSA_{USE,DEF}_ OPERAND, except it will function on either a statement or a PHI node. These should be used when it is appropriate but they are not quite as efficient as the individual FOR_EACH_PHI and FOR_EACH_SSA routines.

```
FOR_EACH_PHI_OR_STMT_USE (use_operand_p, stmt, iter, flags)
  {
     my_code;
  }

FOR_EACH_PHI_OR_STMT_DEF (def_operand_p, phi, iter, flags)
  {
     my_code;
  }
```

12.2.2 Immediate Uses

Immediate use information is now always available. Using the immediate use iterators, you may examine every use of any SSA_NAME. For instance, to change each use of ssa_var to ssa_var2 and call fold_stmt on each stmt after that is done:

```
use_operand_p imm_use_p;
imm_use_iterator iterator;
tree ssa_var, stmt;


FOR_EACH_IMM_USE_STMT (stmt, iterator, ssa_var)
  {
    FOR_EACH_IMM_USE_ON_STMT (imm_use_p, iterator)
      SET_USE (imm_use_p, ssa_var_2);
    fold_stmt (stmt);
  }
```

There are 2 iterators which can be used. FOR_EACH_IMM_USE_FAST is used when the immediate uses are not changed, i.e., you are looking at the uses, but not setting them.

If they do get changed, then care must be taken that things are not changed under the iterators, so use the FOR_EACH_IMM_USE_STMT and FOR_EACH_IMM_USE_ON_STMT iterators. They attempt to preserve the sanity of the use list by moving all the uses for a statement into a controlled position, and then iterating over those uses. Then the optimization can manipulate the stmt when all the uses have been processed. This is a little slower than the FAST version since it adds a placeholder element and must sort through the list a bit for each statement. This placeholder element must be also removed if the loop is terminated early. The macro BREAK_FROM_IMM_USE_SAFE is provided to do this :

```
FOR_EACH_IMM_USE_STMT (stmt, iterator, ssa_var)
  {
    if (stmt == last_stmt)
      BREAK_FROM_SAFE_IMM_USE (iter);

    FOR_EACH_IMM_USE_ON_STMT (imm_use_p, iterator)
      SET_USE (imm_use_p, ssa_var_2);
```

```
    fold_stmt (stmt);
  }
```

There are checks in `verify_ssa` which verify that the immediate use list is up to date, as well as checking that an optimization didn't break from the loop without using this macro. It is safe to simply 'break'; from a `FOR_EACH_IMM_USE_FAST` traverse.

Some useful functions and macros:

1. `has_zero_uses (ssa_var)` : Returns true if there are no uses of `ssa_var`.

2. `has_single_use (ssa_var)` : Returns true if there is only a single use of `ssa_var`.

3. `single_imm_use (ssa_var, use_operand_p *ptr, tree *stmt)` : Returns true if there is only a single use of `ssa_var`, and also returns the use pointer and statement it occurs in, in the second and third parameters.

4. `num_imm_uses (ssa_var)` : Returns the number of immediate uses of `ssa_var`. It is better not to use this if possible since it simply utilizes a loop to count the uses.

5. `PHI_ARG_INDEX_FROM_USE (use_p)` : Given a use within a `PHI` node, return the index number for the use. An assert is triggered if the use isn't located in a `PHI` node.

6. `USE_STMT (use_p)` : Return the statement a use occurs in.

Note that uses are not put into an immediate use list until their statement is actually inserted into the instruction stream via a `bsi_*` routine.

It is also still possible to utilize lazy updating of statements, but this should be used only when absolutely required. Both alias analysis and the dominator optimizations currently do this.

When lazy updating is being used, the immediate use information is out of date and cannot be used reliably. Lazy updating is achieved by simply marking statements modified via calls to `gimple_set_modified` instead of `update_stmt`. When lazy updating is no longer required, all the modified statements must have `update_stmt` called in order to bring them up to date. This must be done before the optimization is finished, or `verify_ssa` will trigger an abort.

This is done with a simple loop over the instruction stream:

```
block_stmt_iterator bsi;
basic_block bb;
FOR_EACH_BB (bb)
  {
    for (bsi = bsi_start (bb); !bsi_end_p (bsi); bsi_next (&bsi))
      update_stmt_if_modified (bsi_stmt (bsi));
  }
```

12.3 Static Single Assignment

Most of the tree optimizers rely on the data flow information provided by the Static Single Assignment (SSA) form. We implement the SSA form as described in *R. Cytron, J. Ferrante, B. Rosen, M. Wegman, and K. Zadeck. Efficiently Computing Static Single Assignment Form and the Control Dependence Graph. ACM Transactions on Programming Languages and Systems, 13(4):451-490, October 1991.*

The SSA form is based on the premise that program variables are assigned in exactly one location in the program. Multiple assignments to the same variable create new versions of that variable. Naturally, actual programs are seldom in SSA form initially because variables tend to be assigned multiple times. The compiler modifies the program representation so that every time a variable is assigned in the code, a new version of the variable is created. Different versions of the same variable are distinguished by subscripting the variable name with its version number. Variables used in the right-hand side of expressions are renamed so that their version number matches that of the most recent assignment.

We represent variable versions using `SSA_NAME` nodes. The renaming process in 'tree-ssa.c' wraps every real and virtual operand with an `SSA_NAME` node which contains the version number and the statement that created the `SSA_NAME`. Only definitions and virtual definitions may create new `SSA_NAME` nodes.

Sometimes, flow of control makes it impossible to determine the most recent version of a variable. In these cases, the compiler inserts an artificial definition for that variable called *PHI function* or *PHI node*. This new definition merges all the incoming versions of the variable to create a new name for it. For instance,

```
if (...)
  a_1 = 5;
else if (...)
  a_2 = 2;
else
  a_3 = 13;

# a_4 = PHI <a_1, a_2, a_3>
return a_4;
```

Since it is not possible to determine which of the three branches will be taken at runtime, we don't know which of a_1, a_2 or a_3 to use at the return statement. So, the SSA renamer creates a new version a_4 which is assigned the result of "merging" a_1, a_2 and a_3. Hence, PHI nodes mean "one of these operands. I don't know which".

The following functions can be used to examine PHI nodes

`gimple_phi_result (`*phi*`)`   [Function]
> Returns the `SSA_NAME` created by PHI node *phi* (i.e., *phi*'s LHS).

`gimple_phi_num_args (`*phi*`)`   [Function]
> Returns the number of arguments in *phi*. This number is exactly the number of incoming edges to the basic block holding *phi*.

`gimple_phi_arg (`*phi*`, `*i*`)`   [Function]
> Returns *i*th argument of *phi*.

`gimple_phi_arg_edge (`*phi*`, `*i*`)`   [Function]
> Returns the incoming edge for the *i*th argument of *phi*.

`gimple_phi_arg_def (`*phi*`, `*i*`)`   [Function]
> Returns the `SSA_NAME` for the *i*th argument of *phi*.

12.3.1 Preserving the SSA form

Some optimization passes make changes to the function that invalidate the SSA property. This can happen when a pass has added new symbols or changed the program so that variables that were previously aliased aren't anymore. Whenever something like this happens, the affected symbols must be renamed into SSA form again. Transformations that emit new code or replicate existing statements will also need to update the SSA form.

Since GCC implements two different SSA forms for register and virtual variables, keeping the SSA form up to date depends on whether you are updating register or virtual names. In both cases, the general idea behind incremental SSA updates is similar: when new SSA names are created, they typically are meant to replace other existing names in the program.

For instance, given the following code:

```
1  L0:
2  x_1 = PHI (0, x_5)
3  if (x_1 < 10)
4    if (x_1 > 7)
5      y_2 = 0
6    else
7      y_3 = x_1 + x_7
8    endif
9    x_5 = x_1 + 1
10   goto L0;
11 endif
```

Suppose that we insert new names x_10 and x_11 (lines 4 and 8).

```
1  L0:
2  x_1 = PHI (0, x_5)
3  if (x_1 < 10)
4    x_10 = ...
5    if (x_1 > 7)
6      y_2 = 0
7    else
8      x_11 = ...
9      y_3 = x_1 + x_7
10   endif
11   x_5 = x_1 + 1
12   goto L0;
13 endif
```

We want to replace all the uses of x_1 with the new definitions of x_10 and x_11. Note that the only uses that should be replaced are those at lines 5, 9 and 11. Also, the use of x_7 at line 9 should *not* be replaced (this is why we cannot just mark symbol x for renaming).

Additionally, we may need to insert a PHI node at line 11 because that is a merge point for x_10 and x_11. So the use of x_1 at line 11 will be replaced with the new PHI node. The insertion of PHI nodes is optional. They are not strictly necessary to preserve the SSA form, and depending on what the caller inserted, they may not even be useful for the optimizers.

Updating the SSA form is a two step process. First, the pass has to identify which names need to be updated and/or which symbols need to be renamed into SSA form for the first time. When new names are introduced to replace existing names in the program, the mapping between the old and the new names are registered by calling register_new_name_mapping (note that if your pass creates new code by duplicating basic blocks, the call to tree_duplicate_bb will set up the necessary mappings automatically).

After the replacement mappings have been registered and new symbols marked for renaming, a call to update_ssa makes the registered changes. This can be done with an explicit call or by creating TODO flags in the tree_opt_pass structure for your pass. There are several TODO flags that control the behavior of update_ssa:

- `TODO_update_ssa`. Update the SSA form inserting PHI nodes for newly exposed symbols and virtual names marked for updating. When updating real names, only insert PHI nodes for a real name O_j in blocks reached by all the new and old definitions for O_j. If the iterated dominance frontier for O_j is not pruned, we may end up inserting PHI nodes in blocks that have one or more edges with no incoming definition for O_j. This would lead to uninitialized warnings for O_j's symbol.

- `TODO_update_ssa_no_phi`. Update the SSA form without inserting any new PHI nodes at all. This is used by passes that have either inserted all the PHI nodes themselves or passes that need only to patch use-def and def-def chains for virtuals (e.g., DCE).

- `TODO_update_ssa_full_phi`. Insert PHI nodes everywhere they are needed. No pruning of the IDF is done. This is used by passes that need the PHI nodes for O_j even if it means that some arguments will come from the default definition of O_j's symbol (e.g., `pass_linear_transform`).

  WARNING: If you need to use this flag, chances are that your pass may be doing something wrong. Inserting PHI nodes for an old name where not all edges carry a new replacement may lead to silent codegen errors or spurious uninitialized warnings.

- `TODO_update_ssa_only_virtuals`. Passes that update the SSA form on their own may want to delegate the updating of virtual names to the generic updater. Since FUD chains are easier to maintain, this simplifies the work they need to do. NOTE: If this flag is used, any OLD->NEW mappings for real names are explicitly destroyed and only the symbols marked for renaming are processed.

12.3.2 Examining `SSA_NAME` nodes

The following macros can be used to examine `SSA_NAME` nodes

`SSA_NAME_DEF_STMT (var)` [Macro]

> Returns the statement s that creates the `SSA_NAME` var. If s is an empty statement (i.e., `IS_EMPTY_STMT (s)` returns `true`), it means that the first reference to this variable is a USE or a VUSE.

`SSA_NAME_VERSION (var)` [Macro]

> Returns the version number of the `SSA_NAME` object var.

12.3.3 Walking the dominator tree

`void walk_dominator_tree (walk_data, bb)` [Tree SSA function]

> This function walks the dominator tree for the current CFG calling a set of callback functions defined in *struct dom_walk_data* in 'domwalk.h'. The call back functions you need to define give you hooks to execute custom code at various points during traversal:
>
> 1. Once to initialize any local data needed while processing *bb* and its children. This local data is pushed into an internal stack which is automatically pushed and popped as the walker traverses the dominator tree.
> 2. Once before traversing all the statements in the *bb*.
> 3. Once for every statement inside *bb*.
> 4. Once after traversing all the statements and before recursing into *bb*'s dominator children.

5. It then recurses into all the dominator children of *bb*.

6. After recursing into all the dominator children of *bb* it can, optionally, traverse every statement in *bb* again (i.e., repeating steps 2 and 3).

7. Once after walking the statements in *bb* and *bb*'s dominator children. At this stage, the block local data stack is popped.

12.4 Alias analysis

Alias analysis in GIMPLE SSA form consists of two pieces. First the virtual SSA web ties conflicting memory accesses and provides a SSA use-def chain and SSA immediate-use chains for walking possibly dependent memory accesses. Second an alias-oracle can be queried to disambiguate explicit and implicit memory references.

1. Memory SSA form.

   All statements that may use memory have exactly one accompanied use of a virtual SSA name that represents the state of memory at the given point in the IL.

   All statements that may define memory have exactly one accompanied definition of a virtual SSA name using the previous state of memory and defining the new state of memory after the given point in the IL.

   ```
   int i;
   int foo (void)
   {
     # .MEM_3 = VDEF <.MEM_2(D)>
     i = 1;
     # VUSE <.MEM_3>
     return i;
   }
   ```

   The virtual SSA names in this case are .MEM_2(D) and .MEM_3. The store to the global variable i defines .MEM_3 invalidating .MEM_2(D). The load from i uses that new state .MEM_3.

   The virtual SSA web serves as constraints to SSA optimizers preventing illegitimate code-motion and optimization. It also provides a way to walk related memory statements.

2. Points-to and escape analysis.

   Points-to analysis builds a set of constraints from the GIMPLE SSA IL representing all pointer operations and facts we do or do not know about pointers. Solving this set of constraints yields a conservatively correct solution for each pointer variable in the program (though we are only interested in SSA name pointers) as to what it may possibly point to.

   This points-to solution for a given SSA name pointer is stored in the `pt_solution` sub-structure of the `SSA_NAME_PTR_INFO` record. The following accessor functions are available:

   - `pt_solution_includes`
   - `pt_solutions_intersect`

   Points-to analysis also computes the solution for two special set of pointers, `ESCAPED` and `CALLUSED`. Those represent all memory that has escaped the scope of analysis or that is used by pure or nested const calls.

3. Type-based alias analysis

   Type-based alias analysis is frontend dependent though generic support is provided by the middle-end in `alias.c`. TBAA code is used by both tree optimizers and RTL optimizers.

   Every language that wishes to perform language-specific alias analysis should define a function that computes, given a `tree` node, an alias set for the node. Nodes in different alias sets are not allowed to alias. For an example, see the C front-end function `c_get_alias_set`.

4. Tree alias-oracle

   The tree alias-oracle provides means to disambiguate two memory references and memory references against statements. The following queries are available:

   - `refs_may_alias_p`
   - `ref_maybe_used_by_stmt_p`
   - `stmt_may_clobber_ref_p`

   In addition to those two kind of statement walkers are available walking statements related to a reference ref. `walk_non_aliased_vuses` walks over dominating memory defining statements and calls back if the statement does not clobber ref providing the non-aliased VUSE. The walk stops at the first clobbering statement or if asked to. `walk_aliased_vdefs` walks over dominating memory defining statements and calls back on each statement clobbering ref providing its aliasing VDEF. The walk stops if asked to.

12.5 Memory model

The memory model used by the middle-end models that of the C/C++ languages. The middle-end has the notion of an effective type of a memory region which is used for type-based alias analysis.

The following is a refinement of ISO C99 6.5/6, clarifying the block copy case to follow common sense and extending the concept of a dynamic effective type to objects with a declared type as required for C++.

```
The effective type of an object for an access to its stored value is
the declared type of the object or the effective type determined by
a previous store to it.  If a value is stored into an object through
an lvalue having a type that is not a character type, then the
type of the lvalue becomes the effective type of the object for that
access and for subsequent accesses that do not modify the stored value.
If a value is copied into an object using memcpy or memmove,
or is copied as an array of character type, then the effective type
of the modified object for that access and for subsequent accesses that
do not modify the value is undetermined.  For all other accesses to an
object, the effective type of the object is simply the type of the
lvalue used for the access.
```

13 RTL Representation

The last part of the compiler work is done on a low-level intermediate representation called Register Transfer Language. In this language, the instructions to be output are described, pretty much one by one, in an algebraic form that describes what the instruction does.

RTL is inspired by Lisp lists. It has both an internal form, made up of structures that point at other structures, and a textual form that is used in the machine description and in printed debugging dumps. The textual form uses nested parentheses to indicate the pointers in the internal form.

13.1 RTL Object Types

RTL uses five kinds of objects: expressions, integers, wide integers, strings and vectors. Expressions are the most important ones. An RTL expression ("RTX", for short) is a C structure, but it is usually referred to with a pointer; a type that is given the typedef name `rtx`.

An integer is simply an `int`; their written form uses decimal digits. A wide integer is an integral object whose type is `HOST_WIDE_INT`; their written form uses decimal digits.

A string is a sequence of characters. In core it is represented as a `char *` in usual C fashion, and it is written in C syntax as well. However, strings in RTL may never be null. If you write an empty string in a machine description, it is represented in core as a null pointer rather than as a pointer to a null character. In certain contexts, these null pointers instead of strings are valid. Within RTL code, strings are most commonly found inside `symbol_ref` expressions, but they appear in other contexts in the RTL expressions that make up machine descriptions.

In a machine description, strings are normally written with double quotes, as you would in C. However, strings in machine descriptions may extend over many lines, which is invalid C, and adjacent string constants are not concatenated as they are in C. Any string constant may be surrounded with a single set of parentheses. Sometimes this makes the machine description easier to read.

There is also a special syntax for strings, which can be useful when C code is embedded in a machine description. Wherever a string can appear, it is also valid to write a C-style brace block. The entire brace block, including the outermost pair of braces, is considered to be the string constant. Double quote characters inside the braces are not special. Therefore, if you write string constants in the C code, you need not escape each quote character with a backslash.

A vector contains an arbitrary number of pointers to expressions. The number of elements in the vector is explicitly present in the vector. The written form of a vector consists of square brackets ('[...]') surrounding the elements, in sequence and with whitespace separating them. Vectors of length zero are not created; null pointers are used instead.

Expressions are classified by *expression codes* (also called RTX codes). The expression code is a name defined in '`rtl.def`', which is also (in uppercase) a C enumeration constant. The possible expression codes and their meanings are machine-independent. The code of an RTX can be extracted with the macro `GET_CODE (x)` and altered with `PUT_CODE (x, newcode)`.

The expression code determines how many operands the expression contains, and what kinds of objects they are. In RTL, unlike Lisp, you cannot tell by looking at an operand what kind of object it is. Instead, you must know from its context—from the expression code of the containing expression. For example, in an expression of code `subreg`, the first operand is to be regarded as an expression and the second operand as an integer. In an expression of code `plus`, there are two operands, both of which are to be regarded as expressions. In a `symbol_ref` expression, there is one operand, which is to be regarded as a string.

Expressions are written as parentheses containing the name of the expression type, its flags and machine mode if any, and then the operands of the expression (separated by spaces).

Expression code names in the 'md' file are written in lowercase, but when they appear in C code they are written in uppercase. In this manual, they are shown as follows: `const_int`.

In a few contexts a null pointer is valid where an expression is normally wanted. The written form of this is `(nil)`.

13.2 RTL Classes and Formats

The various expression codes are divided into several *classes*, which are represented by single characters. You can determine the class of an RTX code with the macro `GET_RTX_CLASS` (*code*). Currently, 'rtl.def' defines these classes:

RTX_OBJ   An RTX code that represents an actual object, such as a register (`REG`) or a memory location (`MEM`, `SYMBOL_REF`). `LO_SUM`) is also included; instead, `SUBREG` and `STRICT_LOW_PART` are not in this class, but in class `x`.

RTX_CONST_OBJ

     An RTX code that represents a constant object. `HIGH` is also included in this class.

RTX_COMPARE

     An RTX code for a non-symmetric comparison, such as `GEU` or `LT`.

RTX_COMM_COMPARE

     An RTX code for a symmetric (commutative) comparison, such as `EQ` or `ORDERED`.

RTX_UNARY

     An RTX code for a unary arithmetic operation, such as `NEG`, `NOT`, or `ABS`. This category also includes value extension (sign or zero) and conversions between integer and floating point.

RTX_COMM_ARITH

     An RTX code for a commutative binary operation, such as `PLUS` or `AND`. `NE` and `EQ` are comparisons, so they have class `<`.

RTX_BIN_ARITH

     An RTX code for a non-commutative binary operation, such as `MINUS`, `DIV`, or `ASHIFTRT`.

RTX_BITFIELD_OPS

> An RTX code for a bit-field operation. Currently only `ZERO_EXTRACT` and `SIGN_EXTRACT`. These have three inputs and are lvalues (so they can be used for insertion as well). See Section 13.11 [Bit-Fields], page 261.

RTX_TERNARY

> An RTX code for other three input operations. Currently only `IF_THEN_ELSE`, `VEC_MERGE`, `SIGN_EXTRACT`, `ZERO_EXTRACT`, and `FMA`.

RTX_INSN   An RTX code for an entire instruction: `INSN`, `JUMP_INSN`, and `CALL_INSN`. See Section 13.19 [Insns], page 271.

RTX_MATCH

> An RTX code for something that matches in insns, such as `MATCH_DUP`. These only occur in machine descriptions.

RTX_AUTOINC

> An RTX code for an auto-increment addressing mode, such as `POST_INC`. 'XEXP (x, 0)' gives the auto-modified register.

RTX_EXTRA

> All other RTX codes. This category includes the remaining codes used only in machine descriptions (`DEFINE_*`, etc.). It also includes all the codes describing side effects (`SET`, `USE`, `CLOBBER`, etc.) and the non-insns that may appear on an insn chain, such as `NOTE`, `BARRIER`, and `CODE_LABEL`. `SUBREG` is also part of this class.

For each expression code, 'rtl.def' specifies the number of contained objects and their kinds using a sequence of characters called the *format* of the expression code. For example, the format of subreg is 'ei'.

These are the most commonly used format characters:

e   An expression (actually a pointer to an expression).

i   An integer.

w   A wide integer.

s   A string.

E   A vector of expressions.

A few other format characters are used occasionally:

u   'u' is equivalent to 'e' except that it is printed differently in debugging dumps. It is used for pointers to insns.

n   'n' is equivalent to 'i' except that it is printed differently in debugging dumps. It is used for the line number or code number of a `note` insn.

S   'S' indicates a string which is optional. In the RTL objects in core, 'S' is equivalent to 's', but when the object is read, from an 'md' file, the string value of this operand may be omitted. An omitted string is taken to be the null string.

V   'V' indicates a vector which is optional. In the RTL objects in core, 'V' is
                     equivalent to 'E', but when the object is read from an 'md' file, the vector value
                     of this operand may be omitted. An omitted vector is effectively the same as a
                     vector of no elements.

B   'B' indicates a pointer to basic block structure.

0   '0' means a slot whose contents do not fit any normal category. '0' slots are
                     not printed at all in dumps, and are often used in special ways by small parts
                     of the compiler.

There are macros to get the number of operands and the format of an expression code:

GET_RTX_LENGTH (*code*)
                     Number of operands of an RTX of code *code*.

GET_RTX_FORMAT (*code*)
                     The format of an RTX of code *code*, as a C string.

Some classes of RTX codes always have the same format. For example, it is safe to assume
that all comparison operations have format **ee**.

1   All codes of this class have format **e**.

<
c
2   All codes of these classes have format **ee**.

b
3   All codes of these classes have format **eee**.

i   All codes of this class have formats that begin with **iuueiee**. See Section 13.19
                     [Insns], page 271. Note that not all RTL objects linked onto an insn chain are
                     of class **i**.

o
m
x   You can make no assumptions about the format of these codes.

13.3 Access to Operands

Operands of expressions are accessed using the macros **XEXP**, **XINT**, **XWINT** and **XSTR**. Each
of these macros takes two arguments: an expression-pointer (RTX) and an operand number
(counting from zero). Thus,

        XEXP (*x*, 2)

accesses operand 2 of expression *x*, as an expression.

        XINT (*x*, 2)

accesses the same operand as an integer. **XSTR**, used in the same fashion, would access it as
a string.

Any operand can be accessed as an integer, as an expression or as a string. You must
choose the correct method of access for the kind of value actually stored in the operand.
You would do this based on the expression code of the containing expression. That is also
how you would know how many operands there are.

For example, if x is a `subreg` expression, you know that it has two operands which can be correctly accessed as `XEXP (x, 0)` and `XINT (x, 1)`. If you did `XINT (x, 0)`, you would get the address of the expression operand but cast as an integer; that might occasionally be useful, but it would be cleaner to write `(int) XEXP (x, 0)`. `XEXP (x, 1)` would also compile without error, and would return the second, integer operand cast as an expression pointer, which would probably result in a crash when accessed. Nothing stops you from writing `XEXP (x, 28)` either, but this will access memory past the end of the expression with unpredictable results.

Access to operands which are vectors is more complicated. You can use the macro `XVEC` to get the vector-pointer itself, or the macros `XVECEXP` and `XVECLEN` to access the elements and length of a vector.

`XVEC (exp, idx)`

> Access the vector-pointer which is operand number *idx* in *exp*.

`XVECLEN (exp, idx)`

> Access the length (number of elements) in the vector which is in operand number *idx* in *exp*. This value is an `int`.

`XVECEXP (exp, idx, eltnum)`

> Access element number *eltnum* in the vector which is in operand number *idx* in *exp*. This value is an RTX.
>
> It is up to you to make sure that *eltnum* is not negative and is less than `XVECLEN (exp, idx)`.

All the macros defined in this section expand into lvalues and therefore can be used to assign the operands, lengths and vector elements as well as to access them.

13.4 Access to Special Operands

Some RTL nodes have special annotations associated with them.

MEM

> `MEM_ALIAS_SET (x)`
>
> > If 0, x is not in any alias set, and may alias anything. Otherwise, x can only alias MEMs in a conflicting alias set. This value is set in a language-dependent manner in the front-end, and should not be altered in the back-end. In some front-ends, these numbers may correspond in some way to types, or other language-level entities, but they need not, and the back-end makes no such assumptions. These set numbers are tested with `alias_sets_conflict_p`.
>
> `MEM_EXPR (x)`
>
> > If this register is known to hold the value of some user-level declaration, this is that tree node. It may also be a `COMPONENT_REF`, in which case this is some field reference, and `TREE_OPERAND (x, 0)` contains the declaration, or another `COMPONENT_REF`, or null if there is no compile-time object associated with the reference.

MEM_OFFSET_KNOWN_P (x)

> True if the offset of the memory reference from `MEM_EXPR` is known. '`MEM_OFFSET` (x)' provides the offset if so.

MEM_OFFSET (x)

> The offset from the start of `MEM_EXPR`. The value is only valid if '`MEM_OFFSET_KNOWN_P` (x)' is true.

MEM_SIZE_KNOWN_P (x)

> True if the size of the memory reference is known. '`MEM_SIZE` (x)' provides its size if so.

MEM_SIZE (x)

> The size in bytes of the memory reference. This is mostly relevant for `BLKmode` references as otherwise the size is implied by the mode. The value is only valid if '`MEM_SIZE_KNOWN_P` (x)' is true.

MEM_ALIGN (x)

> The known alignment in bits of the memory reference.

MEM_ADDR_SPACE (x)

> The address space of the memory reference. This will commonly be zero for the generic address space.

REG

ORIGINAL_REGNO (x)

> This field holds the number the register "originally" had; for a pseudo register turned into a hard reg this will hold the old pseudo register number.

REG_EXPR (x)

> If this register is known to hold the value of some user-level declaration, this is that tree node.

REG_OFFSET (x)

> If this register is known to hold the value of some user-level declaration, this is the offset into that logical storage.

SYMBOL_REF

SYMBOL_REF_DECL (x)

> If the `symbol_ref` x was created for a `VAR_DECL` or a `FUNCTION_DECL`, that tree is recorded here. If this value is null, then x was created by back end code generation routines, and there is no associated front end symbol table entry.
>
> `SYMBOL_REF_DECL` may also point to a tree of class '`c`', that is, some sort of constant. In this case, the `symbol_ref` is an entry in the per-file constant pool; again, there is no associated front end symbol table entry.

SYMBOL_REF_CONSTANT (x)

> If '`CONSTANT_POOL_ADDRESS_P` (x)' is true, this is the constant pool entry for x. It is null otherwise.

SYMBOL_REF_DATA (*x*)

> A field of opaque type used to store SYMBOL_REF_DECL or SYMBOL_REF_CONSTANT.

SYMBOL_REF_FLAGS (*x*)

> In a symbol_ref, this is used to communicate various predicates about the symbol. Some of these are common enough to be computed by common code, some are specific to the target. The common bits are:

> SYMBOL_FLAG_FUNCTION
>
> > Set if the symbol refers to a function.

> SYMBOL_FLAG_LOCAL
>
> > Set if the symbol is local to this "module". See TARGET_BINDS_LOCAL_P.

> SYMBOL_FLAG_EXTERNAL
>
> > Set if this symbol is not defined in this translation unit. Note that this is not the inverse of SYMBOL_FLAG_LOCAL.

> SYMBOL_FLAG_SMALL
>
> > Set if the symbol is located in the small data section. See TARGET_IN_SMALL_DATA_P.

> SYMBOL_REF_TLS_MODEL (*x*)
>
> > This is a multi-bit field accessor that returns the tls_model to be used for a thread-local storage symbol. It returns zero for non-thread-local symbols.

> SYMBOL_FLAG_HAS_BLOCK_INFO
>
> > Set if the symbol has SYMBOL_REF_BLOCK and SYMBOL_REF_BLOCK_OFFSET fields.

> SYMBOL_FLAG_ANCHOR
>
> > Set if the symbol is used as a section anchor. "Section anchors" are symbols that have a known position within an object_block and that can be used to access nearby members of that block. They are used to implement '-fsection-anchors'.
> >
> > If this flag is set, then SYMBOL_FLAG_HAS_BLOCK_INFO will be too.

> Bits beginning with SYMBOL_FLAG_MACH_DEP are available for the target's use.

SYMBOL_REF_BLOCK (*x*)

> If 'SYMBOL_REF_HAS_BLOCK_INFO_P (*x*)', this is the 'object_block' structure to which the symbol belongs, or NULL if it has not been assigned a block.

SYMBOL_REF_BLOCK_OFFSET (x)

> If 'SYMBOL_REF_HAS_BLOCK_INFO_P (x)', this is the offset of x from the first object in 'SYMBOL_REF_BLOCK (x)'. The value is negative if x has not yet been assigned to a block, or it has not been given an offset within that block.

13.5 Flags in an RTL Expression

RTL expressions contain several flags (one-bit bit-fields) that are used in certain types of expression. Most often they are accessed with the following macros, which expand into lvalues.

CONSTANT_POOL_ADDRESS_P (x)

> Nonzero in a symbol_ref if it refers to part of the current function's constant pool. For most targets these addresses are in a .rodata section entirely separate from the function, but for some targets the addresses are close to the beginning of the function. In either case GCC assumes these addresses can be addressed directly, perhaps with the help of base registers. Stored in the unchanging field and printed as '/u'.

RTL_CONST_CALL_P (x)

> In a call_insn indicates that the insn represents a call to a const function. Stored in the unchanging field and printed as '/u'.

RTL_PURE_CALL_P (x)

> In a call_insn indicates that the insn represents a call to a pure function. Stored in the return_val field and printed as '/i'.

RTL_CONST_OR_PURE_CALL_P (x)

> In a call_insn, true if RTL_CONST_CALL_P or RTL_PURE_CALL_P is true.

RTL_LOOPING_CONST_OR_PURE_CALL_P (x)

> In a call_insn indicates that the insn represents a possibly infinite looping call to a const or pure function. Stored in the call field and printed as '/c'. Only true if one of RTL_CONST_CALL_P or RTL_PURE_CALL_P is true.

INSN_ANNULLED_BRANCH_P (x)

> In a jump_insn, call_insn, or insn indicates that the branch is an annulling one. See the discussion under sequence below. Stored in the unchanging field and printed as '/u'.

INSN_DELETED_P (x)

> In an insn, call_insn, jump_insn, code_label, jump_table_data, barrier, or note, nonzero if the insn has been deleted. Stored in the volatil field and printed as '/v'.

INSN_FROM_TARGET_P (x)

> In an insn or jump_insn or call_insn in a delay slot of a branch, indicates that the insn is from the target of the branch. If the branch insn has INSN_ANNULLED_BRANCH_P set, this insn will only be executed if the branch is taken. For annulled branches with INSN_FROM_TARGET_P clear, the insn will be executed only if the branch is not taken. When INSN_ANNULLED_BRANCH_P is not set, this insn will always be executed. Stored in the in_struct field and printed as '/s'.

LABEL_PRESERVE_P (*x*)

> In a `code_label` or `note`, indicates that the label is referenced by code or data not visible to the RTL of a given function. Labels referenced by a non-local goto will have this bit set. Stored in the `in_struct` field and printed as '/s'.

LABEL_REF_NONLOCAL_P (*x*)

> In `label_ref` and `reg_label` expressions, nonzero if this is a reference to a non-local label. Stored in the `volatil` field and printed as '/v'.

MEM_KEEP_ALIAS_SET_P (*x*)

> In `mem` expressions, 1 if we should keep the alias set for this mem unchanged when we access a component. Set to 1, for example, when we are already in a non-addressable component of an aggregate. Stored in the `jump` field and printed as '/j'.

MEM_VOLATILE_P (*x*)

> In `mem`, `asm_operands`, and `asm_input` expressions, nonzero for volatile memory references. Stored in the `volatil` field and printed as '/v'.

MEM_NOTRAP_P (*x*)

> In `mem`, nonzero for memory references that will not trap. Stored in the `call` field and printed as '/c'.

MEM_POINTER (*x*)

> Nonzero in a `mem` if the memory reference holds a pointer. Stored in the `frame_related` field and printed as '/f'.

REG_FUNCTION_VALUE_P (*x*)

> Nonzero in a `reg` if it is the place in which this function's value is going to be returned. (This happens only in a hard register.) Stored in the `return_val` field and printed as '/i'.

REG_POINTER (*x*)

> Nonzero in a `reg` if the register holds a pointer. Stored in the `frame_related` field and printed as '/f'.

REG_USERVAR_P (*x*)

> In a `reg`, nonzero if it corresponds to a variable present in the user's source code. Zero for temporaries generated internally by the compiler. Stored in the `volatil` field and printed as '/v'.
>
> The same hard register may be used also for collecting the values of functions called by this one, but `REG_FUNCTION_VALUE_P` is zero in this kind of use.

RTX_FRAME_RELATED_P (*x*)

> Nonzero in an `insn`, `call_insn`, `jump_insn`, `barrier`, or `set` which is part of a function prologue and sets the stack pointer, sets the frame pointer, or saves a register. This flag should also be set on an instruction that sets up a temporary register to use in place of the frame pointer. Stored in the `frame_related` field and printed as '/f'.
>
> In particular, on RISC targets where there are limits on the sizes of immediate constants, it is sometimes impossible to reach the register save area directly from

the stack pointer. In that case, a temporary register is used that is near enough to the register save area, and the Canonical Frame Address, i.e., DWARF2's logical frame pointer, register must (temporarily) be changed to be this temporary register. So, the instruction that sets this temporary register must be marked as `RTX_FRAME_RELATED_P`.

If the marked instruction is overly complex (defined in terms of what `dwarf2out_frame_debug_expr` can handle), you will also have to create a `REG_FRAME_RELATED_EXPR` note and attach it to the instruction. This note should contain a simple expression of the computation performed by this instruction, i.e., one that `dwarf2out_frame_debug_expr` can handle.

This flag is required for exception handling support on targets with RTL prologues.

`MEM_READONLY_P` (*x*)

Nonzero in a `mem`, if the memory is statically allocated and read-only.

Read-only in this context means never modified during the lifetime of the program, not necessarily in ROM or in write-disabled pages. A common example of the later is a shared library's global offset table. This table is initialized by the runtime loader, so the memory is technically writable, but after control is transferred from the runtime loader to the application, this memory will never be subsequently modified.

Stored in the `unchanging` field and printed as '/u'.

`SCHED_GROUP_P` (*x*)

During instruction scheduling, in an `insn`, `call_insn`, `jump_insn` or `jump_table_data`, indicates that the previous insn must be scheduled together with this insn. This is used to ensure that certain groups of instructions will not be split up by the instruction scheduling pass, for example, `use` insns before a `call_insn` may not be separated from the `call_insn`. Stored in the `in_struct` field and printed as '/s'.

`SET_IS_RETURN_P` (*x*)

For a `set`, nonzero if it is for a return. Stored in the `jump` field and printed as '/j'.

`SIBLING_CALL_P` (*x*)

For a `call_insn`, nonzero if the insn is a sibling call. Stored in the `jump` field and printed as '/j'.

`STRING_POOL_ADDRESS_P` (*x*)

For a `symbol_ref` expression, nonzero if it addresses this function's string constant pool. Stored in the `frame_related` field and printed as '/f'.

`SUBREG_PROMOTED_UNSIGNED_P` (*x*)

Returns a value greater then zero for a `subreg` that has `SUBREG_PROMOTED_VAR_P` nonzero if the object being referenced is kept zero-extended, zero if it is kept sign-extended, and less then zero if it is extended some other way via the `ptr_extend` instruction. Stored in the `unchanging` field and `volatil` field, printed as '/u' and '/v'. This macro may only be used to get the value it may not be used to change the value. Use `SUBREG_PROMOTED_UNSIGNED_SET` to change the value.

`SUBREG_PROMOTED_UNSIGNED_SET` (x)

> Set the `unchanging` and `volatil` fields in a `subreg` to reflect zero, sign, or other extension. If `volatil` is zero, then `unchanging` as nonzero means zero extension and as zero means sign extension. If `volatil` is nonzero then some other type of extension was done via the `ptr_extend` instruction.

`SUBREG_PROMOTED_VAR_P` (x)

> Nonzero in a `subreg` if it was made when accessing an object that was promoted to a wider mode in accord with the `PROMOTED_MODE` machine description macro (see Section 17.5 [Storage Layout], page 444). In this case, the mode of the `subreg` is the declared mode of the object and the mode of `SUBREG_REG` is the mode of the register that holds the object. Promoted variables are always either sign- or zero-extended to the wider mode on every assignment. Stored in the `in_struct` field and printed as '/s'.

`SYMBOL_REF_USED` (x)

> In a `symbol_ref`, indicates that x has been used. This is normally only used to ensure that x is only declared external once. Stored in the `used` field.

`SYMBOL_REF_WEAK` (x)

> In a `symbol_ref`, indicates that x has been declared weak. Stored in the `return_val` field and printed as '/i'.

`SYMBOL_REF_FLAG` (x)

> In a `symbol_ref`, this is used as a flag for machine-specific purposes. Stored in the `volatil` field and printed as '/v'.

> Most uses of `SYMBOL_REF_FLAG` are historic and may be subsumed by `SYMBOL_REF_FLAGS`. Certainly use of `SYMBOL_REF_FLAGS` is mandatory if the target requires more than one bit of storage.

`PREFETCH_SCHEDULE_BARRIER_P` (x)

> In a `prefetch`, indicates that the prefetch is a scheduling barrier. No other INSNs will be moved over it. Stored in the `volatil` field and printed as '/v'.

These are the fields to which the above macros refer:

`call`

> In a `mem`, 1 means that the memory reference will not trap.
>
> In a `call`, 1 means that this pure or const call may possibly infinite loop.
>
> In an RTL dump, this flag is represented as '/c'.

`frame_related`

> In an `insn` or `set` expression, 1 means that it is part of a function prologue and sets the stack pointer, sets the frame pointer, saves a register, or sets up a temporary register to use in place of the frame pointer.
>
> In `reg` expressions, 1 means that the register holds a pointer.
>
> In `mem` expressions, 1 means that the memory reference holds a pointer.
>
> In `symbol_ref` expressions, 1 means that the reference addresses this function's string constant pool.

In an RTL dump, this flag is represented as '/f'.

in_struct

In `reg` expressions, it is 1 if the register has its entire life contained within the test expression of some loop.

In `subreg` expressions, 1 means that the `subreg` is accessing an object that has had its mode promoted from a wider mode.

In `label_ref` expressions, 1 means that the referenced label is outside the innermost loop containing the insn in which the `label_ref` was found.

In `code_label` expressions, it is 1 if the label may never be deleted. This is used for labels which are the target of non-local gotos. Such a label that would have been deleted is replaced with a `note` of type `NOTE_INSN_DELETED_LABEL`.

In an `insn` during dead-code elimination, 1 means that the insn is dead code.

In an `insn` or `jump_insn` during reorg for an insn in the delay slot of a branch, 1 means that this insn is from the target of the branch.

In an `insn` during instruction scheduling, 1 means that this insn must be scheduled as part of a group together with the previous insn.

In an RTL dump, this flag is represented as '/s'.

return_val

In `reg` expressions, 1 means the register contains the value to be returned by the current function. On machines that pass parameters in registers, the same register number may be used for parameters as well, but this flag is not set on such uses.

In `symbol_ref` expressions, 1 means the referenced symbol is weak.

In `call` expressions, 1 means the call is pure.

In an RTL dump, this flag is represented as '/i'.

jump

In a `mem` expression, 1 means we should keep the alias set for this mem unchanged when we access a component.

In a `set`, 1 means it is for a return.

In a `call_insn`, 1 means it is a sibling call.

In an RTL dump, this flag is represented as '/j'.

unchanging

In `reg` and `mem` expressions, 1 means that the value of the expression never changes.

In `subreg` expressions, it is 1 if the `subreg` references an unsigned object whose mode has been promoted to a wider mode.

In an `insn` or `jump_insn` in the delay slot of a branch instruction, 1 means an annulling branch should be used.

In a `symbol_ref` expression, 1 means that this symbol addresses something in the per-function constant pool.

In a `call_insn` 1 means that this instruction is a call to a const function.

In an RTL dump, this flag is represented as '/u'.

used This flag is used directly (without an access macro) at the end of RTL generation for a function, to count the number of times an expression appears in insns. Expressions that appear more than once are copied, according to the rules for shared structure (see Section 13.21 [Sharing], page 280).

For a **reg**, it is used directly (without an access macro) by the leaf register renumbering code to ensure that each register is only renumbered once.

In a **symbol_ref**, it indicates that an external declaration for the symbol has already been written.

volatil In a **mem**, **asm_operands**, or **asm_input** expression, it is 1 if the memory reference is volatile. Volatile memory references may not be deleted, reordered or combined.

In a **symbol_ref** expression, it is used for machine-specific purposes.

In a **reg** expression, it is 1 if the value is a user-level variable. 0 indicates an internal compiler temporary.

In an **insn**, 1 means the insn has been deleted.

In **label_ref** and **reg_label** expressions, 1 means a reference to a non-local label.

In **prefetch** expressions, 1 means that the containing insn is a scheduling barrier.

In an RTL dump, this flag is represented as '/v'.

13.6 Machine Modes

A machine mode describes a size of data object and the representation used for it. In the C code, machine modes are represented by an enumeration type, **machine_mode**, defined in 'machmode.def'. Each RTL expression has room for a machine mode and so do certain kinds of tree expressions (declarations and types, to be precise).

In debugging dumps and machine descriptions, the machine mode of an RTL expression is written after the expression code with a colon to separate them. The letters 'mode' which appear at the end of each machine mode name are omitted. For example, (reg:SI 38) is a **reg** expression with machine mode SImode. If the mode is VOIDmode, it is not written at all.

Here is a table of machine modes. The term "byte" below refers to an object of BITS_PER_UNIT bits (see Section 17.5 [Storage Layout], page 444).

BImode "Bit" mode represents a single bit, for predicate registers.

QImode "Quarter-Integer" mode represents a single byte treated as an integer.

HImode "Half-Integer" mode represents a two-byte integer.

PSImode "Partial Single Integer" mode represents an integer which occupies four bytes but which doesn't really use all four. On some machines, this is the right mode to use for pointers.

SImode "Single Integer" mode represents a four-byte integer.

PDImode   "Partial Double Integer" mode represents an integer which occupies eight bytes but which doesn't really use all eight. On some machines, this is the right mode to use for certain pointers.

DImode   "Double Integer" mode represents an eight-byte integer.

TImode   "Tetra Integer" (?) mode represents a sixteen-byte integer.

OImode   "Octa Integer" (?) mode represents a thirty-two-byte integer.

XImode   "Hexadeca Integer" (?) mode represents a sixty-four-byte integer.

QFmode   "Quarter-Floating" mode represents a quarter-precision (single byte) floating point number.

HFmode   "Half-Floating" mode represents a half-precision (two byte) floating point number.

TQFmode   "Three-Quarter-Floating" (?) mode represents a three-quarter-precision (three byte) floating point number.

SFmode   "Single Floating" mode represents a four byte floating point number. In the common case, of a processor with IEEE arithmetic and 8-bit bytes, this is a single-precision IEEE floating point number; it can also be used for double-precision (on processors with 16-bit bytes) and single-precision VAX and IBM types.

DFmode   "Double Floating" mode represents an eight byte floating point number. In the common case, of a processor with IEEE arithmetic and 8-bit bytes, this is a double-precision IEEE floating point number.

XFmode   "Extended Floating" mode represents an IEEE extended floating point number. This mode only has 80 meaningful bits (ten bytes). Some processors require such numbers to be padded to twelve bytes, others to sixteen; this mode is used for either.

SDmode   "Single Decimal Floating" mode represents a four byte decimal floating point number (as distinct from conventional binary floating point).

DDmode   "Double Decimal Floating" mode represents an eight byte decimal floating point number.

TDmode   "Tetra Decimal Floating" mode represents a sixteen byte decimal floating point number all 128 of whose bits are meaningful.

TFmode   "Tetra Floating" mode represents a sixteen byte floating point number all 128 of whose bits are meaningful. One common use is the IEEE quad-precision format.

QQmode   "Quarter-Fractional" mode represents a single byte treated as a signed fractional number. The default format is "s.7".

HQmode   "Half-Fractional" mode represents a two-byte signed fractional number. The default format is "s.15".

SQmode   "Single Fractional" mode represents a four-byte signed fractional number. The default format is "s.31".

DQmode   "Double Fractional" mode represents an eight-byte signed fractional number. The default format is "s.63".

TQmode   "Tetra Fractional" mode represents a sixteen-byte signed fractional number. The default format is "s.127".

UQQmode   "Unsigned Quarter-Fractional" mode represents a single byte treated as an unsigned fractional number. The default format is ".8".

UHQmode   "Unsigned Half-Fractional" mode represents a two-byte unsigned fractional number. The default format is ".16".

USQmode   "Unsigned Single Fractional" mode represents a four-byte unsigned fractional number. The default format is ".32".

UDQmode   "Unsigned Double Fractional" mode represents an eight-byte unsigned fractional number. The default format is ".64".

UTQmode   "Unsigned Tetra Fractional" mode represents a sixteen-byte unsigned fractional number. The default format is ".128".

HAmode   "Half-Accumulator" mode represents a two-byte signed accumulator. The default format is "s8.7".

SAmode   "Single Accumulator" mode represents a four-byte signed accumulator. The default format is "s16.15".

DAmode   "Double Accumulator" mode represents an eight-byte signed accumulator. The default format is "s32.31".

TAmode   "Tetra Accumulator" mode represents a sixteen-byte signed accumulator. The default format is "s64.63".

UHAmode   "Unsigned Half-Accumulator" mode represents a two-byte unsigned accumulator. The default format is "8.8".

USAmode   "Unsigned Single Accumulator" mode represents a four-byte unsigned accumulator. The default format is "16.16".

UDAmode   "Unsigned Double Accumulator" mode represents an eight-byte unsigned accumulator. The default format is "32.32".

UTAmode   "Unsigned Tetra Accumulator" mode represents a sixteen-byte unsigned accumulator. The default format is "64.64".

CCmode   "Condition Code" mode represents the value of a condition code, which is a machine-specific set of bits used to represent the result of a comparison operation. Other machine-specific modes may also be used for the condition code. These modes are not used on machines that use cc0 (see Section 17.15 [Condition Code], page 521).

BLKmode   "Block" mode represents values that are aggregates to which none of the other modes apply. In RTL, only memory references can have this mode, and only if they appear in string-move or vector instructions. On machines which have no such instructions, BLKmode will not appear in RTL.

VOIDmode   Void mode means the absence of a mode or an unspecified mode. For example,
             RTL expressions of code `const_int` have mode `VOIDmode` because they can be
             taken to have whatever mode the context requires. In debugging dumps of
             RTL, `VOIDmode` is expressed by the absence of any mode.

QCmode, HCmode, SCmode, DCmode, XCmode, TCmode
             These modes stand for a complex number represented as a pair of floating
             point values. The floating point values are in `QFmode`, `HFmode`, `SFmode`, `DFmode`,
             `XFmode`, and `TFmode`, respectively.

CQImode, CHImode, CSImode, CDImode, CTImode, COImode
             These modes stand for a complex number represented as a pair of integer values.
             The integer values are in `QImode`, `HImode`, `SImode`, `DImode`, `TImode`, and `OImode`,
             respectively.

BND32mode BND64mode
             These modes stand for bounds for pointer of 32 and 64 bit size respectively.
             Mode size is double pointer mode size.

The machine description defines `Pmode` as a C macro which expands into the machine
mode used for addresses. Normally this is the mode whose size is `BITS_PER_WORD`, `SImode`
on 32-bit machines.

The only modes which a machine description *must* support are `QImode`, and the modes
corresponding to `BITS_PER_WORD`, `FLOAT_TYPE_SIZE` and `DOUBLE_TYPE_SIZE`. The compiler
will attempt to use `DImode` for 8-byte structures and unions, but this can be prevented by
overriding the definition of `MAX_FIXED_MODE_SIZE`. Alternatively, you can have the compiler
use `TImode` for 16-byte structures and unions. Likewise, you can arrange for the C type
`short int` to avoid using `HImode`.

Very few explicit references to machine modes remain in the compiler and these few
references will soon be removed. Instead, the machine modes are divided into mode classes.
These are represented by the enumeration type `enum mode_class` defined in 'machmode.h'.
The possible mode classes are:

MODE_INT   Integer modes. By default these are `BImode`, `QImode`, `HImode`, `SImode`, `DImode`,
             `TImode`, and `OImode`.

MODE_PARTIAL_INT
             The "partial integer" modes, `PQImode`, `PHImode`, `PSImode` and `PDImode`.

MODE_FLOAT
             Floating point modes. By default these are `QFmode`, `HFmode`, `TQFmode`, `SFmode`,
             `DFmode`, `XFmode` and `TFmode`.

MODE_DECIMAL_FLOAT
             Decimal floating point modes. By default these are `SDmode`, `DDmode` and `TDmode`.

MODE_FRACT
             Signed fractional modes. By default these are `QQmode`, `HQmode`, `SQmode`, `DQmode`
             and `TQmode`.

MODE_UFRACT
             Unsigned fractional modes. By default these are `UQQmode`, `UHQmode`, `USQmode`,
             `UDQmode` and `UTQmode`.

MODE_ACCUM

> Signed accumulator modes. By default these are HAmode, SAmode, DAmode and TAmode.

MODE_UACCUM

> Unsigned accumulator modes. By default these are UHAmode, USAmode, UDAmode and UTAmode.

MODE_COMPLEX_INT

> Complex integer modes. (These are not currently implemented).

MODE_COMPLEX_FLOAT

> Complex floating point modes. By default these are QCmode, HCmode, SCmode, DCmode, XCmode, and TCmode.

MODE_FUNCTION

> Algol or Pascal function variables including a static chain. (These are not currently implemented).

MODE_CC Modes representing condition code values. These are CCmode plus any CC_MODE modes listed in the 'machine-modes.def'. See Section 16.12 [Jump Patterns], page 390, also see Section 17.15 [Condition Code], page 521.

MODE_POINTER_BOUNDS

> Pointer bounds modes. Used to represent values of pointer bounds type. Operations in these modes may be executed as NOPs depending on hardware features and environment setup.

MODE_RANDOM

> This is a catchall mode class for modes which don't fit into the above classes. Currently VOIDmode and BLKmode are in MODE_RANDOM.

Here are some C macros that relate to machine modes:

GET_MODE (x)

> Returns the machine mode of the RTX x.

PUT_MODE (x, newmode)

> Alters the machine mode of the RTX x to be newmode.

NUM_MACHINE_MODES

> Stands for the number of machine modes available on the target machine. This is one greater than the largest numeric value of any machine mode.

GET_MODE_NAME (m)

> Returns the name of mode m as a string.

GET_MODE_CLASS (m)

> Returns the mode class of mode m.

GET_MODE_WIDER_MODE (m)

> Returns the next wider natural mode. For example, the expression GET_MODE_WIDER_MODE (QImode) returns HImode.

GET_MODE_SIZE (m)

> Returns the size in bytes of a datum of mode m.

GET_MODE_BITSIZE (*m*)

> Returns the size in bits of a datum of mode *m*.

GET_MODE_IBIT (*m*)

> Returns the number of integral bits of a datum of fixed-point mode *m*.

GET_MODE_FBIT (*m*)

> Returns the number of fractional bits of a datum of fixed-point mode *m*.

GET_MODE_MASK (*m*)

> Returns a bitmask containing 1 for all bits in a word that fit within mode *m*. This macro can only be used for modes whose bitsize is less than or equal to HOST_BITS_PER_INT.

GET_MODE_ALIGNMENT (*m*)

> Return the required alignment, in bits, for an object of mode *m*.

GET_MODE_UNIT_SIZE (*m*)

> Returns the size in bytes of the subunits of a datum of mode *m*. This is the same as GET_MODE_SIZE except in the case of complex modes. For them, the unit size is the size of the real or imaginary part.

GET_MODE_NUNITS (*m*)

> Returns the number of units contained in a mode, i.e., GET_MODE_SIZE divided by GET_MODE_UNIT_SIZE.

GET_CLASS_NARROWEST_MODE (*c*)

> Returns the narrowest mode in mode class *c*.

The following 3 variables are defined on every target. They can be used to allocate buffers that are guaranteed to be large enough to hold any value that can be represented on the target. The first two can be overridden by defining them in the target's mode.def file, however, the value must be a constant that can determined very early in the compilation process. The third symbol cannot be overridden.

BITS_PER_UNIT

> The number of bits in an addressable storage unit (byte). If you do not define this, the default is 8.

MAX_BITSIZE_MODE_ANY_INT

> The maximum bitsize of any mode that is used in integer math. This should be overridden by the target if it uses large integers as containers for larger vectors but otherwise never uses the contents to compute integer values.

MAX_BITSIZE_MODE_ANY_MODE

> The bitsize of the largest mode on the target.

The global variables byte_mode and word_mode contain modes whose classes are MODE_INT and whose bitsizes are either BITS_PER_UNIT or BITS_PER_WORD, respectively. On 32-bit machines, these are QImode and SImode, respectively.

13.7 Constant Expression Types

The simplest RTL expressions are those that represent constant values.

`(const_int i)`

> This type of expression represents the integer value *i*. *i* is customarily accessed with the macro `INTVAL` as in `INTVAL (exp)`, which is equivalent to `XWINT (exp, 0)`.
>
> Constants generated for modes with fewer bits than in `HOST_WIDE_INT` must be sign extended to full width (e.g., with `gen_int_mode`). For constants for modes with more bits than in `HOST_WIDE_INT` the implied high order bits of that constant are copies of the top bit. Note however that values are neither inherently signed nor inherently unsigned; where necessary, signedness is determined by the rtl operation instead.
>
> There is only one expression object for the integer value zero; it is the value of the variable `const0_rtx`. Likewise, the only expression for integer value one is found in `const1_rtx`, the only expression for integer value two is found in `const2_rtx`, and the only expression for integer value negative one is found in `constm1_rtx`. Any attempt to create an expression of code `const_int` and value zero, one, two or negative one will return `const0_rtx`, `const1_rtx`, `const2_rtx` or `constm1_rtx` as appropriate.
>
> Similarly, there is only one object for the integer whose value is `STORE_FLAG_VALUE`. It is found in `const_true_rtx`. If `STORE_FLAG_VALUE` is one, `const_true_rtx` and `const1_rtx` will point to the same object. If `STORE_FLAG_VALUE` is −1, `const_true_rtx` and `constm1_rtx` will point to the same object.

`(const_double:m i0 i1 ...)`

> This represents either a floating-point constant of mode *m* or (on older ports that do not define `TARGET_SUPPORTS_WIDE_INT`) an integer constant too large to fit into `HOST_BITS_PER_WIDE_INT` bits but small enough to fit within twice that number of bits. In the latter case, *m* will be `VOIDmode`. For integral values constants for modes with more bits than twice the number in `HOST_WIDE_INT` the implied high order bits of that constant are copies of the top bit of `CONST_DOUBLE_HIGH`. Note however that integral values are neither inherently signed nor inherently unsigned; where necessary, signedness is determined by the rtl operation instead.
>
> On more modern ports, `CONST_DOUBLE` only represents floating point values. New ports define `TARGET_SUPPORTS_WIDE_INT` to make this designation.
>
> If *m* is `VOIDmode`, the bits of the value are stored in *i0* and *i1*. *i0* is customarily accessed with the macro `CONST_DOUBLE_LOW` and *i1* with `CONST_DOUBLE_HIGH`.
>
> If the constant is floating point (regardless of its precision), then the number of integers used to store the value depends on the size of `REAL_VALUE_TYPE` (see Section 17.22 [Floating Point], page 580). The integers represent a floating point number, but not precisely in the target machine's or host machine's floating point format. To convert them to the precise bit pattern used by the target machine, use the macro `REAL_VALUE_TO_TARGET_DOUBLE` and friends (see Section 17.20.2 [Data Output], page 548).

`(const_wide_int:m nunits elt0 ...)`

> This contains an array of HOST_WIDE_INTs that is large enough to hold any constant that can be represented on the target. This form of rtl is only used on targets that define TARGET_SUPPORTS_WIDE_INT to be nonzero and then CONST_DOUBLEs are only used to hold floating-point values. If the target leaves TARGET_SUPPORTS_WIDE_INT defined as 0, CONST_WIDE_INTs are not used and CONST_DOUBLEs are as they were before.
>
> The values are stored in a compressed format. The higher-order 0s or -1s are not represented if they are just the logical sign extension of the number that is represented.

CONST_WIDE_INT_VEC (`code`)

> Returns the entire array of HOST_WIDE_INTs that are used to store the value. This macro should be rarely used.

CONST_WIDE_INT_NUNITS (`code`)

> The number of HOST_WIDE_INTs used to represent the number. Note that this generally is smaller than the number of HOST_WIDE_INTs implied by the mode size.

CONST_WIDE_INT_NUNITS (`code,i`)

> Returns the ith element of the array. Element 0 is contains the low order bits of the constant.

`(const_fixed:m ...)`

> Represents a fixed-point constant of mode m. The operand is a data structure of type `struct fixed_value` and is accessed with the macro CONST_FIXED_VALUE. The high part of data is accessed with CONST_FIXED_VALUE_HIGH; the low part is accessed with CONST_FIXED_VALUE_LOW.

`(const_vector:m [x0 x1 ...])`

> Represents a vector constant. The square brackets stand for the vector containing the constant elements. $x0$, $x1$ and so on are the `const_int`, `const_double` or `const_fixed` elements.
>
> The number of units in a `const_vector` is obtained with the macro CONST_VECTOR_NUNITS as in CONST_VECTOR_NUNITS (`v`).
>
> Individual elements in a vector constant are accessed with the macro CONST_VECTOR_ELT as in CONST_VECTOR_ELT (`v`, `n`) where v is the vector constant and n is the element desired.

`(const_string str)`

> Represents a constant string with value `str`. Currently this is used only for insn attributes (see Section 16.19 [Insn Attributes], page 405) since constant strings in C are placed in memory.

`(symbol_ref:mode symbol)`

> Represents the value of an assembler label for data. `symbol` is a string that describes the name of the assembler label. If it starts with a '*', the label is the rest of `symbol` not including the '*'. Otherwise, the label is `symbol`, usually prefixed with '_'.

The `symbol_ref` contains a mode, which is usually `Pmode`. Usually that is the only mode for which a symbol is directly valid.

`(label_ref:`*`mode label`*`)`

Represents the value of an assembler label for code. It contains one operand, an expression, which must be a `code_label` or a `note` of type `NOTE_INSN_DELETED_LABEL` that appears in the instruction sequence to identify the place where the label should go.

The reason for using a distinct expression type for code label references is so that jump optimization can distinguish them.

The `label_ref` contains a mode, which is usually `Pmode`. Usually that is the only mode for which a label is directly valid.

`(const:`*`m exp`*`)`

Represents a constant that is the result of an assembly-time arithmetic computation. The operand, *exp*, is an expression that contains only constants (`const_int`, `symbol_ref` and `label_ref` expressions) combined with `plus` and `minus`. However, not all combinations are valid, since the assembler cannot do arbitrary arithmetic on relocatable symbols.

m should be `Pmode`.

`(high:`*`m exp`*`)`

Represents the high-order bits of *exp*, usually a `symbol_ref`. The number of bits is machine-dependent and is normally the number of bits specified in an instruction that initializes the high order bits of a register. It is used with `lo_sum` to represent the typical two-instruction sequence used in RISC machines to reference a global memory location.

m should be `Pmode`.

The macro `CONST0_RTX (`*`mode`*`)` refers to an expression with value 0 in mode *mode*. If mode *mode* is of mode class `MODE_INT`, it returns `const0_rtx`. If mode *mode* is of mode class `MODE_FLOAT`, it returns a `CONST_DOUBLE` expression in mode *mode*. Otherwise, it returns a `CONST_VECTOR` expression in mode *mode*. Similarly, the macro `CONST1_RTX (`*`mode`*`)` refers to an expression with value 1 in mode *mode* and similarly for `CONST2_RTX`. The `CONST1_RTX` and `CONST2_RTX` macros are undefined for vector modes.

13.8 Registers and Memory

Here are the RTL expression types for describing access to machine registers and to main memory.

`(reg:`*`m n`*`)`   For small values of the integer *n* (those that are less than `FIRST_PSEUDO_REGISTER`), this stands for a reference to machine register number *n*: a *hard register*. For larger values of *n*, it stands for a temporary value or *pseudo register*. The compiler's strategy is to generate code assuming an unlimited number of such pseudo registers, and later convert them into hard registers or into memory references.

m is the machine mode of the reference. It is necessary because machines can generally refer to each register in more than one mode. For example, a register may contain a full word but there may be instructions to refer to it as a half word or as a single byte, as well as instructions to refer to it as a floating point number of various precisions.

Even for a register that the machine can access in only one mode, the mode must always be specified.

The symbol `FIRST_PSEUDO_REGISTER` is defined by the machine description, since the number of hard registers on the machine is an invariant characteristic of the machine. Note, however, that not all of the machine registers must be general registers. All the machine registers that can be used for storage of data are given hard register numbers, even those that can be used only in certain instructions or can hold only certain types of data.

A hard register may be accessed in various modes throughout one function, but each pseudo register is given a natural mode and is accessed only in that mode. When it is necessary to describe an access to a pseudo register using a nonnatural mode, a `subreg` expression is used.

A `reg` expression with a machine mode that specifies more than one word of data may actually stand for several consecutive registers. If in addition the register number specifies a hardware register, then it actually represents several consecutive hardware registers starting with the specified one.

Each pseudo register number used in a function's RTL code is represented by a unique `reg` expression.

Some pseudo register numbers, those within the range of `FIRST_VIRTUAL_REGISTER` to `LAST_VIRTUAL_REGISTER` only appear during the RTL generation phase and are eliminated before the optimization phases. These represent locations in the stack frame that cannot be determined until RTL generation for the function has been completed. The following virtual register numbers are defined:

`VIRTUAL_INCOMING_ARGS_REGNUM`

> This points to the first word of the incoming arguments passed on the stack. Normally these arguments are placed there by the caller, but the callee may have pushed some arguments that were previously passed in registers.

> When RTL generation is complete, this virtual register is replaced by the sum of the register given by `ARG_POINTER_REGNUM` and the value of `FIRST_PARM_OFFSET`.

`VIRTUAL_STACK_VARS_REGNUM`

> If `FRAME_GROWS_DOWNWARD` is defined to a nonzero value, this points to immediately above the first variable on the stack. Otherwise, it points to the first variable on the stack.

> `VIRTUAL_STACK_VARS_REGNUM` is replaced with the sum of the register given by `FRAME_POINTER_REGNUM` and the value `STARTING_FRAME_OFFSET`.

VIRTUAL_STACK_DYNAMIC_REGNUM

> This points to the location of dynamically allocated memory on the stack immediately after the stack pointer has been adjusted by the amount of memory desired.
>
> This virtual register is replaced by the sum of the register given by STACK_POINTER_REGNUM and the value STACK_DYNAMIC_OFFSET.

VIRTUAL_OUTGOING_ARGS_REGNUM

> This points to the location in the stack at which outgoing arguments should be written when the stack is pre-pushed (arguments pushed using push insns should always use STACK_POINTER_REGNUM).
>
> This virtual register is replaced by the sum of the register given by STACK_POINTER_REGNUM and the value STACK_POINTER_OFFSET.

(subreg:*m1* reg:*m2* *bytenum*)

> subreg expressions are used to refer to a register in a machine mode other than its natural one, or to refer to one register of a multi-part reg that actually refers to several registers.
>
> Each pseudo register has a natural mode. If it is necessary to operate on it in a different mode, the register must be enclosed in a subreg.
>
> There are currently three supported types for the first operand of a subreg:
>
> - pseudo registers This is the most common case. Most subregs have pseudo regs as their first operand.
>
> - mem subregs of mem were common in earlier versions of GCC and are still supported. During the reload pass these are replaced by plain mems. On machines that do not do instruction scheduling, use of subregs of mem are still used, but this is no longer recommended. Such subregs are considered to be register_operands rather than memory_operands before and during reload. Because of this, the scheduling passes cannot properly schedule instructions with subregs of mem, so for machines that do scheduling, subregs of mem should never be used. To support this, the combine and recog passes have explicit code to inhibit the creation of subregs of mem when INSN_SCHEDULING is defined.
>
>   The use of subregs of mem after the reload pass is an area that is not well understood and should be avoided. There is still some code in the compiler to support this, but this code has possibly rotted. This use of subregs is discouraged and will most likely not be supported in the future.
>
> - hard registers It is seldom necessary to wrap hard registers in subregs; such registers would normally reduce to a single reg rtx. This use of subregs is discouraged and may not be supported in the future.
>
> subregs of subregs are not supported. Using simplify_gen_subreg is the recommended way to avoid this problem.
>
> subregs come in two distinct flavors, each having its own usage and rules:
>
> Paradoxical subregs
>
> > When *m1* is strictly wider than *m2*, the subreg expression is called *paradoxical*. The canonical test for this class of subreg is:

```
GET_MODE_SIZE (m1) > GET_MODE_SIZE (m2)
```

Paradoxical **subreg**s can be used as both lvalues and rvalues. When used as an lvalue, the low-order bits of the source value are stored in *reg* and the high-order bits are discarded. When used as an rvalue, the low-order bits of the **subreg** are taken from *reg* while the high-order bits may or may not be defined.

The high-order bits of rvalues are defined in the following circumstances:

- **subreg**s of **mem** When *m2* is smaller than a word, the macro **LOAD_EXTEND_OP**, can control how the high-order bits are defined.

- **subreg** of **reg**s The upper bits are defined when **SUBREG_PROMOTED_VAR_P** is true. **SUBREG_PROMOTED_UNSIGNED_P** describes what the upper bits hold. Such subregs usually represent local variables, register variables and parameter pseudo variables that have been promoted to a wider mode.

bytenum is always zero for a paradoxical **subreg**, even on big-endian targets.

For example, the paradoxical **subreg**:

```
(set (subreg:SI (reg:HI x) 0) y)
```

stores the lower 2 bytes of *y* in *x* and discards the upper 2 bytes. A subsequent:

```
(set z (subreg:SI (reg:HI x) 0))
```

would set the lower two bytes of *z* to *y* and set the upper two bytes to an unknown value assuming **SUBREG_PROMOTED_VAR_P** is false.

Normal subregs

When *m1* is at least as narrow as *m2* the **subreg** expression is called *normal*.

Normal **subreg**s restrict consideration to certain bits of *reg*. There are two cases. If *m1* is smaller than a word, the **subreg** refers to the least-significant part (or *lowpart*) of one word of *reg*. If *m1* is word-sized or greater, the **subreg** refers to one or more complete words.

When used as an lvalue, **subreg** is a word-based accessor. Storing to a **subreg** modifies all the words of *reg* that overlap the **subreg**, but it leaves the other words of *reg* alone.

When storing to a normal **subreg** that is smaller than a word, the other bits of the referenced word are usually left in an undefined state. This laxity makes it easier to generate efficient code for such instructions. To represent an instruction that preserves all the bits outside of those in the **subreg**, use **strict_low_part** or **zero_extract** around the **subreg**.

bytenum must identify the offset of the first byte of the **subreg** from the start of *reg*, assuming that *reg* is laid out in memory order. The memory order of bytes is defined by two target macros, `WORDS_BIG_ENDIAN` and `BYTES_BIG_ENDIAN`:

- `WORDS_BIG_ENDIAN`, if set to 1, says that byte number zero is part of the most significant word; otherwise, it is part of the least significant word.

- `BYTES_BIG_ENDIAN`, if set to 1, says that byte number zero is the most significant byte within a word; otherwise, it is the least significant byte within a word.

On a few targets, `FLOAT_WORDS_BIG_ENDIAN` disagrees with `WORDS_BIG_ENDIAN`. However, most parts of the compiler treat floating point values as if they had the same endianness as integer values. This works because they handle them solely as a collection of integer values, with no particular numerical value. Only real.c and the runtime libraries care about `FLOAT_WORDS_BIG_ENDIAN`.

Thus,

        (subreg:HI (reg:SI x) 2)

on a `BYTES_BIG_ENDIAN`, 'UNITS_PER_WORD == 4' target is the same as

        (subreg:HI (reg:SI x) 0)

on a little-endian, 'UNITS_PER_WORD == 4' target. Both `subreg`s access the lower two bytes of register x.

A `MODE_PARTIAL_INT` mode behaves as if it were as wide as the corresponding `MODE_INT` mode, except that it has an unknown number of undefined bits. For example:

        (subreg:PSI (reg:SI 0) 0)

accesses the whole of '(reg:SI 0)', but the exact relationship between the `PSImode` value and the `SImode` value is not defined. If we assume 'UNITS_PER_WORD <= 4', then the following two `subreg`s:

        (subreg:PSI (reg:DI 0) 0)
        (subreg:PSI (reg:DI 0) 4)

represent independent 4-byte accesses to the two halves of '(reg:DI 0)'. Both `subreg`s have an unknown number of undefined bits.

If 'UNITS_PER_WORD <= 2' then these two `subreg`s:

        (subreg:HI (reg:PSI 0) 0)
        (subreg:HI (reg:PSI 0) 2)

represent independent 2-byte accesses that together span the whole of '(reg:PSI 0)'. Storing to the first `subreg` does not affect the value of the second, and vice versa. '(reg:PSI 0)' has an unknown number of undefined bits, so the assignment:

        (set (subreg:HI (reg:PSI 0) 0) (reg:HI 4))

does not guarantee that '(subreg:HI (reg:PSI 0) 0)' has the value '(reg:HI 4)'.

The rules above apply to both pseudo *reg*s and hard *reg*s. If the semantics are not correct for particular combinations of *m1*, *m2* and hard *reg*, the target-specific code must ensure that those combinations are never used. For example:

CANNOT_CHANGE_MODE_CLASS (*m2*, *m1*, *class*)

must be true for every class *class* that includes *reg*.

The first operand of a `subreg` expression is customarily accessed with the `SUBREG_REG` macro and the second operand is customarily accessed with the `SUBREG_BYTE` macro.

It has been several years since a platform in which `BYTES_BIG_ENDIAN` not equal to `WORDS_BIG_ENDIAN` has been tested. Anyone wishing to support such a platform in the future may be confronted with code rot.

(scratch:*m*)

> This represents a scratch register that will be required for the execution of a single instruction and not used subsequently. It is converted into a `reg` by either the local register allocator or the reload pass.
>
> `scratch` is usually present inside a `clobber` operation (see Section 13.15 [Side Effects], page 264).

(cc0)

> This refers to the machine's condition code register. It has no operands and may not have a machine mode. There are two ways to use it:
>
> - To stand for a complete set of condition code flags. This is best on most machines, where each comparison sets the entire series of flags.
>
>   With this technique, (cc0) may be validly used in only two contexts: as the destination of an assignment (in test and compare instructions) and in comparison operators comparing against zero (`const_int` with value zero; that is to say, `const0_rtx`).
>
> - To stand for a single flag that is the result of a single condition. This is useful on machines that have only a single flag bit, and in which comparison instructions must specify the condition to test.
>
>   With this technique, (cc0) may be validly used in only two contexts: as the destination of an assignment (in test and compare instructions) where the source is a comparison operator, and as the first operand of `if_then_else` (in a conditional branch).
>
> There is only one expression object of code cc0; it is the value of the variable `cc0_rtx`. Any attempt to create an expression of code cc0 will return `cc0_rtx`.
>
> Instructions can set the condition code implicitly. On many machines, nearly all instructions set the condition code based on the value that they compute or store. It is not necessary to record these actions explicitly in the RTL because the machine description includes a prescription for recognizing the instructions that do so (by means of the macro `NOTICE_UPDATE_CC`). See Section 17.15 [Condition Code], page 521. Only instructions whose sole purpose is to set the condition code, and instructions that use the condition code, need mention (cc0).
>
> On some machines, the condition code register is given a register number and a `reg` is used instead of (cc0). This is usually the preferable approach if only a small subset of instructions modify the condition code. Other machines store condition codes in general registers; in such cases a pseudo register should be used.

Some machines, such as the SPARC and RS/6000, have two sets of arithmetic
instructions, one that sets and one that does not set the condition code. This
is best handled by normally generating the instruction that does not set the
condition code, and making a pattern that both performs the arithmetic and
sets the condition code register (which would not be (cc0) in this case). For
examples, search for 'addcc' and 'andcc' in 'sparc.md'.

(pc)
This represents the machine's program counter. It has no operands and may
not have a machine mode. (pc) may be validly used only in certain specific
contexts in jump instructions.

There is only one expression object of code pc; it is the value of the variable
pc_rtx. Any attempt to create an expression of code pc will return pc_rtx.

All instructions that do not jump alter the program counter implicitly by in-
crementing it, but there is no need to mention this in the RTL.

(mem:*m* *addr* *alias*)
This RTX represents a reference to main memory at an address represented by
the expression *addr*. *m* specifies how large a unit of memory is accessed. *alias*
specifies an alias set for the reference. In general two items are in different alias
sets if they cannot reference the same memory address.

The construct (mem:BLK (scratch)) is considered to alias all other memories.
Thus it may be used as a memory barrier in epilogue stack deallocation patterns.

(concat*m* *rtx* *rtx*)
This RTX represents the concatenation of two other RTXs. This is used for
complex values. It should only appear in the RTL attached to declarations and
during RTL generation. It should not appear in the ordinary insn chain.

(concatn*m* [*rtx* ...])
This RTX represents the concatenation of all the *rtx* to make a single value.
Like concat, this should only appear in declarations, and not in the insn chain.

13.9 RTL Expressions for Arithmetic

Unless otherwise specified, all the operands of arithmetic expressions must be valid for
mode *m*. An operand is valid for mode *m* if it has mode *m*, or if it is a const_int or
const_double and *m* is a mode of class MODE_INT.

For commutative binary operations, constants should be placed in the second operand.

(plus:*m* *x* *y*)
(ss_plus:*m* *x* *y*)
(us_plus:*m* *x* *y*)
These three expressions all represent the sum of the values represented by *x*
and *y* carried out in machine mode *m*. They differ in their behavior on overflow
of integer modes. plus wraps round modulo the width of *m*; ss_plus saturates
at the maximum signed value representable in *m*; us_plus saturates at the
maximum unsigned value.

(lo_sum:*m* *x* *y*)
This expression represents the sum of *x* and the low-order bits of *y*. It is used
with high (see Section 13.7 [Constants], page 247) to represent the typical

two-instruction sequence used in RISC machines to reference a global memory location.

The number of low order bits is machine-dependent but is normally the number of bits in a `Pmode` item minus the number of bits set by `high`.

m should be `Pmode`.

`(minus:`*m x y*`)`
`(ss_minus:`*m x y*`)`
`(us_minus:`*m x y*`)`

These three expressions represent the result of subtracting *y* from *x*, carried out in mode *M*. Behavior on overflow is the same as for the three variants of `plus` (see above).

`(compare:`*m x y*`)`

Represents the result of subtracting *y* from *x* for purposes of comparison. The result is computed without overflow, as if with infinite precision.

Of course, machines can't really subtract with infinite precision. However, they can pretend to do so when only the sign of the result will be used, which is the case when the result is stored in the condition code. And that is the *only* way this kind of expression may validly be used: as a value to be stored in the condition codes, either (`cc0`) or a register. See Section 13.10 [Comparisons], page 259.

The mode *m* is not related to the modes of *x* and *y*, but instead is the mode of the condition code value. If (`cc0`) is used, it is `VOIDmode`. Otherwise it is some mode in class `MODE_CC`, often `CCmode`. See Section 17.15 [Condition Code], page 521. If *m* is `VOIDmode` or `CCmode`, the operation returns sufficient information (in an unspecified format) so that any comparison operator can be applied to the result of the `COMPARE` operation. For other modes in class `MODE_CC`, the operation only returns a subset of this information.

Normally, *x* and *y* must have the same mode. Otherwise, `compare` is valid only if the mode of *x* is in class `MODE_INT` and *y* is a `const_int` or `const_double` with mode `VOIDmode`. The mode of *x* determines what mode the comparison is to be done in; thus it must not be `VOIDmode`.

If one of the operands is a constant, it should be placed in the second operand and the comparison code adjusted as appropriate.

A `compare` specifying two `VOIDmode` constants is not valid since there is no way to know in what mode the comparison is to be performed; the comparison must either be folded during the compilation or the first operand must be loaded into a register while its mode is still known.

`(neg:`*m x*`)`
`(ss_neg:`*m x*`)`
`(us_neg:`*m x*`)`

These two expressions represent the negation (subtraction from zero) of the value represented by *x*, carried out in mode *m*. They differ in the behavior on overflow of integer modes. In the case of `neg`, the negation of the operand may be a number not representable in mode *m*, in which case it is truncated to *m*. `ss_neg` and `us_neg` ensure that an out-of-bounds result saturates to the maximum or minimum signed or unsigned value.

(mult:*m* *x* *y*)

(ss_mult:*m* *x* *y*)

(us_mult:*m* *x* *y*)

> Represents the signed product of the values represented by *x* and *y* carried out in machine mode *m*. `ss_mult` and `us_mult` ensure that an out-of-bounds result saturates to the maximum or minimum signed or unsigned value.
>
> Some machines support a multiplication that generates a product wider than the operands. Write the pattern for this as
>
> > (mult:*m* (sign_extend:*m* *x*) (sign_extend:*m* *y*))
>
> where *m* is wider than the modes of *x* and *y*, which need not be the same.
>
> For unsigned widening multiplication, use the same idiom, but with `zero_extend` instead of `sign_extend`.

(fma:*m* *x* *y* *z*)

> Represents the `fma`, `fmaf`, and `fmal` builtin functions, which compute '*x* * *y* + *z*' without doing an intermediate rounding step.

(div:*m* *x* *y*)

(ss_div:*m* *x* *y*)

> Represents the quotient in signed division of *x* by *y*, carried out in machine mode *m*. If *m* is a floating point mode, it represents the exact quotient; otherwise, the integerized quotient. `ss_div` ensures that an out-of-bounds result saturates to the maximum or minimum signed value.
>
> Some machines have division instructions in which the operands and quotient widths are not all the same; you should represent such instructions using `truncate` and `sign_extend` as in,
>
> > (truncate:*m1* (div:*m2* *x* (sign_extend:*m2* *y*)))

(udiv:*m* *x* *y*)

(us_div:*m* *x* *y*)

> Like `div` but represents unsigned division. `us_div` ensures that an out-of-bounds result saturates to the maximum or minimum unsigned value.

(mod:*m* *x* *y*)

(umod:*m* *x* *y*)

> Like `div` and `udiv` but represent the remainder instead of the quotient.

(smin:*m* *x* *y*)

(smax:*m* *x* *y*)

> Represents the smaller (for `smin`) or larger (for `smax`) of *x* and *y*, interpreted as signed values in mode *m*. When used with floating point, if both operands are zeros, or if either operand is NaN, then it is unspecified which of the two operands is returned as the result.

(umin:*m* *x* *y*)

(umax:*m* *x* *y*)

> Like `smin` and `smax`, but the values are interpreted as unsigned integers.

(not:*m x*) Represents the bitwise complement of the value represented by *x*, carried out in mode *m*, which must be a fixed-point machine mode.

(and:*m x y*)

Represents the bitwise logical-and of the values represented by *x* and *y*, carried out in machine mode *m*, which must be a fixed-point machine mode.

(ior:*m x y*)

Represents the bitwise inclusive-or of the values represented by *x* and *y*, carried out in machine mode *m*, which must be a fixed-point mode.

(xor:*m x y*)

Represents the bitwise exclusive-or of the values represented by *x* and *y*, carried out in machine mode *m*, which must be a fixed-point mode.

(ashift:*m x c*)
(ss_ashift:*m x c*)
(us_ashift:*m x c*)

These three expressions represent the result of arithmetically shifting *x* left by *c* places. They differ in their behavior on overflow of integer modes. An `ashift` operation is a plain shift with no special behavior in case of a change in the sign bit; `ss_ashift` and `us_ashift` saturates to the minimum or maximum representable value if any of the bits shifted out differs from the final sign bit.

x have mode *m*, a fixed-point machine mode. *c* be a fixed-point mode or be a constant with mode `VOIDmode`; which mode is determined by the mode called for in the machine description entry for the left-shift instruction. For example, on the VAX, the mode of *c* is `QImode` regardless of *m*.

(lshiftrt:*m x c*)
(ashiftrt:*m x c*)

Like `ashift` but for right shift. Unlike the case for left shift, these two operations are distinct.

(rotate:*m x c*)
(rotatert:*m x c*)

Similar but represent left and right rotate. If *c* is a constant, use `rotate`.

(abs:*m x*)

(ss_abs:*m x*)

Represents the absolute value of *x*, computed in mode *m*. `ss_abs` ensures that an out-of-bounds result saturates to the maximum signed value.

(sqrt:*m x*)

Represents the square root of *x*, computed in mode *m*. Most often *m* will be a floating point mode.

(ffs:*m x*) Represents one plus the index of the least significant 1-bit in *x*, represented as an integer of mode *m*. (The value is zero if *x* is zero.) The mode of *x* must be *m* or `VOIDmode`.

(clrsb:*m x*)

Represents the number of redundant leading sign bits in *x*, represented as an integer of mode *m*, starting at the most significant bit position. This is one less than the number of leading sign bits (either 0 or 1), with no special cases. The mode of x must be m or VOIDmode.

(clz:m x)   Represents the number of leading 0-bits in x, represented as an integer of mode m, starting at the most significant bit position. If x is zero, the value is determined by CLZ_DEFINED_VALUE_AT_ZERO (see Section 17.30 [Misc], page 591). Note that this is one of the few expressions that is not invariant under widening. The mode of x must be m or VOIDmode.

(ctz:m x)   Represents the number of trailing 0-bits in x, represented as an integer of mode m, starting at the least significant bit position. If x is zero, the value is determined by CTZ_DEFINED_VALUE_AT_ZERO (see Section 17.30 [Misc], page 591). Except for this case, ctz(x) is equivalent to ffs(x) - 1. The mode of x must be m or VOIDmode.

(popcount:m x)

Represents the number of 1-bits in x, represented as an integer of mode m. The mode of x must be m or VOIDmode.

(parity:m x)

Represents the number of 1-bits modulo 2 in x, represented as an integer of mode m. The mode of x must be m or VOIDmode.

(bswap:m x)

Represents the value x with the order of bytes reversed, carried out in mode m, which must be a fixed-point machine mode. The mode of x must be m or VOIDmode.

13.10 Comparison Operations

Comparison operators test a relation on two operands and are considered to represent a machine-dependent nonzero value described by, but not necessarily equal to, STORE_FLAG_VALUE (see Section 17.30 [Misc], page 591) if the relation holds, or zero if it does not, for comparison operators whose results have a 'MODE_INT' mode, FLOAT_STORE_FLAG_VALUE (see Section 17.30 [Misc], page 591) if the relation holds, or zero if it does not, for comparison operators that return floating-point values, and a vector of either VECTOR_STORE_FLAG_VALUE (see Section 17.30 [Misc], page 591) if the relation holds, or of zeros if it does not, for comparison operators that return vector results. The mode of the comparison operation is independent of the mode of the data being compared. If the comparison operation is being tested (e.g., the first operand of an if_then_else), the mode must be VOIDmode.

There are two ways that comparison operations may be used. The comparison operators may be used to compare the condition codes (cc0) against zero, as in (eq (cc0) (const_int 0)). Such a construct actually refers to the result of the preceding instruction in which the condition codes were set. The instruction setting the condition code must be adjacent to the instruction using the condition code; only note insns may separate them.

Alternatively, a comparison operation may directly compare two data objects. The mode of the comparison is determined by the operands; they must both be valid for a common machine mode. A comparison with both operands constant would be invalid as the machine mode could not be deduced from it, but such a comparison should never exist in RTL due to constant folding.

In the example above, if (cc0) were last set to (compare x y), the comparison operation is identical to (eq x y). Usually only one style of comparisons is supported on a particular machine, but the combine pass will try to merge the operations to produce the eq shown in case it exists in the context of the particular insn involved.

Inequality comparisons come in two flavors, signed and unsigned. Thus, there are distinct expression codes gt and gtu for signed and unsigned greater-than. These can produce different results for the same pair of integer values: for example, 1 is signed greater-than −1 but not unsigned greater-than, because −1 when regarded as unsigned is actually 0xffffffff which is greater than 1.

The signed comparisons are also used for floating point values. Floating point comparisons are distinguished by the machine modes of the operands.

(eq:m x y)
> STORE_FLAG_VALUE if the values represented by x and y are equal, otherwise 0.

(ne:m x y)
> STORE_FLAG_VALUE if the values represented by x and y are not equal, otherwise 0.

(gt:m x y)
> STORE_FLAG_VALUE if the x is greater than y. If they are fixed-point, the comparison is done in a signed sense.

(gtu:m x y)
> Like gt but does unsigned comparison, on fixed-point numbers only.

(lt:m x y)
(ltu:m x y)
> Like gt and gtu but test for "less than".

(ge:m x y)
(geu:m x y)
> Like gt and gtu but test for "greater than or equal".

(le:m x y)
(leu:m x y)
> Like gt and gtu but test for "less than or equal".

(if_then_else cond then else)
> This is not a comparison operation but is listed here because it is always used in conjunction with a comparison operation. To be precise, cond is a comparison expression. This expression represents a choice, according to cond, between the value represented by then and the one represented by else.
>
> On most machines, if_then_else expressions are valid only to express conditional jumps.

(cond [test1 value1 test2 value2 ...] default)
> Similar to if_then_else, but more general. Each of test1, test2, ... is performed in turn. The result of this expression is the value corresponding to the first nonzero test, or default if none of the tests are nonzero expressions.
>
> This is currently not valid for instruction patterns and is supported only for insn attributes. See Section 16.19 [Insn Attributes], page 405.

13.11 Bit-Fields

Special expression codes exist to represent bit-field instructions.

(sign_extract:*m loc size pos*)

>   This represents a reference to a sign-extended bit-field contained or starting in
>   *loc* (a memory or register reference). The bit-field is *size* bits wide and starts
>   at bit *pos*. The compilation option `BITS_BIG_ENDIAN` says which end of the
>   memory unit *pos* counts from.
>
>   If *loc* is in memory, its mode must be a single-byte integer mode. If *loc* is in a
>   register, the mode to use is specified by the operand of the `insv` or `extv` pattern
>   (see Section 16.9 [Standard Names], page 356) and is usually a full-word integer
>   mode, which is the default if none is specified.
>
>   The mode of *pos* is machine-specific and is also specified in the `insv` or `extv`
>   pattern.
>
>   The mode *m* is the same as the mode that would be used for *loc* if it were a
>   register.
>
>   A `sign_extract` can not appear as an lvalue, or part thereof, in RTL.

(zero_extract:*m loc size pos*)

>   Like `sign_extract` but refers to an unsigned or zero-extended bit-field. The
>   same sequence of bits are extracted, but they are filled to an entire word with
>   zeros instead of by sign-extension.
>
>   Unlike `sign_extract`, this type of expressions can be lvalues in RTL; they may
>   appear on the left side of an assignment, indicating insertion of a value into the
>   specified bit-field.

13.12 Vector Operations

All normal RTL expressions can be used with vector modes; they are interpreted as operating on each part of the vector independently. Additionally, there are a few new expressions
to describe specific vector operations.

(vec_merge:*m vec1 vec2 items*)

>   This describes a merge operation between two vectors. The result is a vector of
>   mode *m*; its elements are selected from either *vec1* or *vec2*. Which elements are
>   selected is described by *items*, which is a bit mask represented by a `const_int`;
>   a zero bit indicates the corresponding element in the result vector is taken from
>   *vec2* while a set bit indicates it is taken from *vec1*.

(vec_select:*m vec1 selection*)

>   This describes an operation that selects parts of a vector. *vec1* is the source
>   vector, and *selection* is a `parallel` that contains a `const_int` for each of the
>   subparts of the result vector, giving the number of the source subpart that
>   should be stored into it. The result mode *m* is either the submode for a single
>   element of *vec1* (if only one subpart is selected), or another vector mode with
>   that element submode (if multiple subparts are selected).

`(vec_concat:m x1 x2)`

> Describes a vector concat operation. The result is a concatenation of the vectors or scalars *x1* and *x2*; its length is the sum of the lengths of the two inputs.

`(vec_duplicate:m x)`

> This operation converts a scalar into a vector or a small vector into a larger one by duplicating the input values. The output vector mode must have the same submodes as the input vector mode or the scalar modes, and the number of output parts must be an integer multiple of the number of input parts.

13.13 Conversions

All conversions between machine modes must be represented by explicit conversion operations. For example, an expression which is the sum of a byte and a full word cannot be written as `(plus:SI (reg:QI 34) (reg:SI 80))` because the `plus` operation requires two operands of the same machine mode. Therefore, the byte-sized operand is enclosed in a conversion operation, as in

    (plus:SI (sign_extend:SI (reg:QI 34)) (reg:SI 80))

The conversion operation is not a mere placeholder, because there may be more than one way of converting from a given starting mode to the desired final mode. The conversion operation code says how to do it.

For all conversion operations, *x* must not be `VOIDmode` because the mode in which to do the conversion would not be known. The conversion must either be done at compile-time or *x* must be placed into a register.

`(sign_extend:m x)`

> Represents the result of sign-extending the value *x* to machine mode *m*. *m* must be a fixed-point mode and *x* a fixed-point value of a mode narrower than *m*.

`(zero_extend:m x)`

> Represents the result of zero-extending the value *x* to machine mode *m*. *m* must be a fixed-point mode and *x* a fixed-point value of a mode narrower than *m*.

`(float_extend:m x)`

> Represents the result of extending the value *x* to machine mode *m*. *m* must be a floating point mode and *x* a floating point value of a mode narrower than *m*.

`(truncate:m x)`

> Represents the result of truncating the value *x* to machine mode *m*. *m* must be a fixed-point mode and *x* a fixed-point value of a mode wider than *m*.

`(ss_truncate:m x)`

> Represents the result of truncating the value *x* to machine mode *m*, using signed saturation in the case of overflow. Both *m* and the mode of *x* must be fixed-point modes.

`(us_truncate:m x)`

> Represents the result of truncating the value *x* to machine mode *m*, using unsigned saturation in the case of overflow. Both *m* and the mode of *x* must be fixed-point modes.

(float_truncate:*m x*)

>   Represents the result of truncating the value *x* to machine mode *m*. *m* must
>   be a floating point mode and *x* a floating point value of a mode wider than *m*.

(float:*m x*)

>   Represents the result of converting fixed point value *x*, regarded as signed, to
>   floating point mode *m*.

(unsigned_float:*m x*)

>   Represents the result of converting fixed point value *x*, regarded as unsigned,
>   to floating point mode *m*.

(fix:*m x*)   When *m* is a floating-point mode, represents the result of converting floating
>   point value *x* (valid for mode *m*) to an integer, still represented in floating point
>   mode *m*, by rounding towards zero.

>   When *m* is a fixed-point mode, represents the result of converting floating point
>   value *x* to mode *m*, regarded as signed. How rounding is done is not specified, so
>   this operation may be used validly in compiling C code only for integer-valued
>   operands.

(unsigned_fix:*m x*)

>   Represents the result of converting floating point value *x* to fixed point mode
>   *m*, regarded as unsigned. How rounding is done is not specified.

(fract_convert:*m x*)

>   Represents the result of converting fixed-point value *x* to fixed-point mode *m*,
>   signed integer value *x* to fixed-point mode *m*, floating-point value *x* to fixed-
>   point mode *m*, fixed-point value *x* to integer mode *m* regarded as signed, or
>   fixed-point value *x* to floating-point mode *m*. When overflows or underflows
>   happen, the results are undefined.

(sat_fract:*m x*)

>   Represents the result of converting fixed-point value *x* to fixed-point mode *m*,
>   signed integer value *x* to fixed-point mode *m*, or floating-point value *x* to fixed-
>   point mode *m*. When overflows or underflows happen, the results are saturated
>   to the maximum or the minimum.

(unsigned_fract_convert:*m x*)

>   Represents the result of converting fixed-point value *x* to integer mode *m* re-
>   garded as unsigned, or unsigned integer value *x* to fixed-point mode *m*. When
>   overflows or underflows happen, the results are undefined.

(unsigned_sat_fract:*m x*)

>   Represents the result of converting unsigned integer value *x* to fixed-point mode
>   *m*. When overflows or underflows happen, the results are saturated to the
>   maximum or the minimum.

13.14 Declarations

Declaration expression codes do not represent arithmetic operations but rather state assertions about their operands.

`(strict_low_part (subreg:m (reg:n r) 0))`

> This expression code is used in only one context: as the destination operand of a `set` expression. In addition, the operand of this expression must be a non-paradoxical `subreg` expression.
>
> The presence of `strict_low_part` says that the part of the register which is meaningful in mode n, but is not part of mode m, is not to be altered. Normally, an assignment to such a subreg is allowed to have undefined effects on the rest of the register when m is less than a word.

13.15 Side Effect Expressions

The expression codes described so far represent values, not actions. But machine instructions never produce values; they are meaningful only for their side effects on the state of the machine. Special expression codes are used to represent side effects.

The body of an instruction is always one of these side effect codes; the codes described above, which represent values, appear only as the operands of these.

`(set lval x)`

> Represents the action of storing the value of x into the place represented by *lval*. *lval* must be an expression representing a place that can be stored in: `reg` (or `subreg`, `strict_low_part` or `zero_extract`), `mem`, `pc`, `parallel`, or `cc0`.
>
> If *lval* is a `reg`, `subreg` or `mem`, it has a machine mode; then x must be valid for that mode.
>
> If *lval* is a `reg` whose machine mode is less than the full width of the register, then it means that the part of the register specified by the machine mode is given the specified value and the rest of the register receives an undefined value. Likewise, if *lval* is a `subreg` whose machine mode is narrower than the mode of the register, the rest of the register can be changed in an undefined way.
>
> If *lval* is a `strict_low_part` of a subreg, then the part of the register specified by the machine mode of the `subreg` is given the value x and the rest of the register is not changed.
>
> If *lval* is a `zero_extract`, then the referenced part of the bit-field (a memory or register reference) specified by the `zero_extract` is given the value x and the rest of the bit-field is not changed. Note that `sign_extract` can not appear in *lval*.
>
> If *lval* is (cc0), it has no machine mode, and x may be either a `compare` expression or a value that may have any mode. The latter case represents a "test" instruction. The expression `(set (cc0) (reg:m n))` is equivalent to `(set (cc0) (compare (reg:m n) (const_int 0)))`. Use the former expression to save space during the compilation.
>
> If *lval* is a `parallel`, it is used to represent the case of a function returning a structure in multiple registers. Each element of the `parallel` is an `expr_list` whose first operand is a `reg` and whose second operand is a `const_int` representing the offset (in bytes) into the structure at which the data in that register corresponds. The first element may be null to indicate that the structure is also passed partly in memory.

If *lval* is (pc), we have a jump instruction, and the possibilities for *x* are very limited. It may be a `label_ref` expression (unconditional jump). It may be an `if_then_else` (conditional jump), in which case either the second or the third operand must be (pc) (for the case which does not jump) and the other of the two must be a `label_ref` (for the case which does jump). *x* may also be a `mem` or (plus:SI (pc) *y*), where *y* may be a `reg` or a `mem`; these unusual patterns are used to represent jumps through branch tables.

If *lval* is neither (cc0) nor (pc), the mode of *lval* must not be VOIDmode and the mode of *x* must be valid for the mode of *lval*.

lval is customarily accessed with the `SET_DEST` macro and *x* with the `SET_SRC` macro.

(return)   As the sole expression in a pattern, represents a return from the current function, on machines where this can be done with one instruction, such as VAXen. On machines where a multi-instruction "epilogue" must be executed in order to return from the function, returning is done by jumping to a label which precedes the epilogue, and the `return` expression code is never used.

Inside an `if_then_else` expression, represents the value to be placed in `pc` to return to the caller.

Note that an insn pattern of (**return**) is logically equivalent to (**set** (pc) (**return**)), but the latter form is never used.

(simple_return)

Like (**return**), but truly represents only a function return, while (**return**) may represent an insn that also performs other functions of the function epilogue. Like (**return**), this may also occur in conditional jumps.

(call *function nargs*)

Represents a function call. *function* is a `mem` expression whose address is the address of the function to be called. *nargs* is an expression which can be used for two purposes: on some machines it represents the number of bytes of stack argument; on others, it represents the number of argument registers.

Each machine has a standard machine mode which *function* must have. The machine description defines macro `FUNCTION_MODE` to expand into the requisite mode name. The purpose of this mode is to specify what kind of addressing is allowed, on machines where the allowed kinds of addressing depend on the machine mode being addressed.

(clobber *x*)

Represents the storing or possible storing of an unpredictable, undescribed value into *x*, which must be a `reg`, `scratch`, `parallel` or `mem` expression.

One place this is used is in string instructions that store standard values into particular hard registers. It may not be worth the trouble to describe the values that are stored, but it is essential to inform the compiler that the registers will be altered, lest it attempt to keep data in them across the string instruction.

If *x* is (mem:BLK (const_int 0)) or (mem:BLK (scratch)), it means that all memory locations must be presumed clobbered. If *x* is a `parallel`, it has the same meaning as a `parallel` in a `set` expression.

Note that the machine description classifies certain hard registers as "call-clobbered". All function call instructions are assumed by default to clobber these registers, so there is no need to use `clobber` expressions to indicate this fact. Also, each function call is assumed to have the potential to alter any memory location, unless the function is declared `const`.

If the last group of expressions in a `parallel` are each a `clobber` expression whose arguments are `reg` or `match_scratch` (see Section 16.4 [RTL Template], page 305) expressions, the combiner phase can add the appropriate `clobber` expressions to an insn it has constructed when doing so will cause a pattern to be matched.

This feature can be used, for example, on a machine that whose multiply and add instructions don't use an MQ register but which has an add-accumulate instruction that does clobber the MQ register. Similarly, a combined instruction might require a temporary register while the constituent instructions might not.

When a `clobber` expression for a register appears inside a `parallel` with other side effects, the register allocator guarantees that the register is unoccupied both before and after that insn if it is a hard register clobber. For pseudo-register clobber, the register allocator and the reload pass do not assign the same hard register to the clobber and the input operands if there is an insn alternative containing the '&' constraint (see Section 16.8.4 [Modifiers], page 321) for the clobber and the hard register is in register classes of the clobber in the alternative. You can clobber either a specific hard register, a pseudo register, or a `scratch` expression; in the latter two cases, GCC will allocate a hard register that is available there for use as a temporary.

For instructions that require a temporary register, you should use `scratch` instead of a pseudo-register because this will allow the combiner phase to add the `clobber` when required. You do this by coding (`clobber` (`match_scratch` ...)). If you do clobber a pseudo register, use one which appears nowhere else—generate a new one each time. Otherwise, you may confuse CSE.

There is one other known use for clobbering a pseudo register in a `parallel`: when one of the input operands of the insn is also clobbered by the insn. In this case, using the same pseudo register in the clobber and elsewhere in the insn produces the expected results.

(use x)   Represents the use of the value of x. It indicates that the value in x at this point in the program is needed, even though it may not be apparent why this is so. Therefore, the compiler will not attempt to delete previous instructions whose only effect is to store a value in x. x must be a `reg` expression.

In some situations, it may be tempting to add a `use` of a register in a `parallel` to describe a situation where the value of a special register will modify the behavior of the instruction. A hypothetical example might be a pattern for an addition that can either wrap around or use saturating addition depending on the value of a special control register:

```
(parallel [(set (reg:SI 2) (unspec:SI [(reg:SI 3)
                                        (reg:SI 4)] 0))
           (use (reg:SI 1))])
```

This will not work, several of the optimizers only look at expressions locally; it is very likely that if you have multiple insns with identical inputs to the `unspec`, they will be optimized away even if register 1 changes in between.

This means that `use` can *only* be used to describe that the register is live. You should think twice before adding `use` statements, more often you will want to use `unspec` instead. The `use` RTX is most commonly useful to describe that a fixed register is implicitly used in an insn. It is also safe to use in patterns where the compiler knows for other reasons that the result of the whole pattern is variable, such as '`movmemm`' or '`call`' patterns.

During the reload phase, an insn that has a `use` as pattern can carry a reg_equal note. These `use` insns will be deleted before the reload phase exits.

During the delayed branch scheduling phase, *x* may be an insn. This indicates that *x* previously was located at this place in the code and its data dependencies need to be taken into account. These `use` insns will be deleted before the delayed branch scheduling phase exits.

`(parallel [x0 x1 ...])`

Represents several side effects performed in parallel. The square brackets stand for a vector; the operand of `parallel` is a vector of expressions. *x0*, *x1* and so on are individual side effect expressions—expressions of code `set`, `call`, `return`, `simple_return`, `clobber` or `use`.

"In parallel" means that first all the values used in the individual side-effects are computed, and second all the actual side-effects are performed. For example,

```
(parallel [(set (reg:SI 1) (mem:SI (reg:SI 1)))
           (set (mem:SI (reg:SI 1)) (reg:SI 1))])
```

says unambiguously that the values of hard register 1 and the memory location addressed by it are interchanged. In both places where (`reg:SI 1`) appears as a memory address it refers to the value in register 1 *before* the execution of the insn.

It follows that it is *incorrect* to use `parallel` and expect the result of one `set` to be available for the next one. For example, people sometimes attempt to represent a jump-if-zero instruction this way:

```
(parallel [(set (cc0) (reg:SI 34))
           (set (pc) (if_then_else
                         (eq (cc0) (const_int 0))
                         (label_ref ...)
                         (pc)))])
```

But this is incorrect, because it says that the jump condition depends on the condition code value *before* this instruction, not on the new value that is set by this instruction.

Peephole optimization, which takes place together with final assembly code output, can produce insns whose patterns consist of a `parallel` whose elements are the operands needed to output the resulting assembler code—often `reg`, `mem` or constant expressions. This would not be well-formed RTL at any other stage in compilation, but it is OK then because no further optimization remains to be done. However, the definition of the macro `NOTICE_UPDATE_CC`, if any, must deal with such insns if you define any peephole optimizations.

`(cond_exec [cond expr])`

> Represents a conditionally executed expression. The *expr* is executed only if the *cond* is nonzero. The *cond* expression must not have side-effects, but the *expr* may very well have side-effects.

`(sequence [insns ...])`

> Represents a sequence of insns. If a **sequence** appears in the chain of insns, then each of the *insns* that appears in the sequence must be suitable for appearing in the chain of insns, i.e. must satisfy the `INSN_P` predicate.
>
> After delay-slot scheduling is completed, an insn and all the insns that reside in its delay slots are grouped together into a **sequence**. The insn requiring the delay slot is the first insn in the vector; subsequent insns are to be placed in the delay slot.
>
> `INSN_ANNULLED_BRANCH_P` is set on an insn in a delay slot to indicate that a branch insn should be used that will conditionally annul the effect of the insns in the delay slots. In such a case, `INSN_FROM_TARGET_P` indicates that the insn is from the target of the branch and should be executed only if the branch is taken; otherwise the insn should be executed only if the branch is not taken. See Section 16.19.8 [Delay Slots], page 413.
>
> Some back ends also use **sequence** objects for purposes other than delay-slot groups. This is not supported in the common parts of the compiler, which treat such sequences as delay-slot groups.
>
> DWARF2 Call Frame Address (CFA) adjustments are sometimes also expressed using **sequence** objects as the value of a `RTX_FRAME_RELATED_P` note. This only happens if the CFA adjustments cannot be easily derived from the pattern of the instruction to which the note is attached. In such cases, the value of the note is used instead of best-guesing the semantics of the instruction. The back end can attach notes containing a **sequence** of **set** patterns that express the effect of the parent instruction.

These expression codes appear in place of a side effect, as the body of an insn, though strictly speaking they do not always describe side effects as such:

`(asm_input s)`

> Represents literal assembler code as described by the string *s*.

`(unspec [operands ...] index)`
`(unspec_volatile [operands ...] index)`

> Represents a machine-specific operation on *operands*. *index* selects between multiple machine-specific operations. **unspec_volatile** is used for volatile operations and operations that may trap; **unspec** is used for other operations.
>
> These codes may appear inside a **pattern** of an insn, inside a **parallel**, or inside an expression.

`(addr_vec:m [lr0 lr1 ...])`

> Represents a table of jump addresses. The vector elements *lr0*, etc., are `label_ref` expressions. The mode *m* specifies how much space is given to each address; normally *m* would be `Pmode`.

`(addr_diff_vec:`*m* *base* `[`*lr0 lr1* `...]` *min max flags*`)`

> Represents a table of jump addresses expressed as offsets from *base*. The vector elements *lr0*, etc., are `label_ref` expressions and so is *base*. The mode *m* specifies how much space is given to each address-difference. *min* and *max* are set up by branch shortening and hold a label with a minimum and a maximum address, respectively. *flags* indicates the relative position of *base*, *min* and *max* to the containing insn and of *min* and *max* to *base*. See rtl.def for details.

`(prefetch:`*m* *addr rw locality*`)`

> Represents prefetch of memory at address *addr*. Operand *rw* is 1 if the prefetch is for data to be written, 0 otherwise; targets that do not support write prefetches should treat this as a normal prefetch. Operand *locality* specifies the amount of temporal locality; 0 if there is none or 1, 2, or 3 for increasing levels of temporal locality; targets that do not support locality hints should ignore this.
>
> This insn is used to minimize cache-miss latency by moving data into a cache before it is accessed. It should use only non-faulting data prefetch instructions.

13.16 Embedded Side-Effects on Addresses

Six special side-effect expression codes appear as memory addresses.

`(pre_dec:`*m* *x*`)`

> Represents the side effect of decrementing *x* by a standard amount and represents also the value that *x* has after being decremented. *x* must be a `reg` or `mem`, but most machines allow only a `reg`. *m* must be the machine mode for pointers on the machine in use. The amount *x* is decremented by is the length in bytes of the machine mode of the containing memory reference of which this expression serves as the address. Here is an example of its use:
>
>   (mem:DF (pre_dec:SI (reg:SI 39)))
>
> This says to decrement pseudo register 39 by the length of a `DFmode` value and use the result to address a `DFmode` value.

`(pre_inc:`*m* *x*`)`

> Similar, but specifies incrementing *x* instead of decrementing it.

`(post_dec:`*m* *x*`)`

> Represents the same side effect as `pre_dec` but a different value. The value represented here is the value *x* has *before* being decremented.

`(post_inc:`*m* *x*`)`

> Similar, but specifies incrementing *x* instead of decrementing it.

`(post_modify:`*m* *x y*`)`

> Represents the side effect of setting *x* to *y* and represents *x* before *x* is modified. *x* must be a `reg` or `mem`, but most machines allow only a `reg`. *m* must be the machine mode for pointers on the machine in use.
>
> The expression *y* must be one of three forms: `(plus:`*m* *x z*`)`, `(minus:`*m* *x z*`)`, or `(plus:`*m* *x i*`)`, where *z* is an index register and *i* is a constant.
>
> Here is an example of its use:

```
(mem:SF (post_modify:SI (reg:SI 42) (plus (reg:SI 42)
                                          (reg:SI 48))))
```

> This says to modify pseudo register 42 by adding the contents of pseudo register 48 to it, after the use of what ever 42 points to.

(pre_modify:*m x expr*)
> Similar except side effects happen before the use.

These embedded side effect expressions must be used with care. Instruction patterns may not use them. Until the 'flow' pass of the compiler, they may occur only to represent pushes onto the stack. The 'flow' pass finds cases where registers are incremented or decremented in one instruction and used as an address shortly before or after; these cases are then transformed to use pre- or post-increment or -decrement.

If a register used as the operand of these expressions is used in another address in an insn, the original value of the register is used. Uses of the register outside of an address are not permitted within the same insn as a use in an embedded side effect expression because such insns behave differently on different machines and hence must be treated as ambiguous and disallowed.

An instruction that can be represented with an embedded side effect could also be represented using `parallel` containing an additional `set` to describe how the address register is altered. This is not done because machines that allow these operations at all typically allow them wherever a memory address is called for. Describing them as additional parallel stores would require doubling the number of entries in the machine description.

13.17 Assembler Instructions as Expressions

The RTX code `asm_operands` represents a value produced by a user-specified assembler instruction. It is used to represent an `asm` statement with arguments. An `asm` statement with a single output operand, like this:

```
asm ("foo %1,%2,%0" : "=a" (outputvar) : "g" (x + y), "di" (*z));
```

is represented using a single `asm_operands` RTX which represents the value that is stored in `outputvar`:

```
(set rtx-for-outputvar
     (asm_operands "foo %1,%2,%0" "a" 0
                   [rtx-for-addition-result rtx-for-*z]
                   [(asm_input:m1 "g")
                    (asm_input:m2 "di")]))
```

Here the operands of the `asm_operands` RTX are the assembler template string, the output-operand's constraint, the index-number of the output operand among the output operands specified, a vector of input operand RTX's, and a vector of input-operand modes and constraints. The mode *m1* is the mode of the sum x+y; *m2* is that of *z.

When an `asm` statement has multiple output values, its insn has several such `set` RTX's inside of a `parallel`. Each `set` contains an `asm_operands`; all of these share the same assembler template and vectors, but each contains the constraint for the respective output operand. They are also distinguished by the output-operand index number, which is 0, 1, ... for successive output operands.

13.18 Variable Location Debug Information in RTL

Variable tracking relies on `MEM_EXPR` and `REG_EXPR` annotations to determine what user variables memory and register references refer to.

Variable tracking at assignments uses these notes only when they refer to variables that live at fixed locations (e.g., addressable variables, global non-automatic variables). For variables whose location may vary, it relies on the following types of notes.

(var_location:*mode var exp stat*)

> Binds variable **var**, a tree, to value *exp*, an RTL expression. It appears only in `NOTE_INSN_VAR_LOCATION` and `DEBUG_INSNs`, with slightly different meanings. *mode*, if present, represents the mode of *exp*, which is useful if it is a modeless expression. *stat* is only meaningful in notes, indicating whether the variable is known to be initialized or uninitialized.

(debug_expr:*mode decl*)

> Stands for the value bound to the `DEBUG_EXPR_DECL` *decl*, that points back to it, within value expressions in `VAR_LOCATION` nodes.

13.19 Insns

The RTL representation of the code for a function is a doubly-linked chain of objects called *insns*. Insns are expressions with special codes that are used for no other purpose. Some insns are actual instructions; others represent dispatch tables for **switch** statements; others represent labels to jump to or various sorts of declarative information.

In addition to its own specific data, each insn must have a unique id-number that distinguishes it from all other insns in the current function (after delayed branch scheduling, copies of an insn with the same id-number may be present in multiple places in a function, but these copies will always be identical and will only appear inside a **sequence**), and chain pointers to the preceding and following insns. These three fields occupy the same position in every insn, independent of the expression code of the insn. They could be accessed with `XEXP` and `XINT`, but instead three special macros are always used:

INSN_UID (*i*)

> Accesses the unique id of insn *i*.

PREV_INSN (*i*)

> Accesses the chain pointer to the insn preceding *i*. If *i* is the first insn, this is a null pointer.

NEXT_INSN (*i*)

> Accesses the chain pointer to the insn following *i*. If *i* is the last insn, this is a null pointer.

The first insn in the chain is obtained by calling **get_insns**; the last insn is the result of calling **get_last_insn**. Within the chain delimited by these insns, the `NEXT_INSN` and `PREV_INSN` pointers must always correspond: if *insn* is not the first insn,

```
NEXT_INSN (PREV_INSN (insn)) == insn
```

is always true and if *insn* is not the last insn,

```
PREV_INSN (NEXT_INSN (insn)) == insn
```

is always true.

After delay slot scheduling, some of the insns in the chain might be **sequence** expressions, which contain a vector of insns. The value of `NEXT_INSN` in all but the last of these insns is the next insn in the vector; the value of `NEXT_INSN` of the last insn in the vector is the same as the value of `NEXT_INSN` for the **sequence** in which it is contained. Similar rules apply for `PREV_INSN`.

This means that the above invariants are not necessarily true for insns inside **sequence** expressions. Specifically, if *insn* is the first insn in a **sequence**, `NEXT_INSN (PREV_INSN (insn))` is the insn containing the **sequence** expression, as is the value of `PREV_INSN (NEXT_INSN (insn))` if *insn* is the last insn in the **sequence** expression. You can use these expressions to find the containing **sequence** expression.

Every insn has one of the following expression codes:

insn
: The expression code `insn` is used for instructions that do not jump and do not do function calls. **sequence** expressions are always contained in insns with code `insn` even if one of those insns should jump or do function calls.

  Insns with code `insn` have four additional fields beyond the three mandatory ones listed above. These four are described in a table below.

jump_insn
: The expression code `jump_insn` is used for instructions that may jump (or, more generally, may contain `label_ref` expressions to which `pc` can be set in that instruction). If there is an instruction to return from the current function, it is recorded as a `jump_insn`.

  `jump_insn` insns have the same extra fields as `insn` insns, accessed in the same way and in addition contain a field `JUMP_LABEL` which is defined once jump optimization has completed.

  For simple conditional and unconditional jumps, this field contains the `code_label` to which this insn will (possibly conditionally) branch. In a more complex jump, `JUMP_LABEL` records one of the labels that the insn refers to; other jump target labels are recorded as `REG_LABEL_TARGET` notes. The exception is `addr_vec` and `addr_diff_vec`, where `JUMP_LABEL` is `NULL_RTX` and the only way to find the labels is to scan the entire body of the insn.

  Return insns count as jumps, but their `JUMP_LABEL` is `RETURN` or `SIMPLE_RETURN`.

call_insn
: The expression code `call_insn` is used for instructions that may do function calls. It is important to distinguish these instructions because they imply that certain registers and memory locations may be altered unpredictably.

  `call_insn` insns have the same extra fields as `insn` insns, accessed in the same way and in addition contain a field `CALL_INSN_FUNCTION_USAGE`, which contains a list (chain of `expr_list` expressions) containing `use`, `clobber` and sometimes `set` expressions that denote hard registers and `mem`s used or clobbered by the called function.

A `mem` generally points to a stack slot in which arguments passed to the libcall by reference (see Section 17.9.7 [Register Arguments], page 489) are stored. If the argument is caller-copied (see Section 17.9.7 [Register Arguments], page 489), the stack slot will be mentioned in `clobber` and `use` entries; if it's callee-copied, only a `use` will appear, and the `mem` may point to addresses that are not stack slots.

Registers occurring inside a `clobber` in this list augment registers specified in `CALL_USED_REGISTERS` (see Section 17.7.1 [Register Basics], page 459).

If the list contains a `set` involving two registers, it indicates that the function returns one of its arguments. Such a `set` may look like a no-op if the same register holds the argument and the return value.

`code_label`

A `code_label` insn represents a label that a jump insn can jump to. It contains two special fields of data in addition to the three standard ones. `CODE_LABEL_NUMBER` is used to hold the *label number*, a number that identifies this label uniquely among all the labels in the compilation (not just in the current function). Ultimately, the label is represented in the assembler output as an assembler label, usually of the form '`Ln`' where *n* is the label number.

When a `code_label` appears in an RTL expression, it normally appears within a `label_ref` which represents the address of the label, as a number.

Besides as a `code_label`, a label can also be represented as a `note` of type `NOTE_INSN_DELETED_LABEL`.

The field `LABEL_NUSES` is only defined once the jump optimization phase is completed. It contains the number of times this label is referenced in the current function.

The field `LABEL_KIND` differentiates four different types of labels: `LABEL_NORMAL`, `LABEL_STATIC_ENTRY`, `LABEL_GLOBAL_ENTRY`, and `LABEL_WEAK_ENTRY`. The only labels that do not have type `LABEL_NORMAL` are *alternate entry points* to the current function. These may be static (visible only in the containing translation unit), global (exposed to all translation units), or weak (global, but can be overridden by another symbol with the same name).

Much of the compiler treats all four kinds of label identically. Some of it needs to know whether or not a label is an alternate entry point; for this purpose, the macro `LABEL_ALT_ENTRY_P` is provided. It is equivalent to testing whether '`LABEL_KIND (label) == LABEL_NORMAL`'. The only place that cares about the distinction between static, global, and weak alternate entry points, besides the front-end code that creates them, is the function `output_alternate_entry_point`, in '`final.c`'.

To set the kind of a label, use the `SET_LABEL_KIND` macro.

`jump_table_data`

A `jump_table_data` insn is a placeholder for the jump-table data of a `casesi` or `tablejump` insn. They are placed after a `tablejump_p` insn. A `jump_table_data` insn is not part o a basic blockm but it is associated with the basic block that ends with the `tablejump_p` insn. The `PATTERN` of a `jump_table_data` is always either an `addr_vec` or an `addr_diff_vec`, and a `jump_table_data` insn is always preceded by a `code_label`. The `tablejump_p` insn refers to that `code_label` via its `JUMP_LABEL`.

`barrier`   Barriers are placed in the instruction stream when control cannot flow past them. They are placed after unconditional jump instructions to indicate that the jumps are unconditional and after calls to `volatile` functions, which do not return (e.g., `exit`). They contain no information beyond the three standard fields.

`note`   `note` insns are used to represent additional debugging and declarative information. They contain two nonstandard fields, an integer which is accessed with the macro `NOTE_LINE_NUMBER` and a string accessed with `NOTE_SOURCE_FILE`.

If `NOTE_LINE_NUMBER` is positive, the note represents the position of a source line and `NOTE_SOURCE_FILE` is the source file name that the line came from. These notes control generation of line number data in the assembler output.

Otherwise, `NOTE_LINE_NUMBER` is not really a line number but a code with one of the following values (and `NOTE_SOURCE_FILE` must contain a null pointer):

`NOTE_INSN_DELETED`
> Such a note is completely ignorable. Some passes of the compiler delete insns by altering them into notes of this kind.

`NOTE_INSN_DELETED_LABEL`
> This marks what used to be a `code_label`, but was not used for other purposes than taking its address and was transformed to mark that no code jumps to it.

`NOTE_INSN_BLOCK_BEG`
`NOTE_INSN_BLOCK_END`
> These types of notes indicate the position of the beginning and end of a level of scoping of variable names. They control the output of debugging information.

`NOTE_INSN_EH_REGION_BEG`
`NOTE_INSN_EH_REGION_END`
> These types of notes indicate the position of the beginning and end of a level of scoping for exception handling. `NOTE_EH_HANDLER` identifies which region is associated with these notes.

`NOTE_INSN_FUNCTION_BEG`
> Appears at the start of the function body, after the function prologue.

`NOTE_INSN_VAR_LOCATION`
> This note is used to generate variable location debugging information. It indicates that the user variable in its `VAR_LOCATION` operand is at the location given in the RTL expression, or holds a value that can be computed by evaluating the RTL expression from that static point in the program up to the next such note for the same user variable.

These codes are printed symbolically when they appear in debugging dumps.

debug_insn

>The expression code debug_insn is used for pseudo-instructions that hold debugging information for variable tracking at assignments (see '-fvar-tracking-assignments' option). They are the RTL representation of GIMPLE_DEBUG statements (Section 11.8.7 [GIMPLE_DEBUG], page 199), with a VAR_LOCATION operand that binds a user variable tree to an RTL representation of the value in the corresponding statement. A DEBUG_EXPR in it stands for the value bound to the corresponding DEBUG_EXPR_DECL.

>Throughout optimization passes, binding information is kept in pseudo-instruction form, so that, unlike notes, it gets the same treatment and adjustments that regular instructions would. It is the variable tracking pass that turns these pseudo-instructions into var location notes, analyzing control flow, value equivalences and changes to registers and memory referenced in value expressions, propagating the values of debug temporaries and determining expressions that can be used to compute the value of each user variable at as many points (ranges, actually) in the program as possible.

>Unlike NOTE_INSN_VAR_LOCATION, the value expression in an INSN_VAR_LOCATION denotes a value at that specific point in the program, rather than an expression that can be evaluated at any later point before an overriding VAR_LOCATION is encountered. E.g., if a user variable is bound to a REG and then a subsequent insn modifies the REG, the note location would keep mapping the user variable to the register across the insn, whereas the insn location would keep the variable bound to the value, so that the variable tracking pass would emit another location note for the variable at the point in which the register is modified.

The machine mode of an insn is normally VOIDmode, but some phases use the mode for various purposes.

The common subexpression elimination pass sets the mode of an insn to QImode when it is the first insn in a block that has already been processed.

The second Haifa scheduling pass, for targets that can multiple issue, sets the mode of an insn to TImode when it is believed that the instruction begins an issue group. That is, when the instruction cannot issue simultaneously with the previous. This may be relied on by later passes, in particular machine-dependent reorg.

Here is a table of the extra fields of insn, jump_insn and call_insn insns:

PATTERN (i)

>An expression for the side effect performed by this insn. This must be one of the following codes: set, call, use, clobber, return, simple_return, asm_input, asm_output, addr_vec, addr_diff_vec, trap_if, unspec, unspec_volatile, parallel, cond_exec, or sequence. If it is a parallel, each element of the parallel must be one these codes, except that parallel expressions cannot be nested and addr_vec and addr_diff_vec are not permitted inside a parallel expression.

INSN_CODE (*i*)

> An integer that says which pattern in the machine description matches this insn, or −1 if the matching has not yet been attempted.

> Such matching is never attempted and this field remains −1 on an insn whose pattern consists of a single use, clobber, asm_input, addr_vec or addr_diff_vec expression.

> Matching is also never attempted on insns that result from an asm statement. These contain at least one asm_operands expression. The function asm_noperands returns a non-negative value for such insns.

> In the debugging output, this field is printed as a number followed by a symbolic representation that locates the pattern in the 'md' file as some small positive or negative offset from a named pattern.

LOG_LINKS (*i*)

> A list (chain of insn_list expressions) giving information about dependencies between instructions within a basic block. Neither a jump nor a label may come between the related insns. These are only used by the schedulers and by combine. This is a deprecated data structure. Def-use and use-def chains are now preferred.

REG_NOTES (*i*)

> A list (chain of expr_list, insn_list and int_list expressions) giving miscellaneous information about the insn. It is often information pertaining to the registers used in this insn.

The LOG_LINKS field of an insn is a chain of insn_list expressions. Each of these has two operands: the first is an insn, and the second is another insn_list expression (the next one in the chain). The last insn_list in the chain has a null pointer as second operand. The significant thing about the chain is which insns appear in it (as first operands of insn_list expressions). Their order is not significant.

This list is originally set up by the flow analysis pass; it is a null pointer until then. Flow only adds links for those data dependencies which can be used for instruction combination. For each insn, the flow analysis pass adds a link to insns which store into registers values that are used for the first time in this insn.

The REG_NOTES field of an insn is a chain similar to the LOG_LINKS field but it includes expr_list and int_list expressions in addition to insn_list expressions. There are several kinds of register notes, which are distinguished by the machine mode, which in a register note is really understood as being an enum reg_note. The first operand *op* of the note is data whose meaning depends on the kind of note.

The macro REG_NOTE_KIND (*x*) returns the kind of register note. Its counterpart, the macro PUT_REG_NOTE_KIND (*x, newkind*) sets the register note type of *x* to be *newkind*.

Register notes are of three classes: They may say something about an input to an insn, they may say something about an output of an insn, or they may create a linkage between two insns. There are also a set of values that are only used in LOG_LINKS.

These register notes annotate inputs to an insn:

REG_DEAD   The value in *op* dies in this insn; that is to say, altering the value immediately after this insn would not affect the future behavior of the program.

It does not follow that the register *op* has no useful value after this insn since *op* is not necessarily modified by this insn. Rather, no subsequent instruction uses the contents of *op*.

REG_UNUSED

> The register *op* being set by this insn will not be used in a subsequent insn. This differs from a `REG_DEAD` note, which indicates that the value in an input will not be used subsequently. These two notes are independent; both may be present for the same register.

REG_INC   The register *op* is incremented (or decremented; at this level there is no distinction) by an embedded side effect inside this insn. This means it appears in a `post_inc`, `pre_inc`, `post_dec` or `pre_dec` expression.

REG_NONNEG

> The register *op* is known to have a nonnegative value when this insn is reached. This is used so that decrement and branch until zero instructions, such as the m68k dbra, can be matched.
>
> The `REG_NONNEG` note is added to insns only if the machine description has a 'decrement_and_branch_until_zero' pattern.

REG_LABEL_OPERAND

> This insn uses *op*, a `code_label` or a `note` of type `NOTE_INSN_DELETED_LABEL`, but is not a `jump_insn`, or it is a `jump_insn` that refers to the operand as an ordinary operand. The label may still eventually be a jump target, but if so in an indirect jump in a subsequent insn. The presence of this note allows jump optimization to be aware that *op* is, in fact, being used, and flow optimization to build an accurate flow graph.

REG_LABEL_TARGET

> This insn is a `jump_insn` but not an `addr_vec` or `addr_diff_vec`. It uses *op*, a `code_label` as a direct or indirect jump target. Its purpose is similar to that of `REG_LABEL_OPERAND`. This note is only present if the insn has multiple targets; the last label in the insn (in the highest numbered insn-field) goes into the `JUMP_LABEL` field and does not have a `REG_LABEL_TARGET` note. See Section 13.19 [Insns], page 271.

REG_CROSSING_JUMP

> This insn is a branching instruction (either an unconditional jump or an indirect jump) which crosses between hot and cold sections, which could potentially be very far apart in the executable. The presence of this note indicates to other optimizations that this branching instruction should not be "collapsed" into a simpler branching construct. It is used when the optimization to partition basic blocks into hot and cold sections is turned on.

REG_SETJMP

> Appears attached to each `CALL_INSN` to `setjmp` or a related function.

The following notes describe attributes of outputs of an insn:

`REG_EQUIV`
`REG_EQUAL`

This note is only valid on an insn that sets only one register and indicates that that register will be equal to *op* at run time; the scope of this equivalence differs between the two types of notes. The value which the insn explicitly copies into the register may look different from *op*, but they will be equal at run time. If the output of the single `set` is a `strict_low_part` or `zero_extract` expression, the note refers to the register that is contained in its first operand.

For `REG_EQUIV`, the register is equivalent to *op* throughout the entire function, and could validly be replaced in all its occurrences by *op*. ("Validly" here refers to the data flow of the program; simple replacement may make some insns invalid.) For example, when a constant is loaded into a register that is never assigned any other value, this kind of note is used.

When a parameter is copied into a pseudo-register at entry to a function, a note of this kind records that the register is equivalent to the stack slot where the parameter was passed. Although in this case the register may be set by other insns, it is still valid to replace the register by the stack slot throughout the function.

A `REG_EQUIV` note is also used on an instruction which copies a register parameter into a pseudo-register at entry to a function, if there is a stack slot where that parameter could be stored. Although other insns may set the pseudo-register, it is valid for the compiler to replace the pseudo-register by stack slot throughout the function, provided the compiler ensures that the stack slot is properly initialized by making the replacement in the initial copy instruction as well. This is used on machines for which the calling convention allocates stack space for register parameters. See `REG_PARM_STACK_SPACE` in Section 17.9.6 [Stack Arguments], page 486.

In the case of `REG_EQUAL`, the register that is set by this insn will be equal to *op* at run time at the end of this insn but not necessarily elsewhere in the function. In this case, *op* is typically an arithmetic expression. For example, when a sequence of insns such as a library call is used to perform an arithmetic operation, this kind of note is attached to the insn that produces or copies the final value.

These two notes are used in different ways by the compiler passes. `REG_EQUAL` is used by passes prior to register allocation (such as common subexpression elimination and loop optimization) to tell them how to think of that value. `REG_EQUIV` notes are used by register allocation to indicate that there is an available substitute expression (either a constant or a `mem` expression for the location of a parameter on the stack) that may be used in place of a register if insufficient registers are available.

Except for stack homes for parameters, which are indicated by a `REG_EQUIV` note and are not useful to the early optimization passes and pseudo registers that are equivalent to a memory location throughout their entire life, which is not detected until later in the compilation, all equivalences are initially indicated by an attached `REG_EQUAL` note. In the early stages of register allocation, a

REG_EQUAL note is changed into a REG_EQUIV note if *op* is a constant and the insn represents the only set of its destination register.

Thus, compiler passes prior to register allocation need only check for REG_EQUAL notes and passes subsequent to register allocation need only check for REG_EQUIV notes.

These notes describe linkages between insns. They occur in pairs: one insn has one of a pair of notes that points to a second insn, which has the inverse note pointing back to the first insn.

REG_CC_SETTER
REG_CC_USER

> On machines that use cc0, the insns which set and use cc0 set and use cc0 are adjacent. However, when branch delay slot filling is done, this may no longer be true. In this case a REG_CC_USER note will be placed on the insn setting cc0 to point to the insn using cc0 and a REG_CC_SETTER note will be placed on the insn using cc0 to point to the insn setting cc0.

These values are only used in the LOG_LINKS field, and indicate the type of dependency that each link represents. Links which indicate a data dependence (a read after write dependence) do not use any code, they simply have mode VOIDmode, and are printed without any descriptive text.

REG_DEP_TRUE

> This indicates a true dependence (a read after write dependence).

REG_DEP_OUTPUT

> This indicates an output dependence (a write after write dependence).

REG_DEP_ANTI

> This indicates an anti dependence (a write after read dependence).

These notes describe information gathered from gcov profile data. They are stored in the REG_NOTES field of an insn.

REG_BR_PROB

> This is used to specify the ratio of branches to non-branches of a branch insn according to the profile data. The note is represented as an int_list expression whose integer value is between 0 and REG_BR_PROB_BASE. Larger values indicate a higher probability that the branch will be taken.

REG_BR_PRED

> These notes are found in JUMP insns after delayed branch scheduling has taken place. They indicate both the direction and the likelihood of the JUMP. The format is a bitmask of ATTR_FLAG_* values.

REG_FRAME_RELATED_EXPR

> This is used on an RTX_FRAME_RELATED_P insn wherein the attached expression is used in place of the actual insn pattern. This is done in cases where the pattern is either complex or misleading.

For convenience, the machine mode in an insn_list or expr_list is printed using these symbolic codes in debugging dumps.

The only difference between the expression codes `insn_list` and `expr_list` is that the first operand of an `insn_list` is assumed to be an insn and is printed in debugging dumps as the insn's unique id; the first operand of an `expr_list` is printed in the ordinary way as an expression.

13.20 RTL Representation of Function-Call Insns

Insns that call subroutines have the RTL expression code `call_insn`. These insns must satisfy special rules, and their bodies must use a special RTL expression code, `call`.

A `call` expression has two operands, as follows:

```
(call (mem:fm addr) nbytes)
```

Here *nbytes* is an operand that represents the number of bytes of argument data being passed to the subroutine, *fm* is a machine mode (which must equal as the definition of the `FUNCTION_MODE` macro in the machine description) and *addr* represents the address of the subroutine.

For a subroutine that returns no value, the `call` expression as shown above is the entire body of the insn, except that the insn might also contain `use` or `clobber` expressions.

For a subroutine that returns a value whose mode is not `BLKmode`, the value is returned in a hard register. If this register's number is *r*, then the body of the call insn looks like this:

```
(set (reg:m r)
     (call (mem:fm addr) nbytes))
```

This RTL expression makes it clear (to the optimizer passes) that the appropriate register receives a useful value in this insn.

When a subroutine returns a `BLKmode` value, it is handled by passing to the subroutine the address of a place to store the value. So the call insn itself does not "return" any value, and it has the same RTL form as a call that returns nothing.

On some machines, the call instruction itself clobbers some register, for example to contain the return address. `call_insn` insns on these machines should have a body which is a `parallel` that contains both the `call` expression and `clobber` expressions that indicate which registers are destroyed. Similarly, if the call instruction requires some register other than the stack pointer that is not explicitly mentioned in its RTL, a `use` subexpression should mention that register.

Functions that are called are assumed to modify all registers listed in the configuration macro `CALL_USED_REGISTERS` (see Section 17.7.1 [Register Basics], page 459) and, with the exception of `const` functions and library calls, to modify all of memory.

Insns containing just `use` expressions directly precede the `call_insn` insn to indicate which registers contain inputs to the function. Similarly, if registers other than those in `CALL_USED_REGISTERS` are clobbered by the called function, insns containing a single `clobber` follow immediately after the call to indicate which registers.

13.21 Structure Sharing Assumptions

The compiler assumes that certain kinds of RTL expressions are unique; there do not exist two distinct objects representing the same value. In other cases, it makes an opposite assumption: that no RTL expression object of a certain kind appears in more than one place in the containing structure.

These assumptions refer to a single function; except for the RTL objects that describe global variables and external functions, and a few standard objects such as small integer constants, no RTL objects are common to two functions.

- Each pseudo-register has only a single **reg** object to represent it, and therefore only a single machine mode.

- For any symbolic label, there is only one **symbol_ref** object referring to it.

- All **const_int** expressions with equal values are shared.

- There is only one **pc** expression.

- There is only one **cc0** expression.

- There is only one **const_double** expression with value 0 for each floating point mode. Likewise for values 1 and 2.

- There is only one **const_vector** expression with value 0 for each vector mode, be it an integer or a double constant vector.

- No **label_ref** or **scratch** appears in more than one place in the RTL structure; in other words, it is safe to do a tree-walk of all the insns in the function and assume that each time a **label_ref** or **scratch** is seen it is distinct from all others that are seen.

- Only one **mem** object is normally created for each static variable or stack slot, so these objects are frequently shared in all the places they appear. However, separate but equal objects for these variables are occasionally made.

- When a single **asm** statement has multiple output operands, a distinct **asm_operands** expression is made for each output operand. However, these all share the vector which contains the sequence of input operands. This sharing is used later on to test whether two **asm_operands** expressions come from the same statement, so all optimizations must carefully preserve the sharing if they copy the vector at all.

- No RTL object appears in more than one place in the RTL structure except as described above. Many passes of the compiler rely on this by assuming that they can modify RTL objects in place without unwanted side-effects on other insns.

- During initial RTL generation, shared structure is freely introduced. After all the RTL for a function has been generated, all shared structure is copied by **unshare_all_rtl** in 'emit-rtl.c', after which the above rules are guaranteed to be followed.

- During the combiner pass, shared structure within an insn can exist temporarily. However, the shared structure is copied before the combiner is finished with the insn. This is done by calling **copy_rtx_if_shared**, which is a subroutine of **unshare_all_rtl**.

13.22 Reading RTL

To read an RTL object from a file, call **read_rtx**. It takes one argument, a stdio stream, and returns a single RTL object. This routine is defined in 'read-rtl.c'. It is not available in the compiler itself, only the various programs that generate the compiler back end from the machine description.

People frequently have the idea of using RTL stored as text in a file as an interface between a language front end and the bulk of GCC. This idea is not feasible.

GCC was designed to use RTL internally only. Correct RTL for a given program is very dependent on the particular target machine. And the RTL does not contain all the information about the program.

The proper way to interface GCC to a new language front end is with the "tree" data structure, described in the files 'tree.h' and 'tree.def'. The documentation for this structure (see Chapter 10 [GENERIC], page 133) is incomplete.

14 Control Flow Graph

A control flow graph (CFG) is a data structure built on top of the intermediate code representation (the RTL or `GIMPLE` instruction stream) abstracting the control flow behavior of a function that is being compiled. The CFG is a directed graph where the vertices represent basic blocks and edges represent possible transfer of control flow from one basic block to another. The data structures used to represent the control flow graph are defined in 'basic-block.h'.

In GCC, the representation of control flow is maintained throughout the compilation process, from constructing the CFG early in `pass_build_cfg` to `pass_free_cfg` (see 'passes.def'). The CFG takes various different modes and may undergo extensive manipulations, but the graph is always valid between its construction and its release. This way, transfer of information such as data flow, a measured profile, or the loop tree, can be propagated through the passes pipeline, and even from `GIMPLE` to `RTL`.

Often the CFG may be better viewed as integral part of instruction chain, than structure built on the top of it. Updating the compiler's intermediate representation for instructions can not be easily done without proper maintenance of the CFG simultaneously.

14.1 Basic Blocks

A basic block is a straight-line sequence of code with only one entry point and only one exit. In GCC, basic blocks are represented using the `basic_block` data type.

Special basic blocks represent possible entry and exit points of a function. These blocks are called `ENTRY_BLOCK_PTR` and `EXIT_BLOCK_PTR`. These blocks do not contain any code.

The `BASIC_BLOCK` array contains all basic blocks in an unspecified order. Each `basic_block` structure has a field that holds a unique integer identifier `index` that is the index of the block in the `BASIC_BLOCK` array. The total number of basic blocks in the function is `n_basic_blocks`. Both the basic block indices and the total number of basic blocks may vary during the compilation process, as passes reorder, create, duplicate, and destroy basic blocks. The index for any block should never be greater than `last_basic_block`. The indices 0 and 1 are special codes reserved for `ENTRY_BLOCK` and `EXIT_BLOCK`, the indices of `ENTRY_BLOCK_PTR` and `EXIT_BLOCK_PTR`.

Two pointer members of the `basic_block` structure are the pointers `next_bb` and `prev_bb`. These are used to keep doubly linked chain of basic blocks in the same order as the underlying instruction stream. The chain of basic blocks is updated transparently by the provided API for manipulating the CFG. The macro `FOR_EACH_BB` can be used to visit all the basic blocks in lexicographical order, except `ENTRY_BLOCK` and `EXIT_BLOCK`. The macro `FOR_ALL_BB` also visits all basic blocks in lexicographical order, including `ENTRY_BLOCK` and `EXIT_BLOCK`.

The functions `post_order_compute` and `inverted_post_order_compute` can be used to compute topological orders of the CFG. The orders are stored as vectors of basic block indices. The `BASIC_BLOCK` array can be used to iterate each basic block by index. Dominator traversals are also possible using `walk_dominator_tree`. Given two basic blocks A and B, block A dominates block B if A is *always* executed before B.

Each `basic_block` also contains pointers to the first instruction (the *head*) and the last instruction (the *tail*) or *end* of the instruction stream contained in a basic block. In fact, since the `basic_block` data type is used to represent blocks in both major intermediate representations of GCC (GIMPLE and RTL), there are pointers to the head and end of a basic block for both representations, stored in intermediate representation specific data in the `il` field of `struct basic_block_def`.

For RTL, these pointers are `BB_HEAD` and `BB_END`.

In the RTL representation of a function, the instruction stream contains not only the "real" instructions, but also *notes* or *insn notes* (to distinguish them from *reg notes*). Any function that moves or duplicates the basic blocks needs to take care of updating of these notes. Many of these notes expect that the instruction stream consists of linear regions, so updating can sometimes be tedious. All types of insn notes are defined in '`insn-notes.def`'.

In the RTL function representation, the instructions contained in a basic block always follow a `NOTE_INSN_BASIC_BLOCK`, but zero or more `CODE_LABEL` nodes can precede the block note. A basic block ends with a control flow instruction or with the last instruction before the next `CODE_LABEL` or `NOTE_INSN_BASIC_BLOCK`. By definition, a `CODE_LABEL` cannot appear in the middle of the instruction stream of a basic block.

In addition to notes, the jump table vectors are also represented as "pseudo-instructions" inside the insn stream. These vectors never appear in the basic block and should always be placed just after the table jump instructions referencing them. After removing the table-jump it is often difficult to eliminate the code computing the address and referencing the vector, so cleaning up these vectors is postponed until after liveness analysis. Thus the jump table vectors may appear in the insn stream unreferenced and without any purpose. Before any edge is made *fall-thru*, the existence of such construct in the way needs to be checked by calling `can_fallthru` function.

For the GIMPLE representation, the PHI nodes and statements contained in a basic block are in a `gimple_seq` pointed to by the basic block intermediate language specific pointers. Abstract containers and iterators are used to access the PHI nodes and statements in a basic blocks. These iterators are called *GIMPLE statement iterators* (GSIs). Grep for `^gsi` in the various '`gimple-*`' and '`tree-*`' files. There is a `gimple_stmt_iterator` type for iterating over all kinds of statement, and a `gphi_iterator` subclass for iterating over PHI nodes. The following snippet will pretty-print all PHI nodes the statements of the current function in the GIMPLE representation.

```
    basic_block bb;

FOR_EACH_BB (bb)
  {
    gphi_iterator pi;
    gimple_stmt_iterator si;

    for (pi = gsi_start_phis (bb); !gsi_end_p (pi); gsi_next (&pi))
      {
        gphi *phi = pi.phi ();
        print_gimple_stmt (dump_file, phi, 0, TDF_SLIM);
      }
    for (si = gsi_start_bb (bb); !gsi_end_p (si); gsi_next (&si))
      {
        gimple stmt = gsi_stmt (si);
        print_gimple_stmt (dump_file, stmt, 0, TDF_SLIM);
      }
  }
```

14.2 Edges

Edges represent possible control flow transfers from the end of some basic block A to the head of another basic block B. We say that A is a predecessor of B, and B is a successor of A. Edges are represented in GCC with the **edge** data type. Each **edge** acts as a link between two basic blocks: The **src** member of an edge points to the predecessor basic block of the **dest** basic block. The members **preds** and **succs** of the **basic_block** data type point to type-safe vectors of edges to the predecessors and successors of the block.

When walking the edges in an edge vector, *edge iterators* should be used. Edge iterators are constructed using the **edge_iterator** data structure and several methods are available to operate on them:

ei_start   This function initializes an **edge_iterator** that points to the first edge in a vector of edges.

ei_last   This function initializes an **edge_iterator** that points to the last edge in a vector of edges.

ei_end_p   This predicate is **true** if an **edge_iterator** represents the last edge in an edge vector.

ei_one_before_end_p

This predicate is **true** if an **edge_iterator** represents the second last edge in an edge vector.

ei_next   This function takes a pointer to an **edge_iterator** and makes it point to the next edge in the sequence.

ei_prev   This function takes a pointer to an **edge_iterator** and makes it point to the previous edge in the sequence.

ei_edge   This function returns the **edge** currently pointed to by an **edge_iterator**.

ei_safe_safe

This function returns the **edge** currently pointed to by an **edge_iterator**, but returns **NULL** if the iterator is pointing at the end of the sequence. This function has been provided for existing code makes the assumption that a **NULL** edge indicates the end of the sequence.

The convenience macro **FOR_EACH_EDGE** can be used to visit all of the edges in a sequence of predecessor or successor edges. It must not be used when an element might be removed during the traversal, otherwise elements will be missed. Here is an example of how to use the macro:

```
edge e;
edge_iterator ei;

FOR_EACH_EDGE (e, ei, bb->succs)
  {
     if (e->flags & EDGE_FALLTHRU)
       break;
  }
```

There are various reasons why control flow may transfer from one block to another. One possibility is that some instruction, for example a **CODE_LABEL**, in a linearized instruction stream just always starts a new basic block. In this case a *fall-thru* edge links the basic block to the first following basic block. But there are several other reasons why edges may be created. The `flags` field of the `edge` data type is used to store information about the type of edge we are dealing with. Each edge is of one of the following types:

jump   No type flags are set for edges corresponding to jump instructions. These edges are used for unconditional or conditional jumps and in RTL also for table jumps. They are the easiest to manipulate as they may be freely redirected when the flow graph is not in SSA form.

fall-thru   Fall-thru edges are present in case where the basic block may continue execution to the following one without branching. These edges have the `EDGE_FALLTHRU` flag set. Unlike other types of edges, these edges must come into the basic block immediately following in the instruction stream. The function `force_nonfallthru` is available to insert an unconditional jump in the case that redirection is needed. Note that this may require creation of a new basic block.

exception handling

Exception handling edges represent possible control transfers from a trapping instruction to an exception handler. The definition of "trapping" varies. In C++, only function calls can throw, but for Java and Ada, exceptions like division by zero or segmentation fault are defined and thus each instruction possibly throwing this kind of exception needs to be handled as control flow instruction. Exception edges have the `EDGE_ABNORMAL` and `EDGE_EH` flags set.

When updating the instruction stream it is easy to change possibly trapping instruction to non-trapping, by simply removing the exception edge. The opposite conversion is difficult, but should not happen anyway. The edges can be eliminated via `purge_dead_edges` call.

In the RTL representation, the destination of an exception edge is specified by `REG_EH_REGION` note attached to the insn. In case of a trapping call the `EDGE_ABNORMAL_CALL` flag is set too. In the `GIMPLE` representation, this extra flag is not set.

In the RTL representation, the predicate `may_trap_p` may be used to check whether instruction still may trap or not. For the tree representation, the `tree_could_trap_p` predicate is available, but this predicate only checks for possible memory traps, as in dereferencing an invalid pointer location.

sibling calls

Sibling calls or tail calls terminate the function in a non-standard way and thus an edge to the exit must be present. `EDGE_SIBCALL` and `EDGE_ABNORMAL` are set in such case. These edges only exist in the RTL representation.

computed jumps

Computed jumps contain edges to all labels in the function referenced from the code. All those edges have `EDGE_ABNORMAL` flag set. The edges used to represent computed jumps often cause compile time performance problems, since functions consisting of many taken labels and many computed jumps may have *very* dense flow graphs, so these edges need to be handled with special care. During the earlier stages of the compilation process, GCC tries to avoid such dense flow graphs by factoring computed jumps. For example, given the following series of jumps,

```
goto *x;
[ ... ]

goto *x;
[ ... ]

goto *x;
[ ... ]
```

factoring the computed jumps results in the following code sequence which has a much simpler flow graph:

```
goto y;
[ ... ]

goto y;
[ ... ]

goto y;
[ ... ]

y:
    goto *x;
```

However, the classic problem with this transformation is that it has a runtime cost in there resulting code: An extra jump. Therefore, the computed jumps are un-factored in the later passes of the compiler (in the pass called `pass_duplicate_computed_gotos`). Be aware of that when you work on passes in that area. There have been numerous examples already where the compile time for code with unfactored computed jumps caused some serious headaches.

nonlocal goto handlers

GCC allows nested functions to return into caller using a `goto` to a label passed to as an argument to the callee. The labels passed to nested functions contain special code to cleanup after function call. Such sections of code are referred to as "nonlocal goto receivers". If a function contains such nonlocal goto receivers, an edge from the call to the label is created with the `EDGE_ABNORMAL` and `EDGE_ABNORMAL_CALL` flags set.

function entry points

By definition, execution of function starts at basic block 0, so there is always an edge from the `ENTRY_BLOCK_PTR` to basic block 0. There is no `GIMPLE` representation for alternate entry points at this moment. In RTL, alternate entry points are specified by `CODE_LABEL` with `LABEL_ALTERNATE_NAME` defined. This feature is currently used for multiple entry point prologues and is limited to post-reload passes only. This can be used by back-ends to emit alternate prologues for functions called from different contexts. In future full support for multiple entry functions defined by Fortran 90 needs to be implemented.

function exits

In the pre-reload representation a function terminates after the last instruction in the insn chain and no explicit return instructions are used. This corresponds to the fall-thru edge into exit block. After reload, optimal RTL epilogues are used that use explicit (conditional) return instructions that are represented by edges with no flags set.

14.3 Profile information

In many cases a compiler must make a choice whether to trade speed in one part of code for speed in another, or to trade code size for code speed. In such cases it is useful to know information about how often some given block will be executed. That is the purpose for maintaining profile within the flow graph. GCC can handle profile information obtained through *profile feedback*, but it can also estimate branch probabilities based on statics and heuristics.

The feedback based profile is produced by compiling the program with instrumentation, executing it on a train run and reading the numbers of executions of basic blocks and edges back to the compiler while re-compiling the program to produce the final executable. This method provides very accurate information about where a program spends most of its time on the train run. Whether it matches the average run of course depends on the choice of train data set, but several studies have shown that the behavior of a program usually changes just marginally over different data sets.

When profile feedback is not available, the compiler may be asked to attempt to predict the behavior of each branch in the program using a set of heuristics (see 'predict.def' for details) and compute estimated frequencies of each basic block by propagating the probabilities over the graph.

Each basic_block contains two integer fields to represent profile information: frequency and count. The frequency is an estimation how often is basic block executed within a function. It is represented as an integer scaled in the range from 0 to BB_FREQ_BASE. The most frequently executed basic block in function is initially set to BB_FREQ_BASE and the rest of frequencies are scaled accordingly. During optimization, the frequency of the most frequent basic block can both decrease (for instance by loop unrolling) or grow (for instance by cross-jumping optimization), so scaling sometimes has to be performed multiple times.

The count contains hard-counted numbers of execution measured during training runs and is nonzero only when profile feedback is available. This value is represented as the host's widest integer (typically a 64 bit integer) of the special type gcov_type.

Most optimization passes can use only the frequency information of a basic block, but a few passes may want to know hard execution counts. The frequencies should always match the counts after scaling, however during updating of the profile information numerical error may accumulate into quite large errors.

Each edge also contains a branch probability field: an integer in the range from 0 to REG_BR_PROB_BASE. It represents probability of passing control from the end of the src basic block to the dest basic block, i.e. the probability that control will flow along this edge. The EDGE_FREQUENCY macro is available to compute how frequently a given edge is taken. There is a count field for each edge as well, representing same information as for a basic block.

The basic block frequencies are not represented in the instruction stream, but in the RTL representation the edge frequencies are represented for conditional jumps (via the REG_BR_

PROB macro) since they are used when instructions are output to the assembly file and the flow graph is no longer maintained.

The probability that control flow arrives via a given edge to its destination basic block is called *reverse probability* and is not directly represented, but it may be easily computed from frequencies of basic blocks.

Updating profile information is a delicate task that can unfortunately not be easily integrated with the CFG manipulation API. Many of the functions and hooks to modify the CFG, such as `redirect_edge_and_branch`, do not have enough information to easily update the profile, so updating it is in the majority of cases left up to the caller. It is difficult to uncover bugs in the profile updating code, because they manifest themselves only by producing worse code, and checking profile consistency is not possible because of numeric error accumulation. Hence special attention needs to be given to this issue in each pass that modifies the CFG.

It is important to point out that `REG_BR_PROB_BASE` and `BB_FREQ_BASE` are both set low enough to be possible to compute second power of any frequency or probability in the flow graph, it is not possible to even square the `count` field, as modern CPUs are fast enough to execute 2^32 operations quickly.

14.4 Maintaining the CFG

An important task of each compiler pass is to keep both the control flow graph and all profile information up-to-date. Reconstruction of the control flow graph after each pass is not an option, since it may be very expensive and lost profile information cannot be reconstructed at all.

GCC has two major intermediate representations, and both use the `basic_block` and `edge` data types to represent control flow. Both representations share as much of the CFG maintenance code as possible. For each representation, a set of *hooks* is defined so that each representation can provide its own implementation of CFG manipulation routines when necessary. These hooks are defined in '`cfghooks.h`'. There are hooks for almost all common CFG manipulations, including block splitting and merging, edge redirection and creating and deleting basic blocks. These hooks should provide everything you need to maintain and manipulate the CFG in both the RTL and `GIMPLE` representation.

At the moment, the basic block boundaries are maintained transparently when modifying instructions, so there rarely is a need to move them manually (such as in case someone wants to output instruction outside basic block explicitly).

In the RTL representation, each instruction has a `BLOCK_FOR_INSN` value that represents pointer to the basic block that contains the instruction. In the `GIMPLE` representation, the function `gimple_bb` returns a pointer to the basic block containing the queried statement.

When changes need to be applied to a function in its `GIMPLE` representation, *GIMPLE statement iterators* should be used. These iterators provide an integrated abstraction of the flow graph and the instruction stream. Block statement iterators are constructed using the `gimple_stmt_iterator` data structure and several modifiers are available, including the following:

`gsi_start`

> This function initializes a `gimple_stmt_iterator` that points to the first non-empty statement in a basic block.

gsi_last   This function initializes a `gimple_stmt_iterator` that points to the last statement in a basic block.

gsi_end_p

This predicate is `true` if a `gimple_stmt_iterator` represents the end of a basic block.

gsi_next   This function takes a `gimple_stmt_iterator` and makes it point to its successor.

gsi_prev   This function takes a `gimple_stmt_iterator` and makes it point to its predecessor.

gsi_insert_after

This function inserts a statement after the `gimple_stmt_iterator` passed in. The final parameter determines whether the statement iterator is updated to point to the newly inserted statement, or left pointing to the original statement.

gsi_insert_before

This function inserts a statement before the `gimple_stmt_iterator` passed in. The final parameter determines whether the statement iterator is updated to point to the newly inserted statement, or left pointing to the original statement.

gsi_remove

This function removes the `gimple_stmt_iterator` passed in and rechains the remaining statements in a basic block, if any.

In the RTL representation, the macros `BB_HEAD` and `BB_END` may be used to get the head and end `rtx` of a basic block. No abstract iterators are defined for traversing the insn chain, but you can just use `NEXT_INSN` and `PREV_INSN` instead. See Section 13.19 [Insns], page 271.

Usually a code manipulating pass simplifies the instruction stream and the flow of control, possibly eliminating some edges. This may for example happen when a conditional jump is replaced with an unconditional jump, but also when simplifying possibly trapping instruction to non-trapping while compiling Java. Updating of edges is not transparent and each optimization pass is required to do so manually. However only few cases occur in practice. The pass may call `purge_dead_edges` on a given basic block to remove superfluous edges, if any.

Another common scenario is redirection of branch instructions, but this is best modeled as redirection of edges in the control flow graph and thus use of `redirect_edge_and_branch` is preferred over more low level functions, such as `redirect_jump` that operate on RTL chain only. The CFG hooks defined in 'cfghooks.h' should provide the complete API required for manipulating and maintaining the CFG.

It is also possible that a pass has to insert control flow instruction into the middle of a basic block, thus creating an entry point in the middle of the basic block, which is impossible by definition: The block must be split to make sure it only has one entry point, i.e. the head of the basic block. The CFG hook `split_block` may be used when an instruction in the middle of a basic block has to become the target of a jump or branch instruction.

For a global optimizer, a common operation is to split edges in the flow graph and insert instructions on them. In the RTL representation, this can be easily done using the `insert_insn_on_edge` function that emits an instruction "on the edge", caching it for a later `commit_edge_insertions` call that will take care of moving the inserted instructions off the edge into the instruction stream contained in a basic block. This includes the creation of new basic blocks where needed. In the `GIMPLE` representation, the equivalent functions are `gsi_insert_on_edge` which inserts a block statement iterator on an edge, and `gsi_commit_edge_inserts` which flushes the instruction to actual instruction stream.

While debugging the optimization pass, the `verify_flow_info` function may be useful to find bugs in the control flow graph updating code.

14.5 Liveness information

Liveness information is useful to determine whether some register is "live" at given point of program, i.e. that it contains a value that may be used at a later point in the program. This information is used, for instance, during register allocation, as the pseudo registers only need to be assigned to a unique hard register or to a stack slot if they are live. The hard registers and stack slots may be freely reused for other values when a register is dead.

Liveness information is available in the back end starting with `pass_df_initialize` and ending with `pass_df_finish`. Three flavors of live analysis are available: With `LR`, it is possible to determine at any point `P` in the function if the register may be used on some path from `P` to the end of the function. With `UR`, it is possible to determine if there is a path from the beginning of the function to `P` that defines the variable. `LIVE` is the intersection of the `LR` and `UR` and a variable is live at `P` if there is both an assignment that reaches it from the beginning of the function and a use that can be reached on some path from `P` to the end of the function.

In general `LIVE` is the most useful of the three. The macros `DF_[LR,UR,LIVE]_[IN,OUT]` can be used to access this information. The macros take a basic block number and return a bitmap that is indexed by the register number. This information is only guaranteed to be up to date after calls are made to `df_analyze`. See the file `df-core.c` for details on using the dataflow.

The liveness information is stored partly in the RTL instruction stream and partly in the flow graph. Local information is stored in the instruction stream: Each instruction may contain `REG_DEAD` notes representing that the value of a given register is no longer needed, or `REG_UNUSED` notes representing that the value computed by the instruction is never used. The second is useful for instructions computing multiple values at once.

15   Analysis and Representation of Loops

GCC provides extensive infrastructure for work with natural loops, i.e., strongly connected components of CFG with only one entry block. This chapter describes representation of loops in GCC, both on GIMPLE and in RTL, as well as the interfaces to loop-related analyses (induction variable analysis and number of iterations analysis).

15.1   Loop representation

This chapter describes the representation of loops in GCC, and functions that can be used to build, modify and analyze this representation. Most of the interfaces and data structures are declared in 'cfgloop.h'. Loop structures are analyzed and this information disposed or updated at the discretion of individual passes. Still most of the generic CFG manipulation routines are aware of loop structures and try to keep them up-to-date. By this means an increasing part of the compilation pipeline is setup to maintain loop structure across passes to allow attaching meta information to individual loops for consumption by later passes.

In general, a natural loop has one entry block (header) and possibly several back edges (latches) leading to the header from the inside of the loop. Loops with several latches may appear if several loops share a single header, or if there is a branching in the middle of the loop. The representation of loops in GCC however allows only loops with a single latch. During loop analysis, headers of such loops are split and forwarder blocks are created in order to disambiguate their structures. Heuristic based on profile information and structure of the induction variables in the loops is used to determine whether the latches correspond to sub-loops or to control flow in a single loop. This means that the analysis sometimes changes the CFG, and if you run it in the middle of an optimization pass, you must be able to deal with the new blocks. You may avoid CFG changes by passing LOOPS_MAY_HAVE_MULTIPLE_LATCHES flag to the loop discovery, note however that most other loop manipulation functions will not work correctly for loops with multiple latch edges (the functions that only query membership of blocks to loops and subloop relationships, or enumerate and test loop exits, can be expected to work).

Body of the loop is the set of blocks that are dominated by its header, and reachable from its latch against the direction of edges in CFG. The loops are organized in a containment hierarchy (tree) such that all the loops immediately contained inside loop L are the children of L in the tree. This tree is represented by the struct loops structure. The root of this tree is a fake loop that contains all blocks in the function. Each of the loops is represented in a struct loop structure. Each loop is assigned an index (num field of the struct loop structure), and the pointer to the loop is stored in the corresponding field of the larray vector in the loops structure. The indices do not have to be continuous, there may be empty (NULL) entries in the larray created by deleting loops. Also, there is no guarantee on the relative order of a loop and its subloops in the numbering. The index of a loop never changes.

The entries of the larray field should not be accessed directly. The function get_loop returns the loop description for a loop with the given index. number_of_loops function returns number of loops in the function. To traverse all loops, use FOR_EACH_LOOP macro. The flags argument of the macro is used to determine the direction of traversal and the set of loops visited. Each loop is guaranteed to be visited exactly once, regardless of the changes to the loop tree, and the loops may be removed during the traversal. The newly created loops are never traversed, if they need to be visited, this must be done separately after their creation. The `FOR_EACH_LOOP` macro allocates temporary variables. If the `FOR_EACH_LOOP` loop were ended using break or goto, they would not be released; `FOR_EACH_LOOP_BREAK` macro must be used instead.

Each basic block contains the reference to the innermost loop it belongs to (`loop_father`). For this reason, it is only possible to have one `struct loops` structure initialized at the same time for each CFG. The global variable `current_loops` contains the `struct loops` structure. Many of the loop manipulation functions assume that dominance information is up-to-date.

The loops are analyzed through `loop_optimizer_init` function. The argument of this function is a set of flags represented in an integer bitmask. These flags specify what other properties of the loop structures should be calculated/enforced and preserved later:

- `LOOPS_MAY_HAVE_MULTIPLE_LATCHES`: If this flag is set, no changes to CFG will be performed in the loop analysis, in particular, loops with multiple latch edges will not be disambiguated. If a loop has multiple latches, its latch block is set to NULL. Most of the loop manipulation functions will not work for loops in this shape. No other flags that require CFG changes can be passed to loop_optimizer_init.

- `LOOPS_HAVE_PREHEADERS`: Forwarder blocks are created in such a way that each loop has only one entry edge, and additionally, the source block of this entry edge has only one successor. This creates a natural place where the code can be moved out of the loop, and ensures that the entry edge of the loop leads from its immediate super-loop.

- `LOOPS_HAVE_SIMPLE_LATCHES`: Forwarder blocks are created to force the latch block of each loop to have only one successor. This ensures that the latch of the loop does not belong to any of its sub-loops, and makes manipulation with the loops significantly easier. Most of the loop manipulation functions assume that the loops are in this shape. Note that with this flag, the "normal" loop without any control flow inside and with one exit consists of two basic blocks.

- `LOOPS_HAVE_MARKED_IRREDUCIBLE_REGIONS`: Basic blocks and edges in the strongly connected components that are not natural loops (have more than one entry block) are marked with `BB_IRREDUCIBLE_LOOP` and `EDGE_IRREDUCIBLE_LOOP` flags. The flag is not set for blocks and edges that belong to natural loops that are in such an irreducible region (but it is set for the entry and exit edges of such a loop, if they lead to/from this region).

- `LOOPS_HAVE_RECORDED_EXITS`: The lists of exits are recorded and updated for each loop. This makes some functions (e.g., `get_loop_exit_edges`) more efficient. Some functions (e.g., `single_exit`) can be used only if the lists of exits are recorded.

These properties may also be computed/enforced later, using functions `create_preheaders`, `force_single_succ_latches`, `mark_irreducible_loops` and `record_loop_exits`. The properties can be queried using `loops_state_satisfies_p`.

The memory occupied by the loops structures should be freed with `loop_optimizer_finalize` function. When loop structures are setup to be preserved across passes this function reduces the information to be kept up-to-date to a minimum (only `LOOPS_MAY_HAVE_MULTIPLE_LATCHES` set).

The CFG manipulation functions in general do not update loop structures. Specialized versions that additionally do so are provided for the most common tasks. On GIMPLE, `cleanup_tree_cfg_loop` function can be used to cleanup CFG while updating the loops structures if `current_loops` is set.

At the moment loop structure is preserved from the start of GIMPLE loop optimizations until the end of RTL loop optimizations. During this time a loop can be tracked by its `struct loop` and number.

15.2 Loop querying

The functions to query the information about loops are declared in 'cfgloop.h'. Some of the information can be taken directly from the structures. `loop_father` field of each basic block contains the innermost loop to that the block belongs. The most useful fields of loop structure (that are kept up-to-date at all times) are:

- `header`, `latch`: Header and latch basic blocks of the loop.

- `num_nodes`: Number of basic blocks in the loop (including the basic blocks of the sub-loops).

- `outer`, `inner`, `next`: The super-loop, the first sub-loop, and the sibling of the loop in the loops tree.

There are other fields in the loop structures, many of them used only by some of the passes, or not updated during CFG changes; in general, they should not be accessed directly.

The most important functions to query loop structures are:

- `loop_depth`: The depth of the loop in the loops tree, i.e., the number of super-loops of the loop.

- `flow_loops_dump`: Dumps the information about loops to a file.

- `verify_loop_structure`: Checks consistency of the loop structures.

- `loop_latch_edge`: Returns the latch edge of a loop.

- `loop_preheader_edge`: If loops have preheaders, returns the preheader edge of a loop.

- `flow_loop_nested_p`: Tests whether loop is a sub-loop of another loop.

- `flow_bb_inside_loop_p`: Tests whether a basic block belongs to a loop (including its sub-loops).

- `find_common_loop`: Finds the common super-loop of two loops.

- `superloop_at_depth`: Returns the super-loop of a loop with the given depth.

- `tree_num_loop_insns`, `num_loop_insns`: Estimates the number of insns in the loop, on GIMPLE and on RTL.

- `loop_exit_edge_p`: Tests whether edge is an exit from a loop.

- `mark_loop_exit_edges`: Marks all exit edges of all loops with `EDGE_LOOP_EXIT` flag.

- `get_loop_body`, `get_loop_body_in_dom_order`, `get_loop_body_in_bfs_order`: Enumerates the basic blocks in the loop in depth-first search order in reversed CFG, ordered by dominance relation, and breath-first search order, respectively.

- `single_exit`: Returns the single exit edge of the loop, or `NULL` if the loop has more than one exit. You can only use this function if LOOPS_HAVE_MARKED_SINGLE_EXITS property is used.

- `get_loop_exit_edges`: Enumerates the exit edges of a loop.

- `just_once_each_iteration_p`: Returns true if the basic block is executed exactly once during each iteration of a loop (that is, it does not belong to a sub-loop, and it dominates the latch of the loop).

15.3 Loop manipulation

The loops tree can be manipulated using the following functions:

- `flow_loop_tree_node_add`: Adds a node to the tree.
- `flow_loop_tree_node_remove`: Removes a node from the tree.
- `add_bb_to_loop`: Adds a basic block to a loop.
- `remove_bb_from_loops`: Removes a basic block from loops.

Most low-level CFG functions update loops automatically. The following functions handle some more complicated cases of CFG manipulations:

- `remove_path`: Removes an edge and all blocks it dominates.
- `split_loop_exit_edge`: Splits exit edge of the loop, ensuring that PHI node arguments remain in the loop (this ensures that loop-closed SSA form is preserved). Only useful on GIMPLE.

Finally, there are some higher-level loop transformations implemented. While some of them are written so that they should work on non-innermost loops, they are mostly untested in that case, and at the moment, they are only reliable for the innermost loops:

- `create_iv`: Creates a new induction variable. Only works on GIMPLE. `standard_iv_increment_position` can be used to find a suitable place for the iv increment.
- `duplicate_loop_to_header_edge`, `tree_duplicate_loop_to_header_edge`: These functions (on RTL and on GIMPLE) duplicate the body of the loop prescribed number of times on one of the edges entering loop header, thus performing either loop unrolling or loop peeling. `can_duplicate_loop_p` (`can_unroll_loop_p` on GIMPLE) must be true for the duplicated loop.
- `loop_version`, `tree_ssa_loop_version`: These function create a copy of a loop, and a branch before them that selects one of them depending on the prescribed condition. This is useful for optimizations that need to verify some assumptions in runtime (one of the copies of the loop is usually left unchanged, while the other one is transformed in some way).
- `tree_unroll_loop`: Unrolls the loop, including peeling the extra iterations to make the number of iterations divisible by unroll factor, updating the exit condition, and removing the exits that now cannot be taken. Works only on GIMPLE.

15.4 Loop-closed SSA form

Throughout the loop optimizations on tree level, one extra condition is enforced on the SSA form: No SSA name is used outside of the loop in that it is defined. The SSA form satisfying this condition is called "loop-closed SSA form" – LCSSA. To enforce LCSSA, PHI nodes must be created at the exits of the loops for the SSA names that are used outside of them. Only the real operands (not virtual SSA names) are held in LCSSA, in order to save memory.

There are various benefits of LCSSA:

- Many optimizations (value range analysis, final value replacement) are interested in the values that are defined in the loop and used outside of it, i.e., exactly those for that we create new PHI nodes.

- In induction variable analysis, it is not necessary to specify the loop in that the analysis should be performed – the scalar evolution analysis always returns the results with respect to the loop in that the SSA name is defined.

- It makes updating of SSA form during loop transformations simpler. Without LCSSA, operations like loop unrolling may force creation of PHI nodes arbitrarily far from the loop, while in LCSSA, the SSA form can be updated locally. However, since we only keep real operands in LCSSA, we cannot use this advantage (we could have local updating of real operands, but it is not much more efficient than to use generic SSA form updating for it as well; the amount of changes to SSA is the same).

However, it also means LCSSA must be updated. This is usually straightforward, unless you create a new value in loop and use it outside, or unless you manipulate loop exit edges (functions are provided to make these manipulations simple). `rewrite_into_loop_closed_ssa` is used to rewrite SSA form to LCSSA, and `verify_loop_closed_ssa` to check that the invariant of LCSSA is preserved.

15.5 Scalar evolutions

Scalar evolutions (SCEV) are used to represent results of induction variable analysis on GIMPLE. They enable us to represent variables with complicated behavior in a simple and consistent way (we only use it to express values of polynomial induction variables, but it is possible to extend it). The interfaces to SCEV analysis are declared in 'tree-scalar-evolution.h'. To use scalar evolutions analysis, `scev_initialize` must be used. To stop using SCEV, `scev_finalize` should be used. SCEV analysis caches results in order to save time and memory. This cache however is made invalid by most of the loop transformations, including removal of code. If such a transformation is performed, `scev_reset` must be called to clean the caches.

Given an SSA name, its behavior in loops can be analyzed using the `analyze_scalar_evolution` function. The returned SCEV however does not have to be fully analyzed and it may contain references to other SSA names defined in the loop. To resolve these (potentially recursive) references, `instantiate_parameters` or `resolve_mixers` functions must be used. `instantiate_parameters` is useful when you use the results of SCEV only for some analysis, and when you work with whole nest of loops at once. It will try replacing all SSA names by their SCEV in all loops, including the super-loops of the current loop, thus providing a complete information about the behavior of the variable in the loop nest. `resolve_mixers` is useful if you work with only one loop at a time, and if you possibly need to create code based on the value of the induction variable. It will only resolve the SSA names defined in the current loop, leaving the SSA names defined outside unchanged, even if their evolution in the outer loops is known.

The SCEV is a normal tree expression, except for the fact that it may contain several special tree nodes. One of them is `SCEV_NOT_KNOWN`, used for SSA names whose value cannot be expressed. The other one is `POLYNOMIAL_CHREC`. Polynomial chrec has three arguments – base, step and loop (both base and step may contain further polynomial chrecs). Type of the expression and of base and step must be the same. A variable has evolution `POLYNOMIAL_`

`CHREC(base, step, loop)` if it is (in the specified loop) equivalent to `x_1` in the following example

```
while (...)
  {
    x_1 = phi (base, x_2);
    x_2 = x_1 + step;
  }
```

Note that this includes the language restrictions on the operations. For example, if we compile C code and `x` has signed type, then the overflow in addition would cause undefined behavior, and we may assume that this does not happen. Hence, the value with this SCEV cannot overflow (which restricts the number of iterations of such a loop).

In many cases, one wants to restrict the attention just to affine induction variables. In this case, the extra expressive power of SCEV is not useful, and may complicate the optimizations. In this case, `simple_iv` function may be used to analyze a value – the result is a loop-invariant base and step.

15.6 IV analysis on RTL

The induction variable on RTL is simple and only allows analysis of affine induction variables, and only in one loop at once. The interface is declared in 'cfgloop.h'. Before analyzing induction variables in a loop L, `iv_analysis_loop_init` function must be called on L. After the analysis (possibly calling `iv_analysis_loop_init` for several loops) is finished, `iv_analysis_done` should be called. The following functions can be used to access the results of the analysis:

- `iv_analyze`: Analyzes a single register used in the given insn. If no use of the register in this insn is found, the following insns are scanned, so that this function can be called on the insn returned by get_condition.

- `iv_analyze_result`: Analyzes result of the assignment in the given insn.

- `iv_analyze_expr`: Analyzes a more complicated expression. All its operands are analyzed by `iv_analyze`, and hence they must be used in the specified insn or one of the following insns.

The description of the induction variable is provided in `struct rtx_iv`. In order to handle subregs, the representation is a bit complicated; if the value of the `extend` field is not `UNKNOWN`, the value of the induction variable in the i-th iteration is

```
delta + mult * extend_{extend_mode} (subreg_{mode} (base + i * step)),
```

with the following exception: if `first_special` is true, then the value in the first iteration (when i is zero) is `delta + mult * base`. However, if `extend` is equal to `UNKNOWN`, then `first_special` must be false, `delta` 0, `mult` 1 and the value in the i-th iteration is

```
subreg_{mode} (base + i * step)
```

The function `get_iv_value` can be used to perform these calculations.

15.7 Number of iterations analysis

Both on GIMPLE and on RTL, there are functions available to determine the number of iterations of a loop, with a similar interface. The number of iterations of a loop in GCC is defined as the number of executions of the loop latch. In many cases, it is not possible to determine the number of iterations unconditionally – the determined number is correct only if some assumptions are satisfied. The analysis tries to verify these conditions using the information contained in the program; if it fails, the conditions are returned together with the result. The following information and conditions are provided by the analysis:

- `assumptions`: If this condition is false, the rest of the information is invalid.
- `noloop_assumptions` on RTL, `may_be_zero` on GIMPLE: If this condition is true, the loop exits in the first iteration.
- `infinite`: If this condition is true, the loop is infinite. This condition is only available on RTL. On GIMPLE, conditions for finiteness of the loop are included in `assumptions`.
- `niter_expr` on RTL, `niter` on GIMPLE: The expression that gives number of iterations. The number of iterations is defined as the number of executions of the loop latch.

Both on GIMPLE and on RTL, it necessary for the induction variable analysis framework to be initialized (SCEV on GIMPLE, loop-iv on RTL). On GIMPLE, the results are stored to **struct tree_niter_desc** structure. Number of iterations before the loop is exited through a given exit can be determined using **number_of_iterations_exit** function. On RTL, the results are returned in **struct niter_desc** structure. The corresponding function is named **check_simple_exit**. There are also functions that pass through all the exits of a loop and try to find one with easy to determine number of iterations – **find_loop_niter** on GIMPLE and **find_simple_exit** on RTL. Finally, there are functions that provide the same information, but additionally cache it, so that repeated calls to number of iterations are not so costly – **number_of_latch_executions** on GIMPLE and **get_simple_loop_desc** on RTL.

Note that some of these functions may behave slightly differently than others – some of them return only the expression for the number of iterations, and fail if there are some assumptions. The function **number_of_latch_executions** works only for single-exit loops. The function **number_of_cond_exit_executions** can be used to determine number of executions of the exit condition of a single-exit loop (i.e., the **number_of_latch_executions** increased by one).

On GIMPLE, below constraint flags affect semantics of some APIs of number of iterations analyzer:

- `LOOP_C_INFINITE`: If this constraint flag is set, the loop is known to be infinite. APIs like **number_of_iterations_exit** can return false directly without doing any analysis.
- `LOOP_C_FINITE`: If this constraint flag is set, the loop is known to be finite, in other words, loop's number of iterations can be computed with **assumptions** be true.

Generally, the constraint flags are set/cleared by consumers which are loop optimizers. It's also the consumers' responsibility to set/clear constraints correctly. Failing to do that might result in hard to track down bugs in scev/niter consumers. One typical use case is vectorizer: it drives number of iterations analyzer by setting `LOOP_C_FINITE` and vectorizes possibly infinite loop by versioning loop with analysis result. In return, constraints set by consumers can also help number of iterations analyzer in following optimizers. For example, **niter** of a loop versioned under **assumptions** is valid unconditionally.

Other constraints may be added in the future, for example, a constraint indicating that loops' latch must roll thus **may_be_zero** would be false unconditionally.

15.8 Data Dependency Analysis

The code for the data dependence analysis can be found in 'tree-data-ref.c' and its interface and data structures are described in 'tree-data-ref.h'. The function that computes the data dependences for all the array and pointer references for a given loop is compute_data_dependences_for_loop. This function is currently used by the linear loop transform and the vectorization passes. Before calling this function, one has to allocate two vectors: a first vector will contain the set of data references that are contained in the analyzed loop body, and the second vector will contain the dependence relations between the data references. Thus if the vector of data references is of size n, the vector containing the dependence relations will contain n*n elements. However if the analyzed loop contains side effects, such as calls that potentially can interfere with the data references in the current analyzed loop, the analysis stops while scanning the loop body for data references, and inserts a single chrec_dont_know in the dependence relation array.

The data references are discovered in a particular order during the scanning of the loop body: the loop body is analyzed in execution order, and the data references of each statement are pushed at the end of the data reference array. Two data references syntactically occur in the program in the same order as in the array of data references. This syntactic order is important in some classical data dependence tests, and mapping this order to the elements of this array avoids costly queries to the loop body representation.

Three types of data references are currently handled: ARRAY_REF, INDIRECT_REF and COMPONENT_REF. The data structure for the data reference is data_reference, where data_reference_p is a name of a pointer to the data reference structure. The structure contains the following elements:

- base_object_info: Provides information about the base object of the data reference and its access functions. These access functions represent the evolution of the data reference in the loop relative to its base, in keeping with the classical meaning of the data reference access function for the support of arrays. For example, for a reference a.b[i][j], the base object is a.b and the access functions, one for each array subscript, are: {i_init, + i_step}_1, {j_init, +, j_step}_2.

- first_location_in_loop: Provides information about the first location accessed by the data reference in the loop and about the access function used to represent evolution relative to this location. This data is used to support pointers, and is not used for arrays (for which we have base objects). Pointer accesses are represented as a one-dimensional access that starts from the first location accessed in the loop. For example:

```
for1 i
  for2 j
    *((int *)p + i + j) = a[i][j];
```

The access function of the pointer access is {0, + 4B}_for2 relative to p + i. The access functions of the array are {i_init, + i_step}_for1 and {j_init, +, j_step}_for2 relative to a.

Usually, the object the pointer refers to is either unknown, or we can't prove that the access is confined to the boundaries of a certain object.

Two data references can be compared only if at least one of these two representations has all its fields filled for both data references.

The current strategy for data dependence tests is as follows: If both `a` and `b` are represented as arrays, compare `a.base_object` and `b.base_object`; if they are equal, apply dependence tests (use access functions based on base_objects). Else if both `a` and `b` are represented as pointers, compare `a.first_location` and `b.first_location`; if they are equal, apply dependence tests (use access functions based on first location). However, if `a` and `b` are represented differently, only try to prove that the bases are definitely different.

- Aliasing information.
- Alignment information.

The structure describing the relation between two data references is `data_dependence_relation` and the shorter name for a pointer to such a structure is `ddr_p`. This structure contains:

- a pointer to each data reference,
- a tree node **are_dependent** that is set to **chrec_known** if the analysis has proved that there is no dependence between these two data references, **chrec_dont_know** if the analysis was not able to determine any useful result and potentially there could exist a dependence between these data references, and **are_dependent** is set to NULL_TREE if there exist a dependence relation between the data references, and the description of this dependence relation is given in the **subscripts**, **dir_vects**, and **dist_vects** arrays,
- a boolean that determines whether the dependence relation can be represented by a classical distance vector,
- an array **subscripts** that contains a description of each subscript of the data references. Given two array accesses a subscript is the tuple composed of the access functions for a given dimension. For example, given `A[f1][f2][f3]` and `B[g1][g2][g3]`, there are three subscripts: `(f1, g1)`, `(f2, g2)`, `(f3, g3)`.
- two arrays **dir_vects** and **dist_vects** that contain classical representations of the data dependences under the form of direction and distance dependence vectors,
- an array of loops **loop_nest** that contains the loops to which the distance and direction vectors refer to.

Several functions for pretty printing the information extracted by the data dependence analysis are available: **dump_ddrs** prints with a maximum verbosity the details of a data dependence relations array, **dump_dist_dir_vectors** prints only the classical distance and direction vectors for a data dependence relations array, and **dump_data_references** prints the details of the data references contained in a data reference array.

16 Machine Descriptions

A machine description has two parts: a file of instruction patterns ('.md' file) and a C header file of macro definitions.

The '.md' file for a target machine contains a pattern for each instruction that the target machine supports (or at least each instruction that is worth telling the compiler about). It may also contain comments. A semicolon causes the rest of the line to be a comment, unless the semicolon is inside a quoted string.

See the next chapter for information on the C header file.

16.1 Overview of How the Machine Description is Used

There are three main conversions that happen in the compiler:

1. The front end reads the source code and builds a parse tree.

2. The parse tree is used to generate an RTL insn list based on named instruction patterns.

3. The insn list is matched against the RTL templates to produce assembler code.

For the generate pass, only the names of the insns matter, from either a named define_insn or a define_expand. The compiler will choose the pattern with the right name and apply the operands according to the documentation later in this chapter, without regard for the RTL template or operand constraints. Note that the names the compiler looks for are hard-coded in the compiler—it will ignore unnamed patterns and patterns with names it doesn't know about, but if you don't provide a named pattern it needs, it will abort.

If a define_insn is used, the template given is inserted into the insn list. If a define_expand is used, one of three things happens, based on the condition logic. The condition logic may manually create new insns for the insn list, say via emit_insn(), and invoke DONE. For certain named patterns, it may invoke FAIL to tell the compiler to use an alternate way of performing that task. If it invokes neither DONE nor FAIL, the template given in the pattern is inserted, as if the define_expand were a define_insn.

Once the insn list is generated, various optimization passes convert, replace, and rearrange the insns in the insn list. This is where the define_split and define_peephole patterns get used, for example.

Finally, the insn list's RTL is matched up with the RTL templates in the define_insn patterns, and those patterns are used to emit the final assembly code. For this purpose, each named define_insn acts like it's unnamed, since the names are ignored.

16.2 Everything about Instruction Patterns

A define_insn expression is used to define instruction patterns to which insns may be matched. A define_insn expression contains an incomplete RTL expression, with pieces to be filled in later, operand constraints that restrict how the pieces can be filled in, and an output template or C code to generate the assembler output.

A define_insn is an RTL expression containing four or five operands:

1. An optional name. The presence of a name indicate that this instruction pattern can perform a certain standard job for the RTL-generation pass of the compiler. This pass

knows certain names and will use the instruction patterns with those names, if the
names are defined in the machine description.

The absence of a name is indicated by writing an empty string where the name should
go. Nameless instruction patterns are never used for generating RTL code, but they
may permit several simpler insns to be combined later on.

Names that are not thus known and used in RTL-generation have no effect; they are
equivalent to no name at all.

For the purpose of debugging the compiler, you may also specify a name beginning
with the '*' character. Such a name is used only for identifying the instruction in RTL
dumps; it is equivalent to having a nameless pattern for all other purposes. Names
beginning with the '*' character are not required to be unique.

2. The *RTL template*: This is a vector of incomplete RTL expressions which describe
   the semantics of the instruction (see Section 16.4 [RTL Template], page 305). It is
   incomplete because it may contain `match_operand`, `match_operator`, and `match_dup`
   expressions that stand for operands of the instruction.

   If the vector has multiple elements, the RTL template is treated as a `parallel` expression.

3. The condition: This is a string which contains a C expression. When the compiler
   attempts to match RTL against a pattern, the condition is evaluated. If the condition
   evaluates to `true`, the match is permitted. The condition may be an empty string,
   which is treated as always `true`.

   For a named pattern, the condition may not depend on the data in the insn being
   matched, but only the target-machine-type flags. The compiler needs to test these
   conditions during initialization in order to learn exactly which named instructions are
   available in a particular run.

   For nameless patterns, the condition is applied only when matching an individual insn,
   and only after the insn has matched the pattern's recognition template. The insn's
   operands may be found in the vector `operands`.

   For an insn where the condition has once matched, it cannot later be used to control
   register allocation by excluding certain register or value combinations.

4. The *output template* or *output statement*: This is either a string, or a fragment of C
   code which returns a string.

   When simple substitution isn't general enough, you can specify a piece of C code to
   compute the output. See Section 16.6 [Output Statement], page 310.

5. The *insn attributes*: This is an optional vector containing the values of attributes for
   insns matching this pattern (see Section 16.19 [Insn Attributes], page 405).

16.3 Example of `define_insn`

Here is an example of an instruction pattern, taken from the machine description for the
68000/68020.

```
(define_insn "tstsi"
  [(set (cc0)
        (match_operand:SI 0 "general_operand" "rm"))]
  ""
```

```
    "*
{
  if (TARGET_68020 || ! ADDRESS_REG_P (operands[0]))
    return \"tstl %0\";
  return \"cmpl #0,%0\";
}")
```

This can also be written using braced strings:

```
(define_insn "tstsi"
  [(set (cc0)
        (match_operand:SI 0 "general_operand" "rm"))]
  ""
{
  if (TARGET_68020 || ! ADDRESS_REG_P (operands[0]))
    return "tstl %0";
  return "cmpl #0,%0";
})
```

This describes an instruction which sets the condition codes based on the value of a general operand. It has no condition, so any insn with an RTL description of the form shown may be matched to this pattern. The name 'tstsi' means "test a SImode value" and tells the RTL generation pass that, when it is necessary to test such a value, an insn to do so can be constructed using this pattern.

The output control string is a piece of C code which chooses which output template to return based on the kind of operand and the specific type of CPU for which code is being generated.

'"rm"' is an operand constraint. Its meaning is explained below.

16.4 RTL Template

The RTL template is used to define which insns match the particular pattern and how to find their operands. For named patterns, the RTL template also says how to construct an insn from specified operands.

Construction involves substituting specified operands into a copy of the template. Matching involves determining the values that serve as the operands in the insn being matched. Both of these activities are controlled by special expression types that direct matching and substitution of the operands.

(match_operand:*m n predicate constraint*)

> This expression is a placeholder for operand number *n* of the insn. When constructing an insn, operand number *n* will be substituted at this point. When matching an insn, whatever appears at this position in the insn will be taken as operand number *n*; but it must satisfy *predicate* or this instruction pattern will not match at all.

> Operand numbers must be chosen consecutively counting from zero in each instruction pattern. There may be only one match_operand expression in the pattern for each operand number. Usually operands are numbered in the order of appearance in match_operand expressions. In the case of a define_expand, any operand numbers used only in match_dup expressions have higher values than all other operand numbers.

predicate is a string that is the name of a function that accepts two arguments, an expression and a machine mode. See Section 16.7 [Predicates], page 311. During matching, the function will be called with the putative operand as the expression and m as the mode argument (if m is not specified, `VOIDmode` will be used, which normally causes *predicate* to accept any mode). If it returns zero, this instruction pattern fails to match. *predicate* may be an empty string; then it means no test is to be done on the operand, so anything which occurs in this position is valid.

Most of the time, *predicate* will reject modes other than m—but not always. For example, the predicate `address_operand` uses m as the mode of memory ref that the address should be valid for. Many predicates accept `const_int` nodes even though their mode is `VOIDmode`.

constraint controls reloading and the choice of the best register class to use for a value, as explained later (see Section 16.8 [Constraints], page 316). If the constraint would be an empty string, it can be omitted.

People are often unclear on the difference between the constraint and the predicate. The predicate helps decide whether a given insn matches the pattern. The constraint plays no role in this decision; instead, it controls various decisions in the case of an insn which does match.

(`match_scratch:`*m n constraint*)

This expression is also a placeholder for operand number n and indicates that operand must be a `scratch` or `reg` expression.

When matching patterns, this is equivalent to

> (`match_operand:`*m n* `"scratch_operand"` *constraint*)

but, when generating RTL, it produces a (`scratch:`m) expression.

If the last few expressions in a `parallel` are `clobber` expressions whose operands are either a hard register or `match_scratch`, the combiner can add or delete them when necessary. See Section 13.15 [Side Effects], page 264.

(`match_dup` *n*)

This expression is also a placeholder for operand number n. It is used when the operand needs to appear more than once in the insn.

In construction, `match_dup` acts just like `match_operand`: the operand is substituted into the insn being constructed. But in matching, `match_dup` behaves differently. It assumes that operand number n has already been determined by a `match_operand` appearing earlier in the recognition template, and it matches only an identical-looking expression.

Note that `match_dup` should not be used to tell the compiler that a particular register is being used for two operands (example: `add` that adds one register to another; the second register is both an input operand and the output operand). Use a matching constraint (see Section 16.8.1 [Simple Constraints], page 316) for those. `match_dup` is for the cases where one operand is used in two places in the template, such as an instruction that computes both a quotient and a remainder, where the opcode takes two input operands but the RTL template has to refer to each of those twice; once for the quotient pattern and once for the remainder pattern.

`(match_operator:`*m n predicate* `[`*operands...*`])`

> This pattern is a kind of placeholder for a variable RTL expression code.
>
> When constructing an insn, it stands for an RTL expression whose expression code is taken from that of operand *n*, and whose operands are constructed from the patterns *operands*.
>
> When matching an expression, it matches an expression if the function *predicate* returns nonzero on that expression *and* the patterns *operands* match the operands of the expression.
>
> Suppose that the function `commutative_operator` is defined as follows, to match any expression whose operator is one of the commutative arithmetic operators of RTL and whose mode is *mode*:

```
int
commutative_integer_operator (x, mode)
    rtx x;
    machine_mode mode;
{
  enum rtx_code code = GET_CODE (x);
  if (GET_MODE (x) != mode)
    return 0;
  return (GET_RTX_CLASS (code) == RTX_COMM_ARITH
          || code == EQ || code == NE);
}
```

> Then the following pattern will match any RTL expression consisting of a commutative operator applied to two general operands:

```
(match_operator:SI 3 "commutative_operator"
  [(match_operand:SI 1 "general_operand" "g")
   (match_operand:SI 2 "general_operand" "g")])
```

> Here the vector `[`*operands...*`]` contains two patterns because the expressions to be matched all contain two operands.
>
> When this pattern does match, the two operands of the commutative operator are recorded as operands 1 and 2 of the insn. (This is done by the two instances of `match_operand`.) Operand 3 of the insn will be the entire commutative expression: use `GET_CODE (operands[3])` to see which commutative operator was used.
>
> The machine mode *m* of `match_operator` works like that of `match_operand`: it is passed as the second argument to the predicate function, and that function is solely responsible for deciding whether the expression to be matched "has" that mode.
>
> When constructing an insn, argument 3 of the gen-function will specify the operation (i.e. the expression code) for the expression to be made. It should be an RTL expression, whose expression code is copied into a new expression whose operands are arguments 1 and 2 of the gen-function. The subexpressions of argument 3 are not used; only its expression code matters.
>
> When `match_operator` is used in a pattern for matching an insn, it usually best if the operand number of the `match_operator` is higher than that of the actual operands of the insn. This improves register allocation because the register allocator often looks at operands 1 and 2 of insns to see if it can do register tying.

There is no way to specify constraints in `match_operator`. The operand of the insn which corresponds to the `match_operator` never has any constraints because it is never reloaded as a whole. However, if parts of its *operands* are matched by `match_operand` patterns, those parts may have constraints of their own.

`(match_op_dup:m n[operands...])`

Like `match_dup`, except that it applies to operators instead of operands. When constructing an insn, operand number *n* will be substituted at this point. But in matching, `match_op_dup` behaves differently. It assumes that operand number *n* has already been determined by a `match_operator` appearing earlier in the recognition template, and it matches only an identical-looking expression.

`(match_parallel n predicate [subpat...])`

This pattern is a placeholder for an insn that consists of a `parallel` expression with a variable number of elements. This expression should only appear at the top level of an insn pattern.

When constructing an insn, operand number *n* will be substituted at this point. When matching an insn, it matches if the body of the insn is a `parallel` expression with at least as many elements as the vector of *subpat* expressions in the `match_parallel`, if each *subpat* matches the corresponding element of the `parallel`, *and* the function *predicate* returns nonzero on the `parallel` that is the body of the insn. It is the responsibility of the predicate to validate elements of the `parallel` beyond those listed in the `match_parallel`.

A typical use of `match_parallel` is to match load and store multiple expressions, which can contain a variable number of elements in a `parallel`. For example,

```
(define_insn ""
  [(match_parallel 0 "load_multiple_operation"
     [(set (match_operand:SI 1 "gpc_reg_operand" "=r")
           (match_operand:SI 2 "memory_operand" "m"))
      (use (reg:SI 179))
      (clobber (reg:SI 179))])]
  ""
  "loadm 0,0,%1,%2")
```

This example comes from 'a29k.md'. The function `load_multiple_operation` is defined in 'a29k.c' and checks that subsequent elements in the `parallel` are the same as the `set` in the pattern, except that they are referencing subsequent registers and memory locations.

An insn that matches this pattern might look like:

```
(parallel
 [(set (reg:SI 20) (mem:SI (reg:SI 100)))
  (use (reg:SI 179))
  (clobber (reg:SI 179))
  (set (reg:SI 21)
       (mem:SI (plus:SI (reg:SI 100)
                        (const_int 4))))
  (set (reg:SI 22)
       (mem:SI (plus:SI (reg:SI 100)
                        (const_int 8))))])
```

```
(match_par_dup n [subpat...])
```
        Like `match_op_dup`, but for `match_parallel` instead of `match_operator`.

16.5 Output Templates and Operand Substitution

The *output template* is a string which specifies how to output the assembler code for an instruction pattern. Most of the template is a fixed string which is output literally. The character '%' is used to specify where to substitute an operand; it can also be used to identify places where different variants of the assembler require different syntax.

In the simplest case, a '%' followed by a digit *n* says to output operand *n* at that point in the string.

'%' followed by a letter and a digit says to output an operand in an alternate fashion. Four letters have standard, built-in meanings described below. The machine description macro `PRINT_OPERAND` can define additional letters with nonstandard meanings.

'%c*digit*' can be used to substitute an operand that is a constant value without the syntax that normally indicates an immediate operand.

'%n*digit*' is like '%c*digit*' except that the value of the constant is negated before printing.

'%a*digit*' can be used to substitute an operand as if it were a memory reference, with the actual operand treated as the address. This may be useful when outputting a "load address" instruction, because often the assembler syntax for such an instruction requires you to write the operand as if it were a memory reference.

'%l*digit*' is used to substitute a `label_ref` into a jump instruction.

'%=' outputs a number which is unique to each instruction in the entire compilation. This is useful for making local labels to be referred to more than once in a single template that generates multiple assembler instructions.

'%' followed by a punctuation character specifies a substitution that does not use an operand. Only one case is standard: '%%' outputs a '%' into the assembler code. Other nonstandard cases can be defined in the `PRINT_OPERAND` macro. You must also define which punctuation characters are valid with the `PRINT_OPERAND_PUNCT_VALID_P` macro.

The template may generate multiple assembler instructions. Write the text for the instructions, with '\;' between them.

When the RTL contains two operands which are required by constraint to match each other, the output template must refer only to the lower-numbered operand. Matching operands are not always identical, and the rest of the compiler arranges to put the proper RTL expression for printing into the lower-numbered operand.

One use of nonstandard letters or punctuation following '%' is to distinguish between different assembler languages for the same machine; for example, Motorola syntax versus MIT syntax for the 68000. Motorola syntax requires periods in most opcode names, while MIT syntax does not. For example, the opcode 'movel' in MIT syntax is 'move.l' in Motorola syntax. The same file of patterns is used for both kinds of output syntax, but the character sequence '%.' is used in each place where Motorola syntax wants a period. The `PRINT_OPERAND` macro for Motorola syntax defines the sequence to output a period; the macro for MIT syntax defines it to do nothing.

As a special case, a template consisting of the single character # instructs the compiler to first split the insn, and then output the resulting instructions separately. This helps eliminate redundancy in the output templates. If you have a `define_insn` that needs to emit multiple assembler instructions, and there is a matching `define_split` already defined, then you can simply use `#` as the output template instead of writing an output template that emits the multiple assembler instructions.

If the macro `ASSEMBLER_DIALECT` is defined, you can use construct of the form '{option0|option1|option2}' in the templates. These describe multiple variants of assembler language syntax. See Section 17.20.7 [Instruction Output], page 564.

16.6 C Statements for Assembler Output

Often a single fixed template string cannot produce correct and efficient assembler code for all the cases that are recognized by a single instruction pattern. For example, the opcodes may depend on the kinds of operands; or some unfortunate combinations of operands may require extra machine instructions.

If the output control string starts with a '@', then it is actually a series of templates, each on a separate line. (Blank lines and leading spaces and tabs are ignored.) The templates correspond to the pattern's constraint alternatives (see Section 16.8.2 [Multi-Alternative], page 320). For example, if a target machine has a two-address add instruction 'addr' to add into a register and another 'addm' to add a register to memory, you might write this pattern:

```
(define_insn "addsi3"
  [(set (match_operand:SI 0 "general_operand" "=r,m")
        (plus:SI (match_operand:SI 1 "general_operand" "0,0")
                 (match_operand:SI 2 "general_operand" "g,r")))]
  ""
  "@
   addr %2,%0
   addm %2,%0")
```

If the output control string starts with a '*', then it is not an output template but rather a piece of C program that should compute a template. It should execute a `return` statement to return the template-string you want. Most such templates use C string literals, which require doublequote characters to delimit them. To include these doublequote characters in the string, prefix each one with '\'.

If the output control string is written as a brace block instead of a double-quoted string, it is automatically assumed to be C code. In that case, it is not necessary to put in a leading asterisk, or to escape the doublequotes surrounding C string literals.

The operands may be found in the array `operands`, whose C data type is `rtx []`.

It is very common to select different ways of generating assembler code based on whether an immediate operand is within a certain range. Be careful when doing this, because the result of `INTVAL` is an integer on the host machine. If the host machine has more bits in an `int` than the target machine has in the mode in which the constant will be used, then some of the bits you get from `INTVAL` will be superfluous. For proper results, you must carefully disregard the values of those bits.

It is possible to output an assembler instruction and then go on to output or compute more of them, using the subroutine `output_asm_insn`. This receives two arguments: a template-string and a vector of operands. The vector may be `operands`, or it may be another array of `rtx` that you declare locally and initialize yourself.

When an insn pattern has multiple alternatives in its constraints, often the appearance of the assembler code is determined mostly by which alternative was matched. When this is so, the C code can test the variable `which_alternative`, which is the ordinal number of the alternative that was actually satisfied (0 for the first, 1 for the second alternative, etc.).

For example, suppose there are two opcodes for storing zero, 'clrreg' for registers and 'clrmem' for memory locations. Here is how a pattern could use `which_alternative` to choose between them:

```
(define_insn ""
  [(set (match_operand:SI 0 "general_operand" "=r,m")
        (const_int 0))]
  ""
  {
  return (which_alternative == 0
          ? "clrreg %0" : "clrmem %0");
  })
```

The example above, where the assembler code to generate was *solely* determined by the alternative, could also have been specified as follows, having the output control string start with a '@':

```
(define_insn ""
  [(set (match_operand:SI 0 "general_operand" "=r,m")
        (const_int 0))]
  ""
  "@
   clrreg %0
   clrmem %0")
```

If you just need a little bit of C code in one (or a few) alternatives, you can use '*' inside of a '@' multi-alternative template:

```
(define_insn ""
  [(set (match_operand:SI 0 "general_operand" "=r,<,m")
        (const_int 0))]
  ""
  "@
   clrreg %0
   * return stack_mem_p (operands[0]) ? \"push 0\" : \"clrmem %0\";
   clrmem %0")
```

16.7 Predicates

A predicate determines whether a `match_operand` or `match_operator` expression matches, and therefore whether the surrounding instruction pattern will be used for that combination of operands. GCC has a number of machine-independent predicates, and you can define machine-specific predicates as needed. By convention, predicates used with `match_operand` have names that end in '_operand', and those used with `match_operator` have names that end in '_operator'.

All predicates are boolean functions (in the mathematical sense) of two arguments: the RTL expression that is being considered at that position in the instruction pattern, and the machine mode that the `match_operand` or `match_operator` specifies. In this section, the first argument is called *op* and the second argument *mode*. Predicates can be called from C as ordinary two-argument functions; this can be useful in output templates or other machine-specific code.

Operand predicates can allow operands that are not actually acceptable to the hardware, as long as the constraints give reload the ability to fix them up (see Section 16.8 [Constraints], page 316). However, GCC will usually generate better code if the predicates specify the requirements of the machine instructions as closely as possible. Reload cannot fix up operands that must be constants ("immediate operands"); you must use a predicate that allows only constants, or else enforce the requirement in the extra condition.

Most predicates handle their *mode* argument in a uniform manner. If *mode* is VOIDmode (unspecified), then *op* can have any mode. If *mode* is anything else, then *op* must have the same mode, unless *op* is a CONST_INT or integer CONST_DOUBLE. These RTL expressions always have VOIDmode, so it would be counterproductive to check that their mode matches. Instead, predicates that accept CONST_INT and/or integer CONST_DOUBLE check that the value stored in the constant will fit in the requested mode.

Predicates with this behavior are called *normal*. genrecog can optimize the instruction recognizer based on knowledge of how normal predicates treat modes. It can also diagnose certain kinds of common errors in the use of normal predicates; for instance, it is almost always an error to use a normal predicate without specifying a mode.

Predicates that do something different with their *mode* argument are called *special*. The generic predicates address_operand and pmode_register_operand are special predicates. genrecog does not do any optimizations or diagnosis when special predicates are used.

16.7.1 Machine-Independent Predicates

These are the generic predicates available to all back ends. They are defined in 'recog.c'. The first category of predicates allow only constant, or *immediate*, operands.

immediate_operand   [Function]
    This predicate allows any sort of constant that fits in *mode*. It is an appropriate choice for instructions that take operands that must be constant.

const_int_operand   [Function]
    This predicate allows any CONST_INT expression that fits in *mode*. It is an appropriate choice for an immediate operand that does not allow a symbol or label.

const_double_operand   [Function]
    This predicate accepts any CONST_DOUBLE expression that has exactly *mode*. If *mode* is VOIDmode, it will also accept CONST_INT. It is intended for immediate floating point constants.

The second category of predicates allow only some kind of machine register.

register_operand   [Function]
    This predicate allows any REG or SUBREG expression that is valid for *mode*. It is often suitable for arithmetic instruction operands on a RISC machine.

pmode_register_operand   [Function]
    This is a slight variant on register_operand which works around a limitation in the machine-description reader.

        (match_operand n "pmode_register_operand" *constraint*)

    means exactly what

```
(match_operand:P n "register_operand" constraint)
```

would mean, if the machine-description reader accepted ':P' mode suffixes. Unfortunately, it cannot, because Pmode is an alias for some other mode, and might vary with machine-specific options. See Section 17.30 [Misc], page 591.

scratch_operand   [Function]

This predicate allows hard registers and SCRATCH expressions, but not pseudo-registers. It is used internally by match_scratch; it should not be used directly.

The third category of predicates allow only some kind of memory reference.

memory_operand   [Function]

This predicate allows any valid reference to a quantity of mode *mode* in memory, as determined by the weak form of GO_IF_LEGITIMATE_ADDRESS (see Section 17.13 [Addressing Modes], page 513).

address_operand   [Function]

This predicate is a little unusual; it allows any operand that is a valid expression for the *address* of a quantity of mode *mode*, again determined by the weak form of GO_IF_LEGITIMATE_ADDRESS. To first order, if '(mem:*mode* (*exp*))' is acceptable to memory_operand, then *exp* is acceptable to address_operand. Note that *exp* does not necessarily have the mode *mode*.

indirect_operand   [Function]

This is a stricter form of memory_operand which allows only memory references with a general_operand as the address expression. New uses of this predicate are discouraged, because general_operand is very permissive, so it's hard to tell what an indirect_operand does or does not allow. If a target has different requirements for memory operands for different instructions, it is better to define target-specific predicates which enforce the hardware's requirements explicitly.

push_operand   [Function]

This predicate allows a memory reference suitable for pushing a value onto the stack. This will be a MEM which refers to stack_pointer_rtx, with a side-effect in its address expression (see Section 13.16 [Incdec], page 269); which one is determined by the STACK_PUSH_CODE macro (see Section 17.9.1 [Frame Layout], page 475).

pop_operand   [Function]

This predicate allows a memory reference suitable for popping a value off the stack. Again, this will be a MEM referring to stack_pointer_rtx, with a side-effect in its address expression. However, this time STACK_POP_CODE is expected.

The fourth category of predicates allow some combination of the above operands.

nonmemory_operand   [Function]

This predicate allows any immediate or register operand valid for *mode*.

nonimmediate_operand   [Function]

This predicate allows any register or memory operand valid for *mode*.

`general_operand`   [Function]

>   This predicate allows any immediate, register, or memory operand valid for *mode*.

Finally, there are two generic operator predicates.

`comparison_operator`   [Function]

>   This predicate matches any expression which performs an arithmetic comparison in
>   *mode*; that is, `COMPARISON_P` is true for the expression code.

`ordered_comparison_operator`   [Function]

>   This predicate matches any expression which performs an arithmetic comparison in
>   *mode* and whose expression code is valid for integer modes; that is, the expression
>   code will be one of `eq`, `ne`, `lt`, `ltu`, `le`, `leu`, `gt`, `gtu`, `ge`, `geu`.

16.7.2 Defining Machine-Specific Predicates

Many machines have requirements for their operands that cannot be expressed precisely
using the generic predicates. You can define additional predicates using `define_predicate`
and `define_special_predicate` expressions. These expressions have three operands:

- The name of the predicate, as it will be referred to in `match_operand` or `match_operator` expressions.

- An RTL expression which evaluates to true if the predicate allows the operand *op*, false
  if it does not. This expression can only use the following RTL codes:

  `MATCH_OPERAND`

  >   When written inside a predicate expression, a `MATCH_OPERAND` expression
  >   evaluates to true if the predicate it names would allow *op*. The operand
  >   number and constraint are ignored. Due to limitations in `genrecog`, you
  >   can only refer to generic predicates and predicates that have already been
  >   defined.

  `MATCH_CODE`

  >   This expression evaluates to true if *op* or a specified subexpression of *op*
  >   has one of a given list of RTX codes.
  >
  >   The first operand of this expression is a string constant containing a
  >   comma-separated list of RTX code names (in lower case). These are the
  >   codes for which the `MATCH_CODE` will be true.
  >
  >   The second operand is a string constant which indicates what subexpres-
  >   sion of *op* to examine. If it is absent or the empty string, *op* itself is
  >   examined. Otherwise, the string constant must be a sequence of digits
  >   and/or lowercase letters. Each character indicates a subexpression to ex-
  >   tract from the current expression; for the first character this is *op*, for the
  >   second and subsequent characters it is the result of the previous character.
  >   A digit n extracts 'XEXP (e, n)'; a letter l extracts 'XVECEXP (e, 0, n)'
  >   where n is the alphabetic ordinal of l (0 for 'a', 1 for 'b', and so on). The
  >   `MATCH_CODE` then examines the RTX code of the subexpression extracted
  >   by the complete string. It is not possible to extract components of an
  >   `rtvec` that is not at position 0 within its RTX object.

MATCH_TEST

> This expression has one operand, a string constant containing a C expression. The predicate's arguments, *op* and *mode*, are available with those names in the C expression. The MATCH_TEST evaluates to true if the C expression evaluates to a nonzero value. MATCH_TEST expressions must not have side effects.

AND
IOR
NOT
IF_THEN_ELSE

> The basic 'MATCH_' expressions can be combined using these logical operators, which have the semantics of the C operators '&&', '||', '!', and '? :' respectively. As in Common Lisp, you may give an AND or IOR expression an arbitrary number of arguments; this has exactly the same effect as writing a chain of two-argument AND or IOR expressions.

- An optional block of C code, which should execute 'return true' if the predicate is found to match and 'return false' if it does not. It must not have any side effects. The predicate arguments, *op* and *mode*, are available with those names.

  If a code block is present in a predicate definition, then the RTL expression must evaluate to true *and* the code block must execute 'return true' for the predicate to allow the operand. The RTL expression is evaluated first; do not re-check anything in the code block that was checked in the RTL expression.

The program genrecog scans define_predicate and define_special_predicate expressions to determine which RTX codes are possibly allowed. You should always make this explicit in the RTL predicate expression, using MATCH_OPERAND and MATCH_CODE.

Here is an example of a simple predicate definition, from the IA64 machine description:

```
;; True if op is a SYMBOL_REF which refers to the sdata section.
(define_predicate "small_addr_symbolic_operand"
  (and (match_code "symbol_ref")
       (match_test "SYMBOL_REF_SMALL_ADDR_P (op)")))
```

And here is another, showing the use of the C block.

```
;; True if op is a register operand that is (or could be) a GR reg.
(define_predicate "gr_register_operand"
  (match_operand 0 "register_operand")
{
  unsigned int regno;
  if (GET_CODE (op) == SUBREG)
    op = SUBREG_REG (op);

  regno = REGNO (op);
  return (regno >= FIRST_PSEUDO_REGISTER || GENERAL_REGNO_P (regno));
})
```

Predicates written with define_predicate automatically include a test that *mode* is VOIDmode, or *op* has the same mode as *mode*, or *op* is a CONST_INT or CONST_DOUBLE. They do *not* check specifically for integer CONST_DOUBLE, nor do they test that the value of either kind of constant fits in the requested mode. This is because target-specific predicates that take constants usually have to do more stringent value checks anyway. If you need the exact same treatment of `CONST_INT` or `CONST_DOUBLE` that the generic predicates provide, use a `MATCH_OPERAND` subexpression to call `const_int_operand`, `const_double_operand`, or `immediate_operand`.

Predicates written with `define_special_predicate` do not get any automatic mode checks, and are treated as having special mode handling by `genrecog`.

The program `genpreds` is responsible for generating code to test predicates. It also writes a header file containing function declarations for all machine-specific predicates. It is not necessary to declare these predicates in '*cpu-protos.h*'.

16.8 Operand Constraints

Each `match_operand` in an instruction pattern can specify constraints for the operands allowed. The constraints allow you to fine-tune matching within the set of operands allowed by the predicate.

Constraints can say whether an operand may be in a register, and which kinds of register; whether the operand can be a memory reference, and which kinds of address; whether the operand may be an immediate constant, and which possible values it may have. Constraints can also require two operands to match. Side-effects aren't allowed in operands of inline `asm`, unless '<' or '>' constraints are used, because there is no guarantee that the side-effects will happen exactly once in an instruction that can update the addressing register.

16.8.1 Simple Constraints

The simplest kind of constraint is a string full of letters, each of which describes one kind of operand that is permitted. Here are the letters that are allowed:

whitespace

    Whitespace characters are ignored and can be inserted at any position except the first. This enables each alternative for different operands to be visually aligned in the machine description even if they have different number of constraints and modifiers.

'm'

    A memory operand is allowed, with any kind of address that the machine supports in general. Note that the letter used for the general memory constraint can be re-defined by a back end using the `TARGET_MEM_CONSTRAINT` macro.

'o'

    A memory operand is allowed, but only if the address is *offsettable*. This means that adding a small integer (actually, the width in bytes of the operand, as determined by its machine mode) may be added to the address and the result is also a valid memory address.

    For example, an address which is constant is offsettable; so is an address that is the sum of a register and a constant (as long as a slightly larger constant is also within the range of address-offsets supported by the machine); but an autoincrement or autodecrement address is not offsettable. More complicated indirect/indexed addresses may or may not be offsettable depending on the other addressing modes that the machine supports.

    Note that in an output operand which can be matched by another operand, the constraint letter 'o' is valid only when accompanied by both '<' (if the target machine has predecrement addressing) and '>' (if the target machine has preincrement addressing).

'V'   A memory operand that is not offsettable. In other words, anything that would fit the 'm' constraint but not the 'o' constraint.

'<'   A memory operand with autodecrement addressing (either predecrement or postdecrement) is allowed. In inline **asm** this constraint is only allowed if the operand is used exactly once in an instruction that can handle the side-effects. Not using an operand with '<' in constraint string in the inline **asm** pattern at all or using it in multiple instructions isn't valid, because the side-effects wouldn't be performed or would be performed more than once. Furthermore, on some targets the operand with '<' in constraint string must be accompanied by special instruction suffixes like %U0 instruction suffix on PowerPC or %P0 on IA-64.

'>'   A memory operand with autoincrement addressing (either preincrement or postincrement) is allowed. In inline **asm** the same restrictions as for '<' apply.

'r'   A register operand is allowed provided that it is in a general register.

'i'   An immediate integer operand (one with constant value) is allowed. This includes symbolic constants whose values will be known only at assembly time or later.

'n'   An immediate integer operand with a known numeric value is allowed. Many systems cannot support assembly-time constants for operands less than a word wide. Constraints for these operands should use 'n' rather than 'i'.

'I', 'J', 'K', ... 'P'
            Other letters in the range 'I' through 'P' may be defined in a machine-dependent fashion to permit immediate integer operands with explicit integer values in specified ranges. For example, on the 68000, 'I' is defined to stand for the range of values 1 to 8. This is the range permitted as a shift count in the shift instructions.

'E'   An immediate floating operand (expression code `const_double`) is allowed, but only if the target floating point format is the same as that of the host machine (on which the compiler is running).

'F'   An immediate floating operand (expression code `const_double` or `const_vector`) is allowed.

'G', 'H'   'G' and 'H' may be defined in a machine-dependent fashion to permit immediate floating operands in particular ranges of values.

's'   An immediate integer operand whose value is not an explicit integer is allowed.

            This might appear strange; if an insn allows a constant operand with a value not known at compile time, it certainly must allow any known value. So why use 's' instead of 'i'? Sometimes it allows better code to be generated.

            For example, on the 68000 in a fullword instruction it is possible to use an immediate operand; but if the immediate value is between −128 and 127, better code results from loading the value into a register and using the register. This is because the load into the register can be done with a 'moveq' instruction. We arrange for this to happen by defining the letter 'K' to mean "any integer outside the range −128 to 127", and then specifying 'Ks' in the operand constraints.

'g'   Any register, memory or immediate integer operand is allowed, except for registers that are not general registers.

'X'   Any operand whatsoever is allowed, even if it does not satisfy `general_operand`. This is normally used in the constraint of a `match_scratch` when certain alternatives will not actually require a scratch register.

'0', '1', '2', ... '9'

An operand that matches the specified operand number is allowed. If a digit is used together with letters within the same alternative, the digit should come last.

This number is allowed to be more than a single digit. If multiple digits are encountered consecutively, they are interpreted as a single decimal integer. There is scant chance for ambiguity, since to-date it has never been desirable that '10' be interpreted as matching either operand 1 *or* operand 0. Should this be desired, one can use multiple alternatives instead.

This is called a *matching constraint* and what it really means is that the assembler has only a single operand that fills two roles considered separate in the RTL insn. For example, an add insn has two input operands and one output operand in the RTL, but on most CISC machines an add instruction really has only two operands, one of them an input-output operand:

```
addl #35,r12
```

Matching constraints are used in these circumstances. More precisely, the two operands that match must include one input-only operand and one output-only operand. Moreover, the digit must be a smaller number than the number of the operand that uses it in the constraint.

For operands to match in a particular case usually means that they are identical-looking RTL expressions. But in a few special cases specific kinds of dissimilarity are allowed. For example, *x as an input operand will match *x++ as an output operand. For proper results in such cases, the output template should always use the output-operand's number when printing the operand.

'p'   An operand that is a valid memory address is allowed. This is for "load address" and "push address" instructions.

'p' in the constraint must be accompanied by `address_operand` as the predicate in the `match_operand`. This predicate interprets the mode specified in the `match_operand` as the mode of the memory reference for which the address would be valid.

other-letters

Other letters can be defined in machine-dependent fashion to stand for particular classes of registers or other arbitrary operand types. 'd', 'a' and 'f' are defined on the 68000/68020 to stand for data, address and floating point registers.

In order to have valid assembler code, each operand must satisfy its constraint. But a failure to do so does not prevent the pattern from applying to an insn. Instead, it directs the compiler to modify the code so that the constraint will be satisfied. Usually this is done by copying an operand into a register.

Contrast, therefore, the two instruction patterns that follow:

```
(define_insn ""
  [(set (match_operand:SI 0 "general_operand" "=r")
        (plus:SI (match_dup 0)
                 (match_operand:SI 1 "general_operand" "r")))]
  ""
  "...")
```

which has two operands, one of which must appear in two places, and

```
(define_insn ""
  [(set (match_operand:SI 0 "general_operand" "=r")
        (plus:SI (match_operand:SI 1 "general_operand" "0")
                 (match_operand:SI 2 "general_operand" "r")))]
  ""
  "...")
```

which has three operands, two of which are required by a constraint to be identical. If we are considering an insn of the form

```
(insn n prev next
  (set (reg:SI 3)
       (plus:SI (reg:SI 6) (reg:SI 109)))
  ...)
```

the first pattern would not apply at all, because this insn does not contain two identical subexpressions in the right place. The pattern would say, "That does not look like an add instruction; try other patterns". The second pattern would say, "Yes, that's an add instruction, but there is something wrong with it". It would direct the reload pass of the compiler to generate additional insns to make the constraint true. The results might look like this:

```
(insn n2 prev n
  (set (reg:SI 3) (reg:SI 6))
  ...)

(insn n n2 next
  (set (reg:SI 3)
       (plus:SI (reg:SI 3) (reg:SI 109)))
  ...)
```

It is up to you to make sure that each operand, in each pattern, has constraints that can handle any RTL expression that could be present for that operand. (When multiple alternatives are in use, each pattern must, for each possible combination of operand expressions, have at least one alternative which can handle that combination of operands.) The constraints don't need to *allow* any possible operand—when this is the case, they do not constrain—but they must at least point the way to reloading any possible operand so that it will fit.

- If the constraint accepts whatever operands the predicate permits, there is no problem: reloading is never necessary for this operand.

  For example, an operand whose constraints permit everything except registers is safe provided its predicate rejects registers.

An operand whose predicate accepts only constant values is safe provided its constraints include the letter 'i'. If any possible constant value is accepted, then nothing less than 'i' will do; if the predicate is more selective, then the constraints may also be more selective.

- Any operand expression can be reloaded by copying it into a register. So if an operand's constraints allow some kind of register, it is certain to be safe. It need not permit all classes of registers; the compiler knows how to copy a register into another register of the proper class in order to make an instruction valid.

- A nonoffsettable memory reference can be reloaded by copying the address into a register. So if the constraint uses the letter 'o', all memory references are taken care of.

- A constant operand can be reloaded by allocating space in memory to hold it as preinitialized data. Then the memory reference can be used in place of the constant. So if the constraint uses the letters 'o' or 'm', constant operands are not a problem.

- If the constraint permits a constant and a pseudo register used in an insn was not allocated to a hard register and is equivalent to a constant, the register will be replaced with the constant. If the predicate does not permit a constant and the insn is rerecognized for some reason, the compiler will crash. Thus the predicate must always recognize any objects allowed by the constraint.

If the operand's predicate can recognize registers, but the constraint does not permit them, it can make the compiler crash. When this operand happens to be a register, the reload pass will be stymied, because it does not know how to copy a register temporarily into memory.

If the predicate accepts a unary operator, the constraint applies to the operand. For example, the MIPS processor at ISA level 3 supports an instruction which adds two registers in SImode to produce a DImode result, but only if the registers are correctly sign extended. This predicate for the input operands accepts a sign_extend of an SImode register. Write the constraint to indicate the type of register that is required for the operand of the sign_extend.

16.8.2 Multiple Alternative Constraints

Sometimes a single instruction has multiple alternative sets of possible operands. For example, on the 68000, a logical-or instruction can combine register or an immediate value into memory, or it can combine any kind of operand into a register; but it cannot combine one memory location into another.

These constraints are represented as multiple alternatives. An alternative can be described by a series of letters for each operand. The overall constraint for an operand is made from the letters for this operand from the first alternative, a comma, the letters for this operand from the second alternative, a comma, and so on until the last alternative. All operands for a single instruction must have the same number of alternatives. Here is how it is done for fullword logical-or on the 68000:

```
(define_insn "iorsi3"
  [(set (match_operand:SI 0 "general_operand" "=m,d")
        (ior:SI (match_operand:SI 1 "general_operand" "%0,0")
                (match_operand:SI 2 "general_operand" "dKs,dmKs")))]
  ...)
```

The first alternative has '`m`' (memory) for operand 0, '`0`' for operand 1 (meaning it must match operand 0), and '`dKs`' for operand 2. The second alternative has '`d`' (data register) for operand 0, '`0`' for operand 1, and '`dmKs`' for operand 2. The '`=`' and '`%`' in the constraints apply to all the alternatives; their meaning is explained in the next section (see Section 16.8.3 [Class Preferences], page 321).

If all the operands fit any one alternative, the instruction is valid. Otherwise, for each alternative, the compiler counts how many instructions must be added to copy the operands so that that alternative applies. The alternative requiring the least copying is chosen. If two alternatives need the same amount of copying, the one that comes first is chosen. These choices can be altered with the '`?`' and '`!`' characters:

?   Disparage slightly the alternative that the '`?`' appears in, as a choice when no alternative applies exactly. The compiler regards this alternative as one unit more costly for each '`?`' that appears in it.

!   Disparage severely the alternative that the '`!`' appears in. This alternative can still be used if it fits without reloading, but if reloading is needed, some other alternative will be used.

^   This constraint is analogous to '`?`' but it disparages slightly the alternative only if the operand with the '`^`' needs a reload.

$ This constraint is analogous to '`!`' but it disparages severely the alternative only if the operand with the '`$`' needs a reload.

When an insn pattern has multiple alternatives in its constraints, often the appearance of the assembler code is determined mostly by which alternative was matched. When this is so, the C code for writing the assembler code can use the variable `which_alternative`, which is the ordinal number of the alternative that was actually satisfied (0 for the first, 1 for the second alternative, etc.). See Section 16.6 [Output Statement], page 310.

16.8.3 Register Class Preferences

The operand constraints have another function: they enable the compiler to decide which kind of hardware register a pseudo register is best allocated to. The compiler examines the constraints that apply to the insns that use the pseudo register, looking for the machine-dependent letters such as '`d`' and '`a`' that specify classes of registers. The pseudo register is put in whichever class gets the most "votes". The constraint letters '`g`' and '`r`' also vote: they vote in favor of a general register. The machine description says which registers are considered general.

Of course, on some machines all registers are equivalent, and no register classes are defined. Then none of this complexity is relevant.

16.8.4 Constraint Modifier Characters

Here are constraint modifier characters.

'`=`'   Means that this operand is written to by this instruction: the previous value is discarded and replaced by new data.

'`+`'   Means that this operand is both read and written by the instruction.

When the compiler fixes up the operands to satisfy the constraints, it needs to know which operands are read by the instruction and which are written by it. '=' identifies an operand which is only written; '+' identifies an operand that is both read and written; all other operands are assumed to only be read.

If you specify '=' or '+' in a constraint, you put it in the first character of the constraint string.

'&'   Means (in a particular alternative) that this operand is an *earlyclobber* operand, which is written before the instruction is finished using the input operands. Therefore, this operand may not lie in a register that is read by the instruction or as part of any memory address.

'&' applies only to the alternative in which it is written. In constraints with multiple alternatives, sometimes one alternative requires '&' while others do not. See, for example, the 'movdf' insn of the 68000.

A operand which is read by the instruction can be tied to an earlyclobber operand if its only use as an input occurs before the early result is written. Adding alternatives of this form often allows GCC to produce better code when only some of the read operands can be affected by the earlyclobber. See, for example, the 'mulsi3' insn of the ARM.

Furthermore, if the *earlyclobber* operand is also a read/write operand, then that operand is written only after it's used.

'&' does not obviate the need to write '=' or '+'. As *earlyclobber* operands are always written, a read-only *earlyclobber* operand is ill-formed and will be rejected by the compiler.

'%'   Declares the instruction to be commutative for this operand and the following operand. This means that the compiler may interchange the two operands if that is the cheapest way to make all operands fit the constraints. '%' applies to all alternatives and must appear as the first character in the constraint. Only read-only operands can use '%'.

This is often used in patterns for addition instructions that really have only two operands: the result must go in one of the arguments. Here for example, is how the 68000 halfword-add instruction is defined:

```
(define_insn "addhi3"
  [(set (match_operand:HI 0 "general_operand" "=m,r")
        (plus:HI (match_operand:HI 1 "general_operand" "%0,0")
                 (match_operand:HI 2 "general_operand" "di,g")))]
  ...)
```

GCC can only handle one commutative pair in an asm; if you use more, the compiler may fail. Note that you need not use the modifier if the two alternatives are strictly identical; this would only waste time in the reload pass. The modifier is not operational after register allocation, so the result of define_peephole2 and define_splits performed after reload cannot rely on '%' to make the intended insn match.

'#'   Says that all following characters, up to the next comma, are to be ignored as a constraint. They are significant only for choosing register preferences.

'*'   Says that the following character should be ignored when choosing register
            preferences. '*' has no effect on the meaning of the constraint as a constraint,
            and no effect on reloading. For LRA '*' additionally disparages slightly the
            alternative if the following character matches the operand.

            Here is an example: the 68000 has an instruction to sign-extend a halfword
            in a data register, and can also sign-extend a value by copying it into an ad-
            dress register. While either kind of register is acceptable, the constraints on
            an address-register destination are less strict, so it is best if register allocation
            makes an address register its goal. Therefore, '*' is used so that the 'd' con-
            straint letter (for data register) is ignored when computing register preferences.

```
(define_insn "extendhisi2"
  [(set (match_operand:SI 0 "general_operand" "=*d,a")
        (sign_extend:SI
          (match_operand:HI 1 "general_operand" "0,g")))]
  ...)
```

16.8.5 Constraints for Particular Machines

Whenever possible, you should use the general-purpose constraint letters in **asm** arguments,
since they will convey meaning more readily to people reading your code. Failing that, use
the constraint letters that usually have very similar meanings across architectures. The
most commonly used constraints are 'm' and 'r' (for memory and general-purpose registers
respectively; see Section 16.8.1 [Simple Constraints], page 316), and 'I', usually the letter
indicating the most common immediate-constant format.

Each architecture defines additional constraints. These constraints are used by the compiler itself for instruction generation, as well as for **asm** statements; therefore, some of the
constraints are not particularly useful for **asm**. Here is a summary of some of the machine-
dependent constraints available on some particular machines; it includes both constraints
that are useful for **asm** and constraints that aren't. The compiler source file mentioned in
the table heading for each architecture is the definitive reference for the meanings of that
architecture's constraints.

AArch64 family—'`config/aarch64/constraints.md`'

k	The stack pointer register (SP)
w	Floating point or SIMD vector register
I	Integer constant that is valid as an immediate operand in an ADD instruction
J	Integer constant that is valid as an immediate operand in a SUB instruction (once negated)
K	Integer constant that can be used with a 32-bit logical instruction
L	Integer constant that can be used with a 64-bit logical instruction
M	Integer constant that is valid as an immediate operand in a 32-bit MOV pseudo instruction. The MOV may be assembled to one of several different machine instructions depending on the value
N	Integer constant that is valid as an immediate operand in a 64-bit MOV pseudo instruction

S	An absolute symbolic address or a label reference
Y	Floating point constant zero
Z	Integer constant zero
Ush	The high part (bits 12 and upwards) of the pc-relative address of a symbol within 4GB of the instruction
Q	A memory address which uses a single base register with no offset
Ump	A memory address suitable for a load/store pair instruction in SI, DI, SF and DF modes

ARC — 'config/arc/constraints.md'

q	Registers usable in ARCompact 16-bit instructions: `r0-r3`, `r12-r15`. This constraint can only match when the '-mq' option is in effect.
e	Registers usable as base-regs of memory addresses in ARCompact 16-bit memory instructions: `r0-r3`, `r12-r15`, `sp`. This constraint can only match when the '-mq' option is in effect.
D	ARC FPX (dpfp) 64-bit registers. D0, D1.
I	A signed 12-bit integer constant.
Cal	constant for arithmetic/logical operations. This might be any constant that can be put into a long immediate by the assmbler or linker without involving a PIC relocation.
K	A 3-bit unsigned integer constant.
L	A 6-bit unsigned integer constant.
CnL	One's complement of a 6-bit unsigned integer constant.
CmL	Two's complement of a 6-bit unsigned integer constant.
M	A 5-bit unsigned integer constant.
O	A 7-bit unsigned integer constant.
P	A 8-bit unsigned integer constant.
H	Any const_double value.

ARM family — 'config/arm/constraints.md'

h	In Thumb state, the core registers `r8-r15`.
k	The stack pointer register.
l	In Thumb State the core registers `r0-r7`. In ARM state this is an alias for the `r` constraint.
t	VFP floating-point registers `s0-s31`. Used for 32 bit values.
w	VFP floating-point registers `d0-d31` and the appropriate subset `d0-d15` based on command line options. Used for 64 bit values only. Not valid for Thumb1.

y	The iWMMX co-processor registers.
z	The iWMMX GR registers.
G	The floating-point constant 0.0
I	Integer that is valid as an immediate operand in a data processing instruction. That is, an integer in the range 0 to 255 rotated by a multiple of 2
J	Integer in the range −4095 to 4095
K	Integer that satisfies constraint 'I' when inverted (ones complement)
L	Integer that satisfies constraint 'I' when negated (twos complement)
M	Integer in the range 0 to 32
Q	A memory reference where the exact address is in a single register ("m" is preferable for **asm** statements)
R	An item in the constant pool
S	A symbol in the text segment of the current file
Uv	A memory reference suitable for VFP load/store insns (reg+constant offset)
Uy	A memory reference suitable for iWMMXt load/store instructions.
Uq	A memory reference suitable for the ARMv4 ldrsb instruction.

AVR family—'`config/avr/constraints.md`'

l	Registers from r0 to r15
a	Registers from r16 to r23
d	Registers from r16 to r31
w	Registers from r24 to r31. These registers can be used in 'adiw' command
e	Pointer register (r26–r31)
b	Base pointer register (r28–r31)
q	Stack pointer register (SPH:SPL)
t	Temporary register r0
x	Register pair X (r27:r26)
y	Register pair Y (r29:r28)
z	Register pair Z (r31:r30)
I	Constant greater than −1, less than 64
J	Constant greater than −64, less than 1

K	Constant integer 2
L	Constant integer 0
M	Constant that fits in 8 bits
N	Constant integer -1
O	Constant integer 8, 16, or 24
P	Constant integer 1
G	A floating point constant 0.0
Q	A memory address based on Y or Z pointer with displacement.

Blackfin family—'`config/bfin/constraints.md`'

a	P register
d	D register
z	A call clobbered P register.
qn	A single register. If n is in the range 0 to 7, the corresponding D register. If it is A, then the register P0.
D	Even-numbered D register
W	Odd-numbered D register
e	Accumulator register.
A	Even-numbered accumulator register.
B	Odd-numbered accumulator register.
b	I register
v	B register
f	M register
c	Registers used for circular buffering, i.e. I, B, or L registers.
C	The CC register.
t	LT0 or LT1.
k	LC0 or LC1.
u	LB0 or LB1.
x	Any D, P, B, M, I or L register.
y	Additional registers typically used only in prologues and epilogues: RETS, RETN, RETI, RETX, RETE, ASTAT, SEQSTAT and USP.
w	Any register except accumulators or CC.
Ksh	Signed 16 bit integer (in the range -32768 to 32767)
Kuh	Unsigned 16 bit integer (in the range 0 to 65535)

Ks7	Signed 7 bit integer (in the range -64 to 63)
Ku7	Unsigned 7 bit integer (in the range 0 to 127)
Ku5	Unsigned 5 bit integer (in the range 0 to 31)
Ks4	Signed 4 bit integer (in the range -8 to 7)
Ks3	Signed 3 bit integer (in the range -3 to 4)
Ku3	Unsigned 3 bit integer (in the range 0 to 7)
Pn	Constant n, where n is a single-digit constant in the range 0 to 4.
PA	An integer equal to one of the MACFLAG_XXX constants that is suitable for use with either accumulator.
PB	An integer equal to one of the MACFLAG_XXX constants that is suitable for use only with accumulator A1.
M1	Constant 255.
M2	Constant 65535.
J	An integer constant with exactly a single bit set.
L	An integer constant with all bits set except exactly one.
H	
Q	Any SYMBOL_REF.

CR16 Architecture—'config/cr16/cr16.h'

b	Registers from r0 to r14 (registers without stack pointer)
t	Register from r0 to r11 (all 16-bit registers)
p	Register from r12 to r15 (all 32-bit registers)
I	Signed constant that fits in 4 bits
J	Signed constant that fits in 5 bits
K	Signed constant that fits in 6 bits
L	Unsigned constant that fits in 4 bits
M	Signed constant that fits in 32 bits
N	Check for 64 bits wide constants for add/sub instructions
G	Floating point constant that is legal for store immediate

Epiphany—'config/epiphany/constraints.md'

U16	An unsigned 16-bit constant.
K	An unsigned 5-bit constant.
L	A signed 11-bit constant.
Cm1	A signed 11-bit constant added to -1. Can only match when the '-m1reg-*reg*' option is active.

Cl1   Left-shift of −1, i.e., a bit mask with a block of leading ones, the rest being a block of trailing zeroes. Can only match when the '-m1reg-*reg*' option is active.

Cr1   Right-shift of −1, i.e., a bit mask with a trailing block of ones, the rest being zeroes. Or to put it another way, one less than a power of two. Can only match when the '-m1reg-*reg*' option is active.

Cal   Constant for arithmetic/logical operations. This is like i, except that for position independent code, no symbols / expressions needing relocations are allowed.

Csy   Symbolic constant for call/jump instruction.

Rcs   The register class usable in short insns. This is a register class constraint, and can thus drive register allocation. This constraint won't match unless '-mprefer-short-insn-regs' is in effect.

Rsc   The the register class of registers that can be used to hold a sibcall call address. I.e., a caller-saved register.

Rct   Core control register class.

Rgs   The register group usable in short insns. This constraint does not use a register class, so that it only passively matches suitable registers, and doesn't drive register allocation.

Car   Constant suitable for the addsi3_r pattern. This is a valid offset For byte, halfword, or word addressing.

Rra   Matches the return address if it can be replaced with the link register.

Rcc   Matches the integer condition code register.

Sra   Matches the return address if it is in a stack slot.

Cfm   Matches control register values to switch fp mode, which are encapsulated in UNSPEC_FP_MODE.

FRV—'config/frv/frv.h'

a   Register in the class ACC_REGS (acc0 to acc7).

b   Register in the class EVEN_ACC_REGS (acc0 to acc7).

c   Register in the class CC_REGS (fcc0 to fcc3 and icc0 to icc3).

d   Register in the class GPR_REGS (gr0 to gr63).

e   Register in the class EVEN_REGS (gr0 to gr63). Odd registers are excluded not in the class but through the use of a machine mode larger than 4 bytes.

f   Register in the class FPR_REGS (fr0 to fr63).

h   Register in the class FEVEN_REGS (fr0 to fr63). Odd registers are excluded not in the class but through the use of a machine mode larger than 4 bytes.

l	Register in the class `LR_REG` (the `lr` register).
q	Register in the class `QUAD_REGS` (`gr2` to `gr63`). Register numbers not divisible by 4 are excluded not in the class but through the use of a machine mode larger than 8 bytes.
t	Register in the class `ICC_REGS` (`icc0` to `icc3`).
u	Register in the class `FCC_REGS` (`fcc0` to `fcc3`).
v	Register in the class `ICR_REGS` (`cc4` to `cc7`).
w	Register in the class `FCR_REGS` (`cc0` to `cc3`).
x	Register in the class `QUAD_FPR_REGS` (`fr0` to `fr63`). Register numbers not divisible by 4 are excluded not in the class but through the use of a machine mode larger than 8 bytes.
z	Register in the class `SPR_REGS` (`lcr` and `lr`).
A	Register in the class `QUAD_ACC_REGS` (`acc0` to `acc7`).
B	Register in the class `ACCG_REGS` (`accg0` to `accg7`).
C	Register in the class `CR_REGS` (`cc0` to `cc7`).
G	Floating point constant zero
I	6-bit signed integer constant
J	10-bit signed integer constant
L	16-bit signed integer constant
M	16-bit unsigned integer constant
N	12-bit signed integer constant that is negative—i.e. in the range of -2048 to -1
O	Constant zero
P	12-bit signed integer constant that is greater than zero—i.e. in the range of 1 to 2047.

FT32—'`config/ft32/constraints.md`'

A	An absolute address
B	An offset address
W	A register indirect memory operand
e	An offset address.
f	An offset address.
O	The constant zero or one
I	A 16-bit signed constant ($-32768 \ldots 32767$)
w	A bitfield mask suitable for bext or bins
x	An inverted bitfield mask suitable for bext or bins

L	A 16-bit unsigned constant, multiple of 4 (0 ... 65532)
S	A 20-bit signed constant (−524288 ... 524287)
b	A constant for a bitfield width (1 ... 16)
KA	A 10-bit signed constant (−512 ... 511)

Hewlett-Packard PA-RISC—'config/pa/pa.h'

a	General register 1
f	Floating point register
q	Shift amount register
x	Floating point register (deprecated)
y	Upper floating point register (32-bit), floating point register (64-bit)
Z	Any register
I	Signed 11-bit integer constant
J	Signed 14-bit integer constant
K	Integer constant that can be deposited with a `zdepi` instruction
L	Signed 5-bit integer constant
M	Integer constant 0
N	Integer constant that can be loaded with a `ldil` instruction
O	Integer constant whose value plus one is a power of 2
P	Integer constant that can be used for `and` operations in `depi` and `extru` instructions
S	Integer constant 31
U	Integer constant 63
G	Floating-point constant 0.0
A	A `lo_sum` data-linkage-table memory operand
Q	A memory operand that can be used as the destination operand of an integer store instruction
R	A scaled or unscaled indexed memory operand
T	A memory operand for floating-point loads and stores
W	A register indirect memory operand

Intel IA-64—'config/ia64/ia64.h'

a	General register `r0` to `r3` for `addl` instruction
b	Branch register
c	Predicate register ('c' as in "conditional")

d	Application register residing in M-unit
e	Application register residing in I-unit
f	Floating-point register
m	Memory operand. If used together with '<' or '>', the operand can have postincrement and postdecrement which require printing with '%Pn' on IA-64.
G	Floating-point constant 0.0 or 1.0
I	14-bit signed integer constant
J	22-bit signed integer constant
K	8-bit signed integer constant for logical instructions
L	8-bit adjusted signed integer constant for compare pseudo-ops
M	6-bit unsigned integer constant for shift counts
N	9-bit signed integer constant for load and store postincrements
O	The constant zero
P	0 or −1 for dep instruction
Q	Non-volatile memory for floating-point loads and stores
R	Integer constant in the range 1 to 4 for shladd instruction
S	Memory operand except postincrement and postdecrement. This is now roughly the same as 'm' when not used together with '<' or '>'.

M32C—'config/m32c/m32c.c'

Rsp Rfb Rsb	'$sp', '$fb', '$sb'.
Rcr	Any control register, when they're 16 bits wide (nothing if control registers are 24 bits wide)
Rcl	Any control register, when they're 24 bits wide.
R0w R1w R2w R3w	$r0, $r1, $r2, $r3.
R02	$r0 or $r2, or $r2r0 for 32 bit values.
R13	$r1 or $r3, or $r3r1 for 32 bit values.
Rdi	A register that can hold a 64 bit value.
Rhl	$r0 or $r1 (registers with addressable high/low bytes)
R23	$r2 or $r3

Raa	Address registers
Raw	Address registers when they're 16 bits wide.
Ral	Address registers when they're 24 bits wide.
Rqi	Registers that can hold QI values.
Rad	Registers that can be used with displacements ($a0, $a1, $sb).
Rsi	Registers that can hold 32 bit values.
Rhi	Registers that can hold 16 bit values.
Rhc	Registers chat can hold 16 bit values, including all control registers.
Rra	$r0 through R1, plus $a0 and $a1.
Rfl	The flags register.
Rmm	The memory-based pseudo-registers $mem0 through $mem15.
Rpi	Registers that can hold pointers (16 bit registers for r8c, m16c; 24 bit registers for m32cm, m32c).
Rpa	Matches multiple registers in a PARALLEL to form a larger register. Used to match function return values.
Is3	$-8 \ldots 7$
IS1	$-128 \ldots 127$
IS2	$-32768 \ldots 32767$
IU2	$0 \ldots 65535$
In4	$-8 \ldots -1$ or $1 \ldots 8$
In5	$-16 \ldots -1$ or $1 \ldots 16$
In6	$-32 \ldots -1$ or $1 \ldots 32$
IM2	$-65536 \ldots -1$
Ilb	An 8 bit value with exactly one bit set.
Ilw	A 16 bit value with exactly one bit set.
Sd	The common src/dest memory addressing modes.
Sa	Memory addressed using $a0 or $a1.
Si	Memory addressed with immediate addresses.
Ss	Memory addressed using the stack pointer ($sp).
Sf	Memory addressed using the frame base register ($fb).
Ss	Memory addressed using the small base register ($sb).
S1	$r1h

MicroBlaze—'config/microblaze/constraints.md'

d	A general register (r0 to r31).

z	A status register (**rmsr**, **$fcc1** to **$fcc7**).

MIPS—'config/mips/constraints.md'

d	A general-purpose register. This is equivalent to **r** unless generating MIPS16 code, in which case the MIPS16 register set is used.
f	A floating-point register (if available).
h	Formerly the **hi** register. This constraint is no longer supported.
l	The **lo** register. Use this register to store values that are no bigger than a word.
x	The concatenated **hi** and **lo** registers. Use this register to store doubleword values.
c	A register suitable for use in an indirect jump. This will always be **$25** for '**-mabicalls**'.
v	Register **$3**. Do not use this constraint in new code; it is retained only for compatibility with glibc.
y	Equivalent to **r**; retained for backwards compatibility.
z	A floating-point condition code register.
I	A signed 16-bit constant (for arithmetic instructions).
J	Integer zero.
K	An unsigned 16-bit constant (for logic instructions).
L	A signed 32-bit constant in which the lower 16 bits are zero. Such constants can be loaded using **lui**.
M	A constant that cannot be loaded using **lui**, **addiu** or **ori**.
N	A constant in the range −65535 to −1 (inclusive).
O	A signed 15-bit constant.
P	A constant in the range 1 to 65535 (inclusive).
G	Floating-point zero.
R	An address that can be used in a non-macro load or store.
ZC	A memory operand whose address is formed by a base register and offset that is suitable for use in instructions with the same addressing mode as **ll** and **sc**.
ZD	An address suitable for a **prefetch** instruction, or for any other instruction with the same addressing mode as **prefetch**.

Motorola 680x0—'config/m68k/constraints.md'

a	Address register
d	Data register
f	68881 floating-point register, if available

I	Integer in the range 1 to 8
J	16-bit signed number
K	Signed number whose magnitude is greater than 0x80
L	Integer in the range −8 to −1
M	Signed number whose magnitude is greater than 0x100
N	Range 24 to 31, rotatert:SI 8 to 1 expressed as rotate
O	16 (for rotate using swap)
P	Range 8 to 15, rotatert:HI 8 to 1 expressed as rotate
R	Numbers that mov3q can handle
G	Floating point constant that is not a 68881 constant
S	Operands that satisfy 'm' when -mpcrel is in effect
T	Operands that satisfy 's' when -mpcrel is not in effect
Q	Address register indirect addressing mode
U	Register offset addressing
W	const_call_operand
Cs	symbol_ref or const
Ci	const_int
C0	const_int 0
Cj	Range of signed numbers that don't fit in 16 bits
Cmvq	Integers valid for mvq
Capsw	Integers valid for a moveq followed by a swap
Cmvz	Integers valid for mvz
Cmvs	Integers valid for mvs
Ap	push_operand
Ac	Non-register operands allowed in clr

Moxie—'config/moxie/constraints.md'

A	An absolute address
B	An offset address
W	A register indirect memory operand
I	A constant in the range of 0 to 255.
N	A constant in the range of 0 to −255.

MSP430–'config/msp430/constraints.md'

R12	Register R12.

R13	Register R13.
K	Integer constant 1.
L	Integer constant -1^20..1^19.
M	Integer constant 1-4.
Ya	Memory references which do not require an extended MOVX instruction.
Yl	Memory reference, labels only.
Ys	Memory reference, stack only.

NDS32—'config/nds32/constraints.md'

w	LOW register class $r0 to $r7 constraint for V3/V3M ISA.
l	LOW register class $r0 to $r7.
d	MIDDLE register class $r0 to $r11, $r16 to $r19.
h	HIGH register class $r12 to $r14, $r20 to $r31.
t	Temporary assist register $ta (i.e. $r15).
k	Stack register $sp.
Iu03	Unsigned immediate 3-bit value.
In03	Negative immediate 3-bit value in the range of -7–0.
Iu04	Unsigned immediate 4-bit value.
Is05	Signed immediate 5-bit value.
Iu05	Unsigned immediate 5-bit value.
In05	Negative immediate 5-bit value in the range of -31–0.
Ip05	Unsigned immediate 5-bit value for movpi45 instruction with range 16–47.
Iu06	Unsigned immediate 6-bit value constraint for addri36.sp instruction.
Iu08	Unsigned immediate 8-bit value.
Iu09	Unsigned immediate 9-bit value.
Is10	Signed immediate 10-bit value.
Is11	Signed immediate 11-bit value.
Is15	Signed immediate 15-bit value.
Iu15	Unsigned immediate 15-bit value.
Ic15	A constant which is not in the range of imm15u but ok for bclr instruction.
Ie15	A constant which is not in the range of imm15u but ok for bset instruction.

It15   A constant which is not in the range of imm15u but ok for btgl instruction.

Ii15   A constant whose compliment value is in the range of imm15u and ok for bitci instruction.

Is16   Signed immediate 16-bit value.

Is17   Signed immediate 17-bit value.

Is19   Signed immediate 19-bit value.

Is20   Signed immediate 20-bit value.

Ihig   The immediate value that can be simply set high 20-bit.

Izeb   The immediate value 0xff.

Izeh   The immediate value 0xffff.

Ixls   The immediate value 0x01.

Ix11   The immediate value 0x7ff.

Ibms   The immediate value with power of 2.

Ifex   The immediate value with power of 2 minus 1.

U33   Memory constraint for 333 format.

U45   Memory constraint for 45 format.

U37   Memory constraint for 37 format.

Nios II family—'config/nios2/constraints.md'

I   Integer that is valid as an immediate operand in an instruction taking a signed 16-bit number. Range −32768 to 32767.

J   Integer that is valid as an immediate operand in an instruction taking an unsigned 16-bit number. Range 0 to 65535.

K   Integer that is valid as an immediate operand in an instruction taking only the upper 16-bits of a 32-bit number. Range 32-bit numbers with the lower 16-bits being 0.

L   Integer that is valid as an immediate operand for a shift instruction. Range 0 to 31.

M   Integer that is valid as an immediate operand for only the value 0. Can be used in conjunction with the format modifier z to use r0 instead of 0 in the assembly output.

N   Integer that is valid as an immediate operand for a custom instruction opcode. Range 0 to 255.

P   An immediate operand for R2 andchi/andci instructions.

S   Matches immediates which are addresses in the small data section and therefore can be added to gp as a 16-bit immediate to re-create their 32-bit value.

U	Matches constants suitable as an operand for the rdprs and cache instructions.
v	A memory operand suitable for Nios II R2 load/store exclusive instructions.
w	A memory operand suitable for load/store IO and cache instructions.
T	A const wrapped UNSPEC expression, representing a supported PIC or TLS relocation.

PDP-11—'config/pdp11/constraints.md'

a	Floating point registers AC0 through AC3. These can be loaded from/to memory with a single instruction.
d	Odd numbered general registers (R1, R3, R5). These are used for 16-bit multiply operations.
f	Any of the floating point registers (AC0 through AC5).
G	Floating point constant 0.
I	An integer constant that fits in 16 bits.
J	An integer constant whose low order 16 bits are zero.
K	An integer constant that does not meet the constraints for codes 'I' or 'J'.
L	The integer constant 1.
M	The integer constant −1.
N	The integer constant 0.
O	Integer constants −4 through −1 and 1 through 4; shifts by these amounts are handled as multiple single-bit shifts rather than a single variable-length shift.
Q	A memory reference which requires an additional word (address or offset) after the opcode.
R	A memory reference that is encoded within the opcode.

PowerPC and IBM RS6000—'config/rs6000/constraints.md'

b	Address base register
d	Floating point register (containing 64-bit value)
f	Floating point register (containing 32-bit value)
v	Altivec vector register
wa	Any VSX register if the -mvsx option was used or NO_REGS.
	When using any of the register constraints (wa, wd, wf, wg, wh, wi, wj, wk, wl, wm, wo, wp, wq, ws, wt, wu, wv, ww, or wy) that take VSX registers, you must use %x<n> in the template so that the

correct register is used. Otherwise the register number output in the assembly file will be incorrect if an Altivec register is an operand of a VSX instruction that expects VSX register numbering.

```
asm ("xvadddp %x0,%x1,%x2" : "=wa" (v1) : "wa" (v2), "wa" (v3));
```

is correct, but:

```
asm ("xvadddp %0,%1,%2" : "=wa" (v1) : "wa" (v2), "wa" (v3));
```

is not correct.

If an instruction only takes Altivec registers, you do not want to use %x<n>.

```
asm ("xsaddqp %0,%1,%2" : "=v" (v1) : "v" (v2), "v" (v3));
```

is correct because the `xsaddqp` instruction only takes Altivec registers, while:

```
asm ("xsaddqp %x0,%x1,%x2" : "=v" (v1) : "v" (v2), "v" (v3));
```

is incorrect.

wb	Altivec register if '-mcpu=power9' is used or NO_REGS.
wd	VSX vector register to hold vector double data or NO_REGS.
we	VSX register if the '-mcpu=power9' and '-m64' options were used or NO_REGS.
wf	VSX vector register to hold vector float data or NO_REGS.
wg	If '-mmfpgpr' was used, a floating point register or NO_REGS.
wh	Floating point register if direct moves are available, or NO_REGS.
wi	FP or VSX register to hold 64-bit integers for VSX insns or NO_REGS.
wj	FP or VSX register to hold 64-bit integers for direct moves or NO_REGS.
wk	FP or VSX register to hold 64-bit doubles for direct moves or NO_REGS.
wl	Floating point register if the LFIWAX instruction is enabled or NO_REGS.
wm	VSX register if direct move instructions are enabled, or NO_REGS.
wn	No register (NO_REGS).
wo	VSX register to use for ISA 3.0 vector instructions, or NO_REGS.
wp	VSX register to use for IEEE 128-bit floating point TFmode, or NO_REGS.
wq	VSX register to use for IEEE 128-bit floating point, or NO_REGS.
wr	General purpose register if 64-bit instructions are enabled or NO_REGS.
ws	VSX vector register to hold scalar double values or NO_REGS.

wt	VSX vector register to hold 128 bit integer or NO_REGS.
wu	Altivec register to use for float/32-bit int loads/stores or NO_REGS.
wv	Altivec register to use for double loads/stores or NO_REGS.
ww	FP or VSX register to perform float operations under '-mvsx' or NO_REGS.
wx	Floating point register if the STFIWX instruction is enabled or NO_REGS.
wy	FP or VSX register to perform ISA 2.07 float ops or NO_REGS.
wz	Floating point register if the LFIWZX instruction is enabled or NO_REGS.
wB	Signed 5-bit constant integer that can be loaded into an altivec register.
wD	Int constant that is the element number of the 64-bit scalar in a vector.
wE	Vector constant that can be loaded with the XXSPLTIB instruction.
wF	Memory operand suitable for power9 fusion load/stores.
wG	Memory operand suitable for TOC fusion memory references.
wH	Altivec register if '-mvsx-small-integer'.
wI	Floating point register if '-mvsx-small-integer'.
wJ	FP register if '-mvsx-small-integer' and '-mpower9-vector'.
wK	Altivec register if '-mvsx-small-integer' and '-mpower9-vector'.
wL	Int constant that is the element number that the MFVSRLD instruction. targets.
wM	Match vector constant with all 1's if the XXLORC instruction is available.
wO	A memory operand suitable for the ISA 3.0 vector d-form instructions.
wQ	A memory address that will work with the lq and stq instructions.
wS	Vector constant that can be loaded with XXSPLTIB & sign extension.
h	'MQ', 'CTR', or 'LINK' register
c	'CTR' register
l	'LINK' register
x	'CR' register (condition register) number 0

y	'CR' register (condition register)
z	'XER[CA]' carry bit (part of the XER register)
I	Signed 16-bit constant
J	Unsigned 16-bit constant shifted left 16 bits (use 'L' instead for SImode constants)
K	Unsigned 16-bit constant
L	Signed 16-bit constant shifted left 16 bits
M	Constant larger than 31
N	Exact power of 2
O	Zero
P	Constant whose negation is a signed 16-bit constant
G	Floating point constant that can be loaded into a register with one instruction per word
H	Integer/Floating point constant that can be loaded into a register using three instructions
m	Memory operand. Normally, m does not allow addresses that update the base register. If '<' or '>' constraint is also used, they are allowed and therefore on PowerPC targets in that case it is only safe to use 'm<>' in an asm statement if that asm statement accesses the operand exactly once. The asm statement must also use '%U<opno>' as a placeholder for the "update" flag in the corresponding load or store instruction. For example: `asm ("st%U0 %1,%0" : "=m<>" (mem) : "r" (val));` is correct but: `asm ("st %1,%0" : "=m<>" (mem) : "r" (val));` is not.
es	A "stable" memory operand; that is, one which does not include any automodification of the base register. This used to be useful when 'm' allowed automodification of the base register, but as those are now only allowed when '<' or '>' is used, 'es' is basically the same as 'm' without '<' and '>'.
Q	Memory operand that is an offset from a register (it is usually better to use 'm' or 'es' in asm statements)
Z	Memory operand that is an indexed or indirect from a register (it is usually better to use 'm' or 'es' in asm statements)
R	AIX TOC entry
a	Address operand that is an indexed or indirect from a register ('p' is preferable for asm statements)
U	System V Release 4 small data area reference

W	Vector constant that does not require memory
j	Vector constant that is all zeros.

RL78—'config/rl78/constraints.md'

Int3	An integer constant in the range 1 ... 7.
Int8	An integer constant in the range 0 ... 255.
J	An integer constant in the range −255 ... 0
K	The integer constant 1.
L	The integer constant -1.
M	The integer constant 0.
N	The integer constant 2.
O	The integer constant -2.
P	An integer constant in the range 1 ... 15.
Qbi	The built-in compare types–eq, ne, gtu, ltu, geu, and leu.
Qsc	The synthetic compare types–gt, lt, ge, and le.
Wab	A memory reference with an absolute address.
Wbc	A memory reference using BC as a base register, with an optional offset.
Wca	A memory reference using AX, BC, DE, or HL for the address, for calls.
Wcv	A memory reference using any 16-bit register pair for the address, for calls.
Wd2	A memory reference using DE as a base register, with an optional offset.
Wde	A memory reference using DE as a base register, without any offset.
Wfr	Any memory reference to an address in the far address space.
Wh1	A memory reference using HL as a base register, with an optional one-byte offset.
Whb	A memory reference using HL as a base register, with B or C as the index register.
Whl	A memory reference using HL as a base register, without any offset.
Ws1	A memory reference using SP as a base register, with an optional one-byte offset.
Y	Any memory reference to an address in the near address space.
A	The AX register.
B	The BC register.

D	The `DE` register.
R	`A` through `L` registers.
S	The `SP` register.
T	The `HL` register.
Z08W	The 16-bit `R8` register.
Z10W	The 16-bit `R10` register.
Zint	The registers reserved for interrupts (`R24` to `R31`).
a	The `A` register.
b	The `B` register.
c	The `C` register.
d	The `D` register.
e	The `E` register.
h	The `H` register.
l	The `L` register.
v	The virtual registers.
w	The `PSW` register.
x	The `X` register.

RX—'`config/rx/constraints.md`'

Q	An address which does not involve register indirect addressing or pre/post increment/decrement addressing.
Symbol	A symbol reference.
Int08	A constant in the range −256 to 255, inclusive.
Sint08	A constant in the range −128 to 127, inclusive.
Sint16	A constant in the range −32768 to 32767, inclusive.
Sint24	A constant in the range −8388608 to 8388607, inclusive.
Uint04	A constant in the range 0 to 15, inclusive.

S/390 and zSeries—'`config/s390/s390.h`'

a	Address register (general purpose register except r0)
c	Condition code register
d	Data register (arbitrary general purpose register)
f	Floating-point register
I	Unsigned 8-bit constant (0–255)
J	Unsigned 12-bit constant (0–4095)

K   Signed 16-bit constant (−32768–32767)

L   Value appropriate as displacement.

            (0..4095)
                        for short displacement

            (−524288..524287)
                        for long displacement

M   Constant integer with a value of 0x7fffffff.

N   Multiple letter constraint followed by 4 parameter letters.

            0..9:   number of the part counting from most to least signif-
                        icant

            H,Q: mode of the part

            D,S,H: mode of the containing operand

            0,F: value of the other parts (F—all bits set)

            The constraint matches if the specified part of a constant has a
            value different from its other parts.

Q   Memory reference without index register and with short displace-
            ment.

R   Memory reference with index register and short displacement.

S   Memory reference without index register but with long displace-
            ment.

T   Memory reference with index register and long displacement.

U   Pointer with short displacement.

W   Pointer with long displacement.

Y   Shift count operand.

SPARC—'config/sparc/sparc.h'

f   Floating-point register on the SPARC-V8 architecture and lower
            floating-point register on the SPARC-V9 architecture.

e   Floating-point register. It is equivalent to 'f' on the SPARC-V8
            architecture and contains both lower and upper floating-point reg-
            isters on the SPARC-V9 architecture.

c   Floating-point condition code register.

d   Lower floating-point register. It is only valid on the SPARC-V9
            architecture when the Visual Instruction Set is available.

b   Floating-point register. It is only valid on the SPARC-V9 architec-
            ture when the Visual Instruction Set is available.

h   64-bit global or out register for the SPARC-V8+ architecture.

C   The constant all-ones, for floating-point.

A   Signed 5-bit constant

D   A vector constant

I   Signed 13-bit constant

J   Zero

K   32-bit constant with the low 12 bits clear (a constant that can be loaded with the `sethi` instruction)

L   A constant in the range supported by `movcc` instructions (11-bit signed immediate)

M   A constant in the range supported by `movrcc` instructions (10-bit signed immediate)

N   Same as 'K', except that it verifies that bits that are not in the lower 32-bit range are all zero. Must be used instead of 'K' for modes wider than `SImode`

O   The constant 4096

G   Floating-point zero

H   Signed 13-bit constant, sign-extended to 32 or 64 bits

P   The constant -1

Q   Floating-point constant whose integral representation can be moved into an integer register using a single sethi instruction

R   Floating-point constant whose integral representation can be moved into an integer register using a single mov instruction

S   Floating-point constant whose integral representation can be moved into an integer register using a high/lo_sum instruction sequence

T   Memory address aligned to an 8-byte boundary

U   Even register

W   Memory address for 'e' constraint registers

w   Memory address with only a base register

Y   Vector zero

SPU—'config/spu/spu.h'

a   An immediate which can be loaded with the il/ila/ilh/ilhu instructions. const_int is treated as a 64 bit value.

c   An immediate for and/xor/or instructions. const_int is treated as a 64 bit value.

d   An immediate for the `iohl` instruction. const_int is treated as a 64 bit value.

f	An immediate which can be loaded with `fsmbi`.
A	An immediate which can be loaded with the il/ila/ilh/ilhu instructions. const_int is treated as a 32 bit value.
B	An immediate for most arithmetic instructions. const_int is treated as a 32 bit value.
C	An immediate for and/xor/or instructions. const_int is treated as a 32 bit value.
D	An immediate for the `iohl` instruction. const_int is treated as a 32 bit value.
I	A constant in the range [−64, 63] for shift/rotate instructions.
J	An unsigned 7-bit constant for conversion/nop/channel instructions.
K	A signed 10-bit constant for most arithmetic instructions.
M	A signed 16 bit immediate for `stop`.
N	An unsigned 16-bit constant for `iohl` and `fsmbi`.
O	An unsigned 7-bit constant whose 3 least significant bits are 0.
P	An unsigned 3-bit constant for 16-byte rotates and shifts
R	Call operand, reg, for indirect calls
S	Call operand, symbol, for relative calls.
T	Call operand, const_int, for absolute calls.
U	An immediate which can be loaded with the il/ila/ilh/ilhu instructions. const_int is sign extended to 128 bit.
W	An immediate for shift and rotate instructions. const_int is treated as a 32 bit value.
Y	An immediate for and/xor/or instructions. const_int is sign extended as a 128 bit.
Z	An immediate for the `iohl` instruction. const_int is sign extended to 128 bit.

TI C6X family—'`config/c6x/constraints.md`'

a	Register file A (A0–A31).
b	Register file B (B0–B31).
A	Predicate registers in register file A (A0–A2 on C64X and higher, A1 and A2 otherwise).
B	Predicate registers in register file B (B0–B2).
C	A call-used register in register file B (B0–B9, B16–B31).
Da	Register file A, excluding predicate registers (A3–A31, plus A0 if not C64X or higher).

Db	Register file B, excluding predicate registers (B3–B31).
Iu4	Integer constant in the range $0 \ldots 15$.
Iu5	Integer constant in the range $0 \ldots 31$.
In5	Integer constant in the range $-31 \ldots 0$.
Is5	Integer constant in the range $-16 \ldots 15$.
I5x	Integer constant that can be the operand of an ADDA or a SUBA insn.
IuB	Integer constant in the range $0 \ldots 65535$.
IsB	Integer constant in the range $-32768 \ldots 32767$.
IsC	Integer constant in the range $-2^{20} \ldots 2^{20} - 1$.
Jc	Integer constant that is a valid mask for the clr instruction.
Js	Integer constant that is a valid mask for the set instruction.
Q	Memory location with A base register.
R	Memory location with B base register.
S0	On C64x+ targets, a GP-relative small data reference.
S1	Any kind of SYMBOL_REF, for use in a call address.
Si	Any kind of immediate operand, unless it matches the S0 constraint.
T	Memory location with B base register, but not using a long offset.
W	A memory operand with an address that can't be used in an unaligned access.
Z	Register B14 (aka DP).

TILE-Gx—'`config/tilegx/constraints.md`'

R00	
R01	
R02	
R03	
R04	
R05	
R06	
R07	
R08	
R09	
R10	Each of these represents a register constraint for an individual register, from r0 to r10.
I	Signed 8-bit integer constant.
J	Signed 16-bit integer constant.

K	Unsigned 16-bit integer constant.
L	Integer constant that fits in one signed byte when incremented by one (−129 ... 126).
m	Memory operand. If used together with '<' or '>', the operand can have postincrement which requires printing with '%In' and '%in' on TILE-Gx. For example:

```
asm ("st_add %I0,%1,%i0" : "=m<>" (*mem) : "r" (val));
```

M	A bit mask suitable for the BFINS instruction.
N	Integer constant that is a byte tiled out eight times.
O	The integer zero constant.
P	Integer constant that is a sign-extended byte tiled out as four shorts.
Q	Integer constant that fits in one signed byte when incremented (−129 ... 126), but excluding -1.
S	Integer constant that has all 1 bits consecutive and starting at bit 0.
T	A 16-bit fragment of a got, tls, or pc-relative reference.
U	Memory operand except postincrement. This is roughly the same as 'm' when not used together with '<' or '>'.
W	An 8-element vector constant with identical elements.
Y	A 4-element vector constant with identical elements.
Z0	The integer constant 0xffffffff.
Z1	The integer constant 0xffffffff00000000.

TILEPro—'config/tilepro/constraints.md'

R00	
R01	
R02	
R03	
R04	
R05	
R06	
R07	
R08	
R09	
R10	Each of these represents a register constraint for an individual register, from r0 to r10.
I	Signed 8-bit integer constant.
J	Signed 16-bit integer constant.
K	Nonzero integer constant with low 16 bits zero.

L   Integer constant that fits in one signed byte when incremented by
                one (−129 . . . 126).

m   Memory operand. If used together with '<' or '>', the operand can
                have postincrement which requires printing with '%In' and '%in' on
                TILEPro. For example:

                        asm ("swadd %I0,%1,%i0" : "=m<>" (mem) : "r" (val));

M   A bit mask suitable for the MM instruction.

N   Integer constant that is a byte tiled out four times.

O   The integer zero constant.

P   Integer constant that is a sign-extended byte tiled out as two shorts.

Q   Integer constant that fits in one signed byte when incremented
                (−129 . . . 126), but excluding -1.

T   A symbolic operand, or a 16-bit fragment of a got, tls, or pc-relative
                reference.

U   Memory operand except postincrement. This is roughly the same
                as 'm' when not used together with '<' or '>'.

W   A 4-element vector constant with identical elements.

Y   A 2-element vector constant with identical elements.

Visium—'config/visium/constraints.md'

b   EAM register mdb

c   EAM register mdc

f   Floating point register

k   Register for sibcall optimization

l   General register, but not r29, r30 and r31

t   Register r1

u   Register r2

v   Register r3

G   Floating-point constant 0.0

J   Integer constant in the range 0 .. 65535 (16-bit immediate)

K   Integer constant in the range 1 .. 31 (5-bit immediate)

L   Integer constant in the range −65535 .. −1 (16-bit negative imme-
                diate)

M   Integer constant −1

O   Integer constant 0

P   Integer constant 32

x86 family—'config/i386/constraints.md'

R	Legacy register—the eight integer registers available on all i386 processors (a, b, c, d, si, di, bp, sp).
q	Any register accessible as rl. In 32-bit mode, a, b, c, and d; in 64-bit mode, any integer register.
Q	Any register accessible as rh: a, b, c, and d.
l	Any register that can be used as the index in a base+index memory access: that is, any general register except the stack pointer.
a	The a register.
b	The b register.
c	The c register.
d	The d register.
S	The si register.
D	The di register.

A   The a and d registers. This class is used for instructions that return double word results in the ax:dx register pair. Single word values will be allocated either in ax or dx. For example on i386 the following implements rdtsc:

```
unsigned long long rdtsc (void)
{
  unsigned long long tick;
  __asm__ __volatile__("rdtsc":"=A"(tick));
  return tick;
}
```

This is not correct on x86-64 as it would allocate tick in either ax or dx. You have to use the following variant instead:

```
unsigned long long rdtsc (void)
{
  unsigned int tickl, tickh;
  __asm__ __volatile__("rdtsc":"=a"(tickl),"=d"(tickh));
  return ((unsigned long long)tickh << 32)|tickl;
}
```

f	Any 80387 floating-point (stack) register.
t	Top of 80387 floating-point stack (%st(0)).
u	Second from top of 80387 floating-point stack (%st(1)).
y	Any MMX register.
x	Any SSE register.
Yz	First SSE register (%xmm0).
Y2	Any SSE register, when SSE2 is enabled.
Yi	Any SSE register, when SSE2 and inter-unit moves are enabled.

Ym	Any MMX register, when inter-unit moves are enabled.
I	Integer constant in the range 0 ... 31, for 32-bit shifts.
J	Integer constant in the range 0 ... 63, for 64-bit shifts.
K	Signed 8-bit integer constant.
L	0xFF or 0xFFFF, for andsi as a zero-extending move.
M	0, 1, 2, or 3 (shifts for the lea instruction).
N	Unsigned 8-bit integer constant (for in and out instructions).
O	Integer constant in the range 0 ... 127, for 128-bit shifts.
G	Standard 80387 floating point constant.
C	SSE constant zero operand.
e	32-bit signed integer constant, or a symbolic reference known to fit that range (for immediate operands in sign-extending x86-64 instructions).
Z	32-bit unsigned integer constant, or a symbolic reference known to fit that range (for immediate operands in zero-extending x86-64 instructions).

Xstormy16—‘config/stormy16/stormy16.h’

a	Register r0.
b	Register r1.
c	Register r2.
d	Register r8.
e	Registers r0 through r7.
t	Registers r0 and r1.
y	The carry register.
z	Registers r8 and r9.
I	A constant between 0 and 3 inclusive.
J	A constant that has exactly one bit set.
K	A constant that has exactly one bit clear.
L	A constant between 0 and 255 inclusive.
M	A constant between −255 and 0 inclusive.
N	A constant between −3 and 0 inclusive.
O	A constant between 1 and 4 inclusive.
P	A constant between −4 and −1 inclusive.
Q	A memory reference that is a stack push.

R	A memory reference that is a stack pop.
S	A memory reference that refers to a constant address of known value.
T	The register indicated by Rx (not implemented yet).
U	A constant that is not between 2 and 15 inclusive.
Z	The constant 0.

Xtensa—'`config/xtensa/constraints.md`'

a	General-purpose 32-bit register
b	One-bit boolean register
A	MAC16 40-bit accumulator register
I	Signed 12-bit integer constant, for use in MOVI instructions
J	Signed 8-bit integer constant, for use in ADDI instructions
K	Integer constant valid for BccI instructions
L	Unsigned constant valid for BccUI instructions

16.8.6 Disable insn alternatives using the `enabled` attribute

There are three insn attributes that may be used to selectively disable instruction alternatives:

`enabled`   Says whether an alternative is available on the current subtarget.

`preferred_for_size`
Says whether an enabled alternative should be used in code that is optimized for size.

`preferred_for_speed`
Says whether an enabled alternative should be used in code that is optimized for speed.

All these attributes should use (`const_int 1`) to allow an alternative or (`const_int 0`) to disallow it. The attributes must be a static property of the subtarget; they cannot for example depend on the current operands, on the current optimization level, on the location of the insn within the body of a loop, on whether register allocation has finished, or on the current compiler pass.

The `enabled` attribute is a correctness property. It tells GCC to act as though the disabled alternatives were never defined in the first place. This is useful when adding new instructions to an existing pattern in cases where the new instructions are only available for certain cpu architecture levels (typically mapped to the `-march=` command-line option).

In contrast, the `preferred_for_size` and `preferred_for_speed` attributes are strong optimization hints rather than correctness properties. `preferred_for_size` tells GCC which alternatives to consider when adding or modifying an instruction that GCC wants to optimize for size. `preferred_for_speed` does the same thing for speed. Note that things like code motion can lead to cases where code optimized for size uses alternatives that are not preferred for size, and similarly for speed.

Although `define_insns` can in principle specify the `enabled` attribute directly, it is often clearer to have subsidiary attributes for each architectural feature of interest. The `define_insns` can then use these subsidiary attributes to say which alternatives require which features. The example below does this for `cpu_facility`.

E.g. the following two patterns could easily be merged using the `enabled` attribute:

```
(define_insn "*movdi_old"
  [(set (match_operand:DI 0 "register_operand" "=d")
        (match_operand:DI 1 "register_operand" " d"))]
  "!TARGET_NEW"
  "lgr %0,%1")

(define_insn "*movdi_new"
  [(set (match_operand:DI 0 "register_operand" "=d,f,d")
        (match_operand:DI 1 "register_operand" " d,d,f"))]
  "TARGET_NEW"
  "@
   lgr  %0,%1
   ldgr %0,%1
   lgdr %0,%1")
```

to:

```
(define_insn "*movdi_combined"
  [(set (match_operand:DI 0 "register_operand" "=d,f,d")
        (match_operand:DI 1 "register_operand" " d,d,f"))]
  ""
  "@
   lgr  %0,%1
   ldgr %0,%1
   lgdr %0,%1"
  [(set_attr "cpu_facility" "*,new,new")])
```

with the `enabled` attribute defined like this:

```
(define_attr "cpu_facility" "standard,new" (const_string "standard"))

(define_attr "enabled" ""
  (cond [(eq_attr "cpu_facility" "standard") (const_int 1)
         (and (eq_attr "cpu_facility" "new")
              (ne (symbol_ref "TARGET_NEW") (const_int 0)))
         (const_int 1)]
        (const_int 0)))
```

16.8.7 Defining Machine-Specific Constraints

Machine-specific constraints fall into two categories: register and non-register constraints. Within the latter category, constraints which allow subsets of all possible memory or address operands should be specially marked, to give `reload` more information.

Machine-specific constraints can be given names of arbitrary length, but they must be entirely composed of letters, digits, underscores ('_'), and angle brackets ('< >'). Like C identifiers, they must begin with a letter or underscore.

In order to avoid ambiguity in operand constraint strings, no constraint can have a name that begins with any other constraint's name. For example, if x is defined as a constraint name, xy may not be, and vice versa. As a consequence of this rule, no constraint may begin with one of the generic constraint letters: 'E F V X g i m n o p r s'.

Register constraints correspond directly to register classes. See Section 17.8 [Register Classes], page 465. There is thus not much flexibility in their definitions.

define_register_constraint *name regclass docstring*   [MD Expression]
> All three arguments are string constants. *name* is the name of the constraint, as it will appear in **match_operand** expressions. If *name* is a multi-letter constraint its length shall be the same for all constraints starting with the same letter. *regclass* can be either the name of the corresponding register class (see Section 17.8 [Register Classes], page 465), or a C expression which evaluates to the appropriate register class. If it is an expression, it must have no side effects, and it cannot look at the operand. The usual use of expressions is to map some register constraints to NO_REGS when the register class is not available on a given subarchitecture.
>
> *docstring* is a sentence documenting the meaning of the constraint. Docstrings are explained further below.

Non-register constraints are more like predicates: the constraint definition gives a boolean expression which indicates whether the constraint matches.

define_constraint *name docstring exp*   [MD Expression]
> The *name* and *docstring* arguments are the same as for **define_register_constraint**, but note that the docstring comes immediately after the name for these expressions. *exp* is an RTL expression, obeying the same rules as the RTL expressions in predicate definitions. See Section 16.7.2 [Defining Predicates], page 314, for details. If it evaluates true, the constraint matches; if it evaluates false, it doesn't. Constraint expressions should indicate which RTL codes they might match, just like predicate expressions.
>
> **match_test** C expressions have access to the following variables:
>
> *op*   The RTL object defining the operand.
>
> *mode*   The machine mode of *op*.
>
> *ival*   'INTVAL (op)', if *op* is a const_int.
>
> *hval*   'CONST_DOUBLE_HIGH (op)', if *op* is an integer const_double.
>
> *lval*   'CONST_DOUBLE_LOW (op)', if *op* is an integer const_double.
>
> *rval*   'CONST_DOUBLE_REAL_VALUE (op)',   if   *op*   is   a   floating-point const_double.
>
> The **val* variables should only be used once another piece of the expression has verified that *op* is the appropriate kind of RTL object.

Most non-register constraints should be defined with **define_constraint**. The remaining two definition expressions are only appropriate for constraints that should be handled specially by **reload** if they fail to match.

`define_memory_constraint` *name docstring exp*   [MD Expression]

> Use this expression for constraints that match a subset of all memory operands: that is, `reload` can make them match by converting the operand to the form '(mem (reg *X*))', where *X* is a base register (from the register class specified by `BASE_REG_CLASS`, see Section 17.8 [Register Classes], page 465).
>
> For example, on the S/390, some instructions do not accept arbitrary memory references, but only those that do not make use of an index register. The constraint letter 'Q' is defined to represent a memory address of this type. If 'Q' is defined with `define_memory_constraint`, a 'Q' constraint can handle any memory operand, because `reload` knows it can simply copy the memory address into a base register if required. This is analogous to the way an 'o' constraint can handle any memory operand.
>
> The syntax and semantics are otherwise identical to `define_constraint`.

`define_special_memory_constraint` *name docstring exp*   [MD Expression]

> Use this expression for constraints that match a subset of all memory operands: that is, `reload` can not make them match by reloading the address as it is described for `define_memory_constraint` or such address reload is undesirable with the performance point of view.
>
> For example, `define_special_memory_constraint` can be useful if specifically aligned memory is necessary or desirable for some insn operand.
>
> The syntax and semantics are otherwise identical to `define_constraint`.

`define_address_constraint` *name docstring exp*   [MD Expression]

> Use this expression for constraints that match a subset of all address operands: that is, `reload` can make the constraint match by converting the operand to the form '(reg *X*)', again with *X* a base register.
>
> Constraints defined with `define_address_constraint` can only be used with the `address_operand` predicate, or machine-specific predicates that work the same way. They are treated analogously to the generic 'p' constraint.
>
> The syntax and semantics are otherwise identical to `define_constraint`.

For historical reasons, names beginning with the letters 'G H' are reserved for constraints that match only `const_doubles`, and names beginning with the letters 'I J K L M N O P' are reserved for constraints that match only `const_ints`. This may change in the future. For the time being, constraints with these names must be written in a stylized form, so that `genpreds` can tell you did it correctly:

```
(define_constraint "[GHIJKLMNOP]..."
  "doc..."
  (and (match_code "const_int")   ; const_double for G/H
       condition...))             ; usually a match_test
```

It is fine to use names beginning with other letters for constraints that match `const_doubles` or `const_ints`.

Each docstring in a constraint definition should be one or more complete sentences, marked up in Texinfo format. *They are currently unused.* In the future they will be copied into the GCC manual, in Section 16.8.5 [Machine Constraints], page 323, replacing the hand-maintained tables currently found in that section. Also, in the future the compiler may use this to give more helpful diagnostics when poor choice of **asm** constraints causes a reload failure.

If you put the pseudo-Texinfo directive '**@internal**' at the beginning of a docstring, then (in the future) it will appear only in the internals manual's version of the machine-specific constraint tables. Use this for constraints that should not appear in **asm** statements.

16.8.8 Testing constraints from C

It is occasionally useful to test a constraint from C code rather than implicitly via the constraint string in a **match_operand**. The generated file '**tm_p.h**' declares a few interfaces for working with constraints. At present these are defined for all constraints except **g** (which is equivalent to **general_operand**).

Some valid constraint names are not valid C identifiers, so there is a mangling scheme for referring to them from C. Constraint names that do not contain angle brackets or underscores are left unchanged. Underscores are doubled, each '**<**' is replaced with '**_l**', and each '**>**' with '**_g**'. Here are some examples:

Original	Mangled
x	x
P42x	P42x
P4_x	P4__x
P4>x	P4_gx
P4>>	P4_g_g
P4_g>	P4__g_g

Throughout this section, the variable c is either a constraint in the abstract sense, or a constant from **enum constraint_num**; the variable m is a mangled constraint name (usually as part of a larger identifier).

constraint_num   [Enum]
>   For each constraint except **g**, there is a corresponding enumeration constant: '**CONSTRAINT_**' plus the mangled name of the constraint. Functions that take an **enum constraint_num** as an argument expect one of these constants.

inline bool satisfies_constraint_m (*rtx exp*)   [Function]
>   For each non-register constraint m except **g**, there is one of these functions; it returns **true** if *exp* satisfies the constraint. These functions are only visible if '**rtl.h**' was included before '**tm_p.h**'.

bool constraint_satisfied_p (*rtx exp, enum constraint_num c*)   [Function]
>   Like the **satisfies_constraint_**m functions, but the constraint to test is given as an argument, c. If c specifies a register constraint, this function will always return **false**.

enum reg_class reg_class_for_constraint (*enum constraint_num*   [Function]
> c)
>   Returns the register class associated with c. If c is not a register constraint, or those registers are not available for the currently selected subtarget, returns **NO_REGS**.

Here is an example use of **satisfies_constraint_**m. In peephole optimizations (see Section 16.18 [Peephole Definitions], page 401), operand constraint strings are ignored, so if there are relevant constraints, they must be tested in the C condition. In the example, the optimization is applied if operand 2 does *not* satisfy the 'K' constraint. (This is a simplified version of a peephole definition from the i386 machine description.)

```
(define_peephole2
  [(match_scratch:SI 3 "r")
   (set (match_operand:SI 0 "register_operand" "")
        (mult:SI (match_operand:SI 1 "memory_operand" "")
                 (match_operand:SI 2 "immediate_operand" "")))]

  "!satisfies_constraint_K (operands[2])"

  [(set (match_dup 3) (match_dup 1))
   (set (match_dup 0) (mult:SI (match_dup 3) (match_dup 2)))]

  "")
```

16.9 Standard Pattern Names For Generation

Here is a table of the instruction names that are meaningful in the RTL generation pass of the compiler. Giving one of these names to an instruction pattern tells the RTL generation pass that it can use the pattern to accomplish a certain task.

'movm'   Here m stands for a two-letter machine mode name, in lowercase. This instruction pattern moves data with that machine mode from operand 1 to operand 0. For example, 'movsi' moves full-word data.

If operand 0 is a `subreg` with mode m of a register whose own mode is wider than m, the effect of this instruction is to store the specified value in the part of the register that corresponds to mode m. Bits outside of m, but which are within the same target word as the `subreg` are undefined. Bits which are outside the target word are left unchanged.

This class of patterns is special in several ways. First of all, each of these names up to and including full word size *must* be defined, because there is no other way to copy a datum from one place to another. If there are patterns accepting operands in larger modes, 'movm' must be defined for integer modes of those sizes.

Second, these patterns are not used solely in the RTL generation pass. Even the reload pass can generate move insns to copy values from stack slots into temporary registers. When it does so, one of the operands is a hard register and the other is an operand that can need to be reloaded into a register.

Therefore, when given such a pair of operands, the pattern must generate RTL which needs no reloading and needs no temporary registers—no registers other than the operands. For example, if you support the pattern with a `define_expand`, then in such a case the `define_expand` mustn't call `force_reg` or any other such function which might generate new pseudo registers.

This requirement exists even for subword modes on a RISC machine where fetching those modes from memory normally requires several insns and some temporary registers.

During reload a memory reference with an invalid address may be passed as an operand. Such an address will be replaced with a valid address later in the reload pass. In this case, nothing may be done with the address except to use it as it stands. If it is copied, it will not be replaced with a valid address. No attempt should be made to make such an address into a valid address and no routine (such as `change_address`) that will do so may be called. Note that `general_operand` will fail when applied to such an address.

The global variable `reload_in_progress` (which must be explicitly declared if required) can be used to determine whether such special handling is required.

The variety of operands that have reloads depends on the rest of the machine description, but typically on a RISC machine these can only be pseudo registers that did not get hard registers, while on other machines explicit memory references will get optional reloads.

If a scratch register is required to move an object to or from memory, it can be allocated using `gen_reg_rtx` prior to life analysis.

If there are cases which need scratch registers during or after reload, you must provide an appropriate secondary_reload target hook.

The macro `can_create_pseudo_p` can be used to determine if it is unsafe to create new pseudo registers. If this variable is nonzero, then it is unsafe to call `gen_reg_rtx` to allocate a new pseudo.

The constraints on a 'mov*m*' must permit moving any hard register to any other hard register provided that `HARD_REGNO_MODE_OK` permits mode *m* in both registers and `TARGET_REGISTER_MOVE_COST` applied to their classes returns a value of 2.

It is obligatory to support floating point 'mov*m*' instructions into and out of any registers that can hold fixed point values, because unions and structures (which have modes `SImode` or `DImode`) can be in those registers and they may have floating point members.

There may also be a need to support fixed point 'mov*m*' instructions in and out of floating point registers. Unfortunately, I have forgotten why this was so, and I don't know whether it is still true. If `HARD_REGNO_MODE_OK` rejects fixed point values in floating point registers, then the constraints of the fixed point 'mov*m*' instructions must be designed to avoid ever trying to reload into a floating point register.

'`reload_in`*m*'
'`reload_out`*m*'

> These named patterns have been obsoleted by the target hook `secondary_reload`.
>
> Like 'mov*m*', but used when a scratch register is required to move between operand 0 and operand 1. Operand 2 describes the scratch register. See the discussion of the `SECONDARY_RELOAD_CLASS` macro in see Section 17.8 [Register Classes], page 465.
>
> There are special restrictions on the form of the `match_operands` used in these patterns. First, only the predicate for the reload operand is examined, i.e., `reload_in` examines operand 1, but not the predicates for operand 0 or 2. Second, there may be only one alternative in the constraints. Third, only a

single register class letter may be used for the constraint; subsequent constraint
letters are ignored. As a special exception, an empty constraint string matches
the **ALL_REGS** register class. This may relieve ports of the burden of defining
an **ALL_REGS** constraint letter just for these patterns.

'movstrict*m*'

Like 'mov*m*' except that if operand 0 is a **subreg** with mode *m* of a register
whose natural mode is wider, the 'movstrict*m*' instruction is guaranteed not
to alter any of the register except the part which belongs to mode *m*.

'movmisalign*m*'

This variant of a move pattern is designed to load or store a value from a
memory address that is not naturally aligned for its mode. For a store, the
memory will be in operand 0; for a load, the memory will be in operand 1.
The other operand is guaranteed not to be a memory, so that it's easy to tell
whether this is a load or store.

This pattern is used by the autovectorizer, and when expanding a **MISALIGNED_**
INDIRECT_REF expression.

'load_multiple'

Load several consecutive memory locations into consecutive registers. Operand
0 is the first of the consecutive registers, operand 1 is the first memory location,
and operand 2 is a constant: the number of consecutive registers.

Define this only if the target machine really has such an instruction; do not
define this if the most efficient way of loading consecutive registers from memory
is to do them one at a time.

On some machines, there are restrictions as to which consecutive registers can
be stored into memory, such as particular starting or ending register numbers
or only a range of valid counts. For those machines, use a **define_expand** (see
Section 16.15 [Expander Definitions], page 394) and make the pattern fail if the
restrictions are not met.

Write the generated insn as a **parallel** with elements being a **set** of one register
from the appropriate memory location (you may also need **use** or **clobber**
elements). Use a **match_parallel** (see Section 16.4 [RTL Template], page 305)
to recognize the insn. See 'rs6000.md' for examples of the use of this insn
pattern.

'store_multiple'

Similar to 'load_multiple', but store several consecutive registers into consecutive memory locations. Operand 0 is the first of the consecutive memory
locations, operand 1 is the first register, and operand 2 is a constant: the
number of consecutive registers.

'vec_load_lanes*mn*'

Perform an interleaved load of several vectors from memory operand 1 into
register operand 0. Both operands have mode *m*. The register operand is
viewed as holding consecutive vectors of mode *n*, while the memory operand
is a flat array that contains the same number of elements. The operation is
equivalent to:

```
int c = GET_MODE_SIZE (m) / GET_MODE_SIZE (n);
for (j = 0; j < GET_MODE_NUNITS (n); j++)
  for (i = 0; i < c; i++)
    operand0[i][j] = operand1[j * c + i];
```

For example, 'vec_load_lanestiv4hi' loads 8 16-bit values from memory into a register of mode 'TI'. The register contains two consecutive vectors of mode 'V4HI'.

This pattern can only be used if:

```
TARGET_ARRAY_MODE_SUPPORTED_P (n, c)
```

is true. GCC assumes that, if a target supports this kind of instruction for some mode n, it also supports unaligned loads for vectors of mode n.

This pattern is not allowed to FAIL.

'vec_store_lanes*mn*'

Equivalent to 'vec_load_lanes*mn*', with the memory and register operands reversed. That is, the instruction is equivalent to:

```
int c = GET_MODE_SIZE (m) / GET_MODE_SIZE (n);
for (j = 0; j < GET_MODE_NUNITS (n); j++)
  for (i = 0; i < c; i++)
    operand0[j * c + i] = operand1[i][j];
```

for a memory operand 0 and register operand 1.

This pattern is not allowed to FAIL.

'vec_set*m*'

Set given field in the vector value. Operand 0 is the vector to modify, operand 1 is new value of field and operand 2 specify the field index.

'vec_extract*m*'

Extract given field from the vector value. Operand 1 is the vector, operand 2 specify field index and operand 0 place to store value into.

'vec_init*m*'

Initialize the vector to given values. Operand 0 is the vector to initialize and operand 1 is parallel containing values for individual fields.

'vec_cmp*mn*'

Output a vector comparison. Operand 0 of mode n is the destination for predicate in operand 1 which is a signed vector comparison with operands of mode m in operands 2 and 3. Predicate is computed by element-wise evaluation of the vector comparison with a truth value of all-ones and a false value of all-zeros.

'vec_cmpu*mn*'

Similar to vec_cmp*mn* but perform unsigned vector comparison.

'vec_cmpeq*mn*'

Similar to vec_cmp*mn* but perform equality or non-equality vector comparison only. If vec_cmp*mn* or vec_cmpu*mn* instruction pattern is supported, it will be preferred over vec_cmpeq*mn*, so there is no need to define this instruction pattern if the others are supported.

'vcond*mn*' Output a conditional vector move. Operand 0 is the destination to receive a combination of operand 1 and operand 2, which are of mode m, dependent on the outcome of the predicate in operand 3 which is a signed vector comparison with operands of mode n in operands 4 and 5. The modes m and n should have the same size. Operand 0 will be set to the value *op1 & msk | op2 & ~msk* where *msk* is computed by element-wise evaluation of the vector comparison with a truth value of all-ones and a false value of all-zeros.

'vcondu*mn*'

Similar to vcond*mn* but performs unsigned vector comparison.

'vcondeq*mn*'

Similar to vcond*mn* but performs equality or non-equality vector comparison only. If vcond*mn* or vcondu*mn* instruction pattern is supported, it will be preferred over vcondeq*mn*, so there is no need to define this instruction pattern if the others are supported.

'vcond_mask_*mn*'

Similar to vcond*mn* but operand 3 holds a pre-computed result of vector comparison.

'maskload*mn*'

Perform a masked load of vector from memory operand 1 of mode m into register operand 0. Mask is provided in register operand 2 of mode n.

This pattern is not allowed to FAIL.

'maskstore*mn*'

Perform a masked store of vector from register operand 1 of mode m into memory operand 0. Mask is provided in register operand 2 of mode n.

This pattern is not allowed to FAIL.

'vec_perm*m*'

Output a (variable) vector permutation. Operand 0 is the destination to receive elements from operand 1 and operand 2, which are of mode m. Operand 3 is the *selector*. It is an integral mode vector of the same width and number of elements as mode m.

The input elements are numbered from 0 in operand 1 through $2 * N - 1$ in operand 2. The elements of the selector must be computed modulo $2 * N$. Note that if rtx_equal_p(operand1, operand2), this can be implemented with just operand 1 and selector elements modulo N.

In order to make things easy for a number of targets, if there is no 'vec_perm' pattern for mode m, but there is for mode q where q is a vector of QImode of the same width as m, the middle-end will lower the mode m VEC_PERM_EXPR to mode q.

'vec_perm_const*m*'

Like 'vec_perm' except that the permutation is a compile-time constant. That is, operand 3, the *selector*, is a CONST_VECTOR.

Some targets cannot perform a permutation with a variable selector, but can efficiently perform a constant permutation. Further, the target hook vec_perm_ok is queried to determine if the specific constant permutation is available efficiently; the named pattern is never expanded without vec_perm_ok returning true.

There is no need for a target to supply both 'vec_perm*m*' and 'vec_perm_const*m*' if the former can trivially implement the operation with, say, the vector constant loaded into a register.

'push*m*1'   Output a push instruction. Operand 0 is value to push. Used only when PUSH_ROUNDING is defined. For historical reason, this pattern may be missing and in such case an mov expander is used instead, with a MEM expression forming the push operation. The mov expander method is deprecated.

'add*m*3'   Add operand 2 and operand 1, storing the result in operand 0. All operands must have mode *m*. This can be used even on two-address machines, by means of constraints requiring operands 1 and 0 to be the same location.

'ssadd*m*3', 'usadd*m*3'
'sub*m*3', 'sssub*m*3', 'ussub*m*3'
'mul*m*3', 'ssmul*m*3', 'usmul*m*3'
'div*m*3', 'ssdiv*m*3'
'udiv*m*3', 'usdiv*m*3'
'mod*m*3', 'umod*m*3'
'umin*m*3', 'umax*m*3'
'and*m*3', 'ior*m*3', 'xor*m*3'
        Similar, for other arithmetic operations.

'addv*m*4'   Like add*m*3 but takes a code_label as operand 3 and emits code to jump to it if signed overflow occurs during the addition. This pattern is used to implement the built-in functions performing signed integer addition with overflow checking.

'subv*m*4', 'mulv*m*4'
        Similar, for other signed arithmetic operations.

'uaddv*m*4'   Like addv*m*4 but for unsigned addition. That is to say, the operation is the same as signed addition but the jump is taken only on unsigned overflow.

'usubv*m*4', 'umulv*m*4'
        Similar, for other unsigned arithmetic operations.

'addptr*m*3'
        Like add*m*3 but is guaranteed to only be used for address calculations. The expanded code is not allowed to clobber the condition code. It only needs to be defined if add*m*3 sets the condition code. If adds used for address calculations and normal adds are not compatible it is required to expand a distinct pattern (e.g. using an unspec). The pattern is used by LRA to emit address calculations. add*m*3 is used if addptr*m*3 is not defined.

'fma*m*4'   Multiply operand 2 and operand 1, then add operand 3, storing the result in operand 0 without doing an intermediate rounding step. All operands must have mode *m*. This pattern is used to implement the fma, fmaf, and fmal builtin functions from the ISO C99 standard.

'fms*m*4'   Like fma*m*4, except operand 3 subtracted from the product instead of added to the product. This is represented in the rtl as

        (fma:*m* *op1* *op2* (neg:*m* *op3*))

'fnma*m*4'   Like `fma*m*4` except that the intermediate product is negated before being added
                to operand 3. This is represented in the rtl as
                        (fma:*m* (neg:*m* *op1*) *op2* *op3*)

'fnms*m*4'   Like `fms*m*4` except that the intermediate product is negated before subtracting
                operand 3. This is represented in the rtl as
                        (fma:*m* (neg:*m* *op1*) *op2* (neg:*m* *op3*))

'smin*m*3', 'smax*m*3'
                Signed minimum and maximum operations. When used with floating point, if
                both operands are zeros, or if either operand is NaN, then it is unspecified which
                of the two operands is returned as the result.

'fmin*m*3', 'fmax*m*3'
                IEEE-conformant minimum and maximum operations. If one operand is a quiet
                NaN, then the other operand is returned. If both operands are quiet NaN, then a
                quiet NaN is returned. In the case when gcc supports signaling NaN (-fsignaling-
                nans) an invalid floating point exception is raised and a quiet NaN is returned.

                All operands have mode *m*, which is a scalar or vector floating-point mode.
                These patterns are not allowed to FAIL.

'reduc_smin_scal_*m*', 'reduc_smax_scal_*m*'
                Find the signed minimum/maximum of the elements of a vector. The vector is
                operand 1, and operand 0 is the scalar result, with mode equal to the mode of
                the elements of the input vector.

'reduc_umin_scal_*m*', 'reduc_umax_scal_*m*'
                Find the unsigned minimum/maximum of the elements of a vector. The vector
                is operand 1, and operand 0 is the scalar result, with mode equal to the mode
                of the elements of the input vector.

'reduc_plus_scal_*m*'
                Compute the sum of the elements of a vector. The vector is operand 1, and
                operand 0 is the scalar result, with mode equal to the mode of the elements of
                the input vector.

'sdot_prod*m*'
'udot_prod*m*'
                Compute the sum of the products of two signed/unsigned elements. Operand 1
                and operand 2 are of the same mode. Their product, which is of a wider mode,
                is computed and added to operand 3. Operand 3 is of a mode equal or wider
                than the mode of the product. The result is placed in operand 0, which is of
                the same mode as operand 3.

'ssad*m*'

'usad*m*'   Compute the sum of absolute differences of two signed/unsigned elements.
                Operand 1 and operand 2 are of the same mode. Their absolute difference,
                which is of a wider mode, is computed and added to operand 3. Operand 3 is
                of a mode equal or wider than the mode of the absolute difference. The result
                is placed in operand 0, which is of the same mode as operand 3.

'widen_ssum*m*3'

'widen_usum*m*3'

>   Operands 0 and 2 are of the same mode, which is wider than the mode of
>   operand 1. Add operand 1 to operand 2 and place the widened result in operand
>   0. (This is used express accumulation of elements into an accumulator of a wider
>   mode.)

'vec_shr_*m*'

>   Whole vector right shift in bits, i.e. towards element 0. Operand 1 is a vector
>   to be shifted. Operand 2 is an integer shift amount in bits. Operand 0 is where
>   the resulting shifted vector is stored. The output and input vectors should have
>   the same modes.

'vec_pack_trunc_*m*'

>   Narrow (demote) and merge the elements of two vectors. Operands 1 and 2
>   are vectors of the same mode having N integral or floating point elements of
>   size S. Operand 0 is the resulting vector in which 2*N elements of size N/2 are
>   concatenated after narrowing them down using truncation.

'vec_pack_ssat_*m*', 'vec_pack_usat_*m*'

>   Narrow (demote) and merge the elements of two vectors. Operands 1 and 2 are
>   vectors of the same mode having N integral elements of size S. Operand 0 is the
>   resulting vector in which the elements of the two input vectors are concatenated
>   after narrowing them down using signed/unsigned saturating arithmetic.

'vec_pack_sfix_trunc_*m*', 'vec_pack_ufix_trunc_*m*'

>   Narrow, convert to signed/unsigned integral type and merge the elements of two
>   vectors. Operands 1 and 2 are vectors of the same mode having N floating point
>   elements of size S. Operand 0 is the resulting vector in which 2*N elements of
>   size N/2 are concatenated.

'vec_unpacks_hi_*m*', 'vec_unpacks_lo_*m*'

>   Extract and widen (promote) the high/low part of a vector of signed integral or
>   floating point elements. The input vector (operand 1) has N elements of size S.
>   Widen (promote) the high/low elements of the vector using signed or floating
>   point extension and place the resulting N/2 values of size 2*S in the output
>   vector (operand 0).

'vec_unpacku_hi_*m*', 'vec_unpacku_lo_*m*'

>   Extract and widen (promote) the high/low part of a vector of unsigned inte-
>   gral elements. The input vector (operand 1) has N elements of size S. Widen
>   (promote) the high/low elements of the vector using zero extension and place
>   the resulting N/2 values of size 2*S in the output vector (operand 0).

'vec_unpacks_float_hi_*m*', 'vec_unpacks_float_lo_*m*'

'vec_unpacku_float_hi_*m*', 'vec_unpacku_float_lo_*m*'

>   Extract, convert to floating point type and widen the high/low part of a vector
>   of signed/unsigned integral elements. The input vector (operand 1) has N
>   elements of size S. Convert the high/low elements of the vector using floating
>   point conversion and place the resulting N/2 values of size 2*S in the output
>   vector (operand 0).

'`vec_widen_umult_hi_m`', '`vec_widen_umult_lo_m`'
'`vec_widen_smult_hi_m`', '`vec_widen_smult_lo_m`'
'`vec_widen_umult_even_m`', '`vec_widen_umult_odd_m`'
'`vec_widen_smult_even_m`', '`vec_widen_smult_odd_m`'

> Signed/Unsigned widening multiplication. The two inputs (operands 1 and 2) are vectors with N signed/unsigned elements of size S. Multiply the high/low or even/odd elements of the two vectors, and put the N/2 products of size 2*S in the output vector (operand 0). A target shouldn't implement even/odd pattern pair if it is less efficient than lo/hi one.

'`vec_widen_ushiftl_hi_m`', '`vec_widen_ushiftl_lo_m`'
'`vec_widen_sshiftl_hi_m`', '`vec_widen_sshiftl_lo_m`'

> Signed/Unsigned widening shift left. The first input (operand 1) is a vector with N signed/unsigned elements of size S. Operand 2 is a constant. Shift the high/low elements of operand 1, and put the N/2 results of size 2*S in the output vector (operand 0).

'`mulhisi3`'

> Multiply operands 1 and 2, which have mode `HImode`, and store a `SImode` product in operand 0.

'`mulqihi3`', '`mulsidi3`'

> Similar widening-multiplication instructions of other widths.

'`umulqihi3`', '`umulhisi3`', '`umulsidi3`'

> Similar widening-multiplication instructions that do unsigned multiplication.

'`usmulqihi3`', '`usmulhisi3`', '`usmulsidi3`'

> Similar widening-multiplication instructions that interpret the first operand as unsigned and the second operand as signed, then do a signed multiplication.

'`smulm3_highpart`'

> Perform a signed multiplication of operands 1 and 2, which have mode m, and store the most significant half of the product in operand 0. The least significant half of the product is discarded.

'`umulm3_highpart`'

> Similar, but the multiplication is unsigned.

'`maddmn4`'   Multiply operands 1 and 2, sign-extend them to mode n, add operand 3, and store the result in operand 0. Operands 1 and 2 have mode m and operands 0 and 3 have mode n. Both modes must be integer or fixed-point modes and n must be twice the size of m.

> In other words, `maddmn4` is like `mulmn3` except that it also adds operand 3.

> These instructions are not allowed to `FAIL`.

'`umaddmn4`'

> Like `maddmn4`, but zero-extend the multiplication operands instead of sign-extending them.

'`ssmaddmn4`'

> Like `maddmn4`, but all involved operations must be signed-saturating.

'usmadd*mn*4'

Like **umadd*mn*4**, but all involved operations must be unsigned-saturating.

'msub*mn*4'   Multiply operands 1 and 2, sign-extend them to mode *n*, subtract the result from operand 3, and store the result in operand 0. Operands 1 and 2 have mode *m* and operands 0 and 3 have mode *n*. Both modes must be integer or fixed-point modes and *n* must be twice the size of *m*.

In other words, **msub*mn*4** is like **mul*mn*3** except that it also subtracts the result from operand 3.

These instructions are not allowed to **FAIL**.

'umsub*mn*4'

Like **msub*mn*4**, but zero-extend the multiplication operands instead of sign-extending them.

'ssmsub*mn*4'

Like **msub*mn*4**, but all involved operations must be signed-saturating.

'usmsub*mn*4'

Like **umsub*mn*4**, but all involved operations must be unsigned-saturating.

'divmod*m*4'

Signed division that produces both a quotient and a remainder. Operand 1 is divided by operand 2 to produce a quotient stored in operand 0 and a remainder stored in operand 3.

For machines with an instruction that produces both a quotient and a remainder, provide a pattern for 'divmod*m*4' but do not provide patterns for 'div*m*3' and 'mod*m*3'. This allows optimization in the relatively common case when both the quotient and remainder are computed.

If an instruction that just produces a quotient or just a remainder exists and is more efficient than the instruction that produces both, write the output routine of 'divmod*m*4' to call **find_reg_note** and look for a **REG_UNUSED** note on the quotient or remainder and generate the appropriate instruction.

'udivmod*m*4'

Similar, but does unsigned division.

'ashl*m*3', 'ssashl*m*3', 'usashl*m*3'

Arithmetic-shift operand 1 left by a number of bits specified by operand 2, and store the result in operand 0. Here *m* is the mode of operand 0 and operand 1; operand 2's mode is specified by the instruction pattern, and the compiler will convert the operand to that mode before generating the instruction. The shift or rotate expander or instruction pattern should explicitly specify the mode of the operand 2, it should never be **VOIDmode**. The meaning of out-of-range shift counts can optionally be specified by **TARGET_SHIFT_TRUNCATION_MASK**. See [TARGET_SHIFT_TRUNCATION_MASK], page 593. Operand 2 is always a scalar type.

'ashr*m*3', 'lshr*m*3', 'rotl*m*3', 'rotr*m*3'

Other shift and rotate instructions, analogous to the **ashl*m*3** instructions. Operand 2 is always a scalar type.

'vashl*m*3', 'vashr*m*3', 'vlshr*m*3', 'vrotl*m*3', 'vrotr*m*3'
: Vector shift and rotate instructions that take vectors as operand 2 instead of a scalar type.

'bswap*m*2'   Reverse the order of bytes of operand 1 and store the result in operand 0.

'neg*m*2', 'ssneg*m*2', 'usneg*m*2'
: Negate operand 1 and store the result in operand 0.

'negv*m*3'   Like `negm2` but takes a `code_label` as operand 2 and emits code to jump to it if signed overflow occurs during the negation.

'abs*m*2'   Store the absolute value of operand 1 into operand 0.

'sqrt*m*2'   Store the square root of operand 1 into operand 0. Both operands have mode m, which is a scalar or vector floating-point mode.

This pattern is not allowed to `FAIL`.

'rsqrt*m*2' Store the reciprocal of the square root of operand 1 into operand 0. Both operands have mode m, which is a scalar or vector floating-point mode.

On most architectures this pattern is only approximate, so either its C condition or the `TARGET_OPTAB_SUPPORTED_P` hook should check for the appropriate math flags. (Using the C condition is more direct, but using `TARGET_OPTAB_SUPPORTED_P` can be useful if a target-specific built-in also uses the 'rsqrt*m*2' pattern.)

This pattern is not allowed to `FAIL`.

'fmod*m*3'   Store the remainder of dividing operand 1 by operand 2 into operand 0, rounded towards zero to an integer. All operands have mode m, which is a scalar or vector floating-point mode.

This pattern is not allowed to `FAIL`.

'remainder*m*3'
: Store the remainder of dividing operand 1 by operand 2 into operand 0, rounded to the nearest integer. All operands have mode m, which is a scalar or vector floating-point mode.

This pattern is not allowed to `FAIL`.

'scalb*m*3' Raise `FLT_RADIX` to the power of operand 2, multiply it by operand 1, and store the result in operand 0. All operands have mode m, which is a scalar or vector floating-point mode.

This pattern is not allowed to `FAIL`.

'ldexp*m*3' Raise 2 to the power of operand 2, multiply it by operand 1, and store the result in operand 0. Operands 0 and 1 have mode m, which is a scalar or vector floating-point mode. Operand 2's mode has the same number of elements as m and each element is wide enough to store an `int`. The integers are signed.

This pattern is not allowed to `FAIL`.

'cos*m*2'   Store the cosine of operand 1 into operand 0. Both operands have mode m, which is a scalar or vector floating-point mode.

This pattern is not allowed to `FAIL`.

'sinm2'   Store the sine of operand 1 into operand 0. Both operands have mode m, which
                 is a scalar or vector floating-point mode.

                 This pattern is not allowed to FAIL.

'sincosm3'

                 Store the cosine of operand 2 into operand 0 and the sine of operand 2 into
                 operand 1. All operands have mode m, which is a scalar or vector floating-
                 point mode.

                 Targets that can calculate the sine and cosine simultaneously can implement
                 this pattern as opposed to implementing individual sinm2 and cosm2 patterns.
                 The sin and cos built-in functions will then be expanded to the sincosm3
                 pattern, with one of the output values left unused.

'tanm2'   Store the tangent of operand 1 into operand 0. Both operands have mode m,
                 which is a scalar or vector floating-point mode.

                 This pattern is not allowed to FAIL.

'asinm2'   Store the arc sine of operand 1 into operand 0. Both operands have mode m,
                 which is a scalar or vector floating-point mode.

                 This pattern is not allowed to FAIL.

'acosm2'   Store the arc cosine of operand 1 into operand 0. Both operands have mode m,
                 which is a scalar or vector floating-point mode.

                 This pattern is not allowed to FAIL.

'atanm2'   Store the arc tangent of operand 1 into operand 0. Both operands have mode
                 m, which is a scalar or vector floating-point mode.

                 This pattern is not allowed to FAIL.

'expm2'   Raise e (the base of natural logarithms) to the power of operand 1 and store the
                 result in operand 0. Both operands have mode m, which is a scalar or vector
                 floating-point mode.

                 This pattern is not allowed to FAIL.

'expm1m2'   Raise e (the base of natural logarithms) to the power of operand 1, subtract
                 1, and store the result in operand 0. Both operands have mode m, which is a
                 scalar or vector floating-point mode.

                 For inputs close to zero, the pattern is expected to be more accurate than a
                 separate expm2 and subm3 would be.

                 This pattern is not allowed to FAIL.

'exp10m2'   Raise 10 to the power of operand 1 and store the result in operand 0. Both
                 operands have mode m, which is a scalar or vector floating-point mode.

                 This pattern is not allowed to FAIL.

'exp2m2'   Raise 2 to the power of operand 1 and store the result in operand 0. Both
                 operands have mode m, which is a scalar or vector floating-point mode.

                 This pattern is not allowed to FAIL.

'logm2'   Store the natural logarithm of operand 1 into operand 0. Both operands have
              mode m, which is a scalar or vector floating-point mode.

              This pattern is not allowed to FAIL.

'log1pm2'   Add 1 to operand 1, compute the natural logarithm, and store the result in
              operand 0. Both operands have mode m, which is a scalar or vector floating-
              point mode.

              For inputs close to zero, the pattern is expected to be more accurate than a
              separate addm3 and logm2 would be.

              This pattern is not allowed to FAIL.

'log10m2'   Store the base-10 logarithm of operand 1 into operand 0. Both operands have
              mode m, which is a scalar or vector floating-point mode.

              This pattern is not allowed to FAIL.

'log2m2'   Store the base-2 logarithm of operand 1 into operand 0. Both operands have
              mode m, which is a scalar or vector floating-point mode.

              This pattern is not allowed to FAIL.

'logbm2'   Store the base-FLT_RADIX logarithm of operand 1 into operand 0. Both
              operands have mode m, which is a scalar or vector floating-point mode.

              This pattern is not allowed to FAIL.

'significandm2'
              Store the significand of floating-point operand 1 in operand 0. Both operands
              have mode m, which is a scalar or vector floating-point mode.

              This pattern is not allowed to FAIL.

'powm3'   Store the value of operand 1 raised to the exponent operand 2 into operand 0.
              All operands have mode m, which is a scalar or vector floating-point mode.

              This pattern is not allowed to FAIL.

'atan2m3'   Store the arc tangent (inverse tangent) of operand 1 divided by operand 2 into
              operand 0, using the signs of both arguments to determine the quadrant of the
              result. All operands have mode m, which is a scalar or vector floating-point
              mode.

              This pattern is not allowed to FAIL.

'floorm2'   Store the largest integral value not greater than operand 1 in operand 0.
              Both operands have mode m, which is a scalar or vector floating-point mode.
              If '-ffp-int-builtin-inexact' is in effect, the "inexact" exception may be
              raised for noninteger operands; otherwise, it may not.

              This pattern is not allowed to FAIL.

'btruncm2'
              Round operand 1 to an integer, towards zero, and store the result in operand 0.
              Both operands have mode m, which is a scalar or vector floating-point mode.
              If '-ffp-int-builtin-inexact' is in effect, the "inexact" exception may be
              raised for noninteger operands; otherwise, it may not.

              This pattern is not allowed to FAIL.

'roundm2'   Round operand 1 to the nearest integer, rounding away from zero in the event of a tie, and store the result in operand 0. Both operands have mode m, which is a scalar or vector floating-point mode. If '-ffp-int-builtin-inexact' is in effect, the "inexact" exception may be raised for noninteger operands; otherwise, it may not.

This pattern is not allowed to FAIL.

'ceilm2'   Store the smallest integral value not less than operand 1 in operand 0. Both operands have mode m, which is a scalar or vector floating-point mode. If '-ffp-int-builtin-inexact' is in effect, the "inexact" exception may be raised for noninteger operands; otherwise, it may not.

This pattern is not allowed to FAIL.

'nearbyintm2'
             Round operand 1 to an integer, using the current rounding mode, and store the result in operand 0. Do not raise an inexact condition when the result is different from the argument. Both operands have mode m, which is a scalar or vector floating-point mode.

This pattern is not allowed to FAIL.

'rintm2'   Round operand 1 to an integer, using the current rounding mode, and store the result in operand 0. Raise an inexact condition when the result is different from the argument. Both operands have mode m, which is a scalar or vector floating-point mode.

This pattern is not allowed to FAIL.

'lrintmn2'
             Convert operand 1 (valid for floating point mode m) to fixed point mode n as a signed number according to the current rounding mode and store in operand 0 (which has mode n).

'lroundmn2'
             Convert operand 1 (valid for floating point mode m) to fixed point mode n as a signed number rounding to nearest and away from zero and store in operand 0 (which has mode n).

'lfloormn2'
             Convert operand 1 (valid for floating point mode m) to fixed point mode n as a signed number rounding down and store in operand 0 (which has mode n).

'lceilmn2'
             Convert operand 1 (valid for floating point mode m) to fixed point mode n as a signed number rounding up and store in operand 0 (which has mode n).

'copysignm3'
             Store a value with the magnitude of operand 1 and the sign of operand 2 into operand 0. All operands have mode m, which is a scalar or vector floating-point mode.

This pattern is not allowed to FAIL.

'ffsm2'   Store into operand 0 one plus the index of the least significant 1-bit of operand
                 1. If operand 1 is zero, store zero.

                 m is either a scalar or vector integer mode. When it is a scalar, operand 1 has
                 mode *m* but operand 0 can have whatever scalar integer mode is suitable for the
                 target. The compiler will insert conversion instructions as necessary (typically
                 to convert the result to the same width as int). When *m* is a vector, both
                 operands must have mode *m*.

                 This pattern is not allowed to FAIL.

'clrsbm2'   Count leading redundant sign bits. Store into operand 0 the number of redun-
                 dant sign bits in operand 1, starting at the most significant bit position. A
                 redundant sign bit is defined as any sign bit after the first. As such, this count
                 will be one less than the count of leading sign bits.

                 m is either a scalar or vector integer mode. When it is a scalar, operand 1 has
                 mode *m* but operand 0 can have whatever scalar integer mode is suitable for the
                 target. The compiler will insert conversion instructions as necessary (typically
                 to convert the result to the same width as int). When *m* is a vector, both
                 operands must have mode *m*.

                 This pattern is not allowed to FAIL.

'clzm2'   Store into operand 0 the number of leading 0-bits in operand 1, starting at the
                 most significant bit position. If operand 1 is 0, the CLZ_DEFINED_VALUE_AT_
                 ZERO (see Section 17.30 [Misc], page 591) macro defines if the result is undefined
                 or has a useful value.

                 m is either a scalar or vector integer mode. When it is a scalar, operand 1 has
                 mode *m* but operand 0 can have whatever scalar integer mode is suitable for the
                 target. The compiler will insert conversion instructions as necessary (typically
                 to convert the result to the same width as int). When *m* is a vector, both
                 operands must have mode *m*.

                 This pattern is not allowed to FAIL.

'ctzm2'   Store into operand 0 the number of trailing 0-bits in operand 1, starting at the
                 least significant bit position. If operand 1 is 0, the CTZ_DEFINED_VALUE_AT_
                 ZERO (see Section 17.30 [Misc], page 591) macro defines if the result is undefined
                 or has a useful value.

                 m is either a scalar or vector integer mode. When it is a scalar, operand 1 has
                 mode *m* but operand 0 can have whatever scalar integer mode is suitable for the
                 target. The compiler will insert conversion instructions as necessary (typically
                 to convert the result to the same width as int). When *m* is a vector, both
                 operands must have mode *m*.

                 This pattern is not allowed to FAIL.

'popcountm2'
                 Store into operand 0 the number of 1-bits in operand 1.

                 m is either a scalar or vector integer mode. When it is a scalar, operand 1 has
                 mode *m* but operand 0 can have whatever scalar integer mode is suitable for the
                 target. The compiler will insert conversion instructions as necessary (typically

to convert the result to the same width as `int`). When m is a vector, both operands must have mode m.

This pattern is not allowed to `FAIL`.

'parity*m*2'

Store into operand 0 the parity of operand 1, i.e. the number of 1-bits in operand 1 modulo 2.

m is either a scalar or vector integer mode. When it is a scalar, operand 1 has mode m but operand 0 can have whatever scalar integer mode is suitable for the target. The compiler will insert conversion instructions as necessary (typically to convert the result to the same width as `int`). When m is a vector, both operands must have mode m.

This pattern is not allowed to `FAIL`.

'one_cmpl*m*2'

Store the bitwise-complement of operand 1 into operand 0.

'movmem*m*'   Block move instruction. The destination and source blocks of memory are the first two operands, and both are `mem:BLK`s with an address in mode `Pmode`.

The number of bytes to move is the third operand, in mode m. Usually, you specify `Pmode` for m. However, if you can generate better code knowing the range of valid lengths is smaller than those representable in a full Pmode pointer, you should provide a pattern with a mode corresponding to the range of values you can handle efficiently (e.g., `QImode` for values in the range 0–127; note we avoid numbers that appear negative) and also a pattern with `Pmode`.

The fourth operand is the known shared alignment of the source and destination, in the form of a `const_int` rtx. Thus, if the compiler knows that both source and destination are word-aligned, it may provide the value 4 for this operand.

Optional operands 5 and 6 specify expected alignment and size of block respectively. The expected alignment differs from alignment in operand 4 in a way that the blocks are not required to be aligned according to it in all cases. This expected alignment is also in bytes, just like operand 4. Expected size, when unknown, is set to (`const_int -1`).

Descriptions of multiple `movmem`m patterns can only be beneficial if the patterns for smaller modes have fewer restrictions on their first, second and fourth operands. Note that the mode m in `movmem`m does not impose any restriction on the mode of individually moved data units in the block.

These patterns need not give special consideration to the possibility that the source and destination strings might overlap.

'movstr'   String copy instruction, with `stpcpy` semantics. Operand 0 is an output operand in mode `Pmode`. The addresses of the destination and source strings are operands 1 and 2, and both are `mem:BLK`s with addresses in mode `Pmode`. The execution of the expansion of this pattern should store in operand 0 the address in which the `NUL` terminator was stored in the destination string.

This patern has also several optional operands that are same as in `setmem`.

'setmem*m*'   Block set instruction. The destination string is the first operand, given as a
                mem:BLK whose address is in mode Pmode. The number of bytes to set is the
                second operand, in mode *m*. The value to initialize the memory with is the
                third operand. Targets that only support the clearing of memory should reject
                any value that is not the constant 0. See 'movmem*m*' for a discussion of the choice
                of mode.

                The fourth operand is the known alignment of the destination, in the form of
                a const_int rtx. Thus, if the compiler knows that the destination is word-
                aligned, it may provide the value 4 for this operand.

                Optional operands 5 and 6 specify expected alignment and size of block re-
                spectively. The expected alignment differs from alignment in operand 4 in a
                way that the blocks are not required to be aligned according to it in all cases.
                This expected alignment is also in bytes, just like operand 4. Expected size,
                when unknown, is set to (const_int -1). Operand 7 is the minimal size of the
                block and operand 8 is the maximal size of the block (NULL if it can not be
                represented as CONST_INT). Operand 9 is the probable maximal size (i.e. we
                can not rely on it for correctness, but it can be used for choosing proper code
                sequence for a given size).

                The use for multiple setmem*m* is as for movmem*m*.

'cmpstrn*m*'

                String compare instruction, with five operands. Operand 0 is the output; it
                has mode *m*. The remaining four operands are like the operands of 'movmem*m*'.
                The two memory blocks specified are compared byte by byte in lexicographic
                order starting at the beginning of each string. The instruction is not allowed to
                prefetch more than one byte at a time since either string may end in the first
                byte and reading past that may access an invalid page or segment and cause
                a fault. The comparison terminates early if the fetched bytes are different or
                if they are equal to zero. The effect of the instruction is to store a value in
                operand 0 whose sign indicates the result of the comparison.

'cmpstr*m*'   String compare instruction, without known maximum length. Operand 0 is the
                output; it has mode *m*. The second and third operand are the blocks of memory
                to be compared; both are mem:BLK with an address in mode Pmode.

                The fourth operand is the known shared alignment of the source and destination,
                in the form of a const_int rtx. Thus, if the compiler knows that both source
                and destination are word-aligned, it may provide the value 4 for this operand.

                The two memory blocks specified are compared byte by byte in lexicographic
                order starting at the beginning of each string. The instruction is not allowed to
                prefetch more than one byte at a time since either string may end in the first
                byte and reading past that may access an invalid page or segment and cause
                a fault. The comparison will terminate when the fetched bytes are different or
                if they are equal to zero. The effect of the instruction is to store a value in
                operand 0 whose sign indicates the result of the comparison.

'cmpmem*m*'   Block compare instruction, with five operands like the operands of 'cmpstr*m*'.
                The two memory blocks specified are compared byte by byte in lexicographic
                order starting at the beginning of each block. Unlike 'cmpstr*m*' the instruction

can prefetch any bytes in the two memory blocks. Also unlike 'cmpstr*m*' the comparison will not stop if both bytes are zero. The effect of the instruction is to store a value in operand 0 whose sign indicates the result of the comparison.

'strlen*m*'   Compute the length of a string, with three operands. Operand 0 is the result (of mode *m*), operand 1 is a mem referring to the first character of the string, operand 2 is the character to search for (normally zero), and operand 3 is a constant describing the known alignment of the beginning of the string.

'float*mn*2'
Convert signed integer operand 1 (valid for fixed point mode *m*) to floating point mode *n* and store in operand 0 (which has mode *n*).

'floatuns*mn*2'
Convert unsigned integer operand 1 (valid for fixed point mode *m*) to floating point mode *n* and store in operand 0 (which has mode *n*).

'fix*mn*2'   Convert operand 1 (valid for floating point mode *m*) to fixed point mode *n* as a signed number and store in operand 0 (which has mode *n*). This instruction's result is defined only when the value of operand 1 is an integer.

If the machine description defines this pattern, it also needs to define the ftrunc pattern.

'fixuns*mn*2'
Convert operand 1 (valid for floating point mode *m*) to fixed point mode *n* as an unsigned number and store in operand 0 (which has mode *n*). This instruction's result is defined only when the value of operand 1 is an integer.

'ftrunc*m*2'
Convert operand 1 (valid for floating point mode *m*) to an integer value, still represented in floating point mode *m*, and store it in operand 0 (valid for floating point mode *m*).

'fix_trunc*mn*2'
Like 'fix*mn*2' but works for any floating point value of mode *m* by converting the value to an integer.

'fixuns_trunc*mn*2'
Like 'fixuns*mn*2' but works for any floating point value of mode *m* by converting the value to an integer.

'trunc*mn*2'
Truncate operand 1 (valid for mode *m*) to mode *n* and store in operand 0 (which has mode *n*). Both modes must be fixed point or both floating point.

'extend*mn*2'
Sign-extend operand 1 (valid for mode *m*) to mode *n* and store in operand 0 (which has mode *n*). Both modes must be fixed point or both floating point.

'zero_extend*mn*2'
Zero-extend operand 1 (valid for mode *m*) to mode *n* and store in operand 0 (which has mode *n*). Both modes must be fixed point.

'fract*mn*2'
> Convert operand 1 of mode m to mode n and store in operand 0 (which has mode n). Mode m and mode n could be fixed-point to fixed-point, signed integer to fixed-point, fixed-point to signed integer, floating-point to fixed-point, or fixed-point to floating-point. When overflows or underflows happen, the results are undefined.

'satfract*mn*2'
> Convert operand 1 of mode m to mode n and store in operand 0 (which has mode n). Mode m and mode n could be fixed-point to fixed-point, signed integer to fixed-point, or floating-point to fixed-point. When overflows or underflows happen, the instruction saturates the results to the maximum or the minimum.

'fractuns*mn*2'
> Convert operand 1 of mode m to mode n and store in operand 0 (which has mode n). Mode m and mode n could be unsigned integer to fixed-point, or fixed-point to unsigned integer. When overflows or underflows happen, the results are undefined.

'satfractuns*mn*2'
> Convert unsigned integer operand 1 of mode m to fixed-point mode n and store in operand 0 (which has mode n). When overflows or underflows happen, the instruction saturates the results to the maximum or the minimum.

'extv*m*'
> Extract a bit-field from register operand 1, sign-extend it, and store it in operand 0. Operand 2 specifies the width of the field in bits and operand 3 the starting bit, which counts from the most significant bit if 'BITS_BIG_ENDIAN' is true and from the least significant bit otherwise.
>
> Operands 0 and 1 both have mode m. Operands 2 and 3 have a target-specific mode.

'extv*m*isalign*m*'
> Extract a bit-field from memory operand 1, sign extend it, and store it in operand 0. Operand 2 specifies the width in bits and operand 3 the starting bit. The starting bit is always somewhere in the first byte of operand 1; it counts from the most significant bit if 'BITS_BIG_ENDIAN' is true and from the least significant bit otherwise.
>
> Operand 0 has mode m while operand 1 has BLK mode. Operands 2 and 3 have a target-specific mode.
>
> The instruction must not read beyond the last byte of the bit-field.

'extzv*m*'
> Like 'extv*m*' except that the bit-field value is zero-extended.

'extzv*m*isalign*m*'
> Like 'extv*m*isalign*m*' except that the bit-field value is zero-extended.

'insv*m*'
> Insert operand 3 into a bit-field of register operand 0. Operand 1 specifies the width of the field in bits and operand 2 the starting bit, which counts from the most significant bit if 'BITS_BIG_ENDIAN' is true and from the least significant bit otherwise.

Operands 0 and 3 both have mode *m*. Operands 1 and 2 have a target-specific mode.

'insvmisalign*m*'

>   Insert operand 3 into a bit-field of memory operand 0. Operand 1 specifies the width of the field in bits and operand 2 the starting bit. The starting bit is always somewhere in the first byte of operand 0; it counts from the most significant bit if 'BITS_BIG_ENDIAN' is true and from the least significant bit otherwise.
>
>   Operand 3 has mode *m* while operand 0 has BLK mode. Operands 1 and 2 have a target-specific mode.
>
>   The instruction must not read or write beyond the last byte of the bit-field.

'extv'

>   Extract a bit-field from operand 1 (a register or memory operand), where operand 2 specifies the width in bits and operand 3 the starting bit, and store it in operand 0. Operand 0 must have mode word_mode. Operand 1 may have mode byte_mode or word_mode; often word_mode is allowed only for registers. Operands 2 and 3 must be valid for word_mode.
>
>   The RTL generation pass generates this instruction only with constants for operands 2 and 3 and the constant is never zero for operand 2.
>
>   The bit-field value is sign-extended to a full word integer before it is stored in operand 0.
>
>   This pattern is deprecated; please use 'extv*m*' and extvmisalign*m* instead.

'extzv'

>   Like 'extv' except that the bit-field value is zero-extended.
>
>   This pattern is deprecated; please use 'extzv*m*' and extzvmisalign*m* instead.

'insv'

>   Store operand 3 (which must be valid for word_mode) into a bit-field in operand 0, where operand 1 specifies the width in bits and operand 2 the starting bit. Operand 0 may have mode byte_mode or word_mode; often word_mode is allowed only for registers. Operands 1 and 2 must be valid for word_mode.
>
>   The RTL generation pass generates this instruction only with constants for operands 1 and 2 and the constant is never zero for operand 1.
>
>   This pattern is deprecated; please use 'insv*m*' and insvmisalign*m* instead.

'mov*mode*cc'

>   Conditionally move operand 2 or operand 3 into operand 0 according to the comparison in operand 1. If the comparison is true, operand 2 is moved into operand 0, otherwise operand 3 is moved.
>
>   The mode of the operands being compared need not be the same as the operands being moved. Some machines, sparc64 for example, have instructions that conditionally move an integer value based on the floating point condition codes and vice versa.
>
>   If the machine does not have conditional move instructions, do not define these patterns.

'add*mode*cc'

>   Similar to 'mov*mode*cc' but for conditional addition. Conditionally move operand 2 or (operands 2 + operand 3) into operand 0 according to the

comparison in operand 1. If the comparison is false, operand 2 is moved into operand 0, otherwise (operand 2 + operand 3) is moved.

'negmodecc'

Similar to 'movmodecc' but for conditional negation. Conditionally move the negation of operand 2 or the unchanged operand 3 into operand 0 according to the comparison in operand 1. If the comparison is true, the negation of operand 2 is moved into operand 0, otherwise operand 3 is moved.

'notmodecc'

Similar to 'negmodecc' but for conditional complement. Conditionally move the bitwise complement of operand 2 or the unchanged operand 3 into operand 0 according to the comparison in operand 1. If the comparison is true, the complement of operand 2 is moved into operand 0, otherwise operand 3 is moved.

'cstoremode4'

Store zero or nonzero in operand 0 according to whether a comparison is true. Operand 1 is a comparison operator. Operand 2 and operand 3 are the first and second operand of the comparison, respectively. You specify the mode that operand 0 must have when you write the match_operand expression. The compiler automatically sees which mode you have used and supplies an operand of that mode.

The value stored for a true condition must have 1 as its low bit, or else must be negative. Otherwise the instruction is not suitable and you should omit it from the machine description. You describe to the compiler exactly which value is stored by defining the macro STORE_FLAG_VALUE (see Section 17.30 [Misc], page 591). If a description cannot be found that can be used for all the possible comparison operators, you should pick one and use a define_expand to map all results onto the one you chose.

These operations may FAIL, but should do so only in relatively uncommon cases; if they would FAIL for common cases involving integer comparisons, it is best to restrict the predicates to not allow these operands. Likewise if a given comparison operator will always fail, independent of the operands (for floating-point modes, the ordered_comparison_operator predicate is often useful in this case).

If this pattern is omitted, the compiler will generate a conditional branch—for example, it may copy a constant one to the target and branching around an assignment of zero to the target—or a libcall. If the predicate for operand 1 only rejects some operators, it will also try reordering the operands and/or inverting the result value (e.g. by an exclusive OR). These possibilities could be cheaper or equivalent to the instructions used for the 'cstoremode4' pattern followed by those required to convert a positive result from STORE_FLAG_VALUE to 1; in this case, you can and should make operand 1's predicate reject some operators in the 'cstoremode4' pattern, or remove the pattern altogether from the machine description.

'cbranch*mode*4'

> Conditional branch instruction combined with a compare instruction. Operand 0 is a comparison operator. Operand 1 and operand 2 are the first and second operands of the comparison, respectively. Operand 3 is the `code_label` to jump to.

'jump'
> A jump inside a function; an unconditional branch. Operand 0 is the `code_label` to jump to. This pattern name is mandatory on all machines.

'call'
> Subroutine call instruction returning no value. Operand 0 is the function to call; operand 1 is the number of bytes of arguments pushed as a `const_int`; operand 2 is the number of registers used as operands.
>
> On most machines, operand 2 is not actually stored into the RTL pattern. It is supplied for the sake of some RISC machines which need to put this information into the assembler code; they can put it in the RTL instead of operand 1.
>
> Operand 0 should be a `mem` RTX whose address is the address of the function. Note, however, that this address can be a `symbol_ref` expression even if it would not be a legitimate memory address on the target machine. If it is also not a valid argument for a call instruction, the pattern for this operation should be a `define_expand` (see Section 16.15 [Expander Definitions], page 394) that places the address into a register and uses that register in the call instruction.

'call_value'
> Subroutine call instruction returning a value. Operand 0 is the hard register in which the value is returned. There are three more operands, the same as the three operands of the 'call' instruction (but with numbers increased by one).
>
> Subroutines that return `BLKmode` objects use the 'call' insn.

'call_pop', 'call_value_pop'
> Similar to 'call' and 'call_value', except used if defined and if `RETURN_POPS_ARGS` is nonzero. They should emit a `parallel` that contains both the function call and a `set` to indicate the adjustment made to the frame pointer.
>
> For machines where `RETURN_POPS_ARGS` can be nonzero, the use of these patterns increases the number of functions for which the frame pointer can be eliminated, if desired.

'untyped_call'
> Subroutine call instruction returning a value of any type. Operand 0 is the function to call; operand 1 is a memory location where the result of calling the function is to be stored; operand 2 is a `parallel` expression where each element is a `set` expression that indicates the saving of a function return value into the result block.
>
> This instruction pattern should be defined to support `__builtin_apply` on machines where special instructions are needed to call a subroutine with arbitrary arguments or to save the value returned. This instruction pattern is required on machines that have multiple registers that can hold a return value (i.e. `FUNCTION_VALUE_REGNO_P` is true for more than one register).

'return'
> Subroutine return instruction. This instruction pattern name should be defined only if a single instruction can do all the work of returning from a function.

Like the 'movm' patterns, this pattern is also used after the RTL generation phase. In this case it is to support machines where multiple instructions are usually needed to return from a function, but some class of functions only requires one instruction to implement a return. Normally, the applicable functions are those which do not need to save any registers or allocate stack space.

It is valid for this pattern to expand to an instruction using simple_return if no epilogue is required.

'simple_return'

Subroutine return instruction. This instruction pattern name should be defined only if a single instruction can do all the work of returning from a function on a path where no epilogue is required. This pattern is very similar to the return instruction pattern, but it is emitted only by the shrink-wrapping optimization on paths where the function prologue has not been executed, and a function return should occur without any of the effects of the epilogue. Additional uses may be introduced on paths where both the prologue and the epilogue have executed.

For such machines, the condition specified in this pattern should only be true when reload_completed is nonzero and the function's epilogue would only be a single instruction. For machines with register windows, the routine leaf_function_p may be used to determine if a register window push is required.

Machines that have conditional return instructions should define patterns such as

```
(define_insn ""
  [(set (pc)
        (if_then_else (match_operator
                          0 "comparison_operator"
                          [(cc0) (const_int 0)])
                      (return)
                      (pc)))]
  "condition"
  "...")
```

where *condition* would normally be the same condition specified on the named 'return' pattern.

'untyped_return'

Untyped subroutine return instruction. This instruction pattern should be defined to support __builtin_return on machines where special instructions are needed to return a value of any type.

Operand 0 is a memory location where the result of calling a function with __builtin_apply is stored; operand 1 is a parallel expression where each element is a set expression that indicates the restoring of a function return value from the result block.

'nop'   No-op instruction. This instruction pattern name should always be defined to output a no-op in assembler code. (const_int 0) will do as an RTL pattern.

'indirect_jump'

An instruction to jump to an address which is operand zero. This pattern name is mandatory on all machines.

'casesi'   Instruction to jump through a dispatch table, including bounds checking. This instruction takes five operands:

1. The index to dispatch on, which has mode SImode.

2. The lower bound for indices in the table, an integer constant.

3. The total range of indices in the table—the largest index minus the smallest one (both inclusive).

4. A label that precedes the table itself.

5. A label to jump to if the index has a value outside the bounds.

The table is an addr_vec or addr_diff_vec inside of a jump_table_data. The number of elements in the table is one plus the difference between the upper bound and the lower bound.

'tablejump'

Instruction to jump to a variable address. This is a low-level capability which can be used to implement a dispatch table when there is no 'casesi' pattern.

This pattern requires two operands: the address or offset, and a label which should immediately precede the jump table. If the macro CASE_VECTOR_PC_RELATIVE evaluates to a nonzero value then the first operand is an offset which counts from the address of the table; otherwise, it is an absolute address to jump to. In either case, the first operand has mode Pmode.

The 'tablejump' insn is always the last insn before the jump table it uses. Its assembler code normally has no need to use the second operand, but you should incorporate it in the RTL pattern so that the jump optimizer will not delete the table as unreachable code.

'decrement_and_branch_until_zero'

Conditional branch instruction that decrements a register and jumps if the register is nonzero. Operand 0 is the register to decrement and test; operand 1 is the label to jump to if the register is nonzero. See Section 16.13 [Looping Patterns], page 391.

This optional instruction pattern is only used by the combiner, typically for loops reversed by the loop optimizer when strength reduction is enabled.

'doloop_end'

Conditional branch instruction that decrements a register and jumps if the register is nonzero. Operand 0 is the register to decrement and test; operand 1 is the label to jump to if the register is nonzero. See Section 16.13 [Looping Patterns], page 391.

This optional instruction pattern should be defined for machines with low-overhead looping instructions as the loop optimizer will try to modify suitable loops to utilize it. The target hook TARGET_CAN_USE_DOLOOP_P controls the conditions under which low-overhead loops can be used.

'doloop_begin'

Companion instruction to doloop_end required for machines that need to perform some initialization, such as loading a special counter register. Operand

1 is the associated `doloop_end` pattern and operand 0 is the register that it decrements.

If initialization insns do not always need to be emitted, use a `define_expand` (see Section 16.15 [Expander Definitions], page 394) and make it fail.

'`canonicalize_funcptr_for_compare`'

Canonicalize the function pointer in operand 1 and store the result into operand 0.

Operand 0 is always a `reg` and has mode `Pmode`; operand 1 may be a `reg`, `mem`, `symbol_ref`, `const_int`, etc and also has mode `Pmode`.

Canonicalization of a function pointer usually involves computing the address of the function which would be called if the function pointer were used in an indirect call.

Only define this pattern if function pointers on the target machine can have different values but still call the same function when used in an indirect call.

'`save_stack_block`'
'`save_stack_function`'
'`save_stack_nonlocal`'
'`restore_stack_block`'
'`restore_stack_function`'
'`restore_stack_nonlocal`'

Most machines save and restore the stack pointer by copying it to or from an object of mode `Pmode`. Do not define these patterns on such machines.

Some machines require special handling for stack pointer saves and restores. On those machines, define the patterns corresponding to the non-standard cases by using a `define_expand` (see Section 16.15 [Expander Definitions], page 394) that produces the required insns. The three types of saves and restores are:

1. '`save_stack_block`' saves the stack pointer at the start of a block that allocates a variable-sized object, and '`restore_stack_block`' restores the stack pointer when the block is exited.

2. '`save_stack_function`' and '`restore_stack_function`' do a similar job for the outermost block of a function and are used when the function allocates variable-sized objects or calls `alloca`. Only the epilogue uses the restored stack pointer, allowing a simpler save or restore sequence on some machines.

3. '`save_stack_nonlocal`' is used in functions that contain labels branched to by nested functions. It saves the stack pointer in such a way that the inner function can use '`restore_stack_nonlocal`' to restore the stack pointer. The compiler generates code to restore the frame and argument pointer registers, but some machines require saving and restoring additional data such as register window information or stack backchains. Place insns in these patterns to save and restore any such required data.

When saving the stack pointer, operand 0 is the save area and operand 1 is the stack pointer. The mode used to allocate the save area defaults to `Pmode` but you can override that choice by defining the `STACK_SAVEAREA_MODE` macro (see

Section 17.5 [Storage Layout], page 444). You must specify an integral mode, or `VOIDmode` if no save area is needed for a particular type of save (either because no save is needed or because a machine-specific save area can be used). Operand 0 is the stack pointer and operand 1 is the save area for restore operations. If 'save_stack_block' is defined, operand 0 must not be `VOIDmode` since these saves can be arbitrarily nested.

A save area is a `mem` that is at a constant offset from `virtual_stack_vars_rtx` when the stack pointer is saved for use by nonlocal gotos and a `reg` in the other two cases.

'allocate_stack'

Subtract (or add if `STACK_GROWS_DOWNWARD` is undefined) operand 1 from the stack pointer to create space for dynamically allocated data.

Store the resultant pointer to this space into operand 0. If you are allocating space from the main stack, do this by emitting a move insn to copy `virtual_stack_dynamic_rtx` to operand 0. If you are allocating the space elsewhere, generate code to copy the location of the space to operand 0. In the latter case, you must ensure this space gets freed when the corresponding space on the main stack is free.

Do not define this pattern if all that must be done is the subtraction. Some machines require other operations such as stack probes or maintaining the back chain. Define this pattern to emit those operations in addition to updating the stack pointer.

'check_stack'

If stack checking (see Section 17.9.3 [Stack Checking], page 481) cannot be done on your system by probing the stack, define this pattern to perform the needed check and signal an error if the stack has overflowed. The single operand is the address in the stack farthest from the current stack pointer that you need to validate. Normally, on platforms where this pattern is needed, you would obtain the stack limit from a global or thread-specific variable or register.

'probe_stack_address'

If stack checking (see Section 17.9.3 [Stack Checking], page 481) can be done on your system by probing the stack but without the need to actually access it, define this pattern and signal an error if the stack has overflowed. The single operand is the memory address in the stack that needs to be probed.

'probe_stack'

If stack checking (see Section 17.9.3 [Stack Checking], page 481) can be done on your system by probing the stack but doing it with a "store zero" instruction is not valid or optimal, define this pattern to do the probing differently and signal an error if the stack has overflowed. The single operand is the memory reference in the stack that needs to be probed.

'nonlocal_goto'

Emit code to generate a non-local goto, e.g., a jump from one function to a label in an outer function. This pattern has four arguments, each representing a value to be used in the jump. The first argument is to be loaded into the frame pointer, the second is the address to branch to (code to dispatch to the actual label), the third is the address of a location where the stack is saved, and the last is the address of the label, to be placed in the location for the incoming static chain.

On most machines you need not define this pattern, since GCC will already generate the correct code, which is to load the frame pointer and static chain, restore the stack (using the 'restore_stack_nonlocal' pattern, if defined), and jump indirectly to the dispatcher. You need only define this pattern if this code will not work on your machine.

'nonlocal_goto_receiver'

This pattern, if defined, contains code needed at the target of a nonlocal goto after the code already generated by GCC. You will not normally need to define this pattern. A typical reason why you might need this pattern is if some value, such as a pointer to a global table, must be restored when the frame pointer is restored. Note that a nonlocal goto only occurs within a unit-of-translation, so a global table pointer that is shared by all functions of a given module need not be restored. There are no arguments.

'exception_receiver'

This pattern, if defined, contains code needed at the site of an exception handler that isn't needed at the site of a nonlocal goto. You will not normally need to define this pattern. A typical reason why you might need this pattern is if some value, such as a pointer to a global table, must be restored after control flow is branched to the handler of an exception. There are no arguments.

'builtin_setjmp_setup'

This pattern, if defined, contains additional code needed to initialize the jmp_buf. You will not normally need to define this pattern. A typical reason why you might need this pattern is if some value, such as a pointer to a global table, must be restored. Though it is preferred that the pointer value be recalculated if possible (given the address of a label for instance). The single argument is a pointer to the jmp_buf. Note that the buffer is five words long and that the first three are normally used by the generic mechanism.

'builtin_setjmp_receiver'

This pattern, if defined, contains code needed at the site of a built-in setjmp that isn't needed at the site of a nonlocal goto. You will not normally need to define this pattern. A typical reason why you might need this pattern is if some value, such as a pointer to a global table, must be restored. It takes one argument, which is the label to which builtin_longjmp transferred control; this pattern may be emitted at a small offset from that label.

'builtin_longjmp'

This pattern, if defined, performs the entire action of the longjmp. You will not normally need to define this pattern unless you also define builtin_setjmp_setup. The single argument is a pointer to the jmp_buf.

'eh_return'

> This pattern, if defined, affects the way `__builtin_eh_return`, and thence the call frame exception handling library routines, are built. It is intended to handle non-trivial actions needed along the abnormal return path.
>
> The address of the exception handler to which the function should return is passed as operand to this pattern. It will normally need to copied by the pattern to some special register or memory location. If the pattern needs to determine the location of the target call frame in order to do so, it may use `EH_RETURN_STACKADJ_RTX`, if defined; it will have already been assigned.
>
> If this pattern is not defined, the default action will be to simply copy the return address to `EH_RETURN_HANDLER_RTX`. Either that macro or this pattern needs to be defined if call frame exception handling is to be used.

'prologue'

> This pattern, if defined, emits RTL for entry to a function. The function entry is responsible for setting up the stack frame, initializing the frame pointer register, saving callee saved registers, etc.
>
> Using a prologue pattern is generally preferred over defining `TARGET_ASM_FUNCTION_PROLOGUE` to emit assembly code for the prologue.
>
> The `prologue` pattern is particularly useful for targets which perform instruction scheduling.

'window_save'

> This pattern, if defined, emits RTL for a register window save. It should be defined if the target machine has register windows but the window events are decoupled from calls to subroutines. The canonical example is the SPARC architecture.

'epilogue'

> This pattern emits RTL for exit from a function. The function exit is responsible for deallocating the stack frame, restoring callee saved registers and emitting the return instruction.
>
> Using an epilogue pattern is generally preferred over defining `TARGET_ASM_FUNCTION_EPILOGUE` to emit assembly code for the epilogue.
>
> The `epilogue` pattern is particularly useful for targets which perform instruction scheduling or which have delay slots for their return instruction.

'sibcall_epilogue'

> This pattern, if defined, emits RTL for exit from a function without the final branch back to the calling function. This pattern will be emitted before any sibling call (aka tail call) sites.
>
> The `sibcall_epilogue` pattern must not clobber any arguments used for parameter passing or any stack slots for arguments passed to the current function.

'trap'   This pattern, if defined, signals an error, typically by causing some kind of signal to be raised. Among other places, it is used by the Java front end to signal 'invalid array index' exceptions.

'ctrap*MM4*'

> Conditional trap instruction. Operand 0 is a piece of RTL which performs a comparison, and operands 1 and 2 are the arms of the comparison. Operand 3 is the trap code, an integer.
>
> A typical `ctrap` pattern looks like
>
> ```
> (define_insn "ctrapsi4"
>   [(trap_if (match_operator 0 "trap_operator"
>              [(match_operand 1 "register_operand")
>               (match_operand 2 "immediate_operand")])
>             (match_operand 3 "const_int_operand" "i"))]
>   ""
>   "...")
> ```

'prefetch'

> This pattern, if defined, emits code for a non-faulting data prefetch instruction. Operand 0 is the address of the memory to prefetch. Operand 1 is a constant 1 if the prefetch is preparing for a write to the memory address, or a constant 0 otherwise. Operand 2 is the expected degree of temporal locality of the data and is a value between 0 and 3, inclusive; 0 means that the data has no temporal locality, so it need not be left in the cache after the access; 3 means that the data has a high degree of temporal locality and should be left in all levels of cache possible; 1 and 2 mean, respectively, a low or moderate degree of temporal locality.
>
> Targets that do not support write prefetches or locality hints can ignore the values of operands 1 and 2.

'blockage'

> This pattern defines a pseudo insn that prevents the instruction scheduler and other passes from moving instructions and using register equivalences across the boundary defined by the blockage insn. This needs to be an UNSPEC_VOLATILE pattern or a volatile ASM.

'memory_barrier'

> If the target memory model is not fully synchronous, then this pattern should be defined to an instruction that orders both loads and stores before the instruction with respect to loads and stores after the instruction. This pattern has no operands.

'sync_compare_and_swap*mode*'

> This pattern, if defined, emits code for an atomic compare-and-swap operation. Operand 1 is the memory on which the atomic operation is performed. Operand 2 is the "old" value to be compared against the current contents of the memory location. Operand 3 is the "new" value to store in the memory if the compare succeeds. Operand 0 is the result of the operation; it should contain the contents of the memory before the operation. If the compare succeeds, this should obviously be a copy of operand 2.
>
> This pattern must show that both operand 0 and operand 1 are modified.
>
> This pattern must issue any memory barrier instructions such that all memory operations before the atomic operation occur before the atomic operation and all memory operations after the atomic operation occur after the atomic operation.

For targets where the success or failure of the compare-and-swap operation is available via the status flags, it is possible to avoid a separate compare operation and issue the subsequent branch or store-flag operation immediately after the compare-and-swap. To this end, GCC will look for a MODE_CC set in the output of sync_compare_and_swap*mode*; if the machine description includes such a set, the target should also define special cbranchcc4 and/or cstorecc4 instructions. GCC will then be able to take the destination of the MODE_CC set and pass it to the cbranchcc4 or cstorecc4 pattern as the first operand of the comparison (the second will be (const_int 0)).

For targets where the operating system may provide support for this operation via library calls, the sync_compare_and_swap_optab may be initialized to a function with the same interface as the __sync_val_compare_and_swap_n built-in. If the entire set of __sync builtins are supported via library calls, the target can initialize all of the optabs at once with init_sync_libfuncs. For the purposes of C++11 std::atomic::is_lock_free, it is assumed that these library calls do *not* use any kind of interruptable locking.

'sync_add*mode*', 'sync_sub*mode*'
'sync_ior*mode*', 'sync_and*mode*'
'sync_xor*mode*', 'sync_nand*mode*'

These patterns emit code for an atomic operation on memory. Operand 0 is the memory on which the atomic operation is performed. Operand 1 is the second operand to the binary operator.

This pattern must issue any memory barrier instructions such that all memory operations before the atomic operation occur before the atomic operation and all memory operations after the atomic operation occur after the atomic operation.

If these patterns are not defined, the operation will be constructed from a compare-and-swap operation, if defined.

'sync_old_add*mode*', 'sync_old_sub*mode*'
'sync_old_ior*mode*', 'sync_old_and*mode*'
'sync_old_xor*mode*', 'sync_old_nand*mode*'

These patterns emit code for an atomic operation on memory, and return the value that the memory contained before the operation. Operand 0 is the result value, operand 1 is the memory on which the atomic operation is performed, and operand 2 is the second operand to the binary operator.

This pattern must issue any memory barrier instructions such that all memory operations before the atomic operation occur before the atomic operation and all memory operations after the atomic operation occur after the atomic operation.

If these patterns are not defined, the operation will be constructed from a compare-and-swap operation, if defined.

'sync_new_add*mode*', 'sync_new_sub*mode*'
'sync_new_ior*mode*', 'sync_new_and*mode*'
'sync_new_xor*mode*', 'sync_new_nand*mode*'

These patterns are like their sync_old_*op* counterparts, except that they return the value that exists in the memory location after the operation, rather than before the operation.

'`sync_lock_test_and_set`*mode*'

> This pattern takes two forms, based on the capabilities of the target. In either case, operand 0 is the result of the operand, operand 1 is the memory on which the atomic operation is performed, and operand 2 is the value to set in the lock.
>
> In the ideal case, this operation is an atomic exchange operation, in which the previous value in memory operand is copied into the result operand, and the value operand is stored in the memory operand.
>
> For less capable targets, any value operand that is not the constant 1 should be rejected with `FAIL`. In this case the target may use an atomic test-and-set bit operation. The result operand should contain 1 if the bit was previously set and 0 if the bit was previously clear. The true contents of the memory operand are implementation defined.
>
> This pattern must issue any memory barrier instructions such that the pattern as a whole acts as an acquire barrier, that is all memory operations after the pattern do not occur until the lock is acquired.
>
> If this pattern is not defined, the operation will be constructed from a compare-and-swap operation, if defined.

'`sync_lock_release`*mode*'

> This pattern, if defined, releases a lock set by `sync_lock_test_and_set`*mode*. Operand 0 is the memory that contains the lock; operand 1 is the value to store in the lock.
>
> If the target doesn't implement full semantics for `sync_lock_test_and_set`*mode*, any value operand which is not the constant 0 should be rejected with `FAIL`, and the true contents of the memory operand are implementation defined.
>
> This pattern must issue any memory barrier instructions such that the pattern as a whole acts as a release barrier, that is the lock is released only after all previous memory operations have completed.
>
> If this pattern is not defined, then a `memory_barrier` pattern will be emitted, followed by a store of the value to the memory operand.

'`atomic_compare_and_swap`*mode*'

> This pattern, if defined, emits code for an atomic compare-and-swap operation with memory model semantics. Operand 2 is the memory on which the atomic operation is performed. Operand 0 is an output operand which is set to true or false based on whether the operation succeeded. Operand 1 is an output operand which is set to the contents of the memory before the operation was attempted. Operand 3 is the value that is expected to be in memory. Operand 4 is the value to put in memory if the expected value is found there. Operand 5 is set to 1 if this compare and swap is to be treated as a weak operation. Operand 6 is the memory model to be used if the operation is a success. Operand 7 is the memory model to be used if the operation fails.
>
> If memory referred to in operand 2 contains the value in operand 3, then operand 4 is stored in memory pointed to by operand 2 and fencing based on the memory model in operand 6 is issued.

If memory referred to in operand 2 does not contain the value in operand 3, then fencing based on the memory model in operand 7 is issued.

If a target does not support weak compare-and-swap operations, or the port elects not to implement weak operations, the argument in operand 5 can be ignored. Note a strong implementation must be provided.

If this pattern is not provided, the `__atomic_compare_exchange` built-in functions will utilize the legacy `sync_compare_and_swap` pattern with an `__ATOMIC_SEQ_CST` memory model.

'`atomic_load`*mode*'

> This pattern implements an atomic load operation with memory model semantics. Operand 1 is the memory address being loaded from. Operand 0 is the result of the load. Operand 2 is the memory model to be used for the load operation.
>
> If not present, the `__atomic_load` built-in function will either resort to a normal load with memory barriers, or a compare-and-swap operation if a normal load would not be atomic.

'`atomic_store`*mode*'

> This pattern implements an atomic store operation with memory model semantics. Operand 0 is the memory address being stored to. Operand 1 is the value to be written. Operand 2 is the memory model to be used for the operation.
>
> If not present, the `__atomic_store` built-in function will attempt to perform a normal store and surround it with any required memory fences. If the store would not be atomic, then an `__atomic_exchange` is attempted with the result being ignored.

'`atomic_exchange`*mode*'

> This pattern implements an atomic exchange operation with memory model semantics. Operand 1 is the memory location the operation is performed on. Operand 0 is an output operand which is set to the original value contained in the memory pointed to by operand 1. Operand 2 is the value to be stored. Operand 3 is the memory model to be used.
>
> If this pattern is not present, the built-in function `__atomic_exchange` will attempt to preform the operation with a compare and swap loop.

'`atomic_add`*mode*', '`atomic_sub`*mode*'
'`atomic_or`*mode*', '`atomic_and`*mode*'
'`atomic_xor`*mode*', '`atomic_nand`*mode*'

> These patterns emit code for an atomic operation on memory with memory model semantics. Operand 0 is the memory on which the atomic operation is performed. Operand 1 is the second operand to the binary operator. Operand 2 is the memory model to be used by the operation.
>
> If these patterns are not defined, attempts will be made to use legacy `sync` patterns, or equivalent patterns which return a result. If none of these are available a compare-and-swap loop will be used.

'atomic_fetch_add*mode*', 'atomic_fetch_sub*mode*'
'atomic_fetch_or*mode*', 'atomic_fetch_and*mode*'
'atomic_fetch_xor*mode*', 'atomic_fetch_nand*mode*'

>These patterns emit code for an atomic operation on memory with memory
>model semantics, and return the original value. Operand 0 is an output operand
>which contains the value of the memory location before the operation was per-
>formed. Operand 1 is the memory on which the atomic operation is performed.
>Operand 2 is the second operand to the binary operator. Operand 3 is the
>memory model to be used by the operation.

>If these patterns are not defined, attempts will be made to use legacy **sync**
>patterns. If none of these are available a compare-and-swap loop will be used.

'atomic_add_fetch*mode*', 'atomic_sub_fetch*mode*'
'atomic_or_fetch*mode*', 'atomic_and_fetch*mode*'
'atomic_xor_fetch*mode*', 'atomic_nand_fetch*mode*'

>These patterns emit code for an atomic operation on memory with mem-
>ory model semantics and return the result after the operation is performed.
>Operand 0 is an output operand which contains the value after the operation.
>Operand 1 is the memory on which the atomic operation is performed. Operand
>2 is the second operand to the binary operator. Operand 3 is the memory model
>to be used by the operation.

>If these patterns are not defined, attempts will be made to use legacy **sync**
>patterns, or equivalent patterns which return the result before the operation
>followed by the arithmetic operation required to produce the result. If none of
>these are available a compare-and-swap loop will be used.

'atomic_test_and_set'

>This pattern emits code for **__builtin_atomic_test_and_set**. Operand 0 is
>an output operand which is set to true if the previous previous contents of the
>byte was "set", and false otherwise. Operand 1 is the **QImode** memory to be
>modified. Operand 2 is the memory model to be used.

>The specific value that defines "set" is implementation defined, and is normally
>based on what is performed by the native atomic test and set instruction.

'atomic_bit_test_and_set*mode*'
'atomic_bit_test_and_complement*mode*'
'atomic_bit_test_and_reset*mode*'

>These patterns emit code for an atomic bitwise operation on memory with mem-
>ory model semantics, and return the original value of the specified bit. Operand
>0 is an output operand which contains the value of the specified bit from the
>memory location before the operation was performed. Operand 1 is the memory
>on which the atomic operation is performed. Operand 2 is the bit within the
>operand, starting with least significant bit. Operand 3 is the memory model to
>be used by the operation. Operand 4 is a flag - it is **const1_rtx** if operand 0
>should contain the original value of the specified bit in the least significant bit
>of the operand, and **const0_rtx** if the bit should be in its original position in
>the operand. **atomic_bit_test_and_set*mode*** atomically sets the specified bit
>after remembering its original value, **atomic_bit_test_and_complement*mode***

inverts the specified bit and `atomic_bit_test_and_reset`*mode* clears the specified bit.

If these patterns are not defined, attempts will be made to use `atomic_fetch_or`*mode*, `atomic_fetch_xor`*mode* or `atomic_fetch_and`*mode* instruction patterns, or their `sync` counterparts. If none of these are available a compare-and-swap loop will be used.

'`mem_thread_fence`*mode*'

This pattern emits code required to implement a thread fence with memory model semantics. Operand 0 is the memory model to be used.

If this pattern is not specified, all memory models except `__ATOMIC_RELAXED` will result in issuing a `sync_synchronize` barrier pattern.

'`mem_signal_fence`*mode*'

This pattern emits code required to implement a signal fence with memory model semantics. Operand 0 is the memory model to be used.

This pattern should impact the compiler optimizers the same way that mem_signal_fence does, but it does not need to issue any barrier instructions.

If this pattern is not specified, all memory models except `__ATOMIC_RELAXED` will result in issuing a `sync_synchronize` barrier pattern.

'`get_thread_pointer`*mode*'
'`set_thread_pointer`*mode*'

These patterns emit code that reads/sets the TLS thread pointer. Currently, these are only needed if the target needs to support the `__builtin_thread_pointer` and `__builtin_set_thread_pointer` builtins.

The get/set patterns have a single output/input operand respectively, with *mode* intended to be `Pmode`.

'`stack_protect_set`'

This pattern, if defined, moves a `ptr_mode` value from the memory in operand 1 to the memory in operand 0 without leaving the value in a register afterward. This is to avoid leaking the value some place that an attacker might use to rewrite the stack guard slot after having clobbered it.

If this pattern is not defined, then a plain move pattern is generated.

'`stack_protect_test`'

This pattern, if defined, compares a `ptr_mode` value from the memory in operand 1 with the memory in operand 0 without leaving the value in a register afterward and branches to operand 2 if the values were equal.

If this pattern is not defined, then a plain compare pattern and conditional branch pattern is used.

'`clear_cache`'

This pattern, if defined, flushes the instruction cache for a region of memory. The region is bounded to by the Pmode pointers in operand 0 inclusive and operand 1 exclusive.

If this pattern is not defined, a call to the library function `__clear_cache` is used.

16.10 When the Order of Patterns Matters

Sometimes an insn can match more than one instruction pattern. Then the pattern that appears first in the machine description is the one used. Therefore, more specific patterns (patterns that will match fewer things) and faster instructions (those that will produce better code when they do match) should usually go first in the description.

In some cases the effect of ordering the patterns can be used to hide a pattern when it is not valid. For example, the 68000 has an instruction for converting a fullword to floating point and another for converting a byte to floating point. An instruction converting an integer to floating point could match either one. We put the pattern to convert the fullword first to make sure that one will be used rather than the other. (Otherwise a large integer might be generated as a single-byte immediate quantity, which would not work.) Instead of using this pattern ordering it would be possible to make the pattern for convert-a-byte smart enough to deal properly with any constant value.

16.11 Interdependence of Patterns

In some cases machines support instructions identical except for the machine mode of one or more operands. For example, there may be "sign-extend halfword" and "sign-extend byte" instructions whose patterns are

```
(set (match_operand:SI 0 ...)
     (extend:SI (match_operand:HI 1 ...)))

(set (match_operand:SI 0 ...)
     (extend:SI (match_operand:QI 1 ...)))
```

Constant integers do not specify a machine mode, so an instruction to extend a constant value could match either pattern. The pattern it actually will match is the one that appears first in the file. For correct results, this must be the one for the widest possible mode (HImode, here). If the pattern matches the QImode instruction, the results will be incorrect if the constant value does not actually fit that mode.

Such instructions to extend constants are rarely generated because they are optimized away, but they do occasionally happen in nonoptimized compilations.

If a constraint in a pattern allows a constant, the reload pass may replace a register with a constant permitted by the constraint in some cases. Similarly for memory references. Because of this substitution, you should not provide separate patterns for increment and decrement instructions. Instead, they should be generated from the same pattern that supports register-register add insns by examining the operands and generating the appropriate machine instruction.

16.12 Defining Jump Instruction Patterns

GCC does not assume anything about how the machine realizes jumps. The machine description should define a single pattern, usually a define_expand, which expands to all the required insns.

Usually, this would be a comparison insn to set the condition code and a separate branch insn testing the condition code and branching or not according to its value. For many machines, however, separating compares and branches is limiting, which is why the more flexible approach with one **define_expand** is used in GCC. The machine description becomes clearer for architectures that have compare-and-branch instructions but no condition code. It also works better when different sets of comparison operators are supported by different kinds of conditional branches (e.g. integer vs. floating-point), or by conditional branches with respect to conditional stores.

Two separate insns are always used if the machine description represents a condition code register using the legacy RTL expression (cc0), and on most machines that use a separate condition code register (see Section 17.15 [Condition Code], page 521). For machines that use (cc0), in fact, the set and use of the condition code must be separate and adjacent[1], thus allowing flags in **cc_status** to be used (see Section 17.15 [Condition Code], page 521) and so that the comparison and branch insns could be located from each other by using the functions **prev_cc0_setter** and **next_cc0_user**.

Even in this case having a single entry point for conditional branches is advantageous, because it handles equally well the case where a single comparison instruction records the results of both signed and unsigned comparison of the given operands (with the branch insns coming in distinct signed and unsigned flavors) as in the x86 or SPARC, and the case where there are distinct signed and unsigned compare instructions and only one set of conditional branch instructions as in the PowerPC.

16.13 Defining Looping Instruction Patterns

Some machines have special jump instructions that can be utilized to make loops more efficient. A common example is the 68000 'dbra' instruction which performs a decrement of a register and a branch if the result was greater than zero. Other machines, in particular digital signal processors (DSPs), have special block repeat instructions to provide low-overhead loop support. For example, the TI TMS320C3x/C4x DSPs have a block repeat instruction that loads special registers to mark the top and end of a loop and to count the number of loop iterations. This avoids the need for fetching and executing a 'dbra'-like instruction and avoids pipeline stalls associated with the jump.

GCC has three special named patterns to support low overhead looping. They are 'decrement_and_branch_until_zero', 'doloop_begin', and 'doloop_end'. The first pattern, 'decrement_and_branch_until_zero', is not emitted during RTL generation but may be emitted during the instruction combination phase. This requires the assistance of the loop optimizer, using information collected during strength reduction, to reverse a loop to count down to zero. Some targets also require the loop optimizer to add a **REG_NONNEG** note to indicate that the iteration count is always positive. This is needed if the target performs a signed loop termination test. For example, the 68000 uses a pattern similar to the following for its **dbra** instruction:

---

[1] **note** insns can separate them, though.

```
(define_insn "decrement_and_branch_until_zero"
  [(set (pc)
        (if_then_else
          (ge (plus:SI (match_operand:SI 0 "general_operand" "+d*am")
                       (const_int -1))
              (const_int 0))
          (label_ref (match_operand 1 "" ""))
          (pc)))
   (set (match_dup 0)
        (plus:SI (match_dup 0)
                 (const_int -1)))]
  "find_reg_note (insn, REG_NONNEG, 0)"
  "...")
```

Note that since the insn is both a jump insn and has an output, it must deal with its own reloads, hence the 'm' constraints. Also note that since this insn is generated by the instruction combination phase combining two sequential insns together into an implicit parallel insn, the iteration counter needs to be biased by the same amount as the decrement operation, in this case −1. Note that the following similar pattern will not be matched by the combiner.

```
(define_insn "decrement_and_branch_until_zero"
  [(set (pc)
        (if_then_else
          (ge (match_operand:SI 0 "general_operand" "+d*am")
              (const_int 1))
          (label_ref (match_operand 1 "" ""))
          (pc)))
   (set (match_dup 0)
        (plus:SI (match_dup 0)
                 (const_int -1)))]
  "find_reg_note (insn, REG_NONNEG, 0)"
  "...")
```

The other two special looping patterns, 'doloop_begin' and 'doloop_end', are emitted by the loop optimizer for certain well-behaved loops with a finite number of loop iterations using information collected during strength reduction.

The 'doloop_end' pattern describes the actual looping instruction (or the implicit looping operation) and the 'doloop_begin' pattern is an optional companion pattern that can be used for initialization needed for some low-overhead looping instructions.

Note that some machines require the actual looping instruction to be emitted at the top of the loop (e.g., the TMS320C3x/C4x DSPs). Emitting the true RTL for a looping instruction at the top of the loop can cause problems with flow analysis. So instead, a dummy doloop insn is emitted at the end of the loop. The machine dependent reorg pass checks for the presence of this doloop insn and then searches back to the top of the loop, where it inserts the true looping insn (provided there are no instructions in the loop which would cause problems). Any additional labels can be emitted at this point. In addition, if the desired special iteration counter register was not allocated, this machine dependent reorg pass could emit a traditional compare and jump instruction pair.

The essential difference between the 'decrement_and_branch_until_zero' and the 'doloop_end' patterns is that the loop optimizer allocates an additional pseudo register for the latter as an iteration counter. This pseudo register cannot be used within the loop (i.e., general induction variables cannot be derived from it), however, in many cases the loop induction variable may become redundant and removed by the flow pass.

16.14 Canonicalization of Instructions

There are often cases where multiple RTL expressions could represent an operation performed by a single machine instruction. This situation is most commonly encountered with logical, branch, and multiply-accumulate instructions. In such cases, the compiler attempts to convert these multiple RTL expressions into a single canonical form to reduce the number of insn patterns required.

In addition to algebraic simplifications, following canonicalizations are performed:

- For commutative and comparison operators, a constant is always made the second operand. If a machine only supports a constant as the second operand, only patterns that match a constant in the second operand need be supplied.

- For associative operators, a sequence of operators will always chain to the left; for instance, only the left operand of an integer `plus` can itself be a `plus`. `and`, `ior`, `xor`, `plus`, `mult`, `smin`, `smax`, `umin`, and `umax` are associative when applied to integers, and sometimes to floating-point.

- For these operators, if only one operand is a `neg`, `not`, `mult`, `plus`, or `minus` expression, it will be the first operand.

- In combinations of `neg`, `mult`, `plus`, and `minus`, the `neg` operations (if any) will be moved inside the operations as far as possible. For instance, `(neg (mult A B))` is canonicalized as `(mult (neg A) B)`, but `(plus (mult (neg B) C) A)` is canonicalized as `(minus A (mult B C))`.

- For the `compare` operator, a constant is always the second operand if the first argument is a condition code register or `(cc0)`.

- An operand of `neg`, `not`, `mult`, `plus`, or `minus` is made the first operand under the same conditions as above.

- `(ltu (plus a b) b)` is converted to `(ltu (plus a b) a)`. Likewise with `geu` instead of `ltu`.

- `(minus x (const_int n))` is converted to `(plus x (const_int -n))`.

- Within address computations (i.e., inside `mem`), a left shift is converted into the appropriate multiplication by a power of two.

- De Morgan's Law is used to move bitwise negation inside a bitwise logical-and or logical-or operation. If this results in only one operand being a `not` expression, it will be the first one.

  A machine that has an instruction that performs a bitwise logical-and of one operand with the bitwise negation of the other should specify the pattern for that instruction as

  ```
  (define_insn ""
    [(set (match_operand:m 0 ...)
          (and:m (not:m (match_operand:m 1 ...))
                 (match_operand:m 2 ...)))]
    "..."
    "...")
  ```

  Similarly, a pattern for a "NAND" instruction should be written

  ```
  (define_insn ""
    [(set (match_operand:m 0 ...)
          (ior:m (not:m (match_operand:m 1 ...))
  ```

```
                (not:m (match_operand:m 2 ...)))))]
   "..."
   "...")
```

In both cases, it is not necessary to include patterns for the many logically equivalent RTL expressions.

- The only possible RTL expressions involving both bitwise exclusive-or and bitwise negation are (xor:*m x y*) and (not:*m* (xor:*m x y*)).

- The sum of three items, one of which is a constant, will only appear in the form

   (plus:*m* (plus:*m x y*) *constant*)

- Equality comparisons of a group of bits (usually a single bit) with zero will be written using **zero_extract** rather than the equivalent **and** or **sign_extract** operations.

- (sign_extend:*m1* (mult:*m2* (sign_extend:*m2 x*) (sign_extend:*m2 y*)))   is converted to (mult:*m1* (sign_extend:*m1 x*) (sign_extend:*m1 y*)), and likewise for **zero_extend**.

- (sign_extend:*m1* (mult:*m2* (ashiftrt:*m2 x s*) (sign_extend:*m2 y*))) is converted to (mult:*m1* (sign_extend:*m1* (ashiftrt:*m2 x s*)) (sign_extend:*m1 y*)), and likewise for patterns using **zero_extend** and **lshiftrt**. If the second operand of **mult** is also a shift, then that is extended also. This transformation is only applied when it can be proven that the original operation had sufficient precision to prevent overflow.

Further canonicalization rules are defined in the function **commutative_operand_precedence** in 'gcc/rtlanal.c'.

16.15 Defining RTL Sequences for Code Generation

On some target machines, some standard pattern names for RTL generation cannot be handled with single insn, but a sequence of RTL insns can represent them. For these target machines, you can write a **define_expand** to specify how to generate the sequence of RTL.

A **define_expand** is an RTL expression that looks almost like a **define_insn**; but, unlike the latter, a **define_expand** is used only for RTL generation and it can produce more than one RTL insn.

A **define_expand** RTX has four operands:

- The name. Each **define_expand** must have a name, since the only use for it is to refer to it by name.

- The RTL template. This is a vector of RTL expressions representing a sequence of separate instructions. Unlike **define_insn**, there is no implicit surrounding **PARALLEL**.

- The condition, a string containing a C expression. This expression is used to express how the availability of this pattern depends on subclasses of target machine, selected by command-line options when GCC is run. This is just like the condition of a **define_insn** that has a standard name. Therefore, the condition (if present) may not depend on the data in the insn being matched, but only the target-machine-type flags. The compiler needs to test these conditions during initialization in order to learn exactly which named instructions are available in a particular run.

- The preparation statements, a string containing zero or more C statements which are to be executed before RTL code is generated from the RTL template.

Usually these statements prepare temporary registers for use as internal operands in the RTL template, but they can also generate RTL insns directly by calling routines such as `emit_insn`, etc. Any such insns precede the ones that come from the RTL template.

- Optionally, a vector containing the values of attributes. See Section 16.19 [Insn Attributes], page 405.

Every RTL insn emitted by a `define_expand` must match some `define_insn` in the machine description. Otherwise, the compiler will crash when trying to generate code for the insn or trying to optimize it.

The RTL template, in addition to controlling generation of RTL insns, also describes the operands that need to be specified when this pattern is used. In particular, it gives a predicate for each operand.

A true operand, which needs to be specified in order to generate RTL from the pattern, should be described with a `match_operand` in its first occurrence in the RTL template. This enters information on the operand's predicate into the tables that record such things. GCC uses the information to preload the operand into a register if that is required for valid RTL code. If the operand is referred to more than once, subsequent references should use `match_dup`.

The RTL template may also refer to internal "operands" which are temporary registers or labels used only within the sequence made by the `define_expand`. Internal operands are substituted into the RTL template with `match_dup`, never with `match_operand`. The values of the internal operands are not passed in as arguments by the compiler when it requests use of this pattern. Instead, they are computed within the pattern, in the preparation statements. These statements compute the values and store them into the appropriate elements of `operands` so that `match_dup` can find them.

There are two special macros defined for use in the preparation statements: `DONE` and `FAIL`. Use them with a following semicolon, as a statement.

`DONE`   Use the `DONE` macro to end RTL generation for the pattern. The only RTL insns resulting from the pattern on this occasion will be those already emitted by explicit calls to `emit_insn` within the preparation statements; the RTL template will not be generated.

`FAIL`   Make the pattern fail on this occasion. When a pattern fails, it means that the pattern was not truly available. The calling routines in the compiler will try other strategies for code generation using other patterns.

              Failure is currently supported only for binary (addition, multiplication, shifting, etc.) and bit-field (`extv`, `extzv`, and `insv`) operations.

If the preparation falls through (invokes neither `DONE` nor `FAIL`), then the `define_expand` acts like a `define_insn` in that the RTL template is used to generate the insn.

The RTL template is not used for matching, only for generating the initial insn list. If the preparation statement always invokes `DONE` or `FAIL`, the RTL template may be reduced to a simple list of operands, such as this example:

```
(define_expand "addsi3"
  [(match_operand:SI 0 "register_operand" "")
   (match_operand:SI 1 "register_operand" "")
   (match_operand:SI 2 "register_operand" "")]
```

```
     ""
      "
   {
      handle_add (operands[0], operands[1], operands[2]);
      DONE;
   }")
```

Here is an example, the definition of left-shift for the SPUR chip:

```
(define_expand "ashlsi3"
   [(set (match_operand:SI 0 "register_operand" "")
         (ashift:SI
           (match_operand:SI 1 "register_operand" "")
           (match_operand:SI 2 "nonmemory_operand" "")))]
     ""
      "
   {
      if (GET_CODE (operands[2]) != CONST_INT
          || (unsigned) INTVAL (operands[2]) > 3)
        FAIL;
   }")
```

This example uses `define_expand` so that it can generate an RTL insn for shifting when the shift-count is in the supported range of 0 to 3 but fail in other cases where machine insns aren't available. When it fails, the compiler tries another strategy using different patterns (such as, a library call).

If the compiler were able to handle nontrivial condition-strings in patterns with names, then it would be possible to use a `define_insn` in that case. Here is another case (zero-extension on the 68000) which makes more use of the power of `define_expand`:

```
(define_expand "zero_extendhisi2"
   [(set (match_operand:SI 0 "general_operand" "")
         (const_int 0))
    (set (strict_low_part
           (subreg:HI
             (match_dup 0)
             0))
         (match_operand:HI 1 "general_operand" ""))]
     ""
   "operands[1] = make_safe_from (operands[1], operands[0]);")
```

Here two RTL insns are generated, one to clear the entire output operand and the other to copy the input operand into its low half. This sequence is incorrect if the input operand refers to [the old value of] the output operand, so the preparation statement makes sure this isn't so. The function `make_safe_from` copies the `operands[1]` into a temporary register if it refers to `operands[0]`. It does this by emitting another RTL insn.

Finally, a third example shows the use of an internal operand. Zero-extension on the SPUR chip is done by `and`-ing the result against a halfword mask. But this mask cannot be represented by a `const_int` because the constant value is too large to be legitimate on this machine. So it must be copied into a register with `force_reg` and then the register used in the `and`.

```
(define_expand "zero_extendhisi2"
   [(set (match_operand:SI 0 "register_operand" "")
         (and:SI (subreg:SI
                    (match_operand:HI 1 "register_operand" "")
                    0)
```

```
                        (match_dup 2)))]
   ""
   "operands[2]
       = force_reg (SImode, GEN_INT (65535)); ")
```

Note: If the `define_expand` is used to serve a standard binary or unary arithmetic operation or a bit-field operation, then the last insn it generates must not be a `code_label`, `barrier` or `note`. It must be an `insn`, `jump_insn` or `call_insn`. If you don't need a real insn at the end, emit an insn to copy the result of the operation into itself. Such an insn will generate no code, but it can avoid problems in the compiler.

16.16 Defining How to Split Instructions

There are two cases where you should specify how to split a pattern into multiple insns. On machines that have instructions requiring delay slots (see Section 16.19.8 [Delay Slots], page 413) or that have instructions whose output is not available for multiple cycles (see Section 16.19.9 [Processor pipeline description], page 414), the compiler phases that optimize these cases need to be able to move insns into one-instruction delay slots. However, some insns may generate more than one machine instruction. These insns cannot be placed into a delay slot.

Often you can rewrite the single insn as a list of individual insns, each corresponding to one machine instruction. The disadvantage of doing so is that it will cause the compilation to be slower and require more space. If the resulting insns are too complex, it may also suppress some optimizations. The compiler splits the insn if there is a reason to believe that it might improve instruction or delay slot scheduling.

The insn combiner phase also splits putative insns. If three insns are merged into one insn with a complex expression that cannot be matched by some `define_insn` pattern, the combiner phase attempts to split the complex pattern into two insns that are recognized. Usually it can break the complex pattern into two patterns by splitting out some subexpression. However, in some other cases, such as performing an addition of a large constant in two insns on a RISC machine, the way to split the addition into two insns is machine-dependent.

The `define_split` definition tells the compiler how to split a complex insn into several simpler insns. It looks like this:

```
(define_split
  [insn-pattern]
  "condition"
  [new-insn-pattern-1
   new-insn-pattern-2
   ...]
  "preparation-statements")
```

insn-pattern is a pattern that needs to be split and *condition* is the final condition to be tested, as in a `define_insn`. When an insn matching *insn-pattern* and satisfying *condition* is found, it is replaced in the insn list with the insns given by *new-insn-pattern-1*, *new-insn-pattern-2*, etc.

The *preparation-statements* are similar to those statements that are specified for `define_expand` (see Section 16.15 [Expander Definitions], page 394) and are executed before the new RTL is generated to prepare for the generated code or emit some insns whose pattern is not fixed. Unlike those in `define_expand`, however, these statements must not generate

any new pseudo-registers. Once reload has completed, they also must not allocate any space
in the stack frame.

Patterns are matched against *insn-pattern* in two different circumstances. If an insn
needs to be split for delay slot scheduling or insn scheduling, the insn is already known
to be valid, which means that it must have been matched by some `define_insn` and, if
`reload_completed` is nonzero, is known to satisfy the constraints of that `define_insn`. In
that case, the new insn patterns must also be insns that are matched by some `define_insn`
and, if `reload_completed` is nonzero, must also satisfy the constraints of those definitions.

As an example of this usage of `define_split`, consider the following example from
'a29k.md', which splits a `sign_extend` from HImode to SImode into a pair of shift insns:

```
(define_split
  [(set (match_operand:SI 0 "gen_reg_operand" "")
        (sign_extend:SI (match_operand:HI 1 "gen_reg_operand" "")))]
  ""
  [(set (match_dup 0)
        (ashift:SI (match_dup 1)
                   (const_int 16)))
   (set (match_dup 0)
        (ashiftrt:SI (match_dup 0)
                     (const_int 16)))]
  "
{ operands[1] = gen_lowpart (SImode, operands[1]); }")
```

When the combiner phase tries to split an insn pattern, it is always the case that the
pattern is *not* matched by any `define_insn`. The combiner pass first tries to split a single
`set` expression and then the same `set` expression inside a `parallel`, but followed by a
`clobber` of a pseudo-reg to use as a scratch register. In these cases, the combiner expects
exactly two new insn patterns to be generated. It will verify that these patterns match
some `define_insn` definitions, so you need not do this test in the `define_split` (of course,
there is no point in writing a `define_split` that will never produce insns that match).

Here is an example of this use of `define_split`, taken from 'rs6000.md':

```
(define_split
  [(set (match_operand:SI 0 "gen_reg_operand" "")
        (plus:SI (match_operand:SI 1 "gen_reg_operand" "")
                 (match_operand:SI 2 "non_add_cint_operand" "")))]
  ""
  [(set (match_dup 0) (plus:SI (match_dup 1) (match_dup 3)))
   (set (match_dup 0) (plus:SI (match_dup 0) (match_dup 4)))]
  "
{
  int low = INTVAL (operands[2]) & 0xffff;
  int high = (unsigned) INTVAL (operands[2]) >> 16;

  if (low & 0x8000)
    high++, low |= 0xffff0000;

  operands[3] = GEN_INT (high << 16);
  operands[4] = GEN_INT (low);
}")
```

Here the predicate `non_add_cint_operand` matches any `const_int` that is *not* a valid
operand of a single add insn. The add with the smaller displacement is written so that it
can be substituted into the address of a subsequent operation.

An example that uses a scratch register, from the same file, generates an equality comparison of a register and a large constant:

```
(define_split
  [(set (match_operand:CC 0 "cc_reg_operand" "")
        (compare:CC (match_operand:SI 1 "gen_reg_operand" "")
                    (match_operand:SI 2 "non_short_cint_operand" "")))
   (clobber (match_operand:SI 3 "gen_reg_operand" ""))]
  "find_single_use (operands[0], insn, 0)
   && (GET_CODE (*find_single_use (operands[0], insn, 0)) == EQ
       || GET_CODE (*find_single_use (operands[0], insn, 0)) == NE)"
  [(set (match_dup 3) (xor:SI (match_dup 1) (match_dup 4)))
   (set (match_dup 0) (compare:CC (match_dup 3) (match_dup 5)))]
  "
{
  /* Get the constant we are comparing against, C, and see what it
     looks like sign-extended to 16 bits.  Then see what constant
     could be XOR'ed with C to get the sign-extended value.  */

  int c = INTVAL (operands[2]);
  int sextc = (c << 16) >> 16;
  int xorv = c ^ sextc;

  operands[4] = GEN_INT (xorv);
  operands[5] = GEN_INT (sextc);
}")
```

To avoid confusion, don't write a single define_split that accepts some insns that match some define_insn as well as some insns that don't. Instead, write two separate define_split definitions, one for the insns that are valid and one for the insns that are not valid.

The splitter is allowed to split jump instructions into sequence of jumps or create new jumps in while splitting non-jump instructions. As the central flowgraph and branch prediction information needs to be updated, several restriction apply.

Splitting of jump instruction into sequence that over by another jump instruction is always valid, as compiler expect identical behavior of new jump. When new sequence contains multiple jump instructions or new labels, more assistance is needed. Splitter is required to create only unconditional jumps, or simple conditional jump instructions. Additionally it must attach a REG_BR_PROB note to each conditional jump. A global variable split_branch_probability holds the probability of the original branch in case it was a simple conditional jump, −1 otherwise. To simplify recomputing of edge frequencies, the new sequence is required to have only forward jumps to the newly created labels.

For the common case where the pattern of a define_split exactly matches the pattern of a define_insn, use define_insn_and_split. It looks like this:

```
(define_insn_and_split
  [insn-pattern]
  "condition"
  "output-template"
  "split-condition"
  [new-insn-pattern-1
   new-insn-pattern-2
   ...]
  "preparation-statements"
  [insn-attributes])
```

insn-pattern, *condition*, *output-template*, and *insn-attributes* are used as in `define_insn`. The *new-insn-pattern* vector and the *preparation-statements* are used as in a `define_split`. The *split-condition* is also used as in `define_split`, with the additional behavior that if the condition starts with '`&&`', the condition used for the split will be the constructed as a logical "and" of the split condition with the insn condition. For example, from i386.md:

```
(define_insn_and_split "zero_extendhisi2_and"
  [(set (match_operand:SI 0 "register_operand" "=r")
     (zero_extend:SI (match_operand:HI 1 "register_operand" "0")))
   (clobber (reg:CC 17))]
  "TARGET_ZERO_EXTEND_WITH_AND && !optimize_size"
  "#"
  "&& reload_completed"
  [(parallel [(set (match_dup 0)
                   (and:SI (match_dup 0) (const_int 65535)))
              (clobber (reg:CC 17))])]
  ""
  [(set_attr "type" "alu1")])
```

In this case, the actual split condition will be '`TARGET_ZERO_EXTEND_WITH_AND && !optimize_size && reload_completed`'.

The `define_insn_and_split` construction provides exactly the same functionality as two separate `define_insn` and `define_split` patterns. It exists for compactness, and as a maintenance tool to prevent having to ensure the two patterns' templates match.

16.17 Including Patterns in Machine Descriptions.

The `include` pattern tells the compiler tools where to look for patterns that are in files other than in the file '`.md`'. This is used only at build time and there is no preprocessing allowed.

It looks like:

```
(include
   pathname)
```

For example:

```
(include "filestuff")
```

Where *pathname* is a string that specifies the location of the file, specifies the include file to be in '`gcc/config/target/filestuff`'. The directory '`gcc/config/target`' is regarded as the default directory.

Machine descriptions may be split up into smaller more manageable subsections and placed into subdirectories.

By specifying:

```
(include "BOGUS/filestuff")
```

the include file is specified to be in '`gcc/config/target/BOGUS/filestuff`'.

Specifying an absolute path for the include file such as;

```
(include "/u2/BOGUS/filestuff")
```

is permitted but is not encouraged.

16.17.1 RTL Generation Tool Options for Directory Search

The '-I*dir*' option specifies directories to search for machine descriptions. For example:

```
genrecog -I/p1/abc/proc1 -I/p2/abcd/pro2 target.md
```

Add the directory *dir* to the head of the list of directories to be searched for header files. This can be used to override a system machine definition file, substituting your own version, since these directories are searched before the default machine description file directories. If you use more than one '-I' option, the directories are scanned in left-to-right order; the standard default directory come after.

16.18 Machine-Specific Peephole Optimizers

In addition to instruction patterns the 'md' file may contain definitions of machine-specific peephole optimizations.

The combiner does not notice certain peephole optimizations when the data flow in the program does not suggest that it should try them. For example, sometimes two consecutive insns related in purpose can be combined even though the second one does not appear to use a register computed in the first one. A machine-specific peephole optimizer can detect such opportunities.

There are two forms of peephole definitions that may be used. The original define_peephole is run at assembly output time to match insns and substitute assembly text. Use of define_peephole is deprecated.

A newer define_peephole2 matches insns and substitutes new insns. The peephole2 pass is run after register allocation but before scheduling, which may result in much better code for targets that do scheduling.

16.18.1 RTL to Text Peephole Optimizers

A definition looks like this:

```
(define_peephole
  [insn-pattern-1
   insn-pattern-2
   ...]
  "condition"
  "template"
  "optional-insn-attributes")
```

The last string operand may be omitted if you are not using any machine-specific information in this machine description. If present, it must obey the same rules as in a define_insn.

In this skeleton, *insn-pattern-1* and so on are patterns to match consecutive insns. The optimization applies to a sequence of insns when *insn-pattern-1* matches the first one, *insn-pattern-2* matches the next, and so on.

Each of the insns matched by a peephole must also match a define_insn. Peepholes are checked only at the last stage just before code generation, and only optionally. Therefore, any insn which would match a peephole but no `define_insn` will cause a crash in code generation in an unoptimized compilation, or at various optimization stages.

The operands of the insns are matched with `match_operands`, `match_operator`, and `match_dup`, as usual. What is not usual is that the operand numbers apply to all the insn patterns in the definition. So, you can check for identical operands in two insns by using `match_operand` in one insn and `match_dup` in the other.

The operand constraints used in `match_operand` patterns do not have any direct effect on the applicability of the peephole, but they will be validated afterward, so make sure your constraints are general enough to apply whenever the peephole matches. If the peephole matches but the constraints are not satisfied, the compiler will crash.

It is safe to omit constraints in all the operands of the peephole; or you can write constraints which serve as a double-check on the criteria previously tested.

Once a sequence of insns matches the patterns, the *condition* is checked. This is a C expression which makes the final decision whether to perform the optimization (we do so if the expression is nonzero). If *condition* is omitted (in other words, the string is empty) then the optimization is applied to every sequence of insns that matches the patterns.

The defined peephole optimizations are applied after register allocation is complete. Therefore, the peephole definition can check which operands have ended up in which kinds of registers, just by looking at the operands.

The way to refer to the operands in *condition* is to write `operands[i]` for operand number *i* (as matched by (`match_operand i ...`)). Use the variable `insn` to refer to the last of the insns being matched; use `prev_active_insn` to find the preceding insns.

When optimizing computations with intermediate results, you can use *condition* to match only when the intermediate results are not used elsewhere. Use the C expression `dead_or_set_p (insn, op)`, where *insn* is the insn in which you expect the value to be used for the last time (from the value of `insn`, together with use of `prev_nonnote_insn`), and *op* is the intermediate value (from `operands[i]`).

Applying the optimization means replacing the sequence of insns with one new insn. The *template* controls ultimate output of assembler code for this combined insn. It works exactly like the template of a `define_insn`. Operand numbers in this template are the same ones used in matching the original sequence of insns.

The result of a defined peephole optimizer does not need to match any of the insn patterns in the machine description; it does not even have an opportunity to match them. The peephole optimizer definition itself serves as the insn pattern to control how the insn is output.

Defined peephole optimizers are run as assembler code is being output, so the insns they produce are never combined or rearranged in any way.

Here is an example, taken from the 68000 machine description:

```
(define_peephole
  [(set (reg:SI 15) (plus:SI (reg:SI 15) (const_int 4)))
   (set (match_operand:DF 0 "register_operand" "=f")
        (match_operand:DF 1 "register_operand" "ad"))]
  "FP_REG_P (operands[0]) && ! FP_REG_P (operands[1])"
{
  rtx xoperands[2];
  xoperands[1] = gen_rtx_REG (SImode, REGNO (operands[1]) + 1);
```

```
#ifdef MOTOROLA
  output_asm_insn ("move.l %1,(sp)", xoperands);
  output_asm_insn ("move.l %1,-(sp)", operands);
  return "fmove.d (sp)+,%0";
#else
  output_asm_insn ("movel %1,sp@", xoperands);
  output_asm_insn ("movel %1,sp@-", operands);
  return "fmoved sp@+,%0";
#endif
})
```

The effect of this optimization is to change

```
jbsr _foobar
addql #4,sp
movel d1,sp@-
movel d0,sp@-
fmoved sp@+,fp0
```

into

```
jbsr _foobar
movel d1,sp@
movel d0,sp@-
fmoved sp@+,fp0
```

insn-pattern-1 and so on look *almost* like the second operand of `define_insn`. There is one important difference: the second operand of `define_insn` consists of one or more RTX's enclosed in square brackets. Usually, there is only one: then the same action can be written as an element of a `define_peephole`. But when there are multiple actions in a `define_insn`, they are implicitly enclosed in a `parallel`. Then you must explicitly write the `parallel`, and the square brackets within it, in the `define_peephole`. Thus, if an insn pattern looks like this,

```
(define_insn "divmodsi4"
  [(set (match_operand:SI 0 "general_operand" "=d")
        (div:SI (match_operand:SI 1 "general_operand" "0")
                (match_operand:SI 2 "general_operand" "dmsK")))
   (set (match_operand:SI 3 "general_operand" "=d")
        (mod:SI (match_dup 1) (match_dup 2)))]
  "TARGET_68020"
  "divsl%.l %2,%3:%0")
```

then the way to mention this insn in a peephole is as follows:

```
(define_peephole
  [...
   (parallel
    [(set (match_operand:SI 0 "general_operand" "=d")
          (div:SI (match_operand:SI 1 "general_operand" "0")
                  (match_operand:SI 2 "general_operand" "dmsK")))
     (set (match_operand:SI 3 "general_operand" "=d")
          (mod:SI (match_dup 1) (match_dup 2)))])
   ...]
  ...)
```

16.18.2 RTL to RTL Peephole Optimizers

The `define_peephole2` definition tells the compiler how to substitute one sequence of instructions for another sequence, what additional scratch registers may be needed and what their lifetimes must be.

```
(define_peephole2
  [insn-pattern-1
   insn-pattern-2
   ...]
  "condition"
  [new-insn-pattern-1
   new-insn-pattern-2
   ...]
  "preparation-statements")
```

The definition is almost identical to `define_split` (see Section 16.16 [Insn Splitting], page 397) except that the pattern to match is not a single instruction, but a sequence of instructions.

It is possible to request additional scratch registers for use in the output template. If appropriate registers are not free, the pattern will simply not match.

Scratch registers are requested with a `match_scratch` pattern at the top level of the input pattern. The allocated register (initially) will be dead at the point requested within the original sequence. If the scratch is used at more than a single point, a `match_dup` pattern at the top level of the input pattern marks the last position in the input sequence at which the register must be available.

Here is an example from the IA-32 machine description:

```
(define_peephole2
  [(match_scratch:SI 2 "r")
   (parallel [(set (match_operand:SI 0 "register_operand" "")
                   (match_operator:SI 3 "arith_or_logical_operator"
                     [(match_dup 0)
                      (match_operand:SI 1 "memory_operand" "")]))
              (clobber (reg:CC 17))])]
  "! optimize_size && ! TARGET_READ_MODIFY"
  [(set (match_dup 2) (match_dup 1))
   (parallel [(set (match_dup 0)
                   (match_op_dup 3 [(match_dup 0) (match_dup 2)]))
              (clobber (reg:CC 17))])]
  "")
```

This pattern tries to split a load from its use in the hopes that we'll be able to schedule around the memory load latency. It allocates a single `SImode` register of class `GENERAL_REGS` (`"r"`) that needs to be live only at the point just before the arithmetic.

A real example requiring extended scratch lifetimes is harder to come by, so here's a silly made-up example:

```
(define_peephole2
  [(match_scratch:SI 4 "r")
   (set (match_operand:SI 0 "" "") (match_operand:SI 1 "" ""))
   (set (match_operand:SI 2 "" "") (match_dup 1))
   (match_dup 4)
   (set (match_operand:SI 3 "" "") (match_dup 1))]
  "/* determine 1 does not overlap 0 and 2 */"
  [(set (match_dup 4) (match_dup 1))
   (set (match_dup 0) (match_dup 4))
   (set (match_dup 2) (match_dup 4))
   (set (match_dup 3) (match_dup 4))]
  "")
```

If we had not added the (match_dup 4) in the middle of the input sequence, it might have been the case that the register we chose at the beginning of the sequence is killed by the first or second set.

16.19 Instruction Attributes

In addition to describing the instruction supported by the target machine, the 'md' file also defines a group of *attributes* and a set of values for each. Every generated insn is assigned a value for each attribute. One possible attribute would be the effect that the insn has on the machine's condition code. This attribute can then be used by NOTICE_UPDATE_CC to track the condition codes.

16.19.1 Defining Attributes and their Values

The define_attr expression is used to define each attribute required by the target machine. It looks like:

```
(define_attr name list-of-values default)
```

name is a string specifying the name of the attribute being defined. Some attributes are used in a special way by the rest of the compiler. The enabled attribute can be used to conditionally enable or disable insn alternatives (see Section 16.8.6 [Disable Insn Alternatives], page 351). The predicable attribute, together with a suitable define_cond_exec (see Section 16.20 [Conditional Execution], page 420), can be used to automatically generate conditional variants of instruction patterns. The mnemonic attribute can be used to check for the instruction mnemonic (see Section 16.19.7 [Mnemonic Attribute], page 413). The compiler internally uses the names ce_enabled and nonce_enabled, so they should not be used elsewhere as alternative names.

list-of-values is either a string that specifies a comma-separated list of values that can be assigned to the attribute, or a null string to indicate that the attribute takes numeric values.

default is an attribute expression that gives the value of this attribute for insns that match patterns whose definition does not include an explicit value for this attribute. See Section 16.19.4 [Attr Example], page 410, for more information on the handling of defaults. See Section 16.19.6 [Constant Attributes], page 412, for information on attributes that do not depend on any particular insn.

For each defined attribute, a number of definitions are written to the 'insn-attr.h' file. For cases where an explicit set of values is specified for an attribute, the following are defined:

- A '#define' is written for the symbol 'HAVE_ATTR_*name*'.

- An enumerated class is defined for 'attr_*name*' with elements of the form '*upper-name_upper-value*' where the attribute name and value are first converted to upper-case.

- A function 'get_attr_*name*' is defined that is passed an insn and returns the attribute value for that insn.

For example, if the following is present in the 'md' file:

```
(define_attr "type" "branch,fp,load,store,arith" ...)
```

the following lines will be written to the file 'insn-attr.h'.

```
#define HAVE_ATTR_type 1
enum attr_type {TYPE_BRANCH, TYPE_FP, TYPE_LOAD,
                TYPE_STORE, TYPE_ARITH};
extern enum attr_type get_attr_type ();
```

If the attribute takes numeric values, no **enum** type will be defined and the function to obtain the attribute's value will return **int**.

There are attributes which are tied to a specific meaning. These attributes are not free to use for other purposes:

length   The **length** attribute is used to calculate the length of emitted code chunks. This is especially important when verifying branch distances. See Section 16.19.5 [Insn Lengths], page 411.

enabled   The **enabled** attribute can be defined to prevent certain alternatives of an insn definition from being used during code generation. See Section 16.8.6 [Disable Insn Alternatives], page 351.

mnemonic   The **mnemonic** attribute can be defined to implement instruction specific checks in e.g. the pipeline description. See Section 16.19.7 [Mnemonic Attribute], page 413.

For each of these special attributes, the corresponding 'HAVE_ATTR_*name*' '#define' is also written when the attribute is not defined; in that case, it is defined as '0'.

Another way of defining an attribute is to use:

```
(define_enum_attr "attr" "enum" default)
```

This works in just the same way as **define_attr**, except that the list of values is taken from a separate enumeration called *enum* (see [define_enum], page 426). This form allows you to use the same list of values for several attributes without having to repeat the list each time. For example:

```
(define_enum "processor" [
  model_a
  model_b
  ...
])
(define_enum_attr "arch" "processor"
  (const (symbol_ref "target_arch")))
(define_enum_attr "tune" "processor"
  (const (symbol_ref "target_tune")))
```

defines the same attributes as:

```
(define_attr "arch" "model_a,model_b,..."
  (const (symbol_ref "target_arch")))
(define_attr "tune" "model_a,model_b,..."
  (const (symbol_ref "target_tune")))
```

but without duplicating the processor list. The second example defines two separate C enums (**attr_arch** and **attr_tune**) whereas the first defines a single C enum (**processor**).

16.19.2 Attribute Expressions

RTL expressions used to define attributes use the codes described above plus a few specific to attribute definitions, to be discussed below. Attribute value expressions must have one of the following forms:

`(const_int i)`

> The integer *i* specifies the value of a numeric attribute. *i* must be non-negative.
>
> The value of a numeric attribute can be specified either with a `const_int`, or as an integer represented as a string in `const_string`, `eq_attr` (see below), `attr`, `symbol_ref`, simple arithmetic expressions, and `set_attr` overrides on specific instructions (see Section 16.19.3 [Tagging Insns], page 409).

`(const_string value)`

> The string *value* specifies a constant attribute value. If *value* is specified as '"*"', it means that the default value of the attribute is to be used for the insn containing this expression. '"*"' obviously cannot be used in the *default* expression of a `define_attr`.
>
> If the attribute whose value is being specified is numeric, *value* must be a string containing a non-negative integer (normally `const_int` would be used in this case). Otherwise, it must contain one of the valid values for the attribute.

`(if_then_else test true-value false-value)`

> *test* specifies an attribute test, whose format is defined below. The value of this expression is *true-value* if *test* is true, otherwise it is *false-value*.

`(cond [test1 value1 ...] default)`

> The first operand of this expression is a vector containing an even number of expressions and consisting of pairs of *test* and *value* expressions. The value of the `cond` expression is that of the *value* corresponding to the first true *test* expression. If none of the *test* expressions are true, the value of the `cond` expression is that of the *default* expression.

test expressions can have one of the following forms:

`(const_int i)`

> This test is true if *i* is nonzero and false otherwise.

`(not test)`
`(ior test1 test2)`
`(and test1 test2)`

> These tests are true if the indicated logical function is true.

`(match_operand:m n pred constraints)`

> This test is true if operand *n* of the insn whose attribute value is being determined has mode *m* (this part of the test is ignored if *m* is `VOIDmode`) and the function specified by the string *pred* returns a nonzero value when passed operand *n* and mode *m* (this part of the test is ignored if *pred* is the null string).
>
> The *constraints* operand is ignored and should be the null string.

`(match_test c-expr)`

> The test is true if C expression *c-expr* is true. In non-constant attributes, *c-expr* has access to the following variables:
>
> *insn*   The rtl instruction under test.
>
> *which_alternative*
> > The `define_insn` alternative that *insn* matches. See Section 16.6 [Output Statement], page 310.

operands   An array of *insn*'s rtl operands.

c-expr behaves like the condition in a C `if` statement, so there is no need to explicitly convert the expression into a boolean 0 or 1 value. For example, the following two tests are equivalent:

```
(match_test "x & 2")
(match_test "(x & 2) != 0")
```

`(le arith1 arith2)`
`(leu arith1 arith2)`
`(lt arith1 arith2)`
`(ltu arith1 arith2)`
`(gt arith1 arith2)`
`(gtu arith1 arith2)`
`(ge arith1 arith2)`
`(geu arith1 arith2)`
`(ne arith1 arith2)`
`(eq arith1 arith2)`

These tests are true if the indicated comparison of the two arithmetic expressions is true. Arithmetic expressions are formed with **plus**, **minus**, **mult**, **div**, **mod**, **abs**, **neg**, **and**, **ior**, **xor**, **not**, **ashift**, **lshiftrt**, and **ashiftrt** expressions.

const_int and **symbol_ref** are always valid terms (see Section 16.19.5 [Insn Lengths], page 411, for additional forms). **symbol_ref** is a string denoting a C expression that yields an **int** when evaluated by the '**get_attr_...**' routine. It should normally be a global variable.

`(eq_attr name value)`

name is a string specifying the name of an attribute.

value is a string that is either a valid value for attribute *name*, a comma-separated list of values, or '!' followed by a value or list. If *value* does not begin with a '!', this test is true if the value of the *name* attribute of the current insn is in the list specified by *value*. If *value* begins with a '!', this test is true if the attribute's value is *not* in the specified list.

For example,

```
(eq_attr "type" "load,store")
```

is equivalent to

```
(ior (eq_attr "type" "load") (eq_attr "type" "store"))
```

If *name* specifies an attribute of 'alternative', it refers to the value of the compiler variable **which_alternative** (see Section 16.6 [Output Statement], page 310) and the values must be small integers. For example,

```
(eq_attr "alternative" "2,3")
```

is equivalent to

```
(ior (eq (symbol_ref "which_alternative") (const_int 2))
     (eq (symbol_ref "which_alternative") (const_int 3)))
```

Note that, for most attributes, an **eq_attr** test is simplified in cases where the value of the attribute being tested is known for all insns matching a particular pattern. This is by far the most common case.

`(attr_flag` *name*`)`

> The value of an `attr_flag` expression is true if the flag specified by *name* is true for the `insn` currently being scheduled.
>
> *name* is a string specifying one of a fixed set of flags to test. Test the flags `forward` and `backward` to determine the direction of a conditional branch.
>
> This example describes a conditional branch delay slot which can be nullified for forward branches that are taken (annul-true) or for backward branches which are not taken (annul-false).
>
> ```
> (define_delay (eq_attr "type" "cbranch")
>   [(eq_attr "in_branch_delay" "true")
>    (and (eq_attr "in_branch_delay" "true")
>         (attr_flag "forward"))
>    (and (eq_attr "in_branch_delay" "true")
>         (attr_flag "backward"))])
> ```
>
> The `forward` and `backward` flags are false if the current `insn` being scheduled is not a conditional branch.
>
> `attr_flag` is only used during delay slot scheduling and has no meaning to other passes of the compiler.

`(attr` *name*`)`

> The value of another attribute is returned. This is most useful for numeric attributes, as `eq_attr` and `attr_flag` produce more efficient code for non-numeric attributes.

16.19.3 Assigning Attribute Values to Insns

The value assigned to an attribute of an insn is primarily determined by which pattern is matched by that insn (or which `define_peephole` generated it). Every `define_insn` and `define_peephole` can have an optional last argument to specify the values of attributes for matching insns. The value of any attribute not specified in a particular insn is set to the default value for that attribute, as specified in its `define_attr`. Extensive use of default values for attributes permits the specification of the values for only one or two attributes in the definition of most insn patterns, as seen in the example in the next section.

The optional last argument of `define_insn` and `define_peephole` is a vector of expressions, each of which defines the value for a single attribute. The most general way of assigning an attribute's value is to use a `set` expression whose first operand is an `attr` expression giving the name of the attribute being set. The second operand of the `set` is an attribute expression (see Section 16.19.2 [Expressions], page 406) giving the value of the attribute.

When the attribute value depends on the 'alternative' attribute (i.e., which is the applicable alternative in the constraint of the insn), the `set_attr_alternative` expression can be used. It allows the specification of a vector of attribute expressions, one for each alternative.

When the generality of arbitrary attribute expressions is not required, the simpler `set_attr` expression can be used, which allows specifying a string giving either a single attribute value or a list of attribute values, one for each alternative.

The form of each of the above specifications is shown below. In each case, *name* is a string specifying the attribute to be set.

```
(set_attr name value-string)
```
> *value-string* is either a string giving the desired attribute value, or a string
> containing a comma-separated list giving the values for succeeding alternatives.
> The number of elements must match the number of alternatives in the constraint
> of the insn pattern.
>
> Note that it may be useful to specify '*' for some alternative, in which case the
> attribute will assume its default value for insns matching that alternative.

```
(set_attr_alternative name [value1 value2 ...])
```
> Depending on the alternative of the insn, the value will be one of the specified
> values. This is a shorthand for using a `cond` with tests on the 'alternative'
> attribute.

```
(set (attr name) value)
```
> The first operand of this `set` must be the special RTL expression `attr`, whose
> sole operand is a string giving the name of the attribute being set. *value* is the
> value of the attribute.

The following shows three different ways of representing the same attribute value specification:

```
(set_attr "type" "load,store,arith")

(set_attr_alternative "type"
                      [(const_string "load") (const_string "store")
                       (const_string "arith")])

(set (attr "type")
     (cond [(eq_attr "alternative" "1") (const_string "load")
            (eq_attr "alternative" "2") (const_string "store")]
           (const_string "arith")))
```

The `define_asm_attributes` expression provides a mechanism to specify the attributes
assigned to insns produced from an `asm` statement. It has the form:

```
(define_asm_attributes [attr-sets])
```

where *attr-sets* is specified the same as for both the `define_insn` and the `define_peephole`
expressions.

These values will typically be the "worst case" attribute values. For example, they might
indicate that the condition code will be clobbered.

A specification for a `length` attribute is handled specially. The way to compute the length
of an `asm` insn is to multiply the length specified in the expression `define_asm_attributes`
by the number of machine instructions specified in the `asm` statement, determined by counting the number of semicolons and newlines in the string. Therefore, the value of the `length`
attribute specified in a `define_asm_attributes` should be the maximum possible length
of a single machine instruction.

16.19.4 Example of Attribute Specifications

The judicious use of defaulting is important in the efficient use of insn attributes. Typically, insns are divided into *types* and an attribute, customarily called `type`, is used to
represent this value. This attribute is normally used only to define the default value for
other attributes. An example will clarify this usage.

Assume we have a RISC machine with a condition code and in which only full-word operations are performed in registers. Let us assume that we can divide all insns into loads, stores, (integer) arithmetic operations, floating point operations, and branches.

Here we will concern ourselves with determining the effect of an insn on the condition code and will limit ourselves to the following possible effects: The condition code can be set unpredictably (clobbered), not be changed, be set to agree with the results of the operation, or only changed if the item previously set into the condition code has been modified.

Here is part of a sample 'md' file for such a machine:

```
(define_attr "type" "load,store,arith,fp,branch" (const_string "arith"))

(define_attr "cc" "clobber,unchanged,set,change0"
             (cond [(eq_attr "type" "load")
                        (const_string "change0")
                    (eq_attr "type" "store,branch")
                        (const_string "unchanged")
                    (eq_attr "type" "arith")
                        (if_then_else (match_operand:SI 0 "" "")
                                      (const_string "set")
                                      (const_string "clobber"))]
                   (const_string "clobber")))

(define_insn ""
  [(set (match_operand:SI 0 "general_operand" "=r,r,m")
        (match_operand:SI 1 "general_operand" "r,m,r"))]
  ""
  "@
   move %0,%1
   load %0,%1
   store %0,%1"
  [(set_attr "type" "arith,load,store")])
```

Note that we assume in the above example that arithmetic operations performed on quantities smaller than a machine word clobber the condition code since they will set the condition code to a value corresponding to the full-word result.

16.19.5 Computing the Length of an Insn

For many machines, multiple types of branch instructions are provided, each for different length branch displacements. In most cases, the assembler will choose the correct instruction to use. However, when the assembler cannot do so, GCC can when a special attribute, the **length** attribute, is defined. This attribute must be defined to have numeric values by specifying a null string in its **define_attr**.

In the case of the **length** attribute, two additional forms of arithmetic terms are allowed in test expressions:

(match_dup *n*)
> This refers to the address of operand *n* of the current insn, which must be a **label_ref**.

(pc)
> For non-branch instructions and backward branch instructions, this refers to the address of the current insn. But for forward branch instructions, this refers to the address of the next insn, because the length of the current insn is to be computed.

For normal insns, the length will be determined by value of the `length` attribute. In the case of `addr_vec` and `addr_diff_vec` insn patterns, the length is computed as the number of vectors multiplied by the size of each vector.

Lengths are measured in addressable storage units (bytes).

Note that it is possible to call functions via the `symbol_ref` mechanism to compute the length of an insn. However, if you use this mechanism you must provide dummy clauses to express the maximum length without using the function call. You can an example of this in the `pa` machine description for the `call_symref` pattern.

The following macros can be used to refine the length computation:

ADJUST_INSN_LENGTH (*insn, length*)

> If defined, modifies the length assigned to instruction *insn* as a function of the context in which it is used. *length* is an lvalue that contains the initially computed length of the insn and should be updated with the correct length of the insn.
>
> This macro will normally not be required. A case in which it is required is the ROMP. On this machine, the size of an `addr_vec` insn must be increased by two to compensate for the fact that alignment may be required.

The routine that returns `get_attr_length` (the value of the `length` attribute) can be used by the output routine to determine the form of the branch instruction to be written, as the example below illustrates.

As an example of the specification of variable-length branches, consider the IBM 360. If we adopt the convention that a register will be set to the starting address of a function, we can jump to labels within 4k of the start using a four-byte instruction. Otherwise, we need a six-byte sequence to load the address from memory and then branch to it.

On such a machine, a pattern for a branch instruction might be specified as follows:

```
(define_insn "jump"
  [(set (pc)
        (label_ref (match_operand 0 "" "")))]
  ""
{
  return (get_attr_length (insn) == 4
          ? "b %l0" : "l r15,=a(%l0); br r15");
}
  [(set (attr "length")
        (if_then_else (lt (match_dup 0) (const_int 4096))
                      (const_int 4)
                      (const_int 6)))])
```

16.19.6 Constant Attributes

A special form of `define_attr`, where the expression for the default value is a `const` expression, indicates an attribute that is constant for a given run of the compiler. Constant attributes may be used to specify which variety of processor is used. For example,

```
(define_attr "cpu" "m88100,m88110,m88000"
 (const
  (cond [(symbol_ref "TARGET_88100") (const_string "m88100")
         (symbol_ref "TARGET_88110") (const_string "m88110")]
        (const_string "m88000"))))
```

```
(define_attr "memory" "fast,slow"
 (const
  (if_then_else (symbol_ref "TARGET_FAST_MEM")
                (const_string "fast")
                (const_string "slow"))))
```

The routine generated for constant attributes has no parameters as it does not depend on any particular insn. RTL expressions used to define the value of a constant attribute may use the `symbol_ref` form, but may not use either the `match_operand` form or `eq_attr` forms involving insn attributes.

16.19.7 Mnemonic Attribute

The `mnemonic` attribute is a string type attribute holding the instruction mnemonic for an insn alternative. The attribute values will automatically be generated by the machine description parser if there is an attribute definition in the md file:

```
(define_attr "mnemonic" "unknown" (const_string "unknown"))
```

The default value can be freely chosen as long as it does not collide with any of the instruction mnemonics. This value will be used whenever the machine description parser is not able to determine the mnemonic string. This might be the case for output templates containing more than a single instruction as in `"mvcle\t%0,%1,0\;jo\t.-4"`.

The `mnemonic` attribute set is not generated automatically if the instruction string is generated via C code.

An existing `mnemonic` attribute set in an insn definition will not be overriden by the md file parser. That way it is possible to manually set the instruction mnemonics for the cases where the md file parser fails to determine it automatically.

The `mnemonic` attribute is useful for dealing with instruction specific properties in the pipeline description without defining additional insn attributes.

```
(define_attr "ooo_expanded" ""
  (cond [(eq_attr "mnemonic" "dlr,dsgr,d,dsgf,stam,dsgfr,dlgr")
         (const_int 1)]
        (const_int 0)))
```

16.19.8 Delay Slot Scheduling

The insn attribute mechanism can be used to specify the requirements for delay slots, if any, on a target machine. An instruction is said to require a *delay slot* if some instructions that are physically after the instruction are executed as if they were located before it. Classic examples are branch and call instructions, which often execute the following instruction before the branch or call is performed.

On some machines, conditional branch instructions can optionally *annul* instructions in the delay slot. This means that the instruction will not be executed for certain branch outcomes. Both instructions that annul if the branch is true and instructions that annul if the branch is false are supported.

Delay slot scheduling differs from instruction scheduling in that determining whether an instruction needs a delay slot is dependent only on the type of instruction being generated, not on data flow between the instructions. See the next section for a discussion of data-dependent instruction scheduling.

The requirement of an insn needing one or more delay slots is indicated via the `define_delay` expression. It has the following form:

```
(define_delay test
              [delay-1 annul-true-1 annul-false-1
               delay-2 annul-true-2 annul-false-2
               ...])
```

test is an attribute test that indicates whether this `define_delay` applies to a particular insn. If so, the number of required delay slots is determined by the length of the vector specified as the second argument. An insn placed in delay slot *n* must satisfy attribute test *delay-n*. *annul-true-n* is an attribute test that specifies which insns may be annulled if the branch is true. Similarly, *annul-false-n* specifies which insns in the delay slot may be annulled if the branch is false. If annulling is not supported for that delay slot, (nil) should be coded.

For example, in the common case where branch and call insns require a single delay slot, which may contain any insn other than a branch or call, the following would be placed in the 'md' file:

```
(define_delay (eq_attr "type" "branch,call")
              [(eq_attr "type" "!branch,call") (nil) (nil)])
```

Multiple `define_delay` expressions may be specified. In this case, each such expression specifies different delay slot requirements and there must be no insn for which tests in two `define_delay` expressions are both true.

For example, if we have a machine that requires one delay slot for branches but two for calls, no delay slot can contain a branch or call insn, and any valid insn in the delay slot for the branch can be annulled if the branch is true, we might represent this as follows:

```
(define_delay (eq_attr "type" "branch")
   [(eq_attr "type" "!branch,call")
    (eq_attr "type" "!branch,call")
    (nil)])

(define_delay (eq_attr "type" "call")
              [(eq_attr "type" "!branch,call") (nil) (nil)
               (eq_attr "type" "!branch,call") (nil) (nil)])
```

16.19.9 Specifying processor pipeline description

To achieve better performance, most modern processors (super-pipelined, superscalar RISC, and VLIW processors) have many *functional units* on which several instructions can be executed simultaneously. An instruction starts execution if its issue conditions are satisfied. If not, the instruction is stalled until its conditions are satisfied. Such *interlock (pipeline) delay* causes interruption of the fetching of successor instructions (or demands nop instructions, e.g. for some MIPS processors).

There are two major kinds of interlock delays in modern processors. The first one is a data dependence delay determining *instruction latency time*. The instruction execution is not started until all source data have been evaluated by prior instructions (there are more complex cases when the instruction execution starts even when the data are not available but will be ready in given time after the instruction execution start). Taking the data dependence delays into account is simple. The data dependence (true, output, and anti-dependence) delay between two instructions is given by a constant. In most cases this approach is adequate. The second kind of interlock delays is a reservation delay. The reservation delay means that two instructions under execution will be in need of shared processors resources, i.e. buses, internal registers, and/or functional units, which are reserved for some time. Taking this kind of delay into account is complex especially for modern RISC processors.

The task of exploiting more processor parallelism is solved by an instruction scheduler. For a better solution to this problem, the instruction scheduler has to have an adequate description of the processor parallelism (or *pipeline description*). GCC machine descriptions describe processor parallelism and functional unit reservations for groups of instructions with the aid of *regular expressions*.

The GCC instruction scheduler uses a *pipeline hazard recognizer* to figure out the possibility of the instruction issue by the processor on a given simulated processor cycle. The pipeline hazard recognizer is automatically generated from the processor pipeline description. The pipeline hazard recognizer generated from the machine description is based on a deterministic finite state automaton (DFA): the instruction issue is possible if there is a transition from one automaton state to another one. This algorithm is very fast, and furthermore, its speed is not dependent on processor complexity[2].

The rest of this section describes the directives that constitute an automaton-based processor pipeline description. The order of these constructions within the machine description file is not important.

The following optional construction describes names of automata generated and used for the pipeline hazards recognition. Sometimes the generated finite state automaton used by the pipeline hazard recognizer is large. If we use more than one automaton and bind functional units to the automata, the total size of the automata is usually less than the size of the single automaton. If there is no one such construction, only one finite state automaton is generated.

> (define_automaton *automata-names*)

automata-names is a string giving names of the automata. The names are separated by commas. All the automata should have unique names. The automaton name is used in the constructions define_cpu_unit and define_query_cpu_unit.

Each processor functional unit used in the description of instruction reservations should be described by the following construction.

> (define_cpu_unit *unit-names* [*automaton-name*])

unit-names is a string giving the names of the functional units separated by commas. Don't use name 'nothing', it is reserved for other goals.

automaton-name is a string giving the name of the automaton with which the unit is bound. The automaton should be described in construction define_automaton. You should give *automaton-name*, if there is a defined automaton.

The assignment of units to automata are constrained by the uses of the units in insn reservations. The most important constraint is: if a unit reservation is present on a particular cycle of an alternative for an insn reservation, then some unit from the same automaton must be present on the same cycle for the other alternatives of the insn reservation. The rest of the constraints are mentioned in the description of the subsequent constructions.

---

[2] However, the size of the automaton depends on processor complexity. To limit this effect, machine descriptions can split orthogonal parts of the machine description among several automata: but then, since each of these must be stepped independently, this does cause a small decrease in the algorithm's performance.

The following construction describes CPU functional units analogously to `define_cpu_unit`. The reservation of such units can be queried for an automaton state. The instruction scheduler never queries reservation of functional units for given automaton state. So as a rule, you don't need this construction. This construction could be used for future code generation goals (e.g. to generate VLIW insn templates).

> `(define_query_cpu_unit unit-names [automaton-name])`

unit-names is a string giving names of the functional units separated by commas.

automaton-name is a string giving the name of the automaton with which the unit is bound.

The following construction is the major one to describe pipeline characteristics of an instruction.

> `(define_insn_reservation insn-name default_latency`
> `                          condition regexp)`

default_latency is a number giving latency time of the instruction. There is an important difference between the old description and the automaton based pipeline description. The latency time is used for all dependencies when we use the old description. In the automaton based pipeline description, the given latency time is only used for true dependencies. The cost of anti-dependencies is always zero and the cost of output dependencies is the difference between latency times of the producing and consuming insns (if the difference is negative, the cost is considered to be zero). You can always change the default costs for any description by using the target hook `TARGET_SCHED_ADJUST_COST` (see Section 17.17 [Scheduling], page 531).

insn-name is a string giving the internal name of the insn. The internal names are used in constructions `define_bypass` and in the automaton description file generated for debugging. The internal name has nothing in common with the names in `define_insn`. It is a good practice to use insn classes described in the processor manual.

condition defines what RTL insns are described by this construction. You should remember that you will be in trouble if *condition* for two or more different `define_insn_reservation` constructions is TRUE for an insn. In this case what reservation will be used for the insn is not defined. Such cases are not checked during generation of the pipeline hazards recognizer because in general recognizing that two conditions may have the same value is quite difficult (especially if the conditions contain `symbol_ref`). It is also not checked during the pipeline hazard recognizer work because it would slow down the recognizer considerably.

regexp is a string describing the reservation of the cpu's functional units by the instruction. The reservations are described by a regular expression according to the following syntax:

```
regexp = regexp "," oneof
        | oneof

oneof = oneof "|" allof
        | allof

allof = allof "+" repeat
        | repeat

repeat = element "*" number
```

```
                | element

element = cpu_function_unit_name
                | reservation_name
                | result_name
                | "nothing"
                | "(" regexp ")"
```

- ',' is used for describing the start of the next cycle in the reservation.

- '|' is used for describing a reservation described by the first regular expression **or** a reservation described by the second regular expression **or** etc.

- '+' is used for describing a reservation described by the first regular expression **and** a reservation described by the second regular expression **and** etc.

- '*' is used for convenience and simply means a sequence in which the regular expression are repeated *number* times with cycle advancing (see ',').

- 'cpu_function_unit_name' denotes reservation of the named functional unit.

- 'reservation_name' — see description of construction 'define_reservation'.

- 'nothing' denotes no unit reservations.

Sometimes unit reservations for different insns contain common parts. In such case, you can simplify the pipeline description by describing the common part by the following construction

```
(define_reservation reservation-name regexp)
```

reservation-name is a string giving name of *regexp*. Functional unit names and reservation names are in the same name space. So the reservation names should be different from the functional unit names and can not be the reserved name 'nothing'.

The following construction is used to describe exceptions in the latency time for given instruction pair. This is so called bypasses.

```
(define_bypass number out_insn_names in_insn_names
               [guard])
```

number defines when the result generated by the instructions given in string *out_insn_names* will be ready for the instructions given in string *in_insn_names*. Each of these strings is a comma-separated list of filename-style globs and they refer to the names of **define_insn_reservations**. For example:

```
(define_bypass 1 "cpu1_load_*, cpu1_store_*" "cpu1_load_*")
```

defines a bypass between instructions that start with 'cpu1_load_' or 'cpu1_store_' and those that start with 'cpu1_load_'.

guard is an optional string giving the name of a C function which defines an additional guard for the bypass. The function will get the two insns as parameters. If the function returns zero the bypass will be ignored for this case. The additional guard is necessary to recognize complicated bypasses, e.g. when the consumer is only an address of insn 'store' (not a stored value).

If there are more one bypass with the same output and input insns, the chosen bypass is the first bypass with a guard in description whose guard function returns nonzero. If there is no such bypass, then bypass without the guard function is chosen.

The following five constructions are usually used to describe VLIW processors, or more precisely, to describe a placement of small instructions into VLIW instruction slots. They can be used for RISC processors, too.

```
(exclusion_set unit-names unit-names)
(presence_set unit-names patterns)
(final_presence_set unit-names patterns)
(absence_set unit-names patterns)
(final_absence_set unit-names patterns)
```

unit-names is a string giving names of functional units separated by commas.

patterns is a string giving patterns of functional units separated by comma. Currently pattern is one unit or units separated by white-spaces.

The first construction ('`exclusion_set`') means that each functional unit in the first string can not be reserved simultaneously with a unit whose name is in the second string and vice versa. For example, the construction is useful for describing processors (e.g. some SPARC processors) with a fully pipelined floating point functional unit which can execute simultaneously only single floating point insns or only double floating point insns.

The second construction ('`presence_set`') means that each functional unit in the first string can not be reserved unless at least one of pattern of units whose names are in the second string is reserved. This is an asymmetric relation. For example, it is useful for description that VLIW '`slot1`' is reserved after '`slot0`' reservation. We could describe it by the following construction

```
(presence_set "slot1" "slot0")
```

Or '`slot1`' is reserved only after '`slot0`' and unit '`b0`' reservation. In this case we could write

```
(presence_set "slot1" "slot0 b0")
```

The third construction ('`final_presence_set`') is analogous to '`presence_set`'. The difference between them is when checking is done. When an instruction is issued in given automaton state reflecting all current and planned unit reservations, the automaton state is changed. The first state is a source state, the second one is a result state. Checking for '`presence_set`' is done on the source state reservation, checking for '`final_presence_set`' is done on the result reservation. This construction is useful to describe a reservation which is actually two subsequent reservations. For example, if we use

```
(presence_set "slot1" "slot0")
```

the following insn will be never issued (because '`slot1`' requires '`slot0`' which is absent in the source state).

```
(define_reservation "insn_and_nop" "slot0 + slot1")
```

but it can be issued if we use analogous '`final_presence_set`'.

The forth construction ('`absence_set`') means that each functional unit in the first string can be reserved only if each pattern of units whose names are in the second string is not reserved. This is an asymmetric relation (actually '`exclusion_set`' is analogous to this one but it is symmetric). For example it might be useful in a VLIW description to say that '`slot0`' cannot be reserved after either '`slot1`' or '`slot2`' have been reserved. This can be described as:

```
(absence_set "slot0" "slot1, slot2")
```

Or '`slot2`' can not be reserved if '`slot0`' and unit '`b0`' are reserved or '`slot1`' and unit '`b1`' are reserved. In this case we could write

```
(absence_set "slot2" "slot0 b0, slot1 b1")
```

All functional units mentioned in a set should belong to the same automaton.

The last construction ('`final_absence_set`') is analogous to '`absence_set`' but checking is done on the result (state) reservation. See comments for '`final_presence_set`'.

You can control the generator of the pipeline hazard recognizer with the following construction.

```
(automata_option options)
```

options is a string giving options which affect the generated code. Currently there are the following options:

- *no-minimization* makes no minimization of the automaton. This is only worth to do when we are debugging the description and need to look more accurately at reservations of states.

- *time* means printing time statistics about the generation of automata.

- *stats* means printing statistics about the generated automata such as the number of DFA states, NDFA states and arcs.

- *v* means a generation of the file describing the result automata. The file has suffix '`.dfa`' and can be used for the description verification and debugging.

- *w* means a generation of warning instead of error for non-critical errors.

- *no-comb-vect* prevents the automaton generator from generating two data structures and comparing them for space efficiency. Using a comb vector to represent transitions may be better, but it can be very expensive to construct. This option is useful if the build process spends an unacceptably long time in genautomata.

- *ndfa* makes nondeterministic finite state automata. This affects the treatment of operator '`|`' in the regular expressions. The usual treatment of the operator is to try the first alternative and, if the reservation is not possible, the second alternative. The non-deterministic treatment means trying all alternatives, some of them may be rejected by reservations in the subsequent insns.

- *collapse-ndfa* modifies the behavior of the generator when producing an automaton. An additional state transition to collapse a nondeterministic NDFA state to a deterministic DFA state is generated. It can be triggered by passing **const0_rtx** to state_transition. In such an automaton, cycle advance transitions are available only for these collapsed states. This option is useful for ports that want to use the **ndfa** option, but also want to use **define_query_cpu_unit** to assign units to insns issued in a cycle.

- *progress* means output of a progress bar showing how many states were generated so far for automaton being processed. This is useful during debugging a DFA description. If you see too many generated states, you could interrupt the generator of the pipeline hazard recognizer and try to figure out a reason for generation of the huge automaton.

As an example, consider a superscalar RISC machine which can issue three insns (two integer insns and one floating point insn) on the cycle but can finish only two insns. To describe this, we define the following functional units.

```
(define_cpu_unit "i0_pipeline, i1_pipeline, f_pipeline")
(define_cpu_unit "port0, port1")
```

All simple integer insns can be executed in any integer pipeline and their result is ready in two cycles. The simple integer insns are issued into the first pipeline unless it is reserved, otherwise they are issued into the second pipeline. Integer division and multiplication insns can be executed only in the second integer pipeline and their results are ready correspondingly in 8 and 4 cycles. The integer division is not pipelined, i.e. the subsequent integer division insn can not be issued until the current division insn finished. Floating point insns are fully pipelined and their results are ready in 3 cycles. Where the result of a floating point insn is used by an integer insn, an additional delay of one cycle is incurred. To describe all of this we could specify

```
(define_cpu_unit "div")

(define_insn_reservation "simple" 2 (eq_attr "type" "int")
                         "(i0_pipeline | i1_pipeline), (port0 | port1)")

(define_insn_reservation "mult" 4 (eq_attr "type" "mult")
                         "i1_pipeline, nothing*2, (port0 | port1)")

(define_insn_reservation "div" 8 (eq_attr "type" "div")
                         "i1_pipeline, div*7, div + (port0 | port1)")

(define_insn_reservation "float" 3 (eq_attr "type" "float")
                         "f_pipeline, nothing, (port0 | port1))

(define_bypass 4 "float" "simple,mult,div")
```

To simplify the description we could describe the following reservation

```
(define_reservation "finish" "port0|port1")
```

and use it in all `define_insn_reservation` as in the following construction

```
(define_insn_reservation "simple" 2 (eq_attr "type" "int")
                         "(i0_pipeline | i1_pipeline), finish")
```

16.20 Conditional Execution

A number of architectures provide for some form of conditional execution, or predication. The hallmark of this feature is the ability to nullify most of the instructions in the instruction set. When the instruction set is large and not entirely symmetric, it can be quite tedious to describe these forms directly in the '.md' file. An alternative is the `define_cond_exec` template.

```
(define_cond_exec
  [predicate-pattern]
  "condition"
  "output-template"
  "optional-insn-attribues")
```

predicate-pattern is the condition that must be true for the insn to be executed at runtime and should match a relational operator. One can use `match_operator` to match several relational operators at once. Any `match_operand` operands must have no more than one alternative.

condition is a C expression that must be true for the generated pattern to match.

output-template is a string similar to the `define_insn` output template (see Section 16.5 [Output Template], page 309), except that the '*' and '@' special cases do not apply. This is only useful if the assembly text for the predicate is a simple prefix to the main insn. In order to handle the general case, there is a global variable `current_insn_predicate` that will contain the entire predicate if the current insn is predicated, and will otherwise be NULL.

optional-insn-attributes is an optional vector of attributes that gets appended to the insn attributes of the produced cond_exec rtx. It can be used to add some distinguishing attribute to cond_exec rtxs produced that way. An example usage would be to use this attribute in conjunction with attributes on the main pattern to disable particular alternatives under certain conditions.

When `define_cond_exec` is used, an implicit reference to the `predicable` instruction attribute is made. See Section 16.19 [Insn Attributes], page 405. This attribute must be a boolean (i.e. have exactly two elements in its *list-of-values*), with the possible values being `no` and `yes`. The default and all uses in the insns must be a simple constant, not a complex expressions. It may, however, depend on the alternative, by using a comma-separated list of values. If that is the case, the port should also define an `enabled` attribute (see Section 16.8.6 [Disable Insn Alternatives], page 351), which should also allow only `no` and `yes` as its values.

For each `define_insn` for which the `predicable` attribute is true, a new `define_insn` pattern will be generated that matches a predicated version of the instruction. For example,

```
(define_insn "addsi"
  [(set (match_operand:SI 0 "register_operand" "r")
        (plus:SI (match_operand:SI 1 "register_operand" "r")
                 (match_operand:SI 2 "register_operand" "r")))]
  "test1"
  "add %2,%1,%0")

(define_cond_exec
  [(ne (match_operand:CC 0 "register_operand" "c")
       (const_int 0))]
  "test2"
  "(%0)")
```

generates a new pattern

```
(define_insn ""
  [(cond_exec
     (ne (match_operand:CC 3 "register_operand" "c") (const_int 0))
     (set (match_operand:SI 0 "register_operand" "r")
          (plus:SI (match_operand:SI 1 "register_operand" "r")
                   (match_operand:SI 2 "register_operand" "r"))))]
  "(test2) && (test1)"
  "(%3) add %2,%1,%0")
```

16.21 RTL Templates Transformations

For some hardware architectures there are common cases when the RTL templates for the instructions can be derived from the other RTL templates using simple transformations. E.g., 'i386.md' contains an RTL template for the ordinary `sub` instruction— `*subsi_1`, and for the `sub` instruction with subsequent zero-extension—`*subsi_1_zext`. Such cases can be easily implemented by a single meta-template capable of generating a modified case based on the initial one:

```
(define_subst "name"
  [input-template]
  "condition"
  [output-template])
```

input-template is a pattern describing the source RTL template, which will be transformed.

condition is a C expression that is conjunct with the condition from the input-template to generate a condition to be used in the output-template.

output-template is a pattern that will be used in the resulting template.

define_subst mechanism is tightly coupled with the notion of the subst attribute (see Section 16.23.4 [Subst Iterators], page 430). The use of **define_subst** is triggered by a reference to a subst attribute in the transforming RTL template. This reference initiates duplication of the source RTL template and substitution of the attributes with their values. The source RTL template is left unchanged, while the copy is transformed by **define_subst**. This transformation can fail in the case when the source RTL template is not matched against the input-template of the **define_subst**. In such case the copy is deleted.

define_subst can be used only in **define_insn** and **define_expand**, it cannot be used in other expressions (e.g. in **define_insn_and_split**).

16.21.1 `define_subst` Example

To illustrate how **define_subst** works, let us examine a simple template transformation.

Suppose there are two kinds of instructions: one that touches flags and the other that does not. The instructions of the second type could be generated with the following **define_subst**:

```
(define_subst "add_clobber_subst"
  [(set (match_operand:SI 0 "" "")
        (match_operand:SI 1 "" ""))]
  ""
  [(set (match_dup 0)
        (match_dup 1))
   (clobber (reg:CC FLAGS_REG))]
```

This **define_subst** can be applied to any RTL pattern containing **set** of mode SI and generates a copy with clobber when it is applied.

Assume there is an RTL template for a **max** instruction to be used in **define_subst** mentioned above:

```
(define_insn "maxsi"
  [(set (match_operand:SI 0 "register_operand" "=r")
        (max:SI
          (match_operand:SI 1 "register_operand" "r")
          (match_operand:SI 2 "register_operand" "r")))]
  ""
  "max\t{%2, %1, %0|%0, %1, %2}"
  [...])
```

To mark the RTL template for **define_subst** application, subst-attributes are used. They should be declared in advance:

```
(define_subst_attr "add_clobber_name" "add_clobber_subst" "_noclobber" "_clobber")
```

Here 'add_clobber_name' is the attribute name, 'add_clobber_subst' is the name of the corresponding **define_subst**, the third argument ('_noclobber') is the attribute value that would be substituted into the unchanged version of the source RTL template, and the last argument ('_clobber') is the value that would be substituted into the second, transformed, version of the RTL template.

Once the subst-attribute has been defined, it should be used in RTL templates which need to be processed by the **define_subst**. So, the original RTL template should be changed:

```
(define_insn "maxsi<add_clobber_name>"
  [(set (match_operand:SI 0 "register_operand" "=r")
        (max:SI
          (match_operand:SI 1 "register_operand" "r")
          (match_operand:SI 2 "register_operand" "r")))]
  ""
  "max\t{%2, %1, %0|%0, %1, %2}"
  [...])
```

The result of the **define_subst** usage would look like the following:

```
(define_insn "maxsi_noclobber"
  [(set (match_operand:SI 0 "register_operand" "=r")
        (max:SI
          (match_operand:SI 1 "register_operand" "r")
          (match_operand:SI 2 "register_operand" "r")))]
  ""
  "max\t{%2, %1, %0|%0, %1, %2}"
  [...])
(define_insn "maxsi_clobber"
  [(set (match_operand:SI 0 "register_operand" "=r")
        (max:SI
          (match_operand:SI 1 "register_operand" "r")
          (match_operand:SI 2 "register_operand" "r")))
   (clobber (reg:CC FLAGS_REG))]
  ""
  "max\t{%2, %1, %0|%0, %1, %2}"
  [...])
```

16.21.2 Pattern Matching in `define_subst`

All expressions, allowed in `define_insn` or `define_expand`, are allowed in the input-template of `define_subst`, except `match_par_dup`, `match_scratch`, `match_parallel`. The meanings of expressions in the input-template were changed:

`match_operand` matches any expression (possibly, a subtree in RTL-template), if modes of the `match_operand` and this expression are the same, or mode of the `match_operand` is VOIDmode, or this expression is `match_dup`, `match_op_dup`. If the expression is `match_operand` too, and predicate of `match_operand` from the input pattern is not empty, then the predicates are compared. That can be used for more accurate filtering of accepted RTL-templates.

`match_operator` matches common operators (like `plus`, `minus`), `unspec`, `unspec_volatile` operators and `match_operators` from the original pattern if the modes match and `match_operator` from the input pattern has the same number of operands as the operator from the original pattern.

16.21.3 Generation of output template in `define_subst`

If all necessary checks for `define_subst` application pass, a new RTL-pattern, based on the output-template, is created to replace the old template. Like in input-patterns, meanings of some RTL expressions are changed when they are used in output-patterns of a `define_subst`. Thus, `match_dup` is used for copying the whole expression from the original pattern, which matched corresponding `match_operand` from the input pattern.

`match_dup N` is used in the output template to be replaced with the expression from the original pattern, which matched `match_operand N` from the input pattern. As a consequence, `match_dup` cannot be used to point to `match_operand`s from the output pattern, it should always refer to a `match_operand` from the input pattern.

In the output template one can refer to the expressions from the original pattern and create new ones. For instance, some operands could be added by means of standard `match_operand`.

After replacing `match_dup` with some RTL-subtree from the original pattern, it could happen that several `match_operand`s in the output pattern have the same indexes. It is unknown, how many and what indexes would be used in the expression which would replace `match_dup`, so such conflicts in indexes are inevitable. To overcome this issue, `match_operand`s and `match_operator`s, which were introduced into the output pattern, are renumerated when all `match_dup`s are replaced.

Number of alternatives in `match_operand`s introduced into the output template M could differ from the number of alternatives in the original pattern N, so in the resultant pattern there would be N*M alternatives. Thus, constraints from the original pattern would be duplicated N times, constraints from the output pattern would be duplicated M times, producing all possible combinations.

16.22 Constant Definitions

Using literal constants inside instruction patterns reduces legibility and can be a maintenance problem.

To overcome this problem, you may use the `define_constants` expression. It contains a vector of name-value pairs. From that point on, wherever any of the names appears in the MD file, it is as if the corresponding value had been written instead. You may use `define_constants` multiple times; each appearance adds more constants to the table. It is an error to redefine a constant with a different value.

To come back to the a29k load multiple example, instead of

```
(define_insn ""
  [(match_parallel 0 "load_multiple_operation"
     [(set (match_operand:SI 1 "gpc_reg_operand" "=r")
           (match_operand:SI 2 "memory_operand" "m"))
      (use (reg:SI 179))
      (clobber (reg:SI 179))])]
  ""
  "loadm 0,0,%1,%2")
```

You could write:

```
(define_constants [
    (R_BP 177)
    (R_FC 178)
    (R_CR 179)
    (R_Q  180)
])

(define_insn ""
  [(match_parallel 0 "load_multiple_operation"
     [(set (match_operand:SI 1 "gpc_reg_operand" "=r")
           (match_operand:SI 2 "memory_operand" "m"))
      (use (reg:SI R_CR))
      (clobber (reg:SI R_CR))])]
  ""
```

```
"loadm 0,0,%1,%2")
```

The constants that are defined with a define_constant are also output in the insn-codes.h header file as #defines.

You can also use the machine description file to define enumerations. Like the constants defined by **define_constant**, these enumerations are visible to both the machine description file and the main C code.

The syntax is as follows:

```
(define_c_enum "name" [
  value0
  value1
  ...
  valuen
])
```

This definition causes the equivalent of the following C code to appear in 'insn-constants.h':

```
enum name {
  value0 = 0,
  value1 = 1,
  ...
  valuen = n
};
#define NUM_cname_VALUES (n + 1)
```

where *cname* is the capitalized form of *name*. It also makes each *valuei* available in the machine description file, just as if it had been declared with:

```
(define_constants [(valuei i)])
```

Each *valuei* is usually an upper-case identifier and usually begins with *cname*.

You can split the enumeration definition into as many statements as you like. The above example is directly equivalent to:

```
(define_c_enum "name" [value0])
(define_c_enum "name" [value1])
...
(define_c_enum "name" [valuen])
```

Splitting the enumeration helps to improve the modularity of each individual .md file. For example, if a port defines its synchronization instructions in a separate 'sync.md' file, it is convenient to define all synchronization-specific enumeration values in 'sync.md' rather than in the main '.md' file.

Some enumeration names have special significance to GCC:

unspecv   If an enumeration called **unspecv** is defined, GCC will use it when printing out **unspec_volatile** expressions. For example:

```
(define_c_enum "unspecv" [
  UNSPECV_BLOCKAGE
])
```

causes GCC to print '(unspec_volatile ... 0)' as:

```
(unspec_volatile ... UNSPECV_BLOCKAGE)
```

unspec   If an enumeration called **unspec** is defined, GCC will use it when printing out **unspec** expressions. GCC will also use it when printing out **unspec_volatile** expressions unless an **unspecv** enumeration is also defined. You can therefore decide whether to keep separate enumerations for volatile and non-volatile expressions or whether to use the same enumeration for both.

Another way of defining an enumeration is to use `define_enum`:

```
(define_enum "name" [
  value0
  value1
  ...
  valuen
])
```

This directive implies:

```
(define_c_enum "name" [
  cname_cvalue0
  cname_cvalue1
  ...
  cname_cvaluen
])
```

where *cvaluei* is the capitalized form of *valuei*. However, unlike `define_c_enum`, the enumerations defined by `define_enum` can be used in attribute specifications (see [define_enum_attr], page 406).

16.23 Iterators

Ports often need to define similar patterns for more than one machine mode or for more than one rtx code. GCC provides some simple iterator facilities to make this process easier.

16.23.1 Mode Iterators

Ports often need to define similar patterns for two or more different modes. For example:

- If a processor has hardware support for both single and double floating-point arithmetic, the `SFmode` patterns tend to be very similar to the `DFmode` ones.
- If a port uses `SImode` pointers in one configuration and `DImode` pointers in another, it will usually have very similar `SImode` and `DImode` patterns for manipulating pointers.

Mode iterators allow several patterns to be instantiated from one '`.md`' file template. They can be used with any type of rtx-based construct, such as a `define_insn`, `define_split`, or `define_peephole2`.

16.23.1.1 Defining Mode Iterators

The syntax for defining a mode iterator is:

```
(define_mode_iterator name [(mode1 "cond1") ... (moden "condn")])
```

This allows subsequent '`.md`' file constructs to use the mode suffix `:name`. Every construct that does so will be expanded *n* times, once with every use of `:name` replaced by `:mode1`, once with every use replaced by `:mode2`, and so on. In the expansion for a particular *modei*, every C condition will also require that *condi* be true.

For example:

```
(define_mode_iterator P [(SI "Pmode == SImode") (DI "Pmode == DImode")])
```

defines a new mode suffix `:P`. Every construct that uses `:P` will be expanded twice, once with every `:P` replaced by `:SI` and once with every `:P` replaced by `:DI`. The `:SI` version will only apply if `Pmode == SImode` and the `:DI` version will only apply if `Pmode == DImode`.

As with other '.md' conditions, an empty string is treated as "always true". (*mode* "")
can also be abbreviated to *mode*. For example:

```
(define_mode_iterator GPR [SI (DI "TARGET_64BIT")])
```

means that the :DI expansion only applies if TARGET_64BIT but that the :SI expansion
has no such constraint.

Iterators are applied in the order they are defined. This can be significant if two iterators
are used in a construct that requires substitutions. See Section 16.23.1.2 [Substitutions],
page 427.

16.23.1.2 Substitution in Mode Iterators

If an '.md' file construct uses mode iterators, each version of the construct will often need
slightly different strings or modes. For example:

- When a **define_expand** defines several **add*m*3** patterns (see Section 16.9 [Standard
  Names], page 356), each expander will need to use the appropriate mode name for *m*.

- When a **define_insn** defines several instruction patterns, each instruction will often
  use a different assembler mnemonic.

- When a **define_insn** requires operands with different modes, using an iterator for one
  of the operand modes usually requires a specific mode for the other operand(s).

GCC supports such variations through a system of "mode attributes". There are two
standard attributes: **mode**, which is the name of the mode in lower case, and **MODE**, which
is the same thing in upper case. You can define other attributes using:

```
(define_mode_attr name [(mode1 "value1") ... (moden "valuen")])
```

where *name* is the name of the attribute and *valuei* is the value associated with *modei*.

When GCC replaces some *:iterator* with *:mode*, it will scan each string and mode in the
pattern for sequences of the form **<iterator:attr>**, where *attr* is the name of a mode
attribute. If the attribute is defined for *mode*, the whole **<...>** sequence will be replaced
by the appropriate attribute value.

For example, suppose an '.md' file has:

```
(define_mode_iterator P [(SI "Pmode == SImode") (DI "Pmode == DImode")])
(define_mode_attr load [(SI "lw") (DI "ld")])
```

If one of the patterns that uses :P contains the string "<P:load>\t%0,%1", the SI version
of that pattern will use "lw\t%0,%1" and the DI version will use "ld\t%0,%1".

Here is an example of using an attribute for a mode:

```
(define_mode_iterator LONG [SI DI])
(define_mode_attr SHORT [(SI "HI") (DI "SI")])
(define_insn ...
  (sign_extend:LONG (match_operand:<LONG:SHORT> ...)) ...)
```

The *iterator:* prefix may be omitted, in which case the substitution will be attempted
for every iterator expansion.

16.23.1.3 Mode Iterator Examples

Here is an example from the MIPS port. It defines the following modes and attributes
(among others):

```
(define_mode_iterator GPR [SI (DI "TARGET_64BIT")])
(define_mode_attr d [(SI "") (DI "d")])
```

and uses the following template to define both `subsi3` and `subdi3`:

```
(define_insn "sub<mode>3"
  [(set (match_operand:GPR 0 "register_operand" "=d")
        (minus:GPR (match_operand:GPR 1 "register_operand" "d")
                   (match_operand:GPR 2 "register_operand" "d")))]
  ""
  "<d>subu\t%0,%1,%2"
  [(set_attr "type" "arith")
   (set_attr "mode" "<MODE>")])
```

This is exactly equivalent to:

```
(define_insn "subsi3"
  [(set (match_operand:SI 0 "register_operand" "=d")
        (minus:SI (match_operand:SI 1 "register_operand" "d")
                  (match_operand:SI 2 "register_operand" "d")))]
  ""
  "subu\t%0,%1,%2"
  [(set_attr "type" "arith")
   (set_attr "mode" "SI")])

(define_insn "subdi3"
  [(set (match_operand:DI 0 "register_operand" "=d")
        (minus:DI (match_operand:DI 1 "register_operand" "d")
                  (match_operand:DI 2 "register_operand" "d")))]
  ""
  "dsubu\t%0,%1,%2"
  [(set_attr "type" "arith")
   (set_attr "mode" "DI")])
```

16.23.2 Code Iterators

Code iterators operate in a similar way to mode iterators. See Section 16.23.1 [Mode Iterators], page 426.

The construct:

```
(define_code_iterator name [(code1 "cond1") ... (coden "condn")])
```

defines a pseudo rtx code *name* that can be instantiated as *codei* if condition *condi* is true. Each *codei* must have the same rtx format. See Section 13.2 [RTL Classes], page 230.

As with mode iterators, each pattern that uses *name* will be expanded *n* times, once with all uses of *name* replaced by *code1*, once with all uses replaced by *code2*, and so on. See Section 16.23.1.1 [Defining Mode Iterators], page 426.

It is possible to define attributes for codes as well as for modes. There are two standard code attributes: `code`, the name of the code in lower case, and `CODE`, the name of the code in upper case. Other attributes are defined using:

```
(define_code_attr name [(code1 "value1") ... (coden "valuen")])
```

Here's an example of code iterators in action, taken from the MIPS port:

```
(define_code_iterator any_cond [unordered ordered unlt unge uneq ltgt unle ungt
                                eq ne gt ge lt le gtu geu ltu leu])

(define_expand "b<code>"
  [(set (pc)
        (if_then_else (any_cond:CC (cc0)
```

```
                                   (const_int 0))
                    (label_ref (match_operand 0 ""))
                    (pc)))]
     ""
   {
     gen_conditional_branch (operands, <CODE>);
     DONE;
   })
```

This is equivalent to:

```
(define_expand "bunordered"
  [(set (pc)
        (if_then_else (unordered:CC (cc0)
                                    (const_int 0))
                    (label_ref (match_operand 0 ""))
                    (pc)))]
     ""
   {
     gen_conditional_branch (operands, UNORDERED);
     DONE;
   })

(define_expand "bordered"
  [(set (pc)
        (if_then_else (ordered:CC (cc0)
                                  (const_int 0))
                    (label_ref (match_operand 0 ""))
                    (pc)))]
     ""
   {
     gen_conditional_branch (operands, ORDERED);
     DONE;
   })

   ...
```

16.23.3 Int Iterators

Int iterators operate in a similar way to code iterators. See Section 16.23.2 [Code Iterators], page 428.

The construct:

```
(define_int_iterator name [(int1 "cond1") ... (intn "condn")])
```

defines a pseudo integer constant *name* that can be instantiated as *inti* if condition *condi* is true. Each *int* must have the same rtx format. See Section 13.2 [RTL Classes], page 230. Int iterators can appear in only those rtx fields that have 'i' as the specifier. This means that each *int* has to be a constant defined using define_constant or define_c_enum.

As with mode and code iterators, each pattern that uses *name* will be expanded *n* times, once with all uses of *name* replaced by *int1*, once with all uses replaced by *int2*, and so on. See Section 16.23.1.1 [Defining Mode Iterators], page 426.

It is possible to define attributes for ints as well as for codes and modes. Attributes are defined using:

```
(define_int_attr name [(int1 "value1") ... (intn "valuen")])
```

Here's an example of int iterators in action, taken from the ARM port:

```
(define_int_iterator QABSNEG [UNSPEC_VQABS UNSPEC_VQNEG])

(define_int_attr absneg [(UNSPEC_VQABS "abs") (UNSPEC_VQNEG "neg")])

(define_insn "neon_vq<absneg><mode>"
  [(set (match_operand:VDQIW 0 "s_register_operand" "=w")
(unspec:VDQIW [(match_operand:VDQIW 1 "s_register_operand" "w")
       (match_operand:SI 2 "immediate_operand" "i")]
      QABSNEG))]
  "TARGET_NEON"
  "vq<absneg>.<V_s_elem>\t%<V_reg>0, %<V_reg>1"
  [(set_attr "type" "neon_vqneg_vqabs")]
)
```

This is equivalent to:

```
(define_insn "neon_vqabs<mode>"
  [(set (match_operand:VDQIW 0 "s_register_operand" "=w")
(unspec:VDQIW [(match_operand:VDQIW 1 "s_register_operand" "w")
       (match_operand:SI 2 "immediate_operand" "i")]
      UNSPEC_VQABS))]
  "TARGET_NEON"
  "vqabs.<V_s_elem>\t%<V_reg>0, %<V_reg>1"
  [(set_attr "type" "neon_vqneg_vqabs")]
)

(define_insn "neon_vqneg<mode>"
  [(set (match_operand:VDQIW 0 "s_register_operand" "=w")
(unspec:VDQIW [(match_operand:VDQIW 1 "s_register_operand" "w")
       (match_operand:SI 2 "immediate_operand" "i")]
      UNSPEC_VQNEG))]
  "TARGET_NEON"
  "vqneg.<V_s_elem>\t%<V_reg>0, %<V_reg>1"
  [(set_attr "type" "neon_vqneg_vqabs")]
)
```

16.23.4 Subst Iterators

Subst iterators are special type of iterators with the following restrictions: they could not be declared explicitly, they always have only two values, and they do not have explicit dedicated name. Subst-iterators are triggered only when corresponding subst-attribute is used in RTL-pattern.

Subst iterators transform templates in the following way: the templates are duplicated, the subst-attributes in these templates are replaced with the corresponding values, and a new attribute is implicitly added to the given define_insn/define_expand. The name of the added attribute matches the name of define_subst. Such attributes are declared implicitly, and it is not allowed to have a define_attr named as a define_subst.

Each subst iterator is linked to a define_subst. It is declared implicitly by the first appearance of the corresponding define_subst_attr, and it is not allowed to define it explicitly.

Declarations of subst-attributes have the following syntax:

```
(define_subst_attr "name"
  "subst-name"
  "no-subst-value"
```

```
"subst-applied-value")
```

name is a string with which the given subst-attribute could be referred to.

subst-name shows which `define_subst` should be applied to an RTL-template if the given subst-attribute is present in the RTL-template.

no-subst-value is a value with which subst-attribute would be replaced in the first copy of the original RTL-template.

subst-applied-value is a value with which subst-attribute would be replaced in the second copy of the original RTL-template.

GNU Free Documentation License

Version 1.3, 3 November 2008

0. PREAMBLE

The purpose of this License is to make a manual, textbook, or other functional and useful document *free* in the sense of freedom: to assure everyone the effective freedom to copy and redistribute it, with or without modifying it, either commercially or non-commercially. Secondarily, this License preserves for the author and publisher a way to get credit for their work, while not being considered responsible for modifications made by others.

This License is a kind of "copyleft", which means that derivative works of the document must themselves be free in the same sense. It complements the GNU General Public License, which is a copyleft license designed for free software.

We have designed this License in order to use it for manuals for free software, because free software needs free documentation: a free program should come with manuals providing the same freedoms that the software does. But this License is not limited to software manuals; it can be used for any textual work, regardless of subject matter or whether it is published as a printed book. We recommend this License principally for works whose purpose is instruction or reference.

1. APPLICABILITY AND DEFINITIONS

This License applies to any manual or other work, in any medium, that contains a notice placed by the copyright holder saying it can be distributed under the terms of this License. Such a notice grants a world-wide, royalty-free license, unlimited in duration, to use that work under the conditions stated herein. The "Document", below, refers to any such manual or work. Any member of the public is a licensee, and is addressed as "you". You accept the license if you copy, modify or distribute the work in a way requiring permission under copyright law.

A "Modified Version" of the Document means any work containing the Document or a portion of it, either copied verbatim, or with modifications and/or translated into another language.

A "Secondary Section" is a named appendix or a front-matter section of the Document that deals exclusively with the relationship of the publishers or authors of the Document to the Document's overall subject (or to related matters) and contains nothing that could fall directly within that overall subject. (Thus, if the Document is in part a textbook of mathematics, a Secondary Section may not explain any mathematics.) The relationship could be a matter of historical connection with the subject or with related matters, or of legal, commercial, philosophical, ethical or political position regarding them.

The "Invariant Sections" are certain Secondary Sections whose titles are designated, as being those of Invariant Sections, in the notice that says that the Document is released under this License. If a section does not fit the above definition of Secondary then it is not allowed to be designated as Invariant. The Document may contain zero Invariant Sections. If the Document does not identify any Invariant Sections then there are none.

The "Cover Texts" are certain short passages of text that are listed, as Front-Cover Texts or Back-Cover Texts, in the notice that says that the Document is released under this License. A Front-Cover Text may be at most 5 words, and a Back-Cover Text may be at most 25 words.

A "Transparent" copy of the Document means a machine-readable copy, represented in a format whose specification is available to the general public, that is suitable for revising the document straightforwardly with generic text editors or (for images composed of pixels) generic paint programs or (for drawings) some widely available drawing editor, and that is suitable for input to text formatters or for automatic translation to a variety of formats suitable for input to text formatters. A copy made in an otherwise Transparent file format whose markup, or absence of markup, has been arranged to thwart or discourage subsequent modification by readers is not Transparent. An image format is not Transparent if used for any substantial amount of text. A copy that is not "Transparent" is called "Opaque".

Examples of suitable formats for Transparent copies include plain ASCII without markup, Texinfo input format, LaTeX input format, SGML or XML using a publicly available DTD, and standard-conforming simple HTML, PostScript or PDF designed for human modification. Examples of transparent image formats include PNG, XCF and JPG. Opaque formats include proprietary formats that can be read and edited only by proprietary word processors, SGML or XML for which the DTD and/or processing tools are not generally available, and the machine-generated HTML, PostScript or PDF produced by some word processors for output purposes only.

The "Title Page" means, for a printed book, the title page itself, plus such following pages as are needed to hold, legibly, the material this License requires to appear in the title page. For works in formats which do not have any title page as such, "Title Page" means the text near the most prominent appearance of the work's title, preceding the beginning of the body of the text.

The "publisher" means any person or entity that distributes copies of the Document to the public.

A section "Entitled XYZ" means a named subunit of the Document whose title either is precisely XYZ or contains XYZ in parentheses following text that translates XYZ in another language. (Here XYZ stands for a specific section name mentioned below, such as "Acknowledgements", "Dedications", "Endorsements", or "History".) To "Preserve the Title" of such a section when you modify the Document means that it remains a section "Entitled XYZ" according to this definition.

The Document may include Warranty Disclaimers next to the notice which states that this License applies to the Document. These Warranty Disclaimers are considered to be included by reference in this License, but only as regards disclaiming warranties: any other implication that these Warranty Disclaimers may have is void and has no effect on the meaning of this License.

2. VERBATIM COPYING

You may copy and distribute the Document in any medium, either commercially or noncommercially, provided that this License, the copyright notices, and the license notice saying this License applies to the Document are reproduced in all copies, and that you add no other conditions whatsoever to those of this License. You may not use technical measures to obstruct or control the reading or further copying of the copies you make or distribute. However, you may accept compensation in exchange for copies. If you distribute a large enough number of copies you must also follow the conditions in section 3.

You may also lend copies, under the same conditions stated above, and you may publicly display copies.

3. COPYING IN QUANTITY

If you publish printed copies (or copies in media that commonly have printed covers) of the Document, numbering more than 100, and the Document's license notice requires Cover Texts, you must enclose the copies in covers that carry, clearly and legibly, all these Cover Texts: Front-Cover Texts on the front cover, and Back-Cover Texts on the back cover. Both covers must also clearly and legibly identify you as the publisher of these copies. The front cover must present the full title with all words of the title equally prominent and visible. You may add other material on the covers in addition. Copying with changes limited to the covers, as long as they preserve the title of the Document and satisfy these conditions, can be treated as verbatim copying in other respects.

If the required texts for either cover are too voluminous to fit legibly, you should put the first ones listed (as many as fit reasonably) on the actual cover, and continue the rest onto adjacent pages.

If you publish or distribute Opaque copies of the Document numbering more than 100, you must either include a machine-readable Transparent copy along with each Opaque copy, or state in or with each Opaque copy a computer-network location from which the general network-using public has access to download using public-standard network protocols a complete Transparent copy of the Document, free of added material. If you use the latter option, you must take reasonably prudent steps, when you begin distribution of Opaque copies in quantity, to ensure that this Transparent copy will remain thus accessible at the stated location until at least one year after the last time you distribute an Opaque copy (directly or through your agents or retailers) of that edition to the public.

It is requested, but not required, that you contact the authors of the Document well before redistributing any large number of copies, to give them a chance to provide you with an updated version of the Document.

4. MODIFICATIONS

You may copy and distribute a Modified Version of the Document under the conditions of sections 2 and 3 above, provided that you release the Modified Version under precisely this License, with the Modified Version filling the role of the Document, thus licensing distribution and modification of the Modified Version to whoever possesses a copy of it. In addition, you must do these things in the Modified Version:

A. Use in the Title Page (and on the covers, if any) a title distinct from that of the Document, and from those of previous versions (which should, if there were any, be listed in the History section of the Document). You may use the same title as a previous version if the original publisher of that version gives permission.

B. List on the Title Page, as authors, one or more persons or entities responsible for authorship of the modifications in the Modified Version, together with at least five of the principal authors of the Document (all of its principal authors, if it has fewer than five), unless they release you from this requirement.

C. State on the Title page the name of the publisher of the Modified Version, as the publisher.

D. Preserve all the copyright notices of the Document.

E. Add an appropriate copyright notice for your modifications adjacent to the other copyright notices.

F. Include, immediately after the copyright notices, a license notice giving the public permission to use the Modified Version under the terms of this License, in the form shown in the Addendum below.

G. Preserve in that license notice the full lists of Invariant Sections and required Cover Texts given in the Document's license notice.

H. Include an unaltered copy of this License.

I. Preserve the section Entitled "History", Preserve its Title, and add to it an item stating at least the title, year, new authors, and publisher of the Modified Version as given on the Title Page. If there is no section Entitled "History" in the Document, create one stating the title, year, authors, and publisher of the Document as given on its Title Page, then add an item describing the Modified Version as stated in the previous sentence.

J. Preserve the network location, if any, given in the Document for public access to a Transparent copy of the Document, and likewise the network locations given in the Document for previous versions it was based on. These may be placed in the "History" section. You may omit a network location for a work that was published at least four years before the Document itself, or if the original publisher of the version it refers to gives permission.

K. For any section Entitled "Acknowledgements" or "Dedications", Preserve the Title of the section, and preserve in the section all the substance and tone of each of the contributor acknowledgements and/or dedications given therein.

L. Preserve all the Invariant Sections of the Document, unaltered in their text and in their titles. Section numbers or the equivalent are not considered part of the section titles.

M. Delete any section Entitled "Endorsements". Such a section may not be included in the Modified Version.

N. Do not retitle any existing section to be Entitled "Endorsements" or to conflict in title with any Invariant Section.

O. Preserve any Warranty Disclaimers.

If the Modified Version includes new front-matter sections or appendices that qualify as Secondary Sections and contain no material copied from the Document, you may at your option designate some or all of these sections as invariant. To do this, add their titles to the list of Invariant Sections in the Modified Version's license notice. These titles must be distinct from any other section titles.

You may add a section Entitled "Endorsements", provided it contains nothing but endorsements of your Modified Version by various parties—for example, statements of peer review or that the text has been approved by an organization as the authoritative definition of a standard.

You may add a passage of up to five words as a Front-Cover Text, and a passage of up to 25 words as a Back-Cover Text, to the end of the list of Cover Texts in the Modified Version. Only one passage of Front-Cover Text and one of Back-Cover Text may be added by (or through arrangements made by) any one entity. If the Document already includes a cover text for the same cover, previously added by you or by arrangement made by the same entity you are acting on behalf of, you may not add another; but you may replace the old one, on explicit permission from the previous publisher that added the old one.

The author(s) and publisher(s) of the Document do not by this License give permission to use their names for publicity for or to assert or imply endorsement of any Modified Version.

5. COMBINING DOCUMENTS

You may combine the Document with other documents released under this License, under the terms defined in section 4 above for modified versions, provided that you include in the combination all of the Invariant Sections of all of the original documents, unmodified, and list them all as Invariant Sections of your combined work in its license notice, and that you preserve all their Warranty Disclaimers.

The combined work need only contain one copy of this License, and multiple identical Invariant Sections may be replaced with a single copy. If there are multiple Invariant Sections with the same name but different contents, make the title of each such section unique by adding at the end of it, in parentheses, the name of the original author or publisher of that section if known, or else a unique number. Make the same adjustment to the section titles in the list of Invariant Sections in the license notice of the combined work.

In the combination, you must combine any sections Entitled "History" in the various original documents, forming one section Entitled "History"; likewise combine any sections Entitled "Acknowledgements", and any sections Entitled "Dedications". You must delete all sections Entitled "Endorsements."

6. COLLECTIONS OF DOCUMENTS

You may make a collection consisting of the Document and other documents released under this License, and replace the individual copies of this License in the various documents with a single copy that is included in the collection, provided that you follow the rules of this License for verbatim copying of each of the documents in all other respects.

You may extract a single document from such a collection, and distribute it individually under this License, provided you insert a copy of this License into the extracted document, and follow this License in all other respects regarding verbatim copying of that document.

7. AGGREGATION WITH INDEPENDENT WORKS

A compilation of the Document or its derivatives with other separate and independent documents or works, in or on a volume of a storage or distribution medium, is called an "aggregate" if the copyright resulting from the compilation is not used to limit the legal rights of the compilation's users beyond what the individual works permit. When the Document is included in an aggregate, this License does not apply to the other works in the aggregate which are not themselves derivative works of the Document.

If the Cover Text requirement of section 3 is applicable to these copies of the Document, then if the Document is less than one half of the entire aggregate, the Document's Cover Texts may be placed on covers that bracket the Document within the aggregate, or the electronic equivalent of covers if the Document is in electronic form. Otherwise they must appear on printed covers that bracket the whole aggregate.

8. TRANSLATION

Translation is considered a kind of modification, so you may distribute translations of the Document under the terms of section 4. Replacing Invariant Sections with translations requires special permission from their copyright holders, but you may include translations of some or all Invariant Sections in addition to the original versions of these Invariant Sections. You may include a translation of this License, and all the license notices in the Document, and any Warranty Disclaimers, provided that you also include the original English version of this License and the original versions of those notices and disclaimers. In case of a disagreement between the translation and the original version of this License or a notice or disclaimer, the original version will prevail.

If a section in the Document is Entitled "Acknowledgements", "Dedications", or "History", the requirement (section 4) to Preserve its Title (section 1) will typically require changing the actual title.

9. TERMINATION

You may not copy, modify, sublicense, or distribute the Document except as expressly provided under this License. Any attempt otherwise to copy, modify, sublicense, or distribute it is void, and will automatically terminate your rights under this License.

However, if you cease all violation of this License, then your license from a particular copyright holder is reinstated (a) provisionally, unless and until the copyright holder explicitly and finally terminates your license, and (b) permanently, if the copyright holder fails to notify you of the violation by some reasonable means prior to 60 days after the cessation.

Moreover, your license from a particular copyright holder is reinstated permanently if the copyright holder notifies you of the violation by some reasonable means, this is the first time you have received notice of violation of this License (for any work) from that copyright holder, and you cure the violation prior to 30 days after your receipt of the notice.

Termination of your rights under this section does not terminate the licenses of parties who have received copies or rights from you under this License. If your rights have been terminated and not permanently reinstated, receipt of a copy of some or all of the same material does not give you any rights to use it.

10. FUTURE REVISIONS OF THIS LICENSE

The Free Software Foundation may publish new, revised versions of the GNU Free Documentation License from time to time. Such new versions will be similar in spirit to the present version, but may differ in detail to address new problems or concerns. See http://www.gnu.org/copyleft/.

Each version of the License is given a distinguishing version number. If the Document specifies that a particular numbered version of this License "or any later version" applies to it, you have the option of following the terms and conditions either of that specified version or of any later version that has been published (not as a draft) by the Free Software Foundation. If the Document does not specify a version number of this License, you may choose any version ever published (not as a draft) by the Free Software Foundation. If the Document specifies that a proxy can decide which future versions of this License can be used, that proxy's public statement of acceptance of a version permanently authorizes you to choose that version for the Document.

11. RELICENSING

"Massive Multiauthor Collaboration Site" (or "MMC Site") means any World Wide Web server that publishes copyrightable works and also provides prominent facilities for anybody to edit those works. A public wiki that anybody can edit is an example of such a server. A "Massive Multiauthor Collaboration" (or "MMC") contained in the site means any set of copyrightable works thus published on the MMC site.

"CC-BY-SA" means the Creative Commons Attribution-Share Alike 3.0 license published by Creative Commons Corporation, a not-for-profit corporation with a principal place of business in San Francisco, California, as well as future copyleft versions of that license published by that same organization.

"Incorporate" means to publish or republish a Document, in whole or in part, as part of another Document.

An MMC is "eligible for relicensing" if it is licensed under this License, and if all works that were first published under this License somewhere other than this MMC, and subsequently incorporated in whole or in part into the MMC, (1) had no cover texts or invariant sections, and (2) were thus incorporated prior to November 1, 2008.

The operator of an MMC Site may republish an MMC contained in the site under CC-BY-SA on the same site at any time before August 1, 2009, provided the MMC is eligible for relicensing.

ADDENDUM: How to use this License for your documents

To use this License in a document you have written, include a copy of the License in the document and put the following copyright and license notices just after the title page:

```
Copyright (C)  year  your name.
Permission is granted to copy, distribute and/or modify this document
under the terms of the GNU Free Documentation License, Version 1.3
or any later version published by the Free Software Foundation;
with no Invariant Sections, no Front-Cover Texts, and no Back-Cover
Texts.  A copy of the license is included in the section entitled ``GNU
Free Documentation License''.
```

If you have Invariant Sections, Front-Cover Texts and Back-Cover Texts, replace the "with...Texts." line with this:

```
with the Invariant Sections being list their titles, with
the Front-Cover Texts being list, and with the Back-Cover Texts
being list.
```

If you have Invariant Sections without Cover Texts, or some other combination of the three, merge those two alternatives to suit the situation.

If your document contains nontrivial examples of program code, we recommend releasing these examples in parallel under your choice of free software license, such as the GNU General Public License, to permit their use in free software.